*EVERYMAN, I will go with thee,*

*and be thy guide,*

*In thy most need to go by thy side*

## PLUTARCH

Born at Chaeronea in Boeotia about A.D. 46. Lectured in Rome during Domitian's reign, and held high office under Trajan and Hadrian. Retired to his birthplace and died there about 120.

## ARTHUR HUGH CLOUGH

Born at Liverpool in 1819. Educated at Rugby and Balliol, where he met Matthew Arnold. Their friendship is commemorated in the latter's *Thyrsis*. Clough was himself a poet; his principal works, *The Bothie* (1848) and *Amours de Voyage* (1849), are included in the complete edition of his poems by H. F. Lowry and A. L. P. Norrington (1951). He died at Florence in 1861.

# Plutarch's Lives

IN THREE VOLUMES · VOLUME THREE

DRYDEN EDITION REVISED
WITH AN INTRODUCTION BY
ARTHUR HUGH CLOUGH

DENT: LONDON
EVERYMAN'S LIBRARY
DUTTON: NEW YORK

NO. *409*

# CONTENTS

## VOLUME I

## VOLUME II

## VOLUME III

# PHOCION

DEMADES, the orator, when in the height of the power which he obtained at Athens, by advising the state in the interest of Antipater and the Macedonians, being necessitated to write and speak many things below the dignity, and contrary to the character, of the city, was wont to excuse himself by saying he steered only the shipwrecks of the commonwealth. This hardy saying of his might have some appearance of truth, if applied to Phocion's government. For Demades, indeed, was himself the mere wreck of his country, living and ruling so dissolutely, that Antipater took occasion to say of him, when he was now grown old, that he was like a sacrificed beast, all consumed except the tongue and the belly. But Phocion's was a real virtue, only overmatched in the unequal contest with an adverse time, and rendered, by the ill fortunes of Greece, inglorious and obscure. We must not, indeed, allow ourselves to concur with Sophocles in so far diminishing the force of virtue as to say that—

> " When fortune fails, the sense we had before
> Deserts us also, and is ours no more."

Yet thus much, indeed, must be allowed to happen in the conflicts between good men and ill fortune, that instead of due returns of honour and gratitude, obloquy and unjust surmises may often prevail, to weaken, in a considerable degree, the credit of their virtue.

It is commonly said that public bodies are most insulting and contumelious to a good man, when they are puffed up with prosperity and success. But the contrary often happens; afflictions and public calamities naturally embittering and souring the minds and tempers of men, and disposing them to such peevishness and irritability that hardly any word or sentiment of common vigour can be addressed to them, but they will be apt to take offence. He that remonstrates with them on their errors is presumed to be insulting over their misfortunes, and any free-spoken expostulation is construed into contempt. Honey itself is searching in sore and ulcerated parts; and the wisest and most judicious counsels prove provoking to distempered minds, unless offered with those soothing and compliant approaches which made the poet, for instance, characterise agreeable things in general by a word expressive of a grateful and easy touch, exciting nothing of offence or resistance. Inflamed eyes require a retreat into dusky places, amongst colours of the deepest shades, and are unable to endure the brilliancy of light. So fares it in the body politic, in times of distress and humiliation; a certain sensitiveness and soreness of humour prevail, with a weak incapacity of enduring any free and open advice, even when the necessity of affairs most requires such plain dealing, and when the consequences of any single error may be beyond retrieving. At such times the conduct of public affairs is on all hands most hazardous. Those who humour the people are swallowed up in the common ruin; those who endeavour to lead them aright perish the first in their attempt.

Astronomers tell us, the sun's motion is neither exactly parallel with that of the heavens in general, nor yet directly and diametrically opposite, but describing an oblique line, with insensible declination he steers his course in such a gentle, easy curve, as to dispense his light and influence, in his annual revolution, at several seasons in just proportions to the whole creation. So it happens in political affairs; if the motions of rulers be constantly opposite and cross to the tempers and inclinations of the people, they will be resented as arbitrary and harsh; as, on the other side, too much deference, or encouragement, as too often it has been, to popular faults and errors, is full of danger and ruinous consequences. But where concession is the response to willing obedience, and a statesman gratifies his people, that he may the more imperatively recall them to a sense of the common interest, then, indeed, human beings, who are ready enough to serve well and submit to much, if they are not always ordered about and roughly handled, like slaves, may be said to be guided and governed upon the method that leads to safety. Though it must be confessed it is a nice point, and extremely difficult, so to temper this lenity as to preserve the authority of the government. But if such a blessed mixture and temperament may be obtained, it seems to be of all concords and harmonies the most concordant and most harmonious. For thus we are taught even God governs the world, not by irresistible force, but persuasive argument and reason, controlling it into compliance with his eternal purposes.

Cato the younger is a similar instance. His manners were little agreeable or acceptable to the people, and he received very slender marks of their favour; witness his repulse when he sued for the consulship, which he lost, as Cicero says, for acting rather like a citizen in Plato's commonwealth, than among the dregs of Romulus's posterity, the same thing happening to him, in my opinion, as we observe in fruits ripe before their season, which we rather take pleasure in looking at and admiring than actually use; so much was his old-fashioned virtue out of the present mode, among the depraved customs which time and luxury had introduced, that it appeared, indeed, remarkable and wonderful, but was too great and too good to suit the present exigencies, being so out of all proportion to the times. Yet his circumstances were not altogether like Phocion's, who came to the helm when the ship of the state was just upon sinking. Cato's time was, indeed, stormy and tempestuous, yet so, as he was able to assist in managing the sails, and lend his helping hand to those who, which he was not allowed to do, commanded at the helm, others were to blame for the result; yet his courage and virtue made it in spite of all a hard task for fortune to ruin the commonwealth, and it was only with long time and effort and by slow degrees, when he himself had all but succeeded in averting it, that the catastrophe was at last effected.

Phocion and he may be well compared together, not for any mere general resemblances, as though we should say both were good men and great statesmen. For, assuredly, there is difference enough among virtues of the same denomination, as between the bravery of Alcibiades and that of Epaminondas, the prudence of Themistocles and that of Aristides, the justice of Numa and that of Agesilaus. But these men's virtue, even looking to the most minute points of difference, bear the same colour, stamp, and character impressed upon them, so as not to be distinguishable. The mixture is still made in the same exact proportions whether we look at the combination to be found in them, both of lenity on the one hand, with austerity on the other; their boldness upon some occasions, and caution on others; their extreme solicitude for the public, and perfect neglect of themselves; their fixed and immovable bent to all virtuous and honest actions, accompanied with an extreme tenderness and scrupulosity as to doing anything which might appear mean or unworthy; so that we should need a very nice and subtle logic of discrimination to detect and establish the distinctions between them.

As to Cato's extraction, it is confessed by all to have been illustrious, as will be said hereafter, nor was Phocion's, I feel assured, obscure or ignoble. For had he been the son of a turner, as Idomeneus reports, it had certainly not been forgotten to his disparagement by Glaucippus, the son of Hyperides, when heaping up a thousand spiteful things to say against him. Nor, indeed, had it been possible for him, in such circumstances, to have had such a liberal breeding and education in his youth, as to be first Plato's and afterwards Xenocrates's scholar in the Academy, and to have devoted himself from the first to the pursuit of the noblest studies and practices. His countenance was so composed that scarcely was he ever seen by any Athenian either laughing or in tears. He was rarely known, so Duris has recorded, to appear in the public baths, or was observed with his hand exposed outside his cloak, when he wore one. Abroad, and in the camp, he was so hardy in going always thin clad and barefoot, except in a time of excessive and intolerable cold, that the soldiers used to say in merriment, that it was like to be a hard winter when Phocion wore his coat.

Although he was most gentle and humane in his disposition, his aspect was stern and forbidding, so that he was seldom accosted alone by any who were not intimate with him. When Chares once made some remark on his frowning looks, and the Athenians laughed at the jest, " My sullenness," said Phocion, " never yet made any of you sad, but these men's jollities have given you sorrow enough." In like manner Phocion's language, also, was full of instruction, abounding in happy maxims and wise thoughts, but admitted no embellishment to its austere and commanding brevity. Zeno said a philosopher should never speak till his words had been steeped in meaning; and such, it may be said, were Phocion's, crowding the greatest amount of significance into the smallest allowance of space. And to this, probably, Polyeuctus, the Sphettian, referred, when he said that Demosthenes was, indeed, the best orator of his time, but Phocion the most powerful speaker. His oratory, like small coin of great value, was to be estimated, not by its bulk, but its intrinsic worth. He was once observed, it is said, when the theatre was filling with the audience, to walk musing alone behind the scenes, which one of his friends taking notice of said, " Phocion, you seem to be thoughtful." " Yes," replied he, " I am considering how I may shorten what I am going to say to the Athenians."

Even Demosthenes himself, who used to despise the rest of the haranguers, when Phocion stood up, was wont to say quietly to those about him, " Here is the pruning-knife of my periods." This, however, might refer, perhaps, not so much to his eloquence as to the influence of his character, since not only a word, but even a nod from a person who is esteemed, is of more force than a thousand arguments or studied sentences from others.

In his youth he followed Chabrias, the general, from whom he gained many lessons in military knowledge, and in return did something to correct his unequal and capricious humour. For whereas at other times Chabrias was heavy and phlegmatic, in the heat of battle he used to be so fired and transported that he threw himself headlong into danger beyond the forwardest, which indeed, in the end, cost him his life in the island of Chios, he having pressed his own ship foremost to force a landing. But Phocion, being a man of temper as well as courage, had the dexterity at some times to rouse the general, when in his procrastinating mood, to action, and at others to moderate and cool the impetuousness of his unseasonable fury. Upon which account Chabrias, who was a good-natured, kindly-tempered man, loved him much, and procured him commands and opportunities for action, giving himself means to make himself known in Greece, and using his assistance in all his affairs of moment. Particularly the sea-fight of Naxos added not a little to Phocion's reputation, when he had the left squadron committed to him by Chabrias, as in this quarter the battle was sharply contested, and was decided by a speedy victory. And this being the first prosperous sea-battle the city had engaged in with its own force since its captivity, Chabrias won great popularity by it, and Phocion, also, got the reputation of a good commander. The victory was gained at the time of the Great Mysteries, and Chabrias used to keep the commemoration of it by distributing wine among the Athenians, yearly, on the sixteenth day of Boëdromion.

After this, Chabrias sent Phocion to demand their quota of the charges of the war from the islanders, and offered him a guard of twenty ships. Phocion told him, if he intended him to go against them as enemies, that force was insignificant; if as to friends and allies, one vessel was sufficient. So he took his own single galley, and having visited the cities, and treated with the magistrates in an equitable and open manner, he brought back a number of ships, sent by the confederates to Athens, to convey the supplies. Neither did his friendship and attention close with Chabrias's life, but after his decease he carefully maintained it to all that were related to him, and chiefly to his son, Ctesippus, whom he laboured to bring to some good, and although he was a stupid and intractable young fellow, always endeavoured, so far as in him lay, to correct and cover his faults and follies. Once, however, when the youngster was very impertinent and troublesome to him in the camp, interrupting him with idle questions, and putting forward his opinions and suggestions of how the war should be conducted, he could not forbear exclaiming, " O Chabrias, Chabrias, how grateful I show myself for your friendship, in submitting to endure your son! "

Upon looking into public matters, and the way in which they were now conducted, he observed that the administration of affairs was cut and parcelled out, like so much land by allotment, between the military men and the public speakers, so that neither these nor those should interfere with the claims of the others. As the one were to address the assemblies, to draw up votes and prepare motions, men, for example, like Eubulus, Aristophon, Demosthenes, Lycurgus, and Hyperides, and were to push their interests here; so, in the meantime, Diopithes, Menestheus, Leosthenes, and Chares were to make their profit by war and in military commands. Phocion, on the other hand, was desirous to restore and carry out the old system, more complete in itself, and more harmonious and uniform, which prevailed in the times of Pericles, Aristides, and Solon; when statesmen showed themselves, to use Archilochus's words—

> " Mars' and the Muses' friends alike designed,
>   To arts and arms indifferently inclined."

and the presiding goddess of his country was, he did not fail to see, the patroness and protectress of both civil and military wisdom. With these views, while his advice at home was always for peace and quietness, he nevertheless held the office of general more frequently than any of the statesmen, not only of his own times, but of those preceding, never, indeed, promoting or encouraging military expeditions, yet never, on the other hand, shunning or declining, when he was called upon by the public voice. Thus much is well known, that he was no less than forty-five several times chosen general, he being never on any one of those occasions present at the election, but having the command, in his absence, by common suffrage, conferred on him, and he sent for on purpose to undertake it. Insomuch that it amazed those who did not well consider to see the people always prefer

Phocion, who was so far from humouring them or courting their favour, that he always thwarted and opposed them. But so it was, as great men and princes are said to call in their flatterers when dinner has been served, so the Athenians, upon slight occasions, entertained and diverted themselves with their spruce speakers and trim orators, but when it came to action, they were sober and considerate enough to single out the austerest and wisest for public employment, however much he might be opposed to their wishes and sentiments. This, indeed, he made no scruple to admit, when the oracle from Delphi was read, which informed them that the Athenians were all of one mind, a single dissentient only excepted, frankly coming forward and declaring that they need look no further; he was the man; there was no one but he who was dissatisfied with everything they did. And when once he gave his opinion to the people, and was met with the general approbation and applause of the assembly, turning to some of his friends, he asked them, " Have I inadvertently said something foolish? "

Upon occasion of a public festivity, being solicited for his contribution by the example of others, and the people pressing him much, he bade them apply themselves to the wealthy; for his part he should blush to make a present here, rather than a repayment *there*, turning and pointing to Callicles, the money-lender. Being still clamoured upon and importuned, he told them this tale. A certain cowardly fellow setting out for the wars, hearing the ravens croak in his passage, threw down his arms, resolving to wait. Presently he took them and ventured out again, but hearing the same music, once more made a stop. " For," said he, " you may croak till you are tired, but you shall make no dinner upon me."

The Athenians urging him at an unseasonable time to lead them out against the enemy, he peremptorily refused, and being upbraided by them with cowardice and pusillanimity, he told them, " Just now, do what you will, I shall not be brave; and do what I will, you will not be cowards. Nevertheless, we know well enough what we are." And when again, in a time of great danger, the people were very harsh upon him, demanding a strict account how the public money had been employed, and the like, he bade them, " First, good friends, make sure you are safe." After a war, during which they had been very tractable and timorous, when, upon peace being made, they began again to be confident and overbearing, and to cry out upon Phocion, as having lost them the honour of victory, to all their clamour he made only this answer, " My friends, you are fortunate in having a leader who knows you; otherwise, you had long since been undone."

Having a controversy with the Bœotians about boundaries, which he counselled them to decide by negotiation, they inclined to blows. " You had better," said he, " carry on the contest with the weapons in which you excel (your tongues), and not by war, in which you are inferior." Once when he was addressing them, and they would not hear him or let him go on, said he, " You may compel me to act against my wishes, but you shall never force me to speak against my judgment." Among the many public speakers who opposed him, Demosthenes, for example, once told him, " The Athenians, Phocion, will kill you some day when they once are in a rage." " And you," said he, " if they once are in their senses." Polyeuctus, the Sphettian, once on a hot day was urging war with Philip, and being a corpulent man, and out of breath and in a great heat with speaking, took numerous draughts of water as he went on. " Here, indeed," said Phocion, " is a fit man to lead us into a war! What think you he will do when he is carrying his corselet and his shield to meet the enemy, if even here, delivering a prepared speech to you, has almost killed him with exhaustion? " When Lycurgus in the assembly made many reflections on his past conduct, upbraiding him above all for having advised them to deliver up the ten citizens whom Alexander had demanded, he replied that he had been the author of much safe and wholesome counsel, which had not been followed.

There was a man called Archibiades, nicknamed the Lacedæmonian, who used to go about with a huge, over-grown beard, wearing an old threadbare cloak, and affecting a very stern countenance. Phocion once, when attacked in council by the rest, appealed to this man for his support and testimony. And when he got up and began to speak on the popular side, putting his hand to his beard, " O Archibiades," said he, " it is time you should shave." Aristogiton, a common accuser, was a terrible man of war within the assembly, always inflaming the people to battle, but when the muster-roll came to be produced, he appeared limping on a crutch, with a bandage on his leg; Phocion descried him afar off, coming in, and cried out to the clerk, " Put down Aristogiton, too, as lame and worthless."

So that it is a little wonderful, how a man so severe and harsh upon all occasions should, notwithstanding, obtain the name of the Good. Yet, though difficult, it is not, I suppose, impossible for men's tempers, any more than for wines, to be at the same time harsh and agreeable to the taste; just as on the other hand many that are sweet at the first taste are found, on further use, extremely disagreeable and unwholesome. Hyperides, we are told, once said to the people, " Do not ask yourselves, men of Athens, whether or not I am bitter, but whether or not I am paid for being so," as though a covetous purpose were the only thing that should make a harsh temper insupportable, and as if men might not even more justly render themselves obnoxious to popular dislike and censure, by using their power and influence in the indulgence of their own private passions of pride and jealousy, anger and animosity. Phocion never allowed himself from any feeling of personal hostility to do hurt to any fellow-citizen, nor, indeed, reputed any man his enemy, except so far as he could not but contend sharply with such as opposed the measures he urged for the public good; in which argument he was, indeed, a rude, obstinate, and uncompromising adversary. For his general conversation, it was easy, courteous, and obliging to all, to that point that he would befriend his very opponents in their distress, and espouse the cause of those who differed most from him, when they needed his patronage. His friends reproaching him for pleading in behalf of a man of indifferent character, he told them the innocent had no need of an advocate. Aristogiton, the sycophant, whom we mentioned before, having, after sentence passed upon him, sent earnestly to Phocion to speak with him in the prison, his friends dissuaded him from going; "Nay, by your favour," said he, "where should I rather choose to pay Aristogiton a visit? "

As for the allies of the Athenians, and the islanders, whenever any admiral besides Phocion was sent, they treated him as an enemy suspect, barricaded their gates, blocked up their havens, brought in from the country their cattle, slaves, wives, and children, and put them in garrison; but upon Phocion's arrival, they went out to welcome him in their private boats and barges, with streamers and garlands, and received him at landing with every demonstration of joy and pleasure.

When King Philip was effecting his entry into Eubœa, and was bringing over troops from Macedonia, and making himself master of the cities, by means of the tyrants who ruled in them, Plutarch of Eretria sent to request aid of the Athenians for the relief of the island, which was in imminent danger of falling wholly into the hands of the Macedonians. Phocion was sent

thither with a handful of men in comparison, in expectation that
the Eubœans themselves would flock in and join him. But
when he came, he found all things in confusion, the country all
betrayed, the whole ground, as it were, undermined under his
feet, by the secret pensioners of King Philip, so that he was in
the greatest risk imaginable. To secure himself as far as he
could, he seized a small rising ground, which was divided from
the level plains about Tamynæ by a deep watercourse, and here
he enclosed and fortified the choicest of his army. As for the
idle talkers and disorderly bad citizens who ran off from his
camp and made their way back, he bade his officers not regard
them, since here they would have been not only useless and
ungovernable themselves, but an actual hindrance to the rest:
and further, being conscious to themselves of the neglect of
their duty, they would be less ready to misrepresent the action,
or raise a cry against them at their return home. When the
enemy drew nigh, he bade his men stand to their arms, until
he had finished the sacrifice, in which he spent a considerable
time, either by some difficulty of the thing itself, or on purpose
to invite the enemy nearer. Plutarch, interpreting this tardi-
ness as a failure in his courage, fell on alone with the mercenaries,
which the cavalry perceiving, could not be contained, but issuing
also out of the camp, confusedly and in disorder, spurred up to
the enemy. The first who came up were defeated, the rest were
put to the rout. Plutarch himself took to flight, and a body of
the enemy advanced in the hope of carrying the camp, supposing
themselves to have secured the victory. But by this time, the
sacrifice being over, the Athenians within the camp came forward,
and falling upon them put them to flight, and killed the greater
number as they fled among the intrenchments, while Phocion,
ordering his infantry to keep on the watch and rally those who
came in from the previous flight, himself, with a body of his best
men, engaged the enemy in a sharp and bloody fight, in which
all of them behaved with signal courage and gallantry. Thallus,
the son of Cineas, and Glaucus of Polymedes, who fought near
the general, gained the honours of the day. Cleophanes, also,
did good service in the battle. Recovering the cavalry from its
defeat, and with his shouts and encouragement bringing them
up to succour the general, who was in danger, he confirmed the
victory obtained by the infantry. Phocion now expelled
Plutarch from Eretria, and possessed himself of the very
important fort of Zaretra, situated where the island is pinched
in, as it were, by the seas on each side, and its breadth most

reduced to a narrow girth. He released all the Greeks whom he took, out of fear of the public speakers at Athens, thinking they might very likely persuade the people in their anger into committing some act of cruelty.

This affair thus despatched and settled, Phocion set sail homewards, and the allies had soon as good reason to regret the loss of his just and humane dealing as the Athenians that of his experience and courage. Molossus, the commander who took his place, had no better success than to fall alive into the enemy's hands.

Philip, full of great thoughts and designs, now advanced with all his forces into the Hellespont, to seize the Chersonesus and Perinthus, and after them Byzantium. The Athenians raised a force to relieve them, but the popular leaders made it their business to prefer Chares to be general, who, sailing thither, effected nothing worthy of the means placed in his hands. The cities were afraid, and would not receive his ships into their harbours, so that he did nothing but wander about, raising money from their friends, and despised by their enemies. When the people, chafed by the orators, were extremely indignant, and repented having ever sent any help to the Byzantines, Phocion rose and told them they ought not to be angry with the allies for distrusting, but with their generals for being distrusted. "They make you suspected," he said, "even by those who cannot possibly subsist without your succour." The assembly being moved with this speech of his, changed their minds on the sudden, and commanded him immediately to raise another force, and go himself to assist their confederates in the Hellespont; an appointment which, in effect, contributed more than anything to the relief of Byzantium.

For Phocion's name was already honourably known; and an old acquaintance of his, who had been his fellow-student in the Academy, Leon, a man of high renown for virtue among the Byzantines, having vouched for Phocion to the city, they opened their gates to receive him, not permitting him, though he desired it, to encamp without the walls, but entertained him and all the Athenians with perfect reliance, while they, to requite their confidence, behaved among their new hosts soberly and inoffensively, and exerted themselves on all occasions with the greatest zeal and resolution for their defence. Thus King Philip was driven out of the Hellespont, and was despised to boot, whom, till now, it had been thought impossible to match, or even to oppose. Phocion also took some of his ships, and recaptured some of the places he had garrisoned, making besides several inroads into the country, which he plundered and over-ran, until he received a wound from some of the enemy who came to the defence, and, thereupon, sailed away home.

The Megarians at this time privately praying aid of the Athenians, Phocion, fearing lest the Bœotians should hear of it, and anticipate them, called an assembly at sunrise, and brought forward the petition of the Megarians, and immediately after the vote had been put, and carried in their favour, he sounded the trumpet, and led the Athenians straight from the assembly, to arm and put themselves in posture. The Megarians received them joyfully, and he proceeded to fortify Nisæa, and built two new long walls from the city to the arsenal, and so joined it to the sea, so that having now little reason to regard the enemies on the land side, it placed its dependence entirely on the Athenians.

When final hostilities with Philip were now certain, and in Phocion's absence other generals had been nominated, he, on his arrival from the islands, dealt earnestly with the Athenians, that since Philip showed peaceable inclinations towards them, and greatly apprehended the danger, they would consent to a treaty. Being contradicted in this by one of the ordinary frequenters of the courts of justice, a common accuser, who asked him if he durst presume to persuade the Athenians to peace, now their arms were in their hands, " Yes," said he, " though I know that if there be war, I shall be in office over you, and if peace, you over me." But when he could not prevail, and Demosthenes's opinion carried it, advising them to make war as far off from home as possible, and fight the battle out of Attica, " Good friends," said Phocion, " let us not ask where we shall fight, but how we may conquer in the war. That will be the way to keep it at a distance. If we are beaten, it will be quickly at our doors." After the defeat, when the clamourers and incendiaries in the town would have brought up Charidemus to the hustings, to be nominated to the command, the best of the citizens were in a panic, and supporting themselves with the aid of the council of the Areopagus, with entreaties and tears, hardly prevailed upon the people to have Phocion entrusted with the care of the city. He was of opinion, in general, that the fair terms to be expected from Philip should be accepted, yet after Demades had made a motion that the city should receive the common conditions of peace in concurrence with the rest of the states of Greece, he opposed it, till it were known what the particulars

were which Philip demanded. He was overborne in this advice,
under the pressure of the time, but almost immediately after the
Athenians repented it, when they understood that by these
articles they were obliged to furnish Philip both with horse and
shipping. "It was the fear of this," said Phocion, "that occasioned my opposition. But since the thing is done, let us make
the best of it, and not be discouraged. Our forefathers were
sometimes in command, and sometimes under it; and by doing
their duty, whether as rulers or as subjects, saved their own
country and the rest of Greece."

Upon the news of Philip's death, he opposed himself to any
public demonstrations of joy and jubilee, saying it would be
ignoble to show malice upon such an occasion, and that the army
that had fought them at Chæronea was only diminished by a
single man.

When Demosthenes made his invectives against Alexander,
now on his way to attack Thebes, he repeated those verses of
Homer:—

> " Unwise one, wherefore to a second stroke
> His anger be foolhardy to provoke? "

and asked, " Why stimulate his already eager passion for glory?
Why take pains to expose the city to the terrible conflagration
now so near? We, who accepted office to save our fellow-
citizens, will not, however they desire it, be consenting to their
destruction."

After Thebes was lost, and Alexander had demanded Demosthenes, Lycurgus, Hyperides, and Charidemus to be delivered
up, the whole assembly turning their eyes to him, and calling on
him by name to deliver his opinion, at last he rose up, and showing them one of his most intimate friends, whom he loved and
confided in above all others, told them, " You have brought
things amongst you to that pass, that for my part, should he
demand this my friend Nicocles, I would not refuse to give him
up. For as for myself, to have it in my power to sacrifice my
own life and fortune for the common safety, I should think the
greatest of good fortune. Truly," he added, " it pierces my
heart to see those who are fled hither for succour from the desolation of Thebes. Yet it is enough for Greece to have Thebes to
deplore. It will be more for the interest of all that we should
deprecate the conqueror's anger, and intercede for both, than
run the hazard of another battle."

When this was decreed by the people, Alexander is said to

have rejected their first address when it was presented, throwing it from him scornfully, and turning his back upon the deputation, who left him in affright. But the second, which was presented by Phocion, he received, understanding from the older Macedonians how much Philip had admired and esteemed him. And he not only gave him audience and listened to his memorial and petition, but also permitted him to advise him, which he did to this effect, that if his designs were for quietness, he should make peace at once; if glory were his aim, he should make war, not upon Greece, but on the barbarians. With various counsels and suggestions, happily designed to meet the genius and feelings of Alexander, he so won upon him, and softened his temper, that he bade the Athenians not forget their position, as if anything went wrong with him, the supremacy belonged to them. And to Phocion himself, whom he adopted as his friend and guest, he showed a respect, and admitted him to distinctions, which few of those who were continually near his person ever received. Duris, at any rate, tells us, that when he became great, and had conquered Darius, in the heading of all his letters he left off the word *Greeting*, except in those he wrote to Phocion. To him, and to Antipater alone, he condescended to use it. This also is stated by Chares.

As for his munificence to him, it is well known he sent him a present at one time of one hundred talents; and this being brought to Athens, Phocion asked of the bearers how it came to pass that among all the Athenians he alone should be the object of this bounty. Being told that Alexander esteemed him alone a person of honour and worth, " Let him, then," said he, " permit me to continue so and be still so reputed." Following him to his house, and observing his simple and plain way of living, his wife employed in kneading bread with her own hands, himself drawing water to wash his feet, they pressed him to accept it, with some indignation, being ashamed, as they said, that Alexander's friend should live so poorly and pitifully. So Phocion, pointing out to them a poor old fellow, in a dirty worn-out coat, passing by, asked them if they thought him in worse condition than this man. They bade him not mention such a comparison. " Yet," said Phocion, " he, with less to live upon than I, finds it sufficient, and in brief," he continued, " if I do not use this money, what good is there in my having it; and if I do use it, I shall procure an ill name, both for myself and for Alexander, among my countrymen." So the treasure went back again from Athens, to prove to Greece, by a signal example,

that he who could afford to give so magnificent a present, was
yet not so rich as he who could afford to refuse it. And when
Alexander was displeased, and wrote back to him to say that he
could not esteem those his friends who would not be obliged by
him, not even would this induce Phocion to accept the money,
but he begged leave to intercede with him in behalf of Eche-
cratides, the sophist, and Athenodorus, the Imbrian, as also for
Demaratus and Sparton, two Rhodians, who had been arrested
upon some charges, and were in custody at Sardis. This was
instantly granted by Alexander, and they were set at liberty.
Afterwards, when sending Craterus into Macedonia, he commanded him to make him an offer of four cities in Asia, Cius,
Gergithus, Mylasa, and Elæa, any one of which, at his choice,
should be delivered to him; insisting yet more positively with
him, and declaring he should resent it, should he continue
obstinate in his refusal. But Phocion was not to be prevailed
with at all, and, shortly after, Alexander died.

Phocion's house is shown to this day in Melita, ornamented
with small plates of copper, but otherwise plain and homely.
Concerning his wives, of the first of them there is little said,
except that she was sister of Cephisodotus, the statuary. The
other was a matron of no less reputation for her virtues and
simple living among the Athenians than Phocion was for his
probity. It happened once when the people were entertained
with a new tragedy, that the actor, just as he was to enter the
stage to perform the part of a queen, demanded to have a number
of attendants sumptuously dressed, to follow in his train, and
on their not being provided, was sullen and refused to act, keeping the audience waiting, till at last Melanthius, who had to
furnish the chorus, pushed him on the stage, crying out, " What,
don't you know that Phocion's wife is never attended by more
than a single waiting-woman, but you must needs be grand, and
fill our women's heads with vanity ? " This speech of his, spoken
loud enough to be heard, was received with great applause, and
clapped all round the theatre. She herself, when once entertaining a visitor out of Ionia, who showed her all her rich
ornaments, made of gold and set with jewels, her wreaths, necklaces, and the like, " For my part," said she, " all my ornament
is my husband, Phocion, now for the twentieth year in office as
general at Athens."

He had a son named Phocus, who wished to take part in the
games at the great feast of Minerva. He permitted him so to
do, in the contest of leaping, not with any view to the victory,

but in the hope that the training and discipline for it would make him a better man, the youth being in a general way a lover of drinking, and ill-regulated in his habits. On his having succeeded in the sports, many were eager for the honour of his company at banquets in celebration of the victory. Phocion declined all these invitations but one, and when he came to this entertainment and saw the costly preparations, even the water brought to wash the guests' feet being mingled with wine and spices, he reprimanded his son, asking him why he would so far permit his friend to sully the honour of his victory. And in the hope of wholly weaning the young man from such habits and company, he sent him to Lacedæmon, and placed him among the youths then under the course of the Spartan discipline. This the Athenians took offence at, as though he slighted and contemned the education at home; and Demades twitted him with it publicly. "Suppose, Phocion, you and I advise the Athenians to adopt the Spartan constitution. If you like, I am ready to introduce a bill to that effect, and to speak in its favour." "Indeed," said Phocion, "you, with that strong scent of perfumes about you, and with that mantle on your shoulders, are just the very man to speak in honour of Lycurgus, and recommend the Spartan table."

When Alexander wrote to demand a supply of galleys, and the public speakers objected to sending them, Phocion, on the council requesting his opinion, told them freely, "Sirs, I would either have you victorious yourselves, or friends of those who are so." He took up Pytheas, who about this time first began to address the assembly, and already showed himself a confident, talking fellow, by saying that a young slave whom the people had but bought yesterday ought to have the manners to hold his tongue. And when Harpalus, who had fled from Alexander out of Asia, carrying off a large sum of money, came to Attica, and there was a perfect race among the ordinary public men of the assembly who should be the first to take his pay, he distributed amongst these some trifling sums by way of a bait and provocative, but to Phocion he made an offer of no less than seven hundred talents and all manner of other advantages he pleased to demand; with the compliment that he would entirely commit himself and all his affairs to his disposal. Phocion answered sharply, Harpalus should repent of it, if he did not quickly leave off corrupting and debauching the city, which for the time silenced him, and checked his proceedings. But afterwards, when the Athenians were deliberating in council about him, he found those that had received money from him to be his greatest enemies, urging and aggravating matters against him, to prevent themselves being discovered, whereas Phocion, who had never touched his pay, now, so far as the public interest would admit of it, showed some regard to his particular security. This encouraged him once more to try his inclinations, and upon further survey finding that he himself was a fortress, inaccessible on every quarter to the approaches of corruption, he professed a particular friendship to Phocion's son-in-law, Charicles. And admitting him into his confidence in all his affairs, and continually requesting his assistance, he brought him under some suspicion. Upon the occasion, for example, of the death of Pythonice, who was Harpalus's mistress, for whom he had a great fondness, and had a child by her, he resolved to build her a sumptuous monument, and committed the care of it to his friend Charicles. This commission, disreputable enough in itself, was yet futher disparaged by the figure the piece of workmanship made after it was finished. It is yet to be seen in the Hermeum, as you go from Athens to Eleusis, with nothing in its appearance answerable to the sum of thirty talents, with which Charicles is said to have charged Harpalus for its erection. After Harpalus's own decease, his daughter was educated by Phocion and Charicles with great care. But when Charicles was called to account for his dealings with Harpalus, and entreated his father-in-law's protection, begging that he would appear for him in the court, Phocion refused, telling him, " I did not choose you for my son-in-law for any but honourable purposes."

Asclepiades, the son of Hipparchus, brought the first tidings of Alexander's death to Athens, which Demades told them was not to be credited; for were it true, the whole world would ere this have stunk with the dead body. But Phocion, seeing the people eager for an instant revolution, did his best to quiet and repress them. And when numbers of them rushed up to the hustings to speak, and cried out that the news was true, and Alexander was dead, " If he is dead to-day," said he, " he will be so to-morrow and the day after to-morrow equally. So that there is no need to take counsel hastily or before it is safe."

When Leosthenes now had embarked the city in the Lamian war, greatly against Phocion's wishes, to raise a laugh against Phocion, he asked him scoffingly, what the state had been benefited by his having now so many years been general. " It is not a little," said Phocion, " that the citizens have been buried in their own sepulchres." And when Leosthenes continued to speak boldly and boastfully in the assembly, "Young man," he said, "your speeches are like cypress-trees, stately and tall, and no fruit to come of them." When he was then attacked by Hyperides, who asked him when the time would come that he would advise the Athenians to make war, "As soon," said he, "as I find the young men keep their ranks, the rich men contribute their money, and the orators leave off robbing the treasury." Afterwards, when many admired the forces raised, and the preparations for war that were made by Leosthenes, they asked Phocion how he approved of the new levies. "Very well," said he, "for the short course; but what I fear is the long race. Since, however late the war may last, the city has neither money, ships, nor soldiers, but these." The event justified his prognostics. At first all things appeared fair and promising. Leosthenes gained great reputation by worsting the Bœotians in battle, and driving Antipater within the walls of Lamia, and the citizens were so transported with the first successes, that they kept solemn festivities for them, and offered public sacrifices to the gods. So that some, thinking Phocion must now be convinced of his error, asked him whether he would not willingly have been author of these successful actions. "Yes," said he, "most gladly, but also of the former counsel." And when one express after another came from the camp, confirming and magnifying the victories, "When," said he, "will the end of them come?"

Leosthenes, soon after, was killed, and now those who feared lest if Phocion obtained the command he would put an end to the war, arranged with an obscure person in the assembly, who should stand up and profess himself to be a friend and old confidant of Phocion's, and persuade the people to spare him at this time, and reserve him (with whom none could compare) for a more pressing occasion, and now to give Antiphilus the command of the army. This pleased the generality, but Phocion made it appear he was so far from having any friendship with him of old standing, that he had not so much as the least familiarity with him; "Yet now, sir," says he, "give me leave to put you down among the number of my friends and well-wishers, as you have given a piece of advice so much to my advantage."

When the people were eager to make an expedition against the Bœotians, he at first opposed it; and on his friends telling him the people would kill him for always running counter to them, "That will be unjust of them," he said, "if I give them honest advice, if not, it will be just of them." But when he found them persisting and shouting to him to lead them out, he commanded the crier to make proclamation, that all the Athenians under sixty should instantly provide themselves with five days' provision, and follow him from the assembly. This caused a great tumult. Those in years were startled, and clamoured against the order; he demanded wherein he injured them, " For I," says he, " am now fourscore, and am ready to lead you." This succeeded in pacifying them for the present.

But when Micion, with a large force of Macedonians and mercenaries, began to pillage the sea-coast, having made a descent upon Rhamnus, and overrun the neighbouring country, Phocion led out the Athenians to attack him. And when sundry private persons came, intermeddling with his dispositions, and telling him that he ought to occupy such or such a hill, detach the cavalry in this or that direction, engage the enemy on this point or that, " O Hercules," said he, " how many generals have we here, and how few soldiers!" Afterwards, having formed the battle, one who wished to show his bravery advanced out of his post before the rest, but on the enemy's approaching, lost heart, and retired back into his rank. " Young man," said Phocion, " are you not ashamed twice in one day to desert your station, first that on which I had placed you, and secondly that on which you had placed yourself?" However, he entirely routed the enemy, killing Micion and many more on the spot. The Grecian army, also, in Thessaly, after Leonnatus and the Macedonians who came with him out of Asia had arrived and joined Antipater, fought and beat them in a battle. Leonnatus was killed in the fight, Antiphilus commanding the foot, and Menon, the Thessalian, the horse.

But not long after, Craterus crossed from Asia with numerous forces; a pitched battle was fought at Cranon; the Greeks were beaten; though not, indeed, in a signal defeat, nor with any great loss of men. But what with their want of obedience to their commanders, who were young and over-indulgent with them, and what with Antipater's tampering and treating with their separate cities, one by one, the end of it was that the army was dissolved, and the Greeks shamefully surrendered the liberty of their country.

Upon the news of Antipater's now advancing at once against Athens, with all his force, Demosthenes and Hyperides deserted the city, and Demades, who was altogether insolvent for any part of the fines that had been laid upon him by the city, for he had been condemned no less than seven times for introducing bills contrary to the laws, and who had been disfranchised, and was no longer competent to vote in the assembly, laid hold of this season of impunity to bring in a bill for sending ambassadors with plenipotentiary power to Antipater, to treat about a peace. But the people distrusted him, and called upon Phocion to give his opinion, as the person they only and entirely confided in. He told them, " If my former counsels had been prevalent with you, we had not been reduced to deliberate on the question at all." However, the vote passed; and a decree was made, and he with others deputed to go to Antipater, who lay now encamped in the Theban territories, but intended to dislodge immediately, and pass into Attica. Phocion's first request was, that he would make the treaty without moving his camp. And when Craterus declared that it was not fair to ask them to be burdensome to the country of their friends and allies by their stay, when they might rather use that of their enemies for provisions and the support of their army, Antipater, taking him by the hand, said, " We must grant this favour to Phocion." For the rest he bade them return to their principals, and acquaint them that he could only offer them the same terms, namely, to surrender at discretion, which Leosthenes had offered to him when he was shut up in Lamia.

When Phocion had returned to the city and acquainted them with this answer, they made a virtue of necessity and complied, since it would be no better. So Phocion returned to Thebes with the other ambassadors, and among the rest Xenocrates, the philosopher, the reputation of whose virtue and wisdom was so great and famous everywhere, that they conceived there could not be any pride, cruelty, or anger arising in the heart of man, which would not at the mere sight of him be subdued into something of reverence and admiration. But the result, as it happened, was the very opposite, Antipater showed such a want of feeling, and such a dislike of goodness. He saluted every one else, but would not so much as notice Xenocrates. Xenocrates, they tell us, observed upon it, that Antipater, when meditating such cruelty to Athens, did well to be ashamed of seeing him. When he began to speak, he would not hear him, but broke in and rudely interrupted him, until at last he was obliged to be silent. But when Phocion had declared the purport of their embassy, he replied shortly, that he would make peace with the Athenians on these conditions, and no others; that Demosthenes and Hyperides should be delivered up to him; that they should retain their ancient form of government, the franchise being determined by a property qualification; that they should receive a garrison into Munychia, and pay a certain sum for the cost of the war. As things stood, these terms were judged tolerable by the rest of the ambassadors; Xenocrates only said, that if Antipater considered the Athenians slaves, he was treating them fairly; but if free, severely. Phocion pressed him only to spare them the garrison, and used many arguments and entreaties. Antipater replied, " Phocion, we are ready to do you any favour, which will not bring ruin both on ourselves and on you." Others report it differently; that Antipater asked Phocion, supposing he remitted the garrison to the Athenians, would he, Phocion, stand surety for the city's observing the terms and attempting no revolution? And when he hesitated, and did not at once reply, Callimedon, the Carabus, a hot partisan and professed enemy of free states, cried out, " And if he should talk so idly, Antipater, will you be so much abused as to believe him and not carry out your own purpose? " So the Athenians received the garrison, and Menyllus for the governor, a fair-dealing man, and one of Phocion's acquaintance.

But the proceeding seemed sufficiently imperious and arbitrary, indeed rather a spiteful and insulting ostentation of power, than that the possession of the fortress would be of any great importance. The resentment felt upon it was heightened by the time it happened in, for the garrison was brought in on the twentieth of the month of Boëdromion, just at the time of the great festival, when they carry forth Iacchus with solemn pomp from the city to Eleusis; so that the solemnity being disturbed, many began to call to mind instances, both ancient and modern, of divine interventions and intimations. For in old time, upon the occasions of their happiest successes, the presence of the shapes and voices of the mystic ceremonies had been vouchsafed to them, striking terror and amazement into their enemies; but now, at the very season of their celebration, the gods themselves stood witnesses of the saddest oppressions of Greece, the most holy time being profaned, and their greatest jubilee made the unlucky date of their most extreme calamity. Not many years before, they had a warning from the oracle at Dodona, that they should carefully guard the summits of Diana, lest haply strangers should seize them. And about this very time, when they dyed the ribbons and garlands with which they adorn the couches and cars of the procession, instead of a purple, they received only a faint yellow colour; and to make the omen yet greater, all the things that were dyed for common use, took the natural colour. While a candidate for initiation was washing a young pig in the haven of Cantharus, a shark seized him, bit off all his lower parts up to the belly, and devoured them, by which the god gave them manifestly to understand, that having lost the lower town and sea-coast, they should keep only the upper city.

Menyllus was sufficient security that the garrison should behave itself inoffensively. But those who were now excluded from the franchise by poverty amounted to more than twelve thousand; so that both those that remained in the city thought themselves oppressed and shamefully used, and those who on this account left their homes and went away into Thrace, where Antipater offered them a town and some territory to inhabit, regarded themselves only as a colony of slaves and exiles. And when to this was added the deaths of Demosthenes at Calauria, and of Hyperides at Cleonæ, as we have elsewhere related, the citizens began to think with regret of Philip and Alexander, and almost to wish the return of those times. And as, after Antigonus was slain, when those that had taken him off were afflicting and oppressing the people, a countryman in Phrygia, digging in the fields, was asked what he was doing, " I am," said he, fetching a deep sigh, " searching for Antigonus; " so said many that remembered those days, and the contests they had with those kings, whose anger, however great, was yet generous and placable; whereas Antipater, with the counterfeit humility of appearing like a private man, in the meanness of his dress and his homely fare, merely belied his real love of that arbitrary power, which he exercised, as a cruel master and despot, to distress those under his command. Yet Phocion had interest with him to recall many from banishment by his intercession, and prevailed also for those who were driven out, that they might not, like others, be hurried beyond Tænarus, and the mountains of Ceraunia, but remain in Greece, and plant themselves in Peloponnesus, of which number was Agnonides, the sycophant. He was no less studious to manage the affairs within the city with equity and moderation, preferring constantly those that were men of worth and good education to the magistracies, and recommending the busy and turbulent talkers, to whom it was a mortal blow to be excluded from office and public debating, to learn to stay at home, and be content to till their land. And observing that Xenocrates paid his alien-tax as a foreigner, he offered him the freedom of the city, which he refused, saying he could not accept a franchise which he had been sent as an ambassador to deprecate.

Menyllus wished to give Phocion a considerable present of money, who, thanking him, said, neither was Menyllus greater than Alexander, nor his own occasions more urgent to receive it now, than when he refused it from him. And on his pressing him to permit his son Phocus to receive it, he replied, "If my son returns to a right mind, his patrimony is sufficient; if not, all supplies will be insufficient." But to Antipater he answered more sharply, who would have him engaged in something dishonourable. "Antipater," said he, "cannot have me both as his friend and his flatterer." And, indeed, Antipater was wont to say he had two friends at Athens, Phocion and Demades; the one would never suffer him to gratify him at all, the other would never be satisfied. Phocion might well think that poverty a virtue, in which, after having so often been general of the Athenians, and admitted to the friendship of potentates and princes, he had now grown old. Demades, meantime, delighted in lavishing his wealth even in positive transgressions of the law. For there having been an order that no foreigner should be hired to dance in any chorus on the penalty of a fine of one thousand drachmas on the exhibitor, he had the vanity to exhibit an entire chorus of a hundred foreigners, and paid down the penalty of a thousand drachmas a head upon the stage itself. Marrying his son Demeas, he told him with the like vanity, "My son, when I married your mother, it was done so privately it was not known to the next neighbours, but kings and princes give presents at your nuptials."

The garrison in Munychia continued to be felt as a great grievance, and the Athenians did not cease to be importunate upon Phocion, to prevail with Antipater for its removal; but whether he despaired of effecting it, or perhaps observed the people to be more orderly, and public matters more reasonably conducted by the awe that was thus created, he constantly declined the office, and contented himself with obtaining from Antipater the postponement for the present of the payment of the sum of money in which the city was fined. So the people, leaving him off, applied themselves to Demades, who readily undertook the employment, and took along with him his son also into Macedonia; and some superior power, as it seems, so ordering it, he came just at that nick of time when Antipater was already seized with his sickness, and Cassander, taking upon himself the command, had found a letter of Demades's, formerly

written by him to Antigonus in Asia, recommending him to come
and possess himself of the empire of Greece and Macedon, now
hanging, he said (a scoff at Antipater), " by an old and rotten
thread." So when Cassander saw him come, he seized him;
and first brought out the son, and killed him so close before his
face, that the blood ran all over his clothes and person, and
then, after bitterly taunting and upbraiding him with his ingratitude and treachery, despatched him himself.

Antipater being dead, after nominating Polysperchon general-
in-chief and Cassander commander of the cavalry, Cassander at
once set up for himself, and immediately despatched Nicanor to
Menyllus, to succeed him in the command of the garrison, commanding him to possess himself of Munychia before the news of
Antipater's death should be heard; which being done, and some
days after the Athenians hearing the report of it, Phocion was
taxed as privy to it before, and censured heavily for dissembling
it, out of friendship for Nicanor. But he slighted their talk,
and making it his duty to visit and confer continually with
Nicanor, he succeeded in procuring his good-will and kindness
for the Athenians, and induced him even to put himself to
trouble and expense to seek popularity with them, by undertaking the office of presiding at the games.

In the meantime Polysperchon, who was intrusted with the
charge of the king, to countermine Cassander, sent a letter to
the city, declaring, in the name of the king, that he restored
them their democracy, and that the whole Athenian people were
at liberty to conduct their commonwealth according to their
ancient customs and constitutions. The object of these pretences was merely the overthrow of Phocion's influence, as the
event manifested. For Polysperchon's design being to possess
himself of the city, he despaired altogether of bringing it to pass
whilst Phocion retained his credit; and the most certain way
to ruin him would be again to fill the city with a crowd of dis-
franchised citizens, and let loose the tongues of the demagogues
and common accusers.

With this prospect the Athenians were all in excitement, and
Nicanor, wishing to confer with them on the subject, at a meeting of the Council in Piræus, came himself, trusting for the safety
of his person to Phocion. And when Dercyllus, who commanded the guard there, made an attempt to seize him, upon
notice of it beforehand, he made his escape, and there was little
doubt he would now lose no time in righting himself upon the
city for the affront; and when Phocion was found fault with for

letting him get off and not securing him, he defended himself by saying that he had no mistrust of Nicanor, nor the least reason to expect any mischief from him, but should it prove otherwise, for his part he would have them all know, he would rather receive than do the wrong. And so far as he spoke for himself alone, the answer was honourable and high-minded enough, but he who hazards his country's safety, and that, too, when he is her magistrate and chief commander, can scarcely be acquitted, I fear, of transgressing a higher and more sacred obligation of justice, which he owed to his fellow-citizens. For it will not even do to say that he dreaded the involving the city in war, by seizing Nicanor, and hoped by professions of confidence and just-dealing to retain him in the observance of the like; but it was, indeed, his credulity and confidence in him, and an over-weening opinion of his sincerity, that imposed upon him. So that notwithstanding the sundry intimations he had of his making preparations to attack Piræus, sending soldiers over into Salamis, and tampering with and endeavouring to corrupt various residents in Piræus, he would, notwithstanding all this evidence, never be persuaded to believe it. And even when Philomedes of Lampra had got a decree passed, that all the Athenians should stand to their arms, and be ready to follow Phocion their general, he yet sat still and did nothing, until Nicanor actually led his troops out from Munychia, and drew trenches about Piræus; upon which, when Phocion at last would have let out the Athenians, they cried out against him, and slighted his orders.

Alexander, the son of Polysperchon, was at hand with a con-siderable force, and professed to come to give them succour against Nicanor, but intended nothing less, if possible, than to surprise the city, whilst they were in tumult and divided among themselves. For all that had previously been expelled from the city, now coming back with him, made their way into it, and were joined by a mixed multitude of foreigners and dis-franchised persons, and of these a motley and irregular public assembly came together, in which they presently divested Phocion of all power, and chose other generals; and if by chance Alexander had not been spied from the walls, alone in close con-ference with Nicanor, and had not this, which was often repeated, given the Athenians cause of suspicion, the city had not escaped the snare. The orator Agnonides, however, at once fell foul upon Phocion, and impeached him of treason; Callimedon and Charicles, fearing the worst, consulted their own security by flying from the city. Phocion, with a few of his friends that stayed with him, went over to Polysperchon, and out of respect for him, Solon of Platæa, and Dinarchus of Corinth, who were reputed friends and confidants of Polysperchon, accompanied him. But on account of Dinarchus falling ill, they remained several days in Elatea, during which time, upon the persuasion of Agnonides and on the motion of Archestratus, a decree passed that the people should send delegates thither to accuse Phocion. So both parties reached Polysperchon at the same time, who was going through the country with the king, and was then at a small village of Phocis, Pharygæ, under the mountain now called Galate, but then Acrurium.

There Polysperchon, having set up the golden canopy, and seated the king and his company under it, ordered Dinarchus at once to be taken, and tortured, and put to death; and that done, gave audience to the Athenians, who filled the place with noise and tumult, accusing and recriminating on one another, till at last Agnonides came forward, and requested they might all be shut up together in one cage, and conveyed to Athens, there to decide the controversy. At that the king could not forbear smiling, but the company that attended, for their own amusement, Macedonians and strangers, were eager to hear the altercation, and made signs to the delegates to go on with their case at once. But it was no sort of fair hearing. Polysperchon frequently interrupted Phocion, till at last Phocion struck his staff on the grounds and declined to speak further. And when Hegemon said, Polysperchon himself could bear witness to his affection for the people, Polysperchon called out fiercely, " Give over slandering me to the king," and the king starting up was about to have run him through with his javelin, but Polysperchon interposed and hindered him; so that the assembly dissolved.

Phocion, then, and those about him, were seized; those of his friends that were not immediately by him, on seeing this, hid their faces, and saved themselves by flight. The rest Clitus took and brought to Athens, to be submitted to trial; but, in truth, as men already sentenced to die. The manner of conveying them was indeed extremely moving; they were carried in chariots through the Ceramicus, straight to the place of judication, where Clitus secured them till they had convoked an assembly of the people, which was open to all comers, neither foreigners, nor slaves, nor those who had been punished with disfranchisement being refused admittance, but all alike, both men and women, being allowed to come into the court, and even upon the place of speaking. So having read the king's letters, in which he declared he was satisfied himself that these men were traitors, however, they being a free city, he willingly accorded them the grace of trying and judging them according to their own laws, Clitus brought in his prisoners. Every respectable citizen, at the sight of Phocion, covered up his face, and stooped down to conceal his tears. And one of them had the courage to say, that since the king had committed so important a cause to the judgment of the people, it would be well that the strangers, and those of servile condition, should withdraw. But the populace would not endure it, crying out they were oligarchs, and enemies to the liberty of the people, and deserved to be stoned; after which no man durst offer anything further in Phocion's behalf. He was himself with difficulty heard at all, when he put the question, " Do you wish to put us to death lawfully or unlawfully? " Some answered, " According to law." He replied, " How can you, except we have a fair hearing? " But when they were deaf to all he said, approaching nearer, " As to myself," said he, " I admit my guilt, and pronounce my public conduct to have deserved sentence of death. But why, O men of Athens, kill others who have offended in nothing? " The rabble cried out they were his friends, that was enough. Phocion therefore drew back, and said no more.

Then Agnonides read the bill, in accordance with which the people should decide by show of hands whether they judged them guilty, and if so it should be found, the penalty should be death. When this had been read out, some desired it might be added to the sentence, that Phocion should be tortured also, and the rack should be produced with the executioners. But Agnonides perceiving even Clitus to dislike this, and himself thinking it horrid and barbarous, said, " When we catch that slave, Callimedon, men of Athens, we will put him to the rack, but I shall make no motion of the kind in Phocion's case." Upon which one of the better citizens remarked, he was quite right; " If he should torture Phocion, what could we do to you? " So the form of the bill was approved of, and the show of hands called for; upon which, not one man retaining his seat, but all rising up, and some with garlands on their heads, they condemned them all to death.

There were present with Phocion, Nicocles, Thudippus, Hegemon, and Pythocles. Demetrius the Phalerian, Callimedon, Charicles, and some others, were included in the condemnation, being absent.

After the assembly was dismissed, they were carried to the prison; the rest with cries and lamentations, their friends and relatives following and clinging about them, but Phocion looking (as men observed with astonishment at his calmness and magnanimity), just the same as when he had been used to return to his home attended, as general, from the assembly. His enemies ran along by his side, reviling and abusing him. And one of them coming up to him, spat in his face; at which Phocion, turning to the officers, only said, "You should stop this indecency." Thudippus, on their reaching the prison, when he observed the executioner tempering the poison and preparing it for them, gave away to his passion, and began to bemoan his condition and the hard measure he received, thus unjustly to suffer with Phocion. "You cannot be contented," said he, "to die with Phocion?" One of his friends that stood by, asked him if he wished to have anything said to his son. "Yes, by all means," said he, "bid him bear no grudge against the Athenians." Then Nicocles, the dearest and most faithful of his friends, begged to be allowed to drink the poison first. "My friend," said he, "you ask what I am loath and sorrowful to give, but as I never yet in all my life was so thankless as to refuse you, I must gratify you in this also." After they had all drunk of it, the poison ran short; and the executioner refused to prepare more, except they would pay him twelve drachmas, to defray the cost of the quantity required. Some delay was made, and time spent, when Phocion called one of his friends, and observing that a man could not even die at Athens without paying for it, requested him to give the sum.

It was the nineteenth day of the month Munychion, on which it was the usage to have a solemn procession in the city, in honour of Jupiter. The horsemen, as they passed by, some of them threw away their garlands, others stopped, weeping, and casting sorrowful looks towards the prison doors, and all the citizens whose minds were not absolutely debauched by spite and passion, or who had any humanity left, acknowledged it to have been most impiously done, not, at least, to let that day pass, and the city so be kept pure from death and a public execution at the solemn festival. But as if this triumph had been insufficient, the malice of Phocion's enemies went yet further; his dead body was excluded from burial within the boundaries of the country, and none of the Athenians could light a funeral pile to burn the corpse; neither durst any of his friends venture to concern themselves about it. A certain Conopion, a man who used to do these offices for hire, took the body and carried it beyond Eleusis, and procuring fire from over the frontier of Megara, burned it. Phocion's wife, with her servant-maids, being present and assisting at the solemnity, raised there an empty tomb, and performed the customary libations, and gathering up the bones in her lap, and bringing them home by night, dug a place for them by the fireside in her house, saying, "Blessed hearth, to your custody I commit the remains of a good and brave man, and, I beseech you, protect and restore them to the sepulchre of his fathers, when the Athenians return to their right minds."

And, indeed, a very little time and their own sad experience soon informed them what an excellent governor, and how great an example and guardian of justice and of temperance they had bereft themselves of. And now they decreed him a statue of brass, and his bones to be buried honourably at the public charge; and for his accusers, Agnonides they took themselves, and caused him to be put to death. Epicurus and Demophilus, who fled from the city for fear, his son met with, and took his revenge upon them. This son of his, we are told, was in general of an indifferent character, and once when enamoured of a slave girl kept by a common harlot merchant, happened to hear Theodorus, the atheist, arguing in the Lyceum, that if it were a good and honourable thing to buy the freedom of a friend in the masculine, why not also of a friend in the feminine, if, for example, a master, why not also a mistress? So putting the good argument and his passion together, he went off and purchased the girl's freedom. The death which was thus suffered by Phocion revived among the Greeks the memory of that of Socrates, the two cases being so similar, and both equally the sad fault and misfortune of the city.

## CATO THE YOUNGER

THE family of Cato derived its first lustre from his great-grandfather Cato, whose virtue gained him such great reputation and authority among the Romans, as we have written in his life.

This Cato was, by the loss of both his parents, left an orphan, together with his brother Cæpio, and his sister Porcia. He had also a half-sister, Servilia, by the mother's side. As these lived together, and were bred up in the house of Livius Drusus, their uncle by the mother, who, at that time, had a great share in the government, being a very eloquent speaker, a man of the greatest temperance, and yielding in dignity to none of the Romans.

It is said of Cato that even from his infancy, in his speech, his countenance, and all his childish pastimes, he discovered an inflexible temper, unmoved by any passion, and firm in everything. He was resolute in his purposes, much beyond the strength of his age, to go through with whatever he undertook. He was rough and ungentle toward those that flattered him, and still more unyielding to those who threatened him. It was difficult to excite him to laughter, his countenance seldom relaxed even into a smile; he was not quickly or easily provoked to anger, but if once incensed, he was no less difficult to pacify.

When he began to learn, he proved dull, and slow to apprehend, but of what he once received, his memory was remarkably tenacious. And such, in fact, we find generally to be the course of nature; men of fine genius are readily reminded of things, but those who receive with most pains and difficulty, remember best; every new thing they learn, being, as it were, burnt and branded in on their minds. Cato's natural stubbornness and slowness to be persuaded may also have made it more difficult for him to be taught. For to learn is to submit to have something done to one; and persuasion comes soonest to those who have least strength to resist it. Hence young men are sooner persuaded than those that are more in years, and sick men, than those that are well in health. In fine, where there is least previous doubt and difficulty, the new impression is most easily accepted. Yet Cato, they say, was very obedient to his preceptor, and would do whatever he was commanded; but he would also ask the reason, and inquire the cause of everything.

And, indeed, his teacher was a very well-bred man, more ready to instruct than to beat his scholars. His name was Sarpedon.

When Cato was a child, the allies of the Romans sued to be made free citizens of Rome. Pompædius Silo, one of their deputies, a brave soldier and a man of great repute, who had contracted a friendship with Drusus, lodged at his house for several days, in which time being grown familiar with the children, " Well," said he to them, " will you entreat your uncle to befriend us in our business? " Cæpio, smiling, assented, but Cato made no answer, only he looked steadfastly and fiercely on the strangers. Then said Pompædius, " And you, young sir, what say you to us? will not you, as well as your brother, intercede with your uncle in our behalf? " And when Cato continued to give no answer, by his silence and his countenance seeming to deny their petition, Pompædius snatched him up to the window as if he would throw him out, and told him to consent, or he would fling him down, and, speaking in a harsher tone, held his body out of the window, and shook him several times. When Cato had suffered this a good while, unmoved and unalarmed, Pompædius, setting him down, said in an undervoice to his friend, " What a blessing for Italy that he is but a child! If he were a man, I believe we should not gain one voice among the people." Another time, one of his relations, on his birthday, invited Cato and some other children to supper, and some of the company diverted themselves in a separate part of the house, and were at play, the elder and the younger together, their sport being to act the pleadings before the judges, accusing one another, and carrying away the condemned to prison. Among these a very beautiful young child, being bound and carried by a bigger into prison, cried out to Cato, who seeing what was going on, presently ran to the door, and thrusting away those who stood there as a guard, took out the child, and went home in anger, followed by some of his companions.

Cato at length grew so famous among them, that when Sylla designed to exhibit the sacred game of young men riding courses on horseback, which they called Troy, having gotten together the youth of good birth, he appointed two for their leaders. One of them they accepted for his mother's sake, being the son of Metella, the wife of Sylla; but as for the other, Sextus, the nephew of Pompey, they would not be led by him, nor exercise under him. Then Sylla asking whom they would have, they all cried out, Cato; and Sextus willingly yielded the honour to him, as the more worthy.

Sylla, who was a friend of their family, sent at times for Cato and his brother to see them and talk with them; a favour which he showed to very few, after gaining his great power and authority. Sarpedon, full of the advantage it would be, as well for the honour as the safety of his scholars, would often bring Cato to wait upon Sylla at his house, which, for the multitude of those that were being carried off in custody, and tormented there, looked like a place of execution. Cato was then in his fourteenth year, and seeing the heads of men said to be of great distinction brought thither, and observing the secret sighs of those that were present, he asked his preceptor, "Why does nobody kill this man?" "Because," said he, "they fear him, child, more than they hate him." "Why, then," replied Cato, "did you not give me a sword, that I might stab him, and free my country from this slavery?" Sarpedon hearing this, and at the same time seeing his countenance swelling with anger and determination, took care thenceforward to watch him strictly, lest he should hazard any desperate attempt.

While he was yet very young, to some that asked him whom he loved best, he answered, his brother. And being asked, whom next, he replied, his brother, again. So likewise the third time, and still the same, till they left off to ask any further. As he grew in age, this love to his brother grew yet the stronger. When he was about twenty years old, he never supped, never went out of town, nor into the forum, without Cæpio. But when his brother made use of precious ointments and perfumes, Cato declined them; and he was, in all his habits, very strict and austere, so that when Cæpio was admired for his moderation and temperance, he would acknowledge that indeed he might be accounted such, in comparison with some other men, "but," said he, "when I compare myself with Cato, I find myself scarcely different from Sippius," one at that time notorious for his luxurious and effeminate living.

Cato being made priest of Apollo, went to another house, took his portion of their paternal inheritance, amounting to a hundred and twenty talents, and began to live yet more strictly than before. Having gained the intimate acquaintance of Antipater the Tyrian, the Stoic philosopher, he devoted himself to the study, above everything, of moral and political doctrine. And though possessed, as it were, by a kind of inspiration for the pursuit of every virtue, yet what most of all virtue and excellence fixed his affection was that steady and inflexible justice which is not to be wrought upon by favour or compassion. He learned also the art of speaking and debating in public, thinking that political philosophy, like a great city, should maintain for its security the military and warlike element. But he would never recite his exercises before company, nor was he ever heard to declaim. And to one that told him men blamed his silence, "But I hope not my life," he replied, "I will begin to speak, when I have that to say which had not better be unsaid."

The great Porcian Hall, as it was called, had been built and dedicated to the public use by the old Cato, when ædile. Here the tribunes of the people used to transact their business, and because one of the pillars was thought to interfere with the convenience of their seats, they deliberated whether it were best to remove it to another place, or to take it away. This occasion first drew Cato, much against his will, into the forum; for he opposed the demand of the tribunes, and in so doing gave a specimen both of his courage and his powers of speaking, which gained him great admiration. His speech had nothing youthful or refined in it, but was straightforward, full of matter, and rough, at the same time that there was a certain grace about his rough statements which won the attention; and the speaker's character, showing itself in all he said, added to his severe language something that excited feelings of natural pleasure and interest. His voice was full and sounding, and sufficient to be heard by so great a multitude, and its vigour and capacity of endurance quite indefatigable, for he often would speak a whole day and never stop.

When he had carried this cause, he betook himself again to study and retirement. He employed himself in inuring his body to labour and violent exercise; and habituated himself to go bareheaded in the hottest and the coldest weather, and to walk on foot at all seasons. When he went on a journey with any of his friends, though they were on horseback and he on foot, yet he would often join now one, then another, and converse with them on the way. In sickness the patience he showed in supporting, and the abstinence he used for curing, his distempers were admirable. When he had an ague, he would remain alone, and suffer nobody to see him, till he began to recover, and found the fit was over. At supper, when he threw dice for the choice of dishes, and lost, and the company offered him nevertheless his choice, he declined to dispute, as he said, the decision of Venus. At first, he was wont to drink only once after supper, and then go away; but in process of time he grew to drink more,

insomuch that oftentimes he would continue till morning.   This
his friends explained by saying that state affairs and public
business took him up all day, and being desirous of knowledge,
he liked to pass the night at wine in the conversation of philosophers.   Hence, upon one Memmius saying in public, that
Cato spent whole nights in drinking, "You should add,"
replied Cicero, "that he spends whole days in gambling."   And
in general Cato esteemed the customs and manners of men at
that time so corrupt, and a reformation in them so necessary,
that he thought it requisite, in many things, to go contrary to
the ordinary way of the world.   Seeing the lightest and gayest
purple was then most in fashion, he would always wear that
which was the nearest black; and he would often go out of
doors, after his morning meal, without either shoes or tunic;
not that he sought vain-glory from such novelties, but he would
accustom himself to be ashamed only of what deserves shame,
and to despise all other sorts of disgrace.

The estate of one Cato, his cousin, which was worth one
hundred talents, falling to him, he turned it all into ready
money, which he kept by him for any of his friends that should
happen to want, to whom he would lend it without interest.
And for some of them, he suffered his own land and his slaves
to be mortgaged to the public treasury.

When he thought himself of an age fit to marry, having never
before known any woman, he was contracted to Lepida, who
had before been contracted to Metellus Scipio, but on Scipio's
own withdrawal from it, the contract had been dissolved, and
she left at liberty.   Yet Scipio afterwards repenting himself, did
all he could to regain her, before the marriage with Cato was
completed, and succeeded in so doing.   At which Cato was
violently incensed, and resolved at first to go to law about it;
but his friends persuaded him to the contrary.   However, he
was so moved by the heat of youth and passion that he wrote
a quantity of iambic verses against Scipio, in the bitter, sarcastic
style of Archilochus, without, however, his licence and scurrility.
After this, he married Atilia, the daughter of Soranus, the first
but not the only woman he ever knew, less happy thus far than
Lælius, the friend of Scipio, who in the whole course of so long
a life never knew but the one woman, to whom he was united in
his first and only marriage.

In the war of the slaves, which took its name from Spartacus,
their ringleader, Gellius was general, and Cato went a volunteer,
for the sake of his brother Cæpio, who was a tribune in the army.

TALENT.  Fr Talent, L. Talentum
           from Gr ΤΑΛΑΝΤΟΝ
               fr root tal - akin Skr TUL - t.lift
An ancient weight + denomination of moneys

Cato could find here no opportunity to show his zeal or exercise his valour, on account of the ill conduct of the general. However, amidst the corruption and disorders of that army, he showed such a love of discipline, so much bravery upon occasion, and so much courage and wisdom in everything, that it appeared he was in no way inferior to the old Cato. Gellius offered him great rewards, and would have decreed him the first honours; which, however, he refused, saying he had done nothing that deserved them. This made him be thought a man of strange and eccentric temper.

There was a law passed, moreover, that the candidates who stood for any office should not have prompters in their canvass, to tell them the names of the citizens; and Cato, when he sued to be elected tribune, was the only man that obeyed this law. He took great pains to learn by his own knowledge to salute those he had to speak with, and to call them by their names; yet even those who praised him for this, did not do so without some envy and jealousy, for the more they considered the excellence of what he did, the more they were grieved at the difficulty they found to do the like.

Being chosen tribune, he was sent into Macedon to join Rubrius, who was general there. It is said that his wife showing much concern, and weeping at his departure, Munatius, one of Cato's friends, said to her, " Do not trouble yourself, Atilia, I will engage to watch over him for you." " By all means," replied Cato; and when they had gone one day's journey together, " Now," said he to Munatius, after they had supped, " that you may be sure to keep your promise to Atilia, you must not leave me day nor night," and from that time, he ordered two beds to be made in his own chamber, that Munatius might lie there. And so he continued to do, Cato making it his jest to see that he was always there. There went with him fifteen slaves, two freedmen, and four of his friends; these rode on horseback, but Cato always went on foot, yet would he keep by them, and talk with each of them in turn as they went.

When he came to the army, which consisted of several legions, the general gave him the command of one; and as he looked upon it as a small matter, and not worthy a commander, to give evidence of his own signal valour, he resolved to make his soldiers, as far as he could, like himself, not, however, in this relaxing the terrors of his office, but associating reason with his authority. He persuaded and instructed every one in particular, and bestowed rewards or punishments according to desert; and at

length his men were so well disciplined, that it was hard to say
whether they were more peaceable or more warlike, more valiant
or more just; they were alike formidable to their enemies and
courteous to their allies, fearful to do wrong, and forward to gain
honour. And Cato himself acquired in the fullest measure, what
it had been his least desire to seek, glory and good repute; he
was highly esteemed by all men, and entirely beloved by the
soldiers. Whatever he commanded to be done, he himself took
part in the performing; in his apparel, his diet, and mode of
travelling, he was more like a common soldier than an officer;
but in character, high purpose, and wisdom, he far exceeded all
that had the names and titles of commanders, and he made himself, without knowing it, the object of general affection. For the
true love of virtue is in all men produced by the love and respect
they bear to him that teaches it; and those who praise good men,
yet do not love them, may respect their reputation, but do not
really admire, and will never imitate their virtue.

There dwelt at that time in Pergamus, Athenodorus, surnamed
Cordylio, a man of high repute for his knowledge of the Stoic
philosophy, who was now grown old, and had always steadily
refused the friendship and acquaintance of princes and great
men. Cato understood this; so that imagining he should not be
able to prevail with him by sending or writing, and being by the
laws allowed two months' absence from the army, he resolved
to go into Asia to see him in person, trusting to his own good
qualities not to lose his labour. And when he had conversed
with him, and succeeded in persuading him out of his former
resolutions, he returned and brought him to the camp as joyful
and as proud of this victory as if he had done some heroic exploit,
greater than any of those of Pompey or Lucullus, who with
their armies at that time were subduing so many nations and
kingdoms.

While Cato was yet in the service, his brother, on a journey
towards Asia, fell sick at Ænus in Thrace, letters with intelligence of which were immediately despatched to him. The
sea was very rough, and no convenient ship of any size to be
had; so Cato getting into a small trading-vessel, with only two
of his friends, and three servants, set sail from Thessalonica, and
having very narrowly escaped drowning, he arrived at Ænus
just as Cæpio expired. Upon this occasion, he was thought to
have showed himself more a fond brother than a philosopher,
not only in the excess of his grief, bewailing and embracing the
dead body, but also in the extravagant expenses of the funeral,

the vast quantity of rich perfumes and costly garments which were burnt with the corpse, and the monument of Thasian marble, which he erected, at the cost of eight talents, in the public place of the town of Ænus. For there were some who took upon them to cavil at all this, as not consistent with his usual calmness and moderation, not discerning that though he were steadfast, firm, and inflexible to pleasure, fear or foolish entreaties, yet he was full of natural tenderness and brotherly affection. Divers of the cities and princes of the country sent him many presents, to honour the funeral of his brother; but he took none of their money, only the perfumes and ornaments he received, and paid for them also. And afterwards, when the inheritance was divided between him and Cæpio's daughter, he did not require any portion of the funeral expenses to be discharged out of it. Notwithstanding this, it has been affirmed that he made his brother's ashes be passed through a sieve, to find the gold that was melted down when burnt with the body. But he who made this statement appears to have anticipated an exemption for his pen, as much as for his sword, from all question and criticism.

The time of Cato's service in the army being expired, he received, at his departure, not only the prayers and praises, but the tears and embraces of the soldiers, who spread their clothes at his feet and kissed his hand as he passed, an honour which the Romans at that time scarcely paid even to a very few of their generals and commanders-in-chief. Having left the army, he resolved, before he would return home and apply himself to state affairs, to travel in Asia, and observe the manners, the customs, and the strength of every province. He was also unwilling to refuse the kindness of Deiotarus, King of Galatia, who having had great familiarity and friendship with his father, was very desirous to receive a visit from him. Cato's arrangements in his journey were as follows. Early in the morning he sent out his baker and his cook towards the place where he designed to stay the next night; these went soberly and quietly into the town, in which, if there happened to be no friend or acquaintance of Cato or his family, they provided for him in an inn, and gave no disturbance to anybody; but if there were no inn, then and in this case only, they went to the magistrates, and desiring them to help them to lodgings, took without complaint whatever was allotted to them. His servants thus behaving themselves towards the magistrates, without noise and threatening, were often discredited, or neglected by them, so that Cato many times arrived and found nothing provided for him. And it was all the worse when he appeared himself; still less account was taken of him. When they saw him sitting, without saying anything, on his baggage, they set him down at once as a person of no consequence, who did not venture to make any demand. Sometimes, on such occasions, he would call them to him and tell them, " Foolish people, lay aside this inhospitality. All your visitors will not be Catos. Use your courtesy, to take off the sharp edge of power. There are men enough who desire but a pretence, to take from you by force, what you give with such reluctance."

While he travelled in this manner, a diverting accident befell him in Syria. As he was going into Antioch, he saw a great multitude of people outside the gates, ranged in order on either side the way; here the young men with long cloaks, there the children decently dressed; others wore garlands and white garments who were the priests and magistrates. Cato imagining all this could mean nothing but a display in honour of his reception, began to be angry with his servants, who had been sent before, for suffering it to be done; then making his friends alight, he walked along with them on foot. As soon as he came near the gate, an elderly man, who seemed to be master of these ceremonies, with a wand and a garland in his hand, came up to Cato, and without saluting him, asked him where he had left Demetrius, and how soon he thought he would be there. This Demetrius was Pompey's servant, and as at this time the whole world, so to say, had its eyes fixed upon Pompey, this man also was highly honoured, on account of his influence with his master. Upon this Cato's friends fell into such violent laughter, that they could not restrain themselves while they passed through the crowd; and he himself, ashamed and distressed, uttered the words, " Unfortunate city! " and said no more. Afterwards, however, it always made him laugh, when he either told the story or was otherwise reminded of it.

Pompey himself shortly after made the people ashamed of their ignorance and folly in thus neglecting him, for Cato, coming in his journey to Ephesus, went to pay his respects to him, who was the elder man, had gained much honour, and was then general of a great army. Yet Pompey would not receive him sitting, but as soon as he saw him, rose up, and going to meet him, as the more honourable person, gave him his hand, and embraced him with great show of kindness. He said much in commendation of his virtue both at that time when receiving him, and also yet more after he had withdrawn. So that now all men began at once to display their respect for Cato, and discovered in him the very same things for which they despised him before, an admirable mildness of temper and greatness of spirit. And indeed the civility that Pompey himself showed him appeared to come from one that rather respected than loved him; and the general opinion was, that while Cato was there he paid him admiration, but was not sorry when he was gone. For when other young men came to see him he usually urged and entreated them to continue with him. Now he did not at all invite Cato to stay, but as if his own power were lessened by the other's presence, he very willingly allowed him to take his leave. Yet to Cato alone, of all those who went for Rome, he recommended his children and his wife, who was indeed connected by relationship with Cato.

After this, all the cities through which he passed strove and emulated each other in showing him respect and honour. Feasts and entertainments were made for his reception, so that he bade his friends keep strict watch and take care of him, lest he should end by making good what was said by Curio, who though he were his familiar friend, yet disliking the austerity of his temper, asked him one day if, when he left the army, he designed to see Asia, and Cato answering, "Yes, by all means." "You do well," replied Curio, "you will bring back with you a better temper and pleasanter manners;" pretty nearly the very words he used.

Deiotarus, being now an old man, had sent for Cato, to recommend his children and family to his protection; and as soon as he came, brought him presents of all sorts of things, which he begged and entreated him to accept. And his importunities displeased Cato so much, that though he came but in the evening, he stayed only that night, and went away early the next morning. After he was gone one day's journey, he found at Pessinus a yet greater quantity of presents provided for him there, and also letters from Deiotarus entreating him to receive them, or at least to permit his friends to take them, who for his sake deserved some gratification, and could not have much done for them out of Cato's own means. Yet he would not suffer it, though he saw some of them very willing to receive such gifts, and ready to complain of his severity; but he answered, that corruption would never want pretence, and his friends should share with him in whatever he should justly and honestly obtain, and so returned the presents to Deiotarus.

When he took ship for Brundusium, his friends would have persuaded him to put his brother's ashes into another vessel; but he said he would sooner part with his life than leave them, and so set sail. And as it chanced, he, we are told, had a very dangerous passage, though others at the same time went over safely enough.

After he was returned to Rome, he spent his time for the most part either at home, in conversation with Athenodorus, or at the forum, in the service of his friends. Though it was now the time that he should become quæstor, he would not stand for the place till he had studied the laws relating to it, and by inquiry from persons of experience, had attained a distinct understanding of the duty and authority belonging to it. With this knowledge, as soon as he came into the office, he made a great reformation among the clerks and under-officers of the treasury, people who had long practice and familiarity in all the public records and the laws, and, when new magistrates came in year by year so ignorant and unskilful as to be in absolute need of others to teach them what to do, did not submit and give way, but kept the power in their own hands, and were in effect the treasurers themselves. Till Cato, applying himself roundly to the work, showed that he possessed not only the title and honour of a quæstor, but the knowledge and understanding and full authority of his office. So that he used the clerks and under-officers like servants as they were, exposing their corrupt practices, and instructing their ignorance. Being bold, impudent fellows, they flattered the other quæstors his colleagues, and by their means endeavoured to maintain an opposition against him. But he convicted the chiefest of them of a breach of trust in the charge of an inheritance, and turned him out of his place. A second he brought to trial for dishonesty, who was defended by Lutatius Catulus, at that time censor, a man very considerable for his office, but yet more for his character, as he was eminent above all the Romans of that age for his reputed wisdom and integrity. He was also intimate with Cato, and much commended his way of living. So perceiving he could not bring off his client, if he stood a fair trial, he openly began to beg him off. Cato objected to his doing this. And when he continued still to be importunate, " It would be shameful, Catulus," he said, " that the censor, the judge of all our lives, should incur the dishonour of removal by our officers." At this expression, Catulus looked as if he would have made some answer; but he said nothing, and either through anger or shame went away silent, and out of countenance. Nevertheless, the man was not found guilty, for the voices that acquitted him were but one in number less than those that condemned him, and Marcus Lollius, one of Cato's colleagues, who was absent by reason of sickness, was sent for by Catulus, and entreated to come and save the man. So Lollius was brought into court in a chair, and gave his voice also for acquitting him. Yet Cato never after made use of that clerk, and never paid him his salary, nor would he make any account of the vote given by Lollius. Having thus humbled the clerks, and brought them to be at command, he made use of the books and registers as he thought fit, and in a little while gained the treasury a higher name than the senate house itself; and all men said, Cato had made the office of a quæstor equal to the dignity of a consul. When he found many indebted to the state upon old accounts, and the state also in debt to many private persons, he took care that the public might no longer either do or suffer wrong; he strictly and punctually exacted what was due to the treasury, and as freely and speedily paid all those to whom it was indebted. So that the people were filled with sentiments of awe and respect, on seeing those made to pay, who thought to have escaped with their plunder, and others receiving all their due, who despaired of getting anything. And whereas usually those who brought false bills and pretended orders of the senate, could through favour get them accepted, Cato would never be so imposed upon; and in the case of one particular order, on the question arising whether it had passed the senate, he would not believe a great many witnesses that attested it, nor would admit of it, till the consuls came and affirmed it upon oath.

There were at that time a great many whom Sylla had made use of as his agents in the proscription, and to whom he had for their service in putting men to death, given twelve thousand drachmas apiece. These men everybody hated as wicked and polluted wretches, but nobody durst be revenged upon them. Cato called every one to account, as wrongfully possessed of the public money, and exacted it of them, and at the same time sharply reproved them for their unlawful and impious actions. After these proceedings they were presently accused of murder, and being already in a manner prejudged as guilty, they were easily found so, and accordingly suffered; at which the whole people rejoiced and thought themselves now to see the old tyranny finally abolished, and Sylla himself, so to say, brought to punishment.

Cato's assiduity also, and indefatigable diligence, won very much upon the people. He always came first of any of his colleagues to the treasury, and went away the last. He never missed any assembly of the people, or sitting of the senate; being always anxious and on the watch for those who lightly, or as a matter of interest, passed votes in favour of this or that person, for remitting debts or granting away customs that were owing to the state. And at length, having kept the exchequer pure and clear from base informers, and yet having filled it with treasure, he made it appear that the state might be rich without oppressing the people. At first he excited feelings of dislike and irritation in some of his colleagues, but after a while they were well contented with him, since he was perfectly willing that they should cast all the odium on him, when they declined to gratify their friends with the public money, or to give dishonest judgments in passing their accounts; and when hard-pressed by suitors, they could readily answer it was impossible to do anything unless Cato would consent. On the last day of his office, he was honourably attended to his house by almost all the people; but on the way he was informed that several powerful friends were in the treasury with Marcellus, using all their interest with him to pass a certain debt to the public revenue, as if it had been a gift. Marcellus had been one of Cato's friends from his childhood, and so long as Cato was with him, was one of the best of his colleagues in this office, but when alone, was unable to resist the importunity of suitors, and prone to do anybody a kindness. So Cato immediately turned back, and finding that Marcellus had yielded to pass the thing, he took the book, and while Marcellus silently stood by and looked on, struck it out. This done, he brought Marcellus out of the treasury, and took him home with him; who for all this, neither then, nor ever after, complained of him, but always continued his friendship and familiarity with him.

Cato, after he had laid down his office, yet did not cease to keep a watch upon the treasury. He had his servants who continually wrote out the details of the expenditure, and he himself kept always by him certain books, which contained the accounts of the revenue from Sylla's time to his own quæstorship, which he had bought for five talents.

He was always first at the senate, and went out last; and often, while the others were slowly collecting, he would sit and read by himself, holding his gown before his book. He was never once out of town when the senate was to meet. And when afterwards Pompey and his party, finding that he could never be either persuaded or compelled to favour their unjust designs, endeavoured to keep him from the senate, by engaging him in business for his friends, to plead their causes, or arbitrate in their differences, or the like, he quickly discovered the trick, and to defeat it, fairly told all his acquaintance that he would never meddle in any private business when the senate was assembled. Since it was not in the hope of gaining honour or riches, nor out of mere impulse, or by chance that he engaged himself in politics, but he undertook the service of the state as the proper business of an honest man, and therefore he thought himself obliged to be as constant to his public duty as the bee to the honeycomb. To this end, he took care to have his friends and correspondents everywhere, to send him reports of the edicts, decrees, judgments, and all the important proceedings that passed in any of the provinces. Once when Clodius, the seditious orator, to promote his violent and revolutionary projects, traduced to the people some of the priests and priestesses (among whom Fabia, sister to Cicero's wife, Terentia, ran great danger), Cato having boldly interfered, and having made Clodius appear so infamous that he was forced to leave the town, was addressed, when it was over, by Cicero, who came to thank him for what he had done. "You must thank the commonwealth," said he, for whose sake alone he professed to do everything. Thus he gained a great and wonderful reputation; so that an advocate in a cause, where there was only one witness against him, told the judges they ought not to rely upon a single witness, though it were Cato himself. And it was a sort of proverb with many people, if any very unlikely and incredible thing were asserted, to say, they would not believe it, though Cato himself should affirm it. One day a debauched and sumptuous liver talking in the senate about frugality and temperance, Anæus standing up, cried, "Who can endure this, sir, to have you feast like Crassus, build like Lucullus, and talk like Cato." So likewise those who were vicious and dissolute in their manners, yet affected to be grave and severe in their language, were in derision called Catos.

At first, when his friends would have persuaded him to stand to be tribune of the people, he thought it undesirable; for that the power of so great an office ought to be reserved, as the strongest medicines, for occasions of the last necessity. But afterwards in a vacation time, as he was going, accompanied with his books and philosophers, to Lucania, where he had lands with a pleasant residence, they met by the way a great many horses, carriages, and attendants, of whom they understood, that Metellus Nepos was going to Rome, to stand to be tribune of the people. Hereupon Cato stopped, and after a little pause, gave orders to return back immediately; at which the company seeming to wonder, " Don't you know," said he, " how dangerous of itself the madness of Metellus is? and now that he comes armed with the support of Pompey, he will fall like lightning on the state, and bring it to utter disorder; therefore this is no time for idleness and diversion, but we must go and prevent this man in his designs, or bravely die in defence of our liberty." Nevertheless, by the persuasion of his friends, he went first to his country-house, where he stayed but a very little time, and then returned to town.

He arrived in the evening, and went straight the next morning to the forum, where he began to solicit for the tribuneship, in opposition to Metellus. The power of this office consists rather in controlling than performing any business; for though all the rest except any one tribune should be agreed, yet his denial or intercession could put a stop to the whole matter. Cato, at first, had not many that appeared for him; but as soon as his design was known, all the good and distinguished persons of the city quickly came forward to encourage and support him, looking upon him, not as one that desired a favour of them, but one that proposed to do a great favour to his country and all honest men; who had many times refused the same office, when he might have had it without trouble, but now sought it with danger, that he might defend their liberty and their government. It is reported that so great a number flocked about him that he was like to be stifled amidst the press, and could scarce get through the crowd. He was declared tribune, with several others, among whom was Metellus.

When Cato was chosen into this office, observing that the election of consuls was become a matter of purchase, he sharply rebuked the people for this corruption, and in the conclusion of his speech protested he would bring to trial whomever he should find giving money, making an exception only in the case of Silanus, on account of their near connection, he having married Servilia, Cato's sister. He therefore did not prosecute him, but accused Lucius Murena, who had been chosen consul by corrupt means with Silanus. There was a law that the party accused might appoint a person to keep watch upon his accuser, that he might know fairly what means he took in preparing the accusation. He that was set upon Cato by Murena, at first

followed and observed him strictly, yet never found him dealing
any way unfairly or insidiously, but always generously and
candidly going on in the just and open methods of proceeding.
And he so admired Cato's great spirit, and so entirely trusted to
his integrity, that meeting him in the forum, or going to his
house, he would ask him if he designed to do anything that day
in order to the accusation, and if Cato said no, he went away,
relying on his word. When the cause was pleaded, Cicero, who
was then consul and defended Murena, took occasion to be
extremely witty and jocose, in reference to Cato, upon the Stoic
philosophers, and their paradoxes, as they call them, and so
excited great laughter among the judges; upon which Cato,
smiling, said to the standers-by, "What a pleasant consul
we have, my friends." Murena was acquitted, and afterwards
showed himself a man of no ill-feeling or want of sense; for when
he was consul, he always took Cato's advice in the most weighty
affairs and, during all the time of his office, paid him much
honour and respect. Of which not only Murena's prudence, but
also Cato's own behaviour, was the cause; for though he were
terrible and severe as to matters of justice, in the senate, and at
the bar, yet after the thing was over his manner to all men was
perfectly friendly and humane.

Before he entered on the office of tribune, he assisted Cicero,
at that time consul, in many contests that concerned his office,
but most especially in his great and noble acts at the time of
Catiline's conspiracy; which owed their last successful issue to
Cato. Catiline had plotted a dreadful and entire subversion of
the Roman state by sedition and open war, but being convicted
by Cicero, was forced to fly the city. Yet Lentulus and Cethegus
remained, with several others, to carry on the same plot; and
blaming Catiline, as one that wanted courage, and had been
timid and petty in his designs, they themselves resolved to set
the whole town on fire, and utterly to overthrow the empire,
rousing whole nations to revolt and exciting foreign wars. But
the design was discovered by Cicero (as we have written in his
life), and the matter brought before the senate. Silanus, who
spoke first, delivered his opinion, that the conspirators ought to
suffer the last of punishments, and was therein followed by all
who spoke after him; till it came to Cæsar, who being an excellent speaker, and looking upon all changes and commotions in
the state as materials useful for his own purposes, desired rather
to increase than extinguish them; and standing up, he made a
very merciful and persuasive speech, that they ought not to

suffer death without fair trial according to law, and moved that they might be kept in prison. Thus was the house almost wholly turned by Cæsar, apprehending also the anger of the people; insomuch that even Silanus retracted, and said he did not mean to propose death, but imprisonment, for that was the utmost a Roman could suffer.

Upon this they were all inclined to the milder and more merciful opinion, when Cato, standing up, began at once with great passion and vehemence to reproach Silanus for his change of opinion, and to attack Cæsar, who would, he said, ruin the commonwealth by soft words and popular speeches, and was endeavouring to frighten the senate, when he himself ought to fear, and be thankful, if he escaped unpunished or unsuspected, who thus openly and boldly dared to protect the enemies of the state, and while finding no compassion for his own native country, brought, with all its glories, so near to utter ruin, could yet be full of pity for those men who had better never have been born, and whose death must deliver the commonwealth from bloodshed and destruction. This only of all Cato's speeches, it is said, was preserved; for Cicero, the consul, had disposed in various parts of the senate-house, several of the most expert and rapid writers, whom he had taught to make figures comprising numerous words in a few short strokes; as up to that time they had not used those we call shorthand writers, who then, as it is said, established the first example of the art. Thus Cato carried it, and so turned the house again, that it was decreed the conspirators should be put to death.

Not to omit any small matters that may serve to show Cato's temper, and add something to the portraiture of his mind, it is reported, that while Cæsar and he were in the very heat, and the whole senate regarding them two, a little note was brought in to Cæsar which Cato declared to be suspicious, and urging that some seditious act was going on, bade the letter be read. Upon which Cæsar handed the paper to Cato; who, discovering it to be a love-letter from his sister Servilia to Cæsar, by whom she had been corrupted, threw it to him again, saying, "Take it, drunkard," and so went on with his discourse. And, indeed, it seems Cato had but ill-fortune in women; for this lady was ill-spoken of for her familiarity with Cæsar, and the other Servilia, Cato's sister also, was yet more ill-conducted; for being married to Lucullus, one of the greatest men in Rome, and having brought him a son, she was afterwards divorced for incontinency. But what was worst of all, Cato's own wife Atilia was not free from the same fault; and after she had borne him two children, he was forced to put her away for her misconduct. After that, he married Marcia, the daughter of Philippus, a woman of good reputation, who yet has occasioned much discourse; and the life of Cato, like a dramatic piece, has this one scene or passage full of perplexity and doubtful meaning.

It is thus related by Thrasea, who refers to the authority of Munatius, Cato's friend and constant companion. Among many that loved and admired Cato, some were more remarkable and conspicuous than others. Of these was Quintus Hortensius, a man of high repute and approved virtue, who desired not only to live in friendship and familiarity with Cato, but also to unite his whole house and family with him by some sort or other of alliance in marriage. Therefore he set himself to persuade Cato that his daughter Porcia, who was already married to Bibulus, and had borne him two children, might nevertheless be given to him, as a fair plot of land, to bear fruit also for him. " For," said he, " though this in the opinion of men may seem strange, yet in nature it is honest, and profitable for the public that a woman in the prime of her youth should not lie useless, and lose the fruit of her womb, nor, on the other side, should burden and impoverish one man, by bringing him too many children. Also by this communication of families among worthy men, virtue would increase, and be diffused through their posterity; and the commonwealth would be united and cemented by their alliances." Yet if Bibulus would not part with his wife altogether, he would restore her as soon as she had brought him a child, whereby he might be united to both their families. Cato answered, that he loved Hortensius very well, and much approved of uniting their houses, but he thought it strange to speak of marrying his daughter, when she was already given to another. Then Hortensius, turning the discourse, did not hesitate to speak openly and ask for Cato's own wife, for she was young and fruitful, and he had already children enough. Neither can it be thought that Hortensius did this, as imagining Cato did not care for Marcia; for, it is said, she was then with child. Cato, perceiving his earnest desire, did not deny his request, but said that Phillippus, the father of Marcia, ought also to be consulted. Philippus, therefore, being sent for, came; and finding they were well agreed, gave his daughter Marcia to Hortensius in the presence of Cato, who himself also assisted at the marriage. This was done at a later time, but since I was speaking of women, I thought it well to mention it now.

Lentulus and the rest of the conspirators were put to death; but Cæsar, finding so much insinuated and charged against him in the senate, betook himself to the people, and proceeded to stir up the most corrupt and dissolute elements of the state to form a party in his support. Cato, apprehensive of what might ensue, persuaded the senate to win over the poor and unprovided-for multitude by a distribution of corn, the annual charge of which amounted to twelve hundred and fifty talents. This act of humanity and kindness unquestionably dissipated the present danger. But Metellus, coming into his office of tribune, began to hold tumultuous assemblies, and had prepared a decree, that Pompey the Great should presently be called into Italy, with all his forces, to preserve the city from the danger of Catiline's conspiracy. This was the fair pretence; but the true design was to deliver all into the hands of Pompey, and to give him an absolute power. Upon this the senate was assembled, and Cato did not fall sharply upon Metellus, as he often did, but urged his advice in the most reasonable and moderate tone. At last he descended even to entreaty, and extolled the house of Metellus as having always taken part with the nobility. At this Metellus grew the more insolent, and despising Cato, as if he yielded and were afraid, let himself proceed to the most audacious menaces, openly threatening to do whatever he pleased in spite of the senate. Upon this Cato changed his countenance, his voice, and his language; and after many sharp expressions, boldly concluded that, while he lived, Pompey should never come armed into the city. The senate thought them both extravagant, and not well in their safe senses; for the design of Metellus seemed to be mere rage and frenzy, out of excess of mischief bringing all things to ruin and confusion, and Cato's virtue looked like a kind of ecstasy of contention in the cause of what was good and just.

But when the day came for the people to give their voices for the passing this decree, and Metellus beforehand occupied the forum with armed men, strangers, gladiators, and slaves, those that in hopes of change followed Pompey were known to be no small part of the people, and besides, they had great assistance from Cæsar, who was then prætor; and though the best and chiefest men of the city were no less offended at these proceedings than Cato, they seemed rather likely to suffer with him than able to assist him. In the meantime Cato's whole family were in extreme fear and apprehension for him; some of his friends neither ate nor slept all the night, passing the whole time in debating and perplexity; his wife and sisters also bewailed and lamented him. But he himself, void of all fear, and full of assurance, comforted and encouraged them by his own words and conversation with them. After supper he went to rest at his usual hour, and was the next day waked out of a profound sleep by Minucius Thermus, one of his colleagues. So soon as he was up, they two went together into the forum, accompanied by very few, but met by a great many, who bade them have a care of themselves. Cato, therefore, when he saw the temple of Castor and Pollux encompassed with armed men, and the steps guarded by gladiators, and at the top Metellus and Cæsar seated together, turning to his friends, " Behold," said he, " this audacious coward, who has levied a regiment of soldiers against one unarmed naked man; " and so he went on with Thermus. Those who kept the passages gave way to these two only, and would not let anybody else pass. Yet Cato taking Munatius by the hand, with much difficulty pulled him through along with him. Then going directly to Metellus and Cæsar, he sat himself down between them, to prevent their talking to one another, at which they were both amazed and confounded. And those of the honest party, observing the countenance, and admiring the high spirit and boldness of Cato, went nearer, and cried out to him to have courage, exhorting also one another to stand together, and not betray their liberty nor the defender of it.

Then the clerk took out the bill, but Cato forbade him to read it, whereupon Metellus took it, and would have read it himself, but Cato snatched the book away. Yet Metellus, having the decree by heart, began to recite it without book; but Thermus put his hand to his mouth, and stopped his speech. Metellus seeing them fully bent to withstand him, and the people cowed, and inclining to the better side, sent to his house for armed men. And on their rushing in with great noise and terror, all the rest dispersed and ran away, except Cato, who alone stood still, while the other party threw sticks and stones at him from above, until Murena, whom he had formerly accused, came up to protect him, and holding his gown before him, cried out to them to leave off throwing; and, in fine, persuading and pulling him along, he forced him into the temple of Castor and Pollux. Metellus, now seeing the place clear, and all the adverse party fled out of the forum, thought he might easily carry his point; so he commanded the soldiers to retire, and recommencing in an orderly manner, began to proceed to passing the decree. But the other side having recovered themselves, returned very boldly, and with loud shouting, insomuch that Metellus's adherents were

seized with a panic, supposing them to be coming with a reinforcement of armed men, fled every one out of the place.
They being thus dispersed, Cato came in again, and confirmed
the courage, and commended the resolution of the people; so
that now the majority were, by all means, for deposing Metellus
from his office. The senate also being assembled, gave orders
once more for supporting Cato, and resisting the motion, as of a
nature to excite sedition and perhaps civil war in the city.

But Metellus continued still very bold and resolute; and
seeing his party stood greatly in fear of Cato, whom they looked
upon as invincible, he hurried out of the senate into the forum,
and assembled the people, to whom he made a bitter and invidious speech against Cato, crying out, he was forced to fly from
his tyranny, and this conspiracy against Pompey; that the city
would soon repent their having dishonoured so great a man.
And from hence he started to go to Asia, with the intention, as
would be supposed, of laying before Pompey all the injuries that
were done him. Cato was highly extolled for having delivered
the state from this dangerous tribuneship, and having in some
measure defeated, in the person of Metellus, the power of Pompey;
but he was yet more commended when, upon the senate proceeding to disgrace Metellus and depose him from his office, he
altogether opposed and at length diverted the design. The
common people admired his moderation and humanity, in not
trampling wantonly on an enemy whom he had overthrown, and
wiser men acknowledged his prudence and policy in not ex-
asperating Pompey.

Lucullus soon after returned from the war in Asia, the finishing of which, and thereby the glory of the whole, was thus, in all
appearance, taken out of his hands by Pompey. And he was
also not far from losing his triumph, for Caius Memmius traduced
him to the people, and threatened to accuse him; rather, however, out of love to Pompey, than for any particular enmity to
him. But Cato, being allied to Lucullus, who had married his
sister Servilia, and also thinking it a great injustice, opposed
Memmius, thereby exposing himself to much slander and mis-
representation, insomuch that they would have turned him out
of his office, pretending that he used his power tyrannically.
Yet at length Cato so far prevailed against Memmius that he was
forced to let fall the accusations, and abandon the contest. And
Lucullus having thus obtained his triumph, yet more sedulously
cultivated Cato's friendship, which he looked upon as a great
guard and defence for him against Pompey's power.

And now Pompey also returning with glory from the war, and confiding in the good-will of the people, shown in their splendid reception of him, thought he should be denied nothing, and sent therefore to the senate to put off the assembly for the election of consuls, till he could be present to assist Piso, who stood for that office. To this most of the senators were disposed to yield; Cato only not so much thinking that this delay would be of great importance, but, desiring to cut down at once Pompey's high expectations and designs, withstood his request, and so overruled the senate that it was carrried against him. And this not a little disturbed Pompey, who found he should very often fail in his projects unless he could bring over Cato to his interest. He sent, therefore, for Munatius, his friend; and Cato having two nieces that were marriageable, he offered to marry the eldest himself, and take the youngest for his son. Some say they were not his nieces, but his daughters. Munatius proposed the matter to Cato, in presence of his wife and sisters; the women were full of joy at the prospect of an alliance with so great and important a person. But Cato, without delay or balancing, forming his decision at once, answered, " Go, Munatius, go and tell Pompey that Cato is not assailable on the side of the women's chamber; I am grateful indeed for the intended kindness, and so long as his actions are upright, I promise him a friendship more sure than any marriage alliance, but I will not give hostages to Pompey's glory against my country's safety." This answer was very much against the wishes of the women, and to all his friends it seemed somewhat harsh and haughty. But afterwards, when Pompey, endeavouring to get the consulship for one of his friends, gave pay to the people for their votes, and the bribery was notorious, the money being counted out in Pompey's own gardens, Cato then said to the women, they must necessarily have been concerned in the contamination of these misdeeds of Pompey, if they had been allied to his family; and they acknowledged that he did best in refusing it. Yet if we may judge by the event, Cato was much to blame in rejecting that alliance, which thereby fell to Cæsar. And then that match was made, which, uniting his and Pompey's power, had well-nigh ruined the Roman empire, and did destroy the commonwealth. Nothing of which, perhaps, had come to pass, but that Cato was too apprehensive of Pompey's least faults, and did not consider how he forced him into conferring on another man the opportunity of committing the greatest.

These things, however, were yet to come. Lucullus and

Pompey, meantime, had a great dispute concerning their orders and arrangements in Pontus, each endeavouring that his own ordinances might stand. Cato took part with Lucullus, who was manifestly suffering wrong; and Pompey, finding himself the weaker in the senate, had recourse to the people, and to gain votes he proposed a law for dividing the lands among the soldiers. Cato opposing him in this also made the bill be rejected. Upon this he joined himself with Clodius, at that time the most violent of all the demagogues, and entered also into friendship with Cæsar, upon an occasion of which also Cato was the cause. For Cæsar, returning from his government in Spain, at the same time sued to be chosen consul, and yet desired not to lose his triumph. Now the law requiring that those who stood for any office should be present, and yet that whoever expected a triumph should continue without the walls, Cæsar requested the senate that his friends might be permitted to canvass for him in his absence. Many of the senators were willing to consent to it, but Cato opposed it, and perceiving them inclined to favour Cæsar, spent the whole day in speaking, and so prevented the senate from coming to any conclusion. Cæsar, therefore, resolving to let fall his pretensions to the triumph, came into the town, and immediately made a friendship with Pompey, and stood for the consulship. As soon as he was declared consul elect, he married his daughter Julia to Pompey. And having thus combined themselves together against the commonwealth, the one proposed laws for dividing the lands among the poor people, and the other was present to support the proposals. Lucullus, Cicero, and their friends, joined with Bibulus, the other consul, to hinder their passing, and, foremost of them all, Cato, who already looked upon the friendship and alliance of Pompey and Cæsar as very dangerous, declared he did not so much dislike the advantage the people should get by this division of the lands, as he feared the reward these men would gain, by thus courting and cozening the people. And in this he gained over the senate to his opinion, as likewise many who were not senators, who were offended at Cæsar's ill conduct, that he, in the office of consul, should thus basely and dishonouraby flatter the people; practising, to win their favour, the same means that were wont to be used only by the most rash and rebellious tribunes. Cæsar, therefore, and his party, fearing they should not carry it by fair dealing, fell to open force. First a basket of dung was thrown upon Bibulus as he was going to the forum; then they set upon his lictors and broke their rods; at length several darts were thrown, and many men wounded; so that all that were against those laws fled out of the forum, the rest with what haste they could, and Cato, last of all, walking out slowly, often turning back and calling down vengeance upon them.

Thus the other party not only carried their point of dividing the lands, but also ordained that all the senate should swear to confirm this law, and to defend it against whoever should attempt to alter it, inflicting great penalties on those that should refuse the oath. All these senators, seeing the necessity they were in, took the oath, remembering the example of Metellus in old time, who, refusing to swear upon the like occasion, was forced to leave Italy. As for Cato, his wife and children with tears besought him, his friends and familiars persuaded and entreated him, to yield and take the oath; but he that principally prevailed with him was Cicero, the orator, who urged upon him that it was perhaps not even right in itself, that a private man should oppose what the public had decreed; that the thing being already past altering, it were folly and madness to throw himself into danger without the chance of doing his country any good; it would be the greatest of all evils to embrace, as it were, the opportunity to abandon the commonwealth, for whose sake he did everything, and to let it fall into the hands of those who designed nothing but its ruin, as if he were glad to be saved from the trouble of defending it. "For," said he, "though Cato have no need of Rome, yet Rome has need of Cato, and so likewise have all his friends." Of whom Cicero professed he himself was the chief, being at that time aimed at by Clodius, who openly threatened to fall upon him, as soon as ever he should get to be tribune. Thus Cato, they say, moved by the entreaties and the arguments of his friends, went unwillingly to take the oath, which he did the last of all, except only Favonius, one of his intimate acquaintance.

Cæsar, exalted with this success, proposed another law, for dividing almost all the country of Campania among the poor and needy citizens. Nobody durst speak against it but Cato, whom Cæsar therefore pulled from the rostra and dragged to prison: yet Cato did not even thus remit his freedom of speech, but as he went along continued to speak against the law, and advised the people to put down all legislators who proposed the like. The senate and the best of the citizens followed him with sad and dejected looks, showing their grief and indignation by their silence, so that Cæsar could not be ignorant how much they were offended; but for contention's sake he still persisted, expecting

Cato should either supplicate him, or make an appeal. But when he saw that he did not so much as think of doing either, ashamed of what he was doing and of what people thought of it, he himself privately bade one of the tribunes interpose and procure his release. However, having won the multitude by these laws and gratifications, they decreed that Cæsar should have the government of Illyricum, and all Gaul, with an army of four legions, for the space of five years, though Cato still cried out they were, by their own vote, placing a tyrant in their citadel. Publius Clodius, a patrician, who illegally became a plebeian, was declared tribune of the people, as he had promised to do all things according to their pleasure, on condition he might banish Cicero. And for consuls, they set up Calpurnius Piso, the father of Cæsar's wife, and Aulus Gabinius, one of Pompey's creatures, as they tell us, who best knew his life and manners.

Yet when they had thus firmly established all things, having mastered one part of the city by favour, and the other by fear, they themselves were still afraid of Cato, and remembered with vexation what pains and trouble their success over him had cost them, and indeed what shame and disgrace, when at last they were driven to use violence to him. This made Clodius despair of driving Cicero out of Italy while Cato stayed at home. Therefore, having first laid his design, as soon as he came into his office, he sent for Cato, and told him that he looked upon him as the most incorrupt of all the Romans, and was ready to show he did so. "For whereas," said he, "many have applied to be sent to Cyprus on the commission in the case of Ptolemy and have solicited to have the appointment, I think you alone are deserving of it, and I desire to give you the favour of the appointment." Cato at once cried out it was a mere design upon him, and no favour, but an injury. Then Clodius proudly and fiercely answered, "If you will not take it as a kindness, you shall go, though never so unwillingly;" and immediately going into the assembly of the people he made them pass a decree, that Cato should be sent to Cyprus. But they ordered him neither ship, nor soldier, nor any attendant, except two secretaries, one of whom was a thief and a rascal, and the other a retainer to Clodius. Besides, as if Cyprus and Ptolemy were not work sufficient, he was ordered also to restore the refugees of Byzantium. For Clodius was resolved to keep him far enough off whilst himself continued tribune.

Cato, being in this necessity of going away, advised Cicero, who was next to be set upon, to make no resistance, lest he should throw the state into civil war and confusion, but to give way to the times, and thus become once more the preserver of his country. He himself sent forward Canidius, one of his friends, to Cyprus, to persuade Ptolemy to yield, without being forced; which if he did, he should want neither riches nor honour, for the Romans would give him the priesthood of the goddess at Paphos. He himself stayed at Rhodes, making some preparations, and expecting an answer from Cyprus. In the meantime, Ptolemy, King of Egypt, who had left Alexandria, upon some quarrel between him and his subjects, and was sailing for Rome, in hopes that Pompey and Cæsar would send troops to restore him, in his way thither desired to see Cato, to whom he sent, supposing he would come to him. Cato had taken purging medicine at the time when the messenger came, and made answer, that Ptolemy had better come to him, if he thought fit. And when he came, he neither went forward to meet him, nor so much as rose up to him, but saluting him as an ordinary person, bade him sit down. This at once threw Ptolemy into some confusion, who was surprised to see such stern and haughty manners in one who made so plain and unpretending an appearance; but afterwards, when he began to talk about his affairs, he was no less astonished at the wisdom and freedom of his discourse. For Cato blamed his conduct, and pointed out to him what honour and happiness he was abandoning, and what humiliations and troubles he would run himself into; what bribery he must resort to, and what cupidity he would have to satisfy when he came to the leading men at Rome, whom all Egypt turned into silver would scarcely content. He therefore advised him to return home, and be reconciled to his subjects, offering to go along with him, and assist him in composing the differences. And by this language Ptolemy being brought to himself, as it might be out of a fit of madness or delirium, and discerning the truth and wisdom of what Cato said, resolved to follow his advice; but he was again over-persuaded by his friends to the contrary, and so, according to his first design, went to Rome. When he came there, and was forced to wait at the gate of one of the magistrates, he began to lament his folly in having rejected, rather, as it seemed to him, the oracle of a god than the advice merely of a good and wise man.

In the meantime, the other Ptolemy, in Cyprus, very luckily for Cato, poisoned himself. It was reported he had left great riches; therefore, Cato designing to go first to Byzantium, sent his nephew Brutus to Cyprus, as he would not wholly trust Canidius. Then, having reconciled the refugees and the people of Byzantium, he left the city in peace and quietness; and so sailed to Cyprus, where he found a royal treasure of plate, tables, precious stones and purple, all which was to be turned into ready money. And being determined to do everything with the greatest exactness, and to raise the price of everything to the utmost, to this end he was always present at selling the things, and went carefully into all the accounts. Nor would he trust to the usual customs of the market, but looked doubtfully upon all alike, the officers, criers, purchasers, and even his own friends; and so in fine he himself talked with the buyers, and urged them to bid high, and conducted in this manner the greatest part of the sales.

This mistrustfulness offended most of his friends, and in particular, Munatius, the most intimate of them all, became almost irreconcilable. And this afforded Cæsar the subject of his severest censures in the book he wrote against Cato. Yet Munatius himself relates, that the quarrel was not so much occasioned by Cato's mistrust, as by his neglect of him, and by his own jealousy of Canidius. For Munatius also wrote a book concerning Cato, which is the chief authority followed by Thrasea. Munatius says, that coming to Cyprus after the other, and having a very poor lodging provided for him, he went to Cato's house, but was not admitted, because he was engaged in private with Canidius; of which he afterwards complained in very gentle terms to Cato, but received a very harsh answer, that too much love, according to Theophrastus, often causes hatred; "and you," he said, " because you bear me much love, think you receive too little honour, and presently grow angry. I employ Canidius on account of his industry and his fidelity; he has been with me from the first, and I have found him to be trusted." These things were said in private between them two; but Cato afterwards told Canidius what had passed, on being informed of which, Munatius would no more go to sup with him, and when he was invited to give his counsel, refused to come. Then Cato threatened to seize his goods, as was the custom in the case of those who were disobedient; but Munatius not regarding his threats, returned to Rome, and continued a long time thus discontented. But afterwards, when Cato was come back also, Marcia, who as yet lived with him, contrived to have them both invited to sup together at the house of one Barca; Cato came in last of all, when the rest were laid down, and asked, where he should be. Barca answered him, where he pleased; then looking about, he said he would be near Munatius, and went and placed himself next to him; yet he showed him no other mark of kindness all the time they were at table together. But another time, at the entreaty of Marcia, Cato wrote to Munatius that he desired to speak with him. Munatius went to his house in the morning, and was kept by Marcia till all the company was gone; then Cato came, threw both his arms about him, and embraced him very kindly, and they were reconciled. I have the more fully related this passage, for that I think the manners and tempers of men are more clearly discovered by things of this nature, than by great and conspicuous actions.

Cato got together little less than seven thousand talents of silver; but apprehensive of what might happen in so long a voyage by sea, he provided a great many coffers that held two talents and five hundred drachmas apiece; to each of these he fastened a long rope, and to the other end of the rope a piece of cork, so that if the ship should miscarry, it might be discovered whereabout the chests lay under water. Thus all the money, except a very little, was safely transported. But he had made two books, in which all the accounts of his commission were carefully written out, and neither of these was preserved. For his freedman Philargyrus, who had the charge of one of them, setting sail from Cenchreæ, was lost, together with the ship and all her freight. And the other Cato himself kept safe till he came to Corcyra, but there he set up his tent in the market-place, and the sailors, being very cold in the night, made a great many fires, some of which caught the tents, so that they were burnt, and the book lost. And though he had brought with him several of Ptolemy's stewards, who could testify to his integrity, and stop the mouths of enemies and false accusers, yet the loss annoyed him, and he was vexed with himself about the matter, as he had designed them not so much for a proof of his own fidelity, as for a pattern of exactness to others.

The news did not fail to reach Rome that he was coming up the river. All the magistrates, the priests, and the whole senate, with great part of the people, went out to meet him; both the banks of the Tiber were covered with people; so that his entrance was in solemnity and honour not inferior to a triumph. But it was thought somewhat strange, and looked like wilfulness and pride, that when the consuls and prætors appeared, he did not disembark, nor stay to salute them, but rowed up the

stream in a royal galley of six banks of oars, and stopped not till
he brought his vessels to the dock. However, when the money
was carried through the streets, the people much wondered at
the vast quantity of it, and the senate being assembled, decreed
him in honourable terms an extraordinary prætorship, and also
the privilege of appearing at the public spectacles in a robe
faced with purple. Cato declined all these honours, but declaring what diligence and fidelity he had found in Nicias, the
steward of Ptolemy, he requested the senate to give him his
freedom.

Philippus, the father of Marcia, was that year consul, and the
authority and power of the office rested in a manner in Cato;
for the other consul paid him no less regard for his virtue's sake
than Philippus did on account of the connection between them.
And Cicero, now being returned from his banishment, into
which he was driven by Clodius, and having again obtained
great credit among the people, went, in the absence of Clodius,
and by force took away the records of his tribuneship, which
had been laid up in the capitol. Hereupon the senate was
assembled and Clodius complained of Cicero, who answered,
that Clodius was never legally tribune, and therefore whatever
he had done was void, and of no authority. But Cato interrupted him while he spoke, and at last standing up said, that
indeed he in no way justified or approved of Clodius's proceedings: but if they questioned the validity of what had been done
in his tribuneship, they might also question what himself had
done at Cyprus, for the expedition was unlawful, if he that sent
him had no lawful authority: for himself, he thought Clodius
was legally made tribune, who, by permission of the law, was
from a patrician adopted into a plebeian family; if he had done
ill in his office, he ought to be called to account for it; but the
authority of the magistracy ought not to suffer for the faults of
the magistrate. Cicero took this ill, and for a long time dis-
continued his friendship with Cato; but they were afterwards
reconciled.

Pompey and Crassus, by agreement with Cæsar, who crossed
the Alps to see them, had formed a design, that they two should
stand to be chosen consuls a second time, and when they should
be in their office, they would continue to Cæsar his government
for five years more, and take to themselves the greatest provinces, with armies and money to maintain them. This seemed
a plain conspiracy to subvert the constitution and parcel out
the empire. Several men of high character had intended to

stand to be consuls that year, but upon the appearance of these great competitors, they all desisted, except only Lucius Domitius, who had married Porcia, the sister of Cato, and was by him persuaded to stand it out, and not abandon such an undertaking, which, he said, was not merely to gain the consulship, but to save the liberty of Rome. In the meantime, it was the common topic among the more prudent part of the citizens, that they ought not to suffer the power of Pompey and Crassus to be united, which would then be carried beyond all bounds, and become dangerous to the state; that therefore one of them must be denied. For these reasons they took part with Domitius, whom they exhorted and encouraged to go on, assuring him that many who feared openly to appear for him, would privately assist him. Pompey's party fearing this, laid wait for Domitius, and set upon him as he was going before daylight, with torches, into the Field. First, he that bore the light next before Domitius was knocked down and killed; then several others being wounded, all the rest fled, except Cato and Domitius, whom Cato held, though himself were wounded in the arm, and crying out, conjured the others to stay, and not, while they had any breath, forsake the defence of their liberty against those tyrants, who plainly showed with what moderation they were likely to use the power which they endeavoured to gain by such violence. But at length Domitius, also, no longer willing to face the danger, fled to his own house, and so Pompey and Crassus were declared elected.

Nevertheless, Cato would not give over, but resolved to stand himself to be prætor that year, which he thought would be some help to him in his design of opposing them; that he might not act as a private man, when he was to contend with public magistrates. Pompey and Crassus apprehended this; and fearing that the office of prætor in the person of Cato might be equal in authority to that of consul, they assembled the senate unexpectedly, without giving notice to a great many of the senators, and made an order, that those who were chosen prætors should immediately enter upon their office, without attending the usual time, in which, according to law, they might be accused, if they had corrupted the people with gifts. When by this order they had got leave to bribe freely, without being called to account, they set up their own friends and dependants to stand for the prætorship, giving money, and watching the people as they voted. Yet the virtue and reputation of Cato was like to triumph over all these stratagems; for the people generally felt it to be shameful that a price should be paid for the rejection of Cato, who ought rather to be paid himself to take upon him the office. So he carried it by the voices of the first tribe. Hereupon Pompey immediately framed a lie, crying out, it thundered; and straight broke up the assembly, for the Romans religiously observed this as a bad omen, and never concluded any matter after it had thundered. Before the next time, they had distributed larger bribes, and driving also the best men out of the Field, by these foul means they procured Vatinius to be chosen prætor, instead of Cato. It is said, that those who had thus corruptly and dishonestly given their voices hurried, as if it were in flight, out of the Field. The others staying together, and exclaiming at the event, one of the tribunes continued the assembly, and Cato standing up, as it were by inspiration, foretold all the miseries that afterwards befell the state, exhorted them to beware of Pompey and Crassus, who were guilty of such things, and had laid such designs, that they might well fear to have Cato prætor. When he had ended this speech, he was followed to his house by a greater number of people than all the new prætors elect put together.

Caius Trebonius now proposed the law for allotting provinces to the consuls, one of whom was to have Spain and Africa, the other Egypt and Syria, with full power of making war, and carrying it on both by sea and land, as they should think fit. When this was proposed, all others despaired of putting any stop to it, and neither did nor said anything against it. But Cato, before the voting began, went up into the place of speaking, and desiring to be heard, was with much difficulty allowed two hours to speak. Having spent that time in informing them and reasoning with them, and in foretelling to them much that was to come, he was not suffered to speak any longer; but as he was going on, a serjeant came and pulled him down; yet when he was down, he still continued speaking in a loud voice, and finding many to listen to him, and join in his indignation. Then the serjeant took him, and forced him out of the forum; but as soon as he got loose, he returned again to the place of speaking, crying out to the people to stand by him. When he had done thus several times, Trebonius grew very angry, and commanded him to be carried to prison; but the multitude followed him, and listened to the speech which he made to them as he went along; so that Trebonius began to be afraid again, and ordered him to be released. Thus that day was expended, and the business staved off by Cato. But in the days succeeding, many of the citizens being overawed by fears and threats, and others won by gifts and favours, Aquillius, one of the tribunes, they kept by an armed force within the senate-house; Cato, who cried it thundered, they drove out of the forum; many were wounded, and some slain; and at length by open force they passed the law. At this many were so incensed that they got together and were going to throw down the statues of Pompey; but Cato went and diverted them from that design.

Again, another law was proposed, concerning the provinces and legions of Cæsar. Upon this occasion Cato did not apply himself to the people, but appealed to Pompey himself; and told him, he did not consider now that he was setting Cæsar upon his own shoulders, who would shortly grow too weighty for him; and at length, not able to lay down the burden, nor yet to bear it any longer, he would precipitate both it and himself with it upon the commonwealth; and then he would remember Cato's advice, which was no less advantageous to him than just and honest in itself. Thus was Pompey often warned, but still disregarded and slighted it, never mistrusting Cæsar's change, and always confiding in his own power and good fortune.

Cato was made prætor the following year; but, it seems, he did not do more honour and credit to the office by his signal integrity than he disgraced and diminished it by his strange behaviour. For he would often come to the court without his shoes, and sit upon the bench without any undergarment, and in this attire would give judgment in capital causes, and upon persons of the highest rank. It is said, also, he used to drink wine after his morning meal, and then transact the business of his office; but this was wrongfully reported of him. The people were at that time extremely corrupted by the gifts of those who sought offices, and most made a constant trade of selling their voices. Cato was eager utterly to root this corruption out of the commonwealth; he therefore persuaded the senate to make an order, that those who were chosen into any office, though nobody should accuse them, should be obliged to come into the court, and give account upon oath of their proceedings in their election. This was extremely obnoxious to those who stood for the offices, and yet more to those vast numbers who took the bribes. Insomuch that one morning, as Cato was going to the tribunal, a great multitude of people flocked together, and with loud cries and maledictions reviled him, and threw stones at him. Those that were about the tribunal presently fled, and

Cato himself being forced thence, and jostled about in the throng, very narrowly escaped the stones that were thrown at him, and with much difficulty got hold of the rostra; where, standing up with a bold and undaunted countenance, he at once mastered the tumult, and silenced the clamour; and addressing them in fit terms for the occasion, was heard with great attention, and perfectly quelled the sedition. Afterwards, on the senate commending him for this, " But I," said he, " do not commend you for abandoning your prætor in danger, and bringing him no assistance."

In the meantime, the candidates were in great perplexity; for every one dreaded to give money himself, and yet feared lest his competitors should. At length they agreed to lay down one hundred and twenty-five thousand drachmas apiece, and then all of them to canvass fairly and honestly, on condition, that if any one was found to make use of bribery he should forfeit the money. Being thus agreed, they chose Cato to keep the stakes, and arbitrate the matter; to him they brought the sum concluded on, and before him subscribed the agreement. The money he did not choose to have paid for them, but took their securities who stood bound for them. Upon the day of election, he placed himself by the tribune who took the votes, and very watchfully observing all that passed, he discovered one who had broken the agreement, and immediately ordered him to pay his money to the rest. They, however, commending his justice highly, remitted the penalty, as thinking the discovery a sufficient punishment. It raised, however, as much envy against Cato as it gained him reputation, and many were offended at his thus taking upon himself the whole authority of the senate, the courts of judicature, and the magistracies. For there is no virtue, the honour and credit for which procures a man more odium than that of justice; and this, because more than any other, it acquires a man power and authority among the common people. For they only honour the valiant and admire the wise, while in addition they also love just men, and put entire trust and confidence in them. They fear the bold man, and mistrust the clever man, and moreover think them rather beholding to their natural complexion, than to any goodness of their will, for these excellences; they look upon valour as a certain natural strength of the mind, and wisdom as a constitutional acuteness; whereas a man has it in his power to be just, if he have but the will to be so, and therefore injustice is thought the most dishonourable, because it is least excusable.

Cato upon this account was opposed by all the great men, who thought themselves reproved by his virtue. Pompey especially looked upon the increase of Cato's credit as the ruin of his own power, and therefore continually set up men to rail against him. Among these was the seditious Clodius, now again united to Pompey, who declared openly, that Cato had conveyed away a great deal of the treasure that was found in Cyprus; and that he hated Pompey only because he refused to marry his daughter. Cato answered, that although they had allowed him neither horse nor man, he had brought more treasure from Cyprus alone, than Pompey had, after so many wars and triumphs, from the ransacked world; that he never sought the alliance of Pompey; not that he thought him unworthy of being related to him, but because he differed so much from him in things that concerned the commonwealth. " For," said he, " I laid down the province that was given me, when I went out of my prætorship; Pompey, on the contrary, retains many provinces for himself, and he bestows many on others; and but now he sent Cæsar a force of six thousand men into Gaul, which Cæsar never asked the people for, nor had Pompey obtained their consent to give. Men, and horse, and arms, in any number, are become the mutual gifts of private men to one another; and Pompey, keeping the titles of commander and general, hands over the armies and provinces to others to govern, while he himself stays at home to preside at the contests of the canvass, and to stir up tumults at elections; out of the anarchy he thus creates amongst us, seeking, we see well enough, a monarchy for himself." Thus he retorted on Pompey.

He had an intimate friend and admirer of the name of Marcus Favonius, much the same to Cato as we are told Apollodorus, the Phalerian, was in old time to Socrates, whose words used to throw him into perfect transports and ecstasies, getting into his head, like strong wine, and intoxicating him to a sort of frenzy. This Favonius stood to be chosen ædile, and was like to lose it; but Cato, who was there to assist him, observed that all the votes were written in one hand, and discovering the cheat, appealed to the tribunes, who stopped the election. Favonius was afterwards chosen ædile, and Cato, who assisted him in all things that belonged to his office, also undertook the care of the spectacles that were exhibited in the theatre; giving the actors crowns, not of gold, but of wild olive, such as used to be given at the Olympic games; and instead of the magnificent presents that were usually made, he offered to the Greeks beet root, lettuces, radishes, and pears; and to the Romans earthen pots of wine, pork, figs, cucumbers, and little faggots of wood. Some ridiculed Cato for his economy, others looked with respect on this gentle relaxation of his usual rigour and austerity. In fine, Favonius himself mingled with the crowd, and sitting among the spectators, clapped and applauded Cato, bade him bestow rewards on those who did well, and called on the people to pay their honours to him, as for himself he had placed his whole authority in Cato's hands. At the same time, Curio, the colleague of Favonius, gave very magnificent entertainments in another theatre; but the people left his, and went to those of Favonius, which they much applauded, and joined heartily in the diversion, seeing him act the private man, and Cato the master of the shows, who, in fact, did all this in derision of the great expenses that others incurred, and to teach them, that in amusements men ought to seek amusement only, and the display of a decent cheerfulness, not great preparations and costly magnificence, demanding the expenditure of endless care and trouble about things of little concern.

After this, Scipio, Hypsæus, and Milo, stood to be consuls, and that not only with the usual and now recognised disorders of bribery and corruption, but with arms and slaughter, and every appearance of carrying their audacity and desperation to the length of actual civil war. Whereupon it was proposed that Pompey might be empowered to preside over that election. This Cato at first opposed, saying that the laws ought not to seek protection from Pompey, but Pompey from the laws. Yet the confusion lasting a long time, the forum continually, as it were, besieged with three armies, and no possibility appearing of a stop being put to these disorders, Cato at length agreed that, rather than fall into the last extremity, the senate should freely confer all on Pompey; since it was necessary to make use of a lesser illegality as a remedy against the greatest of all, and better to set up a monarchy themselves than to suffer a sedition to continue that must certainly end in one. Bibulus, therefore, a friend of Cato's, moved the senate to create Pompey sole consul; for that either he would re-establish the lawful government, or they should serve under the best master. Cato stood up, and, contrary to all expectation, seconded this motion, concluding that any government was better than mere confusion, and that he did not question but Pompey would deal honourably, and take care of the commonwealth thus committed to his charge. Pompey being hereupon declared consul, invited Cato to see him in the suburbs. When he came, he saluted and embraced him very kindly, acknowledged the favour he had done him, and desired his counsel and assistance, in the management of this office. Cato made answer, that what he had spoken on any former occasion was not out of hate to Pompey, nor what he had now done out of love to him, but all for the good of the commonwealth; that in private, if he asked him, he would freely give his advice; and in public, though he asked him not, he would always speak his opinion. And he did accordingly. For first, when Pompey made severe laws, for punishing and laying great fines on those who had corrupted the people with gifts, Cato advised him to let alone what was already passed, and to provide for the future; for if he should look up past misdemeanours, it would be difficult to know where to stop; and if he would ordain new penalties, it would be unreasonable to punish men by a law, which at that time they had not the opportunity of breaking. Afterwards, when many considerable men, and some of Pompey's own relations, were accused, and he grew remiss, and disinclined to the prosecution, Cato sharply reproved him, and urged him to proceed. Pompey had made a law, also, to forbid the custom of making commendatory orations in behalf of those that were accused; yet he himself wrote one for Munatius Plancus, and sent it while the cause was pleading; upon which Cato, who was sitting as one of the judges, stopped his ears with his hands, and would not hear it read. Whereupon Plancus, before sentence was given, excepted against him, but was condemned notwithstanding. And indeed Cato was a great trouble and perplexity to almost all that were accused of anything, as they feared to have him one of their judges, yet did not dare to demand his exclusion. And many had been condemned because, by refusing him, they seemed to show that they could not trust to their own innocence; and it was a reproach thrown in the teeth of some by their enemies, that they had not accepted Cato for their judge.

In the meanwhile, Cæsar kept close with his forces in Gaul, and continued in arms; and at the same time employed his gifts, his riches, and his friends above all things, to increase his power in the city. And now Cato's old admonitions began to rouse Pompey out of the negligent security in which he lay, into a sort of imagination of danger at hand; but seeing him slow and unwilling, and timorous to undertake any measures of prevention against Cæsar, Cato resolved himself to stand for the consulship, and presently force Cæsar either to lay down his arms or discover his intentions. Both Cato's competitors were persons of good position; Sulpicius, who was one, owed much to Cato's credit and authority in the city, and it was thought unhandsome and ungratefully done, to stand against him; not that Cato himself took it ill, " For it is no wonder," said he, " if a man will not yield to another, in that which he esteems the greatest good." He had persuaded the senate to make an order, that those who stood for offices should themselves ask the people for their votes, and not solicit by others, nor take others about with them to speak for them, in their canvass. And this made the common people very hostile to him, if they were to lose not only the means of receiving money, but also the opportunity of obliging several persons, and so to become by his means both poor and less regarded. Besides this, Cato himself was by nature altogether unfit for the business of canvassing, as he was more anxious to sustain the dignity of his life and character than to obtain the office. Thus by following his own way of soliciting, and not suffering his friends to do those things which take away the multitude, he was rejected and lost the consulship.

But whereas, upon such occasions, not only those who missed the office, but even their friends and relations, used to feel themselves disgraced and humiliated, and observed a sort of mourning for several days after, Cato took it so unconcernedly that he anointed himself, and played at ball in the field, and after breakfasting, went into the forum, as he used to do, without his shoes or his tunic, and there walked about with his acquaintance. Cicero blames him, for that when affairs required such a consul, he would not take more pains, nor condescend to pay some court to the people, as also because that he afterwards neglected to try again; whereas he had stood a second time to be chosen prætor. Cato answered that he lost the prætorship the first time, not by the voice of the people, but by the violence and corrupt dealing of his adversaries; whereas in the election of consuls there had been no foul play. So that he plainly saw the people did not like his manners, which an honest man ought not to alter for their sake; nor yet would a wise man attempt the same thing again, while liable to the same prejudices.

Cæsar was at this time engaged with many warlike nations, and was subduing them at great hazards. Among the rest, it was believed he had set upon the Germans, in a time of truce, and had thus slain three hundred thousand of them. Upon which, some of his friends moved the senate for a public thanksgiving; but Cato declared they ought to deliver Cæsar into the hands of those who had been thus unjustly treated, and so expiate the offence and not bring a curse upon the city; " Yet we have reason," said he, " to thank the gods, for that they spared the commonwealth, and did not take vengeance upon the army, for the madness and folly of the general." Hereupon Cæsar wrote a letter to the senate which was read openly, and was full of reproachful language and accusations against Cato; who, standing up, seemed not at all concerned, and without any heat or passion, but in a calm and, as it were, premeditated discourse, made all Cæsar's charges against him show like mere common scolding and abuse, and in fact a sort of pleasantry and play on Cæsar's part; and proceeding then to go into all Cæsar's political courses, and to explain and reveal (as though he had been not his constant opponent, but his fellow-conspirator) his whole conduct and purpose from its commencement, he concluded by telling the senate, it was not the sons of the Britons or the Gauls they need fear, but Cæsar himself, if they were wise. And this discourse so moved and awakened the senate, that Cæsar's friends repented they had had a letter read, which had given Cato an opportunity of saying so many reasonable things, and such severe truths against him. However, nothing was then decided upon; it was merely said, that it would be well to send him a successor. Upon that, Cæsar's friends required that Pompey also should lay down his arms, and resign his provinces, or else that Cæsar might not be obliged to either. Then Cato cried out, what he had foretold was come to pass; now it was manifest he was using his forces to compel their judgment, and was turning against the state those armies he had got from it by imposture and trickery. But out of the senate-house Cato could do but little, as the people were ever ready to magnify Cæsar; and the senate, though convinced by Cato, were afraid of the people.

But when the news was brought that Cæsar had seized Ariminum, and was marching with his army toward Rome, then all men, even Pompey, and the common people too, cast their eyes on Cato, who had alone foreseen and first clearly declared Cæsar's intentions. He therefore told them, " If you had believed me, or regarded my advice, you would not now have been reduced to stand in fear of one man, or to put all your hopes in one alone." Pompey acknowledged that Cato indeed had spoken most like a prophet, while he himself had acted too much like a friend. And Cato advised the senate to put all into the hands of Pompey; " For those who can raise up great evils," said he, " can best allay them."

Pompey, finding he had not sufficient forces, and that those he could raise were not very resolute, forsook the city. Cato, resolving to follow Pompey into exile, sent his younger son to Munatius, who was then in the country of Brutium, and took his eldest son with him; but wanting somebody to keep his house and take care of his daughters, he took Marcia again, who was now a rich widow, Hortensius being dead, and having left her all his estate. Cæsar afterward made use of this action also, to reproach him with covetousness, and a mercenary design in his marriage. " For," said he, " if he had need of a wife why did he part with her? And if he had not, why did he take her again? Unless he gave her only as a bait to Hortensius; and lent her when she was young, to have her again when she was rich." But in answer to this, we might fairly apply the saying of Euripides—

> " To speak of mysteries—the chief of these
> Surely were cowardice in Hercules."

For it is much the same thing to reproach Hercules for cowardice, and to accuse Cato of covetousness; though otherwise, whether he did altogether right in this marriage, might be disputed. As soon, however, as he had again taken Marcia, he committed his house and his daughters to her, and himself followed Pompey. And it is said, that from that day he never cut his hair, nor shaved his beard, nor wore a garland, but was always full of sadness, grief, and dejectedness for the calamities of his country, and continually showed the same feeling to the last, whatever party had misfortune or success.

The government of Sicily being allotted to him, he passed over to Syracuse; where, understanding that Asinius Pollio was arrived at Messena, with forces from the enemy, Cato sent to him, to know the reason of his coming thither: Pollio, on the other side, called upon him to show reason for the present convulsions. And being at the same time informed how Pompey had quite abandoned Italy, and lay encamped at Dyrrhachium, he spoke of the strangeness and incomprehensibility of the divine government of things; " Pompey, when he did nothing wisely nor honestly, was always successful; and now that he would preserve his country, and defend her liberty, he is altogether unfortunate." As for Asinius, he said, he could drive him out of Sicily, but as there were larger forces coming to his assistance, he would not engage the island in a war. He therefore advised the Syracusans to join the conquering party and provide for their own safety; and so set sail from thence.

When he came to Pompey, he uniformly gave advice to protract the war; as he always hoped to compose matters, and was by no means desirous that they should come to action; for the commonwealth would suffer extremely, and be the certain cause of its own ruin, whoever were conqueror by the sword.  In like manner, he persuaded Pompey and the council to ordain that no city should be sacked that was subject to the people of Rome; and that no Roman should be killed but in the heat of battle; and hereby he got himself great honour, and brought over many to Pompey's party, whom his moderation and humanity attracted.  Afterwards being sent into Asia, to assist those who were raising men and preparing ships in those parts, he took with him his sister Servilia, and a little boy whom she had by Lucullus.  For since her widowhood, she had lived with her brother, and much recovered her reputation, having put herself under his care, followed him in his voyages, and complied with his severe way of living.  Yet Cæsar did not fail to asperse him upon her account also.

Pompey's officers in Asia, it seems, had no great need of Cato; but he brought over the people of Rhodes by his persuasions, and leaving his sister Servilia and her child there, he returned to Pompey, who had now collected very great forces both by sea and land.  And here Pompey, more than in any other act, betrayed his intentions.  For at first he designed to give Cato the command of the navy, which consisted of no less than five hundred ships of war, besides a vast number of light galleys, scouts, and open boats.  But presently bethinking himself, or put in mind by his friends, that Cato's principal and only aim being to free his country from all usurpation, if he were master of such great forces, as soon as ever Cæsar should be conquered, he would certainly call upon Pompey, also, to lay down his arms, and be subject to the laws, he changed his mind, and though he had already mentioned it to Cato, nevertheless made Bibulus admiral.  Notwithstanding this, he had no reason to suppose that Cato's zeal in the cause was in any way diminished.  For before one of the battles at Dyrrhachium, when Pompey himself, we are told, made an address to the soldiers and bade the officers do the like, the men listened to them but coldly and with silence, until Cato, last of all, came forward, and in the language of philosophy, spoke to them, as the occasion required, concerning liberty, manly virtue, death, and a good name; upon all which he delivered himself with strong natural passion, and concluded with calling in the aid of the gods, to whom he directed his speech, as if they were present to behold them fight for their country. And at this the army gave such a shout and showed such excitement that their officers led them on full of hope and confidence to the danger. Cæsar's party were routed and put to flight; but his presiding fortune used the advantage of Pompey's cautiousness and diffidence to render the victory incomplete. But of this we have spoken in the life of Pompey. While, however, all the rest rejoiced, and magnified their success, Cato alone bewailed his country, and cursed that fatal ambition which made so many brave Romans murder one another.

After this Pompey, following Cæsar into Thessaly, left at Dyrrhachium a quantity of munitions, money, and stores, and many of his domestics and relations; the charge of all which he gave to Cato, with the command only of fifteen cohorts. For though he trusted him much, yet he was afraid of him too, knowing full well, that if he had bad success, Cato would be the last to forsake him, but if he conquered, would never let him use his victory at his pleasure. There were, likewise, many persons of high rank that stayed with Cato at Dyrrhachium. When they heard of the overthrow at Pharsalia, Cato resolved with himself, that if Pompey were slain, he would conduct those that were with him into Italy, and then retire as far from the tyranny of Cæsar as he could, and live in exile; but if Pompey were safe, he would keep the army together for him. With this resolution he passed over to Corcyra, where the navy lay; there he would have resigned his command to Cicero, because he had been consul, and himself only a prætor: but Cicero refused it, and was going for Italy. At which Pompey's son being incensed, would rashly and in heat have punished all those who were going away, and in the first place have laid hands on Cicero; but Cato spoke with him in private, and diverted him from that design. And thus he clearly saved the life of Cicero, and rescued several others also from ill-treatment.

Conjecturing that Pompey the Great was fled toward Egypt or Africa, Cato resolved to hasten after him; and having taken all his men aboard, he set sail; but first to those who were not zealous to continue the contest, he gave free liberty to depart. When they came to the coast of Africa they met with Sextus, Pompey's younger son, who told them of the death of his father in Egypt; at which they were all exceedingly grieved, and declared that after Pompey they would follow no other leader but Cato. Out of compassion, therefore, to so many worthy persons, who had given such testimonies of their fidelity, and whom he could not for shame leave in a desert country, amidst so many difficulties, he took upon him the command, and marched toward the city of Cyrene, which presently received him, though not long before they had shut their gates against Labienus. Here he was informed that Scipio, Pompey's father-in-law, was received by King Juba, and that Attius Varus, whom Pompey had made governor of Africa, had joined them with his forces. Cato therefore resolved to march toward them by land, it being now winter; and got together a number of asses to carry water, and furnished himself likewise with plenty of all other provision, and a number of carriages. He took also with him some of those they call Psylli, who cure the biting of serpents, by sucking out the poison with their mouths, and have likewise certain charms, by which they stupefy and lay asleep the serpents.

Thus they marched seven days together, Cato all the time going on foot at the head of his men, and never making use of any horse or chariot. Ever since the battle of Pharsalia, he used to sit at table, and added this to his other ways of mourning, that he never lay down but to sleep.

Having passed the winter in Africa, Cato drew out his army, which amounted to little less than ten thousand. The affairs of Scipio and Varus went very ill, by reason of their dissensions and quarrels among themselves, and their submissions and flatteries to King Juba, who was insupportable for his vanity, and the pride he took in his strength and riches. The first time he came to a conference with Cato, he had ordered his own seat to be placed in the middle, between Scipio and Cato; which Cato observing, took up his chair and set himself on the other side of Scipio, to whom he thus gave the honour of sitting in the middle, though he were his enemy, and had formerly published some scandalous writing against him. There are people who speak as if this were quite an insignificant matter, and who, nevertheless, find fault with Cato, because in Sicily, walking one day with Philostratus, he gave him the middle place, to show his respect for philosophy. However, he now succeeded both in humbling the pride of Juba, who was treating Scipio and Varus much like a pair of satraps under his orders, and also in reconciling them to each other. All the troops desired him to be their leader; Scipio, likewise, and Varus gave way to it, and offered him the command; but he said he would not break those laws which he sought to defend, and he, being but proprietor, ought not to command in the presence of a pro-

consul (for Scipio had been created proconsul), besides that
people took it as a good omen to see a Scipio command in
Africa, and the very name inspired the soldiers with hopes of
success.

Scipio, having taken upon him the command, presently resolved, at the instigation of Juba, to put all the inhabitants of
Utica to the sword, and to raze the city, for having, as they professed, taken part with Cæsar. Cato would by no means suffer
this; but invoking the gods, exclaiming and protesting against
it in the council of war, he with much difficulty delivered the
poor people from this cruelty. And afterwards, upon the
entreaty of the inhabitants, and at the instance of Scipio, Cato
took upon himself the government of Utica, lest, one way or the
other, it should fall into Cæsar's hands; for it was a strong
place, and very advantageous for either party. And it was yet
better provided and more strongly fortified by Cato, who
brought in great store of corn, repaired the walls, erected towers,
and made deep trenches and palisades around the town. The
young men of Utica he lodged among these works, having first
taken their arms from them; the rest of the inhabitants he kept
within the town, and took the greatest care that no injury
should be done nor affront offered them by the Romans. From
hence he sent great quantity of arms, money, and provision to
the camp, and made this city their chief magazine.

He advised Scipio, as he had before done Pompey, by no
means to hazard a battle against a man experienced in war, and
formidable in the field, but to use delay; for time would gradually abate the violence of the crisis, which is the strength of
usurpation. But Scipio out of pride rejected this counsel, and
wrote a letter to Cato, in which he reproached him with
cowardice; and that he could not be content to lie secure himself within walls and trenches, but he must hinder others from
boldly using their own good sense to seize the right opportunity.
In answer to this, Cato wrote word again, that he would take
the horse and foot which he had brought into Africa, and go
over into Italy, to make a diversion there, and draw Cæsar off
from them. But Scipio derided this proposition also. Then
Cato openly let it be seen that he was sorry he had yielded the
command to Scipio, who he saw would not carry on the war
with any wisdom, and if, contrary to all appearance, he should
succeed, he would use his success as unjustly at home. For
Cato had then made up his mind, and so he told his friends, that
he could have but slender hopes in those generals that had so

much boldness and so little conduct; yet if anything should happen beyond expectation, and Cæsar should be overthrown, for his part he would not stay at Rome, but would retire from the cruelty and inhumanity of Scipio, who had already uttered fierce and proud threats against many.

But what Cato had looked for, fell out sooner than he expected. Late in the evening came one from the army, whence he had been three days coming, who brought word there had been a great battle near Thapsus; that all was utterly lost; Cæsar had taken the camps, Scipio and Juba were fled with a few only, and all the rest of the army was lost. This news arriving in time of war, and in the night, so alarmed the people, that they were almost out of their wits, and could scarce keep themselves within the walls of the city. But Cato came forward, and meeting the people in this hurry and clamour, did all he could to comfort and encourage them, and somewhat appeased the fear and amazement they were in, telling them that very likely things were not so bad in truth, but much exaggerated in the report. And so he pacified the tumult for the present. The next morning he sent for the three hundred, whom he used as his council; these were Romans, who were in Africa upon business, in commerce and money-lending; there were also several senators and their sons. They were summoned to meet in the temple of Jupiter. While they were coming together, Cato walked about very quietly and unconcerned, as if nothing new had happened. He had a book in his hand, which he was reading; in this book was an account of what provision he had for war, armour, corn, ammunition, and soldiers.

When they were assembled, he began his discourse; first, as regarded the three hundred themselves, and very much commended the courage and fidelity they had shown, and their having very well served their country with their persons, money, and counsel. Then he entreated them by no means to separate, as if each single man could hope for any safety in forsaking his companions; on the contrary, while they kept together, Cæsar would have less reason to despise them, if they fought against him, and be more forward to pardon them, if they submitted to him. Therefore he advised them to consult among themselves, nor should he find fault whichever course they adopted. If they thought fit to submit to fortune, he would impute their change to necessity; but if they resolved to stand firm, and undertake the danger for the sake of liberty, he should not only commend, but admire their courage, and would himself be their leader and companion too, till they had put to the proof the utmost fortune of their country; which was not Utica or Adrumetum but Rome, and she had often, by her own greatness, raised herself after worse disasters. Besides, as there were many things that would conduce to their safety, so chiefly this, that they were to fight against one whose affairs urgently claimed his presence in various quarters. Spain was already revolted to the younger Pompey; Rome was unaccustomed to the bridle, and impatient of it, and would therefore be ready to rise in insurrection upon any turn of affairs. As for themselves, they ought not to shrink from the danger; and in this might take example from their enemy, who so freely exposes his life to effect the most unrighteous designs, yet never can hope for so happy a conclusion as they may promise themselves; for notwithstanding the uncertainty of war, they will be sure of a most happy life if they succeed, or a most glorious death if they miscarry. However, he said, they ought to deliberate among themselves; and he joined with them in praying the gods that in recompense of their former courage and good-will, they would prosper their present determinations. When Cato had thus spoken, many were moved and encouraged by his arguments, but the greatest part were so animated by the sense of his intrepidity, generosity, and goodness, that they forgot the present danger, and as if he were the only invincible leader, and above all fortune, they entreated him to employ their persons, arms, and estates, as he thought fit; for they esteemed it far better to meet death in following his counsel, than to find their safety in betraying one of so great virtue. One of the assembly proposed the making a decree to set the slaves at liberty; and most of the rest approved the motion. Cato said that it ought not to be done, for it was neither just nor lawful; but if any of their masters would willingly set them free, those that were fit for service should be received. Many promised so to do, whose names he ordered to be enrolled, and then withdrew.

Presently after this he received letters from Juba and Scipio. Juba, with some few of his men, was retired to a mountain, where he waited to hear what Cato would resolve upon; and intended to stay there for him, if he thought fit to leave Utica, or to come to his aid with his troops, if he were besieged. Scipio was on shipboard, near a certain promontory, not far from Utica, expecting an answer upon the same account. But

Cato thought fit to retain the messengers till the three hundred should come to some resolution.

As for the senators that were there, they showed great forwardness, and at once set free their slaves, and furnished them with arms. But the three hundred being men occupied in merchandise and money-lending, much of their substance also consisting in slaves, the enthusiasm that Cato's speech had raised in them did not long continue. As there are substances that easily admit heat, and as suddenly lose it, when the fire is removed, so these men were heated and inflamed while Cato was present; but when they began to reason among themselves, the fear they had of Cæsar soon overcame their reverence for Cato and for virtue. "For who are we," said they, "and who is it we refuse to obey? Is it not that Cæsar who is now invested with all the power of Rome? and which of us is a Scipio, a Pompey, or a Cato? But now that all men make their honour give way to their fear, shall we alone engage for the liberty of Rome, and in Utica declare war against him, before whom Cato and Pompey the Great fled out of Italy? Shall we set free our slaves against Cæsar, who have ourselves no more liberty than he is pleased to allow? No, let us, poor creatures, know ourselves, submit to the victor, and send deputies to implore his mercy." Thus said the most moderate of them; but the greatest part were for seizing the senators, that by securing them they might appease Cæsar's anger. Cato, though he perceived the change, took no notice of it; but wrote to Juba and Scipio to keep away from Utica, because he mistrusted the three hundred.

A considerable body of horse, which had escaped from the late fight, riding up towards Utica, sent three men before to Cato, who yet did not all bring the same message; for one party was for going to Juba, another for joining with Cato, and some again were afraid to go into Utica. When Cato heard this, he ordered Marcus Rubrius to attend upon the three hundred, and quietly take the names of those who, of their own accord, set their slaves at liberty, but by no means to force anybody. Then taking with him the senators, he went out of the town, and met the principal officers of these horsemen, whom he entreated not to abandon so many Roman senators, not to prefer Juba for their commander before Cato, but consult the common safety, and to come into the city, which was impregnable, and well furnished with corn and other provision, sufficient for many years. The senators likewise with tears besought them to stay. Hereupon the officers went to consult their soldiers, and Cato

with the senators sat down upon an embankment, expecting
their resolution. In the meantime comes Rubrius in great disorder, crying out, the three hundred were all in commotion, and
exciting revolt and tumult in the city. At this all the rest fell
into despair, lamenting and bewailing their condition. Cato
endeavoured to comfort them, and sent to the three hundred,
desiring them to have patience. Then the officers of the horse
returned with no very reasonable demands. They said, they
did not desire to serve Juba for his pay, nor should they fear
Cæsar, while they followed Cato, but they dreaded to be shut up
with the Uticans, men of traitorous temper, and Carthaginian
blood; for though they were quiet at present, yet as soon as
Cæsar should appear, without doubt they would conspire together, and betray the Romans. Therefore, if he expected they
should join with him, he must drive out of the town or destroy
all the Uticans, that he might receive them into a place clear
both of enemies and barbarians. This Cato thought utterly
cruel and barbarous; but he mildly answered, he would consult
the three hundred.

Then he returned to the city, where he found the men, not
framing excuses, or dissembling out of reverence to him, but
openly declaring that no one should compel them to make war
against Cæsar; which, they said, they were neither able nor
willing to do. And some there were who muttered words about
retaining the senators till Cæsar's coming; but Cato seemed not
to hear this, as indeed he had the excuse of being a little deaf.
At the same time came one to him and told him the horse were
going away. And now, fearing lest the three hundred should
take some desperate resolution concerning the senators, he presently went out with some of his friends, and seeing they were
gone some way, he took horse, and rode after them. They,
when they saw him coming, were very glad, and received him
very kindly, entreating him to save himself with them. At this
time, it is said, Cato shed tears, while entreating them on behalf
of the senators, and stretching out his hands in supplication.
He turned some of their horses' heads, and laid hold of the men
by their armour, till in fine he prevailed with them out of compassion, to stay only that one day, to procure a safe retreat for
the senators. Having thus persuaded them to go along with
him, some he placed at the gates of the town, and to others
gave the charge of the citadel. The three hundred began to
fear they should suffer for their inconstancy, and sent to Cato,
entreating him by all means to come to them; but the senators

flocking about him, would not suffer him to go, and said they would not trust their guardian and saviour to the hands of perfidious traitors.

For there had never, perhaps, been a time when Cato's virtue appeared more manifestly; and every class of men in Utica could clearly see, with sorrow and admiration, how entirely free was everything that he was doing from any secret motives or any mixture of self-regard; he, namely, who had long before resolved on his own death, was taking such extreme pains, toil, and care, only for the sake of others, that when he had secured their lives, he might put an end to his own. For it was easily perceived that he had determined to die, though he did not let it appear.

Therefore, having pacified the senators, he complied with the request of the three hundred, and went to them alone without any attendance. They gave him many thanks, and entreated him to employ and trust them for the future; and if they were not Catos, and could not aspire to his greatness of mind, they begged he would pity their weakness; and told him they had determined to send to Cæsar and entreat him, chiefly and in the first place, for Cato, and if they could not prevail for him, they would not accept of pardon for themselves, but as long as they had breath, would fight in his defence. Cato commended their good intentions, and advised them to send speedily, for their own safety, but by no means to ask anything in his behalf; for those who are conquered, entreat, and those who have done wrong, beg pardon; for himself, he did not confess to any defeat in all his life, but rather, so far as he had thought fit, he had got the victory, and had conquered Cæsar in all points of justice and honesty. It was Cæsar that ought to be looked upon as one surprised and vanquished; for he was now convicted and found guilty of those designs against his country, which he had so long practised and so constantly denied. When he had thus spoken, he went out of the assembly, and being informed that Cæsar was coming with his whole army, "Ah," said he, " he expects to find us brave men." Then he went to the senators, and urged them to make no delay, but hasten to be gone, while the horsemen were yet in the city. So ordering all the gates to be shut, except one towards the sea, he assigned their several ships to those that were to depart, and gave money and provision to those that wanted; all which he did with great order and exactness, taking care to suppress all tumults, and that no wrong should be done to the people.

Marcus Octavius, coming with two legions, now encamped near Utica, sent to Cato to arrange about the chief command. Cato returned him no answer; but said to his friends, " Can we wonder all has gone ill with us, when our love of office survives even in our very ruin? " In the meantime, word was brought him, that the horse were going away, and were beginning to spoil and plunder the citizens. Cato ran to them, and from the first he met, snatched what they had taken; the rest threw down all they had gotten, and went away silent and ashamed of what they had done. Then he called together all the people of Utica, and requested them, upon the behalf of the three hundred, not to exasperate Cæsar against them, but all to seek their common safety together with them. After that, he went again to the port to see those who were about to embark; and there he embraced and dismissed those of his friends and acquaintance whom he had persuaded to go. As for his son, he did not counsel him to be gone, nor did he think fit to persuade him to forsake his father. But there was one Statyllius, a young man, in the flower of his age, of a brave spirit, and very desirous to imitate the constancy of Cato. Cato entreated him to go away, as he was a noted enemy to Cæsar, but without success. Then Cato looked at Apollonides, the stoic philosopher, and Demetrius, the peripatetic; " It belongs to you to cool the fever of this young man's spirit, and to make him know what is good for him." And thus, in setting his friends upon their way, and in despatching the business of any that applied to him, he spent that night and the greatest part of the next day.

Lucius Cæsar, a kinsman of Cæsar's, being appointed to go deputy for the three hundred, came to Cato, and desired he would assist him to prepare a persuasive speech for them; " And as to you yourself," said he, " it will be an honour for me to kiss the hands and fall at the knees of Cæsar, in your behalf." But Cato would by no means permit him to do any such thing; " For as to myself," said he, " if I would be preserved by Cæsar's favour, I should myself go to him; but I would not be beholden to a tyrant for his acts of tyranny. For it is but usurpation in him to save, as their rightful lord, the lives of men over whom he has no title to reign. But if you please, let us consider what you had best say for the three hundred." And when they had continued some time together, as Lucius was going away, Cato recommended to him his son and the rest of his friends; and taking him by the hand bade him farewell.

Then he retired to his house again, and called together his son and his friends, to whom he conversed on various subjects; among the rest he forbade his son to engage himself in the affairs of state. For to act therein as became him was now impossible; and to do otherwise, would be dishonourable. Toward evening he went into his bath. As he was bathing, he remembered Statyllius and called out aloud, " Apollonides, have you tamed the high spirit of Statyllius, and is he gone without bidding us farewell? " " No," said Apollonides, " I have said much to him, but to little purpose; he is still resolute and unalterable, and declares he is determined to follow your example." At this, it is said, Cato smiled, and answered, " That will soon be tried."

After he had bathed, he went to supper, with a great deal of company; at which he sat up, as he had always used to do ever since the battle of Pharsalia; for since that time he never lay down but when he went to sleep. There supped with him all his own friends and the magistrates of Utica.

After supper, the wine produced a great deal of lively and agreeable discourse, and a whole series of philosophical questions was discussed. At length they came to the strange dogmas of the stoics, called their Paradoxes; and to this in particular, That the good man only is free, and that all wicked men are slaves. The peripatetic, as was to be expected, opposing this, Cato fell upon him very warmly; and somewhat raising his voice, he argued the matter at great length, and urged the point with such vehemence, that it was apparent to everybody he was resolved to put an end to his life, and set himself at liberty. And so, when he had done speaking, there was a great silence and evident dejection. Cato, therefore, to divert them from any suspicion of his design, turned the conversation, and began again to talk of matters of present interest and expectation, showing great concern for those that were at sea, as also for the others, who, travelling by land, were to pass through a dry and barbarous desert.

When the company was broke up, he walked with his friends, as he used to do after supper, gave the necessary orders to the officers of the watch, and going into his chamber, he embraced his son and every one of his friends with more than usual warmth, which again renewed their suspicion of his design. Then laying himself down, he took into his hand Plato's dialogue concerning the soul. Having read more than half the book, he looked up, and missing his sword, which his son had taken away while he was at supper, he called his servant, and asked who had taken away his sword. The servant making no answer, he fell to reading again; and a little after, not seeming importunate, or hasty for it, but as if he would only know what had become of it, he bade it be brought. But having waited some time, when he had read through the book, and still nobody brought the sword, he called up all his servants, and in a louder tone demanded his sword. To one of them he gave such a blow in the mouth, that he hurt his own hand; and now grew more angry, exclaiming that he was betrayed and delivered naked to the enemy by his son and his servants. Then his son, with the rest of his friends, came running into the room, and falling at his feet, began to lament and beseech him. But Cato raising himself, and looking fiercely, " When," said he, " and how did I become deranged, and out of my senses, that thus no one tries to persuade me by reason, or show me what is better, if I am supposed to be ill-advised? Must I be disarmed, and hindered from using my own reason? And you, young man, why do you not bind your father's hands behind him that, when Cæsar comes, he may find me unable to defend myself? To despatch myself I want no sword; I need but hold my breath awhile, or strike my head against the wall."

When he had thus spoken, his son went weeping out of the chamber, and with him all the rest, except Demetrius and Apollonides, to whom, being left alone with him, he began to speak more calmly. " And you," said he, " do you also think to keep a man of my age alive by force, and to sit here and silently watch me? Or do you bring me some reasons to prove, that it will not be base and unworthy for Cato, when he can find his safety no other way, to seek it from his enemy? If so, adduce your arguments, and show cause why we should now unlearn what we formerly were taught, in ord · that rejecting all the convictions in which we lived, we may now by Cæsar's help grow wiser, and be yet more obliged to him than for life only. Not that I have determined aught concerning myself, but I would have it in my power to perform what I shall think fit to resolve; and I shall not fail to take you as my advisers, in holding counsel, as I shall do, with the doctrines which your philosophy teaches; in the meantime, do not trouble yourselves, but go tell my son that he should not compel his father to what he cannot persuade him to." They made him no answer, but went weeping out of the chamber. Then the sword being brought in by a little boy, Cato took it, drew it out, and looked at it; and when he saw the point was good, " Now," said he, " I am master of myself;" and laying down the sword, he took his book again, which, it is related, he read twice over. After this he slept so soundly that he was heard to snore by those that were without.

About midnight, he called up two of his freedmen, Cleanthes, his physician, and Butas, whom he chiefly employed in public business. Him he sent to the port, to see if all his friends had sailed; to the physician he gave his hand to be dressed, as it was swollen with the blow he had struck one of his servants. At this they all rejoiced, hoping that now he designed to live.

Butas, after a while, returned, and brought word they were all gone except Crassus, who had stayed about some business, but was just ready to depart; he said, also, that the wind was high, and the sea very rough. Cato, on hearing this, sighed, out of compassion to those who were at sea, and sent Butas again to see if any of them should happen to return for anything they wanted, and to acquaint him therewith.

Now the birds began to sing, and he again fell into a little slumber. At length Butas came back, and told him all was quiet in the port. Then Cato, laying himself down, as if he would sleep out the rest of the night, bade him shut the door after him. But as soon as Butas was gone out, he took his sword, and stabbed it into his breast; yet not being able to use his hand so well, on account of the swelling, he did not immediately die of the wound; but struggling, fell off the bed, and throwing down a little mathematical table that stood by, made such a noise that the servants, hearing it, cried out. And immediately his son and all his friends came into the chamber, where, seeing him lie weltering in his blood, great part of his bowels out of his body, but himself still alive and able to look at them, they all stood in horror. The physician went to him, and would have put in his bowels, which were not pierced, and sewed up the wound; but Cato, recovering himself, and understanding the intention, thrust away the physician, plucked out his own bowels, and tearing open the wound, immediately expired.

In less time than one would think his own family could have known this accident, all the three hundred were at the door. And a little after, the people of Utica flocked thither, crying out with one voice, he was their benefactor and their saviour, the only free and only undefeated man. At the very same time, they had news that Cæsar was coming; yet neither fear of the present danger, nor desire to flatter the conqueror, nor the commotions and discord among themselves, could divert them from doing honour to Cato. For they sumptuously set out his body, made him a magnificent funeral, and buried him by the seaside, where now stands his statue, holding a sword. And only when this had been done, they returned to consider of preserving themselves and their city.

Cæsar had been informed that Cato stayed at Utica, and did not seek to fly; that he had sent away the rest of the Romans, but himself, with his son and a few of his friends, continued there very unconcernedly, so that he could not imagine what might be his design. But having a great consideration for the man, he hastened thither with his army. When he heard of his death, it is related he said these words, " Cato, I grudge you your death, as you have grudged me the preservation of your life." And, indeed, if Cato would have suffered himself to owe his life to Cæsar, he would not so much impaired his own honour, as augmented the other's glory. What would have been done, of course, we cannot know, but from Cæsar's usual clemency, we may guess what was most likely.

Cato was forty-eight years old when he died. His son suffered no injury from Cæsar; but, it is said, he grew idle, and was thought to be dissipated among women. In Cappadocia, he stayed at the house of Marphadates, one of the royal family there, who had a very handsome wife; and continuing his visit longer than was suitable, he made himself the subject of various epigrams; such as, for example—

> " To-morrow (being the thirtieth day)
> Cato, 'tis thought, will go away; "

> " Porcius and Marphadates, friends so true,
> One *Soul*, they say, suffices for the two,"

that being the name of the woman, and so again,—

> " To Cato's greatness every one confesses,
> A royal Soul he certainly possesses."

But all these stains were entirely wiped off by the bravery of his death. For in the battle of Philippi, where he fought for his country's liberty against Cæsar and Antony, when the ranks were breaking, he, scorning to fly, or to escape unknown, called out to the enemy, showed himself to them in front, and encouraged those of his party who stayed; and at length fell, and left his enemies full of admiration of his valour.

Nor was the daughter of Cato inferior to the rest of her family for sober-living and greatness of spirit. She was married to Brutus, who killed Cæsar; was acquainted with the conspiracy, and ended her life as became one of her birth and virtue. All which is related in the life of Brutus.

Statyllius, who said he would imitate Cato, was at that time hindered by the philosophers, when he would have put an end to his life. He afterwards followed Brutus, to whom he was very faithful and very serviceable, and died in the field of Philippi.

## AGIS

THE fable of Ixion, who, embracing a cloud instead of Juno, begot the Centaurs, has been ingeniously enough supposed to have been invented to represent to us ambitious men, whose minds, doting on glory, which is a mere image of virtue, produce nothing that is genuine or uniform, but only, as might be expected of such a conjunction, misshapen and unnatural actions. Running after their emulations and passions, and carried away by the impulses of the moment, they may say with the herdsmen in the tragedy of Sophocles—

> " We follow these, though born their rightful lords,
> And they command us, though they speak no words."

For this is indeed the true condition of men in public life, who, to gain the vain title of being the people's leaders and governors, are content to make themselves the slaves and followers of all the people's humours and caprices. For as the lookout men at the ship's prow, though they see what is ahead before the men at the helm, yet constantly look back to the pilots there, and obey the orders they give; so these men, steered, as I may say, by popular applause, though they bear the name of governors, are in reality the mere underlings of the multitude. The man who is completely wise and virtuous has no need at all of glory, except so far as it disposes and eases his way to action by the greater trust that it procures him. A young man, I grant, may be permitted, while yet eager for distinction, to pride himself a little in his good deeds; for (as Theophrastus says) his virtues, which are yet tender and, as it were, in the blade, cherished and supported by praises, grow stronger, and take the deeper root.

But when this passion is exorbitant, it is dangerous in all men, and in those who govern a commonwealth, utterly destructive. For in the possession of large power and authority, it transports men to a degree of madness; so that now they no more think what is good, glorious, but will have those actions only esteemed good that are glorious. As Phocion, therefore, answered King Antipater, who sought his approbation of some unworthy action, " I cannot be your flatterer, and your friend," so these men should answer the people, " I cannot govern and obey you." For it may happen to the commonwealth, as to the serpent in the fable, whose tail, rising in rebellion against the head, complained, as of a great grievance, that it was always forced to follow, and required that it should be permitted by turns to lead the way. And taking the command accordingly, it soon inflicted, by its senseless courses, mischiefs in abundance upon itself, while the head was torn and lacerated with following, contrary to nature, a guide that was deaf and blind. And such we see to have been the lot of many, who, submitting to be guided by the inclinations of an uninformed and unreasoning multitude, could neither stop, nor recover themselves out of the confusion.

This is what has occurred to us to say of that glory which depends on the voice of large numbers, considering the sad effects of it in the misfortunes of Caius and Tiberius Gracchus, men of noble nature, and whose generous natural dispositions were improved by the best of educations, and who came to the administration of affairs with the most laudable intentions; yet they were ruined, I cannot say by an immoderate desire of glory, but by a more excusable fear of disgrace. For being excessively beloved and favoured by the people, they thought it a discredit to them not to make full repayment, endeavouring by new public acts to outdo the honours they had received, and again, because of these new kindnesses, incurring yet further distinctions; till the people and they, mutually inflamed, and vying thus with each other in honours and benefits, brought things at last to such a pass that they might say that to engage so far was indeed a folly, but to retreat would now be a shame.

This the reader will easily gather from the story. I will now compare with them two Lacedæmonian popular leaders, the kings Agis and Cleomenes. For they, being desirous also to raise the people, and to restore the noble and just form of government, now long fallen into disuse, incurred the hatred of the rich and powerful, who could not endure to be deprived of the selfish enjoyment to which they were accustomed. These were not indeed brothers by nature, as the two Romans, but they had a kind of brotherly resemblance in their actions and designs, which took a rise from such beginnings and occasions as I am now about to relate.

When the love of gold and silver had once gained admittance into the Lacedæmonian commonwealth, it was quickly followed by avarice and baseness of spirit in the pursuit of it, and by luxury, effeminacy, and prodigality in the use. Then Sparta fell from almost all her former virtue and repute, and so continued till the days of Agis and Leonidas, who both together were kings of the Lacedæmonians.

Agis was of the royal family of Eurypon, son of Eudamidas, and the sixth in descent from Agesilaus, who made the expedition into Asia, and was the greatest man of his time in Greece. Agesilaus left behind him a son called Archidamus, the same who was slain at Mandonium, in Italy, by the Messapians, and who was then succeeded by his eldest son Agis. He being killed by Antipater near Megalopolis, and leaving no issue, was succeeded by his brother Eudamidas; he by a son called Archidamus; and Archidamus by another Eudamidas, the father of this Agis of whom we now treat.

Leonidas, son of Cleonymus, was of the other royal house of the Agiadæ, and the eighth in descent from Pausanias, who defeated Mardonius in the battle of Platæa. Pausanias was succeeded by a son called Plistoanax; and he by another Pausanias who was banished, and lived as a private man at Tegea, while his eldest son, Agesipolis, reigned in his place. He, dying without issue, was succeeded by a younger brother, called Cleombrotus, who left two sons; the elder was Agesipolis, who reigned but a short time, and died without issue; the younger, who then became king, was called Cleomenes, and had also two sons, Acrotatus and Cleonymus. The first died before his father, but left a son called Areus, who succeeded, and being slain at Corinth, left the kingdom to his son Acrotatus. This Acrotatus was defeated, and slain near Megalopolis, in a battle against the tyrant Aristodemus; he left his wife big with child, and on her being delivered of a son, Leonidas, son of the above-named Cleonymus, was made his guardian, and as the young king died before becoming a man, he succeeded in the kingdom.

Leonidas was a king not particularly suitable to his people. For though there were at that time at Sparta a general decline in manners, yet a greater revolt from the old habits appeared in

him than in others. For having lived a long time among the
great lords of Persia, and been a follower of King Seleucus, he
unadvisedly thought to imitate, among Greek institutions and
in a lawful government, the pride and assumption usual in those
courts. Agis, on the contrary, in fineness of nature and elevation
of mind, not only far excelled Leonidas, but in a manner all the
kings that had reigned since the great Agesilaus. For though
he had been bred very tenderly, in abundance and even in
luxury, by his mother Agesistrata and his grandmother Archidamia, who were the wealthiest of the Lacedæmonians, yet,
before the age of twenty, he renounced all indulgence in pleasures.
Withdrawing himself as far as possible from the gaiety and ornament which seemed becoming to the grace of his person, he made
it his pride to appear in the coarse Spartan coat. In his meals,
his bathings, and in all his exercises, he followed the old Laconian
usage, and was often heard to say, he had no desire for the place
of king, if he did not hope by means of that authority to restore
their ancient laws and discipline.

The Lacedæmonians might date the beginning of their corruption from their conquest of Athens, and the influx of gold
and silver among them that thence ensued. Yet, nevertheless,
the number of houses which Lycurgus appointed being still
maintained, and the law remaining in force by which every one
was obliged to leave his lot or portion of land entirely to his son,
a kind of order and equality was thereby preserved, which still
in some degree sustained the state amidst its errors in other
respects. But one Epitadeus happening to be ephor, a man of
great influence, and of a wilful, violent spirit, on some occasion
of a quarrel with his son, proposed a decree, that all men should
have liberty to dispose of their land by gift in their lifetime, or
by their last will and testament. This being promoted by him
to satisfy a passion of revenge, and through covetousness consented to by others, and thus enacted for a law, was the ruin of
the best state of the commonwealth. For the rich men without
scruple drew the estate into their own hands, excluding the
rightful heirs from their succession; and all the wealth being
centred upon the few, the generality were poor and miserable.
Honourable pursuits, for which there was no longer leisure, were
neglected; the state was filled with sordid business, and with
hatred and envy of the rich. There did not remain above seven
hundred of the old Spartan families, of which, perhaps, one
hundred might have estates in land, the rest were destitute alike
of wealth and of honour, were tardy and unperforming in the

defence of their country against its enemies abroad, and eagerly watched the opportunity for change and revolution at home.

Agis, therefore, believing it a glorious action, as in truth it was, to equalise and repeople the state, began to sound the inclinations of the citizens. He found the young men disposed beyond his expectation; they were eager to enter with him upon the contest in the cause of virtue, and to fling aside, for freedom's sake, their old manner of life, as readily as the wrestler does his garment. But the old men, habituated and more confirmed in their vices, were most of them as alarmed at the very name of Lycurgus, as a fugitive slave to be brought back before his offended master. These men could not endure to hear Agis continually deploring the present state of Sparta, and wishing she might be restored to her ancient glory. But on the other side, Lysander, the son of Libys, Mandroclidas, the son of Ecphanes, together with Agesilaus, not only approved his design, but assisted and confirmed him in it. Lysander had a great authority and credit with the people; Mandroclidas was esteemed the ablest Greek of his time to manage an affair and put it in train, and, joined with skill and cunning, had a great degree of boldness. Agesilaus was the king's uncle, by the mother's side; an eloquent man, but covetous and voluptuous, who was not moved by considerations of public good, but rather seemed to be persuaded in it by his son Hippomedon, whose courage and signal actions in war had gained him a high esteem and great influence among the young men of Sparta, though indeed the true motive was, that he had many debts, and hoped by this means to be freed from them.

As soon as Agis had prevailed with his uncle, he endeavoured by his mediation to gain his mother also, who had many friends and followers, and a number of persons in her debt in the city, and took a considerable part in public affairs. At the first proposal she was very averse, and strongly advised her son not to engage in so difficult and so unprofitable an enterprise. But Agesilaus endeavoured to possess her, that the thing was not so difficult as she imagined, and that it might, in all likelihood, redound to the advantage of her family; while the king, her son, besought her not for money's sake to decline assisting his hopes of glory. He told her he could not pretend to equal other kings in riches, the very followers and menials of the satraps and stewards of Seleucus or Ptolemy abounding more in wealth than all the Spartan kings put together; but if by contempt of wealth and pleasure, by simplicity and magnanimity, he could surpass their luxury and abundance; if he could restore their former equality to the Spartans, then he should be a great king indeed. In conclusion, the mother and the grandmother also were so taken, so carried away with the inspiration, as it were, of the young man's noble and generous ambition, that they not only consented, but were ready on all occasions to spur him on to a perseverance, and not only sent to speak on his behalf with the men with whom they had an interest, but addressed the other women also, knowing well that the Lacedæmonian wives had always a great power with their husbands, who used to impart to them their state affairs with greater freedom than the women would communicate with the men in the private business of their families. Which was indeed one of the greatest obstacles to this design; for the money of Sparta being most of it in the women's hands, it was their interest to oppose it, not only as depriving them of those superfluous trifles, in which, through want of better knowledge and experience, they placed their chief felicity, but also because they knew their riches were the main support of their power and credit.

Those, therefore, who were of this faction had recourse to Leonidas, representing to him how it was his part, as the elder and more experienced, to put a stop to the ill-advised projects of a rash young man. Leonidas, though of himself sufficiently inclined to oppose Agis, durst not openly, for fear of the people, who were manifestly desirous of this change; but underhand he did all he could to discredit and thwart the project, and to prejudice the chief magistrates against him, and on all occasions craftily insinuated that it was at the price of letting him usurp arbitrary power that Agis thus proposed to divide the property of the rich among the poor, and that the object of these measures for cancelling debts and dividing the lands, was not to furnish Sparta with citizens, but purchase him a tyrant's body guard.

Agis, nevertheless, little regarding these rumours, procured Lysander's election as ephor; and then took the first occasion of proposing through him his Rhetra to the council, the chief articles of which were these: That every one should be free from their debts: all the lands to be divided into equal portions, those that lay betwixt the watercourse near Pellene and Mount Taygetus, and as far as the cities of Malea and Sellasia, into four thousand five hundred lots, the remainder into fifteen thousand; these last to be shared out among those of the country people who were fit for service as heavy-armed soldiers, the first among the natural-born Spartans, and their number also should be supplied from any among the country people or strangers who had received the proper breeding of freemen, and were of vigorous body and of age for military service. All these were to be divided into fifteen companies, some of four hundred, and some of two, with a diet and discipline agreeable to the laws of Lycurgus.

This decree being proposed in the council of Elders met there with opposition; so that Lysander immediately convoked the great assembly of the people, to whom he, Mandroclidas, and Agesilaus made orations exhorting them that they would not suffer the majesty of Sparta to remain abandoned to contempt, to gratify a few rich men, who lorded it over them; but that they should call to mind the oracles in old times which had forewarned them to beware of the love of money, as the great danger and probable ruin of Sparta, and, moreover, those recently brought from the temple of Pasiphae. This was a famous temple and oracle at Thalamæ; and this Pasiphae, some say, was one of the daughters of Atlas, who had by Jupiter a son called Ammon; others are of opinion it was Cassandra, the daughter of King Priam, who dying in this place, was called Pasiphae, as the *revealer* of oracles to *all* men. Phylarchus says, that this was Daphne, the daughter of Amyclas, who, flyivg from Apollo, was transformed into a laurel, and honoured by that god with the gift of prophecy. But be it as it will, it is certain the people were made to apprehend that this oracle had commanded them to return to their former state of equality settled by Lycurgus. As soon as these had done speaking, Agis stood up, and after a few words, told them he would make the best contribution in his power to the new legislation, which was proposed for their advantage. In the first place, he would divide among them all his patrimony, which was of large extent in tillage and pasture; he would also give six hundred talents in ready money, and his mother, grandmother, and his other friends and relations, who were the richest of the Lacedæmonians, were ready to follow his example.

The people were transported with admiration of the young man's generosity, and with joy that, after three hundred years' interval, at last there had appeared a king worthy of Sparta. But, on the other side, Leonidas was now more than ever averse, being sensible that he and his friends would be obliged to contribute with their riches, and yet all the honour and obligation would redound to Agis. He asked him then before them all, whether Lycurgus were not in his opinion a wise man, and a lover of his country. Agis answering he was, " And when did Lycurgus," replied Leonidas, " cancel debts, or admit strangers to citizenship,—he who thought the commonwealth not secure unless from time to time the city was cleared of all strangers? " To this Agis replied, " It is no wonder that Leonidas, who was brought up and married abroad, and has children by a wife taken out of a Persian court, should know little of Lycurgus or his laws. Lycurgus took away both debts and loans, by taking away money; and objected indeed to the presence of men who were foreign to the manners and customs of the country, not in any case from an ill-will to their persons, but lest the example of their lives and conduct should infect the city with the love of riches, and of delicate and luxurious habits. For it is well known that he himself gladly kept Terpander, Thales, and Pherecydes though they were strangers, because he perceived they were in their poems and in their philosophy of the same mind with him. And you that are wont to praise Ecprepes, who, being ephor, cut with his hatchet two of the nine strings from the instrument of Phrynis the musician, and to commend those who afterwards imitated him, in cutting the strings of Timotheus's harp, with what face can you blame us for designing to cut off superfluity and luxury and display from the commonwealth? Do you think those men were so concerned only about a lute-string, or intended anything else than to check in music that same excess and extravagance which rule in our present lives and manners, and have disturbed and destroyed all the harmony and order of our city? "

From this time forward, as the common people followed Agis, so the rich men adhered to Leonidas. They besought him not to forsake their cause; and with persuasions and entreaties so far prevailed with the council of Elders, whose power consisted in preparing all laws before they were proposed to the people, that the designed Rhetra was rejected, though but by only one vote. Whereupon Lysander, who was still ephor, resolving to be revenged on Leonidas, drew up an information against him, grounded on two old laws: the one forbids any of the blood of Hercules to raise up children by a foreign woman, and the other makes it capital for a Lacedæmonian to leave his country to settle among foreigners. Whilst he set others on to manage this accusation, he with his colleagues went *to observe the sign,* which was a custom they had, and performed in this manner. Every ninth year, the ephors, choosing a starlight night, when there is neither cloud nor moon, sit down together in quiet and silence, and watch the sky. And if they chance to see the shooting of a star, they presently pronounce their king guilty of some offence against the gods, and thereupon he is immediately suspended from all exercise of regal power, till he is relieved by an oracle from Delphi or Olympia.

Lysander, therefore, assured the people he had seen a star shoot, and at the same time Leonidas was cited to answer for himself. Witnesses were produced to testify he had married an Asian woman, bestowed on him by one of King Seleucus's lieutenants: that he had two children by her, but she so disliked and hated him, that against his wishes, flying from her, he was in a manner forced to return to Sparta, where his predecessor dying without issue, he took upon him the government. Lysander, not content with this, persuaded also Cleombrotus to lay claim to the kingdom. He was of the royal family, and son-in-law to Leonidas; who, fearing now the event of this process, fled as a suppliant to the temple of Minerva of the Brazen House, together with his daughter, the wife of Cleombrotus; for she in this occasion resolved to leave her husband, and to follow her father. Leonidas being again cited, and not appearing, they pronounced a sentence of deposition against him, and made Cleombrotus king in his place.

Soon after this revolution, Lysander, his year expiring, went out of his office, and new ephors were chosen, who gave Leonidas assurance of safety, and cited Lysander and Mandroclidas to answer for having, contrary to law, cancelled debts, and designed a new division of lands. They, seeing themselves in danger, had recourse to the two kings, and represented to them how necessary it was for their interest and safety to act with united authority, and bid defiance to the ephors. For, indeed, the power of the ephors, they said, was only grounded on the dissensions of the kings, it being their privilege, when the kings differed in opinion, to add their suffrage to whichever they judged to have given the best advice; but when the two kings were unanimous, none ought or durst resist their authority, the magistrate, whose office it was to stand as umpire when they were at variance, had no call to interfere when they were of one mind. Agis and Cleombrotus, thus persuaded, went together with their friends into the market-place, where removing the ephors from their seats, they placed others in their room, of whom Agesilaus was one; proceeding then to arm a company of young men, and releasing many out of prison; so that those of the contrary faction began to be in great fear of their lives;

but there was no blood spilt. On the contrary, Agis, having notice that Agesilaus had ordered a company of soldiers to lie in wait for Leonidas, to kill him as he fled to Tegea, immediately sent some of his followers to defend him, and to convey him safely into that city.

Thus far all things proceeded prosperously, none daring to oppose; but through the sordid weakness of one man, these promising beginnings were blasted, and a most noble and truly Spartan purpose overthrown and ruined by the love of money. Agesilaus, as we said, was much in debt, though in possession of one of the largest and best estates in land; and while he gladly joined in this design to be quit of his debts, he was not at all willing to part with his land. Therefore he persuaded Agis, that if both these things should be put in execution at the same time, so great and so sudden an alteration might cause some dangerous commotion; but if debts were in the first place cancelled, the rich men would afterwards more easily be prevailed with to part with their land. Lysander, also, was of the same opinion, being deceived in like manner by the craft of Agesilaus; so that all men were presently commanded to bring in their bonds, or deeds of obligation, by the Lacedæmonians called *Claria*, into the market-place, where being laid together in a heap, they set fire to them. The wealthy, money-lending people, one may easily imagine, beheld it with a heavy heart; but Agesilaus told them scoffingly, his eyes had never seen so bright and so pure a flame.

And now the people pressed earnestly for an immediate division of lands; the kings also had ordered it should be done; but Agesilaus, sometimes pretending one difficulty, and sometimes another, delayed the execution, till an occasion happened to call Agis to the wars. The Achæans, in virtue of a defensive treaty of alliance, sent to demand succours, as they expected every day that the Ætolians would attempt to enter Peloponnesus, from the territory of Megara. They had sent Aratus, their general, to collect forces to hinder this incursion. Aratus wrote to the ephors, who immediately gave order that Agis should hasten to their assistance with the Lacedæmonian auxiliaries. Agis was extremely pleased to see the zeal and bravery of those who went with him upon this expedition. They were for the most part young men, and poor; and being just released from their debts and set at liberty, and hoping on their return to receive each man his lot of land, they followed their king with wonderful alacrity. The cities through which they passed were in admiration to see how they marched from one end of Pelo-

ponnesus to the other, without the least disorder, and, in a
manner, without being heard. It gave the Greeks occasion to
discourse with one another, how great might be the temperance
and modesty of a Laconian army in old time, under their famous
captains Agesilaus, Lysander, or Leonidas, since they saw such
discipline and exact obedience under a leader who perhaps was
the youngest man in all the army. They saw also how he was
himself content to fare hardly, ready to undergo any labours,
and not to be distinguished by pomp or richness of habit or arms
from the meanest of his soldiers; and to people in general it was
an object of regard and admiration. But rich men viewed the
innovation with dislike and alarm, lest haply the example might
spread, and work changes to their prejudice in their own
countries as well.

Agis joined Aratus near the city of Corinth, where it was still
a matter of debate whether or no it were expedient to give the
enemy battle. Agis, on this occasion, showed great forwardness
and resolution, yet without temerity or presumption. He declared it was his opinion they ought to fight, thereby to hinder
the enemy from passing the gates of Peloponnesus, but nevertheless he would submit to the judgment of Aratus, not only as
the elder and more experienced captain, but as he was general
of the Achæans, whose forces he would not pretend to command,
but was only come thither to assist them. I am not ignorant
that Baton of Sinope relates it in another manner; he says,
Aratus would have fought, and that Agis was against it; but it
is certain he was mistaken, not having read what Aratus himself wrote in his own justification, that knowing the people had
well-nigh got in their harvest, he thought it much better to let
the enemy pass than put all to the hazard of a battle. And,
therefore, giving thanks to the confederates for their readiness,
he dismissed them. And Agis, not without having gained a
great deal of honour, returned to Sparta, where he found the
people in disorder, and a new revolution imminent, owing to
the ill-government of Agesilaus.

For he, being now one of the ephors, and freed from the fear
which formerly kept him in some restraint, forbore no kind of
oppression which might bring in gain. Among other things, he
exacted a thirteenth month's tax, whereas the usual cycle required at this time no such addition to the year. For these and
other reasons fearing those whom he injured, and knowing how
he was hated by the people, he thought it necessary to maintain
a guard, which always accompanied him to the magistrate's

office. And presuming now on his power, he was grown so insolent, that of the two kings, the one he openly contemned, and if he showed any respect towards Agis, would have it thought rather an effect of his near relationship, than any duty or submission to the royal authority. He gave it out also that he was to continue ephor the ensuing year.

His enemies, therefore, alarmed by this report, lost no time in risking an attempt against him; and openly bringing back Leonidas from Tegea, re-established him in the kingdom, to which even the people, highly incensed for having been defrauded in the promised division of lands, willingly consented. Agesilaus himself would hardly have escaped their fury, if his son, Hippomedon, whose manly virtues made him dear to all, had not saved him out of their hands, and then privately conveyed him from the city.

During the commotion, the two kings fled, Agis to the temple of the Brazen House, and Cleombrotus to that of Neptune. For Leonidas was more incensed against his son-in-law; and leaving Agis alone, went with his soldiers to Cleombrotus's sanctuary, and there with great passion reproached him for having, though he was son-in-law, conspired with his enemies, usurped his throne, and forced him from his country. Cleombrotus, having little to say for himself, sat silent. His wife, Chilonis, the daughter of Leonidas, had chosen to follow her father in his sufferings; for when Cleombrotus usurped the kingdom, she forsook him, and wholly devoted herself to comfort her father in his affliction; whilst he still remained in Sparta, she remained also, as a suppliant, with him, and when he fled, she fled with him, bewailing his misfortune, and extremely displeased with Cleombrotus. But now, upon this turn of fortune, she changed in like manner, and was seen sitting now, as a suppliant, with her husband, embracing him with her arms, and having her two little children beside her. All men were full of wonder at the piety and tender affection of the young woman, who pointing to her robes and her hair, both alike neglected and unattended to, said to Leonidas, " I am not brought, my father, to this condition you see me in, on account of the present misfortunes of Cleombrotus; my mourning habit is long since familiar to me. It was put on to condole with you in your banishment; and now you are restored to your country, and to your kingdom, must I still remain in grief and misery? Or would you have me attired in my royal ornaments, that I may rejoice with you, when you have killed, within my arms, the man to whom you gave me for a wife? Either Cleombrotus must appease you by mine and my children's tears, or he must suffer a punishment greater than you propose for his faults, and shall see me, whom he loves so well, die before him. To what end should I live, or how shall I appear among the Spartan women, when it shall so manifestly be seen, that I have not been able to move to compassion either a husband or a father? I was born, it seems, to participate in the ill-fortune and in the disgrace, both as a wife and a daughter, of those nearest and dearest to me. As for Cleombrotus, I sufficiently surrendered any honourable plea on his behalf, when I forsook him to follow you; but you yourself offer the fairest excuse for his proceedings, by showing to the world that for the sake of a kingdom, it is just to kill a son-in-law, and be regardless of a daughter." Chilonis, having ended this lamentation, rested her face on her husband's head, and looked round with her weeping and woe-begone eyes upon those who stood before her.

Leonidas, touched with compassion, withdrew a while to advise with his friends; then returning, bade Cleombrotus leave the sanctuary and go into banishment; Chilonis, he said, ought to stay with him, it not being just she should forsake a father whose affection had granted to her intercession the life of her husband. But all he could say would not prevail. She rose up immediately, and taking one of her children in her arms, gave the other to her husband; and making her reverence to the altar of the goddess, went out and followed him. So that, in a word, if Cleombrotus were not utterly blinded by ambition, he must surely choose to be banished with so excellent a woman rather than without her to possess a kingdom.

Cleombrotus thus removed, Leonidas proceeded also to displace the ephors, and to choose others in their room; then he began to consider how he might entrap Agis. At first, he endeavoured by fair means to persuade him to leave the sanctuary, and partake with him in the kingdom. The people, he said, would easily pardon the errors of a young man, ambitious of glory, and deceived by the craft of Agesilaus. But finding Agis was suspicious, and not to be prevailed with to quit his sanctuary, he gave up that design; yet what could not then be effected by the dissimulation of an enemy, was soon after brought to pass by the treachery of friends.

Amphares, Damochares, and Arcesilaus often visited Agis, and he was so confident of their fidelity that after a while he was prevailed on to accompany them to the baths, which were not far distant, they constantly returning to see him safe again in the temple. They were all three his familiars; and Amphares had borrowed a great deal of plate and rich household stuff from Agesistrata, and hoped if he could destroy her and the whole family, he might peaceably enjoy those goods. And he, it is said, was the readiest of all to serve the purposes of Leonidas, and being one of the ephors, did all he could to incense the rest of his colleagues against Agis. These men, therefore, finding that Agis would not quit his sanctuary, but on occasion would venture from it to go to the bath, resolved to seize him on the opportunity thus given them. And one day as he was returning, they met and saluted him as formerly, conversing pleasantly by the way, and jesting, as youthful friends might, till coming to the turning of a street which led to the prison, Amphares, by virtue of his office, laid his hand on Agis, and told him, " You must go with me, Agis, before the other ephors, to answer for your misdemeanours." At the same time Damochares, who was a tall, strong man, drew his cloak tight round his neck, and dragged him after by it, whilst the others went behind to thrust him on. So that none of Agis's friends being near to assist him, nor any one by, they easily got him into the prison, where Leonidas was already arrived, with a company of soldiers, who strongly guarded all the avenues; the ephors also came in, with as many of the Elders as they knew to be true to their party, being desirous to proceed with some semblance of justice. And thus they bade him give an account of his actions. To which Agis, smiling at their dissimulation, answered not a word. Amphares told him it was more seasonable to weep, for now the time was come in which he should be punished for his presumption. Another of the ephors, as though he would be more favourable, and offering as it were an excuse, asked him whether he was not forced to what he did by Agesilaus and Lysander. But Agis answered, he had not been constrained by any man, nor had any other intent in what he did but only to follow the example of Lycurgus, and to govern conformably to his laws. The same ephor asked him whether now at least he did not repent his rashness. To which the young man answered that though he were to suffer the extremest penalty for it, yet he could never repent of so just and so glorious a design. Upon this they passed sentence of death on him, and bade the officers carry him to the Dechas, as it is called, a place in the prison where they strangle malefactors. And when the officers would not venture to lay hands on him, and the very mercenary

soldiers declined it, believing it an illegal and a wicked act to
lay violent hands on a king, Demochares, threatening and
reviling them for it, himself thrust him into the room.

For by this time the news of his being seized had reached
many parts of the city, and there was a concourse of people
with lights and torches about the prison gates, and in the midst
of them the mother and the grandmother of Agis, crying out
with a loud voice that their king ought to appear, and to be
heard and judged by the people. But this clamour, instead of
preventing, hastened his death; his enemies fearing, if the
tumult should increase, he might be rescued during the night
out of their hands.

Agis, being now at the point to die, perceived one of the
officers bitterly bewailing his misfortune; " Weep not, friend,"
said he, " for me, who die innocent, by the lawless act of wicked
men. My condition is much better than theirs." As soon as
he had spoken these words, not showing the least sign of fear, he
offered his neck to the noose.

Immediately after he was dead, Amphares went out of the
prison gate, where he found Agesistrata, who, believing him
still the same friend as before, threw herself at his feet. He
gently raised her up, and assured her, she need not fear any
further violence or danger of death for her son, and that if she
pleased she might go in and see him. She begged her mother
might also have the favour to be admitted, and he replied,
nobody should hinder it. When they were entered, he commanded the gate should again be locked, and Archidamia, the
grandmother, to be first introduced. She was now grown very
old, and had lived all her days in the highest repute among her
fellows. As soon as Amphares thought she was despatched,
he told Agesistrata she might now go in if she pleased. She
entered, and beholding her son's body stretched on the ground,
and her mother hanging by the neck, the first thing she did was,
with her own hands, to assist the officers in taking down the
body; then covering it decently, she laid it out by her son's,
whom then embracing and kissing his cheeks, " O my son," said
she, " it was thy too great mercy and goodness which brought
thee and us to ruin." Amphares, who stood watching behind
the door, on hearing this, broke in, and said angrily to her,
" Since you approve so well of your son's actions, it is fit you
should partake in his reward." She, rising up to offer herself to
the noose, said only, " I pray that it may redound to the good
of Sparta."

The three bodies being now exposed to view, and the fact divulged, no fear was strong enough to hinder the people from expressing their abhorrence of what was done, and their detestation of Leonidas and Amphares, the contrivers of it. So wicked and barbarous an act had never been committed in Sparta since first the Dorians inhabited Peloponnesus; the very enemies in war, they said, were always cautious in spilling the blood of a Lacedæmonian king, insomuch that in any combat they would decline, and endeavour to avoid them, from feelings of respect and reverence for their station. And certainly we see that in the many battles fought betwixt the Lacedæmonians and the other Greeks, up to the time of Philip of Macedon, not one of their kings was ever killed, except Cleombrotus by a javelin-wound at the battle of Leuctra. I am not ignorant that the Messenians affirm, Theopompus was also slain by their Aristomenes; but the Lacedæmonians deny it, and say he was only wounded.

Be it as it will, it is certain at least that Agis was the first king put to death in Lacedæmon by the ephors, for having undertaken a design noble in itself and worthy of his country, at a time of life when men's errors usually meet with an easy pardon. And if errors he did commit, his enemies certainly had less reason to blame him than had his friends for that gentle and compassionate temper which made him save the life of Leonidas and believe in other men's professions.

# CLEOMONES

THUS fell Agis. His brother Archidamus was too quick for Leonidas, and saved himself by a timely retreat. But his wife, then mother of a young child, he forced from her own house, and compelled Agiatis, for that was her name, to marry his son Cleomenes, though at that time too young for a wife, because he was unwilling that any one else should have her, being heiress to her father Gylippus's great estate; in person the most youthful and beautiful woman in all Greece and well-conducted in her habits of life. And therefore, they say, she did all she could that she might not be compelled to this new marriage. But being thus united to Cleomenes, she indeed hated Leonidas, but to the youth showed herself a kind and obliging wife. He, as soon as they came together, began to love her very much, and the constant kindness that she still retained for the memory of Agis brought somewhat of the like feeling in the young man for him, so that he would often inquire of her concerning what had passed, and attentively listen to the story of Agis's purpose and design. Now Cleomenes had a generous and great soul; he was as temperate and moderate in his pleasures as Agis, but not so scrupulous, circumspect, and gentle. There was something of heat and passion always goading him on, and an impetuosity and violence in his eagerness to pursue anything which he thought good and just. To have men obey him of their own free-will, he conceived to be the best discipline; but likewise, to subdue resistance, and force them to the better course was, in his opinion, commendable and brave.

This disposition made him dislike the management of the city. The citizens lay dissolved in supine idleness and pleasures, the king let everything take its own way, thankful if nobody gave him any disturbance, nor called him away from the enjoyment of his wealth and luxury. The public interest was neglected, and each man intent upon his private gain. It was dangerous, now Agis was killed, so much as to name such a thing as the exercising and training of their youth: and to speak of the ancient temperance, endurance, and equality, was a sort of treason against the state. It is said also that Cleomenes, whilst a boy, studied philosophy under Sphærus, the Borystenite, who crossed over to Sparta, and spent some time and trouble in instructing the youth. Sphærus was one of the first of Zeno the Citiean's scholars, and it is likely enough that he admired the manly temper of Cleomenes and inflamed his generous ambition. The ancient Leonidas, as story tells, being asked what manner of poet he thought Tyrtæus, replied, " Good to whet young men's courage; " for being filled with a divine fury by his poems, they rushed into any danger. And so the Stoic philosophy is a dangerous incentive to strong and fiery dispositions, but where it combines with a grave and gentle temper, is most successful in leading it to its proper good.

Upon the death of his father Leonidas, he succeeded, and observing the citizens of all sorts to be debauched, the rich neglecting the public good, and intent on their private gain and pleasure, and the poor distressed in their own homes, and therefore without either spirit for war or ambition to be trained up as Spartans, that he had only the name of king, and the ephors all the power, he was resolved to change the posture of affairs. He had a friend whose name was Xenares, his lover (such an affection the Spartans express by the term, being *inspired*, or *imbreathed* with); him he sounded, and of him he would commonly inquire what manner of king Agis was, by what means and by what assistance he began and pursued his designs. Xenares, at first, willingly complied with his request, and told him the whole story, with all the particular circumstances of the actions. But when he observed Cleomenes to be extremely affected at the relation, and more than ordinarily taken with Agis's new model of the government, and begging a repetition of the story, he at first severely chid him, told him he was frantic, and at last left off all sort of familiarity and intercourse, yet he never told any man the cause of their disagreement, but would only say, Cleomenes knew very well. Cleomenes, finding Xenares averse to his designs, and thinking all others to be of the same disposition, consulted with none, but contrived the whole business by himself. And considering that it would be easier to bring about an alteration when the city was at war than when in peace, he engaged the commonwealth in a quarrel with the Achæans, who had given them fair occasions to complain. For Aratus, a man of the greatest power amongst all the Achæans, designed from the very beginning to bring all the Peloponnesians into one common body. And to effect this was the one object of all his many commanderships and his long political course; as he thought this the only means to make them a match for their foreign enemies. Pretty nearly all the rest agreed to his proposals, only the Lacedæmonians, the Eleans, and as many of the Arcadians as inclined to the Spartan interest, remained unpersuaded. And so as soon as Leonidas was dead, he began to attack the Arcadians, and wasted those especially that bordered on Achæa; by this means designing to try the inclinations of the Spartans, and despising Cleomenes as a youth, and of no experience in affairs of state or war. Upon this, the ephors sent Cleomenes to surprise the Athenæum, near Belbina, which is a pass commanding an entrance into Laconia, and was then the subject of litigation with the Megalopolitans. Cleomenes possessed himself of the place, and fortified it, at which action Aratus showed no public resentment, but marched by night to surprise Tegea and Orchomenus. The design failed, for those that were to betray the cities into his hands turned afraid; so Aratus retreated, imagining that his design had been undiscovered. But Cleomenes wrote a sarcastic letter to him, and desired to know, as from a friend, whither he intended to march at night; and Aratus answering, that having heard of his design to fortify Belbina, he meant to march thither to oppose him, Cleomenes rejoined that he did not dispute it, but begged to be informed, if he might be allowed to ask the question, why he carried those torches and ladders with him.

Aratus laughing at the jest, and asking what manner of youth this was, Damocrates, a Spartan exile, replied, " If you have any designs upon the Lacedæmonians, begin before this young eagle's talons are grown." Presently after this, Cleomenes, encamping in Arcadia with a few horse and three hundred foot, received orders from the ephors, who feared to engage in the war, commanding him to return home; but when upon his retreat Aratus took Caphyæ, they commissioned him again. In this expedition he took Methydrium, and overran the country of the Argives; and the Achæans, to oppose him, came out with an army of twenty thousand foot and one thousand horse, under the command of Aristomachus. Cleomenes faced them at Pallantium, and offered battle, but Aratus, being cowed by his bravery, would not suffer the general to engage, but retreated, amidst the reproaches of the Achæans and the derision and scorn of the Spartans, who were not above five thousand. Cleomenes, encouraged by this success, began to speak boldly among the citizens, and reminding them of a sentence of one of their ancient kings, said, it was in vain now that the Spartans asked not how many their enemies were, but where they were. After this, marching to the assistance of the Eleans, whom the Achæans were attacking, falling upon the enemy in their retreat near the Lycæum, he put their whole army to flight, taking a great number of captives, and leaving many dead upon the place; so that it was commonly reported amongst the Greeks that Aratus was slain. But Aratus, making the best advantage of the opportunity, immediately after the defeat marched to Mantinea, and before anybody suspected it, took the city, and put a garrison into it. Upon this, the Lacedæmonians being quite discouraged, and opposing Cleomenes's designs of carrying on the war, he now exerted himself to have Archidamus, the brother of Agis, sent for from Messene, as he, of the other family, had a right to the kingdom; and besides, Cleomenes thought that the power of the ephors would be reduced, when the kingly state was thus filled up, and raised to its proper position. But those that were concerned in the murder of Agis, perceiving the design, and fearing that upon Archidamus's return that they should be called to an account, received him on his coming privately into town, and joined in bringing him home, and presently after murdered him. Whether Cleomenes was against it, as Phylarchus thinks, or whether he was persuaded by his friends, or let him fall into their hands, is uncertain; however, they were most blamed, as having forced his consent.

He, still resolving to new model the state, bribed the ephors to send him out to war; and won the affections of many others by means of his mother Cratesiclea, who spared no cost and was very zealous to promote her son's ambition; and though of herself she had no inclination to marry, yet for his sake she accepted, as her husband, one of the chiefest citizens for wealth and power. Cleomenes, marching forth with the army now under his command, took Leuctra, a place belonging to Megalopolis; and the Achæans quickly coming up to resist him with a good body of men commanded by Aratus, in a battle under the very walls of the city, some part of his army was routed. But whereas Aratus had commanded the Achæans not to pass a deep watercourse, and thus put a stop to the pursuit, Lydiadas, the Megalopolitan, fretting at the orders, and encouraging the horse which he led, and following the routed enemy, got into a place full of vines, hedges, and ditches; and being forced to break his ranks, began to retire in disorder. Cleomenes, observing the advantage, commanded the Tarentines and Cretans to engage him, by whom, after a brave defence, he was routed and slain. The Lacedæmonians, thus encouraged, fell with a great shout upon the Achæans, and routed their whole army. Of the slain, who were very many, the rest Cleomenes delivered up, when the enemy petitioned for them; but the body of Lydiadas he commanded to be brought to him; and then putting on it a purple robe, and a crown upon its head, sent a convoy with it to the gates of Megalopolis. This is that Lydiadas who resigned his power as tyrant, restored liberty to the citizens, and joined the city to the Achæan interest.

Cleomenes, being very much elated by this success, and persuaded that if matters were wholly at his disposal he should soon be too hard for the Achæans, persuaded Magistonus, his mother's husband, that it was expedient for the state to shake off the power of the ephors, and to put all their wealth into one common stock for the whole body; thus Sparta, being restored to its old equality, might aspire again to the command of all Greece. Megistonus liked the design, and engaged two or three more of his friends. About that time, one of the ephors, sleeping in Pasiphæ's temple, dreamed a very surprising dream; for he thought he saw the four chairs removed out of the place where the ephors used to sit and do the business of their office, and one only set there; and whilst he wondered, he heard a voice out of the temple, saying, " This is best for Sparta." The person telling Cleomenes this dream, he was a little troubled at first, fearing that he used this as a trick to sift him, upon some suspicion of his design, but when he was satisfied that the relator spoke truth, he took heart again. And carrying with him those whom he thought would be most against his project, he took Heræa and Alsæa, two towns in league with the Achæans, furnished Orchomenus with provisions, encamped before Mantinea, and with long marches up and down so harassed the Lacedæmonians that many of them at their own request were left behind in Arcadia, while he with the mercenaries went on toward Sparta, and by the way communicated his design to those whom he thought fitted for his purpose, and marched slowly, that he might catch the ephors at supper.

When he was come near the city, he sent Euryclidas to the public table, where the ephors supped, under pretence of carrying some message from him from the army; Therycion, Phœbis, and two of those who had been bred up with Cleomenes, whom they call *mothaces*, followed with a few soldiers; and whilst Euryclidas was delivering his message to the ephors, they ran upon them with their drawn swords, and slew them. The first of them, Agylæus, on receiving the blow, fell, and lay as dead; but in a little time quietly raising himself, and drawing himself out of the room, he crept, without being discovered, into a little building which was dedicated to Fear, and which always used to be shut, but then by chance was open; and being got in, he shut the door, and lay close. The other four were killed, and above ten more that came to their assistance; to those that were quiet they did no harm, stopped none that fled from the city, and spared Agylæus when he came out of the temple the next day.

The Lacedæmonians have not only sacred places dedicated to Fear, but also to Death, Laughter, and the like Passions. Now they worship Fear, not as they do supernatural powers which they dread, esteeming it hurtful, but thinking their polity is chiefly kept up by fear. Therefore the ephors, Aristotle is my author, when they entered upon their government, made proclamation to the people, that they should shave their mustaches and be obedient to the laws, that the laws might not be hard upon them, making, I suppose, this trivial injunction to accustom their youth to obedience even in the smallest matters. And the ancients, I think, did not imagine bravery to be plain fearlessness, but a cautious fear of blame and disgrace. For those that show most timidity towards the laws are most bold against their enemies; and those are least afraid of any danger who are most afraid of a just reproach. Therefore it was well said that—

> " A reverence still attends on fear; "

and by Homer,—

> " Feared you shall be, dear father, and revered; "

and again,—

> " In silence fearing those that bore the sway; "

for the generality of men are most ready to reverence those whom they fear. And, therefore, the Lacedæmonians placed the temple of Fear by the Syssitium of the ephors, having raised that magistracy to almost royal authority.

The next day, Cleomenes proscribed eighty of the citizens whom he thought necessary to banish, and removed all the seats of the ephors, except one, in which he himself designed to sit and give audience; and calling the citizens together he made an apology for his proceedings, saying, that by Lycurgus the counsel of Elders was joined to the kings, and that that model of government had continued a long time, and no other sort of magistrates had been wanted. But afterwards, in the long war with the Messenians, when the kings, having to command the army, found no time to administer justice, they chose some of their friends, and left them to determine the suits of the citizens in their stead. These were called ephors, and at first behaved themselves as servants to the kings; but afterwards, by degrees, they appropriated the power to themselves, and erected a distinct magistracy. An evidence of the truth of this was the custom still observed by the kings, who, when the ephors send for them, refuse, upon the first and the second summons, to go, but upon the third rise up and attend them. And Asteropus, the first that raised the ephors to that height of power, lived a great many years after their institution. So long, therefore, he continued, as they contained themselves within their own proper sphere, it had been better to bear with them than to make a disturbance. But that an upstart introduced power should so far subvert the ancient form of government as to banish some kings, murder others, without hearing their defence, and threaten those who desired to see the best and most divine constitution restored in Sparta, was not to be borne. Therefore, if it had been possible for him without bloodshed to free Lacedæmon from those foreign plagues, luxury, sumptuosity, debts, and usury, and from those yet more ancient evils, poverty and riches, he should have thought himself the happiest king in the world, to have succeeded, like an expert physician, in curing the diseases of his country without pain. But now, in this necessity, Lycurgus's example favoured his proceedings, who being neither king nor magistrate, but a private man, and aiming at the kingdom, came armed into the market-place, so that King Charillus fled in alarm to the altar. He, being a good man, and a lover of his country, readily concurred in Lycurgus's designs, and admitted the revolution in the state. But, by his own actions, Lycurgus had nevertheless borne witness that it was difficult to change the government without force and fear, in the use of which he himself, he said, had been so moderate as to do no more than put out of the way those who opposed themselves to Sparta's happiness and safety. For the rest of the nation, he told them, the whole land was now their common property; debtors should be cleared of their debts, and examination made of those who were not citizens, that the bravest men might thus be made free Spartans, and give aid in arms to save the city, and " we," he said, " may no longer see Laconia, for want of men to defend it, wasted by the Ætolians and Illyrians."

Then he himself first, with his step-father, Megistonus, and his friends, gave up all their wealth into one public stock, and all the other citizens followed the example. The land was divided, and every one that he had banished had a share assigned him; for he promised to restore all as soon as things were settled and in quiet. And completing the number of citizens out of the best and most promising of the country people, he raised a body of four thousand men; and instead of a spear, taught them to use a *sarissa*, with both hands, and to carry their shields by a band, and not by a handle, as before. After this he began to consult about the education of the youth, and the Discipline, as they call it; most of the particulars of which Sphærus, being then at Sparta, assisted in arranging; and in a short time the schools of exercise and the common tables recovered their ancient decency and order, a few out of necessity, but the most voluntarily, returning to that generous and Laconic way of living. And, that the name of monarch might give them no jealousy, he made Euclidas, his brother, partner in the throne; and that was the only time that Sparta had two kings of the same family.

Then, understanding that the Achæans and Aratus imagined that this change had disturbed and shaken his affairs, and that he would not venture out of Sparta and leave the city now unsettled in the midst of so great an alteration, he thought it great and serviceable to his designs to show his enemies the zeal and forwardness of his troops. And, therefore, making an incursion into the territories of Megalopolis, he wasted the country far and wide, and collected considerable booty. And at last, taking a company of actors as they were travelling from Messene, and building a theatre in the enemy's country, and offering a prize of forty minæ in value, he sat spectator a whole day; not that he either desired or needed such amusement, but wishing to show his disregard for his enemies, and by a display of his contempt, to prove the extent of his superiority to them. For his alone, of all the Greek or royal armies, had no stage-players, no jugglers, no dancing or singing women attending it, but was free from all sorts of looseness, wantonness, and festivity; the young men being for the most part at their exercises, and the old men giving them lessons, or, at leisure times, diverting themselves with their native jests, and quick Laconian answers; the good results of which we have noticed in the life of Lycurgus.

He himself instructed all by his example; he was a living pattern of temperance before every man's eyes; and his course of living was neither more stately, nor more expensive, nor in any way more pretentious, than that of his people. And this was a considerable advantage to him in his designs on Greece. For men when they waited upon other kings did not so much admire their wealth, costly furniture, and numerous attendance, as they hated their pride and state, their difficulty of access, and imperious answers to their addresses. But when they came to Cleomenes, who was both really a king and bore that title, and saw no purple, no robes of state upon him, no couches and litters about him for his ease, and that he did not receive requests and return answers after a long delay and difficulty, through a number of messengers and door-keepers, or by memorials, but that he rose and came forward in any dress he might happen to be wearing, to meet those that came to wait upon him, stayed, talked freely and affably with all that had business, they were extremely taken, and won to his service, and professed that he alone was the true son of Hercules. His common every-day's meal was in an ordinary room, very sparing, and after the Laconic manner; and when he entertained ambassadors, or strangers, two more couches were added, and a little better dinner provided by his servants, but no savouring sauces or sweetmeats; only the dishes were larger, and the wine more plentiful. For he reproved one of his friends for entertaining some strangers with nothing but barley bread and black broth, such diet as they usually had in their *phiditia;* saying that upon such occasions, and when they entertained strangers, it was not well to be too exact Laconians. After the table was removed, a stand was brought in with a brass vessel full of wine, two silver bowls, which held about a pint apiece, a few silver cups, of which he that pleased might drink, but wine was not urged on any of the guests. There was no music, nor was any required; for he entertained the company himself, sometimes asking questions, sometimes telling stories; and his conversation was neither too grave or disagreeably serious, nor yet in any way rude or ungraceful in its pleasantry. For he thought those ways of entrapping men by gifts and presents, which other kings use, dishonest and artificial; and it seemed to him to be the most noble method, and most suitable to a king, to win the affections of those that came near him, by personal intercourse and agreeable conversation, since between a friend and a mercenary the only distinction is, that we gain the one by one's character and conversation, the other by one's money.

The Mantineans were the first that requested his aid; and when he entered their city by night, they aided him to expel the Achæan garrison, and put themselves under his protection. He restored them their polity and laws, and the same day marched to Tegea; and a little while after, fetching a compass through Arcadia, he made a descent upon Pheræ, in Achæa, intending to force Aratus to a battle, or bring him into disrepute for refusing to engage, and suffering him to waste the country. Hyperbatas at that time was general, but Aratus had all the power amongst the Achæans, marching forth with their whole strength, and encamping in Dymæ, near the Hecatombæum, Cleomenes came up, and thinking it not advisable to pitch between Dymæ, a city of the enemies, and the camp of the Achæans, he boldly dared the Achæans, and forced them to a battle, and routing their phalanx, slew a great many in the fight, and took many prisoners, and thence marching to Langon, and driving out the Achæan garrison, he restored the city to the Eleans.

The affair of the Achæans being in this unfortunate condition, Aratus, who was wont to take the office every other year, refused the command, though they entreated and urged him to accept it. And this was ill-done, when the storm was high, to put the power out of his own hands, and set another to the helm. Cleomenes at first proposed fair and easy conditions by his ambassadors to the Achæans, but afterwards he sent others, and required the chief command to be settled upon him; in other matters offering to agree to reasonable terms, and to restore their captives and their country. The Achæans were willing to come to an agreement upon those terms, and invited Cleomenes to Lerna, where an assembly was to be held; but it happened that Cleomenes, hastily marching on, and drinking water at a wrong time, brought up a quantity of blood and lost his voice; therefore being unable to continue his journey, he sent the chiefest of the captives to the Achæans, and, putting off the meeting for some time, retired to Lacedæmon.

This ruined the affairs of Greece, which was just beginning in some sort to recover from its disasters, and to show some capability of delivering itself from the insolence and rapacity of the Macedonians. For Aratus (whether fearing or distrusting Cleomenes, or envying his unlooked-for success, or thinking it a disgrace for him who had commanded thirty-three years to have a young man succeed to all his glory and his power, and be head of that government which he had been raising and settling so many years), first endeavoured to keep the Achæans from closing with Cleomenes; but when they would not hearken to him, fearing Cleomenes' daring spirit, and thinking the Lacedæmonians' proposals to be very reasonable, who designed only to reduce Peloponnesus to its own model, upon this he took his last refuge in an action which was unbecoming any of the Greeks, most dishonourable to him, and most unworthy his former bravery and exploits. For he called Antigonus into Greece and filled Peloponnesus with Macedonians, whom he himself, when a youth, having beaten their garrison out of the castle of Corinth, had driven from the same country. And there had been constant suspicion and variance between him and all the kings, and of Antigonus, in particular, he has said a thousand dishonourable things in the commentaries he has left behind him. And though he declares himself how he suffered considerable losses, and underwent great dangers, that he might free Athens from the garrison of the Macedonians, yet, afterwards, he brought the very same men armed into his own country, and his own house, even to the women's apartment. He would not endure that one of the family of Hercules, and king of Sparta, and one that reformed the polity of his country, as it were, from a disordered harmony, and returned it to the plain Doric measure and rule of life of Lycurgus, should be styled head of the Tritæans and Sicyonians; and whilst he fled the barley-cake and coarse coat, and, which were his chief accusations against Cleomenes, the extirpation of wealth and reformation of poverty, he basely subjected himself, together with Achæa, to the diadem and purple, to the imperious commands of the Macedonians and their satraps. That he might not seem to be under Cleomenes, he offered sacrifices, called Antigonea, in honour of Antigonus, and sang pæans himself, with a garland on his head, to the praise of a wasted, consumptive Macedonian. I write this not out of any design to disgrace Aratus, for in many things he showed himself a true lover of Greece, and a great man, but out of pity to the weakness of human nature, which, in characters like this, so worthy and in so many ways disposed to virtue, cannot maintain its honours unblemished by some envious fault.

The Achæans meeting again in assembly at Argos, and Cleomenes having come from Tegea, there were great hopes that all differences would be composed. But Aratus, Antigonus and he having already agreed upon the chief articles of their league, fearing that Cleomenes would carry all before him, and either win or force the multitude to comply with his demands, proposed that, having three hundred hostages put into his hands, he should come alone into the town, or bring his army to the place of exercise, called the Cyllarabium, outside the city, and treat there.

Cleomenes, hearing this, said that he was unjustly dealt with; for they ought to have told him so plainly at first, and not now he was come even to their doors, show their jealousy and deny him admission. And writing a letter to the Achæans about the same subject, the greatest part of which was an accusation of Aratus, while Aratus, on the other side, spoke violently against him to the assembly, he hastily dislodged, and sent a trumpeter to denounce war against the Achæans, not to Argos, but to Ægium, as Aratus writes, that he might not give them notice enough to make provision for their defence. There had also been a movement among the Achæans themselves, and the cities were eager for revolt; the common people expecting a division of the land, and a release from their debts, and the chief men being in many places ill-disposed to Aratus, and some of them angry and indignant with him for having brought the Macedonians into Peloponnesus. Encouraged by these misunderstandings, Cleomenes invaded Achæa, and first took Pellene by surprise, and beat out the Achæan garrison, and afterwards brought over Pheneus and Pentelleum to his side. Now the Achæans, suspecting some treacherous designs at Corinth and Sicyon, sent their horse and mercenaries out of Argos, to have an eye upon those cities, and they themselves went to Argos to celebrate the Nemean games. Cleomenes, advertised of this march, and hoping, as it afterwards fell out, that upon an un-expected advance to the city, now busied in the solemnity of the games, and thronged with numerous spectators, he should raise a considerable terror and confusion amongst them by night, marched with his army to the walls, and taking the quarter of the town called Aspis, which lies above the theatre, well fortified, and hard to be approached, he so terrified them that none offered to resist, but they agreed to accept a garrison, to give twenty citizens for hostages, and to assist the Lacedæmonians, and that he should have the chief command.

This action considerably increased his reputation and his power; for the ancient Spartan kings, though they in many ways endeavoured to effect it, could never bring Argos to be perma-nently theirs. And Pyrrhus, the most experienced captain, though he entered the city by force, could not keep possession, but was slain himself, with a considerable part of his army. Therefore they admired the despatch and contrivance of Cleo-menes; and those that before derided him, for imitating, as they said, Solon and Lycurgus, in releasing the people from their debts, and in equalising the property of the citizens, were now fain to admit that this was the cause of the change in the Spartans. For before they were very low in the world, and so unable to secure their own, that the Ætolians, invading Laconia, brought away fifty thousand slaves; so that one of the elder Spartans is reported to have said, that they had done Laconia a kindness by unburdening it; and yet a little while after, by merely recurring once again to their native customs, and re-entering the track of the ancient discipline, they were able to give, as though it had been under the eyes and conduct of Lycurgus himself, the most signal instances of courage and obedience, raising Sparta to her ancient place as the commanding state of Greece, and recovering all Peloponnesus.

When Argos was captured, and Cleonæ and Phlius came over, as they did at once, to Cleomenes, Aratus was at Corinth, search-ing after some who were reported to favour the Spartan interest. The news, being brought to him, disturbed him very much; for he perceived the city inclining to Cleomenes, and willing to be rid of the Achæans. Therefore he summoned the citizens to meet in the Council Hall, and slipping away without being observed to the gate, he mounted his horse that had been brought for him thither, and fled to Sicyon. And the Corinthians made such haste to Cleomenes at Argos, that, as Aratus says, striving who should be first there, they spoiled all their horses; he adds that Cleomenes was very angry with the Corinthians for letting him escape; and that Megistonus came from Cleomenes to him, desiring him to deliver up the castle at Corinth, which was then garrisoned by the Achæans, and offered him a considerable sum of money, and that he answered that matters were not now in his power, but he in theirs. Thus Aratus himself writes. But Cleomenes, marching from Argos, and taking in the Trœzenians, Epidaurians, and Hermioneans, came to Corinth, and blocked up the castle, which the Achæans would not surrender; and sending for Aratus's friends and stewards, committed his house and estate to their care and management; and sent Tritymallus, the Messenian, to him a second time, desiring that the castle might be equally garrisoned by the Spartans and Achæans, and promising to Aratus himself double the pension that he received from King Ptolemy. But Aratus, refusing the conditions, and sending his own son with the other hostages to Antigonus, and persuading the Achæans to make a decree for delivering the castle into Antigonus's hands, upon this Cleomenes invaded the territory of the Sicyonians, and by a decree of the Corinthians, accepted Aratus's estate as a gift.

In the meantime Antigonus, with a great army, was passing Geranea; and Cleomenes, thinking it more advisable to fortify and garrison, not the isthmus, but the mountains called Onea, and by a war of posts and positions to weary the Macedonians, rather than to venture a set battle with the highly disciplined phalanx, put his design into execution, and very much distressed Antigonus. For he had not brought victuals sufficient for his army; nor was it easy to force a way through whilst Cleomenes guarded the pass. He attempted by night to pass through Lechæum, but failed and lost some men; so that Cleomenes and his army were mightily encouraged, and so flushed with the victory, that they went merrily to supper; and Antigonous was very much dejected, being driven, by the necessity he was in, to most unpromising attempts. He was proposing to march to the promontory of Heræum, and thence transport his army in boats to Sicyon, which would take up a great deal of time, and require much preparation and means. But when it was now evening, some of Aratus's friends came from Argos by sea, and invited him to return, for the Argives would revolt from Cleomenes. Aristoteles was the man that wrought the revolt, and he had no hard task to persuade the common people; for they were all angry with Cleomenes for not releasing them from their debts as they expected. Accordingly, obtaining fifteen hundred of Antigonus's soldiers, Aratus sailed to Epidaurus; but Aristoteles, not staying for his coming, drew out the citizens, and fought against the garrison of the castle; and Timoxenus, with the Achæans from Sicyon, came to his assistance.

Cleomenes heard the news about the second watch of the night, and sending for Megistonus, angrily commanded him to go and set things right at Argos. Megistonus had passed his word for the Argives' loyalty, and had persuaded him not to banish the suspected. Therefore, despatching him with two thousand soldiers, he himself kept watch upon Antigonus, and encouraged the Corinthians, pretending that there was no great matter in the commotions at Argos, but only a little disturbance raised by a few inconsiderable persons. But when Megistonus, entering Argos, was slain, and the garrison could scarce hold out, and frequent messengers came to Cleomenes for succours, he fearing lest the enemy, having taken Argos, should shut up the passes and securely waste Laconia, and besiege Sparta itself, which he had left without forces, dislodged from Corinth, and immediately lost that city; for Antigonus entered it, and garrisoned the town. He turned aside from his direct march, and assaulting the walls of Argos, endeavoured to carry it by a sudden attack; and then, having collected his forces from their march, breaking into the Aspis, he joined the garrison, which still held out against the Achæans; some parts of the city he scaled and took, and his Cretan archers cleared the streets. But when he saw Antigonus with his phalanx descending from the mountains into the plain, and the horse on all sides entering the city, he thought it impossible to maintain his post, and, gathering together all his men, came safely down and made his retreat under the walls, having in so short a time possessed himself of great power, and in one journey, so to say, having made himself master of all Peloponnesus, and now lost all again in as short a time. For some of his allies at once withdrew and forsook him, and others not long after put their cities under Antigonus's protection. His hopes thus defeated, as he was leading back the relics of his forces, messengers from Lacedæmon met him in the evening at Tegea, and brought him news of as great a misfortune as that which he had lately suffered, and this was the death of his wife, to whom he was so attached, and thought so much of her, that even in his most successful expeditions, when he was most prosperous, he could not refrain, but would every now and then come home to Sparta, to visit Agiatis.

This news afflicted him extremely, and he grieved, as a young man would do, for the loss of a very beautiful and excellent wife; yet he did not let his passion disgrace him or impair the greatness of his mind, but keeping his usual voice, his countenance, and his habit, he gave necessary orders to his captains, and took the precautions required for the safety of Tegea. Next morning he came to Sparta, and having at home, with his mother and children, bewailed the loss, and finished his mourning, he at once devoted himself to the public affairs of the state.

Now Ptolemy, the king of Egypt, promised him assistance, but demanded his mother and children for hostages. This, for some considerable time, he was ashamed to discover to his mother; and though he often went to her on purpose, and was just upon the discourse, yet he still refrained, and kept it to himself; so that she began to suspect, and asked his friends, whether Cleomenes had something to say to her, which he was afraid to speak. At last, Cleomenes venturing to tell her, she laughed aloud, and said, " Was this the thing that you had so often a mind to tell me, and were afraid? Make haste and put me on ship-board, and send this carcase where it may be most service-able to Sparta, before age destroys it unprofitably here." There-fore, all things being provided for the voyage, they went by land to Tænarus, and the army waited on them. Cratesiclea, when she was ready to go on board, took Cleomenes aside into Neptune's temple, and embracing him, who was much dejected and ex-tremely discomposed, she said, " Go to, King of Sparta; when we come forth at the door, let none see us weep, or show any passion that is unworthy of Sparta, for that alone is in our own power; as for success or disappointment, those wait on us as the deity decrees." Having thus said, and composed her counten-ance, she went to the ship with her little grandson, and bade the pilot put at once out to sea. When she came to Egypt, and understood that Ptolemy entertained proposals and overtures of peace from Antigonus, and that Cleomenes, though the Achæans invited and urged him to an agreement, was afraid, for her sake, to come to any, without Ptolemy's consent, she wrote to him, advising him to do that which was most becoming and most profitable for Sparta, and not, for the sake of an old woman and a little child, stand always in fear of Ptolemy. This character she maintained in her misfortunes.

Antigonus, having taken Tegea, and plundered Orchomenus and Mantinea, Cleomenes was shut up within the narrow bounds of Laconia; and making such of the helots as could pay five Attic pounds free of Sparta, and, by that means, getting together five hundred talents, and arming two thousand after the Macedonian fashion, that he might make a body fit to oppose Antigonus's Leucaspides, he undertook a great and unexpected enterprise. Megalopolis was at that time a city of itself as great and as powerful as Sparta, and had the forces of the Achæans and of Antigonus encamping beside it; and it was chiefly the Megalopolitans' doing, that Antigonus had been called in to assist the Achæans. Cleomenes, resolving to snatch the city (no other word so well suits so rapid and so surprising an action), ordered his men to take five days' provision, and marched to Sellasia, as if he intended to ravage the country of the Argives; but from thence making a descent into the territories of Megalopolis, and refreshing his army about Rhœteum, he suddenly took the road by Helicus, and advanced directly upon the city. When he was not far off the town, he sent Panteus, with two regiments, to surprise a portion of the wall between two towers, which he learnt to be the most unguarded quarter of the Megalopolitans' fortifications, and with the rest of his forces he followed leisurely. Panteus not only succeeded at that point, but finding a great part of the wall without guards, he at once proceeded to pull it down in some places, and make openings through it in others, and killed all the defenders that he found. Whilst he was thus busied, Cleomenes came up to him, and was got with his army within the city, before the Megalopolitans knew of the surprise. When, after some time, they learned their misfortune, some left the town immediately, taking with them what property they could; others armed and engaged the enemy; and though they were not able to beat them out, yet they gave their citizens time and opportunity safely to retire, so that there were not above one thousand persons taken in the town, all the rest flying, with their wives and children, and escaping to Messene. The greater number, also, of those that armed and fought the enemy were saved, and very few taken, amongst whom were Lysandridas and Thearidas, two men of great power and reputation amongst the Megalopolitans; and therefore the soldiers, as soon as they were taken, brought them to Cleomenes. And Lysandridas, as soon as he saw Cleomenes afar off, cried out, "Now, King of Sparta, it is in your power, by doing a most kingly and a nobler action than you have already performed, to purchase the greatest glory." And Cleomenes, guessing at his meaning, replied, "What, Lysandridas, you will not surely advise me to restore your city to you again?" "It is that which I mean," Lysandridas replied; "and I advise you not to ruin so brave a city, but to fill it with faithful and steadfast friends and allies, by restoring their country to the Megalopolitans, and being the saviour of so considerable a people." Cleomenes paused a while, and then said: "It is very hard to trust so far in these matters; but with us let profit always yield to glory." Having said this, he sent the two men to Messene with a herald from himself, offering the Megalopolitans their city again, if they would forsake the Achæan interest, and be on his side. But though Cleomenes made these generous and humane proposals, Philopœmen would not suffer them to break their league with the Achæans; and accusing Cleomenes to the people, as if his design was not to restore the city, but to take the citizens too, he forced Thearidas and Lysandridas to leave Messene.

This was that Philopœmen who was afterwards chief of the Achæans and a man of the greatest reputation amongst the Greeks, as I have related in his own life. This news coming to Cleomenes, though he had before taken strict care that the city should not be plundered, yet then, being in anger, and out of all patience, he despoiled the place of all the valuables, and sent the statues and pictures to Sparta; and demolishing a great part of the city, he marched away for fear of Antigonus and the Achæans; but they never stirred, for they were at Ægium, at a council of war. There Aratus mounted the speaker's place, and wept a long while, holding his mantle before his face; and at last, the company being amazed, and commanding him to speak, he said, "Megalopolis is destroyed by Cleomenes." The assembly instantly dissolved, the Achæans being astounded at the suddenness and greatness of the loss; and Antigonus, intending to send speedy succours, when he found his forces gather very slowly out of their winter-quarters, sent them orders to continue there still; and he himself marched to Argos with a small body of men. And now the second enterprise of Cleomenes, though it had the look of a desperate and frantic adventure, yet in Polybius's opinion, was done with mature deliberation and great foresight. For knowing very well that the Macedonians were dispersed into their winter-quarters, and that Antigonus

with his friends and a few mercenaries about him wintered in
Argos, upon these considerations he invaded the country of the
Argives, hoping to shame Antigonus to a battle upon unequal
terms, or else if he did not dare to fight, to bring him into
disrepute with the Achæans. And this accordingly happened.
For Cleomenes wasting, plundering, and spoiling the whole
country, the Argives, in grief and anger at the loss, gathered
in crowds at the king's gates, crying out that he should either
fight, or surrender his command to better and braver men. But
Antigonus, as became an experienced captain, accounting it
rather dishonourable foolishly to hazard his army and quit his
security, than merely to be railed at by other people, would not
march out against Cleomenes, but stood firm to his convictions.
Cleomenes, in the meantime, brought his army up to the very
walls, and having without opposition spoiled the country, and
insulted over his enemies, drew off again.

A little while after, being informed that Antigonus designed
a new advance to Tegea, and thence to invade Laconia, he
rapidly took his soldiers, and marching by a side-road, appeared
early in the morning before Argos, and wasted the fields about
it. The corn he did not cut down, as is usual, with reaping hooks
and knives, but beat it down with great wooden staves made
like broadswords, as if, in mere contempt and wanton scorn,
while travelling on his way, without any effort or trouble, he
spoiled and destroyed their harvest. Yet when his soldiers
would have set Cyllabaris, the exercise ground, on fire, he stopped
the attempt, as if he felt that the mischief he had done at
Megalopolis had been the effects of his passion rather than his
wisdom. And when Antigonus, first of all, came hastily back
to Argos, and then occupied the mountains and passes with his
posts, he professed to disregard and despise it all; and sent
heralds to ask for the keys of the temple of Juno, as though he
proposed to offer sacrifice there and then return. And with this
scornful pleasantry upon Antigonus, having sacrificed to the
goddess under the walls of the temple, which was shut, he went
to Phlius; and from thence driving out those that garrisoned
Oligyrtus, he marched down to Orchomenus. And these enterprises not only encouraged the citizens, but made him appear to
the very enemies to be a man worthy of high command, and
capable of great things. For with the strength of one city, not
only to fight the power of the Macedonians and all the Peloponnesians, supported by all the royal treasures, not only to
preserve Laconia from being spoiled, but to waste the enemy's

country, and to take so many and such considerable cities, was an argument of no common skill and genius for command.

But he that first said that money was the sinews of affairs, seems especially in that saying to refer to war. Demades, when the Athenians had voted that their galleys should be launched and equipped for action, but could produce no money, told them, "The baker was wanted first, and the pilot after." And the old Archidamus, in the beginning of the Peloponnesian war, when the allies desired that the amount of their contributions should be determined, is reported to have answered, that war cannot be fed upon so much a day. For as wrestlers, who have thoroughly trained and disciplined their bodies, in time tire down and exhaust the most agile and most skilful combatant, so Antigonus, coming to the war with great resources to spend from, wore out Cleomenes, whose poverty made it difficult for him to provide the merest sufficiency of pay for the mercenaries, or of provisions for the citizens. For, in all other respects, time favoured Cleomenes; for Antigonus's affairs at home began to be disturbed. For the barbarians wasted and overran Macedonia whilst he was absent, and at that particular time a vast army of Illyrians had entered the country; to be freed from whose devastations, the Macedonians sent for Antigonus, and the letters had almost been brought to him before the battle was fought; upon the receipt of which he would at once have marched away home, and left the Achæans to look to themselves. But Fortune, that loves to determine the greatest affairs by a minute, in this conjuncture showed such an exact niceness of time, that immediately after the battle in Sellasia was over, and Cleomenes had lost his army and his city, the messengers came up and called for Antigonus. And this above everything made Cleomenes's misfortune to be pitied; for if he had gone on retreating and had forborne fighting two days longer, there had been no need of hazarding a battle; since upon the departure of the Macedonians, he might have had what conditions he pleased from the Achæans. But now, as was said before, for want of money, being necessitated to trust everything to arms, he was forced with twenty thousand (such is Polybius's account), to engage thirty thousand. And approving himself an admirable commander in this difficulty, his citizens showing an extraordinary courage, and his mercenaries bravery enough, he was overborne by the different way of fighting, and the weight of the heavy-armed phalanx. Phylarchus also affirms that the treachery of some about him was the chief cause of Cleomenes's ruin.

For Antigonus gave orders that the Illyrians and Acarnanians should march round by a secret way, and encompass the other wing, which Euclidas, Cleomenes's brother, commanded; and then drew out the rest of his forces to the battle. And Cleomenes, from a convenient rising, viewing his order, and not seeing any of the Illyrians and Acarnanians, began to suspect that Antigonus had sent them upon some such design; and calling for Damoteles, who was at the head of those specially appointed to such ambush duty, he bade him carefully to look after and discover the enemy's designs upon his rear. But Damoteles, for some say Antigonus had bribed him, telling him that he should not be solicitous about that matter, for all was well enough, but mind and fight those that met him in the front, he was satisfied, and advanced against Antigonus; and by the vigorous charge of his Spartans, made the Macedonian phalanx give ground, and pressed upon them with great advantage about half a mile; but then making a stand, and seeing the danger which the surrounding wing, commanded by his brother Euclidas, was in, he cried out, " Thou art lost, dear brother, thou art lost, thou brave example to our Spartan youth and theme of our matrons' songs." And Euclidas's wing being cut in pieces, and the conquerors from that part falling upon him, he perceived his soldiers to be disordered, and unable to maintain the fight, and therefore provided for his own safety. There fell, we are told, in the battle, besides many of the mercenary soldiers, all the Spartans, six thousand in number, except two hundred.

When Cleomenes came into the city, he advised those citizens that he met to receive Antigonus; and as for himself, he said, which should appear most advantageous to Sparta, whether his life or death, that he would choose. Seeing the women running out to those that had fled with him, taking their arms, and bringing drink to them, he entered into his own house, and his servant, who was a freeborn woman, taken from Megalopolis after his wife's death, offering, as usual, to do the service he needed on returning from war, though he was very thirsty, he refused to drink, and though very weary to sit down; but in his corselet as he was, he laid his arm sideway against a pillar, and leaning his forehead upon his elbow, he rested his body a little while, and ran over in his thoughts all the courses he could take; and then with his friends set out at once for Gythium; where, finding ships which had been got ready for this very purpose, they embarked. Antigonus, taking the city, treated the Lacedæmonians courteously, and in no way offering any insult or offence to the dignity of Sparta, but permitting them to enjoy their own laws and polity, and sacrificing to the gods, dislodged the third day. For he heard that there was a great war in Macedonia, and that the country was devastated by the barbarians. Besides, his malady had now thoroughly settled into a consumption and continual catarrh. Yet he still kept up, and managed to return and deliver his country, and meet there a most glorious death, in a great defeat and vast slaughter of the barbarians. As Phylarchus says, and as is probable in itself, he broke a blood-vessel by shouting in the battle itself. In the schools we used to be told that, after the victory was won, he cried out for joy, " O glorious day! " and presently bringing up a quantity of blood, fell into a fever, which never left him till his death. And thus much concerning Antigonus.

Cleomenes, sailing from Cythera, touched at another island called Ægialia, whence as he was about to depart for Cyrene, one of his friends, Therycion by name, a man of a noble spirit in all enterprises, and bold and lofty in his talk, came privately to him, and said thus: " Sir, death in battle, which is the most glorious, we have let go; though all heard us say that Antigonus should never tread over the King of Sparta, unless dead. And now that course which is next in honour and virtue is presented to us. Whither do we madly sail, flying the evil which is near, to seek that which is at a distance? For if it is not dishonourable for the race of Hercules to serve the successors of Philip and Alexander, we shall save a long voyage by delivering ourselves up to Antigonus, who, probably, is as much better than Ptolemy, as the Macedonians are better than the Egyptians; but if we think it mean to submit to those whose arms have conquered us, why should we choose him for our master, by whom we have not yet been beaten? Is it to acknowledge two superiors instead of one, whilst we run away from Antigonus, and flatter Ptolemy? Or, is it for your mother's sake that you retreat to Egypt? It will indeed by a very fine and very desirable sight for her to show her son to Ptolemy's women, now changed from a prince into an exile and a slave. Are we not still masters of our own swords? And whilst we have Laconia in view, shall we not here free ourselves from this disgraceful misery, and clear ourselves to those who at Sellasia died for the honour and defence of Sparta? Or, shall we sit lazily in Egypt, inquiring what news from Sparta, and whom Antigonus hath been pleased to make governor of Lacedæmon? " Thus spoke Therycion; and this was Cleomenes's reply: " By seeking

death, you coward, the most easy and most ready refuge, you
fancy that you shall appear courageous and brave, though this
flight is baser than the former.   Better men than we have given
way to their enemies, having been betrayed by fortune, or oppressed by multitude; but he that gives way under labour or
distresses, under the ill-opinions or reports of men, yields the
victory to his own effeminacy.   For a voluntary death ought
not to be chosen as a relief from action, but as an exemplary
action itself; and it is base either to live or to die only to ourselves.   That death to which you now invite us, is proposed
only as a release from our present miseries, but carries nothing
of nobleness or profit in it.   And I think it becomes both me and
you not to despair of our country; but when there are no hopes
of that left, those that have an inclination may quickly die."
To this Therycion returned no answer; but as soon as he had an
opportunity of leaving Cleomenes's company, went aside on the
seashore, and ran himself through.

But Cleomenes sailed from Ægialia, landed in Libya, and,
being honourably conducted through the king's country, came
to Alexandria.   When he was first brought to Ptolemy, no more
than common civilities and usual attentions were paid him; but
when, upon trial, he found him a man of deep sense and great
reason, and that his plain Laconic way of conversation carried
with it a noble and becoming grace, that he did nothing unbecoming his birth, nor bent under fortune, and was evidently a
more faithful counsellor than those who made it their business
to please and flatter, he was ashamed, and repented that he had
neglected so great a man, and suffered Antigonus to get so much
power and reputation by ruining him.   He now offered him
many marks of respect and kindness, and gave him hopes that
he would furnish him with ships and money to return to Greece,
and would reinstate him in his kingdom.   He granted him a
yearly pension of four-and-twenty talents; a little part of which
sum supplied his and his friends' thrifty temperance; and the
rest was employed in doing good offices to, and in relieving the
necessities of, the refugees that had fled from Greece, and retired
into Egypt.

But the elder Ptolemy dying before Cleomenes's affairs had
received a full dispatch, and the successor being a loose, voluptuous, and effeminate prince, under the power of his pleasures
and his women, his business was neglected.   For the king was
so besotted with his women and his wine, that the employments
of his most busy and serious hours consisted at the utmost in

celebrating religious feasts in his palace, carrying a timbrel, and taking part in the show; while the greatest affairs of state were managed by Agathoclea, the king's mistress, her mother, and the pimp Œnanthes. At the first, indeed, they seemed to stand in need of Cleomenes; for Ptolemy, being afraid of his brother Magas, who by his mother's means had a great interest among the soldiers, gave Cleomenes a place in his secret councils, and acquainted him with the design of taking off his brother. He, though all were for it, declared his opinion to the contrary, saying, " The king, if it were possible, should have more brothers for the better security and stability of his affairs." And Sosibius, the greatest favourite, replying that they were not secure of the mercenaries whilst Magas was alive, Cleomenes returned, that he need not trouble himself about that matter; for amongst the mercenaries there were above three thousand Peloponnesians, who were his fast friends, and whom he could command at any time with a nod. This discourse made Cleomenes for the present to be looked upon as a man of great influence and assured fidelity; but afterwards, Ptolemy's weakness increasing his fear, and he, as it usually happens, where there is no judgment and wisdom, placing his security in general distrust and suspicion, it rendered Cleomenes suspected to the courtiers, as having too much interest with the mercenaries; and many had this saying in their mouths, that he was a lion amidst a flock of sheep. For, in fact, such he seemed to be in the court, quietly watching and keeping his eye upon all that went on.

He therefore gave up all thought of asking for ships and soldiers from the king. But receiving news that Antigonus was dead, that the Achæans were engaged in a war with the Ætolians, and that the affairs of Peloponnesus, being now in very great distraction and disorder, required and invited his assistance, he desired leave to depart only with his friends, but could not obtain that, the king not so much as hearing his petition, being shut up amongst his women, and wasting his hours in bacchanalian rites and drinking parties. But Sosibius, the chief minister and counsellor of state, thought that Cleomenes, being detained against his will, would grow ungovernable and dangerous, and yet that it was not safe to let him go, being an aspiring, daring man, and well acquainted with the diseases and weakness of the kingdom. For neither could presents and gifts conciliate or content him; but even as Apis, while living in all possible plenty and apparent delight, yet desires to live as nature would provide for him, to range at liberty, and bound about the fields, and can

scarce endure to be under the priests' keeping, so he could not
brook their courtship and soft entertainment, but sat like
Achilles—

> " and languished far,
> Desiring battle and the shout of war."

His affairs standing in this condition, Nicagoras, the Messenian, came to Alexandria, a man that deeply hated Cleomenes,
yet pretended to be his friend; for he had formerly sold Cleomenes a fair estate, but never received the money because Cleomenes was either unable, as it may be, or else, by reason of his
engagement in the wars and other distractions, had no opportunity to pay him. Cleomenes, seeing him landing, for he was
then walking upon the quay, kindly saluted him, and asked what
business brought him to Egypt. Nicagoras returned his compliment, and told him that he came to bring some excellent
war-horses to the king. And Cleomenes, with a smile, subjoined,
" I could wish you had rather brought young boys and music-
girls; for those now are the king's chief occupation." Nicagoras
at the moment smiled at the conceit, but a few days after, he
put Cleomenes in mind of the estate that he had bought of him,
and desired his money, protesting that he would not have
troubled him, if his merchandise had turned out as profitable
as he had thought it would. Cleomenes replied, that he had
nothing left of all that had been given him. At which answer,
Nicagoras, being nettled, told Sosibius Cleomenes's scoff upon
the king. He was delighted to receive the information; but
desiring to have some greater reason to excite the king against
Cleomenes, persuaded Nicagoras to leave a letter written against
Cleomenes, importing that he had a design, if he could have
gotten ships and soldiers, to surprise Cyrene. Nicagoras wrote
such a letter, and left Egypt. Four days after, Sosibius brought
the letter to Ptolemy, pretending it was just then delivered him,
and excited the young man's fear and anger; upon which it
was agreed that Cleomenes should be invited into a large house,
and treated as formerly, but not suffered to go out again.

This usage was grievous to Cleomenes, and another incident
that occurred made him feel his hopes to be yet more entirely
overcast. Ptolemy, the son of Chrysermas, a favourite of the
king's, had always shown civility to Cleomenes; there was a
considerable intimacy between them, and they had been used to
talk freely together about the state. He, upon Cleomenes's
desire, came to him, and spoke to him in fair terms, softening

down his suspicions and excusing the king's conduct. But as he went out again, not knowing that Cleomenes followed him to the door, he severely reprimanded the keepers for their carelessness in looking after " so great and so furious a wild beast." This Cleomenes himself heard, and retiring before Ptolemy perceived it, told his friends what had been said. Upon this they cast off all former hopes and determined for violent proceedings, resolving to be revenged on Ptolemy for his base and unjust dealing, to have satisfaction for the affronts, to die as it became Spartans, and not stay till, like fatted sacrifices, they were butchered. For it was both grievous and dishonourable for Cleomenes, who had scorned to come to terms with Antigonus, a brave warrior, and a man of action, to wait an effeminate king's leisure, till he should lay aside his timbrel and end his dance, and then kill him.

These courses being resolved on, and Ptolemy happening at the same time to make a progress to Canopus, they first spread abroad a report that his freedom was ordered by the king, and, it being the custom for the king to send presents and an entertainment to those whom he would free, Cleomenes's friends made that provision, and sent it into the prison, thus imposing upon the keepers, who thought it had been sent by the king. For he sacrificed, and gave them large portions, and with a garland upon his head, feasted and made merry with his friends. It is said that he began the action sooner than he designed, having understood that a servant who was privy to the plot had gone out to visit a mistress that he loved. This made him afraid of a discovery; and therefore, as soon as it was full noon, and all the keepers sleeping off their wine, he put on his coat, and opening his seam to bare his right shoulder, with his drawn sword in his hand, he issued forth, together with his friends provided in the same manner, making thirteen in all. One of them, by name Hippitas, was lame, and followed the first onset very well, but when he presently perceived that they were more slow in their advances for his sake, he desired them to run him through, and not ruin their enterprise by staying for a useless, unprofitable man. By chance an Alexandrian was then riding by the door; him they threw off, and setting Hippitas on horseback, ran through the streets, and proclaimed liberty to the people. But they, it seems, had courage enough to praise and admire Cleomenes's daring, but not one had the heart to follow and assist him. Three of them fell on Ptolemy, the son of Chrysermas, as he was coming out of the palace, and killed him. Another

Ptolemy, the officer in charge of the city, advancing against them in a chariot, they set upon, dispersed his guards and attendants, and pulling him out of the chariot, killed him upon the place. Then they made toward the castle, designing to break open the prison, release those who were confined, and avail themselves of their numbers; but the keepers were too quick for them, and secured the passages. Being baffled in this attempt, Cleomenes with his company roamed about the city, none joining with him, but all retreating from and flying his approach. Therefore, despairing of success, and saying to his friends, that it was no wonder that women ruled over men that were afraid of liberty, he bade them all die as bravely as became his followers and their own past actions. This said, Hippitas was first, as he desired, run through by one of the younger men, and then each of them readily and resolutely fell upon his own sword, except Fanteus, the same who first surprised Megalopolis. This man, being of a very handsome person, and a great lover of the Spartan discipline, the king had made his dearest friend; and he now bade him, when he had seen him and the rest fallen, die by their example. Fanteus walked over them as they lay, and pricked every one with his dagger, to try whether any was alive; when he pricked Cleomenes in the ankle, and saw him turn upon his back, he kissed him, sat down by him, and when he was quite dead, covered up the body, and then killed himself over it.

Thus fell Cleomenes, after the life which we have narrated, having been King of Sparta sixteen years. The news of their fall being noised through the city, Cratesiclea, though a woman of a great spirit, could not bear up against the weight of this affliction; but embracing Cleomenes's children, broke out into lamentations. But the eldest boy, none suspecting such a spirit in a child, threw himself headlong from the top of the house. He was bruised very much, but not killed by the fall, and was taken up crying, and expressing his resentment for not being permitted to destroy himself. Ptolemy, as soon as an account of the action was brought him, gave order that Cleomenes's body should be flayed and hung up, and that his children, mother, and the women that were with her, should be killed. Amongst these was Panteus's wife, a beautiful and noble-looking woman, who had been but lately married, and suffered these disasters in the height of her love. Her parents would not have her embark with Panteus so shortly after they were married, though she eagerly desired it, but shut her up, and kept her forcibly at home. But a few days after she procured a horse and a little money, and escaping by night, made speed to Tænarus, where she embarked for Egypt, came to her husband, and with him cheerfully endured to live in a foreign country. She gave her hand to Cratesiclea, as she was going with the soldiers to execution, held up her robe, and begged her to be courageous; who of herself was not in the least afraid of death, and desired nothing else but only to be killed before the children. When they were come to the place of execution, the children were first killed before Cratesiclea's eyes, and afterwards she herself, with only these words in her mouth, " O children, whither are you gone? " But Panteus's wife, fastening her dress close about her, and being a strong woman, in silence and perfect composure, looked after every one that was slain, and laid them decently out as far as circumstances would permit; and after all were killed, rearraying her dress, and drawing her clothes close about her, suffering none to come near or be an eye-witness of her fall, besides the executioner, she courageously submitted to the stroke, and wanted nobody to look after her or wind her up after she was dead. Thus in her death the modesty of her mind appeared, and set that guard upon her body which she always kept when alive. And she, in the declining age of the Spartans, showed that women were no unequal rivals of the men, and was an instance of a courage superior to the affronts of fortune.

A few days after, those that watched the hanging body of Cleomenes, saw a large snake winding about his head, and covering his face, so that no bird of prey would fly at it. This made the king superstitiously afraid, and set the women upon several expiations, as if he had been some extraordinary being, and one beloved by the gods, that had been slain. And the Alexandrians made processions to the place, and gave Cleomenes the title of hero, and son of the gods, till the philosophers satisfied them by saying, that as oxen breed bees, putrifying horses breed wasps, and beetles rise from the carcasses of dead asses, so the humours and juices of the marrow of a man's body, coagulating, produce serpents. And this the ancients observing, appropriate a serpent, rather than any other creature, to heroes.

## TIBERIUS GRACCHUS

HAVING completed the first two narratives, we now may proceed to take a view of misfortunes, not less remarkable, in the Roman couple, and with the lives of Agis and Cleomenes, compare these of Tiberius and Caius. They were the sons of Tiberius Gracchus, who though he had been once censor, twice consul, and twice had triumphed, yet was more renowned and esteemed for his virtue than his honours. Upon this account, after the death of Scipio who overthrew Hannibal, he was thought worthy to match with his daughter Cornelia, though there had been no friendship or familiarity between Scipio and him, but rather the contrary. There is a story told that he once found in his bed-chamber a couple of snakes, and that the soothsayers, being consulted concerning the prodigy, advised that he should neither kill them both nor let them both escape; adding, that if the male serpent was killed, Tiberius should die, and if the female, Cornelia. And that therefore Tiberius, who extremely loved his wife, and thought, besides, that it was much more his part, who was an old man, to die, than it was hers, who as yet was but a young woman, killed the male serpent, and let the female escape; and soon after himself died, leaving behind him twelve children borne to him by Cornelia.

Cornelia, taking upon herself all the care of the household and the education of her children, approved herself so discreet a matron, so affectionate a mother, and so constant and noble-spirited a widow, that Tiberius seemed to all men to have done nothing unreasonable in choosing to die for such a woman; who, when King Ptolemy himself proffered her his crown, and would have married her, refused it, and chose rather to live a widow. In this state she continued, and lost all her children, except one daughter, who was married to Scipio the younger, and two sons, Tiberius and Caius, whose lives we are now writing.

These she brought up with such care, that though they were without dispute in natural endowments and dispositions the first among the Romans of their time, yet they seemed to owe their virtues even more to their education than to their birth. And as, in the statues and pictures made of Castor and Pollux, though the brothers resemble one another, yet there is a difference to be perceived in their countenances, between the one, who delighted in the cestus, and the other, that was famous in the course, so between these two noble youths, though there was a strong general likeness in their common love of fortitude and temperance, in their liberality, their eloquence, and their greatness of mind, yet in their actions and administrations of public affairs, a considerable variation showed itself. It will not be amiss before we proceed to mark the difference between them.

Tiberius, in the form and expression of his countenance, and in his gesture and motion, was gentle and composed; but Caius, earnest and vehement. And so in their public speeches to the people, the one spoke in a quiet, orderly manner, standing throughout on the same spot; the other would walk about on the hustings, and in the heat of his orations pull his gown off his shoulders, and was the first of all the Romans that used such gestures; as Cleon is said to have been the first orator among the Athenians that pulled off his cloak and smote his thigh, when addressing the people. Caius's oratory was impetuous and passionate, making everything tell to the utmost, whereas Tiberius was gentle and persuasive, awakening emotions of pity. His diction was pure and carefully correct, while that of Caius was vehement and rich. So likewise in their way of living and at their tables, Tiberius was frugal and plain, Caius, compared with other men, temperate and even austere, but contrasting with his brother in a fondness for new fashions and rarities, as appears in Drusus's charge against him, that he had bought some silver dolphins, to the value of twelve hundred and fifty drachmas for every pound weight.

The same difference that appeared in their diction was observable also in their tempers. The one was mild and reasonable, the other rough and passionate, and to that degree, that often, in the midst of speaking, he was so hurried away by his passion against his judgment, that his voice lost its tone, and he began to pass into mere abusive talking, spoiling his whole speech. As a remedy to this excess, he made use of an ingenious servant of his, one Licinius, who stood constantly behind him with a sort of pitchpipe, or instrument to regulate the voice by, and whenever he perceived his master's tone alter and break with anger, he struck a soft note with his pipe, on hearing which Caius immediately checked the vehemence of his passion and his voice, grew quieter, and allowed himself to be recalled to temper. Such are the differences between the two brothers; but their valour in war against their country's enemies, their justice in the government of its subjects, their care and industry in office, and their self-command in all that regarded their pleasures, were equally remarkable in both.

Tiberius was the elder by nine years; owing to which their actions as public men were divided by the difference of the times in which those of the one and those of the other were performed. And one of the principal causes of the failure of their enterprises was this interval between their careers, and the want of combination of their efforts. The power they would have exercised, had they flourished both together, could scarcely have failed to overcome all resistance. We must therefore give an account of each of them singly, and first of the eldest.

Tiberius, immediately on his attaining manhood, had such a reputation that he was admitted into the college of the augurs, and that in consideration more of his early virtue than of his noble birth. This appeared by what Appius Claudius did, who, though he had been consul and censor, and was now the head of the Roman senate, and had the highest sense of his own place and merit, at a public feast of the augurs, addressed himself openly to Tiberius, and with great expressions of kindness, offered him his daughter in marriage. And when Tiberius gladly accepted, and the agreement had thus been completed, Appius returning home, no sooner had reached his door, but he called to his wife and cried out in a loud voice, " O Antistia, I have contracted our daughter Claudia to a husband." She, being amazed, answered, " But why so suddenly, or what means this haste? Unless you have provided Tiberius Gracchus for her husband." I am not ignorant that some apply this story to Tiberius, the father of the Gracchi, and Scipio Africanus; but most relate it as we have done. And Polybius writes, that after the death of Scipio Africanus, the nearest relations of Cornelia, preferring Tiberius to all other competitors, gave her to him in marriage, not having been engaged or promised to any one by her father.

This young Tiberius, accordingly, serving in Africa under the younger Scipio, who had married his sister, and living there under the same tent with him, soon learned to estimate the noble spirit of his commander, which was so fit to inspire strong feelings of emulation in virtue and desire to prove merit in action, and in a short time he excelled all the young men of the army in obedience and courage; and he was the first that mounted the enemy's wall, as Fannius says, who writes that he himself climbed up with him, and was partaker in the achievement. He was regarded, while he continued with the army, with great affection; and left behind him on his departure a strong desire for his return.

After that expedition, being chosen paymaster, it was his fortune to serve in the war against the Numantines, under the command of Caius Mancinus, the consul, a person of no bad character, but the most unfortunate of all the Roman generals. Notwithstanding, amidst the greatest misfortunes, and in the most unsuccessful enterprises, not only the discretion and valour of Tiberius, but also, which was still more to be admired, the great respect and honour which he showed for his general, were most eminently remarkable; though the general himself, when reduced to straits, forgot his own dignity and office. For being beaten in various great battles, he endeavoured to dislodge by night and leave his camp; which the Numantines perceiving, immediately possessed themselves of his camp, and pursuing that part of the forces which was in flight, slew those that were in the rear, hedged the whole army in on every side, and forced them into difficult ground, whence there could be no possibility of an escape. Mancinus, despairing to make his way through by force, sent a messenger to desire a truce and conditions of peace. But they refused to give their confidence to any one except Tiberius, and required that he should be sent to treat with them. This was not only in regard to the young man's own character, for he had a great reputation amongst the soldiers, but also in remembrance of his father Tiberius, who, in his command against the Spaniards, had reduced great numbers of them to subjection, but granted a peace to the Numantines, and prevailed upon the Romans to keep it punctually and inviolably.

Tiberius was accordingly despatched to the enemy, whom he persuaded to accept of several conditions, and he himself complied with others; and by this means, it is beyond a question, that he saved twenty thousand of the Roman citizens, besides attendants and camp followers. However, the Numantines retained possession of all the property they had found and plundered in the encampment; and amongst other things were Tiberius's books of accounts, containing the whole transactions of his quæstorship, which he was extremely anxious to recover. And therefore, when the army were already upon their march, he returned to Numantia, accompanied with only three or four of his friends; and making his application to the officers of the Numantines, he entreated that they would return him his books, lest his enemies should have it in their power to reproach him with not being able to give an account of the moneys intrusted to him. The Numantines joyfully embraced this opportunity of obliging him, and invited him into the city; as he stood hesitating, they came up and took him by the hands, and begged that he would no longer look upon them as enemies, but believe them to be his friends, and treat them as such. Tiberius thought it well to consent, desirous as he was to have his books returned, and was afraid lest he should disoblige them by showing any distrust. As soon as he entered into the city, they first offered him food, and made every kind of entreaty that he would sit down and eat something in their company. Afterwards they returned his books, and gave him the liberty to take whatever he wished for in the remaining spoils. He, on the other hand, would accept of nothing but some frankincense, which he used in his public sacrifices, and bidding them farewell with every expression of kindness, departed.

When he returned to Rome, he found the whole transaction censured and reproached, as a proceeding that was base and scandalous to the Romans. But the relations and friends of the soldiers, forming a large body among the people, came flocking to Tiberius, whom they acknowledged as the preserver of so many citizens, imputing to the general all the miscarriages which had happened. Those who cried out against what had been done, urged for imitation the example of their ancestors, who stripped and handed over to the Samnites not only the generals who had consented to the terms of release, but also all the quæstors, for example, and tribunes, who had in any way implicated themselves in the agreement, laying the guilt of perjury and breach of conditions on their heads. But, in this affair, the populace, showing an extraordinary kindness and affection for Tiberius, indeed voted that the consul should be stripped and put in irons, and so delivered to the Numantines; but, for the sake of Tiberius, spared all the other officers. It may be probable, also, that Scipio, who at that time was the greatest and most powerful man among the Romans, contributed to save him, though indeed he was also censured for not protecting Mancinus too, and that he did not exert himself to maintain the observance of the articles of peace which had been agreed upon by his kinsman and friend Tiberius. But it may be presumed that the difference between them was for the most part due to ambitious feelings, and to the friends and reasoners who urged on Tiberius, and, as it was, it never amounted to anything that might not have been remedied, or that was really bad. Nor can

I think that Tiberius would ever have met with his misfortunes, if Scipio had been concerned in dealing with his measures; but he was away fighting at Numantia when Tiberius, upon the following occasion, first came forward as a legislator.

Of the land which the Romans gained by conquest from their neighbours, part they sold publicly, and turned the remainder into common; this common land they assigned to such of the citizens as were poor and indigent, for which they were to pay only a small acknowledgment into the public treasury. But when the wealthy men began to offer larger rents, and drive the poorer people out, it was enacted by law that no person whatever should enjoy more than five hundred acres of ground. This act for some time checked the avarice of the richer, and was of great assistance to the poorer people, who retained under it their respective proportions of ground, as they had been formerly rented by them. Afterwards the rich men of the neighbourhood contrived to get these lands again into their possession, under other people's names, and at last would not stick to claim most of them publicly in their own. The poor, who were thus deprived of their farms, were no longer either ready, as they had formerly been, to serve in war or careful in the education of their children; insomuch that in a short time there were comparatively few freemen remaining in all Italy, which swarmed with workhouses full of foreign-born slaves. These the rich men employed in cultivating their ground of which they dispossessed the citizens. Caius Lælius, the intimate friend of Scipio, undertook to reform this abuse; but meeting with opposition from men of authority, and fearing a disturbance, he soon desisted, and received the name of the Wise or the Prudent, both which meanings belong to the Latin word *Sapiens*.

But Tiberius, being elected tribune of the people, entered upon that design without delay, at the instigation, as is most commonly stated, of Diophanes, the rhetorician, and Blossius, the philosopher. Diophanes was a refugee from Mitylene, the other was an Italian, of the city of Cuma, and was educated there under Antipater of Tarsus, who afterwards did him the honour to dedicate some of his philosophical lectures to him.

Some have also charged Cornelia, the mother of Tiberius, with contributing towards it, because she frequently upbraided her sons, that the Romans as yet rather called her the daughter of Scipio, than the mother of the Gracchi. Others again say that Spurius Postumius was the chief occasion. He was a man of the same age with Tiberius, and his rival for reputation as a public speaker; and when Tiberius, at his return from the campaign, found him to have got far beyond him in fame and influence, and to be much looked up to, he thought to outdo him, by attempting a popular enterprise of this difficulty and of such great consequence. But his brother Caius has left it us in writing, that when Tiberius went through Tuscany to Numantia, and found the country almost depopulated, there being hardly any free husbandmen or shepherds, but for the most part only barbarian, imported slaves, he then first conceived the course of policy which in the sequel proved so fatal to his family. Though it is also most certain that the people themselves chiefly excited his zeal and determination in the prosecution of it, by setting up writings upon the porches, walls, and monuments, calling upon him to reinstate the poor citizens in their former possessions.

However, he did not draw up his law without the advice and assistance of those citizens that were then most eminent for their virtue and authority; amongst whom were Crassus, the high-priest, Mucius Scævola, the lawyer, who at that time was consul, and Claudius Appius, his father-in-law. Never did any law appear more moderate and gentle, especially being enacted against such great oppression and avarice. For they who ought to have been severely punished for transgressing the former laws, and should at least have lost all their titles to such lands which they had unjustly usurped, were notwithstanding to receive a price for quitting their unlawful claims, and giving up their lands to those fit owners who stood in need of help. But though this reformation was managed with so much tenderness that, all the former transactions being passed over, the people were only thankful to prevent abuses of the like nature for the future, yet, on the other hand, the moneyed men, and those of great estates, were exasperated, through their covetous feelings against the law itself, and against the lawgiver, through anger and party-spirit. They therefore endeavoured to seduce the people, declaring that Tiberius was designing a general redivision of lands, to overthrow the government, and put all things into confusion.

But they had no success. For Tiberius, maintaining an honourable and just cause, and possessed of eloquence sufficient to have made a less creditable action appear plausible, was no safe or easy antagonist, when, with the people crowding around the hustings, he took his place, and spoke in behalf of the poor. "The savage beasts," said he, "in Italy, have their particular dens, they have their places of repose and refuge; but the men who bear arms, and expose their lives for the safety of their

country, enjoy in the meantime nothing more in it but the air
and light; and, having no houses or settlements of their own,
are constrained to wander from place to place with their wives
and children." He told them that the commanders were guilty
of a ridiculous error, when, at the head of their armies, they
exhorted the common soldiers to fight for their sepulchres and
altars; when not any amongst so many Romans is possessed of
either altar or monument, neither have they any houses of their
own, or hearths of their ancestors to defend. They fought
indeed and were slain, but it was to maintain the luxury and
the wealth of other men. They were styled the masters of the
world, but in the meantime had not one foot of ground which
they could call their own. An harangue of this nature, spoken
to an enthusiastic and sympathising audience, by a person
of commanding spirit and genuine feelings, no adversaries at
that time were competent to oppose. Forbearing, therefore,
all discussion and debate, they addressed themselves to Marcus
Octavius, his fellow-tribune, who being a young man of a steady,
orderly character, and an intimate friend of Tiberius, upon this
account declined at first the task of opposing him; but at length,
over-persuaded with the repeated importunities of numerous
considerable persons, he was prevailed upon to do so, and
hindered the passing of the law; it being the rule that any
tribune has a power to hinder an act, and that all the rest can
effect nothing, if only one of them dissents. Tiberius, irritated
at these proceedings, presently laid aside this milder bill, but at
the same time preferred another; which, as it was more grateful
to the common people, so it was much more severe against the
wrongdoers, commanding them to make an immediate surrender
of all lands which, contrary to former laws, had come into their
possession. Hence there arose daily contentions between him
and Octavius in their orations. However, though they expressed
themselves with the utmost heat and determination, they yet
were never known to descend to any personal reproaches, or
in their passion to let slip any indecent expressions, so as to
derogate from one another.

For not alone—

      " In revellings and Bacchic play,"

but also in contentions and political animosities, a noble
nature and a temperate education stay and compose the mind.
Observing that Octavius himself was an offender against
this law, and detained a great quantity of ground from the

commonalty, Tiberius desired him to forbear opposing him any
further, and proffered, for the public good, though he himself
had but an indifferent estate, to pay a price for Octavius's share
at his own cost and charges. But upon the refusal of this proffer
by Octavius, he then interposed an edict, prohibiting all magistrates to exercise their respective functions, till such time as the
law was either ratified or rejected by public votes. He further
sealed up the gates of Saturn's temple, so that the treasurers
could neither take any money out from thence, nor put any in.
He threatened to impose a severe fine upon those of the prætors
who presumed to disobey his commands, insomuch that all the
officers, for fear of this penalty, intermitted the exercise of their
several jurisdictions. Upon this the rich proprietors put themselves into mourning, and went up and down melancholy and
dejected; they entered also into a conspiracy against Tiberius,
and procured men to murder him; so that he also, with all
men's knowledge, whenever he went abroad, took with him a
sword-staff, such as robbers use, called in Latin a *dolo*.

When the day appointed was come, and the people summoned
to give their votes, the rich men seized upon the voting urns
and carried them away by force; thus all things were in confusion. But when Tiberius's party appeared strong enough to
oppose the contrary faction, and drew together in a body, with
the resolution to do so, Manlius and Fulvius, two of the consular
quality, threw themselves before Tiberius, took him by the
hand, and, with tears in their eyes, begged of him to desist.
Tiberius, considering the mischiefs that were all but now occurring, and having a great respect for two such eminent persons,
demanded of them what they would advise him to do. They
acknowledged themselves unfit to advise in a matter of so great
importance, but earnestly entreated him to leave it to the determination of the senate. But when the senate assembled, and
could not bring the business to any result, through the preva-
lence of the rich faction, he then was driven to a course neither
legal nor fair, and proposed to deprive Octavius of his tribuneship, it being impossible for him in any other way to get the
law brought to the vote. At first he addressed him publicly,
with entreaties couched in the kindest terms, and taking him by
his hands, besought him, that now, in the presence of all the
people, he would take this opportunity to oblige them, in granting only that request which was in itself so just and reasonable,
being but a small recompense in regard of those many dangers
and hardships which they had undergone for the public safety.

Octavius, however, would by no means be persuaded to compliance; upon which Tiberius declared openly, that, seeing they two were united in the same office, and of equal authority, it would be a difficult matter to compose their difference on so weighty a matter without a civil war; and that the only remedy which he knew must be the deposing one of them from their office. He desired, therefore, that Octavius would summon the people to pass their verdict upon him first, averring that he would willingly relinquish his authority if the citizens desired it. Octavius refused; and Tiberius then said he would himself put to the people the question of Octavius's deposition, if upon mature deliberation he did not alter his mind; and after this declaration he adjourned the assembly till the next day.

When the people were met together again, Tiberius placed himself in the rostra, and endeavoured a second time to persuade Octavius. But all being to no purpose, he referred the whole matter to the people, calling on them to vote at once, whether Octavius should be deposed or not; and when seventeen of the thirty-five tribes had already voted against him, and there wanted only the votes of one tribe more for his final deprivation, Tiberius put a short stop to the proceedings, and once more renewed his importunities; he embraced and kissed him before all the assembly, begging with all the earnestness imaginable, that he would neither suffer himself to incur the dishonour, nor him to be reputed the author and promoter of so odious a measure. Octavius, we are told, did seem a little softened and moved with these entreaties; his eyes filled with tears, and he continued silent for a considerable time. But presently looking towards the rich men and proprietors of estates, who stood gathered in a body together, partly for shame, and partly for fear of disgracing himself with them, he boldly bade Tiberius use any severity he pleased. The law for his deprivation being thus voted, Tiberius ordered one of his servants, whom he had made a freeman, to remove Octavius from the rostra, employing his own domestic freed servants in the stead of the public officers. And it made the action seem all the sadder, that Octavius was dragged out in such an ignominious manner. The people immediately assaulted him, whilst the rich men ran in to his assistance. Octavius, with some difficulty, was snatched away and safely conveyed out of the crowd; though a trusty servant of his, who had placed himself in front of his master that he might assist his escape, in keeping off the multitude, had his eyes struck out, much to the displeasure of Tiberius, who ran with all haste, when he perceived the disturbance, to appease the rioters.

This being done, the law concerning the lands was ratified and confirmed, and three commissioners were appointed, to make a survey of the grounds, and see the same equally divided. These were Tiberius himself, Claudius Appius, his father-in-law, and his brother, Caius Gracchus, who at this time was not at Rome, but in the army under the command of Scipio Africanus before Numantia. These things were transacted by Tiberius without any disturbance, none daring to offer any resistance to him; besides which, he gave the appointment as tribune in Octavius's place, not to any person of distinction, but to a certain Mucius, one of his own clients. The great men of the city were therefore utterly offended, and, fearing lest he grew yet more popular, they took all opportunities of affronting him publicly in the senate house. For when he requested, as was usual, to have a tent provided at the public charge for his use, while dividing the lands, though it was a favour commonly granted to persons employed in business of much less importance, it was peremptorily refused to him; and the allowance made him for his daily expenses was fixed to nine obols only. The chief promoter of these affronts was Publius Nasica, who openly abandoned himself to his feelings of hatred against Tiberius, being a large holder of the public lands, and not a little resenting now to be turned out of them by force. The people, on the other hand, were still more and more excited, insomuch that a little after this, it happening that one of Tiberius's friends died suddenly, and his body being marked with malignant-looking spots, they ran, in a tumultuous manner, to his funeral, crying aloud that the man was poisoned. They took the bier upon their shoulders, and stood over it, while it was placed on the pile, and really seemed to have fair grounds for their suspicion of foul play. For the body burst open, and such a quantity of corrupt humours issued out, that the funeral fire was extinguished, and when it was again kindled, the wood still would not burn; insomuch that they were constrained to carry the corpse to another place, where with much difficulty it took fire. Besides this, Tiberius, that he might incense the people yet more, put himself into mourning, brought his children amongst the crowd, and entreated the people to provide for them and their mother, as if he now despaired of his own security.

About this time king Attalus, surnamed Philometor, died, and Eudemus, a Pergammenian, brought his last will to Rome, by which he had made the Roman people his heirs. Tiberius, to please the people, immediately proposed making a law, that all the money which Attalus left should be distributed amongst such poor citizens as were to be sharers of the public lands, for the better enabling them to proceed in stocking and cultivating their ground; and as for the cities that were in the territories of Attalus, he declared that the disposal of them did not at all belong to the senate, but to the people, and that he himself would ask their pleasure herein. By this he offended the senate more than ever he had done before, and Pompeius stood up and acquainted them that he was the next neighbour to Tiberius, and so had the opportunity of knowing that Eudemus, the Perga- menian, had presented Tiberius with a royal diadem and a purple robe, as before long he was to be king of Rome. Quintus Metellus also upbraided him, saying, that when his father was censor, the Romans, whenever he happened to be going home from a supper, used to put out all their lights, lest they should be seen to have indulged themselves in feasting and drinking at unseasonable hours, whereas now the most indigent and audacious of the people were found with their torches at night, following Tiberius home. Titus Annius, a man of no great repute for either justice or temperance, but famous for his skill in putting and answering questions, challenged Tiberius to the proof by wager, declaring him to have deposed a magistrate who by law was sacred and inviolable. Loud clamour ensued, and Tiberius, quitting the senate hastily, called together the people, and summoning Annius to appear, was proceeding to accuse him. But Annius, being no great speaker, nor of any repute compared to him, sheltered himself in his own particular art, and desired that he might propose one or two questions to Tiberius before he entered upon the chief argument. This liberty being granted, and silence proclaimed, Annius proposed his question. " If you," said he, " had a design to disgrace and defame me, and I should apply myself to one of your colleagues for redress, and he should come forward to my assistance, would you for that reason fall into a passion, and depose him? " Tiberius, they say, was so much disconcerted at this question, that, though at other times his assurance as his readiness of speech was always remarkable, yet now he was silent and made no reply.

For the present he dismissed the assembly. But beginning to understand that the course he had taken with Octavius had created offence even among the populace as well as the nobility, because the dignity of the tribunes seemed to be violated, which had always continued till that day sacred and honourable, he made a speech to the people in justification of himself; out of which it may not be improper to collect some particulars, to give an impression of his force and persuasiveness in speaking. " A tribune," he said, " of the people, is sacred indeed, and ought to be inviolable, because in a manner consecrated to be the guardian and protector of them; but if he degenerate so far as to oppress the people, abridge their powers, and take away their liberty of voting, he stands deprived by his own act of honours and immunities, by the neglect of the duty for which the honour was bestowed upon him. Otherwise we should be under the obligation to let a tribune do this pleasure, though he should proceed to destroy the capitol or set fire to the arsenal. He who should make these attempts would be a bad tribune. He who assails the power of the people is no longer a tribune at all. Is it not inconceivable that a tribune should have power to imprison a consul, and the people have no authority to degrade him when he uses that honour which he received from them, to their detriment? For the tribunes, as well as the consuls, hold office by the people's votes. The kingly government, which comprehends all sorts of authority in itself alone, is moreover elevated by the greatest and most religious solemnity imaginable into a condition of sanctity. But the citizens, notwithstanding this, deposed Tarquin, when he acted wrongfully; and for the crime of one single man, the ancient government under which Rome was built was abolished for ever. What is there in all Rome so sacred and venerable as the vestal virgins, to whose care alone the preservation of the eternal fire is committed? yet if one of these transgress she is buried alive; the sanctity which for the gods' sakes is allowed them, is forfeited when they offend against the gods. So likewise a tribune retains not his inviolability, which for the people's sake was accorded to him, when he offends against the people, and attacks the foundations of that authority from whence he derived his own. We esteem him to be legally chosen tribune who is elected only by the majority of votes; and is not therefore the same person much more lawfully degraded when, by a general consent of them all, they agree to depose him? Nothing is so sacred as religious offerings; yet the people were never prohibited to make use of them, but suffered to remove and carry them wherever they pleased; so likewise, as it were some sacred present, they have lawful power to transfer the tribuneship from one man's hands to another's. Nor can that authority be thought inviolable and irremovable which many of those who have held it, have of their own act surrendered and desired to be discharged from."

These were the principal heads of Tiberius's apology. But his friends, apprehending the dangers which seemed to threaten him, and the conspiracy that was gathering head against him, were of opinion that the safest way would be for him to petition that he might be continued tribune for the year ensuing. Upon this consideration he again endeavoured to secure the people's good-will with fresh laws, making the years of serving in the war fewer than formerly, granting liberty of appeal from the judges to the people, and joining to the senators, who were judges at that time, an equal number of citizens of the horsemen's degree, endeavouring as much as in him lay to lessen the power of the senate, rather from passion and partisanship than from any rational regard to equity and the public good. And when it came to the question whether these laws should be passed, and they perceived that the opposite party were strongest, the people as yet being not got together in a full body, they began first of all to gain time by speeches in accusation of some of their fellow-magistrates, and at length adjourned the assembly till the day following.

Tiberius then went down into the market-place amongst the people, and made his addresses to them humbly and with tears in his eyes; and told them he had just reason to suspect that his adversaries would attempt in the night-time to break open his house and murder him. This worked so strongly with the multitude, that several of them pitched tents round about his house, and kept guard all night for the security of his person. By break of day came one of the soothsayers, who prognosticate good or bad success by the pecking of fowls, and threw them something to eat. The soothsayer used his utmost endeavours to fright the fowls out of their coop; but none of them except one would venture out, which fluttered with his left wing, and stretched out its leg, and ran back again into the coop, without eating anything. This put Tiberius in mind of another ill-omen which had formerly happened to him. He had a very costly headpiece, which he made use of when he engaged in any battle, and into this piece of armour two serpents crawled, laid eggs, and brought forth young ones. The remembrance of which made Tiberius more concerned now than otherwise he would have been. However, he went towards the capitol as soon as he understood that the people were assembled there; but before he got out of the house he stumbled upon the threshold with such violence, that he broke the nail of his great toe, insomuch that blood gushed out of his shoes. He was not gone very far before he saw two ravens fighting on the top of a house which stood on his left hand as he passed along; and though he was surrounded with a number of people, a stone struck from its place by one of the ravens, fell just at his foot. This even the boldest men about him felt as check. But Blossius of Cuma, who was present, told him that it would be a shame and an ignominious thing for Tiberius, who was a son of Gracchus, the grandson of Scipio Africanus, and the protector of the Roman people to refuse, for fear of a silly bird, to answer when his countrymen called to him; and that his adversaries would represent it not as a mere matter for their ridicule, but would declaim about it to the people as the mark of a tyrannical temper, which felt a pride in taking liberties with the people. At the same time several messengers came also from his friends, to desire his presence at the capitol, saying that all things went there according to expectation. And indeed Tiberius's first entrance there was in every way successful; as soon as ever he appeared, the people welcomed him with loud acclamations, and as he went up to his place, they repeated their expressions of joy, and gathered in a body around him, so that no one who was not well known to be his friend might approach. Mucius then began to put the business again to the vote; but nothing could be performed in the usual course and order, because of the disturbance caused by those who were on the outside of the crowd, where there was a struggle going on with those of the opposite party, who were pushing on and trying to force their way in and establish themselves among them.

Whilst things were in this confusion, Flavius Flaccus, a senator, standing in a place where he could be seen, but at such a distance from Tiberius that he could not make him hear, signified to him by motions of his hand, that he wished to impart something of consequence to him in private. Tiberius ordered the multitude to make way for him, by which means, though not without some difficulty, Flavius got to him, and informed him that the rich men, in a sitting of the senate, seeing they could not prevail upon the consul to espouse their quarrel, had come to a final determination amongst themselves that he should be assassinated, and to that purpose had a great number of their friends and servants ready armed to accomplish it. Tiberius no sooner communicated this confederacy to those about him, but they immediately tucked up their gowns, broke the halberts which the officers used to keep the crowd off into pieces, and distributed them among themselves, resolving to resist the attack with these. Those who stood at a distance wondered, and asked what was the occasion; Tiberius, knowing that they could not hear him at that distance, lifted his hand to his head wishing to intimate the great danger which he apprehended himself to be in. His adversaries, taking notice of that action, ran off at once to the senate house, and declared that Tiberius desired the people to bestow a crown upon him, as if this were the meaning of his touching his head. This news created general confusion in the senators, and Nasica at once called upon the consul to punish this tyrant, and defend the government. The consul mildly replied, that he would not be the first to do any violence; and as he would not suffer any freeman to be put to death, before sentence had lawfully passed upon him, so neither would he allow any measure to be carried into effect, if by persuasion or compulsion on the part of Tiberius the people had been induced to pass an unlawful vote. But Nasica, rising from his seat, " Since the consul," said he, " regards not the safety of the commonwealth, let every one who will defend the laws, follow me." He then, casting the skirt of his gown over his head, hastened to the capitol; those who bore him company, wrapped their gowns also about their arms, and forced their way after him. And as they were persons of the greatest authority in the city, the common people did not venture to obstruct their passing, but were rather so eager to clear the way for them, that they tumbled over one another in haste. The attendants they brought with them had furnished themselves with clubs and staves from their houses, and they themselves picked up the feet and other fragments of stools and chairs, which were broken by the hasty flight of the common people. Thus armed, they made towards Tiberius, knocking down those whom they found in front of him, and those were soon wholly dispersed and many of them slain. Tiberius tried to save himself by flight. As he was running, he was stopped by one who caught hold of him by the gown; but he threw it off, and fled in his under-garment only. And stumbling over those who before had been knocked down, as he was endeavouring to get up again, Publius Satureius, a tribune, one of his colleagues, was observed to give him the first fatal stroke, by hitting him upon the head with the foot of a stool. The second blow was claimed, as though it had been a deed to be proud of, by Lucius Rufus. And of the rest there

fell above three hundred killed by clubs and staves only, none
by an iron weapon.

This, we are told, was the first sedition amongst the Romans,
since the abrogation of kingly government, that ended in the
effusion of blood. All former quarrels which were neither small
nor about trivial matters, were always amicably composed, by
mutual concessions on either side, the senate yielding for fear of
the commons, and the commons out of respect to the senate.
And it is probable indeed that Tiberius himself might then have
been easily induced, by mere persuasion, to give way, and
certainly, if attacked at all, must have yielded without any
recourse to violence and bloodshed, as he had not at that time
above three thousand men to support him. But it is evident,
that this conspiracy was fomented against him, more out of
the hatred and malice which the rich men had to his person,
than for the reasons which they commonly pretended against
him. In testimony of which, we may adduce the cruelty and
unnatural insults which they used to his dead body. For they
would not suffer his own brother, though he earnestly begged
the favour, to bury him in the night, but threw him, together
with the other corpses, into the river. Neither did their
animosity stop here; for they banished some of his friends
without legal process, and slew as many of the others as they
could lay their hands on; amongst whom Diophanes, the orator,
was slain, and one Caius Villius cruelly murdered by being shut
up in a large tun with vipers and serpents. Blossius of Cuma,
indeed, was carried before the consuls, and examined touching
what had happened, and freely confessed that he had done,
without scruple, whatever Tiberius bade him. " What," cried
Nasica, " then if Tiberius had bidden you burn the capitol,
would you have burnt it? " His first answer was, that Tiberius
never would have ordered any such thing; but being pressed
with the same question by several, he declared, " If Tiberius had
commanded it, it would have been right for me to do it; for he
never would have commanded it, if it had not been for the
people's good." Blossius at this time was pardoned, and afterwards went away to Aristonicus in Asia, and when Aristonicus
was overthrown and ruined, killed himself.

The senate, to soothe the people after these transactions, did
not oppose the division of the public lands, and permitted them
to choose another commissioner in the room of Tiberius. So
they elected Publius Crassus, who was Gracchus's near connection, as his daughter Licinia was married to Caius Gracchus;

although Cornelius Nepos says, that it was not Crassus's
daughter whom Caius married, but Brutus's, who triumphed
for his victories over the Lusitanians: but most writers state it
as we have done.   The people, however, showed evident marks
of their anger at Tiberius's death; and were clearly waiting only
for the opportunity to be revenged, and Nasica was already
threatened with an impeachment.   The senate, therefore, fearing lest some mischief should befall him, sent him ambassador
into Asia, though there was no occasion for his going thither.
For the people did not conceal their indignation, even in the
open streets, but railed at him, whenever they met him abroad
calling him a murderer and a tyrant, one who had polluted the
most holy and religious spot in Rome with the blood of a sacred
and inviolable magistrate.   And so Nasica left Italy, although
he was bound, being the chief priest, to officiate in all principal
sacrifices.   Thus wandering wretchedly and ignominiously from
one place to another, he died in a short time after, not far from
Pergamus.   It is no wonder that the people had su c h an aversion
to Nasica, when even Scipio Africanus, though so much and so
deservedly beloved by the Romans, was in danger of quite losing
the good opinion which the people had of him, only for repeating,
when the news of Tiberius's death was first brought to Numantia,
the verse out of Homer—

" Even so perish all who do the same."

And afterwards, being asked by Caius and Fulvius, in a great
assembly, what he thought of Tiberius's death, he gave an
answer adverse to Tiberius's public actions.   Upon which
account, the people thenceforth used to interrupt him when he
spoke, which, until that time, they had never done, and he, on
the other hand, was induced to speak ill of the people.   But of
this the particulars are given in the life of Scipio.

## CAIUS GRACCHUS

CAIUS GRACCHUS at first, either for fear of his brother's enemies, or designing to render them more odious to the people, absented himself from the public assemblies, and lived quietly in his own house, as if he were not only reduced for the present to live unambitiously, but was disposed in general to pass his life in inaction. And some, indeed, went so far as to say that he disliked his brother's measures, and had wholly abandoned the defence of them. However, he was not but very young, being not so old as Tiberius by nine years; and he was not yet thirty when he was slain.

In some little time, however, he quietly let his temper appear, which was one of an utter antipathy to a lazy retirement and effeminacy, and not the least likely to be contented with a life of eating, drinking, and money-getting. He gave great pains to the study of eloquence, as wings upon which he might aspire to public business; and it was very apparent that he did not intend to pass his days in obscurity. When Vettius, a friend of his, was on his trial, he defended his cause, and the people were in an ecstasy, and transported with joy, finding him master of such eloquence that the other orators seemed like children in comparison, and jealousies and fears on the other hand began to be felt by the powerful citizens; and it was generally spoken of amongst them that they must hinder Caius from being made tribune.

But soon after, it happened that he was elected quæstor, and obliged to attend Orestes, the consul, into Sardinia. This, as it pleased his enemies, so it was not ungrateful to him, being naturally of a warlike character, and as well trained in the art of war as in that of pleading. And, besides, as yet he very much dreaded meddling with state affairs, and appearing publicly in the rostra, which, because of the importunity of the people and his friends, he could not otherwise avoid than by taking this journey. He was therefore most thankful for the opportunity of absenting himself. Notwithstanding which, it is the prevailing opinion that Caius was a far more thorough demagogue, and more ambitious than ever Tiberius had been, of popular applause; yet it is certain that he was borne rather by a sort of necessity than by any purpose of his own into public business. And Cicero, the orator, relates, that when he declined all such concerns, and would have lived privately, his brother appeared to him in a dream, and calling him by his name, said, "Why do you tarry, Caius? There is no escape; one life and one death is appointed for us both, to spend the one and to meet the other in the service of the people."

Caius was no sooner arrived in Sardinia, but he gave exemplary proofs of his high merit; he not only excelled all the young men of his age in his actions against his enemies, in doing justice to his inferiors, and in showing all obedience and respect to his superior officer; but likewise in temperance, frugality, and industry, he surpassed even those who were much older than himself. It happened to be a sharp and sickly winter in Sardinia, insomuch that the general was forced to lay an imposition upon several towns to supply the soldiers with necessary clothes. The cities sent to Rome, petitioning to be excused from that burden; the senate found their request reasonable, and ordered the general to find some other way of new clothing the army. While he was at a loss what course to take in this affair, the soldiers were reduced to great distress; but Caius went from one city to another, and by his mere representations he prevailed with them, that of their own accord they clothed the Roman army. This again being reported to Rome, and seeming to be only an intimation of what was to be expected of him as a popular leader hereafter, raised new jealousies amongst the senators. And, besides, there came ambassadors out of Africa from King Micipsa, to acquaint the senate that their master, out of respect to Caius Gracchus, had sent a considerable quantity of corn to the general in Sardinia; at which the senators were so much offended, that they turned the ambassadors out of the senate house, and made an order that the soldiers should be relieved by sending others in their room; but that Orestes should continue at his post, with whom Caius, also, as they presumed, being his quæstor, would remain. But he, finding how things were carried, immediately in anger took ship for Rome, where his unexpected appearance obtained him the censure not only of his enemies, but also of the people; who thought it strange that a quæstor should leave before his commander. Nevertheless, when some accusation upon this ground was made against him to the censors, he desired leave to defend himself, and did it so effectually, that, when he ended, he was regarded as one who had been very much injured. He made it then appear that he had served twelve years in the army, whereas others are obliged to serve only ten; that he had continued quæstor to the general three years, whereas he might by law have returned at the end of one year; and alone of all who went on the expedition, he had carried out a full and had brought home an empty purse, while others, after drinking up the wine they had carried out with them, brought back the wine-jars filled again with gold and silver from the war.

After this they brought other accusations and writs against him, for exciting insurrection amongst the allies, and being engaged in the conspiracy that was discovered about Fregellæ. But having cleared himself of every suspicion, and proved his entire innocence, he now at once came forward to ask for the tribuneship; in which, though he was universally opposed by all persons of distinction, yet there came such infinite numbers of people from all parts of Italy to vote for Caius, that lodgings for them could not be supplied in the city; and the Field being not large enough to contain the assembly, there were numbers who climbed upon the roofs and the tilings of the houses to use their voices in his favour. However, the nobility so far forced the people to their pleasure and disappointed Caius's hope, that he was not returned the first, as was expected, but the fourth tribune. But when he came to the execution of his office, it was seen presently who was really first tribune, as he was a better orator that any of his contemporaries, and the passion with which he still lamented his brother's death made him the bolder in speaking. He used on all occasions to remind the people of what had happened in that tumult, and laid before them the examples of their ancestors, how they declared war against the Faliscans, only for giving scurrilous language to one Genucius, a tribune of the people; and sentenced Caius Veturius to death, for refusing to give way in the forum to a tribune; " Whereas," said he, " these men did, in the presence of you all, murder Tiberius with clubs, and dragged the slaughtered body through the middle of the city, to be cast into the river. Even his friends, as many as could be taken, were put to death immediately, without any trial, notwithstanding that just and ancient custom, which has always been observed in our city, that whenever any one is accused of a capital crime, and does not make his personal appearance in court, a trumpeter is sent in the morning to his lodging, to summon him by sound of trumpet to appear; and before this ceremony is performed, the judges do not proceed to the vote; so cautious and reserved were our ancestors about business of life and death."

Having moved the people's passion with such addresses (and his voice was of the loudest and strongest), he proposed two laws. The first was, that whoever was turned out of any public office by the people, should be thereby rendered incapable of bearing any office afterwards; the second, that if any magistrate condemn a Roman to be banished without a legal trial, the people be authorised to take cognisance thereof.

One of these laws was manifestly levelled at Marcus Octavius, who, at the instigation of Tiberius, had been deprived of his tribuneship. The other touched Popilius, who, in his prætorship, had banished all Tiberius's friends; whereupon Popilius, being unwilling to stand the hazard of a trial, fled out of Italy. As for the former law, it was withdrawn by Caius himself, who said he yielded in the case of Octavius, at the request of his mother Cornelia. This was very acceptable and pleasing to the people, who had a great veneration for Cornelia, not more for the sake of her father than for that of her children; and they afterwards erected a statue of brass in honour of her, with this inscription, *Cornelia, the mother of the Gracchi.* There are several expressions recorded, in which he used her name perhaps with too much rhetoric, and too little self-respect, in his attacks upon his adversaries. " How," said he, " dare you presume to reflect upon Cornelia, the mother of Tiberius? " And because the person who made the reflections had been suspected of effeminate courses, " With what face," said he, " can you compare Cornelia with yourself? Have you brought forth children as she has done? And yet all Rome knows that she has refrained from the conversation of men longer than you yourself have done." Such was the bitterness he used in his language; and numerous similar expressions might be adduced from his written remains.

Of the laws which he now proposed, with the object of gratifying the people and abridging the power of the senate, the first was concerning the public lands, which were to be divided amongst the poor citizens; another was concerning the common soldiers, that they should be clothed at the public charge, without any diminution of their pay, and that none should be obliged to serve in the army who was not full seventeen years old; another gave the same right to all the Italians in general, of voting at elections, as was enjoyed by the citizens of Rome; a fourth related to the price of corn, which was to be sold at a lower rate than formerly to the poor; and a fifth regulated the courts of justice, greatly reducing the power of the senators. For hitherto, in all causes, senators only sat as judges, and were

therefore much dreaded by the Roman knights and the people.
But Caius joined three hundred ordinary citizens of equestrian
rank with the senators, who were three hundred likewise in
number, and ordained that the judicial authority should be
equally invested in the six hundred. While he was arguing for
the ratification of this law, his behaviour was observed to show
in many respects unusual earnestness, and whereas other popular
leaders had always hitherto, when speaking, turned their faces
towards the senate house, and the place called the comitium,
he, on the contrary, was the first man that in his harangue to
the people turned himself the other way, towards them, and
continued after that time to do so. An insignificant movement
and change of posture, yet it marked no small revolution in
state affairs, the conversion, in a manner, of the whole gover-
ment from an aristocracy to a democracy, his action intimating
that public speakers should address themselves to the people,
not the senate.

When the commonalty ratified this law, and gave him power
to select those of the knights whom he approved of, to be judges,
he was invested with a sort of a kingly power, and the senate
itself submitted to receive his advice in matters of difficulty;
nor did he advise anything that might derogate from the honour
of that body. As, for example, his resolution about the corn
which Fabius the proprietor sent from Spain, was very just and
honourable; for he persuaded the senate to sell the corn, and
return the money to the same provinces which had furnished
them with it; and also that Fabius should be censured for rendering the Roman government odious and insupportable. This
got him extraordinary respect and favour among the provinces.
Besides all this, he proposed measures for the colonisation of
several cities, for making roads, and for building public granaries;
of all which works he himself undertook the management and
superintendence, and was never wanting to give necessary orders
for the despatch of all these different and great undertakings;
and that with such wonderful expedition and diligence, as if he
had been but engaged upon one of them; insomuch that all
persons, even those who hated or feared him, stood amazed to
see what a capacity he had for effecting and completing all he
undertook. As for the people themselves, they were transported
at the very sight, when they saw him surrounded with a crowd
of contractors, artificers, public deputies, military officers,
soldiers, and scholars. All these he treated with an easy familiarity, yet without abandoning his dignity in his gentleness; and

so accommodated his nature to the wants and occasions of every one who addressed him, that those were looked upon as no better than envious detractors, who had represented him as a terrible, assuming, and violent character. He was even a greater master of the popular leader's art in his common talk and his actions, than he was in his public addresses.

His most especial exertions were given to constructing the roads, which he was careful to make beautiful and pleasant, as well as convenient. They were drawn by his directions through the fields, exactly in a straight line, partly paved with hewn stone, and partly laid with solid masses of gravel. When he met with any valleys or deep watercourses crossing the line, he either caused them to be filled up with rubbish, or bridges to be built over them, so well levelled, that all being of an equal height on both sides, the work presented one uniform and beautiful prospect. Besides this, he caused the roads to be all divided into miles (each mile containing little less than eight furlongs), and erected pillars of stone to signify the distance from one place to another. He likewise placed other stones at small distances from one another, on both sides of the way, by the help of which travellers might get easily on horseback without wanting a groom.

For these reasons, the people highly extolled him, and were ready upon all occasions to express their affection towards him. One day, in an oration to them, he declared that he had only one favour to request, which, if they granted, he should think the greatest obligation in the world; yet if it were denied, he would never blame them for the refusal. This expression made the world believe that his ambition was to be consul; and it was generally expected that he wished to be both consul and tribune at the same time. When the day for election of consuls was at hand, and all in great expectation, he appeared in the Field with Caius Fannius, canvassing together with his friends for his election. This was of great effect in Fannius's favour. He was chosen consul, and Caius elected tribune the second time, without his own seeking or petitioning for it, but at the voluntary motion of the people. But when he understood that the senators were his declared enemies, and that Fannius himself was none of the most zealous of friends, he began again to rouse the people with other new laws. He proposed that a colony of Roman citizens might be sent to re-people Tarentum and Capua, and that the Latins should enjoy the same privileges with the citizens of Rome. But the senate, apprehending that he would at last grow too powerful and dangerous, took a new and unusual course to alienate the people's affections from him, by playing the demagogue in opposition to him, and offering favours contrary to all good policy. Livius Drusus was fellow-tribune with Caius, a person of as good a family and as well educated as any amongst the Romans, and noways inferior to those who for their eloquence and riches were the most honoured and most powerful men of that time. To him, therefore, the chief senators made their application, exhorting him to attack Caius, and join in their confederacy against him; which they designed to carry on, not by using any force, or opposing the common people, but by gratifying and obliging them with such unreasonable things as otherwise they would have felt it honourable for them to incur the greatest unpopularity in resisting.

Livius offered to serve the senate with his authority in this business; and proceeded accordingly to bring forward such laws as were in reality neither honourable nor advantageous for the public; his whole design being to outdo Caius in pleasing and cajoling the populace (as if it had been in some comedy), with obsequious flattery and every kind of gratifications; the senate thus letting it be seen plainly that they were not angry with Caius's public measures, but only desirous to ruin him utterly, or at least to lessen his reputation. For when Caius proposed the settlement of only two colonies, and mentioned the better class of citizens for that purpose, they accused him of abusing the people; and yet, on the contrary, were pleased with Drusus, when he proposed the sending out of twelve colonies, each to consist of three thousand persons, and those, too, the most needy that he could find. When Caius divided the public land amongst the poor citizens, and charged them with a small rent, annually to be paid into the exchequer, they were angry at him, as one who sought to gratify the people only for his own interest; yet afterwards they commended Livius, though he exempted them from paying even that little acknowledgment. They were displeased with Caius for offering the Latins an equal right with the Romans of voting at the election of magistrates; but when Livius proposed that it might not be lawful for a Roman captain to scourge a Latin soldier, they promoted the passing of that law. And Livius, in all his speeches to the people, always told them that he proposed no laws but such as were agreeable to the senate, who had a particular regard to the people's advantage. And this truly was the only point in all his proceedings which was of any real service, as it created more kindly feelings towards the senate in the people; and whereas they formerly suspected and hated the principal senators, Livius appeased and mitigated this perverseness and animosity, by his profession that he had done nothing in favour and for the benefit of the commons without their advice and approbation.

But the greatest credit which Drusus got for kindness and justice towards the people was, that he never seemed to propose any law for his own sake, or his own advantage; he committed the charge of seeing the colonies rightly settled to other commissioners; neither did he ever concern himself with the distribution of the moneys; whereas Caius always took the principal part in any important transactions of this kind. Rubrius, another tribune of the people, had proposed to have Carthage again inhabited, which had been demolished by Scipio, and it fell to Caius's lot to see this performed, and for that purpose he sailed to Africa. Drusus took this opportunity of his absence to insinuate himself still more into the people's affections, which he did chiefly by accusing Fulvius, who was a particular friend to Caius, and was appointed a commissioner with him for the division of the lands. Fulvius was a man of a turbulent spirit; and notoriously hated by the senate; and besides, he was suspected by others to have fomented the difference between the citizens and their confederates, and underhand to be inciting the Italians to rebel; though there was little other evidence of the truth of these accusations than his being an unsettled character and of a well-known seditious temper. This was one principal cause of Caius's ruin; for part of the envy which fell upon Fulvius was extended to him. And when Scipio Africanus died suddenly, and no cause of such an unexpected death could be assigned, only some marks of blows upon his body seemed to intimate that he had suffered violence, as is related in the history of his life, the greatest part of the odium attached to Fulvius, because he was his enemy, and that very day had reflected upon Scipio in a public address to the people. Nor was Caius himself clear from suspicion. However, this great outrage, committed too upon the person of the greatest and most considerable man in Rome, was never either punished or inquired into thoroughly, for the populace opposed and hindered any judicial investigation, for fear that Caius should be implicated in the charge if proceedings were carried on. This, however, had happened some time before.

But in Africa, where at present Caius was engaged in the re-

peopling of Carthage, which he named Junonia, many ominous
appearances, which presaged mischief, are reported to have been
sent from the gods. For a sudden gust of wind falling upon the
first standard, and the standard-bearer holding it fast, the staff
broke; another sudden storm blew away the sacrifices, which
were laid upon the altars, and carried them beyond the bounds
laid out for the city, and the wolves came and carried away the
very marks that were set up to show the boundary. Caius, notwithstanding all this, ordered and despatched the whole business
in the space of seventy days, and then returned to Rome, understanding how Fulvius was prosecuted by Drusus, and that the
present juncture of affairs would not suffer him to be absent.
For Lucius Opimius, one who sided with the nobility, and was
of no small authority in the senate, who had formerly sued to be
consul, but was repulsed by Caius's interest, at the time when
Fannius was elected, was in a fair way now of being chosen
consul, having a numerous company of supporters. And it was
generally believed, if he did obtain it, that he would wholly ruin
Caius, whose power was already in a declining condition; and the
people were not so apt to admire his actions as formerly, because
there were so many others who every day contrived new ways
to please them, with which the senate readily complied.

After his return to Rome, he quitted his house on the Palatine
Mount, and went to live near the market-place, endeavouring to
make himself more popular in those parts, where most of the
humble and poorer citizens lived. He then brought forward
the remainder of his proposed laws, as intending to have them
ratified by the popular vote; to support which a vast number
of people collected from all quarters. But the senate persuaded
Fannius, the consul, to command all persons who were not born
Romans to depart the city. A new and unusual proclamation
was thereupon made, prohibiting any of the allies or Confederates
to appear at Rome during that time. Caius, on the contrary,
published an edict, accusing the consul for what he had done,
and setting forth to the Confederates, that if they would continue upon the place, they might be assured of his assistance and
protection. However, he was not so good as his word; for
though he saw one of his own familiar friends and companions
dragged to prison by Fannius's officers, he, notwithstanding,
passed by without assisting him; either because he was afraid
to stand the test of his power, which was already decreased, or
because, as he himself reported, he was unwilling to give his
enemies an opportunity, which they very much desired, of

coming to actual violence and fighting. About that time there happened likewise a difference between him and his fellow-officers upon this occasion. A show of gladiators was to be exhibited before the people in the market-place, and most of the magistrates erected scaffolds round about, with an intention of letting them for advantage. Caius commanded them to take down their scaffolds, that the poor people might see the sport without paying anything. But nobody obeying these orders of his, he gathered together a body of labourers, who worked for him, and overthrew all the scaffolds the very night before the contest was to take place. So that by the next morning the market-place was cleared, and the common people had an opportunity of seeing the pastime. In this, the populace thought he had acted the part of a man; but he much disobliged the tribunes his colleagues, who regarded it as a piece of violent and presumptuous interference.

This was thought to be the chief reason that he failed of being the third time elected tribune; not but that he had the most votes, but because his colleagues out of revenge caused false returns to be made. But as to this matter there was a controversy. Certain it is, he very much resented this repulse, and behaved with unusual arrogance towards some of his adversaries who were joyful at his defeat, telling them that all this was but a false, sardonic mirth, as they little knew how much his actions threw them into obscurity.

As soon as Opimius also was chosen consul, they presently cancelled several of Caius's laws, and especially called in question his proceedings at Carthage, omitting nothing that was likely to irritate him, that from some effect of his passion they might find out a tolerable pretence to put him to death. Caius at first bore these things very patiently; but afterwards, at the instigation of his friends, especially Fulvius, he resolved to put himself at the head of a body of supporters, to oppose the consul by force. They say also that on this occasion his mother, Cornelia, joined in the sedition, and assisted him by sending privately several strangers into Rome, under pretence as if they came to be hired there for harvest-men; for that intimations of this are given in her letters to him. However, it is confidently affirmed by others that Cornelia did not in the least approve of these actions.

When the day came in which Opimius designed to abrogate the laws of Caius, both parties met very early at the capitol; and the consul having performed all the rites usual in their sacrifices, one Quintus Antyllius, an attendant on the consul, carrying out the entrails of the victim, spoke to Fulvius, and his friends who stood about him, " Ye factious citizens, make way for honest men." Some report that, besides this provoking language, he extended his naked arm towards them, as a piece of scorn and contempt. Upon this he was presently killed with the strong stiles which are commonly used in writing, though some say that on this occasion they had been manufactured for this purpose only. This murder caused a sudden consternation in the whole assembly, and the heads of each faction had their different sentiments about it. As for Caius, he was much grieved, and severely reprimanded his own party, because they had given their adversaries a reasonable pretence to proceed against them, which they had so long hoped for. Opimius, immediately seizing the occasion thus offered, was in great delight, and urged the people to revenge; but there happening a great shower of rain on a sudden, it put an end to the business of that day.

Early the next morning, the consul summoned the senate, and whilst he advised with the senators in the senate-house, the corpse of Antyllius was laid upon a bier, and brought through the market-place, being there exposed to open view, just before the senate-house, with a great deal of crying and lamentation. Opimius was not at all ignorant that this was designed to be done; however, he seemed to be surprised, and wondered what the meaning of it should be; the senators, therefore, presently went out to know the occasion of it, and, standing about the corpse, uttered exclamations against the inhuman and barbarous act. The people, meantime, could not but feel resentment and hatred for the senators, remembering how they themselves had not only assassinated Tiberius Gracchus, as he was executing his office in the very capitol, but had also thrown his mangled body into the river; yet now they could honour with their presence and their public lamentations in the forum the corpse of an ordinary hired attendant (who, though he might perhaps die wrongfully, was, however, in a great measure the occasion of it himself), by these means hoping to undermine him who was the only remaining defender and safeguard of the people.

The senators, after some time, withdrew, and presently ordered that Opimius, the consul, should be invested with extraordinary power to protect the commonwealth and suppress all tyrants. This being decreed, he presently commanded the senators to arm themselves, and the Roman knights to be in readiness very early the next morning, and every one of them to be attended with two servants well armed. Fulvius, on the other side, made his preparations and collected the populace. Caius at that time returning from the market-place, made a stop just before his father's statue, and fixing his eyes for some time upon it, remained in a deep contemplation; at length he sighed, shed tears, and departed. This made no small impression upon those who saw it, and they began to upbraid themselves that they should desert and betray so worthy a man as Caius. They therefore went directly to his house, remaining there as a guard about it all night, though in a different manner from those who were a guard to Fulvius; for they passed away the night with shouting and drinking, and Fulvius himself, being the first to get drunk, spoke and acted many things very unbecoming a man of his age and character. On the other side, the party which guarded Caius, were quiet and diligent, relieving one another by turns, and forecasting, as in a public calamity, what the issue of things might be. As soon as daylight appeared, they roused Fulvius, who had not yet slept off the effects of his drinking; and having armed themselves with the weapons hung up in his house, that were formerly taken from the Gauls, whom he conquered in the time of his consulship, they presently, with threats and loud acclamations, made their way towards the Aventine Mount.

Caius could not be persuaded to arm himself, but put on his gown, as if he had been going to the assembly of the people, only with this difference, that under it he had then a short dagger by his side. As he was going out, his wife came running to him at the gate, holding him with one hand, and with the other a young child of his. She bespoke him: " Alas, Caius, I do not now part with you to let you address the people either as a tribune or a lawgiver, nor as if you were going to some honourable war, when, though you might perhaps have en-countered that fate which all must some time or other submit to, yet you had left me this mitigation of my sorrow, that my mourning was respected and honoured. You go now to expose your person to the murderers of Tiberius, unarmed indeed, and rightly so, choosing rather to suffer the worst of injuries than do the least yourself. But even your very death at this time will not be serviceable to the public good. Faction prevails; power and arms are now the only measures of justice. Had your brother fallen before Numantia, the enemy would have given back what then had remained of Tiberius; but such is my hard fate, that I probably must be an humble suppliant to the floods or the waves, that they would somewhere restore to me your relics; for since Tiberius was not spared, what trust can we place either on the laws, or in the gods?" Licinia, thus bewailing, Caius, by degrees getting loose from her embraces, silently withdrew himself, being accompanied by his friends; she, endeavouring to catch him by the gown, fell prostrate upon the earth, lying there for some time speechless. Her servants took her up for dead, and conveyed her to her brother Crassus.

Fulvius, when the people were gathered together in a full body, by the advice of Caius sent his youngest son into the market-place, with a herald's rod in his hand. He, being a very handsome youth, and modestly addressing himself, with tears in his eyes and a becoming bashfulness, offered proposals of agreement to the consul and the whole senate. The greatest part of the assembly were inclinable to accept of the proposals; but Opimius said, that it did not become them to send messengers and capitulate with the senate, but to surrender at discretion to the laws, like loyal citizens, and endeavour to merit their pardon by submission. He commanded the youth not to return, unless they would comply with these conditions. Caius, as it is reported, was very forward to go and clear himself before the senate; but none of his friends consenting to it, Fulvius sent his son a second time to intercede for them, as before. But Opimius, who was resolved that a battle should ensue, caused the youth to be apprehended and committed into custody; and then with a company of his foot-soldiers and some Cretan archers set upon the party under Fulvius. These archers did such execution, and inflicted so many wounds, that a rout and flight quickly ensued. Fulvius fled into an obscure bathing-house; but shortly after being discovered, he and his eldest son were slain together. Caius was not observed to use any violence against any one; but, extremely disliking all these outrages, retired to Diana's temple. There he attempted to kill himself, but was hindered by his faithful friends, Pomponius and Licinius; they took his sword away from him, and were very urgent that he would endeavour to make his escape. It is reported that, falling upon his knee and lifting up his hands, he prayed the goddess that the Roman people, as a punishment for their ingratitude and treachery, might always remain in slavery. For as soon as a proclamation was made of a pardon, the greater part openly deserted him.

Caius, therefore, endeavoured now to make his escape, but was pursued so close by his enemies, as far as the wooden bridge, that from thence he narrowly escaped. There his two trusty friends begged of him to preserve his own person by flight, whilst they in the meantime would keep their post, and maintain the passage; neither could their enemies, until they were both slain, pass the bridge. Caius had no other companion in his flight but one Philocrates, a servant of his. As he ran along, everybody encouraged him, and wished him success, as standers-by may do to those who are engaged in a race, but nobody either lent him any assistance, or would furnish him with a horse, though he asked for one; for his enemies had gained ground, and got very near him. However, he had still time enough to hide himself in a little grove, consecrated to the Furies. In that place, his servant Philocrates having first slain him, presently afterwards killed himself also, and fell dead upon his master. Though some affirm it for a truth, that they were both taken alive by their enemies, and that Philocrates embraced his master so close, that they could not wound Caius until his servant was slain.

They say that when Caius's head was cut off, and carried away by one of his murderers, Septimuleius, Opimius's friend, met him, and forced it from him; because, before the battle began, they had made proclamation, that whoever should bring the head either of Caius or Fulvius, should, as a reward, receive its weight in gold. Septimuleius, therefore, having fixed Caius's head upon the top of his spear, came and presented it to Opimius. They presently brought the scales, and it was found to weigh above seventeen pounds. But in this affair, Septimuleius gave as great signs of his knavery as he had done before of his cruelty; for having taken out the brains, he had filled the skull with lead. There were others who brought the head of Fulvius, too, but, being mean, inconsiderable persons, were turned away without the promised reward. The bodies of these two persons, as well as of the rest who were slain, to the number of three thousand men, were all thrown into the river; their goods were confiscated, and their widows forbidden to put themselves into mourning. They dealt even more severely with Licinia, Caius's wife, and deprived her even of her jointure; and as in addition still to all their inhumanity, they barbarously murdered Fulvius's youngest son; his only crime being, not that he took up arms against them, or that he was present in the battle, but merely that he had come with articles of agreement; for this he was first imprisoned, then slain.

But that which angered the common people most was, that

at this time, in memory of his success, Opimius built the Temple of Concord, as if he gloried and triumphed in the slaughter of so many citizens. Somebody in the night time, under the inscription of the temple added this verse:—

"Folly and Discord Concord's temple built."

Yet this Opimius, the first who, being consul, presumed to usurp the power of a dictator, condemning, without any trial, with three thousand other citizens, Caius Gracchus and Fulvius Flaccus, one of whom had triumphed and been consul, the other far excelled all his contemporaries in virtue and honour, afterwards was found incapable of keeping his hands from thieving: and when he was sent ambassador to Jugurtha, King of Numidia, he was there corrupted by presents, and at his return, being shamefully convicted of it, lost all his honours, and grew old amidst the hatred and the insults of the people; who, though humble, and affrighted at the time, did not fail before long to let everybody see what respect and veneration they had for the memory of the Gracchi. They ordered their statues to be made and set up in public view; they consecrated the places where they were slain, and thither brought the first-fruits of everything, according to the season of the year, to make their offerings. Many came likewise thither to their devotions, and daily worshipped there, as at the temple of the gods.

It is reported that as Cornelia, their mother, bore the loss of her two sons with a noble and undaunted spirit, so, in reference to the holy places in which they were slain, she said, their dead bodies were well worthy of such sepulchres. She removed afterwards, and dwelt near the place called Misenum, not at all altering her former way of living. She had many friends, and hospitably received many strangers at her house; many Greeks and learned men were continually about her; nor was there any foreign prince but received gifts from her and presented her again. Those who were conversant with her, were much interested, when she pleased to entertain them with her recollections of her father Scipio Africanus, and of his habits and way of living. But it was most admirable to hear her make mention of her sons, without any tears or sign of grief, and give the full account of all their deeds and misfortunes, as if she had been relating the history of some ancient heroes. This made some imagine, that age, or the greatness of her afflictions, had made her senseless and devoid of natural feelings. But they who so thought were themselves more truly insensible not to see how

much a noble nature and education avail to conquer any affliction; and though fortune may often be more successful, and
may defeat the efforts of virtue to avert misfortunes, it cannot,
when we incur them, prevent our bearing them reasonably.


## THE COMPARISON OF TIBERIUS AND CAIUS
## GRACCHUS WITH AGIS AND CLEOMENES

HAVING given an account severally of these persons, it remains
only that we should take a view of them in comparison with
one another.

As for the Gracchi, the greatest detractors and their worst
enemies could not but allow that they had a genius to virtue
beyond all other Romans, which was improved also by a generous
education.   Agis and Cleomenes may be supposed to have had
stronger natural gifts, since, though they wanted all the advantages of good education, and were bred up in those very customs,
manners, and habits of living which had for a long time corrupted others, yet they were public examples of temperance and
frugality.   Besides, the Gracchi, happening to live when Rome
had her greatest repute for honour and virtuous actions, might
justly have been ashamed, if they had not also left to the next
generation the noble inheritance of the virtues of their ancestors.
Whereas the other two had parents of different morals, and
though they found their country in a sinking condition, and
debauched, yet that did not quench their forward zeal to what
was just and honourable.

The integrity of the two Romans, and their superiority to
money, was chiefly remarkable in this: that in office and the
administration of public affairs, they kept themselves from
the imputation of unjust gain; whereas Agis might justly be
offended if he had only that mean commendation given him,
that he took nothing wrongfully from any man, seeing he distributed his own fortunes which, in ready money only, amounted
to the value of six hundred talents, amongst his fellow-citizens.
Extortion would have appeared a crime of a strange nature to
him, who esteemed it a piece of covetousness to possess, though
never so justly gotten, greater riches than his neighbours.

Their political actions, also, and the state revolutions they
attempted, were very different in magnitude.   The chief things
in general that the two Romans commonly aimed at, were the
settlement of cities and mending of highways; and, in particular,

the boldest design which Tiberius is famed for, was the recovery of the public lands; and Caius gained his greatest reputation by the addition, for the exercise of judiciary powers, of three hundred of the order of knights to the same number of senators. Whereas the alteration which Agis and Cleomenes made was in a quite different kind. They did not set about removing partial evils and curing petty incidents of disease, which would have been (as Plato says) like cutting off one of the Hydra's heads, the very means to increase the number; but they instituted a thorough reformation, such as would free the country from all its grievances, or rather, to speak more truly, they reversed that former change which had been the cause of all their calamities, and so restored their city to its ancient state.

However, this must be confessed in the behalf of the Gracchi, that their undertakings were always opposed by men of the greatest influence. On the other side, those things which were first attempted by Agis, and afterwards consummated by Cleomenes, were supported by the great and glorious precedent of those ancient laws concerning frugality and levelling which they had themselves received upon the authority of Lycurgus, and he had instituted on that of Apollo. It is also further observable, that from the actions of the Gracchi, Rome received no additions to her former greatness; whereas, under the conduct of Cleomenes, Greece presently saw Sparta exert her sovereign power over all Peloponnesus, and contest the supreme command with the most powerful princes of the time; success in which would have freed Greece from Illyrian and Gaulish violence, and placed her once again under the orderly rule of the sons of Hercules.

From the circumstances of their deaths, also, we may infer some difference in the quality of their courage. The Gracchi, fighting with their fellow-citizens, were both slain as they endeavoured to make their escape; Agis willingly submitted to his fate, rather than any citizen should be in danger of his life. Cleomenes, being shamefully and unjustly treated, made an effort toward revenge, but failing of that, generously fell by his own hand.

On the other side it must be said, that Agis never did a great action worthy a commander, being prevented by an untimely death. And as for those heroic actions of Cleomenes, we may justly compare with them that of Tiberius, when he was the first who attempted to scale the walls of Carthage, which was no mean exploit. We may add the peace which he concluded with the Numantines, by which he saved the lives of twenty thousand Romans, who otherwise had certainly been cut off. And Caius, not only at home, but in war in Sardinia, displayed distinguished courage. So that their early actions were no small argument that afterwards they might have rivalled the best of the Roman commanders, if they had not died so young.

In civil life, Agis showed a lack of determination; he let himself be baffled by the craft of Agesilaus, disappointed the expectations of the citizens as to the division of the lands, and generally left all the designs, which he had deliberately formed and publicly announced, unperformed and unfulfilled through a young man's want of resolution. Cleomenes, on the other hand, proceeded to effect the revolution with only too much boldness and violence, and unjustly slew the Ephors whom he might, by superiority in arms, have gained over to his party, or else might easily have banished, as he did several others of the city. For to use the knife, unless in the extremest necessity, is neither good surgery nor wise policy, but in both cases mere unskilfulness; and in the latter, unjust as well as unfeeling. Of the Gracchi, neither the one nor the other was the first to shed the blood of his fellow-citizens; and Caius is reported to have avoided all manner of resistance, even when his life was aimed at, showing himself always valiant against a foreign enemy, but wholly inactive in a sedition. This was the reason that he went from his own house unarmed, and withdrew when the battle began, and in all respects showed himself anxious rather not to do any harm to others, than not to suffer any himself. Even the very flight of the Gracchi must not be looked upon as an argument of their mean spirit, but an honourable retreat from endangering of others. For if they had stayed, they must either have yielded to those who assailed them, or else have fought them in their own defence.

The greatest crime that can be laid to Tiberius's charge was the deposing of his fellow tribune, and seeking afterwards a second tribuneship for himself. As for the death of Antyllius, it is falsely and unjustly attributed to Caius, for he was slain unknown to him, and much to his grief. On the contrary, Cleomenes (not to mention the murder of the Ephors) set all the slaves at liberty, and governed by himself alone in reality, having a partner only for show; having made choice of his brother Euclidas, who was one of the same family. He prevailed upon Archidamus, who was the right heir to the kingdom of the other line, to venture to return home from Messene; but after his being slain, by not doing anything to revenge his death, confirmed the suspicion that he was privy to it himself. Lycurgus, whose example he professed to imitate, after he had voluntarily settled his kingdom upon Charillus, his brother's son, fearing lest, if the youth should chance to die by accident, he might be suspected for it, travelled a long time, and would not return again to Sparta until Charillus had a son, and an heir to his kingdom. But we have indeed no other Grecian who is worthy to be compared with Lycurgus, and it is clear enough that in the public measures of Cleomenes various acts of considerable audacity and lawlessness may be found.

Those, therefore, who incline to blame their characters may observe, that the two Grecians were disturbers even from their youth, lovers of contest, and aspirants to despotic power; that Tiberius and Caius by nature had an excessive desire after glory and honours. Beyond this, their enemies could find nothing to bring against them; but as soon as the contention began with their adversaries, their heat and passions would so far prevail beyond their natural temper, that by them, as by ill winds, they were driven afterwards to all their rash undertakings. What could be more just and honourable than their first design, had not the power and the faction of the rich, by endeavouring to abrogate that law, engaged them both in those fatal quarrels, the one, for his own preservation, the other, to revenge his brother's death, who was murdered without any law or justice?

From the account, therefore, which has been given, you yourself may perceive the difference; which if it were to be pronounced of every one singly, I should affirm Tiberius to have excelled them all in virtue; that young Agis had been guilty of the fewest misdeeds; and that in action and boldness Caius came far short of Cleomenes.

# DEMOSTHENES

WHOEVER it was, Sosius, that wrote the poem in honour of Alcibiades, upon his winning the chariot-race at the Olympian Games, whether it were Euripides, as is most commonly thought, or some other person, he tells us that to a man's being happy it is in the first place requisite he should be born in " some famous city." But for him that would attain to true happiness, which for the most part is placed in the qualities and disposition of the mind, it is, in my opinion, of no other disadvantage to be of a mean, obscure country, than to be born of a small or plain-looking woman. For it were ridiculous to think that Iulis, a little part of Ceos, which itself is no great island, and Ægina, which an Athenian once said ought to be removed, like a small eyesore, from the port of Piræus, should breed good actors and poets, and yet should never be able to produce a just, temperate, wise, and high-minded man. Other arts, whose end it is to acquire riches or honour, are likely enough to wither and decay in poor and undistinguished towns; but virtue, like a strong and durable plant, may take root and thrive in any place where it can lay hold of an ingenuous nature, and a mind that is industrious. I, for my part, shall desire that for any deficiency of mine in right judgment or action, I myself may be, as in fairness, held accountable, and shall not attribute it to the obscurity of my birthplace.

But if any man undertake to write a history that has to be collected from materials gathered by observation and the reading of works not easy to be got in all places, nor written always in his own language, but many of them foreign and dispersed in other hands, for him, undoubtedly, it is in the first place and above all things most necessary to reside in some city of good note, addicted to liberal arts, and populous; where he may have plenty of all sorts of books, and upon inquiry may hear and inform himself of such particulars as, having escaped the pens of writers, are more faithfully preserved in the memories of men, lest his work be deficient in many things, even those which it can least dispense with.

But for me, I live in a little town, where I am willing to continue, lest it should grow less; and having had no leisure, while I was in Rome and other parts of Italy, to exercise myself in the Roman language, on account of public business and of those who came to be instructed by me in philosophy, it was very late, and in the decline of my age, before I applied myself to the reading of Latin authors. Upon which that which happened to me may seem strange, though it be true; for it was not so much by the knowledge of words that I came to the understanding of things, as by my experience of things I was enabled to follow the meaning of words. But to appreciate the graceful and ready pronunciation of the Roman tongue, to understand the various figures and connection of words, and such other ornaments, in which the beauty of speaking consists, is, I doubt not, an admirable and delightful accomplishment; but it requires a degree of practice and study which is not easy, and will better suit those who have more leisure, and time enough yet before them for the occupation.

And so in this fifth book of my Parallel Lives, in giving an account of Demosthenes and Cicero, my comparison of their natural dispositions and their characters will be formed upon their actions and their lives as statesmen, and I shall not pretend to criticise their orations one against the other, to show which of the two was the more charming or the more powerful speaker. For there, as Ion says—

" We are but like a fish upon dry land; "

a proverb which Cæcilius perhaps forgot, when he employed his always adventurous talents in so ambitious an attempt as a comparison of Demosthenes and Cicero; and, possibly, if it were a thing obvious and easy for every man to *know himself*, the precept had not passed for an oracle.

The divine power seems originally to have designed Demosthenes and Cicero upon the same plan, giving them many similarities in their natural characters, as their passion for distinction and their love of liberty in civil life, and their want of courage in dangers and war, and at the same time also to have added many accidental resemblances. I think there can hardly be found two other orators, who, from small and obscure beginnings, became so great and mighty; who both contested with kings and tyrants; both lost their daughters, were driven out of their country, and returned with honour; who, flying from thence again, were both seized upon by their enemies, and at last ended their lives with the liberty of their countrymen. So that if we were to suppose there had been a trial of skill between nature and fortune, as there is sometimes between artists, it would be hard to judge whether that succeeded best in making them alike in their dispositions and manners, or this in the coincidences of their lives. We will speak of the eldest first.

Demosthenes, the father of Demosthenes, was a citizen of good rank and quality, as Theopompus informs us, surnamed the Sword-maker, because he had a large workhouse, and kept servants skilful in that art at work. But of that which Æschines the orator said of his mother, that she was descended of one Gylon, who fled his country upon an accusation of treason, and of a barbarian woman, I can affirm nothing, whether he spoke true, or slandered and maligned her. This is certain, that Demosthenes, being as yet but seven years old, was left by his father in affluent circumstances, the whole value of his estate being little short of fifteen talents, and that he was wronged by his guardians, part of his fortune being embezzled by them, and the rest neglected; insomuch that even his teachers were defrauded of their salaries. This was the reason that he did not obtain the liberal education that he should have had; besides that, on account of weakness and delicate health, his mother would not let him exert himself, and his teachers forbore to urge him. He was meagre and sickly from the first, and hence had his nickname of Batalus given him, it is said, by the boys, in derision of his appearance; Batalus being, as some tell us, a certain enervated flute-player, in ridicule of whom Antiphanes wrote a play. Others speak of Batalus as a writer of wanton verses and drinking songs. And it would seem that some part of the body, not decent to be named, was at that time called *batalus* by the Athenians. But the name of Argas, which also they say was a nickname of Demosthenes, was given him for his behaviour, as being savage and spiteful, *argas* being one of the poetical words for a snake; or for his disagreeable way of speaking, Argas being the name of a poet who composed very harshly and disagreeably. So much, as Plato says, for such matters.

The first occasion of his eager inclination to oratory, they say, was this. Callistratus, the orator, being to plead in open court for Oropus, the expectation of the issue of that cause was very great, as well for the ability of the orator, who was then at the height of his reputation, as also for the fame of the action itself. Therefore, Demosthenes, having heard the tutors and schoolmasters agreeing among themselves to be present at this trial, with much importunity persuades his tutor to take him along with him to the hearing; who, having some acquaintance with the doorkeepers, procured a place where the boy might sit un-

seen, and hear what was said. Callistratus having got the day,
and being much admired, the boy began to look upon his glory
with a kind of emulation, observing how he was courted on all
hands, and attended on his way by the multitude; but his
wonder was more than all excited by the power of his eloquence,
which seemed able to subdue and win over anything. From
this time, therefore, bidding farewell to other sorts of learning
and study, he now began to exercise himself, and to take pains
in declaiming, as one that meant to be himself also an orator.
He made use of Isæus as his guide to the art of speaking, though
Isocrates at that time was giving lessons; whether, as some say,
because he was an orphan, and was not able to pay Isocrates
his appointed fee of ten minæ, or because he preferred Isæus's
speaking, as being more business-like and effective in actual use.
Hermippus says that he met with certain memoirs without any
author's name, in which it was written that Demosthenes was a
scholar to Plato, and learnt much of his eloquence from him;
and he also mentions Ctesibius, as reporting from Callias of
Syracuse and some others, that Demosthenes secretly obtained
a knowledge of the systems of Isocrates and Alcidamas, and
mastered them thoroughly.

As soon, therefore, as he was grown up to man's estate, he
began to go to law with his guardians, and to write orations
against them; who, in the meantime, had recourse to various
subterfuges and pleas for new trials, and Demosthenes, though
he was thus, as Thucydides says, taught his business in dangers,
and by his own exertions was successful in his suit, was yet
unable for all this to recover so much as a small fraction of his
patrimony. He only attained some degree of confidence in
speaking, and some competent experience in it. And having
got a taste of the honour and power which are acquired by
pleadings, he now ventured to come forth, and to undertake
public business. And, as it is said of Laomedon, the Orcho-
menian, that, by advice of his physician, he used to run long
distances to keep off some disease of his spleen, and by that
means having, through labour and exercise, framed the habit of
his body, he betook himself to the great garland games, and
became one of the best runners at the long race; so it happened
to Demosthenes, who, first venturing upon oratory for the
recovery of his own private property, by this acquired ability
in speaking, and at length, in public business, as it were in the
great games, came to have the pre-eminence of all competitors
in the assembly. But when he first addressed himself to the

people, he met with great discouragements, and was derided for his strange and uncouth style, which was cumbered with long sentences and tortured with formal arguments to a most harsh and disagreeable excess. Besides, he had, it seems, a weakness in his voice, a perplexed and indistinct utterance and a shortness of breath, which, by breaking and disjointing his sentences, much obscured the sense and meaning of what he spoke. So that in the end being quite disheartened, he forsook the assembly; and as he was walking carelessly and sauntering about the Piræus, Eunomus, the Thriasian, then a very old man, seeing him, up-braided him, saying that his diction was very much like that of Pericles, and that he was wanting to himself through cowardice and meanness of spirit, neither bearing up with courage against popular outcry, not fitting his body for action, but suffering it to languish through mere sloth and negligence.

Another time, when the assembly had refused to hear him, and he was going home with his head muffled up, taking it very heavily, they relate that Satyrus, the actor, followed him, and being his familiar acquaintance, entered into conversation with him. To whom, when Demosthenes bemoaned himself, that having been the most industrious of all the pleaders, and having almost spent the whole strength and vigour of his body in that employment, he could not yet find any acceptance with the people, that drunken sots, mariners, and illiterate fellows were heard, and had the hustings for their own, while he himself was despised, "You say true, Demosthenes," replied Satyrus, "but I will quickly remedy the cause of all this, if you will repeat to me some passage out of Euripides or Sophocles." Which when Demosthenes had pronounced, Satyrus presently taking it up after him, gave the same passage, in his rendering of it, such a new form, by accompanying it with the proper mien and gesture, that to Demosthenes it seemed quite another thing. By this, being convinced how much grace and ornament language acquires from action, he began to esteem it a small matter, and as good as nothing for a man to exercise himself in declaiming, if he neglected enunciation and delivery. Hereupon he built himself a place to study in under ground (which was still remaining in our time), and hither he would come constantly every day to form his action and to exercise his voice; and here he would continue, oftentimes without intermission, two or three months together, shaving one half of his head, that so for shame he might not go abroad, though he desired it ever so much.

Nor was this all, but he also made his conversation with people abroad, his common speech, and his business, subservient to his studies, taking from hence occasions and arguments as matter to work upon. For as soon as he was parted from his company, down he would go at once into his study, and run over everything in order that had passed, and the reasons that might be alleged for and against it. Any speeches, also, that he was present at, he would go over again with himself, and reduce into periods; and whatever others spoke to him, or he to them, he would correct, transform, and vary several ways. Hence it was that he was looked upon as a person of no great natural genius, but one who owed all the power and ability he had in speaking to labour and industry. Of the truth of which it was thought to be no small sign that he was very rarely heard to speak upon the occasion, but though he were by name frequently called upon by the people, as he sat in the assembly, yet he would not rise unless he had previously considered the subject, and came prepared for it. So that many of the popular pleaders used to make it a jest against him; and Pytheas once, scoffing at him, said that his arguments smelt of the lamp. To which Demosthenes gave the sharp answer, " It is true, indeed, Pytheas, that your lamp and mine are not conscious of the same things." To others, however, he would not much deny it, but would admit frankly enough, that he neither entirely wrote his speeches beforehand, nor yet spoke wholly extempore. And he would affirm that it was the more truly popular act to use premeditation, such preparation being a kind of respect to the people; whereas, to slight and take no care how what is said is likely to be received by the audience, shows something of an oligarchical temper, and is the course of one that intends force rather than persuasion. Of his want of courage and assurance to speak offhand, they make it also another argument that, when he was at a loss and discomposed, Demades would often rise up on the sudden to support him, but he was never observed to do the same for Demades.

Whence then, may some say, was it, that Æschines speaks of him as a person so much to be wondered at for his boldness in speaking? Or, how could it be, when Python, the Byzantine, with so much confidence and such a torrent of words inveighed against the Athenians, that Demosthenes alone stood up to oppose him? Or when Lamarchus, the Myrinæan, had written a panegyric upon King Philip and Alexander, in which he uttered many things in reproach of the Thebans and Olynthians, and at the Olympic Games recited it publicly, how was it that he, rising up, and recounting historically and demonstratively what benefits and advantages all Greece had received from the Thebans and Chalcidians, and, on the contrary, what mischiefs the flatterers of the Macedonians had brought upon it, so turned the minds of all that were present that the sophist, in alarm at the outcry against him, secretly made his way out of the assembly? But Demosthenes, it should seem, regarded other points in the character of Pericles to be unsuited to him; but his reserve and his sustained manner, and his forbearing to speak on the sudden, or upon every occasion, as being the things to which principally he owed his greatness, these he followed, and endeavoured to imitate, neither wholly neglecting the glory which present occasion offered, nor yet willing too often to expose his faculty to the mercy of chance. For, in fact, the orations which were spoken by him had much more of boldness and confidence in them than those that he wrote, if we may believe Eratosthenes, Demetrius the Phalerian, and the Comedians. Eratosthenes says that often in his speaking he would be transported into a kind of ecstasy, and Demetrius, that he uttered the famous metrical adjuration to the people—

" By the earth, the springs, the rivers, and the streams,"

as a man inspired and beside himself. One of the comedians calls him a *rhopoperperethras*, and another scoffs at him for his use of antithesis:—

" And what he took, took back; a phrase to please,
The very fancy of Demosthenes."

Unless, indeed, this also is meant by Antiphanes for a jest upon the speech on Halonesus, which Demosthenes advised the Athenians not to *take* at Philip's hands, but to *take back*.

All, however, used to consider Demades, in the mere use of his natural gifts, an orator impossible to surpass, and that in what he spoke on the sudden, he excelled all the study and preparation of Demosthenes. And Ariston, the Chian, has recorded a judgment which Theophrastus passed upon the orators; for being asked what kind of orator he accounted Demosthenes, he answered, " Worthy of the city of Athens; " and then what he thought of Demades, he answered, " Above it." And the same philosopher reports that Polyeuctus, the Sphettian, one of the Athenian politicians about that time, was wont to say that Demosthenes was the greatest orator, but Phocion the ablest, as he expressed the most sense in the fewest words. And, indeed, it is related that Demosthenes himself, as often as Phocion stood up to plead against him, would say to his acquaintance, " Here comes the knife to my speech." Yet it does not appear whether he had this feeling for his powers of speaking, or for his life and character, and meant to say that one word or nod from a man who was really trusted would go further than a thousand lengthy periods from others.

Demetrius, the Phalerian, tells us that he was informed by Demosthenes himself, now grown old, that the ways he made use of to remedy his natural bodily infirmities and defects were such as these; his inarticulate and stammering pronunciation he overcame and rendered more distinct by speaking with pebbles in his mouth; his voice he disciplined by declaiming and reciting speeches or verses when he was out of breath, while running or going up steep places; and that in his house he had a large looking-glass, before which he would stand and go through his exercises. It is told that some one once came to request his assistance as a pleader, and related how he had been assaulted and beaten. "Certainly," said Demosthenes, " nothing of the kind can have happened to you." Upon which the other, raising his voice, exclaimed loudly, "What, Demosthenes, nothing has been done to me?" "Ah," replied Demosthenes, " now I hear the voice of one that has been injured and beaten." Of so great consequence towards the gaining of belief did he esteem the tone and action of the speaker. The action which he used himself was wonderfully pleasing to the common people, but by well-educated people, as, for example, by Demetrius, the Phalerian, it was looked upon as mean, humiliating, and unmanly. And Hermippus says of Æsion, that, being asked his opinion concerning the ancient orators, and those of his own time, he answered that it was admirable to see with what composure and in what high style they addressed themselves to the people; but that the orations of Demosthenes, when they are read, certainly appear to be superior in point of construction, and more effective. His written speeches, beyond all question, are characterised by austere tone and by their severity. In his extempore retorts and rejoinders, he allowed himself the use of jest and mockery. When Demades said, " Demosthenes teach me! So might the sow teach Minerva!" he replied, "Was it this Minerva, that was lately found playing the harlot in Collytus?" When a thief, who had the nickname of the Brazen, was attempting to upbraid him for sitting up late, and writing by candle-light, "I know very well," said he, " that you had rather have all lights out; and wonder not, O ye men of Athens, at the many robberies which are committed, since we have thieves of brass and walls of clay." But on these points, though we have much more to mention, we will add nothing at present. We will proceed to take an estimate of his character from his actions and his life as a statesman.

His first entering into public business was much about the time of the Phocian war, as himself affirms, and may be collected from his Philippic orations. For of these, some were made after that action was over, and the earliest of them refer to its concluding events. It is certain that he engaged in the accusation of Midias when he was but two-and-thirty years old, having as yet no interest or reputation as a politician. And this it was, I consider, that induced him to withdraw the action, and accept a sum of money as a compromise. For of himself—

" He was no easy or good-natured man,"

but of a determined disposition, and resolute to see himself righted; however, finding it a hard matter and above his strength to deal with Midias, a man so well secured on all sides with money, eloquence, and friends, he yielded to the entreaties of those who interceded for him. But had he seen any hopes or possibility of prevailing, I cannot believe that three thousand drachmas could have taken off the edge of his revenge. The object which he chose for himself in the commonwealth was noble and just, the defence of the Grecians against Philip; and in this he behaved himself so worthily that he soon grew famous, and excited attention everywhere for his eloquence and courage in speaking. He was admired through all Greece, the King of Persia courted him, and by Philip himself he was more esteemed than all the other orators. His very enemies were forced to confess that they had to do with a man of mark; for such a character even Æschines and Hyperides give him, where they accuse and speak against him.

So that I cannot imagine what ground Theopompus had to say that Demosthenes was of a fickle, unsettled disposition, and could not long continue firm either to the same men or the same affairs; whereas the contrary is most apparent, for the same party and post in politics which he held from the beginning, to these he kept constant to the end; and was so far from leaving them while he lived that he chose rather to forsake his life than his purpose. He was never heard to apologise for shifting sides like Demades, who would say he often spoke against himself, but never against the city; nor as Melanopus, who, being generally against Callistratus, but being often bribed off with money, was wont to tell the people, "The man indeed is my enemy, but we must submit for the good of our country;" nor again as Nicodemus, the Messenian, who having first appeared on Cassander's side, and afterwards taken part with Demetrius, said the two things were not in themselves contrary, it being always most advisable to obey the conqueror. We have nothing of this kind to say against Demosthenes, as one who would turn aside or prevaricate, either in word or deed. There could not have been less variation in his public acts if they had all been played, so to say, from first to last, from the same score. Panætius, the philosopher, said that most of his orations are so written as if they were to prove this one conclusion, that what is honest and virtuous is for itself only to be chosen; as that of the Crown, that against Aristocrates, that for the Immunities, and the Philippics; in all which he persuades his fellow-citizens to pursue not that which seems most pleasant, easy, or profitable; but declares, over and over again, that they ought in the first place to prefer that which is just and honourable before their own safety and preservation. So that if he had kept his hands clean, if his courage for the wars had been answerable to the generosity of his principles, and the dignity of his orations, he might deservedly have his name placed, not in the number of such orators as Mœrocles, Polyeuctus, and Hyperides, but in the highest rank with Cimon, Thucydides, and Pericles.

Certainly amongst those who were contemporary with him, Phocion, though he appeared on the less commendable side in the commonwealth, and was counted as one of the Macedonian party, nevertheless, by his courage and his honesty, procured himself a name not inferior to these of Ephialtes, Aristides, and Cimon. But Demosthenes, being neither fit to be relied on for courage in arms, as Demetrius says, nor on all sides inaccessible to bribery (for how invincible soever he was against the gifts of Philip and the Macedonians, yet elsewhere he lay open to assault, and was overpowered by the gold which came down from Susa and Ecbatana), was therefore esteemed better able to recommend than to imitate the virtues of past times. And yet (excepting only Phocion), even in his life and manners, he far surpassed the other orators of his time. None of them addressed the people so boldly; he attacked the faults, and opposed himself to the unreasonable desires of the multitude, as may be seen in his orations. Theopompus writes, that the

Athenians having by name selected Demosthenes, and called upon him to accuse a certain person, he refused to do it; upon which the assembly being all in an uproar, he rose up and said, " Your counsellor, whether you will or no, O ye men of Athens, you shall always have me; but a sycophant or false accuser, though you would have me, I shall never be." And his conduct in the case of Antiphon was perfectly aristocratical; whom, after he had been acquitted in the assembly, he took and brought before the court of Areopagus, and, setting at naught the displeasure of the people, convicted him there of having promised Philip to burn the arsenal; whereupon the man was condemned by that court, and suffered for it. He accused, also, Theoris, the priestess, amongst other misdemeanours, of having instructed and taught the slaves to deceive and cheat their masters, for which the sentence of death was passed upon her, and she was executed.

The oration which Apollodorus made use of, and by it carried the cause against Timotheus, the general, in an action of debt, it is said was written for him by Demosthenes; as also those against Phormion and Stephanus, in which latter case he was thought to have acted dishonourably, for the speech which Phormion used against Apollodorus was also of his making; he, as it were, having simply furnished two adversaries out of the same shop with weapons to wound one another. Of his orations addressed to the public assemblies, that against Androtion, and those against Timocrates and Aristocrates, were written for others, before he had come forward himself as a politician. They were composed, it seems, when he was but seven or eight and twenty years old. That against Aristogiton, and that for the Immunities, he spoke himself, at the request, as he says, of Ctesippus, the son of Chabrias, but, as some say, out of courtship to the young man's mother. Though, in fact, he did not marry her, for his wife was a woman of Samos, as Demetrius, the Magnesian, writes, in his book on Persons of the same Name. It is not certain whether his oration against Æschines, for Misconduct as Ambassador, was ever spoken; although Idomeneus says that Æschines wanted only thirty voices to condemn him. But this seems not to be correct, at least so far as may be conjectured from both their orations concerning the Crown; for in these, neither of them speaks clearly or directly of it, as a cause that ever came to trial. But let others decide this controversy.

It was evident, even in time of peace, what course Demosthenes would steer in the commonwealth; for whatever was done by the Macedonian, he criticised and found fault with, and upon all occasions was stirring up the people of Athens, and inflaming them against him.    Therefore, in the court of Philip, no man was so much talked of, or of so great account as he; and when he came thither, one of the ten ambassadors who were sent into Macedonia, though all had audience given them, yet his speech was answered with most care and exactness.    But in other respects, Philip entertained him not so honourably as the rest, neither did he show him the same kindness and civility with which he applied himself to the party of Æschines and Philocrates.    So that, when the others commended Philip for his able speaking, his beautiful person, nay, and also for his good companionship in drinking, Demosthenes could not refrain from cavilling at these praises; the first, he said, was a quality which might well enough become a rhetorician, the second a woman, and the last was only the property of a sponge; no one of them was the proper commendation of a prince.

But when things came at last to war, Philip on the one side being not able to live in peace, and the Athenians, on the other side, being stirred up by Demosthenes, the first action he put them upon was the reducing of Eubœa, which, by the treachery of the tyrants, was brought under subjection to Philip.    And on his proposition, the decree was voted, and they crossed over thither and chased the Macedonians out of the island.    The next was the relief of the Byzantines and Perinthians, whom the Macedonians at that time were attacking.    He persuaded the people to lay aside their enmity against these cities, to forget the offences committed by them in the Confederate War, and to send them such succours as eventually saved and secured them.    Not long after, he undertook an embassy through the states of Greece, which he solicited and so far incensed against Philip that, a few only excepted, he brought them all into a general league.    So that, besides the forces composed of the citizens themselves, there was an army consisting of fifteen thousand foot and two thousand horse, and the money to pay these strangers was levied and brought in with great cheerfulness.    On which occasion it was, says Theophrastus, on the allies requesting that their contributions for the war might be ascertained and stated, Crobylus, the orator, made use of the saying, " War can't be fed at so much a day."    Now was all Greece up in arms, and in great expectation what would be the event.    The Eubœans, the Achæans, the Corinthians, the Megarians, the Leucadians, and Corcyræans, their people and their cities, were all joined together in a league.

But the hardest task was yet behind, left for Demosthenes, to draw the Thebans into this confederacy with the rest. Their country bordered next upon Attica, they had great forces for the war, and at that time they were accounted the best soldiers of all Greece, but it was no easy matter to make them break with Philip, who, by many good offices, had so lately obliged them in the Phocian war; especially considering how the subjects of dispute and variance between the two cities were continually renewed and exasperated by petty quarrels, arising out of the proximity of their frontiers.

But after Philip, being now grown high and puffed up with his good success at Amphissa, on a sudden surprised Elatea and possessed himself of Phocis, and the Athenians were in a great consternation, none durst venture to rise up to speak, no one knew what to say, all were at a loss, and the whole assembly in silence and perplexity, in this extremity of affairs Demosthenes was the only man who appeared, his counsel to them being alliance with the Thebans. And having in other ways encouraged the people, and, as his manner was, raised their spirits up with hopes, he, with some others, was sent ambassador to Thebes. To oppose him, as Marsyas says, Philip also sent thither his envoys, Amyntas and Clearchus, two Macedonians, besides Daochus, a Thessalian, and Thrasydæus. Now the Thebans, in their consultations, were well enough aware what suited best with their own interest, but every one had before his eyes the terrors of war, and their losses in the Phocian troubles were still recent: but such was the force and power of the orator, fanning up, as Theopompus says, their courage, and firing their emulation, that, casting away every thought of prudence, fear, or obligation, in a sort of divine possession, they chose the path of honour, to which his words invited them. And this success, thus accomplished by an orator, was thought to be so glorious and of such consequence, that Philip immediately sent heralds to treat and petition for a peace: all Greece was aroused, and up in arms to help. And the commanders-in-chief, not only of Attica, but of Bœotia, applied themselves to Demosthenes, and observed his directions. He managed all the assemblies of the Thebans, no less than those of the Athenians; he was beloved both by the one and by the other, and exercised the same supreme authority with both; and that not by unfair means, or without just cause, as Theopompus professes, but indeed it was no more than was due to his merit.

But there was, it would seem, some divinely ordered fortune, commissioned, in the revolution of things, to put a period at this time to the liberty of Greece, which opposed and thwarted all their actions, and by many signs foretold what should happen. Such were the sad predictions uttered by the Pythian priestess, and this old oracle cited out of the Sibyl's verses:—

> " The battle on Thermodon that shall be
> Safe at a distance I desire to see,
> Far, like an eagle, watching in the air,
> Conquered shall weep, and conqueror perish there."

This Thermodon, they say, is a little rivulet here in our country in Chæronea, running into the Cephisus. But we know of none that is so called at the present time; and can only conjecture that the streamlet which is now called Hæmon, and runs by the Temple of Hercules, where the Grecians were encamped, might perhaps in those days be called Thermodon, and after the fight, being filled with blood and dead bodies, upon this occasion, as we guess, might change its old name for that which it now bears. Yet Duris says that this Thermodon was no river, but that some of the soldiers, as they were pitching their tents and digging trenches about them, found a small stone statue, which, by the inscription, appeared to be the figure of Thermodon, carrying a wounded Amazon in his arms; and that there was another oracle current about it, as follows:—

> " The battle on Thermodon that shall be,
> Fail not, black raven, to attend and see;
> The flesh of men shall there abound for thee."

In fine, it is not easy to determine what is the truth. But of Demosthenes it is said that he had such great confidence in the Grecian forces, and was so excited by the sight of the courage and resolution of so many brave men ready to engage the enemy, that he would by no means endure they should give any heed to oracles, or hearken to prophecies, but gave out that he suspected even the prophetess herself, as if she had been tampered with to speak in favour of Philip. The Thebans he put in mind of Epaminondas, the Athenians of Pericles, who always took their own measures and governed their actions by reason, looking upon things of this kind as mere pretexts for cowardice. Thus far, therefore, Demosthenes acquitted himself like a brave man. But in the fight he did nothing honourable, nor was his performance answerable to his speeches. For he fled, deserting his place disgracefully, and throwing away his arms, not ashamed, as Pytheas observed, to belie the inscription written on his shield, in letters of gold, " With good fortune."

In the meantime Philip, in the first moment of victory, was so transported with joy, that he grew extravagant, and going out after he had drunk largely to visit the dead bodies, he chanted the first words of the decree that had been passed on the motion of Demosthenes—

"The motion of Demosthenes, Demosthenes's son,"

dividing it metrically into feet, and marking the beats.

But when he came to himself, and had well considered the danger he was lately under, he could not forbear from shuddering at the wonderful ability and power of an orator who had made him hazard his life and empire on the issue of a few brief hours. The fame of it also reached even to the court of Persia, and the king sent letters to his lieutenants commanding them to supply Demosthenes with money, and to pay every attention to him, as the only man of all the Grecians who was able to give Philip occupation and find employment for his forces near home, in the troubles of Greece. This afterwards came to the knowledge of Alexander, by certain letters of Demosthenes which he found at Sardis, and by other papers of the Persian officers, stating the large sums which had been given him.

At this time, however, upon the ill-success which now happened to the Grecians, those of the contrary faction in the commonwealth fell foul upon Demosthenes and took the opportunity to frame several informations and indictments against him. But the people not only acquitted him of these accusations, but continued towards him their former respect, and still invited him, as a man that meant well, to take a part in public affairs. Insomuch that when the bones of those who had been slain at Chæronea were brought home to be solemnly interred, Demosthenes was the man they chose to make the funeral oration. They did not show, under the misfortunes which befell them, a base or ignoble mind, as Theopompus writes in his exaggerated style, but on the contrary, by the honour and respect paid to their counsellor, they made it appear that they were noway dissatisfied with the counsels he had given them. The speech, therefore, was spoken by Demosthenes. But the subsequent decrees he would not allow to be passed in his own name, but made use of those of his friends, one after another, looking upon his own as unfortunate and inauspicious; till at length he took courage again after the death of Philip, who did not long outlive his victory at Chæronea. And this, it seems, was that which was foretold in the last verse of the oracle—

"Conquered shall weep, and conqueror perish there."

Demosthenes had secret intelligence of the death of Philip, and laying hold of this opportunity to prepossess the people with courage and better hopes for the future, he came into the assembly with a cheerful countenance, pretending to have had a dream that presaged some great good fortune for Athens; and, not long after, arrived the messengers who brought the news of Philip's death. No sooner had the people received it, but immediately they offered sacrifice to the gods, and decreed that Pausanias should be presented with a crown. Demosthenes appeared publicly in a rich dress, with a chaplet on his head, though it were but the seventh day since the death of his daughter, as is said by Æschines, who upbraids him upon this account, and rails at him as one void of natural affection towards his children. Whereas, indeed, he rather betrays himself to be of a poor, low spirit, and effeminate mind, if he really means to make wailings and lamentation the only signs of a gentle and affectionate nature, and to condemn those who bear such accidents with more temper and less passion. For my own part, I cannot say that the behaviour of the Athenians on this occasion was wise or honourable, to crown themselves with garlands and to sacrifice to the gods for the death of a prince who, in the midst of his success and victories, when they were a conquered people, had used them with so much clemency and humanity. For besides provoking fortune, it was a base thing, and unworthy in itself, to make him a citizen of Athens, and pay him honours while he lived, and yet as soon as he fell by another's hand, to set no bounds to their jollity, to insult over him dead, and to sing triumphant songs of victory, as if by their own valour they had vanquished him. I must at the same time commend the behaviour of Demosthenes, who, leaving tears and lamentations and domestic sorrows to the women, made it his business to attend the interests of the commonwealth. And I think it the duty of him who would be accounted to have a soul truly valiant, and fit for government, that, standing always firm to the common good, and letting private griefs and troubles find their compensation in public blessings, he should maintain the dignity of his character and station, much more than actors who represent the persons of kings and tyrants, who, we see, when they either laugh or weep on the stage, follow, not their own private inclinations, but the course consistent with the subject and with their position. And if, moreover, when our neighbour is in misfortune, it is not our duty to forbear offering any consolation, but rather to say whatever may tend to cheer him, and to invite his attention to any agreeable objects, just as we tell people who are troubled with sore eyes to withdraw their sight from bright and offensive colours to green, and those of a softer mixture, from whence can a man seek, in his own case, better arguments of consolation for afflictions in his family, than from the prosperity of his country, by making public and domestic chances count, so to say, together, and the better fortune of the state obscure and conceal the less happy circumstances of the individual. I have been induced to say so much, because I have known many readers melted by Æschines's language into a soft and unmanly tenderness.

But now to turn to my narrative. The cities of Greece were inspirited once more by the efforts of Demosthenes to form a league together. The Thebans, whom he had provided with arms, set upon their garrison, and slew many of them; the Athenians made preparations to join their forces with them; Demosthenes ruled supreme in the popular assembly, and wrote letters to the Persian officers who commanded under the king in Asia, inciting them to make war upon the Macedonian, calling him child and simpleton. But as soon as Alexander had settled matters in his own country, and came in person with his army into Bœotia, down fell the courage of the Athenians, and Demosthenes was hushed; the Thebans, deserted by them, fought by themselves, and lost their city. After which, the people of Athens, all in distress and great perplexity, resolved to send ambassadors to Alexander, and amongst others, made choice of Demosthenes for one; but his heart failing him for fear of the king's anger, he returned back from Cithæron, and left the embassy. In the meantime, Alexander sent to Athens, requiring ten of their orators to be delivered up to him, as Idomeneus and Duris have reported, but as the most and best historians say, he demanded these eight only,—Demosthenes, Polyeuctus, Ephialtes, Lycurgus, Mœrocles, Demon, Callisthenes, and Charidemus. It was upon this occasion that Demosthenes related to them the fable in which the sheep are said to deliver up their dogs to the wolves; himself and those who with him contended for the people's safety being, in his comparison, the dogs that defended the flock, and Alexander " the Macedonian arch-wolf." He further told them, " As we see corn-masters sell their whole stock by a few grains of wheat which they carry about with them in a dish, as a sample of the rest, so you by delivering up us, who are but a few, do at the same time unawares surrender up yourselves all together with us; " so we find it related in the history of Aristobulus, the Cassandrian. The Athenians were deliberating, and at a loss what to do, when Demades, having agreed with the persons whom Alexander had demanded, for five talents, undertook to go ambassador, and to intercede with the king for them; and, whether it was that he relied on his friendship and kindness, or that he hoped to find him satiated, as a lion glutted with slaughter, he certainly went, and prevailed with him both to pardon the men, and to be reconciled to the city.

So he and his friends, when Alexander went away, were great men, and Demosthenes was quite put aside. Yet when Agis, the Spartan, made his insurrection, he also for a short time attempted a movement in his favour; but he soon shrunk back again, as the Athenians would not take any part in it, and, Agis being slain, the Lacedæmonians were vanquished. During this time it was that the indictment against Ctesiphon, concerning the crown, was brought to trial. The action was commenced a little before the battle in Chæronea, when Chærondas was archon, but it was not proceeded with till about ten years after, Aristophon being then archon. Never was any public cause more celebrated than this, alike for the fame of the orators, and for the generous courage of the judges, who, though at that time the accusers of Demosthenes were in the height of power, and supported by all the favour of the Macedonians, yet would not give judgment against him, but acquitted him so honourably, that Æschines did not obtain the fifth part of their suffrages on his side, so that, immediately after, he left the city, and spent the rest of his life in teaching rhetoric about the island of Rhodes, and upon the continent in Ionia.

It was not long after that Harpalus fled from Alexander, and came to Athens out of Asia; knowing himself guilty of many misdeeds into which his love of luxury had led him, and fearing the king, who was now grown terrible even to his best friends. Yet this man had no sooner addressed himself to the people, and delivered up his goods, his ships, and himself to their disposal, but the other orators of the town had their eyes quickly fixed upon his money, and came in to his assistance, persuading the Athenians to receive and protect their suppliant. Demosthenes at first gave advice to chase him out of the country, and to beware lest they involved their city in a war upon an unnecessary and unjust occasion. But some few days after, as they were taking an account of the treasure, Harpalus, perceiving how much he was pleased with a cup of Persian manufacture, and how curiously he surveyed the sculpture and fashion of it, desired him to poise it in his hand, and consider the weight of the gold. Demosthenes, being amazed to feel how heavy it was, asked him what weight it *came to.* "To you," said Harpalus, smiling, "it shall *come with* twenty talents." And presently after, when night drew on, he sent him the cup with so many talents. Harpalus, it seems, was a person of singular skill to discern a man's covetousness by the air of his countenance, and the look and movements of his eyes. For Demosthenes could not resist the temptation, but admitting the present, like an armed garrison, into the citadel of his house, he surrendered himself up to the interest of Harpalus. The next day, he came into the assembly with his neck swathed about with wool and rollers, and when they called on him to rise up and speak, he made signs as if he had lost his voice. But the wits, turning the matter to ridicule, said that certainly the orator had been seized that night with no other than a silver quinsy. And soon after, the people, becoming aware of the bribery, grew angry, and would not suffer him to speak, or make any apology for himself, but ran him down with noise; and one man stood up, and cried out, "What, ye men of Athens, will you not hear the cup-bearer?" So at length they banished Harpalus out of the city; and fearing lest they should be called to account for the treasure which the orators had purloined, they made a strict inquiry, going from house to house; only Callicles, the son of Arrhenidas, who was newly married, they would not suffer to be searched, out of respect, as Theopompus writes, to the bride, who was within.

Demosthenes resisted the inquisition, and proposed a decree to refer the business to the court of Areopagus, and to punish those whom that court should find guilty. But being himself one of the first whom the court condemned, when he came to the bar, he was fined fifty talents, and committed to prison; where, out of shame of the crime for which he was condemned, and through the weakness of his body, growing incapable of supporting the confinement, he made his escape, by the carelessness of some and by the contrivance of others of the citizens. We are told, at least, that he had not fled far from the city when, finding that he was pursued by some of those who had been his adversaries, he endeavoured to hide himself. But when they called him by his name, and coming up nearer to him, desired he would accept from them some money which they had brought from home as a provision for his journey, and to that purpose only had followed him, when they entreated him to take courage, and to bear up against his misfortune, he burst out

into much greater lamentation, saying, " But how is it possible
to support myself under so heavy an affliction, since I leave a
city in which I have such enemies, as in any other it is not easy
to find friends." He did not show much fortitude in his banishment, spending his time for the most part in Ægina and Trœzen,
and, with tears in his eyes, looking towards the country of
Attica. And there remain upon record some sayings of his,
little resembling those sentiments of generosity and bravery
which he used to express when he had the management of the
commonwealth. For, as he was departing out of the city, it is
reported, he lifted up his hands towards the Acropolis, and said,
" O Lady Minerva, how is it that thou takest delight in three
such fierce untractable beasts, the owl, the snake, and the
people? " The young men that came to visit and converse with
him, he deterred from meddling with state affairs, telling them,
that if at first two ways had been proposed to him, the one
leading to the speaker's stand and the assembly, the other going
direct to destruction, and he could have foreseen the many evils
which attend those who deal in public business, such as fears,
envies, calumnies, and contentions, he would certainly have
taken that which led straight on to his death.

But now happened the death of Alexander, while Demosthenes was in this banishment which we have been speaking of.
And the Grecians were once again up in arms, encouraged by
the brave attempts of Leosthenes, who was then drawing a circumvallation about Antipater, whom he held close besieged in
Lamia. Pytheas, therefore, the orator, and Callimedon, called
the Crab, fled from Athens, and taking sides with Antipater,
went about with his friends and ambassadors to keep the
Grecians from revolting and taking part with the Athenians.
But, on the other side, Demosthenes, associating himself with
the ambassadors that came from Athens, used his utmost endeavours and gave them his best assistance in persuading the
cities to fall unanimously upon the Macedonians, and to drive
them out of Greece. Phylarchus says that in Arcadia there
happened a rencounter between Pytheas and Demosthenes,
which came at last to downright railing, while the one pleaded
for the Macedonians, and the other for the Grecians. Pytheas
said, that as we always suppose there is some disease in the
family to which they bring asses' milk, so wherever there comes
an embassy from Athens that city must needs be indisposed.
And Demosthenes answered him, retorting the comparison:
" Asses' milk is brought to restore health and the Athenians

come for the safety and recovery of the sick." With this conduct the people of Athens were so well pleased that they decreed the recall of Demosthenes from banishment. The decree was brought in by Demon the Pæanian, cousin to Demosthenes. So they sent him a ship to Ægina, and he landed at the port of Piræus, where he was met and joyfully received by all the citizens, not so much as an archon or a priest staying behind. And Demetrius, the Magnesian, says that he lifted up his hands towards heaven, and blessed this day of his happy return, as far more honourable than that of Alcibiades; since he was recalled by his countrymen, not through any force or constraint put upon them, but by their own good-will and free inclinations. There remained only his pecuniary fine, which, according to law, could not be remitted by the people. But they found out a way to elude the law. It was a custom with them to allow a certain quantity of silver to those who were to furnish and adorn the altar for the sacrifice of Jupiter Soter. This office, for that turn, they bestowed on Demosthenes, and for the performance of it ordered him fifty talents, the very sum in which he was condemned.

Yet it was no long time that he enjoyed his country after his return, the attempts of the Greeks being soon all utterly defeated. For the battle of Cranon happened in Metagitnion, in Boëdromion the garrison entered into Munychia, and in the Pyanepsion following died Demosthenes after this manner.

Upon the report that Antipater and Craterus were coming to Athens, Demosthenes with his party took their opportunity to escape privily out of the city; but sentence of death was, upon the motion of Demades, passed upon them by the people. They dispersed themselves, flying some to one place, some to another; and Antipater sent about his soldiers into all quarters to apprehend them. Archias was their captain, and was thence called the exile-hunter. He was a Thurian born, and is reported to have been an actor of tragedies, and they say that Polus, of Ægina, the best actor of his time, was his scholar; but Hermippus reckons Archias among the disciples of Lacritus, the orator, and Demetrius says he spent some time with Anaximenes. This Archias finding Hyperides the orator, Aritonicus of Marathon, and Himeræus, the brother of Demetrius the Phalerian, in Ægina, took them by force out of the temple of Æcus, whither they were fled for safety, and sent them to Antipater, then at Cleonæ, where they were all put to death; and Hyperides, they say, had his tongue cut out.

Demosthenes, he heard, had taken sanctuary at the temple of Neptune in Calauria, and, crossing over thither in some light vessels, as soon as he had landed himself, and the Thracian spearmen that came with him, he endeavoured to persuade Demosthenes to accompany him to Antipater, as if he should meet with no hard usage from him. But Demosthenes, in his sleep the night before, had a strange dream. It seemed to him that he was acting a tragedy, and contended with Archias for the victory; and though he acquitted himself well, and gave good satisfaction to the spectators, yet for want of better furniture and provision for the stage, he lost the day. And so, while Archias was discoursing to him with many expressions of kindness, he sate still in the same posture, and looking up steadfastly upon him, " O Archias," said he, " I am as little affected by your promises now as I used formerly to be by your acting." Archias at this beginning to grow angry and to threaten him, " Now," said Demosthenes, " you speak like the genuine Macedonian oracle; before you were but acting a part. Therefore forbear only a little, while I write a word or two home to my family." Having thus spoken, he withdrew into the temple, and taking a scroll, as if he meant to write, he put the reed into his mouth, and biting it as he was wont to do when he was thoughtful or writing, he held it there some time. Then he bowed down his head and covered it. The soldiers that stood at the door, supposing all this to proceed from want of courage and fear of death, in derision called him effeminate, and faint-hearted, and coward. And Archias drawing near, desired him to rise up, and repeating the same kind of thing he had spoken before, he once more promised to make his peace with Antipater. But Demosthenes, perceiving that now the poison had pierced, and seized his vitals, uncovered his head, and fixing his eyes upon Archias, " Now," said he, " as soon as you please, you may commence the part of Creon in the tragedy, and cast out this body of mine unburied. But, O gracious Neptune, I, for my part, while I am yet alive, will rise up and depart out of this sacred place; though Antipater and the Macedonians have not left so much as thy temple unpolluted." After he had thus spoken and desired to be held up, because already he began to tremble and stagger, as he was going forward, and passing by the altar, he fell down, and with a groan gave up the ghost.

Ariston says that he took the poison out of a reed, as we have shown before. But Pappus, a certain historian whose history was recovered by Hermippus, says, that as he fell near the altar, there was found in his scroll this beginning only of a letter, and nothing more, " Demosthenes to Antipater." And that when his sudden death was much wondered at, the Thracians who guarded the doors reported that he took the poison into his hand out of a rag, and put it in his mouth, and that they imagined it had been gold which he swallowed, but the maid that served him, being examined by the followers of Archias, affirmed that he had worn it in a bracelet for a long time, as an amulet. And Eratosthenes also says that he kept the poison in a hollow ring, and that that ring was the bracelet which he wore about his arm. There are various other statements made by the many authors who have related the story, but there is no need to enter into their discrepancies; yet I must not omit what is said by Demochares, the relation of Demosthenes, who is of opinion it was not by the help of poison that he met with so sudden and so easy a death, but that by the singular favour and providence of the gods he was thus rescued from the cruelty of the Macedonians. He died on the sixteenth of Pyanepsion, the most sad and solemn day of the Thesmophoria, which the women observe by fasting in the temple of the goddess.

Soon after his death, the people of Athens bestowed on him such honours as he had deserved. They erected his statue of brass; they decreed that the eldest of his family should be maintained in the Prytaneum; and on the base of his statue was engraven the famous inscription—

> " Had you for Greece been strong, as wise you were,
> The Macedonian had not conquered her."

For it is simply ridiculous to say, as some have related, that Demosthenes made these verses himself in Calauria, as he was about to take the poison.

A little before he went to Athens, the following incident was said to have happened. A soldier, being summoned to appear before his superior officer, and answer to an accusation brought against him, put that little gold which he had into the hands of Demosthenes's statue. The fingers of this statue were folded one within another, and near it grew a small plane-tree, from which many leaves, either accidentally blown thither by the wind, or placed so on purpose by the man himself, falling together and lying round about the gold, concealed it for a long time. In the end, the soldier returned, and found his treasure entire, and the fame of this incident was spread abroad. And many ingenious persons of the city competed with each other, on this occasion, to vindicate the integrity of Demosthenes in several epigrams which they made on the subject.

As for Demades, he did not long enjoy the new honours he now came in for, divine vengeance for the death of Demosthenes pursuing him into Macedonia, where he was justly put to death by those whom he had basely flattered. They were weary of him before, but at this time the guilt he lay under was manifest and undeniable. For some of his letters were intercepted, in which he had encouraged Perdiccas to fall upon Macedonia, and to save the Grecians, who, he said, hung only by an old rotten thread, meaning Antipater. Of this he was accused by Dinarchus, the Corinthian, and Cassander was so enraged, that he first slew his son in his bosom, and then gave orders to execute him; who might now at last, by his own extreme misfortunes, learn the lesson that traitors who made sale of their country sell themselves first; a truth which Demosthenes had often foretold him, and he would never believe. Thus, Sosius, you have the life of Demosthenes, from such accounts as we have either read or heard concerning him.

# CICERO

IT is generally said, that Helvia, the mother of Cicero, was both well-born and lived a fair life; but of his father nothing is reported but in extremes. For whilst some would have him the son of a fuller, and educated in that trade, others carry back the origin of his family to Tullus Attius, an illustrious king of the Volscians, who waged war not without honour against the Romans. However, he who first of that house was surnamed Cicero seems to have been a person worthy to be remembered; since those who succeeded him not only did not reject, but were fond of that name, though vulgarly made a matter of reproach. For the Latins call a vetch *Cicer*, and a nick or dent at the tip of his nose, which resembled the opening in a vetch, gave him the surname of *Cicero*.

Cicero, whose story I am writing, is said to have replied with spirit to some of his friends, who recommended him to lay aside or change the name when he first stood for office and engaged in politics, that he would make it his endeavour to render the name of Cicero more glorious than that of the Scauri and Catuli.

And when he was quæstor in Sicily, and was making an offering of silver plate to the gods, and had inscribed his two names, Marcus and Tullius, instead of the third, he jestingly told the artificer to engrave the figure of a vetch by them. Thus much is told us about his name.

Of his birth it is reported that his mother was delivered, without pain or labour, on the third of the new Calends, the same day on which now the magistrates of Rome pray and sacrifice for the emperor. It is said, also, that a vision appeared to his nurse, and foretold the child she then suckled should afterwards become a great benefit to the Roman states. To such presages, which might in general be thought mere fancies and idle talk, he himself ere long gave the credit of true prophecies. For as soon as he was of an age to begin to have lessons, he became so distinguished for his talent, and got such a name and reputation amongst the boys, that their fathers would often visit the school that they might see young Cicero, and might be able to say that they themselves had witnessed the quickness and readiness in learning for which he was renowned. And the more rude among them used to be angry with their children, to see them, as they walked together, receiving Cicero with respect into the middle place. And being, as Plato would have the scholar-like and philosophical temper, eager for every kind of learning, and indisposed to no description of knowledge or instruction, he showed, however, a more peculiar propensity to poetry; and there is a poem now extant, made by him when a boy, in tetrameter verse, called Pontius Glaucus. And afterwards, when he applied himself more curiously to these accomplishments, he had the name of being not only the best orator, but also the best poet of Rome. And the glory of his rhetoric still remains, notwithstanding the many new modes in speaking since his time; but his verses are forgotten and out of all repute, so many ingenious poets have followed him.

Leaving his juvenile studies, he became an auditor of Philo the Academic, whom the Romans, above all the other scholars of Clitomachus, admired for his eloquence and loved for his character. He also sought the company of the Mucii, who were eminent statesmen and leaders in the senate, and acquired from them a knowledge of the laws. For some short time he served in arms under Sylla, in the Marsian war. But perceiving the commonwealth running into factions, and from faction all things tending to an absolute monarchy, he betook himself to a retired and contemplative life, and conversing with the learned

Greeks, devoted himself to study, till Sylla had obtained the government, and the commonwealth was in some kind of settlement.

At this time, Chrysogonus, Sylla's emancipated slave, having laid an information about an estate belonging to one who was said to have been put to death by proscription, had bought it himself for two thousand drachmas. And when Roscius, the son and heir of the dead, complained, and demonstrated the estate to be worth two hundred and fifty talents, Sylla took it angrily to have his actions questioned, and preferred a process against Roscius for the murder of his father, Chrysogonus managing the evidence. None of the advocates durst assist him, but, fearing the cruelty of Sylla, avoided the cause. The young man, being thus deserted, came for refuge to Cicero. Cicero's friends encouraged him, saying he was not likely ever to have a fairer and more honourable introduction to public life; he therefore undertook the defence, carried the cause, and got much renown for it.

But fearing Sylla, he travelled into Greece, and gave it out that he did so for the benefit of his health. And indeed he was lean and meagre, and had such a weakness in his stomach that he could take nothing but a spare and thin diet, and that not till late in the evening. His voice was loud and good, but so harsh and unmanaged that in vehemence and heat of speaking he always raised it to so high a tone that there seemed to be reason to fear about his health.

When he came to Athens, he was a hearer of Antiochus of Ascalon, with whose fluency and elegance of diction he was much taken, although he did not approve of his innovations in doctrine. For Antiochus had now fallen off from the New Academy, as they call it, and forsaken the sect of Carneades, whether that he was moved by the argument of manifestness and the senses, or, as some say, had been led by feelings of rivalry and opposition to the followers of Clitomachus and Philo to change his opinions, and in most things to embrace the doctrine of the Stoics. But Cicero rather affected and adhered to the doctrines of the New Academy; and purposed with himself, if he should be disappointed of any employment in the commonwealth, to retire hither from pleading and political affairs, and to pass his life with quiet in the study of philosophy.

But after he had received the news of Sylla's death, and his body, strengthened again by exercise, was come to a vigorous habit, his voice managed and rendered sweet and full to the ear

and pretty well brought into keeping with his general constitution, his friends at Rome earnestly soliciting him by letters, and
Antiochus also urging him to return to public affairs, he again
prepared for use his orator's instrument of rhetoric, and summoned into action his political faculties, diligently exercising
himself in declamations, and attending the most celebrated
rhetoricians of the time. He sailed from Athens for Asia and
Rhodes. Amongst the Asian masters, he conversed with
Xenocles of Adramyttium, Dionysius of Magnesia, and Menippus
of Caria; at Rhodes, he studied oratory with Apollonius, the
son of Molon, and philosophy with Posidonius. Apollonius, we
are told, not understanding Latin, requested Cicero to declaim
in Greek. He complied willingly, thinking that his faults would
thus be better pointed out to him. And after he finished, all
his other hearers were astonished, and contended who should
praise him most, but Apollonius, who had shown no signs of
excitement whilst he was hearing him, so also now, when it was
over, sate musing for some considerable time, without any
remark. And when Cicero was discomposed at this, he said,
" You have my praise and admiration, Cicero, and Greece my
pity and commiseration, since those arts and that eloquence
which are the only glories that remain to her, will now be trans-
ferred by you to Rome."

And now when Cicero, full of expectation, was again bent
upon political affairs, a certain oracle blunted the edge of his
inclination; for consulting the god of Delphi how he should
attain most glory, the Pythoness answered, by making his own
genius and not the opinion of the people the guide of his life;
and therefore at first he passed his time in Rome cautiously, and
was very backward in pretending to public offices, so that he
was at that time in little esteem, and had got the names, so
readily given by low and ignorant people in Rome, of Greek and
Scholar. But when his own desire of fame and the eagerness of
his father and relations had made him take in earnest to pleading, he made no slow or gentle advance to the first place, but
shone out in full lustre at once, and far surpassed all the advocates
of the bar. At first, it is said, he, as well as Demosthenes, was
defective in his delivery, and on that account paid much attention to the instructions, sometimes of Roscius the comedian, and
sometimes of Æsop the tragedian. They tell of this Æsop, that
whilst he was representing on the theatre Atreus deliberating the
revenge of Thyestes, he was so transported beyond himself in
the heat of action, that he struck with his sceptre one of the

servants, who was running across the stage, so violently that he laid him dead upon the place. And such afterwards was Cicero's delivery that it did not a little contribute to render his eloquence persuasive. He used to ridicule loud speakers, saying that they shouted because they could not speak, like lame men who get on horseback because they cannot walk. And his readiness and address in sarcasm, and generally in witty sayings, was thought to suit a pleader very well, and to be highly attractive, but his using it to excess offended many, and gave him the repute of ill-nature.

He was appointed quæstor in a great scarcity of corn, and had Sicily for his province, where, though at first he displeased many, by compelling them to send in their provisions to Rome, yet after they had had experience of his care, justice, and clemency, they honoured him more than ever they did any of their governors before. It happened, also, that some young Romans of good and noble families, charged with neglect of discipline and misconduct in military service, were brought before the prætor in Sicily. Cicero undertook their defence, which he conducted admirably, and got them acquitted. So returning to Rome with a great opinion of himself for these things, a ludicrous incident befell him, as he tells us himself. Meeting an eminent citizen in Campania, whom he accounted his friend, he asked him what the Romans said and thought of his actions, as if the whole city had been filled with the glory of what he had done. His friend asked him in reply, " Where is it you have been, Cicero? " This for the time utterly mortified and cast him down, to perceive that the report of his actions had sunk into the city of Rome as into an immense ocean, without any visible effect or result in reputation. And afterwards considering with himself that the glory he contended for was an infinite thing, and that there was no fixed end nor measure in its pursuit, he abated much of his ambitious thoughts. Nevertheless, he was always excessively pleased with his own praise, and continued to the very last to be passionately fond of glory; which often interfered with the prosecution of his wisest resolutions.

On beginning to apply himself more resolutely to public business, he remarked it as an unreasonable and absurd thing that artificers, using vessels and instruments inanimate, should know the name, place, and use of every one of them, and yet the statesman, whose instruments for carrying out public measures are men, should be negligent and careless in the knowledge of persons. And so he not only acquainted himself with the names, but also knew the particular place where every one of the more eminent citizens dwelt, what lands he possessed, the friends he made use of, and those that were of his neighbourhood, and when he travelled on any road in Italy, he could readily name and show the estates and seats of his friends and acquaintance. Having so small an estate, though a sufficient competency for his own expenses, it was much wondered at that he took neither fees nor gifts from his clients, and more especially that he did not do so when he undertook the prosecution of Verres. This Verres, who had been prætor of Sicily, and stood charged by the Sicilians of many evil practices during his government there, Cicero succeeded in getting condemned, not by speaking, but in a manner by holding his tongue. For the prætors, favouring Verres, had deferred the trial by several adjournments to the last day, in which it was evident there could not be sufficient time for the advocates to be heard, and the cause brought to an issue. Cicero, therefore, came forward, and said there was no need of speeches; and after producing and examining witnesses, he required the judges to proceed to sentence. However, many witty sayings are on record, as having been used by Cicero on the occasion. When a man named Cæcilius, one of the freed slaves, who was said to be given to Jewish practices, would have put by the Sicilians, and undertaken the prosecution of Verres himself, Cicero asked, " What has a Jew to do with swine? " *verres* being the Roman word for a boar. And when Verres began to reproach Cicero with effeminate living, " You ought," replied he, " to use this language at home, to your sons; " Verres having a son who had fallen into disgraceful courses. Hortensius the orator, not daring directly to undertake the defence of Verres, was yet persuaded to appear for him at the laying on of the fine, and received an ivory sphinx for his reward; and when Cicero, in some passage of the speech, obliquely reflected on him, and Hortensius told him he was not skilful in solving riddles, " No," said Cicero, " and yet you have the sphinx in your house! "

Verres was thus convicted; though Cicero, who set the fine at seventy-five myriads, lay under the suspicion of being corrupted by bribery to lessen the sum. But the Sicilians, in testimony of their gratitude, came and brought him all sorts of presents from the island, when he was ædile; of which he made no private profit himself, but used their generosity only to reduce the public price of provisions.

He had a very pleasant seat at Arpi, he had also a farm near

Naples, and another about Pompeii, but neither of any great value. The portion of his wife, Terentia, amounted to ten myriads, and he had a bequest valued at nine myriads of denarii; upon these he lived in a liberal but temperate style with the learned Greeks and Romans that were his familiars. He rarely, if at any time, sat down to meat till sunset, and that not so much on account of business, as for his health and the weakness of his stomach. He was otherwise in the care of his body nice and delicate, appointing himself, for example, a set number of walks and rubbings. And after this manner managing the habit of his body, he brought it in time to be healthful, and capable of supporting many great fatigues and trials. His father's house he made over to his brother, living himself near the Palatine hill, that he might not give the trouble of long journeys to those that made suit to him. And, indeed, there were not fewer daily appearing at his door, to do their court to him, than there were that came to Crassus for his riches, or to Pompey for his power amongst the soldiers, these being at that time the two men of the greatest repute and influence in Rome. Nay, even Pompey himself used to pay court to Cicero, and Cicero's public actions did much to establish Pompey's authority and reputation in the state.

Numerous distinguished competitors stood with him for the prætor's office; but he was chosen before them all, and managed the decision of causes with justice and integrity. It is related that Licinius Macer, a man himself of great power in the city, and supported also by the assistance of Crassus, was accused before him of extortion, and that, in confidence on his own interest and the diligence of his friends, whilst the judges were debating about the sentence, he went to his house, where hastliy trimming his hair and putting on a clean gown as already acquitted, he was setting off again to go to the Forum; but at his hall door meeting Crassus, who told him that he was condemned by all the votes, he went in again, threw himself upon his bed, and died immediately. This verdict was considered very creditable to Cicero, as showing his careful management of the courts of justice. On another occasion, Vatinius, a man of rude manners and often insolent in court to the magistrates, who had large swellings on his neck, came before his tribunal and made some request, and on Cicero's desiring further time to consider it, told him that he himself would have made no question about it had he been prætor. Cicero, turning quickly upon him, answered, " But I, you see, have not the neck that you have."

When there were but two or three days remaining in his office, Manilius was brought before him, and charged with peculation. Manilius had the good opinion and favour of the common people, and was thought to be prosecuted only for Pompey's sake, whose particular friend he was. And therefore, when he asked a space of time before his trial, and Cicero allowed him but one day, and that the next only, the common people grew highly offended, because it had been the custom of the prætors to allow ten days at least to the accused; and the tribunes of the people, having called him before the people and accused him, he, desiring to be heard, said, that as he had always treated the accused with equity and humanity, as far as the law allowed, so he thought it hard to deny the same to Manilius, and that he had studiously appointed that day of which alone, as prætor, he was master, and that it was not the part of those that were desirous to help him to cast the judgment of his cause upon another prætor. These things being said made a wonderful change in the people, and commending him much for it they desired that he himself would undertake the defence of Manilius; which he willingly consented to, and that principally for the sake of Pompey, who was absent. And, accordingly, taking his place before the people again, he delivered a bold invective upon the oligarchical party and on those who were jealous of Pompey.

Yet he was preferred to the consulship no less by the nobles than the common people, for the good of the city; and both parties jointly assisted his promotion, upon the following reasons. The change of government made by Sylla, which at first seemed a senseless one, by time and usage had now come to be considered by the people no unsatisfactory settlement. But there were some that endeavoured to alter and subvert the whole present state of affairs, not from any good motives, but for their own private gain; and Pompey being at this time employed in the wars with the kings of Pontus and Armenia, there was no sufficient force at Rome to suppress any attempts at a revolution. These people had for their head a man of bold, daring, and restless character, Lucius Catiline, who was accused, besides other great offences, of deflowering his virgin daughter, and killing his own brother; for which latter crime, fearing to be prosecuted at law, he persuaded Sylla to set him down, as though he were yet alive, amongst those that were to be put to death by proscription. This man the profligate citizens choosing for their captain, gave faith to one another, amongst other pledges, by sacrificing a man, and eating of his flesh; and a great part of the young men of the city were corrupted by him, he providing for every one pleasures, drink, and women, and profusely supplying the expense of these debauches. Etruria, moreover, had all been excited to revolt, as well as a great part of Gaul within the Alps. But Rome itself was in the most dangerous inclination to change on account of the unequal distribution of wealth and property, those of highest rank and greatest spirit having impoverished themselves by shows, entertainments, ambition of offices, and sumptuous buildings, and the riches of the city having thus fallen into the hands of mean and low-born persons. So that there wanted but a slight impetus to set all in motion, it being in the power of every daring man to overturn a sickly commonwealth.

Catiline, however, being desirous of procuring a strong position to carry out his designs, stood for the consulship, and had great hopes of success, thinking he should be appointed, with Caius Antonius as his colleague, who was a man fit to lead neither in a good cause nor in a bad one, but might be a valuable accession to another's power. These things the greatest part of the good and honest citizens apprehending, put Cicero upon standing for the consulship; whom the people readily receiving, Catiline was put by, so that he and Caius Antonius were chosen, although amongst the competitors he was the only man descended from a father of the equestrian and not of the senatorial order.

Though the designs of Catiline were not yet publicly known, yet considerable preliminary troubles immediately followed upon Cicero's entrance upon the consulship. For, on the one side, those who were disqualified by the laws of Sylla from holding any public offices, being neither inconsiderable in power nor in number, came forward as candidates and caressed the people for them; speaking many things truly and justly against the tyranny of Sylla, only that they disturbed the government at an improper and unseasonable time; on the other hand, the tribunes of the people proposed laws to the same purpose, constituting a commission of ten persons, with unlimited powers, in whom as supreme governors should be vested the right of selling the public lands of all Italy and Syria and Pompey's new conquest, of judging and banishing whom they pleased, of planting colonies, of taking moneys out of the treasury, and of levying and paying what soldiers should be thought needful. And several of the nobility favoured this law, but especially Caius Antonius, Cicero's colleague, in hopes of being one of the ten.

But what gave the greatest fear to the nobles was, that he was thought privy to the conspiracy of Catiline, and not to dislike it because of his great debts.

Cicero, endeavouring in the first place to provide a remedy against this danger, procured a decree assigning to him the province of Macedonia, he himself declining that of Gaul, which was offered to him. And this piece of favour so completely won over Antonius, that he was ready to second and respond to, like a hired player, whatever Cicero said for the good of the country. And now, having made his colleague thus tame and tractable, he could with greater courage attack the conspirators. And, therefore, in the senate, making an oration against the law of the ten commissioners, he so confounded those who proposed it, that they had nothing to reply. And when they again endeavoured, and, having prepared things beforehand, had called the consuls before the assembly of the people, Cicero, fearing nothing, went first out, and commanded the senate to follow him, and not only succeeded in throwing out the law, but so entirely overpowered the tribunes by his oratory, that they abandoned all thought of their other projects.

For Cicero, it may be said, was the one man, above all others, who made the Romans feel how great a charm eloquence lends to what is good, and how invincible justice is, if it be well spoken; and that it is necessary for him who would dexterously govern a commonwealth, in action, always to prefer that which is honest before that which is popular, and in speaking, to free the right and useful measure from everything that may occasion offence. An incident occurred in the theatre, during his consulship, which showed what his speaking could do. For whereas formerly the knights of Rome were mingled in the theatre with the common people, and took their places among them as it happened, Marcus Otho, when he was prætor, was the first who distinguished them from the other citizens, and appointed them a proper seat, which they still enjoy as their special place in the theatre. This the common people took as an indignity done to them, and, therefore, when Otho appeared in the theatre they hissed him; the knights, on the contrary, received him with loud clapping. The people repeated and increased their hissing; the knights continued their clapping. Upon this, turning upon one another, they broke out into insulting words, so that the theatre was in great disorder. Cicero being informed of it, came himself to the theatre, and summoning the people into the temple of Bellona, he so effectually chid and chastised them for it, that again returning into the theatre they received Otho with loud applause, contending with the knights who should give him the greatest demonstrations of honour and respect.

The conspirators with Catiline, at first cowed and disheartened, began presently to take courage again. And assembling themselves together, they exhorted one another boldly to undertake the design before Pompey's return, who, as it was said, was now on his march with his forces for Rome. But the old soldiers of Sylla were Catiline's chief stimulus to action. They had been disbanded all about Italy, but the greatest number and the fiercest of them lay scattered among the cities of Etruria, entertaining themselves with dreams of new plunder and rapine amongst the hoarded riches of Italy. These, having for their leader Manlius, who had served with distinction in the wars under Sylla, joined themselves to Catiline, and came to Rome to assist him with their suffrages at the election. For he again pretended to the consulship, having resolved to kill Cicero in a tumult at the elections. Also, the divine powers seemed to give intimation of the coming troubles, by earthquakes, thunderbolts, and strange appearances. Nor was human evidence wanting certain enough in itself, though not sufficient for the conviction of the noble and powerful Catiline. Therefore Cicero, deferring the day of election, summoned Catiline into the senate, and questioned him as to the charges made against him. Catiline, believing there were many in the senate desirous of change, and to give a specimen of himself to the conspirators present, returned an audacious answer, " What harm," said he, " when I see two bodies, the one lean and consumptive with a head, the other great and strong without one, if I put a head to that body which wants one? " This covert representation of the senate and the people excited yet greater apprehensions in Cicero. He put on armour, and was attended from his house by the noble citizens in a body; and a number of the young men went with him into the Plain. Here, designedly letting his tunic slip partly off from his shoulders, he showed his armour underneath, and discovered his danger to the spectators; who, being much moved at it, gathered round about him for his defence. At length, Catiline was by a general suffrage again put by, and Silanus and Murena chosen consuls.

Not long after this, Catiline's soldiers got together in a body in Etruria, and began to form themselves into companies, the day appointed for the design being near at hand. About midnight, some of the principal and most powerful citizens of Rome,

Marcus Crassus, Marcus Marcellus, and Scipio Metellus went to Cicero's house, where, knocking at the gate, and calling up the porter, they commanded him to awake Cicero, and tell him they were there. The business was this: Crassus's porter after supper had delivered to him letters brought by an unknown person. Some of them were directed to others, but one to Crassus, without a name; this only Crassus read, which informed him that there was a great slaughter intended by Catiline, and advised him to leave the city. The others he did not open, but went with them immediately to Cicero, being affrighted at the danger, and to free himself of the suspicion he lay under for his familiarity with Catiline. Cicero, considering the matter, summoned the senate at break of day. The letters he brought with him, and delivered them to those to whom they were directed, commanding them to read them publicly; they all alike contained an account of the conspiracy. And when Quintus Arrius, a man of prætorian dignity, recounted to them how soldiers were collecting in companies in Etruria, and Manlius stated to be in motion with a large force, hovering about those cities, in expectation of intelligence from Rome, the senate made a decree to place all in the hands of the consuls, who should undertake the conduct of everything, and do their best to save the state. This was not a common thing, but only done by the senate in case of imminent danger.

After Cicero had received this power, he committed all affairs outside to Quintus Metellus, but the management of the city he kept in his own hands. Such a numerous attendance guarded him every day when he went abroad, that the greatest part of the market-place was filled with his train when he entered it. Catiline, impatient of further delay, resolved himself to break forth and go to Manlius, but he commanded Marcius and Cethegus to take their swords, and go early in the morning to Cicero's gates, as if only intending to salute him, and then to fall upon him and slay him. This a noble lady, Fulvia, coming by night, discovered to Cicero, bidding him beware of Cethegus and Marcius. They came by break of day, and being denied entrance, made an outcry and disturbance at the gates, which excited all the more suspicion. But Cicero, going forth, summoned the senate into the temple of Jupiter Stator, which stands at the end of the Sacred Street, going up to the Palatine. And when Catiline with others of his party also came, as intending to make his defence, none of the senators would sit by him, but all of them left the bench where he had placed himself. And when he began to speak, they interrupted him with outcries. At length Cicero, standing up, commanded him to leave the city, for since one governed the commonwealth with words, the other with arms, it was necessary there should be a wall betwixt them. Catiline, therefore, immediately left the town, with three hundred armed men; and assuming, as if he had been a magistrate, the rods, axes, and military ensigns, he went to Manlius, and having got together a body of near twenty thousand men, with these he marched to the several cities, endeavouring to persuade or force them to revolt. So it being now come to open war, Antonius was sent forth to fight him.

The remainder of those in the city whom he had corrupted, Cornelius Lentulus kept together and encouraged. He had the surname Sura, and was a man of a noble family, but a dissolute liver, who for his debauchery was formerly turned out of the senate, and was now holding the office of prætor for the second time, as the custom is with those who desire to regain the dignity of senator. It is said that he got the surname Sura upon this occasion; being quæstor in the time of Sylla, he had lavished away and consumed a great quantity of the public moneys, at which Sylla being provoked, called him to give an account in the senate; he appeared with great coolness and contempt, and said he had no account to give, but they might take this, holding up the calf of his leg, as boys do at ball, when they have missed. Upon which he was surnamed *Sura, sura* being the Roman word for the calf of the leg. Being at another time prosecuted at law, and having bribed some of the judges, he escaped only by two votes, and complained of the needless expense he had gone to in paying for a second, as one would have sufficed to acquit him. This man, such in his own nature, and now inflamed by Catiline, false prophets and fortune-tellers had also corrupted with vain hopes, quoting to him fictitious verses and oracles, and proving from the Sibylline prophecies that there were three of the name Cornelius designed by fate to be monarchs of Rome; two of whom, Cinna and Sylla, had already fulfilled the decree, and that divine fortune was now advancing with the gift of monarchy for the remaining third Cornelius; and that therefore he ought by all means to accept it, and not lose opportunity by delay, as Catiline had done.

Lentulus, therefore, designed no mean or trivial matter, for he had resolved to kill the whole senate, and as many other citizens as he could, to fire the city, and spare nobody, except only Pompey's children, intending to seize and keep them as

pledges of his reconciliation with Pompey. For there was then
a common and strong report that Pompey was on his way home-
ward from his great expedition. The night appointed for the
design was one of the Saturnalia; swords, flax, and sulphur they
carried and hid in the house of Cethegus; and providing one
hundred men, and dividing the city into as many parts, they
had allotted to every one singly his proper place, so that in a
moment, many kindling the fire, the city might be in a flame all
together. Others were appointed to stop up the aqueducts, and
to kill those who should endeavour to carry water to put it out.
Whilst these plans were preparing, it happened there were two
ambassadors from the Allobroges staying in Rome; a nation at
that time in a distressed condition, and very uneasy under the
Roman government. These Lentulus and his party judging
useful instruments to move and seduce Gaul to revolt, admitted
into the conspiracy, and they gave them letters to their own
magistrates, and letters to Catiline; in those they promised
liberty, in these they exhorted Catiline to set all slaves free, and
to bring them along with him to Rome. They sent also to
accompany them to Cataline, one Titus, a native of Croton, who
was to carry those letters to him.

These counsels of inconsidering men, who conversed together
over wine and with women, Cicero watched with sober industry
and forethought, and with most admirable sagacity, having
several emissaries abroad, who observed and traced with him
all that was done, and keeping also a secret correspondence with
many who pretended to join in the conspiracy. He thus knew
all the discourse which passed betwixt them and the strangers;
and lying in wait for them by night, he took the Crotonian with
his letters, the ambassadors of the Allobroges acting secretly in
concert with him.

By break of day, he summoned the senate into the temple of
Concord, where he read the letters and examined the informers.
Junius Silanus further stated that several persons had heard
Cethegus say that three consuls and four prætors were to be
slain. Piso, also, a person of consular dignity, testified other
matters of the like nature; and Caius Sulpicius, one of the
prætors, being sent to Cethegus's house, found there a quantity
of darts and of armour, and a still greater number of swords and
daggers, all recently whetted. At length, the senate decreeing
indemnity to the Crotonian upon his confession of the whole
matter, Lentulus was convicted, abjured his office (for he was
then prætor), and put off his robe edged with purple in the

senate, changing it for another garment more agreeable to his present circumstances. He thereupon, with the rest of his confederates present, was committed to the charge of the prætors in free custody.

It being evening, and the common people in crowds expecting without, Cicero went forth to them, and told them what was done, and then, attended by them, went to the house of a friend and near neighbour; for his own was taken up by the women, who were celebrating with secret rites the feast of the goddess whom the Romans call the Good, and the Greeks the Women's goddess. For a sacrifice is annually performed to her in the consul's house, either by his wife or mother, in the presence of the vestal virgins. And having got into his friend's house privately, a few only being present, he began to deliberate how he should treat these men. The severest, and the only punishment fit for such heinous crimes, he was somewhat shy and fearful of inflicting, as well from the clemency of his nature, as also lest he should be thought to exercise his authority too insolently, and to treat too harshly men of the noblest birth and most powerful friendships in the city; and yet, if he should use them more mildly, he had a dreadful prospect of danger from them. For there was no likelihood, if they suffered less than death, they would be reconciled, but rather, adding new rage to their former wickedness, they would rush into every kind of audacity, while he himself, whose character for courage already did not stand very high with the multitude, would be thought guilty of the greatest cowardice and want of manliness.

Whilst Cicero was doubting what course to take, a portent happened to the women in their sacrificing. For on the altar, where the fire seemed wholly extinguished, a great and bright flame issued forth from the ashes of the burnt wood; at which others were affrighted, but the holy virgins called to Terentia, Cicero's wife, and bade her haste to her husband, and command him to execute what he had resolved for the good of his country, for the goddess had sent a great light to the increase of his safety and glory. Terentia, therefore, as she was otherwise in her own nature neither tender-hearted nor timorous, but a woman eager for distinction (who, as Cicero himself says, would rather thrust herself into his public affairs, than communicate her domestic matters to him), told him these things, and excited him against the conspirators. So also did Quintus his brother, and Publius Nigidius, one of his philosophical friends, whom he often made use of in his greatest and most weighty affairs of state.

The next day, a debate arising in the senate about the punishment of the men, Silanus, being the first who was asked his opinion, said it was fit they should be all sent to the prison, and there suffer the utmost penalty. To him all consented in order till it came to Caius Cæsar, who was afterwards dictator. He was then but a young man, and only at the outset of his career, but had already directed his hopes and policy to that course by which he afterwards changed the Roman state into a monarchy. Of this others foresaw nothing; but Cicero had seen reason for strong suspicion, though without obtaining any sufficient means of proof. And there were some indeed that said that he was very near being discovered, and only just escaped him; others are of opinion that Cicero voluntarily overlooked and neglected the evidence against him, for fear of his friends and power; for it was very evident to everybody that if Cæsar was to be accused with the conspirators, they were more likely to be saved with him, than he to be punished with them.

When, therefore, it came to Cæsar's turn to give his opinion, he stood up and proposed that the conspirators should not be put to death, but their estates confiscated, and their persons confined in such cities in Italy as Cicero should approve, there to be kept in custody till Catiline was conquered. To this sentence, as it was the most moderate, and he that delivered it a most powerful speaker, Cicero himself gave no small weight, for he stood up and, turning the scale on either side, spoke in favour partly of the former, partly of Cæsar's sentence. And all Cicero's friends, judging Cæsar's sentence most expedient for Cicero, because he would incur the less blame if the conspirators were not put to death, chose rather the latter; so that Silanus, also changing his mind, retracted his opinion, and said he had not declared for capital, but only the utmost punishment, which to a Roman senator is imprisonment. The first man who spoke against Cæsar's motion was Catulus Lutatius. Cato followed, and so vehemently urged in his speech the strong suspicion against Cæsar himself, and so filled the senate with anger and resolution, that a decree was passed for the execution of the conspirators. But Cæsar opposed the confiscation of their goods, not thinking it fair that those who rejected the mildest part of his sentence should avail themselves of the severest. And when many insisted upon it, he appealed to the tribunes, but they would do nothing; till Cicero himself yielding, remitted that part of the sentence.

After this, Cicero went out with the senate to the conspirators;

they were not all together in one place, but the several prætors
had them, some one, some another, in custody. And first he
took Lentulus from the Palatine, and brought him by the Sacred
Street, through the middle of the market-place, a circle of the
most eminent citizens encompassing and protecting him. The
people, affrighted at what was doing, passed along in silence,
especially the young men; as if, with fear and trembling, they
were undergoing a rite of initiation into some ancient sacred
mysteries of aristocratic power. Thus passing from the market-
place, and coming to the gaol, he delivered Lentulus to the
officer, and commanded him to execute him; and after him
Cethegus, and so all the rest in order, he brought and delivered
up to execution. And when he saw many of the conspirators
in the market-place, still standing together in companies,
ignorant of what was done, and waiting for the night, supposing
the men were still alive and in a possibility of being rescued,
he called out in a loud voice, and said, " *They did live ;* " for so
the Romans, to avoid inauspicious language, name those that
are dead.

It was now evening, when he returned from the market-place
to his own house, the citizens no longer attending him with
silence, nor in order, but receiving him, as he passed, with
acclamations and applauses, and saluting him as the saviour
and founder of his country. A bright light shone through the
streets from the lamps and torches set up at the doors, and the
women showed lights from the tops of the houses, to honour
Cicero, and to behold him returning home with a splendid train
of the most principal citizens; amongst whom were many who
had conducted great wars, celebrated triumphs, and added to the
possessions of the Roman empire, both by sea and land. These,
as they passed along with him, acknowledged to one another,
that though the Roman people were indebted to several officers
and commanders of that age for riches, spoils, and power, yet to
Cicero alone they owed the safety and security of all these, for
delivering them from so great and imminent a danger. For
though it might seem no wonderful thing to prevent the design,
and punish the conspirators, yet to defeat the greatest of all
conspiracies with so little disturbance, trouble, and commotion,
was very extraordinary. For the greater part of those who had
flocked into Catiline, as soon as they heard the fate of Lentulus
and Cethegus, left and forsook him, and he himself, with his
remaining forces, joining battle with Antonius, was destroyed
with his army.

And yet there were some who were very ready both to speak ill of Cicero, and to do him hurt for these actions; and they had for their leaders some of the magistrates of the ensuing year, as Cæsar, who was one of the prætors, and Metellus and Bestia, the tribunes. These, entering upon their office some few days before Cicero's consulate expired, would not permit him to make any address to the people, but throwing the benches before the rostra, hindered his speaking, telling him he might, if he pleased, make the oath of withdrawal from office, and then come down again. Cicero, accordingly, accepting the conditions, came forward to make his withdrawal; and silence being made, he recited his oath, not in the usual, but in a new and peculiar form, namely, that he had saved his country and preserved the empire; the truth of which oath all the people confirmed with theirs. Cæsar and the tribunes, all the more exasperated by this, endeavoured to create him further trouble, and for this purpose proposed a law for calling Pompey home with his army, to put an end to Cicero's usurpation. But it was a very great advantage for Cicero and the whole commonwealth that Cato was at that time one of the tribunes. For he, being of equal power with the rest, and of greater reputation, could oppose their designs. He easily defeated their other projects, and in an oration to the people so highly extolled Cicero's consulate, that the greatest honours were decreed him, and he was publicly declared the Father of his Country, which title he seems to have obtained, the first man who did so, when Cato gave it to him in this address to the people.

At this time, therefore, his authority was very great in the city; but he created himself much envy, and offended very many, not by any evil action, but because he was always lauding and magnifying himself. For neither senate, nor assembly of the people, nor court of judicature could meet, in which he was not heard to talk of Catiline and Lentulus. Indeed, he also filled his books and writings with his own praises, to such an excess as to render a style, in itself most pleasant and delightful, nauseous and irksome to his hearers; this ungrateful humour, like a disease, always cleaving to him. Nevertheless, though he was intemperately fond of his own glory, he was very free from envying others, and was, on the contrary, most liberally profuse in commending both the ancients and his contemporaries, as any one may see in his writings. And many such sayings of his are also remembered; as that he called Aristotle a river of flowing gold, and said of Plato's Dialogues, that if Jupiter were to speak, it would be in language like theirs. He used to call Theophrastus his special luxury. And being asked which of Demosthenes's orations he liked best, he answered, the longest. And yet some affected imitators of Demosthenes have complained of some words that occur in one of his letters, to the effect that Demosthenes sometimes falls asleep in his speeches; forgetting the many high encomiums he continually passes upon him, and the compliment he paid him when he named the most elaborate of all his orations, those he wrote against Antony, Philippics. And as for the eminent men of his own time, either in eloquence or philosophy, there was not one of them whom he did not, by writing or speaking favourably of him, render more illustrious. He obtained of Cæsar, when in power, the Roman citizenship for Cratippus, the Peripatetic, and got the court of Areopagus, by public decree, to request his stay at Athens, for the instruction of their youth and the honour of their city. There are letters extant from Cicero to Herodes, and others to his son, in which he recommends the study of philosophy under Cratippus. There is one in which he blames Gorgias, the rhetorician, for enticing his son into luxury and drinking, and, therefore, forbids him his company. And this, and one other to Pelops, the Byzantine, are the only two of his Greek epistles which seem to be written in anger. In the first, he justly reflects on Gorgias, if he were what he was thought to be, a dissolute and profligate character; but in the other, he rather meanly expostulates and complains with Pelops for neglecting to procure him a decree of certain honours from the Byzantines.

Another illustration of his love of praise is the way in which sometimes, to make his orations more striking, he neglected decorum and dignity. When Munatius, who had escaped conviction by his advocacy, immediately prosecuted his friend Sabinus, he said in the warmth of his resentment, " Do you suppose you were acquitted for your own merits, Munatius, and was it not that I so darkened the case, that the court could not see your guilt? " When from the rostra he had made a eulogy on Marcus Crassus, with much applause, and within a few days after again as publicly reproached him, Crassus called to him, and said, " Did not you yourself two days ago, in this same place, commend me? " " Yes," said Cicero, " I exercised my eloquence in declaiming upon a bad subject." At another time, Crassus had said that no one of his family had ever lived beyond sixty years of age, and afterwards denied it, and asked, " What should put it into my head to say so? " " It was to gain the people's favour," answered Cicero; " you knew how glad they would be to hear it." When Crassus expressed admiration of the Stoic doctrine, that *the good man is always rich,* " Do you not mean," said Cicero, " their doctrine that *all things belong to the wise ?* " Crassus being generally accused of covetousness. One of Crassus's sons, who was thought so exceedingly like a man of the name of Axius as to throw some suspicion on his mother's honour, made a successful speech in the senate. Cicero, on being asked how he liked it, replied with the Greek words *Axios Crassou.*

When Crassus was about to go into Syria, he desired to leave Cicero rather his friend than his enemy, and, therefore, one day saluting him, told him he would come and sup with him, which the other as courteously received. Within a few days after, on some of Cicero's acquaintances interceding for Vatinius, as desirous of reconciliation and friendship, for he was then his enemy, " What," he replied, " does Vatinius also wish to come and sup with me? " Such was his way with Crassus. When Vatinius, who had swellings in his neck, was pleading a cause, he called him the *tumid* orator; and having been told by some one that Vatinius was dead, on hearing, presently after, that he was alive, " May the rascal perish," said he, " for his news not being true."

Upon Cæsar's bringing forward a law for the division of the lands in Campania amongst the soldiers, many in the senate opposed it; amongst the rest, Lucius Gellius, one of the oldest men in the house, said it should never pass whilst he lived. " Let us postpone it," said Cicero, " Gellius does not ask us to wait long." There was a man of the name of Octavius, sus-pected to be of African descent. He once said, when Cicero was pleading, that he could not hear him; " Yet there are holes," said Cicero, " in your ears." When Metellus Nepos told him that he had ruined more as a witness than he had saved as an advocate, " I admit," said Cicero, " that I have more truth than eloquence." To a young man who was suspected of having given a poisoned cake to his father, and who talked largely of the invectives he meant to deliver against Cicero, " Better these," replied he, " than your cakes." Publius Sextius, having amongst others retained Cicero as his advocate in a certain cause, was yet desirous to say all for himself, and would not allow anybody to speak for him; when he was about to receive his acquittal from the judges, and the ballots were passing, Cicero called to him, " Make haste, Sextius, and use your time;

to-morrow you will be nobody." He cited Publius Cotta to bear testimony in a certain cause, one who affected to be thought a lawyer, though ignorant and unlearned; to whom, when he had said, " I know nothing of the matter," he answered, " You think, perhaps, we ask you about a point of law." To Metellus Nepos, who, in a dispute between them, repeated several times, " Who was your father, Cicero? " he replied, " Your mother has made the answer to such a question in your case more difficult; " Nepos's mother having been of ill-repute. The son, also, was of a giddy, uncertain temper. At one time, he suddenly threw up his office of tribune, and sailed off into Syria to Pompey; and immediately after, with as little reason, came back again. He gave his tutor, Philagrus, a funeral with more than necessary attention, and then set up the stone figure of a crow over his tomb. " This," said Cicero, " is really appropriate; as he did not teach you to speak, but to fly about." When Marcus Appius, in the opening of some speech in a court of justice, said that his friend had desired him to employ industry, eloquence, and fidelity in that cause, Cicero answered, " And how have you had the heart not to accede to any one of his requests? "

To use this sharp raillery against opponents and antagonists in judicial pleading seems allowable rhetoric. But he excited much ill-feeling by his readiness to attack any one for the sake of a jest. A few anecdotes of this kind may be added. Marcus Aquinius, who had two sons-in-law in exile, received from him the name of King Adrastus. Lucius Cotta, an intemperate lover of wine, was censor when Cicero stood for the consulship. Cicero, being thirsty at the election, his friends stood round about him while he was drinking. " You have reason to be afraid," he said, " lest the censor should be angry with me for drinking water." Meeting one day Voconius with his three very ugly daughters, he quoted the verse—

" He reared a race without Apollo's leave."

When Marcus Gellius, who was reputed the son of a slave, had read several letters in the senate with a very shrill and loud voice, " Wonder not," said Cicero, " he comes of the criers." When Faustus Sylla, the son of Sylla the dictator, who had, during his dictatorship, by public bills proscribed and condemned so many citizens, had so far wasted his estate, and got into debt, that he was forced to publish his bills of sale, Cicero told him that he liked these bills much better than those of his father. By this habit he made himself odious with many people.

But Clodius's faction conspired against him upon the following occasion. Clodius was a member of a noble family, in the
flower of his youth, and of a bold and resolute temper. He,
being in love with Pompeia, Cæsar's wife, got privately into his
house in the dress and attire of a music-girl; the women being
at that time offering there the sacrifice which must not be seen
by men, and there was no man present. Clodius, being a youth
and beardless, hoped to get to Pompeia among the women without being taken notice of. But coming into a great house by
night, he missed his way in the passages, and a servant belonging
to Aurelia, Cæsar's mother, spying him wandering up and down,
inquired his name. Thus being necessitated to speak, he told
her he was seeking for one of Pompeia's maids, Abra by name;
and she, perceiving it not to be a woman's voice, shrieked out,
and called in the women; who, shutting the gates, and search-
ing every place, at length found Clodius hidden in the chamber
of the maid with whom he had come in. This matter being
much talked about, Cæsar put away his wife, Pompeia, and
Clodius was prosecuted for profaning the holy rites.

Cicero was at this time his friend, for he had been useful to
him in the conspiracy of Catiline, as one of his forwardest assistants and protectors. But when Clodius rested his defence upon
this point, that he was not then at Rome, but at a distance in
the country, Cicero testified that he had come to his house that
day, and conversed with him on several matters; which thing
was indeed true, although Cicero was thought to testify it not so
much for the truth's sake as to preserve his quiet with Terentia
his wife. For she bore a grudge against Clodius on account of
his sister Clodia's wishing, as it was alleged, to marry Cicero,
and having employed for this purpose the intervention of Tullus,
a very intimate friend of Cicero's; and his frequent visits to
Clodia, who lived in their neighbourhood, and the attentions he
paid to her had excited Terentia's suspicions, and, being a
woman of a violent temper, and having the ascendant over
Cicero, she urged him on to taking a part against Clodius, and
delivering his testimony. Many other good and honest citizens
also gave evidence against him, for perjuries, disorders, bribing
the people, and debauching women. Lucullus proved, by his
women-servants, that he had debauched his youngest sister when
she was Lucullus's wife; and there was a general belief that he
had done the same with his two other sisters, Tertia, whom
Marcius Rex, and Clodia, whom Metellus Celer had married;
the latter of whom was called Quadrantia, because one of her

lovers had deceived her with a purse of small copper money instead of silver, the smallest copper coin being called a *quadrant*. Upon this sister's account, in particular, Clodius's character was attacked. Notwithstanding all this, when the common people united against the accusers and witnesses and the whole party, the judges were affrighted, and a guard was placed about them for their defence; and most of them wrote their sentences on the tablets in such a way that they could not well be read. It was decided, however, that there was a majority for his acquittal, and bribery was reported to have been employed; in reference to which Catulus remarked, when he next met the judges, " You were very right to ask for a guard, to prevent your money being taken from you." And when Clodius upbraided Cicero that the judges had not believed his testimony, " Yes," said he, " five-and-twenty of them trusted me and condemned you, and the other thirty did not trust you, for they did not acquit you till they had got your money."

Cæsar, though cited, did not give his testimony against Clodius, and declared himself not convinced of his wife's adultery, but that he had put her away because it was fit that Cæsar's house should not be only free of the evil fact, but of the fame too.

Clodius, having escaped this danger, and having got himself chosen one of the tribunes, immediately attacked Cicero, heaping up all matters and inciting all persons against him. The common people he gained over with popular laws; to each of the consuls he decreed large provinces, to Piso, Macedonia, and to Gabinius, Syria; he made a strong party among the indigent citizens, to support him in his proceedings, and had always a body of armed slaves about him. Of the three men then in greatest power, Crassus was Cicero's open enemy, Pompey indifferently made advances to both, and Cæsar was going with an army into Gaul. To him, though not his friend (what had occurred in the time of the conspiracy having created suspicions between them), Cicero applied, requesting an appointment as one of his lieutenants in the province. Cæsar accepted him, and Clodius, perceiving that Cicero would thus escape his tribunician authority, professed to be inclinable to a reconciliation, laid the greatest fault upon Terentia, made always a favourable mention of him, and addressed him with kind expressions, as one who felt no hatred or ill-will, but who merely wished to urge his complaints in a moderate and friendly way. By these artifices, he so freed Cicero of all his fears, that he resigned his appointment to Cæsar, and betook himself again to political affairs. At which Cæsar, being exasperated, joined the party of Clodius against him, and wholly alienated Pompey from him; he also himself declared in a public assembly of the people, that he did not think Lentulus and Cethegus, with their accomplices, were fairly and legally put to death without being brought to trial. And this, indeed, was the crime charged upon Cicero, and this impeachment he was summoned to answer. And so, as an accused man, and in danger for the result, he changed his dress, and went round with his hair untrimmed, in the attire of a suppliant, to beg the people's grace. But Clodius met him in every corner, having a band of abusive and daring fellows about him, who derided Cicero for his change of dress and his humiliation, and often, by throwing dirt and stones at him, interrupted his supplication to the people.

However, first of all, almost the whole equestrian order changed their dress with him, and no less than twenty thousand young gentlemen followed him with their hair untrimmed, and supplicating with him to the people. And then the senate met, to pass a decree that the people should change their dress as in time of public sorrow. But the consuls opposing it, and Clodius with armed men besetting the senate-house, many of the senators ran out, crying out and tearing their clothes. But this sight moved neither shame nor pity; Cicero must either fly or determine it by the sword with Clodius. He entreated Pompey to aid him, who was on purpose gone out of the way, and was staying at his country-house in the Alban hills; and first he sent his son-in-law Piso to intercede with him, and afterwards set out to go himself. Of which Pompey being informed, would not stay to see him, being ashamed at the remembrance of the many conflicts in the commonwealth which Cicero had undergone in his behalf, and how much of his policy he had directed for his advantage. But being now Cæsar's son-in-law, at his instance he had set aside all former kindness, and, slipping out at another door, avoided the interview. Thus being forsaken by Pompey, and left alone to himself, he fled to the consuls. Gabinius was rough with him, as usual, but Piso spoke more courteously, desiring him to yield and give place for a while to the fury of Clodius, and to await a change of times, and to be now, as before, his country's saviour from the peril of these troubles and commotions which Clodius was exciting.

Cicero, receiving this answer, consulted with his friends. Lucullus advised him to stay, as being sure to prevail at last;

others to fly, because the people would soon desire him again, when they should have enough of the rage and madness of Clodius. This last Cicero approved. But first he took a statue of Minerva, which had been long set up and greatly honoured in his house, and carrying it to the capitol, there dedicated it, with the inscription, " To Minerva, Patroness of Rome." And receiving an escort from his friends, about the middle of the night he left the city, and went by land through Lucania, intending to reach Sicily.

But as soon as it was publicly known that he was fled, Clodius proposed to the people a decree of exile, and by his own order interdicted him fire and water, prohibiting any within five hundred miles in Italy to receive him into their houses. Most people, out of respect for Cicero, paid no regard to this edict, offering him every attention, and escorting him on his way. But at Hipponium, a city of Lucania now called Vibo, one Vibius, a Sicilian by birth, who, amongst many other instances of Cicero's friendship, had been made head of the state engineers when he was consul, would not receive him into his house, sending him word he would appoint a place in the country for his reception. Caius Vergilius, the prætor of Sicily, who had been on the most intimate terms with him, wrote to him to forbear coming into Sicily. At these things Cicero, being disheartened, went to Brundusium, whence putting forth with a prosperous wind, a contrary gale blowing from the sea carried him back to Italy the next day. He put again to sea, and having reached Dyrrachium, on his coming to shore there, it is reported that an earthquake and a convulsion in the sea happened at the same time, signs which the diviners said intimated that his exile would not be long, for these were prognostics of change. Although many visited him with respect, and the cities of Greece contended which should honour him most, he yet continued disheartened and disconsolate, like an unfortunate lover, often casting his looks back upon Italy; and, indeed, he was become so poor-spirited, so humiliated and dejected by his misfortunes, as none could have expected in a man who had devoted so much of his life to study and learning. And yet he often desired his friends not to call him orator, but philosopher, because he had made philosophy his business, and had only used rhetoric as an instrument for attaining his objects in public life. But the desire of glory has great power in washing the tinctures of philosophy out of the souls of men, and in imprinting the passions of the common people, by custom and

conversation, in the minds of those that take a part in governing them, unless the politician be very careful so to engage in
public affairs as to interest himself only in the affairs themselves,
but not participate in the passions that are consequent to them.

Clodius, having thus driven away Cicero, fell to burning his
farms and villas, and afterwards his city house, and built on
the site of it a temple to Liberty. The rest of his property he
exposed to sale by daily proclamation, but nobody came to buy.
By these courses he became formidable to the noble citizens,
and being followed by the commonalty, whom he had filled with
insolence and licentiousness, he began at last to try his strength
against Pompey, some of whose arrangements in the countries
he conquered, he attacked. The disgrace of this made Pompey
begin to reproach himself for his cowardice in deserting Cicero,
and changing his mind, he now wholly set himself with his
friends to contrive his return. And when Clodius opposed it,
the senate made a vote that no public measure should be ratified
or passed by them till Cicero was recalled. But when Lentulus
was consul, the commotions grew so high upon this matter, that
the tribunes were wounded in the Forum, and Quintus, Cicero's
brother, was left as dead, lying unobserved amongst the slain.
The people began to change in their feelings, and Annius Milo,
one of their tribunes, was the first who took confidence to
summon Clodius to trial for acts of violence. Many of the
common people out of the neighbouring cities formed a party
with Pompey, and he went with them, and drove Clodius out
of the Forum, and summoned the people to pass their vote.
And, it is said, the people never passed any suffrage more
unanimously than this. The senate, also, striving to outdo the
people, sent letters of thanks to those cities which had received
Cicero with respect in his exile, and decreed that his house and
his country-places, which Clodius had destroyed, should be
rebuilt at the public charge.

Thus Cicero returned sixteen months after his exile, and the
cities were so glad, and people so zealous to meet him, that
what he boasted of afterwards, that Italy had brought him on
her shoulders home to Rome, was rather less than the truth.
And Crassus himself, who had been his enemy before his exile,
went then voluntarily to meet him, and was reconciled, to please
his son Publius, as he said, who was Cicero's affectionate admirer.

Cicero had not been long at Rome when, taking the opportunity of Clodius's absence, he went with a great company to
the capitol, and there tore and defaced the tribunician tables,

in which were recorded the acts done in the time of Clodius. And on Clodius calling him in question for this, he answered that he, being of the patrician order, had obtained the office of tribune against law, and therefore nothing done by him was valid. Cato was displeased at this, and opposed Cicero, not that he commended Clodius, but rather disapproved of his whole administration; yet, he contended, it was an irregular and violent course for the senate to vote the illegality of so many decrees and acts, including those of Cato's own government in Cyprus and at Byzantium. This occasioned a breach between Cato and Cicero, which, though it came not to open enmity, yet made a more reserved friendship between them.

After this, Milo killed Clodius, and, being arraigned for the murder, he procured Cicero as his advocate. The senate, fearing lest the questioning of so eminent and high-spirited a citizen as Milo might disturb the peace of the city, committed the superintendence of this and of the other trials to Pompey, who should undertake to maintain the security alike of the city and of the courts of justice. Pompey, therefore, went in the night, and occupying the high grounds about it, surrounded the Forum with soldiers. Milo, fearing lest Cicero, being disturbed by such an unusual sight, should conduct his cause the less successfully, persuaded him to come in a litter into the Forum, and there repose himself till the judges were set and the court filled. For Cicero, it seems, not only wanted courage in arms, but, in his speaking also, began with timidity, and in many cases scarcely left off trembling and shaking when he had got thoroughly into the current and the substance of his speech. Being to defend Licinius Murena against the prosecution of Cato, and being eager to outdo Hortensius, who had made his plea with great applause, he took so little rest that night, and was so disordered with thought and overwatching, that he spoke much worse than usual. And so now, on quitting his litter to commence the cause of Milo, at the sight of Pompey, posted, as it were, and encamped with his troops above, and seeing arms shining round about the Forum, he was so confounded that he could hardly begin his speech for the trembling of his body and hesitance of his tongue; whereas Milo, meantime, was bold and intrepid in his demeanour, disdaining either to let his hair grow or to put on the mourning habit. And this, indeed, seems to have been one principal cause of his condemnation. Cicero, however, was thought not so much to have shown timidity for himself, as anxiety about his friend.

He was made one of the priests, whom the Romans call Augurs, in the room of Crassus the younger, dead in Parthia. Then he was appointed by lot to the province of Cilicia, and set sail thither with twelve thousand foot and two thousand six hundred horse. He had orders to bring back Cappadocia to its allegiance to Ariobarzanes, its king; which settlement he effected very completely without recourse to arms. And perceiving the Cilicians, by the great loss the Romans had suffered in Parthia, and the commotions in Syria, to have become disposed to attempt a revolt, by a gentle course of government he soothed them back into fidelity. He would accept none of the presents that were offered him by the kings; he remitted the charge of public entertainments, but daily at his own house received the ingenious and accomplished persons of the province, not sumptuously, but liberally. His house had no porter, nor was he ever found in bed by any man, but early in the morning, standing or walking before his door, he received those who came to offer their salutations. He is said never once to have ordered any of those under his command to be beaten with rods, or to have their garments rent. He never gave contumelious language in his anger, nor inflicted punishment with reproach. He detected an embezzlement, to a large amount, in the public money, and thus relieved the cities from their burdens, at the same time that he allowed those who made restitution to retain without further punishment their rights as citizens. He engaged too, in war, so far as to give a defeat to the banditti who infested Mount Amanus, for which he was saluted by his army Imperator. To Cæcilius, the orator, who asked him to send him some panthers from Cilicia, to be exhibited on the theatre at Rome, he wrote, in commendation of his own actions, that there were no panthers in Cilicia, for they were all fled to Caria, in anger that in so general a peace they had become the sole objects of attack. On leaving his province, he touched at Rhodes, and tarried for some length of time at Athens, longing much to renew his old studies. He visited the eminent men of learning, and saw his former friends and companions; and after receiving in Greece the honours that were due to him, returned to the city, where everything was now just as it were in a flame, breaking out into a civil war.

When the senate would have decreed him a triumph, he told them he had rather, so differences were accommodated, follow the triumphal chariot of Cæsar. In private, he gave advice to both, writing many letters to Cæsar, and personally entreating

Pompey; doing his best to soothe and bring to reason both the one and the other. But when matters became incurable, and Cæsar was approaching Rome, and Pompey durst not abide it, but, with many honest citizens, left the city, Cicero as yet did not join in the flight, and was reputed to adhere to Cæsar. And it is very evident he was in his thoughts much divided, and wavered painfully between both, for he writes in his epistles, "To which side should I turn? Pompey has the fair and honourable plea for war; and Cæsar, on the other hand, has managed his affairs better, and is more able to secure himself and his friends. So that I know whom I should fly, not whom I should fly to." But when Trebatius, one of Cæsar's friends, by letter signified to him that Cæsar thought it was his most desirable course to join his party, and partake his hopes, but if he considered himself too old a man for this, then he should retire into Greece, and stay quietly there, out of the way of either party, Cicero, wondering that Cæsar had not written himself, gave an angry reply, that he should not do anything unbecoming his past life. Such is the account to be collected from his letters.

But as soon as Cæsar was marched into Spain, he immediately sailed away to join Pompey. And he was welcomed by all but Cato; who, taking him privately, chid him for coming to Pompey. As for himself, he said, it had been indecent to forsake that part in the commonwealth which he had chosen from the beginning; but Cicero might have been more useful to his country and friends, if, remaining neuter, he had attended and used his influence to moderate the result, instead of coming hither to make himself, without reason or necessity, an enemy to Cæsar, and a partner in such great dangers.

By this language, partly, Cicero's feelings were altered, and partly, also, because Pompey made no great use of him. Although, indeed, he was himself the cause of it, by his not denying that he was sorry he had come, by his depreciating Pompey's resources, finding fault underhand with his counsels, and continually indulging in jests and sarcastic remarks on his fellow-soldiers. Though he went about in the camp with a gloomy and melancholy face himself, he was always trying to raise a laugh in others, whether they wished it or not. It may not be amiss to mention a few instances. To Domitius, on his preferring to a command one who was no soldier, and saying, in his defence, that he was a modest and prudent person, he replied, "Why did not you keep him for a tutor for your children?"

On hearing Theophanes, the Lesbian, who was master of the engineers in the army, praised for the admirable way in which he had consoled the Rhodians for the loss of their fleet, " What a thing it is," he said, " to have a Greek in command! " When Cæsar had been acting successfully, and in a manner blockading Pompey, Lentulus was saying it was reported that Cæsar's friends were out of heart; " Because," said Cicero, " they do not wish Cæsar well." To one Marcius, who had just come from Italy, and told them that there was a strong report at Rome that Pompey was blocked up, he said, " And you sailed hither to see it with your own eyes." To Nonius, encouraging them after a defeat to be of good hope, because there were seven eagles still left in Pompey's camp, " Good reason for encouragement," said Cicero, " if we were going to fight with jackdaws." Labienus insisted on some prophecies to the effect that Pompey would gain the victory; " Yes," said Cicero; " and the first step in the campaign has been losing our camp."

After the battle of Pharsalia was over, at which he was not present for want of health, and Pompey was fled, Cato, having considerable forces and a great fleet at Dyrrachium, would have had Cicero commander-in-chief, according to law and the precedence of his consular dignity. And on his refusing the command, and wholly declining to take part in their plans for continuing the war, he was in the greatest danger of being killed, young Pompey and his friends calling him traitor, and drawing their swords upon him; only that Cato interposed, and hardly rescued and brought him out of the camp.

Afterwards, arriving at Brundusium, he tarried there some time in expectation of Cæsar, who was delayed by his affairs in Asia and Egypt. And when it was told him that he was arrived at Tarentum, and was coming thence by land to Brundusium, he hastened towards him, not altogether without hope, and yet in some fear of making experiment of the temper of an enemy and conqueror in the presence of many witnesses. But there was no necessity for him either to speak or do anything unworthy of himself; for Cæsar, as soon as he saw him coming a good way before the rest of the company, came down to meet him, saluted him, and, leading the way, conversed with him alone for some furlongs. And from that time forward he continued to treat him with honour and respect, so that, when Cicero wrote an oration in praise of Cato, Cæsar in writing an answer to it, took occasion to commend Cicero's own life and eloquence, comparing him to Pericles and Theramenes. Cicero's oration was called Cato; Cæsar's, anti-Cato.

So also it is related that when Quintus Ligarius was prosecuted for having been in arms against Cæsar, and Cicero had undertaken his defence, Cæsar said to his friends, " Why might we not as well once more hear a speech from Cicero? Ligarius, there is no question, is a wicked man and an enemy." But when Cicero began to speak, he wonderfully moved him, and proceeded in his speech with such varied pathos, and such a charm of language, that the colour of Cæsar's countenance often changed, and it was evident that all the passions of his soul were in commotion. At length, the orator touching upon the Pharsalian battle, he was so affected that his body trembled, and some of the papers he held dropped out of his hands. And thus he was overpowered, and acquitted Ligarius.

Henceforth, the commonwealth being changed into a monarchy, Cicero withdrew himself from public affairs, and employed his leisure in instructing those young men that would, in philosophy; and by the near intercourse he thus had with some of the noblest and highest in rank, he again began to possess great influence in the city. The work and object to which he set himself was to compose and translate philosophical dialogues and to render logical and physical terms into the Roman idiom. For he it was, as it is said, who first or principally gave Latin names to *phantasia, syncatathesis, epokhe, catalepsis, atamon, ameres, kenon,* and other such technical terms, which, either by metaphors or other means of accommodation, he succeeded in making intelligible and expressible to the Romans. For his recreation, he exercised his dexterity in poetry, and when he was set to it would make five hundred verses in a night. He spent the greatest part of his time at his country-house near Tusculum. He wrote to his friends that he led the life of Laertes either jestingly, as his custom was, or rather from a feeling of ambition for public employment, which made him impatient under the present state of affairs. He rarely went to the city, unless to pay his court to Cæsar. He was commonly the first amongst those who voted him honours, and sought out new terms of praise for himself and for his actions. As, for example, what he said of the statues of Pompey, which had been thrown down, and were afterwards by Cæsar's orders set up again; that Cæsar, by this act of humanity, had indeed set up Pompey's statues, but he had fixed and established his own.

He had a design, it is said, of writing the history of his country, combining with it much of that of Greece, and incorporating in it all the stories and legends of the past that he had collected. But his purposes were interfered with by various public and various private unhappy occurrences and misfortunes; for most of which he was himself in fault. For first of all, he put away his wife Terentia, by whom he had been neglected in the time of the war, and sent away destitute of necessaries for his journey; neither did he find her kind when he returned into Italy, for she did not join him at Brundusium, where he stayed a long time, nor would allow her young daughter, who undertook so long a journey, decent attendance, or the requisite expenses; besides, she left him a naked and empty house, and yet had involved him in many and great debts. These were alleged as the fairest reasons for the divorce. But Terentia, who denied them all, had the most unmistakable defence furnished her by her husband himself, who not long after married a young maiden for the love of her beauty, as Terentia upbraided him; or as Tiro, his emancipated slave, has written, for her riches, to discharge his debts. For the young woman was very rich, and Cicero had the custody of her estate, being left guardian in trust; and being indebted many myriads of money, he was persuaded by friends and relations to marry her, notwithstanding his disparity of age, and to use her money to satisfy his creditors. Antony, who mentions this marriage in his answer to the Philippics, reproaches him for putting away a wife with whom he had lived to old age; adding some happy strokes of sarcasm on Cicero's domestic, inactive, unsoldier-like habits. Not long after this marriage, his daughter di·d in childbed at Lentulus's house, to whom she had been married after the death of Piso, her former husband. The philosophers from all parts came to comfort Cicero; for his grief was so excessive, that he put away his new-married wife, because she seemed to be pleased at the death of Tullia. And thus stood Cicero's domestic affairs at this time.

He had no concern in the design that was now forming against Cæsar, although, in general, he was Brutus's most principal confidant, and one who was as aggrieved at the present, and as desirous of the former state of public affairs, as any other whatsoever. But they feared his temper, as wanting courage, and his old age, in which the most daring dispositions are apt to be timorous.

As soon, therefore, as the act was committed by Brutus and

Cassius, and the friends of Cæsar were got together, so that there was fear the city would again be involved in a civil war, Antony, being consul, convened the senate, and made a short address recommending concord. And Cicero following with various remarks such as the occasion called for, persuaded the senate to imitate the Athenians, and decree an amnesty for what had been done in Cæsar's case, and to bestow provinces on Brutus and Cassius. But neither of these things took effect. For as soon as the common people, of themselves inclined to pity, saw the dead body of Cæsar borne through the market-place, and Antony showing his clothes filled with blood, and pierced through in every part with swords, enraged to a degree of frenzy, they made a search for the murderers, and with fire-brands in their hands ran to their houses to burn them. They, however, being forewarned, avoided this danger; and expecting many more and greater to come, they left the city.

Antony on this was at once in exultation, and every one was in alarm with the prospect that he would make himself sole ruler, and Cicero in more alarm than any one. For Antony, seeing his influence reviving in the commonwealth and knowing how closely he was connected with Brutus, was ill-pleased to have him in the city. Besides, there had been some former jealousy between them, occasioned by the difference of their manners. Cicero, fearing the event, was inclined to go as lieu-tenant with Dolabella into Syria. But Hirtius and Pansa, con-suls elect as successors of Antony, good men and lovers of Cicero, entreated him not to leave them, undertaking to put down Antony if he would stay in Rome. And he, neither distrusting wholly, nor trusting them, let Dolabella go without him, promising Hirtius that he would go and spend his summer at Athens, and return again when he entered upon his office. So he set out on his journey; but some delay occurring in his passage, new intelligence, as often happens, came suddenly from Rome, that Antony had made an astonishing change, and was doing all things and managing all public affairs at the will of the senate, and that there wanted nothing but his presence to bring things to a happy settlement. And therefore, blaming himself for his cowardice, he returned again to Rome, and was not de-ceived in his hopes at the beginning. For such multitudes flocked out to meet him, that the compliments and civilities which were paid him at the gates, and at his entrance into the city, took up almost one whole day's time.

On the morrow, Antony convened the senate, and summoned

Cicero thither. He came not, but kept his bed, pretending to be ill with his journey; but the true reason seemed the fear of some design against him, upon a suspicion and intimation given him on his way to Rome. Antony, however, showed great offence at the affront, and sent soldiers, commanding them to bring him or burn his house; but many interceding and supplicating for him, he was contented to accept sureties. Ever after, when they met, they passed one another with silence, and continued on their guard, till Cæsar, the younger, coming from Apollonia, entered on the first Cæsar's inheritance, and was engaged in a dispute with Antony about two thousand five hundred myriads of money, which Antony detained from the estate.

Upon this, Philippus, who married the mother, and Marcellus, who married the sister of young Cæsar, came with the young man to Cicero, and agreed with him that Cicero should give them the aid of his eloquence and political influence with the senate and people, and Cæsar give Cicero the defence of his riches and arms. For the young man had already a great party of the soldiers of Cæsar about him. And Cicero's readiness to join him was founded, it is said, on some yet stronger motives; for it seems, while Pompey and Cæsar were yet alive, Cicero, in his sleep, had fancied himself engaged in calling some of the sons of the senators into the capitol, Jupiter being about, according to the dream, to declare one of them the chief ruler of Rome. The citizens, running up with curiosity, stood about the temple, and the youths, sitting in their purple-bordered robes, kept silence. On a sudden the doors opened, and the youths, arising one by one in order, passed round the god, who reviewed them all, and, to their sorrow, dismissed them; but when this one was passing by, the god stretched forth his right hand and said, " O ye Romans, this young man, when he shall be lord of Rome, shall put an end to all your civil wars." It is said that Cicero formed from his dream a distinct image of the youth, and retained it afterwards perfectly, but did not know who it was. The next day, going down into the Campus Martius, he met the boys returning from their gymnastic exercises, and the first was he, just as he had appeared to him in his dream. Being astonished at it, he asked him who were his parents. And it proved to be this young Cæsar, whose father was a man of no great eminence, Octavius, and his mother, Attia, Cæsar's sister's daughter; for which reason, Cæsar, who had no children, made him by will the heir of his house and property. From that time, it is said that Cicero studiously noticed the youth when-

ever he met him, and he as kindly received the civility; and by
fortune he happened to be born when Cicero was consul.

These were the reasons spoken of; but it was principally
Cicero's hatred of Antony, and a temper unable to resist honour,
which fastened him to Cæsar, with the purpose of getting the
support of Cæsar's power for his own public designs. For the
young man went so far in his court to him, that he called him
Father; at which Brutus was so highly displeased, that, in his
epistles to Atticus, he reflected on Cicero saying, it was manifest,
by his courting Cæsar for fear of Antony, he did not intend
liberty to his country, but an indulgent master to himself.
Notwithstanding, Brutus took Cicero's son, then studying philosophy at Athens, gave him a command, and employed him in
various ways, with a good result. Cicero's own power at this
time was at the greatest height in the city, and he did whatsoever he pleased; he completely overpowered and drove out
Antony, and sent the two consuls, Hirtius and Pansa, with an
army, to reduce him; and, on the other hand, persuaded the
senate to allow Cæsar the lictors and ensigns of a prætor, as
though he were his country's defender. But after Antony was
defeated in battle, and the consuls slain, the armies united, and
ranged themselves with Cæsar. And the senate, fearing the
young man, and his extraordinary fortune, endeavoured, by
honours and gifts, to call off the soldiers from him, and to lessen
his power; professing there was no further need of arms now
Antony was put to flight.

This giving Cæsar an affright, he privately sends some friends
to entreat and persuade Cicero to procure the consular dignity
for them both together; saying he should manage the affairs as
he pleased, should have the supreme power, and govern the
young man who was only desirous of name and glory. And
Cæsar himself confessed that, in fear of ruin, and in danger of
being deserted, he had seasonably made use of Cicero's ambition,
persuading him to stand with him, and to accept the offer of his
aid and interest for the consulship.

And now, more than at any other time, Cicero let himself be
carried away and deceived, though an old man, by the persuasion of a boy. He joined him in soliciting votes, and procured the good-will of the senate, not without blame at the time
on the part of his friends; and he, too, soon enough after, saw
that he had ruined himself, and betrayed the liberty of his
country. For the young man, once established, and possessed
of the office of consul, bade Cicero farewell; and, reconciling

himself to Antony and Lepidus, joined his power with theirs, and divided the government, like a piece of property, with them. Thus united, they made a schedule of above two hundred persons who were to be put to death. But the greatest contention in all their debates was on the question of Cicero's case. Antony would come to no conditions, unless he should be the first man to he killed. Lepidus held with Antony, and Cæsar opposed them both. They met secretly and by themselves, for three days together, near the town of Bononia. The spot was not far from the camp, with a river surrounding it. Cæsar, it is said, contended earnestly for Cicero the first two days; but on the third day he yielded, and gave him up. The terms of their mutual concessions were these: that Cæsar should desert Cicero, Lepidus his brother Paulus, and Antony, Lucius Cæsar, his uncle by his mother's side. Thus they let their anger and fury take from them the sense of humanity, and demonstrated that no beast is more savage than man when possessed with power answerable to his rage.

Whilst these things were contriving, Cicero was with his brother at his country-house near Tusculum; whence, hearing of the proscriptions, they determined to pass to Astura, a villa of Cicero's near the sea, and to take shipping from thence for Macedonia to Brutus, of whose strength in that province news had already been heard. They travelled together in their separate litters, overwhelmed with sorrow; and often stopping on the way till their litters came together, condoled with one another. But Quintus was the more disheartened when he reflected on his want of means for his journey; for, as he said, he had brought nothing with him from home. And even Cicero himself had but a slender provision. It was judged, therefore, most expedient that Cicero should make what haste he could to fly, and Quintus return home to provide necessaries, and thus resolved, they mutually embraced, and parted with many tears.

Quintus, within a few days after, betrayed by his servants to those who came to search for him, was slain, together with his young son. But Cicero was carried to Astura, where finding a vessel, he immediately went on board her, and sailed as far as Circæum with a prosperous gale; but when the pilots resolved immediately to set sail from thence, whether fearing the sea, or not wholly distrusting the faith of Cæsar, he went on shore, and passed by land a hundred furlongs, as if he was going for Rome. But losing resolution and changing his mind, he again returned to the sea, and there spent the night in fearful and

perplexed thoughts. Sometimes he resolved to go into Cæsar's
house privately, and there kill himself upon the altar of his
household gods, to bring divine vengeance upon him; but the
fear of torture put him off this course. And after passing
through a variety of confused and uncertain counsels, at last he
let his servants carry him by sea to Capitæ, where he had a
house, an agreeable place to retire to in the heat of summer,
when the Etesian winds are so pleasant.

There was at that place a chapel of Apollo, not far from the
seaside, from which a flight of crows rose with a great noise, and
made towards Cicero's vessel, as it rowed to land, and lighting
on both sides of the yard, some croaked, others pecked the ends
of the ropes. This was looked upon by all as an ill-omen; and,
therefore, Cicero went again ashore, and entering his house, lay
down upon his bed to compose himself to rest. Many of the
crows settled about the window, making a dismal cawing; but
one of them alighted upon the bed where Cicero lay covered up,
and with its bill by little and little pecked off the clothes from
his face. His servants, seeing this, blamed themselves that
they should stay to be spectators of their master's murder, and
do nothing in his defence, whilst the brute creatures came to
assist and take care of him in his undeserved affliction; and
therefore, partly by entreaty, partly by force, they took him
up, and carried him in his litter towards the seaside.

But in the meantime the assassins were come with a band of
soldiers, Herennius, a centurion, and Popillius, a tribune, whom
Cicero had formerly defended when prosecuted for the murder
of his father. Finding the doors shut, they broke them open,
and Cicero not appearing, and those within saying they knew
not where he was, it is stated that a youth, who had been
educated by Cicero in the liberal arts and sciences, an emancipated slave of his brother Quintus, Philologus by name, informed
the tribune that the litter was on its way to the sea through the
close and shady walks. The tribune, taking a few with him,
ran to the place where he was to come out. And Cicero, perceiving Herennius running in the walks, commanded his servants
to set down the litter; and stroking his chin, as he used to do,
with his left hand, he looked steadfastly upon his murderers,
his person covered with dust, his beard and hair untrimmed,
and his face worn with his troubles. So that the greatest part
of those that stood by covered their faces whilst Herennius
slew him. And thus was he murdered, stretching forth his neck
out of the litter, being now in his sixty-fourth year. Herennius

cut off his head, and, by Antony's command, his hands also, by which his Philippics were written; for so Cicero styled those orations he wrote against Antony, and so they are called to this day.

When these members of Cicero were brought to Rome, Antony was holding an assembly for the choice of public officers; and when he heard it, and saw them, he cried out, " Now let there be an end of our proscriptions." He commanded his head and hands to be fastened up over the rostra, where the orators spoke; a sight which the Roman people shuddered to behold, and they believed they saw there, not the face of Cicero, but the image of Antony's own soul. And yet amidst these actions he did justice in one thing, by delivering up Philologus to Pomponia, the wife of Quintus; who, having got his body into her power, besides other grievous punishments, made him cut off his own flesh by pieces, and roast and eat it; for so some writers have related. But Tiro, Cicero's emancipated slave, has not so much as mentioned the treachery of Philologus.

Some long time after, Cæsar, I have been told, visiting one of his daughter's sons, found him with a book of Cicero's in his hand. The boy for fear endeavoured to hide it under his gown; which Cæsar perceiving, took it from him, and, turning over a great part of the book standing, gave it him again, and said, " My child, this was a learned man, and a lover of his country." And immediately after he had vanquished Antony, being then consul, he made Cicero's son his colleague in the office; and under that consulship the senate took down all the statues of Antony, and abolished all the other honours that had been given him, and decreed that none of that family should thereafter bear the name of Marcus; and thus the final acts of the punishment of Antony were, by the divine powers, devolved upon the family of Cicero.


## THE COMPARISON OF DEMOSTHENES AND CICERO

THESE are the most memorable circumstances recorded in history of Demosthenes and Cicero which have come to our knowledge. But omitting an exact comparison of their respective faculties in speaking, yet thus much seems fit to be said; that Demosthenes, to make himself a master in rhetoric, applied all the faculties he had, natural or acquired, wholly that way; that he far surpassed in force and strength of eloquence all his contemporaries in political and judicial speaking, in grandeur and majesty all the panegyrical orators, and in accuracy and science all the logicians and rhetoricians of his day; that Cicero was highly educated, and by his diligent study became a most accomplished general scholar in all these branches, having left behind him numerous philosophical treatises of his own on Academic principles; as, indeed, even in his written speeches, both political and judicial, we see him continually trying to show his learning by the way. And one may discover the different temper of each of them in their speeches. For Demosthenes's oratory was without all embellishment and jesting, wholly composed for real effect and seriousness; not smelling of the lamp, as Pytheas scoffingly said, but of the temperance, thoughtfulness, austerity, and grave earnestness of his temper. Whereas Cicero's love of mockery often ran him into scurrility; and in his love of laughing away serious arguments in judicial cases by jests and facetious remarks, with a view to the advantage of his clients, he paid too little regard to what was decent: saying, for example, in his defence of Cælius, that he had done no absurd thing in such plenty and affluence to indulge himself in pleasures, it being a kind of madness not to enjoy the things we possess, especially since the most eminent philosophers have asserted pleasures to be the chiefest good. So also we are told that when Cicero, being consul, undertook the defence of Murena against Cato's prosecution, by way of bantering Cato, he made a long series of jokes upon the absurd *paradoxes*, as they are called, of the Stoic set; so that a loud laughter passing from the crowd to the judges, Cato, with a quiet smile, said to those that sat next him, " My friends, what an amusing consul we have."

And, indeed, Cicero was by natural temper very much disposed to mirth and pleasantry, and always appeared with a smiling and serene countenance. But Demosthenes had constant care and thoughtfulness in his look, and a serious anxiety, which he seldom, if ever, laid aside; and, therefore, was accounted by his enemies, as he himself confessed, morose and ill-mannered.

Also, it is very evident, out of their several writings, that Demosthenes never touched upon his own praises but decently and without offence when there was need of it, and for some weightier end; but upon other occasions modestly and sparingly. But Cicero's immeasurable boasting of himself in his orations argues him guilty of an uncontrollable appetite for distinction, his cry being evermore that arms should give place to the gown, and the soldier's laurel to the tongue. And at last we find him extolling not only his deeds and actions, but his orations also, as well those that were only spoken, as those that were published; as if he were engaged in a boyish trial of skill, who should speak best, with the rhetoricians. Isocrates and Anaximenes, not as one who could claim the task to guide and instruct the Roman nation, the—

" Soldier full-armed, terrific to the foe."

It is necessary, indeed, for a political leader to be an able speaker; but it is an ignoble thing for any man to admire and relish the glory of his own eloquence. And, in this matter, Demosthenes had a more than ordinary gravity and magnificence of mind, accounting his talent in speaking nothing more than a mere accomplishment and matter of practice, the success of which must depend greatly on the good-will and candour of his hearers, and regarding those who pride themselves on such accounts to be men of a low and petty disposition.

The power of persuading and governing the people did, indeed, equally belong to both, so that those who had armies and camps at command stood in need of their assistance; as Charas, Diopithes, and Leosthenes of Demosthenes's, Pompey and young Cæsar of Cicero's, as the latter himself admits in his Memoirs addressed to Agrippa and Mæcenas. But what are thought and commonly said most to demonstrate and try the tempers of men, namely, authority and place, by moving every passion, and discovering every frailty, these are things which Demosthenes never received; nor was he ever in a position to give such proof of himself, having never obtained any eminent office, nor led any of those armies into the field against Philip which he raised by his eloquence. Cicero, on the other hand, was sent quæstor into Sicily, and proconsul into Cilicia and Cappadocia, at a time when avarice was at the height, and the commanders and governors who were employed abroad, as though they thought it a mean thing to steal, set themselves to seize by open force; so that it seemed no heinous matter to take bribes, but he that did it most moderately was in good esteem. And yet he, at this time, gave the most abundant proofs alike of his contempt of riches and of his humanity and good-nature. And at Rome, when he was created consul in name, but indeed received sovereign and dictatorial authority against Catiline and his conspirators, he attested the truth of Plato's prediction, that then the miseries of states would be at an end when, by a

happy fortune, supreme power, wisdom, and justice should be
united in one.

It is said, to the reproach of Demosthenes, that his eloquence
was mercenary; that he privately made orations for Phormion
and Apollodorus, though adversaries in the same cause; that
he was charged with moneys received from the King of Persia,
and condemned for bribes from Harpalus. And should we grant
that all those (and they are not few) who have made these
statements against him have spoken what is untrue, yet that
Demosthenes was not the character to look without desire on
the presents offered him out of respect and gratitude by royal
persons, and that one who lent money on maritime usury was
likely to be thus indifferent, is what we cannot assert. But
that Cicero refused, from the Sicilians when he was quæstor,
from the King of Cappadocia when he was proconsul, and from
his friends at Rome when he was in exile, many presents, though
urged to receive them, has been said already.

Moreover, Demosthenes's banishment was infamous, upon
conviction for bribery; Cicero's very honourable, for ridding
his country of a set of villains. Therefore, when Demosthenes
fled his country, no man regarded it; for Cicero's sake the senate
changed their habit, and put on mourning, and would not be
persuaded to make any act before Cicero's return was decreed.
Cicero, however, passed his exile idly in Macedonia. But the
very exile of Demosthenes made up a great part of the services
he did for his country; for he went through the cities of Greece,
and everywhere, as we have said, joined in the conflict on behalf
of the Grecians, driving out the Macedonian ambassadors, and
approving himself a much better citizen than Themistocles and
Alcibiades did in the like fortune. And, after his return, he
again devoted himself to the same public service, and continued
firm to his opposition to Antipater and the Macedonians.
Whereas Lælius reproached Cicero in the senate for sitting silent
when Cæsar, a beardless youth, asked leave to come forward,
contrary to the law, as a candidate for the consulship; and
Brutus, in his epistles, charges him with nursing and rearing a
greater and more heavy tyranny than that they had removed.

Finally, Cicero's death excites our pity; for an old man to be
miserably carried up and down by his servants, flying and hiding
himself from that death which was, in the course of nature, so
near at hand; and yet at last to be murdered. Demosthenes,
though he seemed at first a little to supplicate, yet, by his preparing and keeping the poison by him, demands our admiration;

and still more admirable was his using it. When the temple of the god no longer afforded him a sanctuary, he took refuge, as it were, at a mightier altar, freeing himself from arms and soldiers, and laughing to scorn the cruelty of Antipater.

## DEMETRIUS

INGENIOUS men have long observed a resemblance between the arts and the bodily senses. And they were first led to do so, I think, by noticing the way in which, both in the arts and with our senses, we examine opposites. Judgment once obtained, the use to which we put it differs in the two cases. Our senses are not meant to pick out black rather than white, to prefer sweet to bitter, or soft and yielding to hard and resisting objects all they have to do is to receive impressions as they occur, and report to the understanding the impressions as received. The arts, on the other hand, which reason institutes expressly to choose and obtain some suitable, and to refuse and get rid of some unsuitable object, have their proper concern in the consideration of the former; though, in a casual and contingent way, they must also, for the very rejection of them, pay attention to the latter. Medicine, to produce health, has to examine disease, and music, to create harmony, must investigate discord; and the supreme arts, of temperance, of justice, and of wisdom, as they are acts of judgment and selection, exercised not on good and just and expedient only, but also on wicked, unjust, and inexpedient objects, do not give their commendations to the mere innocence whose boast is its inexperience of evil, and whose truer name is, by their award, simpleness and ignorance of what all men who live aright should know. The ancient Spartans, at their festivals, used to force their Helots to swallow large quantities of raw wine, and then to expose them at the public tables, to let the young men see what it is to be drunk. And, though I do not think it consistent with humanity or with civil justice to correct one man's morals by corrupting those of another, yet we may, I think, avail ourselves of the cases of those who have fallen into indiscretions, and have, in high stations, made themselves conspicuous for misconduct; and I shall not do ill to introduce a pair or two of such examples among these biographies, not, assuredly, to amuse and divert my readers, or give variety to my theme, but as Ismenias, the Theban, used to show his scholars good and bad performers on the flute, and to tell them, " You should play like this man," and, " You should not play like that," and as Antigenidas used to say, Young people would take greater pleasure in hearing good playing, if first they were set to hear bad, so, in the same manner, it seems to me likely enough that we shall be all the more zealous and more emulous to read, observe, and imitate the better lives, if we are not left in ignorance of the blameworthy and the bad.

For this reason, the following book contains the lives of Demetrius Poliorcetes and Antonius the Triumvir; two persons who have abundantly justified the words of Plato, that great natures produce great vices as well as virtues. Both alike were amorous and intemperate, warlike and munificent, sumptuous in their way of living and overbearing in their manners. And the likeness of their fortunes carried out the resemblance in their characters. Not only were their lives each a series of great successes and great disasters, mighty acquisitions and tremendous losses of power, sudden overthrows followed by unexpected recoveries, but they died, also, Demetrius in actual captivity to his enemies and Antony on the verge of it.

Antigonus had by his wife, Stratonice, the daughter of Corrhæus, two sons; the one of whom, after the name of his uncle, he called Demetrius, the other had that of his grandfather Philip, and died young. This is the most general account, although some have related that Demetrius was not the son of Antigonus, but of his brother; and that his own father dying young, and his mother being afterwards married to Antigonus, he was accounted to be his son.

Demetrius had not the height of his father Antigonus, though he was a tall man. But his countenance was one of such singular beauty and expression that no painter or sculptor ever produced a good likeness of him. It combined grace and strength, dignity with boyish bloom, and, in the midst of youthful heat and passion, what was hardest of all to represent was a certain heroic look and air of kingly greatness. Nor did his character belie his looks, as no one was better able to render himself both loved and feared. For as he was the most easy and agreeable of companions, and the most luxurious and delicate of princes in his drinking and banqueting and daily pleasures, so in action there was never any one that showed a more vehement persistence, or a more passionate energy. Bacchus, skilled in the conduct of war, and after war in giving peace its pleasures and joys, seems to have been his pattern among the gods.

He was wonderfully fond of his father Antigonus; and the tenderness he had for his mother led him, for her sake, to redouble attentions, which it was evident were not so much owing to fear or duty as to the more powerful motives of inclination. It is reported that, returning one day from hunting, he went immediately into the apartment of Antigonus, who was conversing with some ambassadors, and after stepping up and kissing his father, he sat down by him, just as he was, still holding in his hand the javelins which he had brought with him. Whereupon Antigonus, who had just dismissed the ambassadors with their answer, called out in a loud voice to them, as they were going, "Mention, also, that this is the way in which we two live together;" as if to imply to them that it was no slender mark of the power and security of his government that there was so perfect good understanding between himself and his son. Such an unsociable, solitary thing is power, and so much of jealousy and distrust in it, that the first and greatest of the successors of Alexander could make it a thing to glory in that he was not so afraid of his son as to forbid his standing beside him with a weapon in his hand. And, in fact, among all the successors of Alexander, that of Antigonus was the only house which, for many descents, was exempted from crime of this kind; or to state it exactly, Philip was the only one of this family who was guilty of a son's death. All the other families, we may fairly say, afforded frequent examples of fathers who brought their children, husbands their wives, children their mothers, to untimely ends; and that brothers should put brothers to death was assumed, like the postulate of mathematicians, as the common and recognised royal first principle of safety.

Let us here record an example in the early life of Demetrius, showing his natural humane and kindly disposition. It was an adventure which passed betwixt him and Mithridates, the son of Ariobarzanes, who was about the same age with Demetrius, and lived with him, in attendance on Antigonus; and although nothing was said or could be said to his reproach, he fell under suspicion, in consequence of a dream which Antigonus had. Antigonus thought himself in a fair and spacious field, where he sowed golden seed, and saw presently a golden crop come up; of which, however, looking presently again, he saw nothing remain but the stubble, without the ears. And as he stood by in anger and vexation, he heard some voices saying Mithridates had cut the golden harvest and carried it off into Pontus. Antigonus, much discomposed with his dream, first bound his son by an oath not to speak, and then related it to him, adding that he had resolved, in consequence, to lose no time in ridding himself of Mithridates, and making away with him. Demetrius was extremely distressed; and when the young man came, as usual, to pass his time with him, to keep his oath he forbore from saying a word, but, drawing him aside little by little from the company, as soon as they were by themselves, without opening his lips, with the point of his javelin he traced before him the words "Fly, Mithridates." Mithridates took the hint, and fled by night into Cappadocia, where Antigonus's dream about him was quickly brought to its due fulfilment; for he got possession of a large and fertile territory; and from him descended the line of the kings of Pontus, which, in the eighth generation, was reduced by the Romans. This may serve for a specimen of the early goodness and love of justice that was part of Demetrius's natural character.

But as in the elements of the world, Empedocles tells us, out of liking and dislike, there spring up contention and warfare, and all the more, the closer the contact, or the nearer the approach of the objects, even so the perpetual hostilities among the successors of Alexander were aggravated and inflamed, in particular cases, by juxtaposition of interests and of territories; as, for example, in the case of Antigonus and Ptolemy. News came to Antigonus that Ptolemy had crossed from Cyprus and invaded Syria, and was ravaging the country and reducing the cities. Remaining, therefore, himself in Phrygia, he sent Demetrius, now twenty-two years old, to make his first essay as sole commander in an important charge. He, whose youthful heat outran his experience, advancing against an adversary trained in Alexander's school, and practised in many encounters, incurred a great defeat near the town of Gaza, in which eight thousand of his men were taken and five thousand killed. His own tent, also his money, and all his private effects and furniture, were captured. These, however, Ptolemy sent back, together with his friends, accompanying them with the humane and courteous message, that they were not fighting for anything else but honour and dominion. Demetrius accepted the gift, praying only to the gods not to leave him long in Ptolemy's debt, but to let him have an early chance of doing the like to him. He took his disaster, also, with the temper, not of a boy defeated in his attempt, but of an old and long-tried general familiar with reverse of fortune; he busied himself in collecting his men, replenishing his magazines, watching the allegiance of the cities, and drilling his new recruits.

Antigonus received the news of the battle with the remark that Ptolemy had beaten boys and would now have to fight with men. But not to humble the spirit of his son, he acceded to his request, and left him to command on the next occasion.

Not long after, Cilles, Ptolemy's lieutenant, with a powerful army, took the field, and looking upon Demetrius as already defeated by the previous battle, he had in his imagination driven him out of Syria before he saw him. But he quickly found himself deceived; for Demetrius came so unexpectedly upon him that he surprised both the general and his army, making him and seven thousand of the soldiers prisoners of war, and possessing himself of a large amount of treasure. But his joy in the victory was not so much for the prizes he should keep, as for those he could restore; and his thankfulness was less for the wealth and glory than for the means it gave him of requiting his enemy's former generosity. He did not, however, take it into his own hands, but wrote to his father. And on receiving leave to do as he liked, he sent back to Ptolemy Cilles and his friends, loaded with presents. This defeat drove Ptolemy out of Syria, and brought Antigonus from Celænæ to enjoy the victory and the sight of the son who had gained it.

Soon after, Demetrius was sent to bring the Nabathæan Arabs into obedience. And here he got into a district without water, and incurred considerable danger, but by his resolute and composed demeanour he overawed the barbarians, and returned after receiving from them a large amount of booty and seven hundred camels. Not long after, Seleucus, whom Antigonus had formerly chased out of Babylon, but who had afterwards recovered his dominion by his own efforts and maintained himself in it, went with large forces on an expedition to reduce the tribes on the confines of India and the provinces near Mount Caucasus. And Demetrius, conjecturing that he had left Mesopotamia but slenderly guarded in his absence, suddenly passed the Euphrates with his army and made his way into Babylonia unexpectedly; when he succeeded in capturing one of the two citadels, out of which he expelled the garrison of Seleucus, and placed in it seven thousand men of his own. And after allowing his soldiers to enrich themselves with all the spoil they could carry with them out of the country, he retired to the sea, leaving Seleucus more securely master of his dominions than before, as he seemed by this conduct to abandon every claim to a country which he treated like an enemy's.   However, by a rapid advance, he rescued Halicarnassus from Ptolemy, who was besieging it. The glory which this act obtained them inspired both the father and son with a wonderful desire for freeing Greece, which Cassander and Ptolemy had everywhere reduced to slavery. No nobler or juster war was undertaken by any of the kings; the wealth they had gained while humbling, with Greek assistance, the barbarians, being thus employed, for honour's sake and good repute, in helping the Greeks.   When the resolution was taken to begin their attempt with Athens, one of his friends told Antigonus, if they captured Athens, they must keep it safe in their own hands, as by this gangway they might step out from their ships into Greece when they pleased.   But Antigonus would not hear of it; he did not want a better or a steadier gangway than people's good-will; and from Athens, the beacon of the world, the news of their conduct would soon be handed on to all the world's inhabitants.   So Demetrius, with a sum of five thousand talents, and a fleet of two hundred and fifty ships, set sail for Athens, where Demetrius the Phalerian was governing the city for Cassander, with a garrison lodged in the port of Munychia.   By good fortune and skilful management he appeared before Piræus, on the twenty-sixth of Thargelion, before anything had been heard of him.   Indeed, when his ships were seen, they were taken for Ptolemy's, and preparations were commenced for receiving them; till at last, the generals discovering their mistake, hurried down, and all was alarm and confusion, and attempts to push forward preparations to oppose the landing of this hostile force.   For Demetrius, having found the entrances of the port undefended, stood in directly, and was by this time safely inside, before the eyes of everybody, and made signals from his ship, requesting a peaceable hearing. And on leave being given, he caused a herald with a loud voice to make proclamation that he was come thither by the command of his father, with no other design than what he prayed the gods to prosper with success, to give the Athenians their liberty, to expel the garrison, and to restore the ancient laws and constitution of the country.

The people, hearing this, at once threw down their shields, and clapping their hands, with loud acclamations entreated Demetrius to land, calling him their deliverer and benefactor. And the Phalerian and his party, who saw that there was nothing for it but to receive the conqueror, whether he should

perform his promises or not, sent, however, messengers to beg
for his protection; to whom Demetrius gave a kind reception,
and sent back with them Aristodemus of Miletus, one of his
father's friends. The Phalerian, under the change of government, was more afraid of his fellow-citizens than of the enemy;
but Demetrius took precautions for him, and out of respect for
his reputation and character, sent him with a safe conduct to
Thebes, whither he desired to go. For himself, he declared he
would not, in spite of all his curiosity, put his foot in the city
till he had completed his deliverance by driving out the garrison.
So blockading Munychia with a palisade and trench, he sailed
off to attack Megara, where also there was one of Cassander's
garrisons. But, hearing that Cratesipolis, the wife of Alexander,
son of Polysperchon, who was famous for her beauty, was well
disposed to see him, he left his troops near Megara, and set out
with a few light-armed attendants for Patræ, where she was now
staying. And, quitting these also, he pitched his tent apart
from everybody, that the woman might pay her visit without
being seen. This some of the enemy perceived, and suddenly
attacked him; and, in his alarm, he was obliged to disguise
himself in a shabby cloak, and run for it, narrowly escaping the
shame of being made a prisoner, in reward for his foolish passion.
And as it was, his tent and money were taken. Megara, however,
surrendered, and would have been pillaged by the soldiers, but
for the urgent intercession of the Athenians. The garrison was
driven out, and the city restored to independence. While he
was occupied in this, he remembered that Stilpo, the philosopher,
famous for his choice of a life of tranquillity, was residing here.
He, therefore, sent for him, and begged to know whether anything belonging to him had been taken. " No," replied Stilpo,
" I have not met with any one to take away knowledge."
Pretty nearly all the servants in the city had been stolen away;
and so, when Demetrius, renewing his courtesies to Stilpo, on
taking leave of him, said, " I leave your city, Stilpo, a city of
freemen." " Certainly," replied Stilpo, " there is not one serving
man left among us all."

Returning from Megara, he sat down before the citadel of
Munychia, which in a few days he took by assault, and caused the
fortifications to be demolished; and thus having accomplished
his design, upon the request and invitation of the Athenians
he made his entrance into the upper city, where, causing the
people to be summoned, he publicly announced to them that
their ancient constitution was restored, and that they should

receive from his father, Antigonus, a present of one hundred and fifty thousand measures of wheat, and such a supply of timber as would enable them to build a hundred galleys. In this manner did the Athenians recover their popular institutions, after the space of fifteen years from the time of the war of Lamia and the battle before Cranon, during which interval of time the government had been administered nominally as an oligarchy, but really by a single man, Demetrius the Phalerian being so powerful. But the excessive honours which the Athenians bestowed, for these noble and generous acts, upon Demetrius, created offence and disgust. The Athenians were the first who gave Antigonus and Demetrius the title of kings, which hitherto they had made it a point of piety to decline, as the one remaining royal honour still reserved for the lineal descendants of Philip and Alexander, in which none but they could venture to participate. Another name which they received from no people but the Athenians was that of the Tutelar Dieties and Deliverers. And to enhance this flattery, by a common vote it was decreed to change the style of the city, and not to have the years named any longer from the annual archon; a priest of the two Tutelary Divinities, who was to be yearly chosen, was to have this honour, and all public acts and instruments were to bear their date by his name. They decreed, also, that the figures of Antigonus and Demetrius should be woven, with those of the gods, into the pattern of the great robe. They consecrated the spot where Demetrius first alighted from his chariot, and built an altar there, with the name of the Altar of the Descent of Demetrius. They created two new tribes, calling them after the names of these princes, the Antigonid and the Demetriad; and to the Council, which consisted of five hundred persons, fifty being chosen out of every tribe, they added one hundred more to represent these new tribes. But the wildest proposal was one made by Stratocles, the great inventor of all these ingenious and exquisite compliments, enacting that the members of any deputation that the city should send to Demetrius or Antigonus should have the same title as those sent to Delphi or Olympia for the performance of the national sacrifices in behalf of the state at the great Greek festivals. This Stratocles was, in all respects, an audacious and abandoned character, and seemed to have made it his object to copy, by his buffoonery and impertinence, Cleon's old familiarity with the people. His mistress, Phylacion, one day bringing him a dish of brains and neckbones for his dinner, " Oh," said he, " I am to dine upon the things which we statesmen play at ball with." At another time, when the Athenians received their naval defeat near Amorgos, he hastened home before the news could reach the city, and having a chaplet on his head, came riding through the Ceramicus, announcing that they had won a victory, and moved a vote for thanksgivings to the gods, and a distribution of meat among the people in their tribes. Presently after came those who brought home the wrecks from the battle; and when the people exclaimed at what he had done, he came boldly to face the outcry, and asked what harm there had been in giving them two days' pleasure.

Such was Stratocles. And, " adding flame to fire," as Aristophanes says, there was one who, to outdo Stratocles, proposed that it should be decreed that, whensoever Demetrius should honour their city with his presence, they should treat him with the same show of hospitable entertainment with which Ceres and Bacchus are received; and the citizen who exceeded the rest in the splendour and costliness of his reception should have a sum of money granted him from the public purse to make a sacred offering. Finally, they changed the name of the month of Munychion, and called it Demetrion; they gave the name of the Demetrion to the odd day between the end of the old and the beginning of the new month; and turned the feast of Bacchus, the Dionysia, into the Demetria or feast of Demetrius. Most of these changes were marked by the divine displeasure. The sacred robe, in which, according to their decree, the figures of Demetrius and Antigonus had been woven with those of Jupiter and Minerva, was caught by a violent gust of wind, while the procession was conveying it through the Ceramicus, and was torn from the top to the bottom. A crop of hemlock, a plant which scarcely grew anywhere, even in the country thereabouts, sprang up in abundance round the altars which they had erected to these new divinities. They had to omit the solemn procession at the feast of Bacchus, as upon the very day of its celebration there was such a severe and rigorous frost, coming quite out of its time, that not only the vines and figtrees were killed, but almost all the wheat was destroyed in the blade. Accordingly, Philippides, an enemy to Stratocles, attacked him in a comedy, in the following verses:—

> " He for whom frosts that nipped your vines were sent,
> And for whose sins the holy robe was rent,
> Who grants to men the gods' own honours, he,
> Not the poor stage, is now the people's enemy."

Philippides was a great favourite with King Lysimachus, from whom the Athenians received, for his sake, a variety of kindnesses. Lysimachus went so far as to think it a happy omen to meet or see Philippides at the outset of any enterprise or expedition. And, in general, he was well thought of for his own character, as a plain, uninterfering person, with none of the officious, self-important habits of a court. Once, when Lysimachus was solicitous to show him kindness, and asked what he had that he could make him a present of, " Anything," replied Philippides, " but your state secrets." The stage-player, we thought, deserved a place in our narrative quite as well as the public speaker.

But that which exceeded all the former follies and flatteries was the proposal of Dromoclides of Sphettus; who, when there was a debate about sending to the Delphic Oracle to inquire the proper course for the consecration of certain bucklers, moved in the assembly that they should rather send to receive an oracle from Demetrius. I will transcribe the very words of the order, which was in these terms: " May it be happy and propitious. The people of Athens have decreed, that a fit person shall be chosen among the Athenian citizens, who shall be deputed to be sent to the Deliverer; and after he hath duly performed the sacrifices, shall inquire of the Deliverer, in what most religious and decent manner he will please to direct, at the earliest possible time, the consecration of the bucklers; and according to the answer the people shall act." With this befooling they completed the perversion of a mind which even before was not so strong or sound as it should have been.

During his present leisure in Athens, he took to wife Eurydice, a descendant of the ancient Miltiades, who had been married to Opheltas, the ruler of Cyrene, and after his death had come back to Athens. The Athenians took the marriage as a compliment and favour to the city. But Demetrius was very free in these matters, and was the husband of several wives at once; the highest place and honour among all being retained by Phila, who was Antipater's daughter, and had been the wife of Craterus, the one of all the successors of Alexander who left behind him the strongest feelings of attachment among the Macedonians. And for these reasons Antigonus had obliged him to marry her, notwithstanding the disparity of their years, Demetrius being quite a youth, and she much older; and when upon that account he made some difficulty in complying, Antigonus whispered in his ear the maxim from Euripides, broadly substituting a new word for the original, *serve*—

> " Natural or not,
> A man must *wed* where profit will be got."

Any respect, however, which he showed either to Phila or to his other wives did not go so far as to prevent him from consorting with any number of mistresses, and bearing, in this respect, the worst character of all the princes of his time.

A summons now arrived from his father, ordering him to go and fight with Ptolemy in Cyprus, which he was obliged to obey, sorry as he was to abandon Greece. And in quitting this nobler and more glorious enterprise, he sent to Cleonides, Ptolemy's general, who was holding garrisons in Sicyon and Corinth, offering him money to let the cities be independent. But on his refusal, he set sail hastily, taking additional forces with him, and made for Cyprus; where, immediately upon his arrival, he fell upon Menelaus, the brother of Ptolemy, and gave him a defeat. But when Ptolemy himself came in person, with large forces both on land and sea, for some little time nothing took place beyond an interchange of menaces and lofty talk. Ptolemy bade Demetrius sail off before the whole armament came up, if he did not wish to be trampled under foot; and Demetrius offered to let him retire, on condition of his withdrawing his garrisons from Sicyon and Corinth. And not they alone, but all the other potentates and princes of the time, were in anxiety for the uncertain impending issue of the conflict; as it seemed evident that the conqueror's prize would be, not Cyprus or Syria, but the absolute supremacy.

Ptolemy had brought a hundred and fifty galleys with him, and gave orders to Menelaus to sally, in the heat of the battle, out of the harbour of Salamis, and attack with sixty ships the rear of Demetrius, Demetrius, however, opposing to these sixty ten of his galleys, which were a sufficient number to block up the narrow entrance of the harbour, and drawing out his land forces along all the headlands running out into sea, went into action with a hundred and eighty galleys, and, attacking with the utmost boldness and impetuosity, utterly routed Ptolemy, who fled with eight ships, the sole remnant of his fleet, seventy having been taken with all their men, and the rest destroyed in the battle; while the whole multitude of attendants, friends, and women, that had followed in the ships of burden, all the arms, treasure, and military engines fell, without exception, into the hands of Demetrius, and were by him collected and brought into the camp. Among the prisoners was the celebrated Lamia, famed at one time for her skill on the flute, and afterwards renowned as a mistress. And although now upon the wane of her youthful beauty, and though Demetrius was much her junior, she exercised over him so great a charm that all other women seemed to be amorous of Demetrius, but Demetrius amorous only of Lamia. After this signal victory, Demetrius came before Salamis; and Menelaus, unable to make any resistance, surrendered himself and all his fleet, twelve hundred horse, and twelve thousand foot, together with the place. But that which added more than all to the glory and splendour of the success was the humane and generous conduct of Demetrius to the vanquished. For, after he had given honourable funerals to the dead, he bestowed liberty upon the living; and that he might not forget the Athenians, he sent them, as a present, complete arms for twelve hundred men.

To carry this happy news, Aristodemus of Miletus, the most perfect flatterer belonging to the court, was despatched to Antigonus; and he, to enhance the welcome message, was resolved, it would appear, to make his most successful effort. When he crossed from Cyprus, he bade the galley which conveyed him to come to anchor off the land; and, having ordered all the ship's crew to remain aboard, he took the boat, and was set ashore alone. Thus he proceeded to Antigonus, who, one may well imagine, was in suspense enough about the issue, and suffered all the anxieties natural to men engaged in so perilous a struggle. And when he heard that Aristodemus was coming alone, it put him into yet greater trouble; he could scarcely forbear from going out to meet him himself; he sent messenger on messenger, and friend after friend, to inquire what news. But Aristodemus, walking gravely and with a settled countenance, without making any answer, still proceeded quietly onward; until Antigonus, quite alarmed and no longer able to refrain, got up and met him at the gate, whither he came with a crowd of anxious followers now collected and running after him. As soon as he saw Antigonus within hearing stretching out his hands, he accosted him with the loud exclamation, " Hail, King Antigonus! we have defeated Ptolemy by sea, and have taken Cyprus and sixteen thousand eight hundred prisoners." " Welcome, Aristodemus," replied Antigonus, " but, as you chose to torture us so long for your good news, you may wait awhile for the reward of it."

Upon this the people around gave Antigonus and Demetrius,

for the first time, the title of kings. His friends at once set a diadem on the head of Antigonus; and he sent one presently to his son, with a letter addressed to him as King Demetrius. And when this news was told in Egypt, that they might not seem to be dejected with the late defeat, Ptolemy's followers also took occasion to bestow the style of king upon him; and the rest of the successors of Alexander were quick to follow the example. Lysimachus began to wear the diadem, and Seleucus, who had before received the name in all addresses from the barbarians, now also took it upon him in all business with the Greeks. Cassander still retained his usual superscription in his letters, but others, both in writing and speaking, gave him the royal title. Nor was this the mere accession of a name, or introduction of a new fashion. The men's own sentiments about themselves were disturbed, and their feelings elevated; a spirit of pomp and arrogance passed into their habits of life and conversation, as a tragic actor on the stage modifies, with a change of dress, his steps, his voice, his motions in sitting down, his manner in addressing another. The punishments they inflicted were more violent after they had thus laid aside that modest style under which they formerly dissembled their power, and the influence of which had often made them gentler and less exacting to their subjects. A single flattering voice effected a revolution in the world.

Antigonus, extremely elevated with the success of his arms in Cyprus, under the conduct of Demetrius, resolved to push on his good fortune, and to lead his forces in person against Ptolemy by land whilst Demetrius should coast with a great fleet along the shore, to assist him by sea. The issue of the contest was intimated in a dream which Medius, a friend to Antigonus, had at this time in his sleep. He thought he saw Antigonus and his whole army running, as if it had been a race; that, in the first part of the course, he went off showing great strength and speed; gradually, however, his pace slackened, and at the end he saw him come lagging up, tired and almost breathless and quite spent. Antigonus himself met with many difficulties by land; and Demetrius, encountering a great storm at sea, was driven, with the loss of many of his ships, upon a dangerous coast without a harbour. So the expedition returned without effecting anything. Antigonus, now nearly eighty years old, was no longer well able to go through the fatigues of a marching campaign, though rather on account of his great size and corpulence than from loss of strength; and for this reason he left things to his

son, whose fortune and experience appeared sufficient for all
undertakings, and whose luxury and expense and revelry gave
him no concern. For though in peace he vented himself in
pleasures, and, when there was nothing to do, ran headlong into
any excesses, in war he was as sober and abstemious as the most
temperate character. The story is told that once, after Lamia
had gained open supremacy over him, the old man, when
Demetrius coming home from abroad began to kiss him with
unusual warmth, asked him if he took him for Lamia. At
another time, Demetrius, after spending several days in a
debauch, excused himself for his absence, by saying he had had
a violent flux. "So I heard," replied Antigonus; "was it of
Thasian wine, or Chian?" Once he was told his son was ill,
and went to see him. At the door he met some young beauty.
Going in, he sat down by the bed and took his pulse. "The
fever," said Demetrius, "has just left me." "Oh yes," replied
the father, "I met it going out at the door." Demetrius's great
actions made Antigonus treat him thus easily. The Scythians
in their drinking-bouts twang their bows, to keep their courage
awake amidst the dreams of indulgence; but he would resign
his whole being, now to pleasure, and now to action; and though
he never let thoughts of the one intrude upon the pursuit of the
other, yet when the time came for preparing for war, he showed
as much capacity as any man.

And indeed his ability displayed itself even more in preparing
for than in conducting a war. He thought he could never be
too well supplied for every possible occasion, and took a pleasure,
not to be satiated, in great improvements in ship-building and
machines. He did not waste his natural genius and power of
mechanical research on toys and idle fancies, turning, painting,
and playing on the flute, like some kings, Æropus, for example,
King of Macedon, who spent his days in making small lamps
and tables; or Attalus Philometor, whose amusement was to
cultivate poisons, henbane and hellebore, and even hemlock,
aconite, and dorycnium, which he used to sow himself in the
royal gardens, and made it his business to gather the fruits and
collect the juices in their season. The Parthian kings took a
pride in whetting and sharpening with their own hands the
points of their arrows and javelins. But when Demetrius played
the workman, it was like a king, and there was magnificence in
his handicraft. The articles he produced bore marks upon the
face of them not of ingenuity only, but of a great mind and a lofty
purpose. They were such as a king might not only design and

pay for, but use his own hands to make; and while friends might be terrified with their greatness, enemies could be charmed with their beauty; a phrase which is not so pretty to the ear as it is true to the fact. The very people against whom they were to be employed could not forbear running to gaze with admiration upon his galleys of five and six ranges of oars, as they passed along their coasts; and the inhabitants of besieged cities came on their walls to see the spectacles of his famous *City-takers*. Even Lysimachus, of all the kings of his time the greatest enemy of Demetrius, coming to raise the siege of Soli in Cilicia, sent first to desire permission to see his galleys and engines, and, having had his curiosity gratified by a view of them, expressed his admiration and quitted the place. The Rhodians, also, whom he long besieged, begged him, when they concluded a peace, to let them have some of his engines, which they might preserve as a memorial at once of his power and of their own brave resistance.

The quarrel between him and the Rhodians was on account of their being allies to Ptolemy, and in the siege the greatest of all the engines was planted against their walls. The base of it was exactly square, each side containing twenty-four cubits; it rose to a height of thirty-three cubits, growing narrower from the base to the top. Within were several apartments or chambers, which were to be filled with armed men, and in every story the front towards the enemy had windows for discharging missiles of all sorts, the whole being filled with soldiers for every description of fighting. And what was most wonderful was that, notwithstanding its size, when it was moved it never tottered or inclined to one side, but went forward on its base in perfect equilibrium, with a loud noise and great impetus, astounding the minds, and yet at the same time charming the eyes of all the beholders.

Whilst Demetrius was at this same siege, there were brought to him two iron cuirasses from Cyprus, weighing each of them no more than forty pounds, and Zoilus, who had forged them, to show the excellence of their temper, desired that one of them might be tried with a catapult missile, shot out of one of the engines at no greater dstance than six-and-twenty paces; and, upon the experiment, it was found that though the dart exactly hit the cuirass, yet it made no greater impression than such a slight scratch as might be made with the point of a style or graver. Demetrius took this for his own wearing, and gave the other to Alcimus the Epirot, the best soldier and strongest man of all his captains, the only one who used to wear armour to the weight of two talents, one talent being the weight which others thought sufficient. He fell during this siege in a battle near the theatre.

The Rhodians made a brave defence, insomuch that Demetrius saw he was making but little progress, and only persisted out of obstinacy and passion; and the rather because the Rhodians, having captured a ship in which some clothes and furniture, with letters from herself, were coming to him from Phila his wife, had sent on everything to Ptolemy, and had not copied the honourable example of the Athenians, who, having surprised an express sent from King Philip, their enemy, opened all the letters he was charged with, excepting only those directed to Queen Olympias, which they returned with the seal unbroken. Yet, although greatly provoked, Demetrius, into whose power it shortly after came to repay the affront, would not suffer himself to retaliate. Protogenes the Caunian had been making them a painting of the story of Ialysus, which was all but completed, when it was taken by Demetrius in one of the suburbs. The Rhodians sent a herald begging him to be pleased to spare the work and not let it be destroyed; Demetrius's answer to which was that he would rather burn the pictures of his father than a piece of art which had cost so much labour. It is said to have taken Protogenes seven years to paint, and they tell us that Apelles, when he first saw it, was struck dumb with wonder, and called it, on recovering his speech, "a great labour and a wonderful success," adding, however, that it had not the graces which carried his own paintings as it were up to the heavens. This picture, which came with the rest in the general mass to Rome, there perished by fire.

While the Rhodians were thus defending their city to the utmost, Demetrius, who was not sorry for an excuse to retire, found one in the arrival of ambassadors from Athens, by whose mediation terms were made that the Rhodians should bind themselves to aid Antigonus and Demetrius against all enemies, Ptolemy excepted.

The Athenians entreated his help against Cassander, who was besieging the city. So he went thither with a fleet of three hundred and thirty ships, and many soldiers; and not only drove Cassander out of Attica, but pursued him as far as Thermopylæ, routed him and became master of Heraclea, which came over to him voluntarily, and of a body of six thousand

Macedonians, which also joined him. Returning hence, he gave their liberty to all the Greeks on this side Thermopylæ, and made alliance with the Bœotians, took Cenchreæ, and reducing the fortresses of Phyle and Panactum, in which were garrisons of Cassander, restored them to the Athenians. They, in requital, though they had before been so profuse in bestowing honours upon him that one would have thought they had exhausted all the capacities of invention, showed they had still new refinements of adulation to devise for him. They gave him, as his lodging, the back temple in the Parthenon, and here he lived, under the immediate roof, as they meant it to imply, of his hostess, Minerva—no reputable or well-conducted guest to be quartered upon a maiden goddess! When his brother Philip was once put into a house where three young women were living, Antigonus, saying nothing to him, sent for his quartermaster, and told him, in the young man's presence, to find some less crowded lodgings for him.

Demetrius, however, who should, to say the least, have paid the goddess the respect due to an elder sister, for that was the purport of the city's compliment, filled the temple with such pollutions that the place seemed least profaned when his licence confined itself to common women like Chrysis, Lamia, Demo, and Anticyra.

The fair name of the city forbids any further plain particulars; let us only record the severe virtue of the young Damocles, surnamed, and by that surname pointed out to Demetrius, the beautiful; who, to escape importunities, avoided every place of resort, and when at last followed into a private bathing room by Demetrius, seeing none at hand to help or deliver, seized the lid from the cauldron, and, plunging into the boiling water, sought a death untimely and unmerited, but worthy of the country and of the beauty that occasioned it. Not so Cleænetus, the son of Cleomedon, who, to obtain from Demetrius a letter of intercession to the people in behalf of his father, lately condemned in a fine of fifty talents, disgraced himself, and got the city into trouble. In deference to the letter, they remitted the fine, yet they made an edict prohibiting any citizen for the future to bring letters from Demetrius. But being informed that Demetrius resented this as a great indignity, they not only rescinded in alarm the former order, but put some of the proposers and advisers of it to death and banished others, and furthermore enacted and decreed, that whatsoever King Demetrius should in time to come ordain, should be accounted right

towards the gods and just towards men; and when one of the
better class of citizens said Stratocles must be mad to use such
words, Demochares of Leuconoe observed he would be a fool
not to be mad. For Stratocles was well rewarded for his
flatteries; and the saying was remembered against Demochares,
who was soon after sent into banishment. So fared the Athenians, after being relieved of the foreign garrison, and recovering
what was called their liberty.

After this Demetrius marched with his forces into Peloponnesus, where he met with none to oppose him, his enemies flying
before him, and allowing the cities to join him. He received
into friendship all Acte, as it is called, and all Arcadia except
Mantinea. He bought the liberty of Argos, Corinth, and Sicyon,
by paying a hundred talents to their garrisons to evacuate them.
At Argos, during the feast of Juno, which happened at the time,
he presided at the games, and, joining in the festivities with the
multitude of the Greeks assembled there, he celebrated his
marriage with Deidamia, daughter of Æacides, King of the
Molossians, and sister of Pyrrhus. At Sicyon he told the people
they had put the city just outside of the city, and, persuading
them to remove to where they now live, gave their town not
only a new site but a new name, Demetrias, after himself. A
general assembly met on the Isthmus, where he was proclaimed,
by a great concourse of the people, the Commander of Greece,
like Philip and Alexander of old; whose superior he, in the
present height of his prosperity and power, was willing enough
to consider himself; and certainly, in one respect, he outdid
Alexander, who never refused their title to other kings, or took
on himself the style of king of kings, though many kings received
both their title and their authority as such from him; whereas
Demetrius used to ridicule those who gave the name of king to
any except himself and his father; and in his entertainments
was well pleased when his followers, after drinking to him and
his father as kings, went on to drink the healths of Seleucus,
with the title of Master of the Elephants; of Ptolemy, by the
name of High Admiral; of Lysimachus, with the addition of
Treasurer; and of Agathocles, with the style of Governor of the
Island of Sicily. The other kings merely laughed when they
were told of this vanity; Lysimachus alone expressed some
indignation at being considered a eunuch, such being usually
then selected for the office of treasurer. And, in general, there
was a more bitter enmity between him and Lysimachus than
with any of the others. Once, as a scoff at his passion for Lamia,

Lysimachus said he had never before seen a courtesan act a queen's part; to which Demetrius rejoined that his mistress was quite as honest as Lysimachus's own Penelope.

But to proceed. Demetrius being about to return to Athens, signified by letter to the city that he desired immediate admission to the rites of initiation into the Mysteries, and wished to go through all the stages of the ceremony, from first to last, without delay. This was absolutely contrary to the rules, and a thing which had never been allowed before; for the lesser mysteries were celebrated in the month of Anthesterion, and the great solemnity in Boëdromion, and none of the novices were finally admitted till they had completed a year after this latter. Yet all this notwithstanding, when in the public assembly these letters of Demetrius were produced and read, there was not one single person who had the courage to oppose them, except Pythodorus, the torch-bearer. But it signified nothing, for Stratocles at once proposed that the month of Munychion, then current, should by edict be reputed to be the month of Anthesterion; which being voted and done, and Demetrius thereby admitted to the lesser ceremonies, by another vote they turned the same month of Munychion into the other month of Boëdromion; the celebration of the greater mysteries ensued, and Demetrius was fully admitted. These proceedings gave the comedian, Philippides, a new occasion to exercise his wit upon Stratocles—

" ——whose flattering fear
Into one month hath crowded all the year."

And on the vote that Demetrius should lodge in the Parthenon—

" Who turns the temple to a common inn,
And makes the Virgin's house a house of sin."

Of all the disreputable and flagitious acts of which he was guilty in this visit, one that particularly hurt the feelings of the Athenians was that, having given command that they should forthwith raise for his service two hundred and fifty talents, and they to comply with his demands being forced to levy it upon the people with the utmost rigour and severity, when they presented him with the money which they had with such difficulty raised, as if it were a trifling sum, he ordered it to be given to Lamia and the rest of his women, to buy soap. The loss, which was bad enough, was less galling than the shame, and the words more intolerable than the act which they accompanied. Though, indeed, the story is variously reported; and some say it was the Thessalians, and not the Athenians, who were thus treated. Lamia, however, exacted contributions herself to pay for an entertainment she gave to the king, and her banquet was so renowned for its sumptuosity that a description of it was drawn up by the Samian writer, Lynceus. Upon this occasion, one of the comic writers gave Lamia the name of the real *Helepolis;* and Demochares of Soli called Demetrius *Mythus*, because the fable always has its Lamia, and so had he.

And, in truth, his passion for this woman, and the prosperity in which she lived were such as to draw upon him not only the envy and jealousy of all his wives, but the animosity even of his friends. For example, on Lysimachus's showing to some ambassadors from Demetrius the scars of the wounds which he had received upon his thighs and arms by the paws of the lion with which Alexander had shut him up, after hearing his account of the combat, they smiled and answered, that their king, also, was not without his scars, but could show upon his neck the marks of a Lamia, a no less dangerous beast. It was also matter of wonder that, though he had objected so much to Phila on account of her age, he was yet such a slave to Lamia who was so long past her prime. One evening at supper, when she played the flute, Demetrius asked Demo, whom the men called Madness, what she thought of her. Demo answered she thought her an old woman. And when a quantity of sweetmeats were brought in, and the king said again, " See what presents I get from Lamia! " " My old mother," answered Demo, " will send you more, if you will make her your mistress." Another story is told of a criticism passed by Lamia on the famous judgment of Bocchoris. A young Egyptian had long made suit to Thonis, the courtesan, offering a sum of gold for her favour. But before it came to pass, he dreamed one night that he had obtained it, and, satisfied with the shadow, felt no more desire for the substance. Thonis upon this brought an action for the sum. Bocchoris, the judge, on hearing the case, ordered the defendant to bring into court the full amount in a vessel, which he was to move to and fro in his hand, and the shadow of it was to be adjudged to Thonis. The fairness of this sentence Lamia contested, saying the young man's desire might have been satisfied with the dream, but Thonis's desire for the money could not be relieved by the shadow. Thus much for Lamia.

And now the story passes from the comic to the tragic stage in pursuit of the acts and fortunes of its subjects. A general league of the kings, who were now gathering and combining their forces to attack Antigonus, recalled Demetrius from Greece. He was encouraged by finding his father full of a spirit and resolution for the combat that belied his years. Yet it would seem to be true, that if Antigonus could only have borne to make some trifling concessions, and if he had shown any moderation in his passion for empire, he might have maintained for himself till his death and left to his son behind him the first place among the kings. But he was of a violent and haughty spirit; and the insulting words as well as actions in which he allowed himself could not be borne by young and powerful princes, and provoked them into combining against him. Though now when he was told of the confederacy, he could not forbear from saying that this flock of birds would soon be scattered by one stone and a single shout. He took the field at the head of more than seventy thousand foot, and of ten thousand horse, and seventy-five elephants. His enemies had sixty-four thousand foot, five hundred more horse than he, elephants to the number of four hundred, and a hundred and twenty chariots. On their near approach to each other, an alteration began to be observable, not in the purposes, but in the presentiments of Antigonus. For whereas in all former campaigns he had ever shown himself lofty and confident, loud in voice and scornful in speech, often by some joke or mockery on the eve of battle expressing his contempt and displaying his composure, he was now remarked to be thoughtful, silent, and retired. He presented Demetrius to the army, and declared him his successor; and what every one thought stranger than all was that he now conferred alone in his tent with Demetrius; whereas in former time he had never entered into any secret consultations even with him; but had always followed his own advice, made his resolutions, and then given out his commands. Once when Demetrius was a boy and asked him how soon the army would move, he is said to have answered him sharply, " Are you afraid lest you, of all the army, should not hear the trumpet? "

There were now, however, inauspicious signs, which affected his spirits. Demetrius, in a dream, had seen Alexander, completely armed, appear and demand of him what word they intended to give in the time of the battle; and Demetrius answering that he intended the word should be " Jupiter and Victory," " Then," said Alexander, " I will go to your adversaries and find my welcome with them." And on the morning of the combat, as the armies were drawing up, Antigonus, going out of the door of his tent, by some accident or other, stumbled and fell flat upon the ground, hurting himself a good deal. And on recovering his feet, lifting up his hands to heaven, he prayed the gods to grant him, " either victory, or death without knowledge of defeat." When the armies engaged, Demetrius, who commanded the greatest and best part of the cavalry, made a charge on Antiochus, the son of Seleucus, and gloriously routing the enemy, followed the pursuit, in the pride and exultation of success, so eagerly, and so unwisely far, that it fatally lost him the day; for when, perceiving his error, he would have come in to the assistance of his own infantry, he was not able, the enemy with their elephants having cut off his retreat. And on the other hand, Seleucus, observing the main battle of Antigonus left naked of their horse, did not charge, but made a show of charging; and keeping them in alarm and wheeling about and still threatening an attack, he gave opportunity for those who wished it to separate and come over to him; which a large body of them did, the rest taking to flight. But the old King Antigonus still kept his post, and when a strong body of the enemies drew up to charge him, and one of those about him cried out to him, " Sir, they are coming upon you," he only replied, " What else should they do? but Demetrius will come to my rescue." And in this hope he persisted to the last, looking out on every side for his son's approach, until he was borne down by a whole multitude of darts, and fell. His other followers and friends fled, and Thorax of Larissa remained alone by the body.

The battle having been thus decided, the kings who had gained the victory, carving up the whole vast empire that had belonged to Demetrius and Antigonus, like a carcass, into so many portions, added these new gains to their former possessions. As for Demetrius, with five thousand foot and four thousand horse, he fled at his utmost speed to Ephesus, when it was the common opinion he would seize the treasures of the temple to relieve his wants; but he, on the contrary, fearing such an attempt on the part of his soldiers, hastened away, and sailed for Greece, his chief remaining hopes being placed in the fidelity of the Athenians, with whom he had left part of his navy and of his treasures and his wife Deidamia. And in their attachment he had not the least doubt but he should in this his extremity find a safe resource. Accordingly when, upon reaching the Cyclades, he was met by ambassadors from Athens, requesting him not to proceed to the city, as the people had passed a vote to admit no king whatever within their walls, and

had conveyed Deidamia with honourable attendance to Megara,
his anger and surprise overpowered him, and the constancy
quite failed him which he had hitherto shown in a wonderful
degree under his reverses, nothing humiliating or mean-spirited
having as yet been seen in him under all his misfortunes. But
to be thus disappointed in the Athenians, and to find the friendship he had trusted prove, upon trial, thus empty and unreal,
was a great pang to him. And, in truth, an excessive display
of outward honour would seem to be the most uncertain attesta-
tion of the real affection of a people for any king or potentate.
Such shows lose their whole credit as tokens of affection (which
has its virtue in the feelings and moral choice), when we reflect
that they may equally proceed from fear. The same decrees
are voted upon the latter motive as upon the former. And therefore judicious men do not look so much to statues, paintings,
or divine honours that are paid them, as to their own actions
and conduct, judging hence whether they shall trust these as
a genuine, or discredit them as a forced homage. As in fact
nothing is less unusual than for a people, even while offering
compliments, to be disgusted with those who accept them
greedily, or arrogantly, or without respect to the free-will of
the givers.

Demetrius, shamefully used as he thought himself, was in no
condition to revenge the affront. He returned a message of
gentle expostulation, saying, however, that he expected to have
his galleys sent to him, among which was that of thirteen banks
of oars. And this being accorded him, he sailed to the Isthmus,
and, finding his affairs in very ill condition, his garrisons expelled,
and a general secession going on to the enemy, he left Pyrrhus
to attend to Greece, and took his course to the Chersonesus,
where he ravaged the territories of Lysimachus, and by the
booty which he took, maintained and kept together his troops,
which were now once more beginning to recover and to show
some considerable front. Nor did any of the other princes care
to meddle with him on that side; for Lysimachus had quite as
little claim to be loved, and was more to be feared for his power.
But not long after Seleucus sent to treat with Demetrius for a
marriage betwixt himself and Stratonice, daughter of Demetrius by Phila. Seleucus, indeed, had already, by Apama, the
Persian, a son named Antiochus, but he was possessed of
territories that might well satisfy more than one successor, and
he was the rather induced to this alliance with Demetrius,
because Lysimachus had just married himself to one daughter

of King Ptolemy, and his son Agathocles to another. Demetrius, who looked upon the offer as an unexpected piece of good fortune, presently embarked with his daughter, and with his whole fleet sailed for Syria. Having during his voyage to touch several times on the coast, among other places he landed in part of Cilicia, which by the apportionment of the kings after the defeat of Antigonus was allotted to Plistarchus, the brother of Cassander. Plistarchus, who took this descent of Demetrius upon his coasts as an infraction of his rights, and was not sorry to have something to complain of, hastened to expostuate in person with Seleucus for entering separately into relations with Demetrius, the common enemy, without consulting the other kings.

Demetrius, receiving information of this, seized the opportunity, and fell upon the city of Quinda, which he surprised, and took in it twelve hundred talents still remaining of the treasure. With this prize, he hastened back to his galleys, embarked, and set sail. At Rhosus, where his wife Phila was now with him, he was met by Seleucus, and their communications with each other at once were put on a frank, unsuspecting, and kingly footing. First, Seleucus gave a banquet to Demetrius in his tent in the camp; then Demetrius received him in the ship of thirteen banks of oars. Meetings for amusements, conferences, and long visits for general intercourse succeeded, all without attendants or arms; until at length Seleucus took his leave, and in great state conducted Stratonice to Antioch. Demetrius meantime possessed himself of Cilicia, and sent Phila to her brother Cassander, to answer the complaints of Plistarchus. And here his wife Deidamia came by sea out of Greece to meet him, but not long after contracted an illness, of which she died. After her death, Demetrius, by the mediation of Seleucus, became reconciled to Ptolemy, and an agreement was made that he should marry his daughter Ptolemais. Thus far all was handsomely done on the part of Seleucus. But, shortly after, desiring to have the province of Cilicia from Demetrius for a sum of money, and being refused it, he then angrily demanded of him the cities of Tyre and Sidon, which seemed a mere piece of arbitrary dealing, and, indeed, an outrageous thing, that he, who was possessed of all the vast provinces between India and the Syrian sea, should think himself so poorly off as, for the sake of two cities which he coveted, to disturb the peace of his dear connection, already a sufferer under a severe reverse of fortune. However, he did but justify the saying of Plato, that the only certain way to be truly rich is not to have more property, but fewer desires. For whoever is always grasping at more avows that he is still in want, and must be poor in the midst of affluence.

But Demetrius, whose courage did not sink, resolutely sent him answer, that, though he were to lose ten thousand battles like that of Ipsus, he would pay no price for the good-will of such a son-in-law as Seleucus. He reinforced these cities with sufficient garrisons to enable them to make a defence against Seleucus; and, receiving information that Lachares, taking the opportunity of their civil dissensions, had set up himself as a usurper over the Athenians, he imagined that if he made a sudden attempt upon the city, he might now without difficulty get possession of it. He crossed the sea in safety with a large fleet; but passing along the coast of Attica, was met by a violent storm, and lost the greater number of his ships, and a very considerable body of men on board of them. As for him, he escaped, and began to make war in a petty manner with the Athenians, but, finding himself unable to effect his design, he sent back orders for raising another fleet, and, with the troops which he had, marched into Peloponnesus and laid siege to the city of Messena. In attacking which place he was in danger of death; for a missile from an engine struck him in the face, and passed through the cheek into his mouth. He recovered, however, and, as soon as he was in a condition to take the field, won over divers cities which had revolted from him, and made an incursion into Attica, where he took Eleusis and Rhamnus, and wasted the country thereabout. And that he might straiten the Athenians by cutting off all manner of provision, a vessel laden with corn bound thither falling into his hands, he ordered the master and the supercargo to be immediately hanged, thereby to strike a terror into others, that so they might not venture to supply the city with provisions. By which means they were reduced to such extremities that a bushel of salt sold for forty drachmas, and a peck of wheat for three hundred. Ptolemy had sent to their relief a hundred and fifty galleys, which came so near as to be seen off Ægina; but this brief hope was soon extinguished by the arrival of three hundred ships, which came to reinforce Demetrius from Cyprus, Peloponnesus, and other places; upon which Ptolemy's fleet took to flight, and Lachares, the tyrant, ran away, leaving the city to its fate.

And now the Athenians, who before had made it capital for any person to propose a treaty or accommodation with Demetrius, immediately opened the nearest gates to send ambassadors to him, not so much out of hopes of obtaining any honourable conditions from his clemency as out of necessity, to avoid death by famine. For among many frightful instances of the distress they were reduced to, it is said that a father and son were sitting in a room together, having abandoned every hope, when a dead mouse fell from the ceiling; and for this prize they leaped up and came to blows. In this famine, it is also related, the philosopher Epicurus saved his own life, and the lives of his scholars, by a small quantity of beans, which he distributed to them daily by number.

In this condition was the city when Demetrius made his entrance and issued a proclamation that all the inhabitants should assemble in the theatre; which being done, he drew up his soldiers at the back of the stage, occupied the stage itself with his guards, and, presently coming in himself by the actors' passages, when the people's consternation had risen to its height, with his first words he put an end to it. Without any harshness of tone or bitterness of words, he reprehended them in a gentle and friendly way, and declared himself reconciled, adding a present of a hundred thousand bushels of wheat, and appointing as magistrates persons acceptable to the people. So Dromoclides, the orator, seeing the people at a loss how to express their gratitude by any words or acclamations, and ready for anything that would outdo the verbal encomiums of the public speakers, came forward, and moved a decree for delivering Piræus and Munychia into the hands of King Demetrius. This was passed accordingly, and Demetrius, of his own motion, added a third garrison, which he placed in the Museum, as a precaution against any new restiveness on the part of the people, which might give him the trouble of quitting his other enterprises.

He had not long been master of Athens before he had formed designs against Lacedæmon; of which Archidamus, the king, being advertised, came out and met him, but he was overthrown in a battle near Mantinea; after which Demetrius entered Laconia, and, in a second battle near Sparta itself, defeated him again with the loss of two hundred Lacedæmonians slain, and five hundred taken prisoners. And now it was almost impossible for the city, which hitherto had never been captured, to escape his arms. But certainly there never was any king upon whom fortune made such short turns, nor any other life or story so filled with her swift and surprising changes, over and over again, from small things to great, from splendour back to humiliation and from utter weakness once more to power and might. They say in his sadder vicissitudes he used sometimes to apostrophise fortune in the words of Æschylus—

" Thou liftest up, to cast us down again."

And so at this moment, when all things seemed to conspire together to give him his heart's desire of dominion and power, news arrived that Lysimachus had taken all his cities in Asia, that Ptolemy had reduced all Cyprus with the exception of Salamis, and that in Salamis his mother and children were shut up and close besieged; and yet, like the woman in Archilochus—

" Water in one deceitful hand she shows,
While burning fire within her other glows."

The same fortune that drew him off with these disastrous tidings from Sparta, in a moment after opened upon him a new and wonderful prospect, of the following kind. Cassander, King of Macedon, dying, and his eldest son, Philip, who succeeded him, not long surviving his father, the two younger brothers fell at variance concerning the succession. And Antipater having murdered his mother Thessalonica, Alexander, the younger brother, called in to his assistance Pyrrhus out of Epirus, and Demetrius out of the Peloponnese. Pyrrhus arrived first, and, taking in recompense for his succour a large slice of Macedonia, had made Alexander begin to be aware that he had brought upon himself a dangerous neighbour. And, that he might not run a yet worse hazard from Demetrius, whose power and reputation were so great, the young man hurried away to meet him at Dium, whither he, who on receiving his letter had set out on his march, was now come. And, offering his greetings and grateful acknowledgments, he at the same time informed him that his affairs no longer required the presence of his ally, thereupon he invited him to supper. There were not wanting some feelings of suspicion on either side already; and when Demetrius was now on his way to the banquet, some one came and told him that in the midst of the drinking he would be killed. Demetrius showed little concern, but, making only a little less haste, he sent to the principal officers of his army commanding them to draw out the soldiers, and make them stand to their arms, and ordered his retinue (more numerous a good deal than that of Alexander) to attend him into the very room of the entertainment, and not to stir from thence till they saw him rise from the table. Thus

Alexander's servants, finding themselves overpowered, had not courage to attempt anything. And, indeed, Demetrius gave them no opportunity, for he made a very short visit, and pretending to Alexander that he was not at present in health for drinking wine, left early. And the next day he occupied himself in preparations for departing, telling Alexander he had received intelligence that obliged him to leave, and begging him to excuse so sudden a parting; he would hope to see him further when his affairs allowed him leisure. Alexander was only too glad, not only that he was going, but that he was doing so of his own motion, without any offence, and proposed to accompany him into Thessaly. But when they came to Larissa, new invitations passed between them, new professions of good-will, covering new conspiracies; by which Alexander put himself into the power of Demetrius. For as he did not like to use precautions on his own part, for fear Demetrius should take the hint to use them on his, the very thing he meant to do was first done to him. He accepted an invitation, and came to Demetrius's quarters; and when Demetrius, while they were still supping, rose from the table and went forth, the young man rose also, and followed him to the door, where Demetrius, as he passed through, only said to the guards, "Kill him that follows me," and went on; and Alexander was at once despatched by them, together with such of his friends as endeavoured to come to his rescue, one of whom, before he died, said, "You have been one day too quick for us."

The night following was one, as may be supposed, of disorder and confusion. And with the morning, the Macedonians, still in alarm, and fearful of the forces of Demetrius, on finding no violence offered, but only a message sent from Demetrius desiring an interview and opportunity for explanation of his actions, at last began to feel pretty confident again, and prepared to receive him favourably. And when he came, there was no need of much being said; their hatred of Antipater for his murder of his mo her, and the absence of any one better to govern them, soon decided them to proclaim Demetrius King of Macedon. And into Macedonia they at once started and took him. And the Macedonians at home, who had not forgotten or forgiven the wicked deeds committed by Cassander on the family of Alexander, were far from sorry at the change. Any kind recollections that still might subsist of the plain and simple rule of the first Antipater went also to the benefit of Demetrius, whose wife was Phila, his daughter, and his son by her, a boy already old enough to be serving in the army with his father, was the natural successor to the government.

To add to this unexpected good fortune, news arrived that Ptolemy had dismissed his mother and children, bestowing upon them presents and honours; and also that his daughter Stratonice, whom he had married to Seleucus, was remarried to Antiochus, the son of Seleucus, and proclaimed Queen of Upper Asia.

For Antiochus, it appears, had fallen passionately in love with Stratonice, the young queen, who had already made Seleucus the father of a son. He struggled very hard with the beginning of this passion, and at last, resolving with himself that his desires were wholly unlawful, his malady past all cure, and his powers of reason too feeble to act, he determined on death, and thought to bring his life slowly to extinction by neglecting his person and refusing nourishment, under the pretence of being ill. Erasistratus, the physician who attended him, quickly perceived that love was his distemper, but the difficulty was to discover the object. He therefore waited continually in his chamber, and when any of the beauties of the court made their visit to the sick prince, he observed the emotions and alterations in the countenance of Antiochus, and watched for the changes which he knew to be indicative of the inward passions and inclinations of the soul. He took notice that the presence of other women produced no effect upon him; but when Stratonice came, as she often did, alone, or in company with Seleucus, to see him, he observed in him all Sappho's famous symptoms,—his voice faltered, his face flushed up, his eyes glanced stealthily, a sudden sweat broke out on his skin, the beatings of his heart were irregular and violent, and, unable to support the excess of his passion, he would sink into a state of faintness, prostration, and pallor.

Erasistratus, reasoning upon these symptoms, and, upon the probabilities of things, considering that the king's son would hardly, if the object of his passion had been any other, have persisted to death rather than reveal it, felt, however, the difficulty of making a discovery of this nature to Seleucus. But, trusting to the tenderness of Seleucus for the young man, he put on all the assurances he could, and at last, on some opportunity, spoke out and told him the malady was love, a love impossible to gratify or relieve. The king was extremely surprised, and asked, 'Why impossible to relieve?' "The fact is," replied Erasistratus, " he is in love with my wife." " How ! " said Seleucus, " and will our friend Erasistratus refuse to bestow his wife upon my son and only successor, when there is no other way to save his life?" "You," replied Erasistratus, "who are his father, would not do so, if he were in love with Stratonice." "Ah, my friend," answered Seleucus, "would to heaven any means, human or divine, could but convert his present passion to that; it would be well for me to part not only with Stratonice, but with my empire, to save Antiochus." This he said with the greatest passion, shedding tears as he spoke; upon which Erasistratus, taking him by the hand, replied, "In that case, you have no need of Erasistratus; for you, who are the husband, the father, and the king, are the proper physician for your own family." Seleucus, accordingly, summoning a general assembly of his people, declared to them, that he had resolved to make Antiochus king, and Stratonice queen, of all the provinces of Upper Asia, uniting them in marriage; telling them, that he thought he had sufficient power over the prince's will that he should find in him no repugnance to obey his commands; and for Stratonice, he hoped all his friends would endeavour to make her sensible, if she should manifest any reluctance to such a marriage, that she ought to esteem those things just and honourable which had been determined upon by the king as necessary to the general good. In this manner, we are told, was brought about the marriage of Antiochus and Stratonice.

To return to the affairs of Demetrius. Having obtained the crown of Macedon, he presently became master of Thessaly also. And holding the greatest part of Peloponnesus, and, on this side of the Isthmus, the cities of Megara and Athens, he now turned his arms against the Bœotians. They at first made overtures for an accommodation; but Cleonymus of Sparta having ventured with some troops to their assistance, and having made his way into Thebes, and Pisis, the Thespian, who was their first man in power and reputation, animating them to make a brave resistance, they broke off the treaty. No sooner, however, had Demetrius begun to approach the walls with his engines, but Cleonymus in affright secretly withdrew; and the Bœotians, finding themselves abandoned, made their submission. Demetrius placed a garrison in charge of their towns, and, having raised a large sum of money from them, he placed Hieronymus, the historian, in the office of governor and military commander over them, and was thought on the whole to have shown great clemency, more particularly to Pisis, to whom he did no hurt, but spoke with him courteously and kindly, and made him chief magistrate of Thespiæ. Not long after, Lysimachus was taken prisoner by Dromichætes, and Demetrius went off instantly in the hopes of possessing himself of Thrace, thus left without a king. Upon this, the Bœotians revolted again, and news also came that Lysimachus had regained his liberty. So Demetrius, turning back quickly and in anger, found on coming up that his son Antigonus had already defeated the Bœotians in battle, and therefore proceeded to lay siege again to Thebes.

But understanding that Pyrrhus had made an incursion into Thessaly, and that he was advanced as far as Thermopylæ, leaving Antigonus to continue the siege, he marched with the rest of his army to oppose this enemy. Pyrrhus, however, made a quick retreat. So, leaving ten thousand foot and a thousand horse for the protection of Thessaly, he returned to the siege of Thebes, and there brought up his famous City-taker to the attack, which, however, was so laboriously and so slowly moved on account of its bulk and heaviness, that in two months it did not advance two furlongs. In the meantime the citizens made a stout defence, and Demetrius, out of heat and contentiousness very often, more than upon any necessity, sent his soldiers into danger; until at last Antigonus, observing how many men were losing their lives, said to him, " Why, my father, do we go on letting the men be wasted in this way without any need of it? " But Demetrius, in a great passion, interrupted him: " And you, good sir, why do you afflict yourself for the matter? will dead men come to you for rations? " But that the soldiers might see that he valued his own life at no dearer rate than theirs, he exposed himself freely, and was wounded with a javelin through his neck, which put him into great hazard of his life. But, not-withstanding, he continued the siege, and in conclusion took the town again. And after his entrance, when the citizens were in fear and trembling, and expected all the severities which an in-censed conqueror could inflict, he only put to death thirteen and banished some few others, pardoning all the rest. Thus the city of Thebes, which had not yet been ten years restored, in that short space was twice besieged and taken.

Shortly after, the festival of the Pythian Apollo was to be celebrated, and the Ætolians having blocked up all the passages to Delphi, Demetrius held the games and celebrated the feast at Athens, alleging it was great reason those honours should be paid in that place, Apollo being the paternal god of the Athenian people, and the reputed first founder of their race.

From thence Demetrius returned to Macedon, and as he not only was of a restless temper himself, but saw also that the

Macedonians were ever the best subjects when employed in military expeditions, but turbulent and desirous of change in the idleness of peace, he led them against the Ætolians, and, having wasted their country, he left Pantauchus with a great part of his army to complete the conquest, and with the rest he marched in person to find out Pyrrhus, who in like manner was advancing to encounter him. But so it fell out, that by taking different ways the two armies did not meet; but whilst Demetrius entered Epirus, and laid all waste before him, Pyrrhus fell upon Pantauchus, and in a battle in which the two commanders met in person and wounded each other, he gained the victory, and took five thousand prisoners, besides great numbers slain in the field. The worst thing, however, for Demetrius was that Pyrrhus had excited less animosity as an enemy than admiration as a brave man. His taking so large a part with his own hand in the battle had gained him the greatest name and glory among the Macedonians. Many among them began to say that this was the only king in whom there was any likeness to be seen of the great Alexander's courage; the other kings, and particularly Demetrius, did nothing but personate him, like actors on a stage, in his pomp and outward majesty. And Demetrius truly was a perfect play and pageant, with his robes and diadems, his gold-edged purple and his hats with double streamers, his very shoes being of the richest purple felt, embroidered over in gold. One robe in particular, a most superb piece of work, was long in the loom in preparation for him, in which was to be wrought the representation of the universe and the celestial bodies. This, left unfinished when his reverse overtook him, not any one of the kings of Macedon, his successors, though divers of them haughty enough, ever presumed to use.

But it was not this theatric pomp alone which disgusted the Macedonians, but his profuse and luxurious way of living; and, above all, the difficulty of speaking with him or of obtaining access to his presence. For either he would not be seen at all, or, if he did give audience, he was violent and overbearing. Thus he made the envoys of the Athenians, to whom yet he was more attentive than to all the other Grecians, wait two whole years before they could obtain a hearing. And when the Lacedæmonians sent a single person on an embassy to him, he held himself insulted, and asked angrily whether it was the fact that the Lacedæmonians had sent but one ambassador. "Yes," was the happy reply he received, "one ambassador to one king."

Once when in some apparent fit of a more popular and acceptable temper he was riding abroad, a number of people came up and presented their written petitions. He courteously received all these, and put them up in the skirt of his cloak, while the poor people were overjoyed, and followed him close. But when he came upon the bridge of the river Axius, shaking out his cloak, he threw all into the river. This excited very bitter resentment among the Macedonians, who felt themselves to be not governed, but insulted. They called to mind what some of them had seen, and others had heard related of King Philip's unambitious and open, accessible manners. One day when an old woman had assailed him several times in the road, and importuned him to hear her after he had told her he had no time, " If so," cried she, " you have no time to be a king." And this reprimand so stung the king that, after thinking of it a while, he went back into the house, and setting all other matters apart, for several days together he did nothing else but receive, beginning with the old woman, the complaints of all that would come. And to do justice, truly enough, might well be called a king's first business. " Mars," as says Timotheus, " is the tyrant; " but Law, in Pindar's words, the king of all. Homer does not say that kings received at the hands of Jove besieging engines or ships of war, but sentences of justice, to keep and observe; nor is it the most warlike, unjust, and murderous, but the most righteous of kings, that has from him the name of Jupiter's " familiar friend " and scholar. Demetrius's delight was the title most unlike the choice of the king of gods. The divine names were those of the Defender and Keeper, his was that of the Besieger of Cities. The place of virtue was given by him to that which, had he not been as ignorant as he was powerful, he would have known to be vice, and honour by his act was associated with crime. While he lay dangerously ill at Pella, Pyrrhus pretty nearly overran all Macedon, and advanced as far as the city of Edessa. On recovering his health, he quickly drove him out, and came to terms with him, being desirous not to employ his time in a string of petty local conflicts with a neighbour, when all his thoughts were fixed upon another design. This was no less than to endeavour the recovery of the whole empire which his father had possessed; and his preparations were suitable to his hopes and the greatness of the enterprise. He had arranged for the levying of ninety-eight thousand foot and nearly twelve thousand horse; and he had a fleet of five hundred galleys on the stocks, some building at Athens, others at Corinth and Chalcis, and in the neighbourhood of Pella. And he himself was passing evermore from one to another of these places, to give his directions and his assistance to the plans, while all that saw were amazed, not so much at the number, as at the magnitude of the works. Hitherto, there had never been seen a galley with fifteen or sixteen ranges of oars. At a later time, Ptolemy Philopator built one of forty rows, which was two hundred and eighty cubits in length and the height of her to the top of her stern, forty-eight cubits; she had four hundred sailors and four thousand rowers, and afforded room besides for very near three thousand soldiers to fight on her decks. But this, after all, was for show, and not for service, scarcely differing from a fixed edifice ashore, and was not to be moved without extreme toil and peril; whereas these galleys of Demetrius were meant quite as much for fighting as for looking at, were not the less serviceable for their magnificence, and were as wonderful for their speed and general performance as for their size.

These mighty preparations against Asia, the like of which had not been made since Alexander first invaded it, united Seleucus, Ptolemy, and Lysimachus in a confederacy for their defence. They also despatched ambassadors to Pyrrhus, to persuade him to make a diversion by attacking Macedonia; he need not think there was any validity in a treaty which Demetrius had concluded, not as an engagement to be at peace with him, but as a means for enabling himself to make war first upon the enemy of his choice. So when Pyrrhus accepted their proposals, Demetrius, still in the midst of his preparations, was encompassed with war on all sides. Ptolemy, with a mighty navy, invaded Greece; Lysimachus entered Macedonia upon the side of Thrace, and Pyrrhus, from the Epirot border, both of them spoiling and wasting the country. Demetrius, leaving his son to look after Greece, marched to the relief of Macedon, and first of all to oppose Lysimachus. On his way, he received the news that Pyrrhus had taken the city Berœa; and the report quickly getting out among the soldiers, all discipline at once was lost, and the camp was filled with lamentations and tears, anger and execrations on Demetrius; they would stay no longer, they would march off, as they said, to take care of their country, friends, and families; but in reality the intention was to revolt to Lysimachus. Demetrius, therefore, thought it his business to keep them as far away as he could from Lysimachus, who was their own countryman, and for Alexander's sake kindly looked upon by many; they would be ready to fight with Pyrrhus, a new comer and a foreigner, whom they could hardly

prefer to himself. But he found himself under a great mistake
in these conjectures. For when he advanced and pitched his
camp near, the old admiration for Pyrrhus's gallantry in arms
revived again; and as they had been used from time imme-
morial to suppose that the best king was he that was the bravest
soldier, so now they were also told of his generous usage of his
prisoners, and, in short, they were eager to have any one in the
place of Demetrius, and well pleased that the man should be
Pyrrhus. At first, some straggling parties only deserted, but
in a little time the whole army broke out into a universal
mutiny, insomuch that at last some of them went up and told
him openly that if he consulted his own safety he were best to
make haste to be gone, for that the Macedonians were resolved
no longer to hazard their lives for the satisfaction of his luxury
and pleasure. And this was thought fair and moderate language, compared with the fierceness of the rest. So, withdrawing into his tent, and, like an actor rather than a real king,
laying aside his stage-robes of royalty, he put on some common
clothes and stole away. He was no sooner gone but the mutinous
army were fighting and quarrelling for the plunder of his tent,
but Pyrrhus, coming immediately, took possession of the camp
without a blow, after which he, with Lysimachus, parted the
realm of Macedon betwixt them, after Demetrius had securely
held it just seven years.

As for Demetrius, being thus suddenly despoiled of everything, he retired to Cassandrea. His wife Phila, in the passion
of her grief, could not endure to see her hapless husband reduced
to the condition of a private and banished man. She refused
to entertain any further hope, and resolving to quit a fortune
which was never permanent except for calamity, took poison
and died. Demetrius, determining still to hold on by the
wreck, went off to Greece, and collected his friends and officers
there. Menelaus, in the play of Sophocles, to give an image of
his vicissitudes of estate, says—

> " For me, my destiny, alas, is found
>  Whirling upon the gods' swift wheel around,
>  And changing still, and as the moon's fair frame
>  Cannot continue for two nights the same,
>  But out of shadow first a crescent shows,
>  Thence into beauty and perfection grows,
>  And when the form of plenitude it wears,
>  Dwindles again, and wholly disappears."

The simile is yet truer of Demetrius and the phases of his
fortunes, now on the increase, presently on the wane, now filling

up and now falling away. And so, at this time of apparent
entire obscuration and extinction, his light again shone out, and
accessions of strength, little by little, came in to fulfil once more
the measure of his hope. At first he showed himself in the
garb of a private man, and went about the cities without any
of the badges of a king. One who saw him at Thebes applied
to him, not inaptly, the lines of Euripides—

> " Humbled to man, laid by the godhead's pride,
> He comes to Dirce and Ismenus's side."

But ere long his expectations had re-entered the royal track,
and he began once more to have about him the body and form
of empire. The Thebans received back, as his gift, their ancient
constitution. The Athenians had deserted him. They displaced Diphilus, who was that year the priest of the two Tutelar
Deities, and restored the archons, as of old, to mark the year;
and on hearing that Demetrius was not so weak as they had
expected, they sent into Macedonia to beg the protection of
Pyrrhus. Demetrius, in anger, marched to Athens, and laid
close siege to the city. In this distress, they sent out to him
Crates the philosopher, a person of authority and reputation,
who succeeded so far, that what with his entreaties and the
solid reasons which he offered, Demetrius was persuaded to raise
the siege; and, collecting all his ships, he embarked a force of
eleven thousand men with cavalry, and sailed away to Asia, to
Caria and Lydia, to take those provinces from Lysimachus.
Arriving at Miletus, he was met there by Eurydice, the sister
of Phila, who brought along with her Ptolemais, one of her
daughters by King Ptolemy, who had before been affianced to
Demetrius, and with whom he now consummated his marriage.
Immediately after, he proceeded to carry out his project, and
was so fortunate in the beginning that many cities revolted to
him; others, as particularly Sardis, he took by force; and some
generals of Lysimachus, also, came over to him with troops and
money. But when Agathocles, the son of Lysimachus, arrived
with an army, he retreated into Phrygia, with an intention to
pass into Armenia, believing that, if he could once plant his foot
in Armenia, he might set Media in revolt, and gain a position in
Upper Asia, where a fugitive commander might find a hundred
ways of evasion and escape. Agathocles pressed hard upon
him, and many skirmishes and conflicts occurred, in which
Demetrius had still the advantage; but Agathocles straitened
him much in his forage, and his men showed a great dislike to

his purpose, which they suspected, of carrying them far away into Armenia and Media. Famine also pressed upon them, and some mistake occurred in their passage of the river Lycus, in consequence of which a large number were swept away and drowned. Still, however, they could pass their jests, and one of them fixed upon Demetrius's tent-door a paper with the first verse, slightly altered, of the Œdipus:—

> " Child of the blind old man, Antigonus,
>   Into what country are you bringing us? "

But at last, pestilence, as is usual when armies are driven to such necessities as to subsist upon any food they can get, began to assail them as well as famine. So that, having lost eight thousand of his men, with the rest he retreated and came to Tarsus, and because that city was within the dominions of Seleucus, he was anxious to prevent any plundering, and wished to give no sort of offence to Seleucus. But when he perceived it was impossible to restrain the soldiers in their extreme necessity, Agathocles also having blocked up all the avenues of Mount Taurus, he wrote a letter to Seleucus, bewailing first all his own sad fortunes, and proceeding with entreaties and supplications for some compassion on his part towards one nearly connected with him, who was fallen into such calamities as might extort tenderness and pity from his very enemies.

These letters so far moved Seleucus, that he gave orders to the governors of those provinces that they should furnish Demetrius with all things suitable to his royal rank, and with sufficient provisions for his troops. But Patrocles, a person whose judgment was greatly valued, and who was a friend highly trusted by Seleucus, pointed out to him that the expense of maintaining such a body of soldiers was the least important consideration, but that it was contrary to all policy to let Demetrius stay in the country, since he, of all the kings of his time, was the most violent, and most addicted to daring enterprises; and he was now in a condition which might tempt persons of the greatest temper and moderation to unlawful and desperate attempts. Seleucus, excited by this advice, moved with a powerful army towards Cilicia; and Demetrius, astonished at this sudden alteration, betook himself for safety to the most inaccessible places of Mount Taurus; from whence he sent envoys to Seleucus, to request from him that he would permit him the liberty to settle with his army somewhere among the independent barbarian tribes, where he might be able to make himself a petty king, and end his life without further travel and hardship; or, if he refused him this, at any rate to give his troops food during the winter, and not expose him in this distressed and naked condition to the fury of his enemies.

But Seleucus, whose jealousy made him put an ill-construction on all he said, sent him answer, that he would permit him to stay two months and no longer in Cataonia, provided he presently sent him the principal of his friends as hostages for his departure then; and, in the meantime, he fortified all the passages into Syria. So that Demetrius, who saw himself thus, like a wild beast, in the way to be encompassed on all sides in the toils, was driven in desperation to his defence, overran the country, and in several engagements in which Seleucus attacked him, had the advantage of him. Particularly, when he was once assailed by the scythed chariots, he successfully avoided the charge and routed his assailants, and then, expelling the troops that were in guard of the passes, made himself master of the roads leading into Syria. And now, elated himself, and finding his soldiers also animated by these successes, he was resolved to push at all, and to have one deciding blow for the empire with Seleucus; who indeed was in considerable anxiety and distress, being averse to any assistance from Lysimachus, whom he both mistrusted and feared, and shrinking from a battle with Demetrius, whose desperation he knew, and whose fortune he had so often seen suddenly pass from the lowest to the highest.

But Demetrius, in the meanwhile, was taken with a violent sickness, from which he suffered extremely himself, and which ruined all his prospects. His men deserted to the enemy, or dispersed. At last, after forty days, he began to be so far recovered as to be able to rally his remaining forces, and marched as if he directly designed for Cilicia; but in the night, raising his camp without sound of trumpet, he took a countermarch, and, passing the mountain Amanus, he ravaged all the lower country as far as Cyrrhestica.

Upon this, Seleucus advancing towards him and encamping at no great distance, Demetrius set his troops in motion to surprise him by night. And almost to the last moment Seleucus knew nothing, and was lying asleep. Some deserter came with the tidings just so soon that he had time to leap, in great consternation, out of bed, and give the alarm to his men. And as he was putting on his boots to mount his horse, he bade the officers about him look well to it, for they had to meet a furious and terrible wild beast. But Demetrius, by the noise he heard in the camp, finding they had taken the alarm, drew off his troops in haste. With the morning's return he found Seleucus pressing hard upon him; so, sending one of his officers against the other wing, he defeated those that were opposed to himself. But Seleucus, lighting from his horse, pulling off his helmet, and taking a target, advanced to the foremost ranks of the mercenary soldiers, and, showing them who he was, bade them come over and join him, telling them that it was for their sakes only that he had so long forborne coming to extremities. And thereupon, without a blow more, they saluted Seleucus as their king and passed over.

Demetrius, who felt that this was his last change of fortune, and that he had no more vicissitudes to expect, fled to the passes of Amanus, where, with a very few friends and followers, he threw himself into a dense forest, and there waited for the night, purposing, if possible, to make his escape towards Caunus, where he hoped to find his shipping ready to transport him. But upon inquiry, finding that they had not provisions even for that one day, he began to think of some other project. Whilst he was yet in doubt, his friend Sosigenes arrived, who had four hundred pieces of gold about him, and, with this relief, he again entertained hopes of being able to reach the coast, and, as soon as it began to be dark, set forward towards the passes. But, perceiving by the fires that the enemies had occupied them, he gave up all thought of that road, and retreated to his old station in the wood, but not with all his men; for some had deserted, nor were those that remained as willing as they had been. One of them, in fine, ventured to speak out, and say that Demetrius had better give himself up to Seleucus; which Demetrius overhearing, drew out his sword, and would have passed it through his body, but that some of his friends interposed and prevented the attempt, persuading him to do as had been said. So at last he gave way, and sent to Seleucus, to surrender himself at discretion.

Seleucus, when he was told of it, said it was not Demetrius's good fortune that had found out this means for his safety, but his own, which had added to his other honours the opportunity of showing his clemency and generosity. And forthwith he gave order to his domestic officers to prepare a royal pavilion, and all things suitable to give him a splendid reception and entertainment. There was in the attendance of Seleucus one Apollonides, who formerly had been intimate with Demetrius.

He was, therefore, as the fittest person, despatched from the king to meet Demetrius, that he might feel himself more at his ease, and might come with the confidence of being received as a friend and relative. No sooner was this message known, but the courtiers and officers, some few at first, and afterwards almost the whole of them, thinking Demetrius would presently become of great power with the king, hurried off, vying who should be foremost to pay him their respects. The effect of which was that compassion was converted into jealousy, and ill-natured, malicious people could the more easily insinuate to Seleucus that he was giving way to an unwise humanity, the very first sight of Demetrius having been the occasion of a dangerous excitement in the army. So, whilst Apollonides, in great delight, and after him many others, were relating to Demetrius the kind expressions of Seleucus, and he, after so many troubles and calamities, if indeed he had still any sense of his surrender of himself being a disgrace, had now, in confidence on the good hopes held out to him, entirely forgotten all such thoughts, Pausanias with a guard of a thousand horse and foot came and surrounded him; and, dispersing the rest that were with him, carried him not to the presence of Seleucus, but to the Syrian Chersonese, where he was committed to the safe custody of a strong guard. Sufficient attendance and liberal provisions were here allowed him, space for riding and walking, a park with game for hunting, those of his friends and companions in exile who wished it had permission to see him, and messages of kindness, also, from time to time, were brought him from Seleucus, bidding him fear nothing, and intimating that, as soon as Antiochus and Stratonice should arrive, he would receive his liberty.

Demetrius, however, finding himself in this condition, sent letters to those who were with his son, and to his captains and friends at Athens and Corinth, that they should give no manner of credit to any letters written to them in his name, though they were sealed with his own signet, but that, looking upon him as if he were already dead, they should maintain the cities and whatever was left of his power for Antigonus, as his successor. Antigonus received the news of his father's captivity with great sorrow; he put himself into mourning and wrote letters to the rest of the kings, and to Seleucus himself, making entreaties, and offering not only to surrender whatever they had left, but himself to be a hostage for his father. Many cities also and princes joined in interceding for him; only Lysimachus sent and offered a large sum of money to Seleucus to take away his life. But he, who had always shown his aversion to Lysimachus before, thought him only the greater barbarian and monster for it. Nevertheless, he still protracted the time, reserving the favour, as he professed, for the intercession of Antiochus and Stratonice.

Demetrius, who had sustained the first stroke of his misfortune, in time grew so familiar with it, that, by continuance, it became easy. At first he persevered one way or other in taking exercise, in hunting, so far as he had means, and in riding. Little by little, however, after a while, he let himself grow indolent and indisposed for them, and took to dice and drinking, in which he passed most of his time, whether it were to escape the thoughts of his present condition, with which he was haunted when sober, and to drown reflection in drunkenness, or that he acknowledged to himself that this was the real happy life he had long desired and wished for, and had foolishly let himself be seduced away from it by a senseless and vain ambition, which had only brought trouble to himself and others; that highest good which he had thought to obtain by arms and fleets and soldiers he had now discovered unexpectedly in idleness, leisure, and repose. As, indeed, what other end or period is there of all the wars and dangers which hapless princes run into, whose misery and folly it is, not merely that they make luxury and pleasure, instead of virtue and excellence, the object of their lives, but that they do not so much as know where this luxury and pleasure are to be found?

Having thus continued three years a prisoner in Chersonesus, for want of exercise, and by indulging himself in eating and drinking, he fell into a disease, of which he died at the age of fifty-four. Seleucus was ill spoken of, and was himself greatly grieved, that he had yielded so far to his suspicions, and had let himself be so much outdone by the barbarian Dromichætes of Thrace, who had shown so much humanity and such a kingly temper in his treatment of his prisoner Lysimachus.

There was something dramatic and theatrical in the very funeral ceremonies with which Demetrius was honoured. For his son Antigonus, understanding that his remains were coming over from Syria, went with all his fleet to the islands to meet them. They were there presented to him in a golden urn, which he placed in his largest admiral galley. All the cities where they touched in their passage sent chaplets to adorn the urn, and deputed certain of their citizens to follow in mourning, to assist at the funeral solemnity. When the fleet approached the harbour of Corinth, the urn, covered with purple, and a royal diadem upon it, was visible upon the poop, and a troop of young men attended in arms to receive it at landing. Xenophantus, the most famous musician of the day, played on the flute his most solemn measure, to which the rowers, as the ship came in, made loud response, their oars, like the funeral beating of the breast, keeping time with the cadences of the music. But Antigonus, in tears and mourning attire, excited among the spectators gathered on the shore the greatest sorrow and compassion. After crowns and other honours had been offered at Corinth, the remains were conveyed to Demetrias, a city to which Demetrius had given his name, peopled from the inhabitants of the small villages of Iolcus.

Demetrius left no other children by his wife Phila but Antigonus and Stratonice, but he had two other sons, both of his own name, one surnamed the Thin, by an Illyrian mother, and one who ruled in Cyrene, by Ptolemais. He had also, by Deidamia, a son, Alexander, who lived and died in Egypt; and there are some who say that he had a son by Eurydice, named Corrhabus. His family was continued in a succession of kings down to Perseus, the last, from whom the Romans took Macedonia.

And now, the Macedonian drama being ended, let us prepare to see the Roman.

# ANTONY

THE grandfather of Antony was the famous pleader, whom Marius put to death for having taken part with Sylla. His father was Antony, surnamed of Crete, not very famous or distinguished in public life, but a worthy good man, and particularly remarkable for his liberality, as may appear from a single example. He was not very rich, and was for that reason checked in the exercise of his good nature by his wife. A friend that stood in need of money came to borrow of him. Money he had none, but he bade a servant bring him water in a silver basin, with which, when it was brought, he wetted his face, as if he meant to shave, and, sending away the servant upon another errand, gave his friend the basin, desiring him to turn it to his purpose. And when there was, afterwards, a great inquiry for it in the house, and his wife was in a very ill humour, and was going to put the servants one by one to the search, he acknowledged what he had done, and begged her pardon.

His wife was Julia, of the family of the Cæsars, who, for her discretion and fair behaviour, was not inferior to any of her time. Under her, Antony received his education, she being, after the death of his father, remarried to Cornelius Lentulus, who was put to death by Cicero for having been of Catiline's conspiracy. This, probably, was the first ground and occasion of that mortal grudge that Antony bore Cicero. He says, even, that the body of Lentulus was denied burial, till, by application made to Cicero's wife, it was granted to Julia. But this seems to be a manifest error, for none of those that suffered in the consulate of Cicero had the right of burial denied them. Antony grew up a very beautiful youth, but by the worst of misfortunes, he fell into the acquaintance and friendship of Curio, a man abandoned to his pleasures, who, to make Antony's dependence upon him a matter of greater necessity, plunged him into a life of drinking and dissipation, and led him through a course of such extravagance that he ran, at that early age, into debt to the amount of two hundred and fifty talents. For this sum Curio became his surety; on hearing which, the elder Curio, his father, drove Antony out of his house. After this, for some short time he took part with Clodius, the most insolent and outrageous demagogue of the time, in his course of violence and disorder; but getting weary, before long, of his madness, and apprehensive of the powerful party forming against him, he left Italy and travelled into Greece, where he spent his time in military exercises and in the study of eloquence. He took most to what was called the Asiatic taste in speaking, which was then at its height, and was, in many ways, suitable to his ostentations, vaunting temper, full of empty flourishes and unsteady efforts for glory.

After some stay in Greece, he was invited by Gabinius, who had been consul, to make a campaign with him in Syria, which at first he refused, not being willing to serve in a private character, but receiving a commission to command the horse, he went along with him. His first service was against Aristobulus, who had prevailed with the Jews to rebel. Here he was himself the first man to scale the largest of the works, and beat Aristobulus out of all of them; after which he routed, in a pitched battle, an army many times over the number of his, killed almost all of them and took Aristobulus and his son prisoners. This war ended, Gabinius was solicited by Ptolemy to restore him to his kingdom of Egypt, and a promise made of ten thousand talents reward. Most of the officers were against this enterprise, and Gabinius himself did not much like it, though sorely tempted by the ten thousand talents. But Antony, desirous of brave actions, and willing to please Ptolemy, joined in persuading Gabinius to go. And whereas all were of opinion that the most dangerous thing before them was the march to Pelusium, in which they would have to pass over a deep sand, where no fresh water was to be hoped for, along the Acregma and the Serbonian marsh (which the Egyptians call Typhon's breathing-hole, and which is, in probability, water left behind by, or making its way through from, the Red Sea, which is here divided from the Mediterranean by a narrow isthmus), Antony, being ordered thither with the horse, not only made himself master of the passes, but won Pelusium itself, a great city, took the garrison prisoners, and by this means rendered the march secure to the army, and the way to victory not difficult for the general to pursue. The enemy also reaped some benefit of his eagerness for honour. For when Ptolemy, after he had entered Pelusium, in his rage and spite against the Egyptians, designed to put them to the sword, Antony withstood him, and hindered the execution. In all the great and frequent skirmishes and battles he gave continual proofs of his personal valour and military conduct; and once in particular, by wheeling about and attacking the rear of the enemy, he gave the victory to the assailants in the front, and received for this service signal marks of distinction. Nor was his humanity towards the deceased Archelaus less taken notice of. He had been formerly his guest and acquaintance, and, as he was now compelled, he fought him bravely while alive, but on his death, sought out his body and buried it with royal honours. The consequence was that he left behind him a great name among the Alexandrians, and all who were serving in the Roman army looked upon him as a most gallant soldier.

He had also a very good and noble appearance; his beard was well grown, his forehead large, and his nose aquiline, giving him altogether a bold, masculine look that reminded people of the faces of Hercules in paintings and sculptures. It was, moreover, an ancient tradition, that the Antonys were descended from Hercules, by a son of his called Anton; and this opinion he thought to give credit to by the similarity of his person just mentioned, and also by the fashion of his dress. For, whenever he had to appear before large numbers, he wore his tunic girt low about the hips, a broadsword on his side, and over all a large coarse mantle. What might seem to some very insupportable, his vaunting, his raillery, his drinking in public, sitting down by the men as they were taking their food, and eating, as he stood, off the common soldiers' tables, made him the delight and pleasure of the army. In love affairs, also, he was very agreeable: he gained many friends by the assistance he gave them in theirs, and took other people's raillery upon his own with good-humour. And his generous ways, his open and lavish hand in gifts and favours to his friends and fellow-soldiers, did a great deal for him in his first advance to power, and after he had become great, long maintained his fortunes, when a thousand follies were hastening their overthrow. One instance of his liberality I must relate. He had ordered payment to one of his friends of twenty-five myriads of money or *decies*, as the Romans call it, and his steward wondering at the extravagance of the sum, laid all the silver in a heap, as he should pass by. Antony, seeing the heap, asked what it meant; his steward replied, "The money you have ordered to be given to your friend." So, perceiving the man's malice, said he, "I thought the *decies* had been much more; 'tis too little; let it be doubled." This, however, was at a later time.

When the Roman state finally broke up into two hostile factions, the aristocratical party joining Pompey, who was in the city, and the popular side seeking help from Cæsar, who was at the head of an army in Gaul, Curio, the friend of Antony, having changed his party and devoted himself to Cæsar, brought over Antony also to his service. And the influence which he gained with the people by his eloquence and by the money which was supplied by Cæsar, enabled him to make Antony, first, tribune of the people, and then, augur. And Antony's accession to office was at once of the greatest advantage to Cæsar. In the first place, he resisted the consul Marcellus, who was putting under Pompey's orders the troops who were already collected, and was giving him power to raise new levies; he, on the other hand, making an order that they should be sent into Syria to reinforce Bibulus, who was making war with the Parthians, and that no one should give in his name to serve under Pompey. Next, when the senators would not suffer Cæsar's letters to be received or read in the senate, by virtue of his office he read them publicly, and succeeded so well, that many were brought to change their mind; Cæsar's demands, as they appeared in what he wrote, being but just and reasonable. At length, two questions being put in the senate, the one, whether Pompey should dismiss his army, the other, if Cæsar his, some were for the former, for the latter all, except some few, when Antony stood up and put the question, if it would be agreeable to them that both Pompey and Cæsar should dismiss their armies. This proposal met with the greatest approval, they gave him loud acclamations, and called for it to be put to the vote. But when the consuls would not have it so, Cæsar's friends again made some few offers, very fair and equitable, but were strongly opposed by Cato, and Antony himself was commanded to leave the senate by the consul Lentulus. So, leaving them with execrations, and disguising himself in a servant's dress, hiring a carriage with Quintus Cassius, he went straight away to Cæsar, declaring at once, when they reached the camp, that affairs at Rome were conducted without any order or justice, that the privilege of speaking in the senate was denied the tribunes, and that he who spoke for common fair dealing was driven out and in danger of his life.

Upon this, Cæsar set his army in motion, and marched into Italy; and for this reason it is that Cicero writes in his Philippics that Antony was as much the cause of the civil war as Helen was of the Trojan. But this is but a calumny. For Cæsar was not of so slight or weak a temper as to suffer himself to be carried away, by the indignation of the moment, into a civil war with his country, upon the sight of Antony and Cassius seeking refuge in his camp meanly dressed and in a hired carriage, without ever having thought of it or taken any such resolution long before. This was to him, who wanted a pretence of declaring war, a fair and plausible occasion; but the true motive that led him was the same that formerly led Alexander and Cyrus against all mankind, the unquenchable thirst of empire, and the distracted ambition of being the greatest man in the world, which was impracticable for him, unless Pompey were put down. So soon, then, as he had advanced and occupied Rome, and driven Pompey out of Italy, he proposed first to go against the legions that Pompey had in Spain, and then cross over and follow him with the fleet that should be prepared during his absence, in the meantime leaving the government of Rome to Lepidus, as prætor, and the command of the troops and of Italy to Antony, as tribune of the people. Antony was not long in getting the hearts of the soldiers, joining with them in their exercises, and for the most part living amongst them and making them presents to the utmost of his abilities; but with all others he was unpopular enough. He was too lazy to pay attention to the complaints of persons who were injured; he listened impatiently to petitions; and he had an ill name for familiarity with other people's wives. In short, the government of Cæsar (which, so far as he was concerned himself, had the appearance of anything rather than a tyranny) got a bad repute through his friends. And of these friends, Antony, as he had the largest trust, and committed the greatest errors, was thought the most deeply in fault.

Cæsar, however, at his return from Spain, overlooked the charges against him, and had no reason ever to complain, in the employments he gave him in the war, of any want of courage, energy, or military skill. He himself, going aboard at Brundusium, sailed over the Ionian Sea with a few troops and sent back the vessels with orders to Antony and Gabinius to embark the army, and come over with all speed to Macedonia. Gabinius, having no mind to put to sea in the rough, dangerous weather of the winter season, was for marching the army round by the long land route; but Antony, being more afraid lest Cæsar might suffer from the number of his enemies, who pressed him hard, beat back Libo, who was watching with a fleet at the mouth of the haven of Brundusium, by attacking his galleys with a number of small boats, and gaining thus an opportunity, put on board twenty thousand foot and eight hundred horse, and so set out to sea. And, being espied by the enemy and pursued, from this danger he was rescued by a strong south wind, which sprang up and raised so high a sea that the enemy's galleys could make little way. But his own ships were driving before it upon a lee shore of cliffs and rocks running sheer to the water, where there was no hope of escape, when all of a sudden the wind turned about to south-west, and blew from land to the main sea, where Antony, now sailing in security, saw the coast all covered with the wreck of the enemy's fleet. For hither the galleys in pursuit had been carried by the gale, and not a few of them dashed to pieces. Many men and much property fell into Antony's hands; he took also the town of Lissus, and, by the seasonable arrival of so large a reinforcement, gave Cæsar great encouragement.

There was not one of the many engagements that now took place one after another in which he did not signalise himself; twice he stopped the army in its full flight, led them back to a charge, and gained the victory. So that now without reason his reputation, next to Cæsar's, was greatest in the army. And what opinion Cæsar himself had of him well appeared when, for the final battle in Pharsalia, which was to determine everything, he himself chose to lead the right wing, committing the charge of the left to Antony, as to the best officer of all that served under him. After the battle, Cæsar, being created dictator, went in pursuit of Pompey, and sent Antony to Rome, with the character of Master of the Horse, who is in office and power next to the dictator, when present, and in his absence the first, and pretty nearly indeed the sole magistrate. For on the appointment of a dictator, with the one exception of the tribunes, all other magistrates cease to exercise any authority in Rome.

Dolabella, however, who was tribune, being a young man and eager for change, was now for bringing in a general measure for cancelling debts, and wanted Antony, who was his friend, and forward enough to promote any popular project, to take part with him in this step. Asinius and Trebellius were of the contrary opinion, and it so happened, at the same time, Antony was crossed by a terrible suspicion that Dolabella was too familiar with his wife; and in great trouble at this, he parted with her (she being his cousin, and daughter to Caius Antonius, colleague of Cicero), and, taking part with Asinius, came to open hostilities with Dolabella, who had seized on the forum, intending to pass his law by force. Antony, backed by a vote of the senate that Dolabella should be put down by force of arms, went down and attacked him, killing some of his, and losing some of his own men; and by this action lost his favour with the commonalty, while with the better class and with all well-conducted people his general course of life made him, as Cicero says, absolutely odious, utter disgust being excited by his drinking bouts at all hours, his wild expenses, his gross amours, the day spent in sleeping or walking off his debauches, and the night in banquets and at theatres, and in celebrating the nuptials of some comedian or buffoon. It is related that, drinking all night at the wedding of Hippias, the comedian, on the morning, having to harangue the people, he came forward, overcharged as he was, and vomited before them all, one of his friends holding his gown for him. Sergius, the player, was one of the friends who could do most with him; also Cytheris, a woman of the same trade, whom he made much of, and who, when he went his progress, accompanied him in a litter, and had her equipage not in anything inferior to his mother's; while every one, moreover, was scandalised at the sight of the golden cups that he took with him, fitter for the ornaments of a procession than the uses of a journey, at his having pavilions set up, and sumptuous morning repasts laid out by river sides and in groves, at his having chariots drawn by lions, and common women and singing girls quartered upon the houses of serious fathers and mothers of families. And it seemed very unreasonable that Cæsar, out of Italy, should lodge in the open field, and, with great fatigue and danger, pursue the remainder of a hazardous war, whilst others, by favour of his authority, should insult the citizens with their impudent luxury.

All this appears to have aggravated party quarrels in Rome, and to have encouraged the soldiers in acts of licence and rapacity. And, accordingly, when Cæsar came home, he acquitted Dolabella, and, being created the third time consul, took not Antony, but Lepidus, for his colleague. Pompey's house being offered for sale, Antony bought it, and when the price was demanded of him, loudly complained. This, he tells us himself, and because he thought his former services had not been recompensed as they deserved, made him not follow Cæsar with the army into Libya. However, Cæsar, by dealing gently with his errors, seems to have succeeded in curing him of a good deal of his folly and extravagance. He gave up his former courses, and took a wife, Fulvia, the widow of Clodius the demagogue, a woman not born for spinning or housewifery, nor one that could be content with ruling a private husband, but prepared to govern a first magistrate, or give orders to a commander-in-chief. So that Cleopatra had great obligations to her for having taught Antony to be so good a servant, he coming to her hands tame and broken into entire obedience to the commands of a mistress. He used to play all sorts of sportive, boyish tricks, to keep Fulvia in good humour. As, for example, when Cæsar, after his victory in Spain, was on his return, Antony, among the rest, went out to meet him; and, a rumour being spread that Cæsar was killed and the enemy marching into Italy, he returned to Rome, and, disguising himself, came to her by night muffled up as a servant that brought letters from Antony. She, with great impatience, before she received the letter, asks if Antony were well, and instead of an answer he gives her the letter; and, as she was opening it, took her about the neck and kissed her. This little story, of many of the same nature, I give as a specimen.

There was nobody of any rank in Rome that did not go some days' journey to meet Cæsar on his return from Spain; but

Antony was the best received of any, admitted to ride the whole journey with him in his carriage, while behind came Brutus Albinus and Octavian, his niece's son, who afterwards bore his name and reigned so long over the Romans. Cæsar being created, the fifth time, consul, without delay chose Antony for his colleague, but designing himself to give up his own consulate to Dolabella, he acquainted the senate with his resolution. But Antony opposed it with all his might, saying much that was bad against Dolabella, and receiving the like language in return, till Cæsar could bear with the indecency no longer, and deferred the matter to another time. Afterwards, when he came before the people to proclaim Dolabella, Antony cried out that the auspices were unfavourable, so that at last Cæsar, much to Dolabella's vexation, yielded and gave it up. And it is credible that Cæsar was about as much disgusted with the one as the other. When some one was accusing them both to him, "It is not," said he, "these well-fed, long-haired men that I fear, but the pale and the hungry-looking;" meaning Brutus and Cassius, by whose conspiracy he afterwards fell.

And the fairest pretext for that conspiracy was furnished, without his meaning it, by Antony himself. The Romans were celebrating their festival, called the Lupercalia, when Cæsar, in his triumphal habit, and seated above the rostra in the market-place, was a spectator of the sports. The custom is, that many young noblemen and of the magistracy, anointed with oil and having straps of hide in their hands, run about and strike, in sport, at every one they meet. Antony was running with the rest; but, omitting the old ceremony, twining a garland of bay round a diadem, he ran up to the rostra, and, being lifted up by his companions, would have put it upon the head of Cæsar, as if by that ceremony he were declared king. Cæsar seemingly refused, and drew aside to avoid it, and was applauded by the people with great shouts. Again Antony pressed it, and again he declined its acceptance. And so the dispute between them went on for some time, Antony's solicitations receiving but little encouragement from the shouts of a few friends, and Cæsar's refusal being accompanied with the general applause of the people; a curious thing enough, that they should submit with patience to the fact, and yet at the same time dread the name as the destruction of their liberty. Cæsar, very much discomposed at what had passed, got up from his seat, and, laying bare his neck, said he was ready to receive a stroke, if any one of them desired to give it. The crown was at last put on one of his statues, but was taken down by some of the tribunes, who were followed home by the people with shouts of applause. Cæsar, however, resented it, and deposed them.

These passages gave great encouragement to Brutus and Cassius, who, in making choice of trusty friends for such an enterprise, were thinking to engage Antony. The rest approved, except Trebonius, who told them that Antony and he had lodged and travelled together in the last journey they took to meet Cæsar, and that he had let fall several words, in a cautious way, on purpose to sound him; that Antony very well understood him, but did not encourage it; however, he had said nothing of it to Cæsar but had kept the secret faithfully. The conspirators then proposed that Antony should die with him, which Brutus would not consent to, insisting that an action undertaken in defence of right and the laws must be maintained unsullied, and pure of injustice. It was settled that Antony, whose bodily strength and high office made him formidable, should, at Cæsar's entrance into the senate, when the deed was to be done, be amused outside by some of the party in a conversation about some pretended business.

So when all was proceeded with, according to their plan, and Cæsar had fallen in the senate-house, Antony, at the first moment, took a servant's dress, and hid himself. But, understanding that the conspirators had assembled in the Capitol, and had no further design upon any one, he persuaded them to come down, giving them his son as a hostage. That night Cassius supped at Antony's house, and Brutus with Lepidus. Antony then convened the senate, and spoke in favour of an act of oblivion, and the appointment of Brutus and Cassius to provinces. These measures the senate passed; and resolved that all Cæsar's acts should remain in force. Thus Antony went out of the senate with the highest possible reputation and esteem; for it was apparent that he had prevented a civil war, and had composed, in the wisest and most statesmanlike way, questions of the greatest difficulty and embarrassment. But these temperate counsels were soon swept away by the tide of popular applause, and the prospect, if Brutus were overthrown, of being without doubt the ruler-in-chief. As Cæsar's body was conveying to the tomb, Antony, according to the custom, was making his funeral oration in the market-place, and perceiving the people to be infinitely affected with what he had said, he began to mingle with his praises language of commiseration, and horror at what had happened, and, as he was ending his speech, he took the under-clothes of the dead, and held them up, showing them stains of blood and the holes of the many stabs, calling those that had done this act villains and bloody murderers. All which excited the people to such indignation, that they would not defer the funeral, but, making a pile of tables and forms in the very market-place, set fire to it; and every one, taking a brand, ran to the conspirators' houses, to attack them.

Upon this, Brutus and his whole party left the city, and Cæsar's friends joined themselves to Antony. Calpurnia, Cæsar's wife, lodged with him the best part of the property, to the value of four thousand talents; he got also into his hands all Cæsar's papers wherein were contained journals of all he had done, and draughts of what he designed to do, which Antony made good use of; for by this means he appointed what magistrates he pleased, brought whom he would into the senate, recalled some from exile, freed others out of prison, and all this as ordered so by Cæsar. The Romans, in mockery, gave those who were thus benefited the name of Charonites, since, if put to prove their patents, they must have recourse to the papers of the dead. In short, Antony's behaviour in Rome was very absolute, he himself being consul and his two brothers in great place; Caius, the one, being prætor, and Lucius, the other, tribune of the people.

While matters went thus in Rome, the young Cæsar, Cæsar's niece's son, and by testament left his heir, arrived at Rome from Apollonia, where he was when his uncle was killed. The first thing he did was to visit Antony, as his father's friend. He spoke to him concerning the money that was in his hands, and reminded him of the legacy Cæsar had made of seventy-five drachmas to every Roman citizen. Antony, at first, laughing at such discourse from so young a man, told him he wished he were in his health, and that he wanted good counsel and good friends to tell him the burden of being executor to Cæsar would sit very uneasy upon his young shoulders. This was no answer to him; and, when he persisted in demanding the property, Antony went on treating him injuriously both in word and deed, opposed him when he stood for the tribune's office, and, when he was taking steps for the dedication of his father's golden chair, as had been enacted, he threatened to send him to prison if he did not give over soliciting the people. This made the young Cæsar apply himself to Cicero, and all those that hated Antony; by them he was recommended to the senate, while he himself courted the people, and drew together the soldiers from their settlements, till Antony got alarmed, and gave him a meeting in the Capitol, where, after some words, they came to an accommodation.

That night Antony had a very unlucky dream, fancying that his right hand was thunderstruck. And, some few days after, he was informed that Cæsar was plotting to take his life. Cæsar explained, but was not believed, so that the breach was now made as wide as ever; each of them hurried about all through Italy to engage, by great offers, the old soldiers that lay scattered in their settlements, and to be the first to secure the troops that still remained undischarged. Cicero was at this time the man of greatest influence in Rome. He made use of all his art to exasperate the people against Antony, and at length persuaded the senate to declare him a public enemy, to send Cæsar the rods and axes and other marks of honour usually given to prætors, and to issue orders to Hirtius and Pansa, who were the consuls, to drive Antony out of Italy. The armies engaged near Modena, and Cæsar himself was present and took part in the battle. Antony was defeated, but both the consuls were slain. Antony, in his flight, was overtaken by distresses of every kind, and the worst of all of them was famine. But it was his character in calamities to be better than at any other time. Antony, in misfortune, was most nearly a virtuous man. It is common enough for people, when they fall into great disasters, to discern what is right, and what they ought to do; but there are but few who in such extremities have the strength to obey their judgment, either in doing what it approves or avoiding what it condemns; and a good many are so weak as to give way to their habits all the more, and are incapable of using their minds. Antony, on this occasion, was a most wonderful example to his soldiers. He, who had just quitted so much luxury and sumptuous living, made no difficulty now of drinking foul water and feeding on wild fruits and roots. Nay, it is related they ate the very bark of trees, and, in passing over the Alps, lived upon creatures that no one before had ever been willing to touch.

The design was to join the army on the other side the Alps, commanded by Lepidus, who he imagined would stand his friend, he having done him many good offices with Cæsar. On coming up and encamping near at hand, finding he had no sort of encouragement offered him, he resolved to push his fortune and venture all. His hair was long and disordered, nor had he shaved his beard since his defeat; in this guise, and with a dark coloured cloak flung over him, he came into the trenches of Lepidus, and began to address the army. Some were moved at his habit, others at his words, so that Lepidus, not liking it, ordered the trumpets to sound, that he might be heard no longer. This raised in the soldiers yet a greater pity, so that they resolved to confer secretly with him, and dressed Lælius and Clodius in women's clothes, and sent them to see him. They advised him without delay to attack Lepidus's trenches, assuring him that a strong party would receive him, and, if he wished it, would kill Lepidus. Antony, however, had no wish for this, but next morning marched his army to pass over the river that parted the two camps. He was himself the first man that stepped in, and, as he went through towards the other bank, he saw Lepidus's soldiers in great numbers reaching out their hands to help him, and beating down the works to make him way. Being entered into the camp, and finding himself absolute master, he nevertheless treated Lepidus with the greatest civility, and gave him the title of Father, when he spoke to him, and though he had everything at his own command, he left him the honour of being called the general. This fair usage brought over to him Munatius Plancus, who was not far off with a considerable force. Thus in great strength he repassed the Alps, leading with him into Italy seventeen legions and ten thousand horse, besides six legions which he left in garrison under the command of Varius, one of his familiar friends and boon companions, whom they used to call by the nickname of Cotylon.

Cæsar, perceiving that Cicero's wishes were for liberty, had ceased to pay any further regard to him, and was now employing the mediation of his friends to come to a good understanding with Antony. They both met together with Lepidus in a small island, where the conference lasted three days. The empire was soon determined of, it being divided amongst them as if it had been their paternal inheritance. That which gave them all the trouble was to agree who should be put to death, each of them desiring to destroy his enemies and to save his friends. But, in the end, animosity to those they hated carried the day against respect for relations and affection for friends; and Cæsar sacrificed Cicero to Antony, Antony gave up his uncle Lucius Cæsar, and Lepidus received permission to murder his brother Paulus, or, as others say, yielded his brother to them. I do not believe anything ever took place more truly savage or barbarous than this composition, for, in this exchange of blood for blood, they were equally guilty of the lives they surrendered and of those they took; or, indeed, more guilty in the case of their friends, for whose deaths they had not even the justification of hatred. To complete the reconciliation, the soldiery, coming about them, demanded that confirmation should be given to it by some alliance of marriage; Cæsar should marry Clodia, the daughter of Fulvia, wife to Antony. This also being agreed to, three hundred persons were put to death by proscription. Antony gave orders to those that were to kill Cicero to cut off his head and right hand, with which he had written his invectives against him; and, when they were brought before him, he regarded them joyfully, actually bursting out more than once into laughter, and, when he had satiated himself with the sight of them, ordered them to be hung up above the speaker's place in the forum, thinking thus to insult the dead, while in fact he only exposed his own wanton arrogance, and his unworthiness to hold the power that fortune had given him. His uncle, Lucius Cæsar, being closely pursued, took refuge with his sister, who, when the murderers had broken into her house and were pressing into her chamber, met them at the door, and spreading out her hands, cried out several times. "You shall not kill Lucius Cæsar till you first despatch me, who gave your general his birth;" and in this manner she succeeded in getting her brother out of the way, and saving his life.

This triumvirate was very hateful to the Romans, and Antony most of all bore the blame, because he was older than Cæsar, and had greater authority than Lepidus, and withal he was no sooner settled in his affairs, but he turned to his luxurious and dissolute way of living. Besides the ill reputation he gained by his general behaviour, it was some considerable disadvantage to him his living in the house of Pompey the Great, who had been as much admired for his temperance and his sober, citizen-like habits of life, as ever he was for having triumphed three times. They could not without anger see the doors of that house shut against magistrates, officers, and envoys, who were shamefully refused admittance, while it was filled inside with players, jugglers, and drunken flatterers, upon whom were spent the greatest part of the wealth which violence and cruelty procured. For they did not limit themselves to the forfeiture of the estates of such as were proscribed, defrauding the widows and families, nor were they contented with laying on every possible kind of tax and imposition; but hearing that several sums of money were, as well by strangers as citizens of Rome, deposited in the hands of the vestal virgins, they went and took the money away

by force.  When it was manifest that nothing would ever be
enough for Antony, Cæsar at last called for a division of property.
The army was also divided between them, upon their march into
Macedonia to make war with Brutus and Cassius, Lepidus being
left with the command of the city.

However, after they had crossed the sea and engaged in operations of war, encamping in front of the enemy, Antony opposite
Cassius, and Cæsar opposite Brutus, Cæsar did nothing worth
relating, and all the success and victory were Antony's.  In the
first battle, Cæsar was completely routed by Brutus, his camp
taken, he himself very narrowly escaping by flight.  As he himself writes in his Memoirs, he retired before the battle, on account
of a dream which one of his friends had.  But Antony, on the
other hand, defeated Cassius; though some have written that he
was not actually present in the engagement, and only joined
afterwards in the pursuit.  Cassius was killed, at his own entreaty and order, by one of his most trusted freedmen, Pindarus,
not being aware of Brutus's victory.  After a few days' interval,
they fought another battle, in which Brutus lost the day, and
slew himself; and Cæsar being sick, Antony had almost all the
honour of the victory.  Standing over Brutus's dead body, he
uttered a few words of reproach upon him for the death of his
brother Caius, who had been executed by Brutus's order in Macedonia in revenge of Cicero; but, saying presently that Hortensius
was most to blame for it, he gave order for his being slain upon
his brother's tomb, and, throwing his own scarlet mantle, which
was of great value, upon the body of Brutus, he gave charge to
one of his own freedmen to take care of his funeral.  This man,
as Antony came to understand, did not leave the mantle with the
corpse, but kept both it and a good part of the money that should
have been spent in the funeral for himself; for which he had him
put to death.

But Cæsar was conveyed to Rome, no one expecting that he
would long survive.  Antony, purposing to go to the eastern
provinces to lay them under contribution, entered Greece with
a large force.  The promise had been made that every common
soldier should receive for his pay five thousand drachmas; so it
was likely there would be need of pretty severe taxing and
levying to raise money.  However, to the Greeks he showed at
first reason and moderation enough; he gratified his love of
amusement by hearing the learned men dispute, by seeing the
games, and undergoing initiation; and in judicial matters he
was equitable, taking pleasure in being styled a lover of Greece,

but, above all, in being called a lover of Athens, to which city
he made very considerable presents. The people of Megara
wished to let him know that they also had something to show
him, and invited him to come and see their senate-house. So
he went and examined it, and on their asking him how he liked
it, told them it was " not very large, but extremely *ruinous*."
At the same time, he had a survey made of the temple of the
Pythian Apollo as if he had designed to repair it, and indeed he
had declared to the senate his intention so to do.

However, leaving Lucius Censorinus in Greece, he crossed
over into Asia, and there laid his hands on the stores of accumu-
lated wealth, while kings waited at his door, and queens were
rivalling one another, who should make him the greatest presents
or appear most charming in his eyes. Thus, whilst Cæsar in
Rome was wearing out his strength amidst seditions and wars,
Antony, with nothing to do amidst the enjoyments of peace, let
his passions carry him easily back to the old course of life that
was familiar to him. A set of harpers and pipers, Anaxenor
and Xuthus, the dancing-man, Metrodorus, and a whole Bacchic
rout of the like Asiatic exhibitors, far outdoing in licence and
buffoonery the pests that had followed him out of Italy, came
in and possessed the court; the thing was past patience, wealth
of all kinds being wasted on objects like these. The whole of
Asia was like the city in Sophocles, loaded, at one time—

> "————with incense in the air,
> Jubilant songs, and outcries of despair."

When he made his entry into Ephesus, the women met him
dressed up like Bacchantes, and the men and boys like satyrs
and fauns, and throughout the town nothing was to be seen but
spears wreathed about with ivy, harps, flutes, and psalteries,
while Antony in their songs was Bacchus, the Giver of Joy, and
the Gentle. And so indeed he was to some, but to far more the
Devourer and the Savage; for he would deprive persons of worth
and quality of their fortunes to gratify villains and flatterers,
who would sometimes beg the estates of men yet living, pretending they were dead, and, obtaining a grant, take possession.
He gave his cook the house of a Magnesian citizen, as a reward
for a single highly successful supper, and, at last, when he was
proceeding to lay a second whole tribute on Asia, Hybreas,
speaking on behalf of the cities, took courage, and told him
broadly, but aptly enough for Antony's taste, " if you can take
two yearly tributes, you can doubtless give us a couple of
summers and a double harvest time;" and put it to him in the

plainest and boldest way, that Asia had raised two hundred thousand talents for his service: "If this has not been paid to you, ask your collectors for it; if it has, and is all gone, we are ruined men." These words touched Antony to the quick, who was simply ignorant of most things that were done in his name; not that he was so indolent, as he was prone to trust frankly in all about him. For there was much simplicity in his character; he was slow to see his faults, but when he did see them, was extremely repentant, and ready to ask pardon of those he had injured; prodigal in his acts of reparation, and severe in his punishments, but his generosity was much more extravagant than his severity; his raillery was sharp and insulting, but the edge of it was taken off by his readiness to submit to any kind of repartee; for he was as well contented to be rallied, as he was pleased to rally others. And this freedom of speech was, indeed, the cause of many of his disasters. He never imagined those who used so much liberty in their mirth would flatter or deceive him in business of consequence, not knowing how common it is with parasites to mix their flattery with boldness, as confectioners do their sweetmeats with something biting, to prevent the sense of satiety. Their freedoms and impertinences at table were designed expressly to give to their obsequiousness in council the air of being not complaisance, but conviction.

Such being his temper, the last and crowning mischief that could befall him came in the love of Cleopatra, to awaken and kindle to fury passions that as yet lay still and dormant in his nature, and to stifle and finely corrupt any elements that yet made resistance in him of goodness and a sound judgment. He fell into the snare thus. When making preparation for the Parthian war, he sent to command her to make her personal appearance in Cilicia, to answer an accusation, that she had given great assistance, in the late wars, to Cassius. Dellius, who was sent on this message, had no sooner seen her face, and remarked her adroitness and subtlety in speech, but he felt convinced that Antony would not so much as think of giving any molestation to a woman like this; on the contrary, she would be the first in favour with him. So he set himself at once to pay his court to the Egyptian, and gave her his advice, " to go," in the Homeric style, to Cilicia, " in her best attire," and bade her fear nothing from Antony, the gentlest and kindest of soldiers. She had some faith in the words of Dellius, but more in her own attractions; which, having formerly recommended her to Cæsar and the young Cænus Pompey, she did not doubt might prove yet more successful with Antony. Their acquaintance was with her when a girl, young and ignorant of the world, but she was to meet Antony in the time of life when women's beauty is most splendid, and their intellects are in full maturity. She made great preparation for her journey, of money, gifts, and ornaments of value, such as so wealthy a kingdom might afford, but she brought with her her surest hopes in her own magic arts and charms.

She received several letters, both from Antony and from his friends, to summon her, but she took no account of these orders; and at last, as if in mockery of them, she came sailing up the river Cydnus, in a barge with gilded stern and outspread sails of purple, while oars of silver beat time to the music of flutes and fifes and harps. She herself lay all along under a canopy of cloth of gold, dressed as Venus in a picture, and beautiful young boys, like painted Cupids, stood on each side to fan her. Her maids were dressed like sea nymphs and graces, some steering at the rudder, some working at the ropes. The perfumes diffused themselves from the vessel to the shore, which was covered with multitudes, part following the galley up the river on either bank, part running out of the city to see the sight. The market-place was quite emptied, and Antony at last was left alone sitting upon the tribunal; while the word went through all the multitude, that Venus was come to feast with Bacchus, for the common good of Asia. On her arrival, Antony sent to invite her to supper. She thought it fitter he should come to her; so, willing to show his good-humour and courtesy, he complied, and went. He found the preparations to receive him magnificent beyond expression, but nothing so admirable as the great number of lights; for on a sudden there was let down altogether so great a number of branches with lights in them so ingeniously disposed, some in squares, and some in circles, that the whole thing was a spectacle that has seldom been equalled for beauty.

The next day, Antony invited her to supper, and was very desirous to outdo her as well in magnificence as contrivance; but he found he was altogether beaten in both, and was so well convinced of it that he was himself the first to jest and mock at his poverty of wit and his rustic awkwardness. She, perceiving that his raillery was broad and gross, and savoured more of the soldier than the courtier, rejoined in the same taste, and fell into it at once, without any sort of reluctance or reserve. For her actual beauty, it is said, was not in itself so remarkable

that none could be compared with her, or that no one could see
her without being struck by it, but the contact of her presence,
if you lived with her, was irresistible; the attraction of her
person, joining with the charm of her conversation, and the
character that attended all she said or did, was something be-
witching. It was a pleasure merely to hear the sound of her
voice, with which, like an instrument of many strings, she could
pass from one language to another; so that there were few of
the barbarian nations that she answered by an interpreter; to
most of them she spoke herself, as to the Æthiopians, Troglo-
dytes, Hebrews, Arabians, Syrians, Medes, Parthians, and many
others, whose language she had learnt; which was all the more
surprising because most of the kings, her predecessors, scarcely
gave themselves the trouble to acquire the Egyptian tongue,
and several of them quite abandoned the Macedonian.

Antony was so captivated by her that, while Fulvia his wife
maintained his quarrels in Rome against Cæsar by actual force
of arms, and the Parthian troops, commanded by Labienus (the
king's generals having made him commander-in-chief), were
assembled in Mesopotamia, and ready to enter Syria, he could
yet suffer himself to be carried away by her to Alexandria, there
to keep holiday, like a boy, in play and diversion, squandering
and fooling away in enjoyments that most costly, as Antiphon
says, of all valuables, time. They had a sort of company, to
which they gave a particular name, calling it that of the Inimitable Livers. The members entertained one another daily in
turn, with an extravagance of expenditure beyond measure or
belief. Philotas, a physician of Amphissa, who was at that time
a student of medicine in Alexandria, used to tell my grandfather
Lamprias that, having some acquaintance with one of the royal
cooks, he was invited by him, being a young man, to come and
see the sumptuous preparations for supper. So he was taken
into the kitchen, where he admired the prodigious variety of all
things; but particularly, seeing eight wild boars roasting whole,
says he, " Surely you have a great number of guests." The
cook laughed at his simplicity, and told him there were not
above twelve to sup, but that every dish was to be served up
just roasted to a turn, and if anything was but one minute ill-
timed, it was spoiled " And," said he, " maybe Antony will
sup just now, maybe not this hour, maybe he will call for wine,
or begin to talk, and will put it off. So that," he continued,
" it is not one, but many suppers must be had in readiness, as
it is impossible to guess at his hour." This was Philotas's

story; who related besides, that he afterwards came to be one of the medical attendants of Antony's eldest son by Fulvia, and used to be invited pretty often, among other companions, to his table, when he was not supping with his father. One day another physician had talked loudly, and given great disturbance to the company, whose mouth Philotas stopped with this sophistical syllogism: "In some states of fever the patient should take cold water; every one who has a fever is in some state of fever; therefore in a fever cold water should always be taken." The man was quite struck dumb, and Antony's son, very much pleased, laughed aloud, and said, "Philotas, I make you a present of all you see there," pointing to a sideboard covered with plate. Philotas thanked him much, but was far enough from ever imagining that a boy of his age could dispose of things of that value. Soon after, however, the plate was all brought to him, and he was desired to set his mark upon it; and when he put it away from him, and was afraid to accept the present, "What ails the man?" said he that brought it; "do you know that he who gives you this is Antony's son, who is free to give it, if it were all gold? but if you will be advised by me, I would counsel you to accept of the value in money from us; for there may be amongst the rest some antique or famous piece of workmanship, which Antony would be sorry to part with." These anecdotes, my grandfather told us, Philotas used frequently to relate.

To return to Cleopatra; Plato admits four sorts of flattery, but she had a thousand. Were Antony serious or disposed to mirth, she had at any moment some new delight or charm to meet his wishes; at every turn he was upon him, and let him escape her neither by day nor by night. She played at dice with him, drank with him, hunted with him; and when he exercised in arms, she was there to see. At night she would go rambling with him to disturb and torment people at their doors and windows, dressed like a servant-woman, for Antony also went in servant's disguise, and from these expeditions he often came home very scurvily answered, and sometimes even beaten severely, though most people guessed who it was. However, the Alexandrians in general liked it all well enough, and joined good-humouredly and kindly in his frolic and play, saying they were much obliged to Antony for acting his tragic parts at Rome, and keeping his comedy for them. It would be trifling without end to be particular in his follies, but his fishing must not be forgotten. He went out one day to angle with Cleopatra, and, being so unfortunate as to catch nothing in the presence of his mistress, he gave secret orders to the fishermen to dive under water, and put fishes that had been already taken upon his hooks; and these he drew so fast that the Egyptian perceived it. But, feigning great admiration, she told everybody how dexterous Antony was, and invited them next day to come and see him again. So, when a number of them had come on board the fishing-boats, as soon as he had let down his hook, one of her servants was beforehand with his divers, and fixed upon his hook a salted fish from Pontus. Antony, feeling his line give, drew up the prey, and when, as may be imagined, great laughter ensued, " Leave," said Cleopatra, " the fishing-rod, general, to us poor sovereigns of Pharos and Canopus; your game is cities, provinces, and kingdoms."

Whilst he was thus diverting himself and engaged in this boy's play, two despatches arrived; one from Rome, that his brother Lucius and his wife Fulvia, after many quarrels among themselves, had joined in war against Cæsar, and having lost all, had fled out of Italy; the other bringing little better news, that Labienus, at the head of the Parthians, was overrunning Asia, from Euphrates and Syria as far as Lydia and Ionia. So, scarcely at last rousing himself from sleep, and shaking off the fumes of wine, he set out to attack the Parthians, and went as far as Phœnicia; but, upon the receipt of lamentable letters from Fulvia, turned his course with two hundred ships to Italy. And, in his way, receiving such of his friends as fled from Italy, he was given to understand that Fulvia was the sole cause of the war, a woman of a restless spirit and very bold, and withal her hopes were that commotions in Italy would force Antony from Cleopatra. But it happened that Fulvia, as she was coming to meet her husband, fell sick by the way, and died at Sicyon, so that an accommodation was the more easily made. For when he reached Italy, and Cæsar showed no intention of laying anything to his charge, and he on his part shifted the blame of everything on Fulvia, those that were friends to them would not suffer that the time should be spent in looking narrowly into the plea, but made a reconciliation first, and then a partition of the empire between them, taking as their boundary the Ionian Sea, the eastern provinces falling to Antony, to Cæsar the western, and Africa being left to Lepidus. And an agreement was made that every one in their turn, as they thought fit, should make their friends consuls, when they did not choose to take the offices themselves.

These terms were well approved of, but yet it was thought some closer tie would be desirable; and for this, fortune offered occasion. Cæsar had an elder sister, not of the whole blood, for Attia was his mother's name, hers Ancharia. This sister, Octavia, he was extremely attached to, as indeed she was, it is said, quite a wonder of a woman. Her husband, Caius Marcellus, had died not long before, and Antony was now a widower by the death of Fulvia; for, though he did not disavow the passion he had for Cleopatra, yet he disowned anything of marriage, reason as yet, upon this point, still maintaining the debate against the charms of the Egyptian. Everybody concurred in promoting this new alliance, fully expecting that with the beauty, honour, and prudence of Octavia, when her company should, as it was certain it would, have engaged his affections, all would be kept in the safe and happy course of friendship. So, both parties being agreed, they went to Rome to celebrate the nuptials, the senate dispensing with the law by which a widow was not permitted to marry till ten months after the death of her husband.

Sextus Pompeius was in possession of Sicily, and with his ships, under the command of Menas, the pirate, and Menecrates, so infested the Italian coast that no vessels durst venture into those seas. Sextus had behaved with much humanity towards Antony, having received his mother when she fled with Fulvia, and it was therefore judged fit that he also should be received into the peace. They met near the promontory of Misenum, by the mole of the port, Pompey having his fleet at anchor close by, and Antony and Cæsar their troops drawn up all along the shore. There it was concluded that Sextus should quietly enjoy the government of Sicily and Sardinia, he conditioning to scour the seas of all pirates, and to send so much corn every year to Rome.

This agreed on, they invited one another to supper, and by lot it fell to Pompey's turn to give the first entertainment, and Antony, asking where it was to be, " There," said he, pointing to the admiral-galley, a ship of six banks of oars, " that is the only house that Pompey is heir to of his father's." And this he said, reflecting upon Antony, who was then in possession of his father's house. Having fixed the ship on her anchors, and formed a bridgeway from the promontory to conduct on board of her, he gave them a cordial welcome. And when they began to grow warm, and jests were passing freely on Antony and Cleopatra's loves, Menas, the pirate, whispered Pompey, in the

ear, " Shall I," said he, " cut the cables, and make you master
not of Sicily only and Sardinia, but of the whole Roman empire?"
Pompey, having considered a little while, returned him answer,
" Menas, this might have been done without acquainting me;
now we must rest content; I do not break my word." And
so, having been entertained by the other two in their turns, he
set sail for Sicily.

After the treaty was completed, Antony despatched Ventidius
into Asia, to check the advance of the Parthians, while he, as a
compliment to Cæsar, accepted the office of priest to the deceased
Cæsar. And in any state affair and matter of consequence, they
both behaved themselves with much consideration and friendli-
ness for each other. But it annoyed Antony that in all their
amusements, on any trial of skill or fortune, Cæsar should be
constantly victorious. He had with him an Egyptian diviner,
one of those who calculate nativities, who, either to make his
court to Cleopatra, or that by the rules of his art he found it
to be so, openly declared to him that though the fortune that
attended him was bright and glorious, yet it was overshadowed
by Cæsar's; and advised him to keep himself as far distant as
he could from that young man; " for your Genius," said he,
" dreads his; when absent from him yours is proud and brave,
but in his presence unmanly and dejected;" and incidents that
occurred appeared to show that the Egyptian spoke truth. For
whenever they cast lots for any playful purpose, or threw dice,
Antony was still the loser; and repeatedly, when they fought
game-cocks or quails, Cæsar's had the victory. This gave
Antony a secret displeasure, and made him put the more confidence in the skill of his Egyptian. So, leaving the management of his home affairs to Cæsar, he left Italy, and took Octavia,
who had lately borne him a daughter, along with him into
Greece.

Here, whilst he wintered in Athens, he received the first
news of Ventidius's successes over the Parthians, of his having
defeated them in a battle, having slain Labienus and Pharna-
pates, the best general their king, Hyrodes, possessed. For the
celebrating of which he made public feast through Greece, and
for the prizes which were contested at Athens he himself acted
as steward, and, leaving at home the ensigns that are carried
before the general, he made his public appearance in a gown
and white shoes, with the steward's wands marching before;
and he performed his duty in taking the combatants by the
neck, to part them, when they had fought enough.

When the time came for him to set out for the war, he took a garland from the sacred olive, and, in obedience to some oracle, he filled a vessel with the water of the Clepsydra to carry along with him. In this interval, Pacorus, the Parthian king's son, who was marching into Syria with a large army, was met by Ventidius, who gave him battle in the country of Cyrrhestica, slew a large number of his men, and Pacorus among the first. This victory was one of the most renowned achievements of the Romans, and fully avenged their defeats under Crassus, the Parthians being obliged, after the loss of three battles successively, to keep themselves within the bounds of Media and Mesopotamia. Ventidius was not willing to push his good fortune further, for fear of raising some jealousy in Antony, but turning his arms against those that had quitted the Roman interest, he reduced them to their former obedience. Among the rest, he besieged Antiochus, King of Commagene, in the city of Samosata, who made an offer of a thousand talents for his pardon, and a promise of submission to Antony's commands. But Ventidius told him that he must send to Antony, who was already on his march, and had sent word to Ventidius to make no terms with Antiochus, wishing that at any rate this one exploit might be ascribed to him, and that people might not think that all his successes were won by his lieutenants. The siege, however, was long protracted; for when those within found their offers refused, they defended themselves stoutly, till, at last, Antony, finding he was doing nothing, in shame and regret for having refused the first offer, was glad to make an accommodation with Antiochus for three hundred talents. And, having given some orders for the affairs of Syria, he returned to Athens; and, paying Ventidius the honours he well deserved, dismissed him to receive his triumph. He is the only man that has ever yet triumphed for victories obtained over the Parthians; he was of obscure birth, but, by means of Antony's friendship, obtained an opportunity of showing his capacity, and doing great things; and his making such glorious use of it gave new credit to the current observation about Cæsar and Antony, that they were more fortunate in what they did by their lieutenants than in their own persons. For Sossius, also, had great success, and Canidius, whom he left in Armenia, defeated the people there, and also the kings of the Albanians and Iberians, and marched victorious as far as Caucasus, by which means the fame of Antony's arms had become great among the barbarous nations.

He, however, once more, upon some unfavourable stories,

taking offence against Cæsar, set sail with three hundred ships for Italy, and, being refused admittance to the port of Brundusium, made for Tarentum. There his wife Octavia, who came from Greece with him, obtained leave to visit her brother, she being then great with child, having already borne her husband a second daughter; and as she was on her way she met Cæsar, with his two friends Agrippa and Mæcenas, and, taking these two aside, with great entreaties and lamentations she told them, that of the most fortunate woman upon earth, she was in danger of becoming the most unhappy; for as yet every one's eyes were fixed upon her as the wife and sister of the two great commanders, but, if rash counsels should prevail, and war ensue, "I shall be miserable," said she, "without redress; for on what side soever victory falls, I shall be sure to be a loser." Cæsar was overcome by these entreaties, and advanced in a peaceable temper to Tarentum, where those that were present beheld a most stately spectacle; a vast army drawn up by the shore, and as great a fleet in the harbour, all without the occurrence of any act of hostility; nothing but the salutations of friends, and other expressions of joy and kindness, passing from one armament to the other. Antony first entertained Cæsar, this also being a concession on Cæsar's part to his sister; and when at length an agreement was made between them, that Cæsar should give Antony two of his legions to serve him in the Parthian war, and that Antony should in return leave with him a hundred armed galleys, Octavia further obtained of her husband, besides this, twenty light ships for her brother, and of her brother, a thousand foot for her husband. So, having parted good friends, Cæsar went immediatcly to make war with Pompey to conquer Sicily. And Antony, leaving in Cæsar's charge his wife and children, and his children by his former wife Fulvia, set sail for Asia.

But the mischief that thus long had lain still, the passion for Cleopatra, which better thoughts had seemed to have lulled and charmed into oblivion, upon his approach to Syria gathered strength again, and broke out into a flame. And, in fine, like Plato's restive and rebellious horse of the human soul, flinging off all good and wholesome counsel, and breaking fairly loose, he sends Fonteius Capito to bring Cleopatra into Syria. To whom at her arrival he made no small or trifling present, Phœnicia, Cœle-Syria, Cyprus, great part of Cilicia, that side of Judæa which produces balm, that part of Arabia where the Nabathæans extend to the outer sea; profuse gifts which much displeased the Romans. For although he had invested several private persons in great governments and kingdoms, and bereaved many kings of theirs, as Antigonus of Judæa, whose head he caused to be struck off (the first example of that punishment being inflicted on a king), yet nothing stung the Romans like the shame of these honours paid to Cleopatra. Their dissatisfaction was augmented also by his acknowledging as his own the twin children he had by her, giving them the name of Alexander and Cleopatra, and adding, as their surnames, the titles of Sun and Moon. But he, who knew how to put a good colour on the most dishonest action, would say that the greatness of the Roman empire consisted more in giving than in taking kingdoms, and that the way to carry noble blood through the world was by begetting in every place a new line and series of kings; his own ancestor had thus been born of Hercules; Hercules had not limited his hopes of progeny to a single womb, nor feared any law like Solon's or any audit of procreation, but had freely let nature take her will in the foundation and first commencement of many families.

After Phraates had killed his father Hyrodes, and taken possession of his kingdom, many of the Parthians left their country; among the rest Monæses, a man of great distinction and authority, sought refuge with Antony, who, looking on his case as similar to that of Themistocles, and likening his own opulence and magnanimity to those of the former Persian kings, gave him three cities, Larissa, Arethusa, and Hierapolis, which was formerly called Bambyce. But when the King of Parthia soon recalled him, giving him his word and honour for his safety, Antony was not unwilling to give him leave to return, hoping thereby to surprise Phraates, who would believe that peace would continue; for he only made the demand of him that he should send back the Roman ensigns which were taken when Crassus was slain, and the prisoners that remained yet alive. This done, he sent Cleopatra to Egypt, and marched through Arabia and Armenia; and, when his forces came together, and were joined by those of his confederate kings (of whom there were very many, and the most considerable, Artavasdes, King of Armenia, who came at the head of six thousand horse and seven thousand foot), he made a general muster. There appeared sixty thousand Roman foot, ten thousand horse, Spaniards and Gauls, who counted as Romans; and, of other nations, horse and foot thirty thousand. And these great preparations, that put the Indians beyond Bactria into alarm, and made all Asia

shake, were all we are told rendered useless to him because of
Cleopatra. For, in order to pass the winter with her, the war
was pushed on before its due time; and all he did was done
without perfect consideration, as by a man who had no power
of control over his faculties, who, under the effect of some drug
or magic, was still looking back elsewhere, and whose object was
much more to hasten his return than to conquer his enemies.

For, first of all, when he should have taken up his winter-
quarters in Armenia, to refresh his men, who were tired with
long marches, having come at least eight thousand furlongs,
and then having taken the advantage in the beginning of the
spring to invade Media, before the Parthians were out of winter-
quarters, he had not patience to expect his time, but marched
into the province of Atropatene, leaving Armenia on the left
hand, and laid waste all that country. Secondly, his haste was
so great that he left behind the engines absolutely required for
any siege, which followed the camp in three hundred waggons,
and, among the rest, a ram eighty feet long; none of which was
it possible, if lost or damaged, to repair or to make the like, as
the provinces of the Upper Asia produce no trees long or hard
enough for such uses. Nevertheless, he left them all behind, as
a mere impediment to his speed, in the charge of a detachment
under the command of Statianus, the waggon officer. He himself laid siege to Phraata, a principal city of the King of Media,
wherein were that king's wife and children. And when actual
need proved the greatness of his error, in leaving the siege-train
behind him, he had nothing for it but to come up and raise a
mound against the walls, with infinite labour and great loss of
time. Meantime Phraates, coming down with a large army, and
hearing that the waggons were left behind with the battering
engines, sent a strong party of horse, by which Statianus was
surprised, he himself and ten thousand of his men slain, the
engines all broken in pieces, many taken prisoners, and among
the rest King Polemon.

This great miscarriage in the opening of the campaign much
discouraged Antony's army, and Artavasdes, King of Armenia,
deciding that the Roman prospects were bad, withdrew with
all his forces from the camp, although he had been the chief
promoter of the war. The Parthians, encouraged by their
success, came up to the Romans at the siege, and gave them
many affronts; upon which Antony, fearing that the despond-
ency and alarm of his soldiers would only grow worse if he let
them lie idle, taking all the horse, ten legions, and three prætorian

cohorts of heavy infantry, resolved to go out and forage, designing by this means to draw the enemy with more advantage to
a battle. To effect this, he marched a day's journey from his
camp, and finding the Parthians hovering about, in readiness to
attack him while he was in motion, he gave orders for the signal
of battle to be hung out in the encampment, but, at the same
time, pulled down the tents, as if he meant not to fight, but to
lead his men home again; and so he proceeded to lead them
past the enemy, who were drawn up in a half-moon, his orders
being that the horse should charge as soon as the legions were
come up near enough to second them. The Parthians, standing
still while the Romans marched by them, were in great admiration of their army, and of the exact discipline it observed, rank
after rank passing on at equal distances in perfect order and
silence, their pikes all ready in their hands. But when the signal
was given, and the horse turned short upon the Parthians, and
with loud cries charged them, they bravely received them,
though they were at once too near for bowshot; but the legions
coming up with loud shouts and rattling of their arms so
frightened their horses and indeed the men themselves, that
they kept their ground no longer. Antony pressed them hard,
in great hopes that this victory should put an end to the war;
the foot had them in pursuit for fifty furlongs, and the horse
for thrice that distance, and yet, the advantage summed up,
they had but thirty prisoners, and there were but fourscore slain.
So that they were all filled with dejection and discouragement,
to consider that when they were victorious, their advantages
were so small, and that when they were beaten, they lost so
great a number of men as they had done when the carriages
were taken.

The next day, having put the baggage in order, they marched
back to the camp before Phraata, in the way meeting with some
scattering troops of the enemy, and, as they marched further,
with greater parties, at length with the body of the enemy's
army, fresh and in good order, who defied them to battle, and
charged them on every side, and it was not without great
difficulty that they reached the camp. There Antony, finding
that his men had in a panic deserted the defence of the mound,
upon a sally of the Medes, resolved to proceed against them by
decimation, as it is called, which is done by dividing the soldiers
into tens, and, out of every ten, putting one to death, as it
happens by lot. The rest he gave orders should have, instead
of wheat, their rations of corn in barley.

The war was now become grievous to both parties, and the prospect of its continuance yet more fearful to Antony, in respect that he was threatened with famine; for he could no longer forage without wounds and slaughter. And Phraates, on the other side, was full of apprehension that if the Romans were to persist in carrying on the siege, the autumnal equinox being past and the air already closing in for cold, he should be deserted by his soldiers, who would suffer anything ther than wintering in open field. To prevent which, he had recourse to the following deceit: he gave orders to those of his men who had made most acquaintance among the Roman soldiers, not to pursue too close when they met them foraging, but to suffer them to carry off some provision; moreover, that they should praise their valour, and declare that it was not without just reason that their king looked upon the Romans as the bravest men in the world. This done, upon further opportunity, they rode nearer in, and, drawing up their horses by the men, began to revile Antony for his obstinacy; that whereas Phraates desired nothing more than peace, and an occasion to show how ready he was to save the lives of so many brave soldiers, he, on the contrary, gave no opening to any friendly offers, but sat awaiting the arrival of the two fiercest and worst enemies, winter and famine, from whom it would be hard for them to make their escape, even with all the good-will of the Parthians to help them. Antony, having these reports from many hands, began to indulge the hope; nevertheless, he would not send any message to the Parthian till he had put the question to these friendly talkers, whether what they said was said by order of their king. Receiving answer that it was, together with new encouragement to believe them, he sent some of his friends to demand once more the standards and prisoners, lest if he should ask nothing, he might be supposed to be too thankful to have leave to retreat in quiet. The Parthian king made answer that, as for the standards and prisoners, he need not trouble himself: but if he thought fit to retreat, he might do it when he pleased, in peace and safety. Some few days, therefore, being spent in collecting the baggage he set out upon his march. On which occasion, though there was no man of his time like him for addressing a multitude, or for carrying soldiers with him by the force of words, out of shame and sadness he could not find in his heart to speak himself but employed Domitius Ænobarbus. And some of the soldiers resented it, as an undervaluing of them; but the greater number saw the true cause, and pitied it, and thought it rather a reason why they on their side should treat their general with more respect and obedience than ordinary.

Antony had resolved to return by the same way he came, which was through a level country clear of all trees; but a certain Mardian came to him (one that was very conversant with the manners of the Parthians, and whose fidelity to the Romans had been tried at the battle where the machines were lost), and advised him to keep the mountains close on his right hand, and not to expose his men, heavily armed, in a broad, open, riding country, to the attacks of a numerous army of light horse and archers; that Phraates with fair promises had persuaded him from the siege on purpose that he might with more ease cut him off in his retreat; but if so he pleased, he would conduct him by a nearer route, on which moreover he should find the necessaries for his army in greater abundance. Antony upon this began to consider what was best to be done; he was unwilling to seem to have any mistrust of the Parthians after their treaty; but, holding it to be really best to march his army the shorter and more inhabited way, he demanded of the Mardian some assurance of his faith, who offered himself to be bound until the army came safe into Armenia. Two days he conducted the army bound, and, on the third, when Antony had given up all thought of the enemy, and was marching at his ease in no very good order, the Mardian, perceiving the bank of the river broken down, and the water let out and overflowing the road by which they were to pass, saw at once that this was the handiwork of the Parthians, done out of mischief, and to hinder their march: so he advised Antony to be upon his guard, for that the enemy was nigh at hand. And no sooner had he begun to put his men in order, disposing the slingers and dart-men in convenient intervals for sallying out, but the Parthians came pouring in on all sides, fully expecting to encompass them, and throw the whole army into disorder. They were at once attacked by the light troops, whom they galled a good deal with their arrows; but being themselves as warmly entertained with the slings and darts, and many wounded, they made their retreat. Soon after, rallying up afresh, they were beat back by a battalion of Gallic horse, and appeared no more that day.

By their manner of attack Antony, seeing what to do, not only placed the slings and darts as a rear guard, but also lined both flanks with them, and so marched in a square battle, giving order to the horse to charge and beat off the enemy, but not to follow them far as they retired. So that the Parthians, not doing more

mischief for the four ensuing days than they received, began to
abate in their zeal, and, complaining that the winter season was
much advanced, pressed for returning home.

But, on the fifth day, Flavius Gallus, a brave and active officer,
who had a considerable command in the army, came to Antony,
desiring of him some light infantry out of the rear, and some
horse out of the front, with which he would undertake to do some
considerable service.   Which when he had obtained, he beat the
enemy back, not withdrawing, as was usual, at the same time,
and retreating upon the mass of the heavy infantry, but maintaining his own ground, and engaging boldly.   The officers who
commanded in the rear, perceiving how far he was getting from
the body of the army, sent to warn him back, but he took no
notice of them.   It is said that Titius the quæstor snatched the
standards and turned them round, upbraiding Gallus with thus
leading so many brave men to destruction.   But when he on the
other side reviled him again, and commanded the men that were
about him to stand firm, Titius made his retreat, and Gallus,
charging the enemies in the front, was encompassed by a party
that fell upon his rear, which at length perceiving, he sent a
messenger to demand succour.   But the commanders of the
heavy infantry, Canidius amongst others, a particular favourite
of Antony's, seem here to have committed a great oversight.
For, instead of facing about with the whole body, they sent small
parties, and, when they were defeated, they still sent out small
parties, so that by their bad management the rout would have
spread through the whole army, if Antony himself had not
marched from the van at the head of the third legion, and,
passing this through among the fugitives, faced the enemies, and
hindered them from any further pursuit.

In this engagement were killed three thousand, five thousand
were carried back to the camp wounded, amongst the rest Gallus,
shot through the body with four arrows, of which wounds he
died.   Antony went from tent to tent to visit and comfort the
rest of them, and was not able to see his men without tears and
a passion of grief.   They, however, seized his hand with joyful
faces, bidding him go and see to himself and not be concerned
about them, calling him their emperor and their general, and
saying that if he did well they were safe.   For, in short, never
in all these times can history make mention of a general at the
head of a more splendid army; whether you consider strength
and youth, or patience and sufferance in labours and fatigues;
but as for the obedience and affectionate respect they bore their

general, and the unanimous feeling amongst small and great
alike, officers and common soldiers, to prefer his good opinion of
them to their very lives and being, in this part of military excellence it was not possible that they could have been surpassed
by the very Romans of old. For this devotion, as I have said
before, there were many reasons, as the nobility of his family,
his eloquence, his frank and open manners, his liberal and magnificent habits, his familiarity in talking with everybody, and, at
this time particularly, his kindness in visiting and pitying the
sick, joining in all their pains, and furnishing them with all
things necessary, so that the sick and wounded were even more
eager to serve than those that were whole and strong.

Nevertheless, this last victory had so encouraged the enemy
that, instead of their former impatience and weariness, they
began soon to feel contempt for the Romans, staying all night
near the camp, in expectation of plundering their tents and
baggage, which they concluded they must abandon; and in the
morning new forces arrived in large masses, so that their number
was grown to be not less, it is said, than forty thousand horse;
and the king had sent the very guards that attended upon his
own person, as to a sure and unquestioned victory, for he
himself was never present in any fight. Antony, designing to
harangue the soldiers, called for a mourning habit that he might
move them the more, but was dissuaded by his friends; so he
came forward in the general's scarlet cloak, and addressed them,
praising those that had gained the victory, and reproaching
those that had fled, the former answering him with promises of
success, and the latter excusing themselves, and telling him they
were ready to undergo decimation, or any other punishment he
should please to inflict upon them, only entreating that he would
forget and not discompose himself with their faults. At which
he lifted up his hands to heaven, and prayed the gods that, if to
balance the great favours he had received of them any judgment
lay in store, they would pour it upon his head alone, and grant
his soldiers victory.

The next day they took better order for their march, and the
Parthians, who thought they were marching rather to plunder
than to fight, were much taken aback, when they came up and
were received with a shower of missiles, to find the enemy not
disheartened, but fresh and resolute. So that they themselves
began to lose courage. But at the descent of a hill where the
Romans were obliged to pass, they got together, and let fly their
arrows upon them as they moved slowly down. But the full-

armed infantry, facing round, received the light troops within; and those in the first rank knelt on one knee, holding their shields before them, the next rank holding theirs over the first, and so again others over these, much like the tiling of a house, or the rows of seats in a theatre, the whole affording sure defence against arrows, which glanced upon them without doing any harm. The Parthians, seeing the Romans down upon their knees, could not imagine but that it must proceed from weariness; so that they laid down their bows, and, taking their spears, made a fierce onset, when the Romans, with a great cry, leaped upon their feet, striking hand to hand with their javelins, slew the foremost, and put the rest to flight. After this rate it was every day, and the trouble they gave made the marches short; in addition to which famine began to be felt in the camp, for they could get but little corn, and that which they got they were forced to fight for; and, besides this, they were in want of implements to grind it and make bread. For they had left almost all behind, the baggage horses being dead or otherwise employed in carrying the sick and wounded. Provision was so scarce in the army that an Attic quart of wheat sold for fifty drachmas, and barley loaves for their weight in silver. And when they tried vegetables and roots, they found such as are commonly eaten very scarce, so that they were constrained to venture upon any they could get, and, among others, they chanced upon an herb that was mortal, first taking away all sense and understanding. He that had eaten of it remembered nothing in the world, and employed himself only in moving great stones from one place to another, which he did with as much earnestness and industry as if it had been a business of the greatest consequence. Through all the camp there was nothing to be seen but men grubbing upon the ground at stones, which they carried from place to place. But in the end they threw up bile and died, as wine, moreover, which was the one antidote, failed. When Antony saw them die so fast, and the Parthians still in pursuit, he was heard to exclaim several times over, " O, the Ten Thousand! " as if in admiration of the retreat of the Greeks, with Xenophon, who, when they had a longer journey to make from Babylonia, and a more powerful enemy to deal with, nevertheless came home safe.

The Parthians, finding that they could not divide the Roman army, nor break the order of their battle, and that withal they had been so often worsted, once more began to treat the foragers with professions of humanity; they came up to them with their bows unbent, telling them that they were going home to their houses; that this was the end of their retaliation, and that only some Median troops would follow for two or three days, not with any design to annoy them, but for the defence of some of the villages further on. And, saying this, they saluted them and embraced them with a great show of friendship. This made the Romans full of confidence again, and Antony, on hearing of it, was more disposed to take the road through the level country, being told that no water was to be hoped for on that through the mountains. But while he was preparing thus to do, Mithridates came into the camp, a cousin to Monæses, of whom we related that he sought refuge with the Romans, and received in gift from Antony three cities. Upon his arrival, he desired somebody might be brought to him that could speak Syriac or Parthian. One Alexander, of Antioch, a friend of Antony's, was brought to him, to whom the stranger, giving his name, and mentioning Monæses as the person who desired to do the kindness, put the question, did he see that high range of hills, pointing at some distance. He told him, yes. "It is there," said he, "the whole Parthian army lie in wait for your passage; for the great plains come immediately up to them, and they expect that, confiding in their promises, you will leave the way of the mountains, and take the level route. It is true that in passing over the mountains you will suffer the want of water, and the fatigue to which you have become familiar, but if you pass through the plains, Antony must expect the fortune of Crassus."

This said, he departed. Antony, in alarm calling his friends in council, sent for the Mardian guide, who was of the same opinion. He told them that, with or without enemies, the want of any certain track in the plain, and the likelihood of their losing their way, were quite objection enough; the other route was rough and without water, but then it was but for a day. Antony, therefore, changing his mind, marched away upon this road that night, commanding that every one should carry water sufficient for his own use; but most of them being unprovided with vessels, they made shift with their helmets, and some with skins. As soon as they started, the news of it was carried to the Parthians, who followed them, contrary to their custom, through the night, and at sunrise attacked the rear, which was tired with marching and want of sleep, and not in condition to make any considerable defence. For they had got through two hundred and forty furlongs that night, and at the end of such a march to find the enemy at their heels put them out of heart. Besides, having to fight for every step of the way increased their distress from thirst. Those that were in the van came up to a river, the water of which was extremely cool and clear, but brackish and medicinal, and, on being drunk, produced immediate pains in the bowels and a renewed thirst. Of this the Mardian had forewarned them, but they could not forbear, and, beating back those that opposed them, they drank of it. Antony ran from one place to another, begging they would have a little patience, that not far off there was a river of wholesome water, and that the rest of the way was so difficult for the horse that the enemy could pursue them no further; and, saying this, he ordered to sound a retreat to call those back that were engaged, and commanded the tents should be set up, that the soldiers might at any rate refresh themselves in the shade.

But the tents were scarce well put up, and the Parthians beginning, according to their custom, to withdraw, when Mithridates came again to them, and informed Alexander, with whom he had before spoken, that he would do well to advise Antony to stay where he was no longer than needs he must, that, after having refreshed his troops, he should endeavour with all diligence to gain the next river, that the Parthians would not cross it, but so far they were resolved to follow them. Alexander made his report to Antony, who ordered a quantity of gold plate to be carried to Mithridates, who, taking as much as he could well hide under his clothes, went his way. And, upon this advice, Antony, while it was yet day, broke up his camp, and the whole army marched forward without receiving any molestation from the Parthians, though that night by their own doing was in effect the most wretched and terrible that they passed. For some of the men began to kill and plunder those whom they suspected to have any money, ransacked the baggage, and seized the money there. In the end, they laid hands on Antony's own equipage, and broke all his rich tables and cups, dividing the fragments amongst them. Antony, hearing such a noise and such a stirring to and fro all through the army, the belief prevailing that the enemy had routed and cut off a portion of the troops, called for one of his freedmen, then serving as one of his guards, Rhamnus by name, and made him take an oath that whenever he should give him orders, he would run his sword through his body and cut off his head, that he might not fall alive into the hands of the Parthians, nor, when dead, be recognised as the general. While he was in this consternation, and all his friends about him in tears, the Mardian came up and

gave them all new life.  He convinced them, by the coolness and
humidity of the air, which they could feel in breathing it, that
the river which he had spoken of was now not far off, and the
calculation of the time that had been required to reach it came,
he said, to the same result, for the night was almost spent.
And, at the same time, others came with information that all
the confusion in the camp proceeded only from their own
violence and robbery among themselves.  To compose this
tumult, and bring them again into some order after their distraction, he commanded the signal to be given for a halt.

Day began to break, and quiet and regularity were just re-
appearing, when the Parthian arrows began to fly among the
rear, and the light-armed troops were ordered out to battle.
And, being seconded by the heavy infantry, who covered one
another as before described with their shields, they bravely
received the enemy, who did not think convenient to advance
any further, while the van of the army, marching forward
leisurely in this manner, came in sight of the river, and Antony,
drawing up the cavalry on the banks to confront the enemy,
first passed over the sick and wounded.  And, by this time, even
those who were engaged with the enemy had opportunity to
drink at their ease; for the Parthians, on seeing the river, unbent
their bows, and told the Romans they might pass over freely,
and made them great compliments in praise of their valour.
Having crossed without molestation, they rested themselves
awhile, and presently went forward, not giving perfect credit
to the fair words of their enemies.  Six days after this last
battle, they arrived at the river Araxes, which divides Media
and Armenia, and seemed, both by its deepness and the violence
of the current, to be very dangerous to pass.  A report, also,
had crept in amongst them, that the enemy was in ambush,
ready to set upon them as soon as they should be occupied with
their passage.  But when they were got over on the other side,
and found themselves in Armenia, just as if land was now
sighted after a storm at sea, they kissed the ground for joy,
shedding tears and embracing each other in their delight.  But
taking their journey through a land that abounded in all sorts
of plenty, they ate, after their long want, with that excess of
everything they met with that they suffered from dropsies
and dysenteries.

Here Antony, making a review of his army, found that he
had lost twenty thousand foot and four thousand horse, of which
the better half perished, not by the enemy, but by diseases.

Their march was of twenty-seven days from Phraata, during which they had beaten the Parthians in eighteen battles, though with little effect or lasting result, because of their being so unable to pursue. By which it is manifest that it was Artavasdes who lost Antony the benefit of the expedition. For had the sixteen thousand horsemen whom he led away, out of Media, armed in the same style as the Parthians, and accustomed to their manner of fight, been there to follow the pursuit when the Romans put them to flight, it is impossible they could have rallied so often after their defeats, and reappeared again as they did to renew their attacks. For this reason, the whole army was very earnest with Antony to march into Armenia to take revenge. But he, with more reflection, forbore to notice the desertion, and continued all his former courtesies, feeling that the army was wearied out, and in want of all manner of necessaries. Afterwards, however, entering Armenia, with invitations and fair promises he prevailed upon Artavasdes to meet him, when he seized him, bound him, and carried him to Alexandria, and there led him in a triumph; one of the things which most offended the Romans, who felt as if all the honours and solemn observances of their country were, for Cleopatra's sake, handed over to the Egyptians.

This, however, was at an after time. For the present, marching his army in great haste in the depth of winter through continual storms of snow, he lost eight thousand of his men, and came with much diminished numbers to a place called the White Village, between Sidon and Berytus, on the sea-coast, where he waited for the arrival of Cleopatra. And, being impatient of the delay she made, he bethought himself of shortening the time in wine and drunkenness, and yet could not endure the tediousness of a meal, but would start from table and run to see if she were coming. Till at last she same into port, and brought with her clothes and money for the soldiers. Though some say that Antony only received the clothes from her and distributed his own money in her name.

A quarrel presently happening between the King of Media and Phraates of Parthia, beginning, it is said, about the division of the booty that was taken from the Romans, and creating great apprehension in the Median lest he should lose his kingdom. He sent, therefore, ambassadors to Antony, with offers of entering into a confederate war against Phraates. And Antony, full of hopes at being thus asked, as a favour, to accept that one thing, horse and archers, the want of which had hindered his beating the Parthians before, began at once to prepare for a return to

Armenia, there to join the Medes on the Araxes, and begin the war afresh. But Octavia, in Rome, being desirous to see Antony, asked Cæsar's leave to go to him; which he gave her, not so much, say most authors, to gratify his sister, as to obtain a fair pretence to begin the war upon her dishonourable reception. She no sooner arrived at Athens, but by letters from Antony she was informed of his new expedition, and his will that she should await him there. And, though she were much displeased, not being ignorant of the real reason of this usage, yet she wrote to him to know to what place he would be pleased she should send the things she had brought with her for his use; for she had brought clothes for his soldiers, baggage, cattle, money, and presents for his friends and officers, and two thousand chosen soldiers sumptuously armed, to form prætorian cohorts. This message was brought from Octavia to Antony by Niger, one of his friends, who added to it the praises she deserved so well. Cleopatra, feeling her rival already, as it were, at hand, was seized with fear, lest if to her noble life and her high alliance, she once could add the charm of daily habit and affectionate intercourse, she should become irresistible, and be his absolute mistress forever. So she feigned to be dying for love of Antony, bringing her body down by slender diet; when he entered the room, she fixed her eyes upon him in a rapture, and when he left, seemed to languish and half faint away. She took great pains that he should see her in tears, and, as soon as he noticed it, hastily dried them up and turned away, as if it were her wish that he should know nothing of it. All this was acting while he prepared for Media; and Cleopatra's creatures were not slow to forward the design, upbraiding Antony with his unfeeling, hard-hearted temper, thus letting a woman perish whose soul depended upon him and him alone. Octavia, it was true, was his wife, and had been married to him because it was found convenient for the affairs of her brother that it should be so, and she had the honour of the title; but Cleopatra, the sovereign queen of many nations, had been contented with the name of his mistress, nor did she shun or despise the character whilst she might see him, might live with him, and enjoy him; if she were bereaved of this, she would not survive the loss. In fine, they so melted and unmanned him that, fully believing she would die if he forsook her, he put off the war and returned to Alexandria, deferring his Median expedition until next summer, though news came of the Parthians being all in confusion with intestine disputes. Nevertheless, he did some time after go into that country, and made an alliance with the King of Media, by marriage of a son of his by Cleopatra to the king's daughter, who was yet very young; and so returned, with his thoughts taken up about the civil war.

When Octavia returned from Athens, Cæsar, who considered she had been injuriously treated, commanded her to live in a separate house; but she refused to leave the house of her husband, and entreated him, unless he had already resolved, upon other motives, to make war with Antony, that he would on her account let it alone; it would be intolerable to have it said of the two greatest commanders in the world that they had involved the Roman people in a civil war, the one out of passion for, the other out of resentment about, a woman. And her behaviour proved her words to be sincere. She remained in Antony's house as if he were at home in it, and took the noblest and most generous care, not only of his children by her, but of those by Fulvia also. She received all the friends of Antony that came to Rome to seek office or upon any business, and did her utmost to prefer their requests to Cæsar; yet this her honourable deportment did but, without her meaning it, damage the reputation of Antony; the wrong he did to such a woman made him hated. Nor was the division he made among his sons at Alexandria less unpopular; it seemed a theatrical piece of insolence and contempt of his country. For assembling the people in the exercise ground, and causing two golden thrones to be placed on a platform of silver, the one for him and the other for Cleopatra, and at their feet lower thrones for their children, he proclaimed Cleopatra Queen of Egypt, Cyprus, Libya, and Cœle-Syria, and with her conjointly Cæsarion, the reputed son of the former Cæsar, who left Cleopatra with child. His own sons by Cleopatra were to have the style of kings of kings; to Alexander he gave Armenia and Media, with Parthia, so soon as it should be overcome; to Ptolemy, Phœnicia, Syria, and Cilicia. Alexander was brought out before the people in Median costume, the tiara and upright peak, and Ptolemy, in boots and mantle and Macedonian cap done about with the diadem; for this was the habit of the successors of Alexander, as the other was of the Medes and Armenians. And as soon as they had saluted their parents, the one was received by a guard of Macedonians, the other by one of Armenians. Cleopatra was then, as at other times when she appeared in public, dressed in the habit of the goddess Isis, and gave audience to the people under the name of the New Isis.

Cæsar, relating these things in the senate, and often complaining to the people, excited men's minds against Antony, and

Antony also sent messages of accusation against Cæsar. The principal of his charges were these: first, that he had not made any division with him of Sicily, which was lately taken from Pompey; secondly, that he had retained the ships he had lent him for the war; thirdly, that. after deposing Lepidus, their colleague, he had taken for himself the army, governments, and revenues formerly appropriated to him; and lastly, that he had parcelled out almost all Italy amongst his own soldiers, and left nothing for his. Cæsar's answer was as follows: that he had put Lepidus out of government because of his own misconduct; that what he had got in war he would divide with Antony, so soon as Antony gave him a share of Armenia; that Antony's soldiers had no claims in Italy, being in possession of Media and Parthia, the acquisitions which their brave actions under their general had added to the Roman empire.

Antony was in Armenia when this answer came to him, and immediately sent Canidius with sixteen legions towards the sea; but he, in the company of Cleopatra, went to Ephesus, whither ships were coming in from all quarters to form the navy, consisting, vessels of burden included, of eight hundred vessels, of which Cleopatra furnished two hundred, together with twenty thousand talents, and provision for the whole army during the war. Antony, on the advice of Domitius and some others, bade Cleopatra return into Egypt, there to expect the event of the war; but she, dreading some new reconciliation by Octavia's means, prevailed with Canidius, by a large sum of money, to speak in her favour with Antony, pointing out to him that it was not just that one that bore so great a part in the charge of the war should be robbed of her share of glory in the carrying it on; nor would it be politic to disoblige the Egyptians, who were so considerable a part of his naval forces; nor did he see how she was inferior in prudence to any one of the kings that were serving with him; she had long governed a great kingdom by herself alone, and long lived with him, and gained experience in public affairs. These arguments (so the fate that destined all to Cæsar would have it) prevailed; and when all their forces had met, they sailed together to Samos, and held high festivities. For, as it was ordered that all kings, princes, and governors, all nations and cities within the limits of Syria, the Mæotid Lake, Armenia, and Illyria, should bring or cause to be brought all munitions necessary for war, so was it also proclaimed that all stage-players should make their appearance at Samos; so that, while pretty nearly the whole world was filled with groans and lamentations, this one island for some days resounded with piping and harping, theatres filling, and choruses playing. Every city sent an ox as its contribution to the sacrifice, and the kings that accompanied Antony competed who should make the most magnificent feasts and the greatest presents; and men began to ask themselves, what would be done to celebrate the victory, when they went to such an expense of festivity at the opening of the war.

This over, he gave Priene to his players for a habitation, and set sail for Athens, where fresh sports and play-acting employed him. Cleopatra, jealous of the honours Octavia had received at Athens (for Octavia was much beloved by the Athenians), courted the favour of the people with all sorts of attentions. The Athenians, in requital, having decreed her public honours, deputed several of the citizens to wait upon her at her house; amongst whom went Antony as one, he being an Athenian citizen, and he it was that made the speech. He sent orders to Rome to have Octavia removed out of his house. She left it, we are told, accompanied by all his children, except the eldest by Fulvia, who was then with his father, weeping and grieving that she must be looked upon as one of the causes of the war. But the Romans pitied, not so much her, as Antony himself, and more particularly those who had seen Cleopatra, whom they could report to have no way the advantage of Octavia either in youth or in beauty.

The speed and extent of Antony's preparations alarmed Cæsar, who feared he might be forced to fight the decisive battle that summer. For he wanted many necessaries, and the people grudged very much to pay the taxes; freemen being called upon to pay a fourth part of their incomes, and freed slaves an eighth of their property, so that there were loud outcries against him, and disturbances throughout all Italy. And this is looked upon as one of the greatest of Antony's oversights, that he did not then press the war. For he allowed time at once for Cæsar to make his preparations and for the commotions to pass over. For while people were having their money called for, they were mutinous and violent; but, having paid it, they held their peace. Titius and Plancus, men of consular dignity and friends to Antony, having been ill-used by Cleopatra, whom they had most resisted in her design of being present in the war, came over to Cæsar and gave information of the contents of Antony's will, with which they were acquainted. It was deposited in the hands of the vestal virgins, who refused to deliver it up, and sent Cæsar word, if he pleased, he should come and seize it himself, which he did. And, reading it over to himself, he noted those places that were most for his purpose, and, having summoned the senate, read them publicly. Many were scandalised at the proceeding, thinking it out of reason and equity to call a man to account for what was not to be until after his death. Cæsar specially pressed what Antony said in his will about his burial; for he had ordered that even if he died in the city of Rome, his body, after being carried in state through the forum, should be sent to Cleopatra at Alexandria. Calvisius, a dependant of Cæsar's, urged other charges in connection with Cleopatra against Antony; that he had given her the library of Pergamus, containing two hundred thousand distinct volumes; that at a great banquet, in the presence of many guests, he had risen up and rubbed her feet, to fulfil some wager or promise; that he had suffered the Ephesians to salute her as their queen; that he had frequently at the public audience of kings and princes received amorous messages written in tablets made of onyx and crystal, and read them openly on the tribunal; that when Furnius, a man of great authority and eloquence among the Romans, was pleading, Cleopatra happening to pass by in her chair, Antony started up and left them in the middle of their cause, to follow at her side and attend her home.

Calvisius, however, was looked upon as the inventor of most of these stories. Antony's friends went up and down the city to gain him credit, and sent one of themselves, Geminius, to him, to beg him to take heed and not allow himself to be deprived by vote of his authority, and proclaimed a public enemy to the Roman state. But Geminius no sooner arrived in Greece but he was looked upon as one of Octavia's spies; at their suppers he was made a continual butt for mockery, and was put to sit in the least honourable places; all of which he bore very well, seeking only an occasion of speaking with Antony. So at supper, being told to say what business he came about, he answered he would keep the rest for a soberer hour, but one thing he had to say, whether full or fasting, that all would go well if Cleopatra would return to Egypt. And on Antony showing his anger at it, "You have done well, Geminius," said Cleopatra, "to tell your secret without being put to the rack." So Geminius, after a few days, took occasion to make his escape and go to Rome. Many more of Antony's friends were driven from him by the insolent usage they had from Cleopatra's flatterers, amongst whom were Marcus Silanus and Dellius the historian. And Dellius says he was afraid of his life, and that Glaucus, the physician, informed him of Cleopatra's design against him. She was angry with him for having said that Antony's friends were served with sour wine, while at Rome Sarmentus, Cæsar's little page (his *delicia,* as the Romans call it), drank Falernian.

As soon as Cæsar had completed his preparations, he had a decree made declaring war on Cleopatra, and depriving Antony of the authority which he had let a woman exercise in his place. Cæsar added that he had drunk potions that had bereaved him of his senses, and that the generals they would have to fight with would be Mardion the eunuch, Pothinus, Iras, Cleopatra's hair-dressing girl, and Charmion, who were Antony's chief state-councillors.

These prodigies are said to have announced the war. Pisaurum, where Antony had settled a colony, on the Adriatic sea, was swallowed up by an earthquake; sweat ran from one of the marble statues of Antony at Alba for many days together, and though frequently wiped off, did not stop. When he himself was in the city of Patræ, the temple of Hercules was struck by lightning, and, at Athens, the figure of Bacchus was torn by a violent wind out of the Battle of the Giants, and laid flat upon the theatre; with both which deities Antony claimed connection, professing to be descended from Hercules, and from his imitating Bacchus in his way of living having received the name of young Bacchus. The same whirlwind at Athens also brought down, from amongst many others which were not disturbed, the colossal statues of Eumenes and Attalus, which were inscribed with Antony's name. And in Cleopatra's admiral-galley, which was called the Antonias, a most inauspicious omen occurred. Some swallows had built in the stern of the galley, but other swallows came, beat the first away, and destroyed their nests.

When the armaments gathered for the war, Antony had no less than five hundred ships of war, including numerous galleys of eight and ten banks of oars, as richly ornamented as if they were meant for a triumph. He had a hundred thousand foot and twelve thousand horse. He had vassal kings attending, Bocchus of Libya, Tarcondemus of the Upper Cilicia, Archelaus of Cappadocia, Philadelphus of Paphlagonia, Mithridates of Commagene, and Sadalas of Thrace; all these were with him in person. Out of Pontus Polemon sent him considerable forces, as did also Malchus from Arabia, Herod the Jew, and Amyntus, King of Lycaonia and Galatia; also the Median king sent some troops to join him. Cæsar had two hundred and fifty galleys of war, eighty thousand foot, and horse about equal to the enemy. Antony's empire extended from Euphrates and Armenia to the Ionian sea and the Illyrians; Cæsar's, from Illyria to the westward ocean, and from the ocean all along the Tuscan and Sicilian sea. Of Africa, Cæsar had all the coast opposite to Italy, Gaul, and Spain, as far as the Pillars of Hercules, and Antony the provinces from Cyrene to Æthiopia.

But so wholly was he now the mere appendage to the person of Cleopatra that, although he was much superior to the enemy in land-forces, yet, out of complaisance to his mistress, he wished the victory to be gained by sea, and that, too, when he could not but see how, for want of sailors, his captains, all through unhappy Greece, were pressing every description of men, common travellers and ass-drivers, harvest labourers and boys, and for all this the vessels had not their complements, but remained, most of them, ill-manned and badly rowed. Cæsar, on the other side, had ships that were built not for size or show, but for service, not pompous galleys, but light, swift, and perfectly manned; and from his headquarters at Tarentum and Brundusium he sent messages to Antony not to protract the war, but come out with his forces; he would give him secure roadsteads and ports for his fleet, and, for his land army to disembark and pitch their camp, he would leave him as much ground in Italy, inland from the sea, as a horse could traverse in a single course. Antony, on the other side, with the like bold language, challenged him to a single combat, though he were much the older; and, that being refused, proposed to meet him in the Pharsalian fields, where Cæsar and Pompey had fought before. But whilst Antony lay with his fleet near Actium, where now stands Nicopolis, Cæsar seized his opportunity and crossed the Ionian sea, securing himself at a place in Epirus called the Ladle. And when those about Antony were much disturbed, their land forces being a good way off, "Indeed," said Cleopatra, in mockery, "we may well be frightened if Cæsar has got hold of the Ladle!"

On the morrow, Antony, seeing the enemy sailing up, and fearing lest his ships might be taken for want of the soldiers to go on board of them, armed all the rowers, and made a show upon the decks of being in readiness to fight; the oars were mounted as if waiting to be put in motion, and the vessels themselves drawn up to face the enemy on either side of the channel of Actium, as though they were properly manned and ready for an engagement. And Cæsar, deceived by this stratagem, retired. He was also thought to have shown considerable skill in cutting off the water from the enemy by some lines of trenches and forts, water not being plentiful anywhere else, nor very good. And again, his conduct to Domitius was generous, much against the will of Cleopatra. For when he had made his escape in a little boat to Cæsar, having then a fever upon him, although Antony could not but resent it highly, yet he sent after him his whole equipage with his friends and servants; and Domitius, as if he would give a testimony to the world how repentant he had become on his desertion and treachery being thus manifest, died soon after. Among the kings, also, Amyntas and Deiotarus went over to Cæsar. And the fleet was so unfortunate in everything that was undertaken, and so unready on every occasion, that Antony was driven again to put his confidence in the land forces. Canidius, too, who commanded the legions, when he saw how things stood, changed his opinion, and now was of advice that Cleopatra should be sent back, and that, retiring into Thrace or Macedonia, the quarrel should be decided in a land fight. For Dicomes, also, the King of the Getæ, promised to come and join him with a great army, and it would not be any kind of disparagement to him to yield the sea to Cæsar, who, in the Sicilian wars, had had such long practice in ship-fighting; on the contrary, it would be simply ridiculous for Antony, who was by land the most experienced commander living, to make no use of his well-disciplined and numerous infantry, scattering and wasting his forces by parcelling them out in the ships. But for all this, Cleopatra prevailed that a sea-fight should determine all, having already an eye to flight, and ordering all her affairs, not so as to assist in gaining a victory, but to escape with the greatest safety from the first commencement of a defeat.

There were two long walls, extending from the camp to the station of the ships, between which Antony used to pass to and fro without suspecting any danger. But Cæsar, upon the suggestion of a servant that it would not be difficult to surprise him, laid an ambush, which, rising up somewhat too hastily, seized the man that came just before him, he himself escaping narrowly by flight.

When it was resolved to stand to a fight at sea, they set fire to all the Egyptian ships except sixty; and of these the best and largest, from ten banks down to three, he manned with twenty thousand full-armed men and two thousand archers. Here it is related that a foot captain, one that had fought often under Antony, and had his body all mangled with wounds, exclaimed, "O my general, what have our wounds and swords done to displease you, that you should give your confidence to rotten

timbers? Let Egyptians and Phœnicians contend at sea, give
us the land, where we know well how to die upon the spot or
gain the victory." To which he answered nothing, but, by his
look and motion of his hand seeming to bid him be of good
courage, passed forwards, having already, it would seem, no
very sure hopes, since when the masters proposed leaving the
sails behind them, he commanded they should be put aboard,
" For we must not," said he, " let one enemy escape."

That day and the three following the sea was so rough they
could not engage. But on the fifth there was a calm, and they
fought; Antony commanding with Publicola the right, and
Cœlius the left squadron, Marcus Octavius and Marcus Insteius
the centre. Cæsar gave the charge of the left to Agrippa, commanding in person on the right. As for the land forces, Canidius
was general for Antony, Taurus for Cæsar; both armies remaining drawn up in order along the shore. Antony in a small boat
went from one ship to another, encouraging his soldiers, and
bidding them stand firm and fight as steadily on their large ships
as if they were on land. The masters he ordered that they
should receive the enemy lying still as if they were at anchor,
and maintain the entrance of the port, which was a narrow and
difficult passage. Of Cæsar they relate that, leaving his tent
and going round, while it was yet dark, to visit the ships, he
met a man driving an ass, and asked him his name. He answered
him that his own name was " Fortunate, and my ass," says he,
" is called Conqueror." And afterwards, when he disposed the
beaks of the ships in that place in token of his victory, the statue
of this man and his ass in bronze were placed amongst them.
After examining the rest of his fleet, he went in a boat to the
right wing, and looked with much admiration at the enemy
lying perfectly still in the straits, in all appearance as if they
had been at anchor. For some considerable length of time he
actually thought they were so, and kept his own ships at rest,
at a distance of about eight furlongs from them. But about
noon a breeze sprang up from the sea, and Antony's men, weary
of expecting the enemy so long, and trusting to their large tall
vessels, as if they had been invincible, began to advance the left
squadron. Cæsar was overjoyed to see them move, and ordered
his own right squadron to retire, that he might entice them out
to sea as far as he could, his design being to sail round and round,
and so with his light and well-manned galleys to attack these
huge vessels, which their size and their want of men made slow
to move and difficult to manage.

When they engaged, there was no charging or striking of one ship by another, because Antony's, by reason of their great bulk, were incapable of the rapidity required to make the stroke effectual, and on the other side, Cæsar's durst not charge head to head on Antony's, which were all armed with solid masses and spikes of brass; nor did they like even to run in on their sides, which were so strongly built with great squared pieces of timber, fastened together with iron bolts, that their vessels' beaks would easily have been shattered upon them. So that the engagement resembled a land fight, or, to speak yet more properly, the attack and defence of a fortified place; for there were always three or four vessels of Cæsar's about one of Antony's, pressing them with spears, javelins, poles, and several inventions of fire, which they flung among them, Antony's men using catapults also, to pour down missiles from wooden towers. Agrippa drawing out the squadron under his command to out-flank the enemy, Publicola was obliged to observe his motions, and gradually to break off from the middle squadron, where some confusion and alarm ensued, while Arruntius engaged them. But the fortune of the day was still undecided, and the battle equal, when on a sudden Cleopatra's sixty ships were seen hoisting sail and making out to sea in full flight, right through the ships that were engaged. For they were placed behind the great ships, which, in breaking through, they put into disorder. The enemy was astonished to see them sailing off with a fair wind towards Peloponnesus. Here it was that Antony showed to all the world that he was no longer actuated by the thoughts and motives of a commander or a man, or indeed by his own judgment at all, and what was once said as a jest, that the soul of a lover lives in some one else's body, he proved to be a serious truth. For, as if he had been born part of her, and must move with her wheresoever she went, as soon as he saw her ship sailing away, he abandoned all that were fighting and spending their lives for him, and put himself aboard a galley of five banks of oars, taking with him only Alexander of Syria and Scellias, to follow her that had so well begun his ruin and would hereafter accomplish it.

She, perceiving him to follow, gave the signal to come aboard. So, as soon as he came up with them, he was taken into the ship. But without seeing her or letting himself be seen by her, he went forward by himself, and sat alone, without a word, in the ship's prow, covering his face with his two hands. In the meanwhile, some of Cæsar's light Liburnian ships, that were in pursuit, came in sight. But on Antony's commanding to face about, they all gave back except Eurycles the Laconian, who pressed on, shaking a lance from the deck, as if he meant to hurl it at him. Antony, standing at the prow, demanded of him, " Who is this that pursues Antony? " " I am," said he, " Eurycles, the son of Lachares, armed with Cæsar's fortune to revenge my father's death." Lachares had been condemned for a robbery, and beheaded by Antony's orders. However, Eurycles did not attack Antony, but ran with his full force upon the other admiral-galley (for there were two of them), and with the blow turned her round, and took both her and another ship, in which was a quantity of rich plate and furniture. So soon as Eurycles was gone, Antony returned to his posture and sate silent, and thus he remained for three days, either in anger with Cleopatra, or wishing not to upbraid her, at the end of which they touched at Tænarus. Here the women of their company succeeded first in bringing them to speak, and afterwards to eat and sleep together. And, by this time, several of the ships of burden and some of his friends began to come in to him from the rout, bringing news of his fleet's being quite destroyed, but that the land forces, they thought, still stood firm. So that he sent messengers to Canidius to march the army with all speed through Macedonia into Asia. And, designing himself to go from Tænarus into Africa, he gave one of the merchant ships, laden with a large sum of money, and vessels of silver and gold of great value, belonging to the royal collections, to his friends, desiring them to share it amongst them, and provide for their own safety. They refusing his kindness with tears in their eyes, he comforted them with all the goodness and humanity imaginable, entreating them to leave them, and wrote letters in their behalf to Theophilus, his steward, at Corinth, that he would provide for their security, and keep them concealed till such time as they could make their peace with Cæsar. This Theophilus was the father of Hipparchus, who had such interest with Antony, who was the first of all his freedmen that went over to Cæsar, and who settled afterwards at Corinth. In this posture were affairs with Antony.

But at Actium, his fleet, after a long resistance to Cæsar, and suffering the most damage from a heavy sea that set in right ahead, scarcely at four in the afternoon, gave up the contest, with the loss of not more than five thousand men killed, but of three hundred ships taken, as Cæsar himself has recorded. Only a few had known of Antony's flight; and those who were told of it could not at first give any belief to so incredible a thing as that a general who had nineteen entire legions and twelve thousand horse upon the seashore, could abandon all and fly away; and he, above all, who had so often experienced both good and evil fortune, and had in a thousand wars and battles been inured to changes. His soldiers, however, would not give up their desires and expectations, still fancying he would appear from some part or other, and showed such a generous fidelity to his service that, when they were thoroughly assured that he was fled in earnest, they kept themselves in a body seven days, making no account of the messages that Cæsar sent to them. But at last, seeing that Canidius himself, who commanded them, was fled from the camp by night, and that all their officers had quite abandoned them, they gave way, and made their submission to the conqueror. After this, Cæsar set sail for Athens, where he made a settlement with Greece, and distributed what remained of the provision of corn that Antony had made for his army among the cities, which were in a miserable condition, despoiled of their money, their slaves, their horses, and beasts of service. My great-grandfather Nicharchus used to relate that the whole body of the people of our city were put in requisition to carry each one a certain measure of corn upon their shoulders to the seaside near Anticyra, men standing by to quicken them with the lash. They had made one journey of the kind, but when they had just measured out the corn, and were putting it on their backs for a second, news came of Antony's defeat, and so saved Chæronea, for all Antony's purveyors and soldiers fled upon the news, and left them to divide the corn among themselves.

When Antony came into Africa, he sent on Cleopatra from Parætonium into Egypt, and stayed himself in the most entire solitude that he could desire, roaming and wandering about with only two friends, one a Greek, Aristocrates, a rhetorician, and the other a Roman, Lucilius, of whom we have elsewhere spoken, how, at Philippi, to give Brutus time to escape, he suffered himself to be taken by the pursuers, pretending he was Brutus. Antony gave him his life, and on this account he remained true and faithful to him to the last.

But when also the officer who commanded for him in Africa, to whose care he had committed all his forces there, took them over to Cæsar, he resolved to kill himself, but was hindered by his friends. And coming to Alexandria, he found Cleopatra busied in a most bold and wonderful enterprise. Over the small space of land which divides the Red Sea from the sea near Egypt, which may be considered also the boundary between Asia and Africa, and in the narrowest place is not much above three hundred furlongs across, over this neck of land Cleopatra had formed a project of dragging her fleet and setting it afloat in the Arabian Gulf, thus with her soldiers and her treasure to secure herself a home on the other side, where she might live in peace far away from war and slavery. But the first galleys which were carried over being burnt by the Arabians of Petra, and Antony not knowing but that the army before Actium still held together, she desisted from her enterprise, and gave orders for the fortifying all the approaches to Egypt. But Antony, leaving the city and the conversation of his friends, built him a dwelling-place in the water, near Pharos, upon a little mole which he cast up in the sea, and there, secluding himself from the company of mankind, said he desired nothing but to live the life of Timon; as indeed, his case was the same, and the ingratitude and injuries which he suffered from those he had esteemed his friends made him hate and distrust all mankind.

This Timon was a citizen of Athens, and lived much about the Peloponnesian war, as may be seen by the comedies of Aristophanes and Plato, in which he is ridiculed as hater and enemy of mankind. He avoided and repelled the approaches of every one, but embraced with kisses and the greatest show of affection Alcibiades, then in his hot youth. And when Apemantus was astonished, and demanded the reason, he replied that he knew this young man would one day do infinite mischief to the Athenians. He never admitted any one into his company, except at times this Apemantus, who was of the same sort of temper, and was an imitator of his way of life. At the celebration of the festival of flagons, these two kept the feast together, and Apemantus, saying to him, " What a pleasant party, Timon! " " It would be," he answered, " if you were away." One day he got up in a full assembly on the speaker's place, and when there was a dead silence and great wonder at so unusual a sight, he said, " Ye men of Athens, I have a little plot of ground, and in it grows a fig-tree, on which many citizens have been pleased to hang themselves; and now, having resolved to build in that place, I wish to announce it publicly, that any of you who may be desirous may go and hang yourselves before I cut it down." He died and was buried at Halæ, near the sea, where it so happened that, after his burial, a land-slip took place on the point of the shore, and the sea, flowing in, sur-

rounded his tomb, and made it inaccessible to the foot of man.
It bore this incription:—

> " Here am I laid, my life of misery done.
>     Ask not my name, I curse you every one."

And this epitaph was made by himself while yet alive; that
which is more generally known is by Callimachus:—

> " Timon, the misanthrope, am I below.
>     Go, and revile me, traveller, only go."

Thus much of Timon, of whom much more might be said.
Canidius now came, bringing word in person of the loss of the
army before Actium. Then he received news that Herod of
Judæa was gone over to Cæsar with some legions and cohorts,
and that the other kings and princes were in like manner deserting him, and that, out of Egypt, nothing stood by him. All
this, however, seemed not to disturb him, but, as if he were glad
to put away all hope, that with it he might be rid of all care,
and leaving his habitation by the sea, which he called the
Timoneum, he was received by Cleopatra in the palace, and set
the whole city into a course of feasting, drinking, and presents.
The son of Cæsar and Cleopatra was registered among the
youths, and Antyllus, his own son by Fulvia, received the gown
without the purple border given to those that are come of age;
in honour of which the citizens of Alexandria did nothing but
feast and revel for many days. They themselves broke up the
Order of the Inimitable Livers, and constituted another in its
place, not inferior in splendour, luxury, and sumptuosity, calling
it that of the Diers Together. For all those that said they
would die with Antony and Cleopatra gave in their names, for
the present passing their time in all manner of pleasures and a
regular succession of banquets. But Cleopatra was busied in
making a collection of all varieties of poisonous drugs, and,
in order to see which of them were the least painful in the
operation, she had them tried upon prisoners condemned to
die. But, finding that the quick poisons always worked with
sharp pains, and that the less painful were slow, she next tried
venomous animals, and watching with her own eyes whilst
they were applied, one creature to the body of another. This
was her daily practice, and she pretty well satisfied herself that
nothing was comparable to the bite of the asp, which, without
convulsion or groaning, brought on a heavy drowsiness and
lethargy, with a gentle sweat on the face, the senses being
stupefied by degrees; the patient, in appearance, being sensible

of no pain, but rather troubled to be disturbed or awakened like those that are in a profound natural sleep.

At the same time, they sent ambassadors to Cæsar into Asia, Cleopatra asking for the kingdom of Egypt for her children, and Antony, that he might have leave to live as a private man in Egypt, or, if that were thought too much, that he might retire to Athens. In lack of friends, so many having deserted, and others not being trusted, Euphronius, his son's tutor, was sent on this embassy. For Alexas of Laodicea, who, by the recommendation of Timagenes, became acquainted with Antony at Rome, and had been more powerful with him than any Greek, and was, of all the instruments which Cleopatra made use of to persuade Antony, the most violent, and the chief subverter of any good thoughts that from time to time might rise in his mind in Octavia's favour, had been sent before to dissuade Herod from desertion; but betraying his master, stayed with him and, confiding in Herod's interest, had the boldness to come into Cæsar's presence. Herod, however, was not able to help him, for he was immediately put in chains and sent into his own country, where, by Cæsar's orders, he was put to death. This reward of his treason Alexas received while Antony was yet alive.

Cæsar would not listen to any proposals for Antony, but he made answer to Cleopatra, that there was no reasonable favour which she might not expect, if she put Antony to death, or expelled him from Egypt. He sent back with the ambassadors his own freedman, Thyrsus, a man of understanding, and not at all ill-qualified for conveying the messages of a youthful general to a woman so proud of her charms and possessed with the opinion of the power of her beauty. But by the long audiences he received from her, and the special honours which she paid him, Antony's jealousy began to be awakened; he had him seized, whipped, and sent back; writing Cæsar word that the man's busy, impertinent ways had provoked him; in his circumstances he could not be expected to be very patient: "But if it offend you," he added, "you have got my freedman, Hipparchus, with you; hang him up and scourge him to make us even." But Cleopatra, after this, to clear herself, and to allay his jealousies, paid him all the attentions imaginable. When her own birthday came, she kept it as was suitable to their fallen fortunes; but his was observed with the utmost prodigality of splendour and magnificence, so that many of the guests sat down in want, and went home wealthy men. Meantime, continual letters came to Cæsar from Agrippa, telling him his presence was extremely required at Rome.

And so the war was deferred for a season. But, the winter being over, he began his march; he himself by Syria, and his captains through Africa. Pelusium being taken, there went a report as if it had been delivered up to Cæsar by Seleucus, not without the consent of Cleopatra; but she, to justify herself, gave up into Antony's hands the wife and children of Seleucus to be put to death. She had caused to be built, joining to the temple of Isis, several tombs and monuments of wonderful height, and very remarkable for the workmanship; thither she removed her treasure, her gold, silver, emeralds, pearls, ebony, ivory, cinnamon, and, after all, a great quantity of torchwood and tow. Upon which Cæsar began to fear lest she should, in a desperate fit, set all these riches on fire; and, therefore, while he was marching towards the city with his army, he omitted no occasion of giving her new assurances of his good intentions. He took up his position in the Hippodrome, where Antony made a fierce sally upon him, routed the horse, and beat them back into their trenches, and so returned with great satisfaction to the palace, where, meeting Cleopatra, armed as he was, he kissed her, and commended to her favour one of his men, who had most signalised himself in the fight, to whom she made a present of a breastplate and helmet of gold; which he having received went that very night and deserted to Cæsar.

After this, Antony sent a new challenge to Cæsar to fight him hand-to-hand; who made him answer that he might find several other ways to end his life; and he, considering with himself that he could not die more honourably than in battle, resolved to make an effort both by land and sea. At supper, it is said, he bade his servants help him freely, and pour him out wine plentifully, since to-morrow, perhaps, they should not do the same, but be servants to a new master, whilst he should lie on the ground, a dead corpse, and nothing. His friends that were about him wept to hear him talk so; which he perceiving, told them he would not lead them to a battle in which he expected rather an honourable death than either safety or victory. That night, it is related, about the middle of it, when the whole city was in a deep silence and general sadness, expecting the event of the next day, on a sudden was heard the sound of all sorts of instruments, and voices singing in tune, and the cry of a crowd of people shouting and dancing, like a troop of bacchanals on its way. This tumultuous procession seemed to take its

course right through the middle of the city to the gate nearest
the enemy; here it became the loudest, and suddenly passed
out. People who reflected considered this to signify that
Bacchus, the god whom Antony had always made it his study
to copy and imitate, had now forsaken him.

As soon as it was light, he marched his infantry out of the
city, and posted them upon a rising ground, from whence he
saw his fleet make up to the enemy. There he stood in expectation of the event; but as soon as the fleets came near to one
another, his men saluted Cæsar's with their oars; and on their
responding, the whole body of the ships, forming into a single
fleet, rowed up direct to the city. Antony had no sooner seen
this, but the horse deserted him, and went over to Cæsar; and
his foot being defeated, he retired into the city, crying out that
Cleopatra had betrayed him to the enemies he had made for her
sake. She, being afraid lest in his fury and despair he might
do her a mischief, fled to her monument, and letting down the
falling doors, which were strong with bars and bolts, she sent
messengers who should tell Antony she was dead. He, believing it, cried out, " Now, Antony, why delay longer? Fate has
snatched away the only pretext for which you could say you
desired yet to live." Going into his chamber, and there loosen-
ing and opening his coat of armour, " I am not," said he,
" troubled, Cleopatra, to be at present bereaved of you, for I
shall soon be with you; but it distresses me that so great a
general should be found of a tardier courage than a woman."
He had a faithful servant, whose name was Eros; he had
engaged him formerly to kill him when he should think it
necessary, and now he put him to his promise. Eros drew his
sword, as designing to kill him, but, suddenly turning round,
he slew himself. And as he fell dead at his feet, " It is well
done, Eros," said Antony; " you show your master how to do
what you had not the heart to do yourself; and so he ran himself into the belly, and laid himself upon the couch. The wound,
however, was not immediately mortal; and the flow of blood
ceasing when he lay down, presently he came to himself, and
entreated those that were about him to put him out of his pain;
but they all fled out of the chamber, and left him crying out and
struggling, until Diomede, Cleopatra's secretary, came to him,
having orders from her to bring him into the monument.

When he understood she was alive, he eagerly gave order to
the servants to take him up, and in their arms was carried to
the door of the building. Cleopatra would not open the door,

but, looking from a sort of window, she let down ropes and cords, to which Antony was fastened; and she and her two women, the only persons she had allowed to enter the monument, drew him up. Those that were present say that nothing was ever more sad than this spectacle, to see Antony, covered all over with blood and just expiring, thus drawn up, still holding up his hands to her, and lifting up his body with the little force he had left. As, indeed, it was no easy task for the women; and Cleopatra, with all her force, clinging to the rope, and straining with her head to the ground, with difficulty pulled him up, while those below encouraged her with their cries, and joined in all her efforts and anxiety. When she had got him up, she laid him on the bed, tearing all her clothes, which she spread upon him; and, beating her breast with her hands, lacerating herself, and disfiguring her own face with the blood from his wounds, she called him her lord, her husband, her emperor, and seemed to have pretty nearly forgotten all her own evils, she was so intent upon his misfortunes. Antony, stopping her lamentations as well as he could, called for wine to drink, either that he was thirsty, or that he imagined that it might put him the sooner out of pain. When he had drunk, he advised her to bring her own affairs, so far as might be honourably done, to a safe conclusion, and that, among all the friends of Cæsar, she should rely on Proculeius; that she should not pity him in this last turn of fate, but rather rejoice for him in remembrance of his past happiness, who had been of all men the most illustrious and powerful, and in the end had fallen not ignobly, a Roman by a Roman overcome.

Just as he breathed his last, Proculeius arrived from Cæsar; for when Antony gave himself his wound, and was carried into Cleopatra, one of his guards, Dercetæus, took up Antony's sword and hid it; and, when he saw his opportunity, stole away to Cæsar, and brought him the first news of Antony's death, and withal showed him the bloody sword. Cæsar, upon this, retired into the inner part of his tent, and giving some tears to the death of one that had been nearly allied to him in marriage, his colleague in empire, and companion in so many wars and dangers, he came out to his friends, and, bringing with him many letters, he read to them with how much reason and moderation he had always addressed himself to Antony, and in return what overbearing and arrogant answers he received. Then he sent Proculeius to use his utmost endeavours to get Cleopatra alive into his power; for he was afraid of losing a great treasure, and, besides, she would be no small addition to the glory of his triumph. She, however, was careful not to put herself in Proculeius's power; but from within her monument, he standing on the outside of a door, on the level of the ground, which was strongly barred, but so that they might well enough hear one another's voice, she held a conference with him; she demanding that her kingdom might be given to her children, and he binding her to be of good courage, and trust Cæsar in everything.

Having taken particular notice of the place, he returned to Cæsar, and Gallius was sent to parley with her the second time; who, being come to the door, on purpose prolonged the conference, while Proculeius fixed his scaling-ladders in the window through which the women had pulled up Antony. And so entering, with two men to follow him, he went straight down to the door where Cleopatra was discoursing with Gallus. One of the two women who were shut up in the monument with her cried out, "Miserable Cleopatra, you are taken prisoner!" Upon which she turned quick, and, looking at Proculeius, drew out her dagger which she had with her to stab herself. But Proculeius ran up quickly, and seizing her with both his hands, "For shame," said he, "Cleopatra; you wrong yourself and Cæsar much, who would rob him of so fair an occasion of showing his clemency, and would make the world believe the most gentle of commanders to be a faithless and implacable enemy." And so, taking the dagger out of her hand, he also shook her dress to see if there were any poison hid in it. After this, Cæsar sent Epaphroditus, one of his freedmen, with orders to treat her with all the gentleness and civility possible, but to take the strictest precautions to keep her alive.

In the meanwhile, Cæsar made his entry into Alexandria, with Areius the philosopher at his side, holding him by the hand and talking with him; desiring that all his fellow-citizens should see what honour was paid to him, and should look up to him accordingly from the very first moment. Then, entering the exercise ground, he mounted a platform erected for the purpose, and from thence commanded the citizens (who, in great fear and consternation, fell prostrate at his feet) to stand up, and told them that he freely acquitted the people of all blame, first, for the sake of Alexander, who built their city, then for the city's sake itself, which was so large and beautiful; and, thirdly, to gratify his friend Areius.

Such great honour did Areius receive from Cæsar; and by his intercession many lives were saved, amongst the rest that of Philostratus, a man, of all the professors of logic that ever were, the most ready in extempore speaking, but quite destitute of any right to call himself one of the philosophers of the Academy. Cæsar, out of disgust at his character, refused all attention to his entreaties. So, growing a long white beard, and dressing himself in black, he followed behind Areius, shouting out the verse,

" The wise, if they are wise, will save the wise."

Which Cæsar hearing, gave him his pardon, to prevent rather any odium that might attach to Areius, than any harm that Philostratus might suffer.

Of Antony's children, Antyllus, his son by Fulvia, being betrayed by his tutor, Theodorus, was put to death; and while the soldiers were cutting off his head, his tutor contrived to steal a precious jewel which he wore about his neck, and put it in his pocket, and afterwards denied the fact, but was convicted and crucified. Cleopatra's children, with their attendants, had a guard set on them, and were treated very honourably. Cæsarion, who was reputed to be the son of Cæsar the Dictator, was sent by his mother, with a great sum of money, through Æthiopia, to pass into India; but his tutor, a man named Rhodon, about as honest as Theodorus, persuaded him to turn back, for that Cæsar designed to make him king. Cæsar consulting what was best to be done with him, Areius we are told, said,

" Too many *Cæsars* are not well."

So, afterwards, when Cleopatra was dead he was killed.

Many kings and great commanders made petition to Cæsar for the body of Antony, to give him his funeral rites; but he would not take away his corpse from Cleopatra by whose hands he was buried with royal splendour and magnificence, it being granted to her to employ what she pleased on his funeral. In this extremity of grief and sorrow, and having inflamed and ulcerated her breasts with beating them, she fell into a high fever, and was very glad of the occasion, hoping, under this pretext, to abstain from food, and so to die in quiet without interference. She had her own physician, Olympus, to whom she told the truth, and asked his advice and help to put an end to herself, as Olympus himself has told us, in a narrative which he wrote of these events. But Cæsar, suspecting her purpose, took to menacing language about her children, and excited her fears for them, before which engines her purpose shook and gave way, so that she suffered those about her to give her what meat or medicine they pleased.

Some few days after, Cæsar himself came to make her a visit and comfort her. She lay then upon her pallet-bed in undress, and, on his entering, sprang up from off her bed, having nothing on but the one garment next her body, and flung herself at his feet, her hair and face looking wild and disfigured, her voice quivering, and her eyes sunk in her head. The marks of the blows she had given herself were visible about her bosom, and altogether her whole person seemed no less afflicted than her soul. But, for all this, her old charm, and the boldness of her youthful beauty, had not wholly left her, and, in spite of her present condition, still sparkled from within, and let itself appear in all the movements of her countenance. Cæsar, desiring her to repose herself, sat down by her; and, on this opportunity, she said something to justify her actions, attributing what she had done to the necessity she was under, and to her fear of Antony; and when Cæsar, on each point, made his objections, and she found herself confuted, she broke off at once into language of entreaty and deprecation, as if she desired nothing more than to prolong her life. And at last, having by her a list of her treasure, she gave it into his hands; and when Seleucus, one of her stewards, who was by, pointed out that various articles were omitted, and charged her with secreting them, she flew up and caught him by the hair, and struck him several blows on the face. Cæsar smiling and withholding her, " Is it not very hard, Cæsar," said she, " when you do me the honour to visit me in this condition I am in, that I should be accused by one of my own servants of laying by some women's toys, not meant to adorn, be sure, my unhappy self, but that I might have some little present by me to make your Octavia and your Livia, that by their intercession I might hope to find you in some measure disposed to mercy? " Cæsar was pleased to hear her talk thus, being now assured that she was desirous to live. And, therefore, letting her know that the things she had laid by she might dispose of as she pleased, and his usage of her should be honourable above her expectation, he went away, well satisfied that he had overreached her, but, in fact, was himself deceived.

There was a young man of distinction among Cæsar's companions named Cornelius Dolabella. He was not without a certain tenderness for Cleopatra, and sent her word privately, as she had besought him to do, that Cæsar was about to return through Syria, and that she and her children were to be sent on within three days. When she understood this, she made her request to Cæsar that he would be pleased to permit her to make oblations to the departed Antony; which being granted, she ordered herself to be carried to the place where he was buried, and there, accompanied by her women, she embraced his tomb with tears in her eyes, and spoke in this manner: " O, dearest Antony," said she, " it is not long since that with these hands I buried you; then they were free, now I am a captive, and pay these last duties to you with a guard upon me, for fear that my just griefs and sorrows should impair my servile body, and make it less fit to appear in their triumph over you.   No further offerings or libations expect from me; these are the last honours that Cleopatra can pay your memory, for she is to be hurried away far from you.   Nothing could part us whilst we lived, but death seems to threaten to divide us.   You, a Roman born, have found a grave in Egypt; I, an Egyptian, am to seek that favour, and none but that, in your country.   But if the gods below, with whom you now are, either can or will do anything (since those above have betrayed us), suffer not your living wife to be abandoned; let me not be led in triumph to your shame, but hide me and bury me here with you, since, amongst all my bitter misfortunes, nothing has afflicted me like this brief time that I have lived away from you."

Having made these lamentations, crowning the tomb with garlands and kissing it, she gave orders to prepare her a bath, and, coming out of the bath, she lay down and made a sumptuous meal.   And a country fellow brought her a little basket, which the guards intercepting and asking what it was, the fellow put the leaves which lay uppermost aside, and showed them it was full of figs; and on their admiring the largeness and beauty of the figs, he laughed, and invited them to take some, which they refused, and, suspecting nothing, bade him carry them in.   After her repast, Cleopatra sent to Cæsar a letter which she had written and sealed; and, putting everybody out of the monument but her two women, she shut the doors.   Cæsar, opening her letter, and finding pathetic prayers and entreaties that she might be buried in the same tomb with Antony, soon guessed what was doing.   At first he was going himself in all haste, but, changing his mind, he sent others to see.   The thing had been quickly done.   The messengers came at full speed, and found the guards apprehensive of nothing; but on opening the doors they saw her stone-dead, lying upon a bed of gold, set out in all her royal ornaments.   Iras, one of her women, lay dying at her feet, and Charmion, just ready to fall, scarce able to hold up her head, was adjusting her mistress's diadem.   And when one that came in

said angrily, " Was this well done of your lady, Charmion? "
" Extremely well," she answered, " and as became the descendant of so many kings; " and as she said this, she fell down dead
by the bedside.

Some relate that an asp was brought in amongst those figs and
covered with the leaves, and that Cleopatra had arranged that it
might settle on her before she knew, but, when she took away
some of the figs and saw it, she said, " So here it is," and held
out her bare arm to be bitten.   Others say that it was kept in a
vase, and that she vexed and pricked it with a golden spindle
till it seized her arm.   But what really took place is known to no
one, since it was also said that she carried poison in a hollow
bodkin, about which she wound her hair; yet there was not so
much as a spot found, or any symptom of poison upon her body,
nor was the asp seen within the monument; only something like
the trail of it was said to have been noticed on the sand by the
sea, on the part towards which the building faced and where the
windows were.   Some relate that two faint puncture-marks were
found on Cleopatra's arm, and to this account Cæsar seems to
have given credit; for in his triumph there was carried a figure
of Cleopatra, with an asp clinging to her.   Such are the various
accounts.   But Cæsar, though much disappointed by her death,
yet could not but admire the greatness of her spirit, and gave
order that her body should be buried by Antony with royal
splendour and magnificence.   Her women, also, received honourable burial by his directions.   Cleopatra had lived nine-and-thirty
years, during twenty-two of which she had reigned as queen, and
for fourteen had been Antony's partner in his empire.   Antony,
according to some authorities, was fifty-three, according to
others, fifty-six years old.   His statues were all thrown down,
but those of Cleopatra were left untouched; for Archibius, one
of her friends, gave Cæsar two thousand talents to save them
from the fate of Antony's.

Antony left by his three wives seven children, of whom only
Antyllus, the eldest, was put to death by Cæsar; Octavia took
the rest, and brought them up with her own.   Cleopatra, his
daughter by Cleopatra, was given in marriage to Juba, the most
accomplished of kings; and Antony, his son by Fulvia, attained
such high favour that, whereas Agrippa was considered to hold
the first place with Cæsar, and the sons of Livia the second, the
third, without dispute, was possessed by Antony.   Octavia, also,
having had by her first husband, Marcellus, two daughters, and
one son named Marcellus, this son Cæsar adopted, and gave him

his daughter in marriage; as did Octavia one of the daughters to Agrippa. But Marcellus dying almost immediately after his marriage, she, perceiving that her brother was at a loss to find elsewhere any sure friend to be his son-in-law, was the first to recommend that Agrippa should put away her daughter and marry Julia. To this Cæsar first, and then Agrippa himself, gave assent; so Agrippa married Julia, and Octavia, receiving her daughter, married her to the young Antony. Of the two daughters whom Octavia had borne to Antony, the one was married to Domitius Ahenobarbus; and the other, Antonia, famous for her beauty and discretion, was married to Drusus, the son of Livia, and stepson to Cæsar. Of these parents were born Germanicus and Claudius. Claudius reigned later; and of the children of Germanicus, Caius, after a reign of distinction, was killed with his wife and child; Agrippina, after bearing a son Lucius Domitius, to Ahenobarbus, was married to Claudius Cæsar, who adopted Domitius, giving him the name of Nero Germanicus. He was emperor in our time, and put his mother to death, and with his madness and folly came not far from ruining the Roman empire, being Antony's descendant in the fifth generation.

## THE COMPARISON OF DEMETRIUS AND ANTONY

As both are great examples of the vicissitudes of fortune, let us first consider in what way they attained their power and glory. Demetrius hired a kingdom already won for him by Antigonus, the most powerful of the Successors, who, before Demetrius grew to be a man, traversed with his armies and subdued the greater part of Asia. Antony's father was well enough in other respects, but was no warrior, and could bequeath no great legacy of reputation to his son, who had the boldness, nevertheless, to take upon him the government, to which birth give him no claim, which had been held by Cæsar, and became the inheritor of his great labours. And such power did he attain, with only himself to thank for it, that, in a division of the whole empire into two portions, he took and received the nobler one; and, absent himself, by his mere subalterns and lieutenants often defeated the Parthians, and drove the barbarous nations of the Caucasus back to the Caspian Sea. Those very things that procured him ill-repute bear witness to his greatness. Antigonus considered

Antipater's daughter Phila, in spite of the disparity of her years, an advantageous match for Demetrius. Antony was thought disgraced by his marriage with Cleopatra, a queen superior in power and glory to all, except Arsaces, who were kings in her time. Antony was so great as to be thought by others worthy of higher things than his own desires.

As regards the right and justice of their aims at empire, Demetrius need not be blamed for seeking to rule a people that had always had a king to rule them. Antony, who enslaved the Roman people, just liberated from the rule of Cæsar, followed a cruel and tyrannical object. His greatest and most illustrious work, his successful war with Brutus and Cassius, was done to crush the liberties of his country and of his fellow-citizens. Demetrius, till he was driven to extremity, went on, without intermission, maintaining liberty in Greece, and expelling the foreign garrisons from the cities; not like Antony, whose boast was to have slain in Macedonia those who had set up liberty in Rome. As for the profusion and magnificence of his gifts, one point for which Antony is lauded, Demetrius so far outdid them that what he gave to his enemies was far more than Antony ever gave to his friends. Antony was renowned for giving Brutus honourable burial; Demetrius did so to all the enemy's dead, and sent the prisoners back to Ptolemy with money and presents.

Both were insolent in prosperity, and abandoned themselves to luxuries and enjoyments. Yet it cannot be said that Demetrius, in his revellings and dissipations, ever let slip the time for action; pleasures with him attended only the superabundance of his ease, and his Lamia, like that of the fable, belonged only to his playful, half-waking, half-sleeping hours. When war demanded his attention, his spear was not wreathed with ivy, nor his helmet redolent of unguents; he did not come out to battle from the women's chamber, but, hushing the bacchanal shouts and putting an end to the orgies, he became at once, as Euripides calls it, " the minister of the unpriestly Mars; " and, in short, he never once incurred disaster through indolence or self-indulgence. Whereas Antony, like Hercules in the picture where Omphale is seen removing his club and stripping him of his lion's skin, was over and over again disarmed by Cleopatra, and beguiled away, while great actions and enterprises of the first necessity fell, as it were, from his hands, to go with her to the seashore of Canopus and Taphosiris, and play about. And in the end, like another Paris, he left the battle to fly to her arms; or rather, to say the truth, Paris fled when he was already beaten; Antony fled first, and, following Cleopatra, abandoned his victory.

There was no law to prevent Demetrius from marrying several wives; from the time of Philip and Alexander it had become usual with Macedonian kings, and he did no more than was done by Lysimachus and Ptolemy. And those he married he treated honourably. But Antony, first of all, in marrying two wives at once, did a thing which no Roman had ever allowed himself; and then he drove away his lawful Roman wife to please the foreign and unlawful woman. And so Demetrius incurred no harm at all; Antony procured his ruin by his marriage. On the other hand, no licentious act of Antony's can be charged with that impiety which marks those of Demetrius. Historical writers tell us that the very dogs are excluded from the whole Acropolis because of their gross, uncleanly habits. The very Parthenon itself saw Demetrius consorting with harlots and debauching free women of Athens. The vice of cruelty, also, remote as it seems from the indulgence of voluptuous desires, must be attributed to him, who, in the pursuit of his pleasures, allowed or, to say more truly, compelled the death of the most beautiful and most chaste of the Athenians, who found no way but this to escape his violence. In one word, Antony himself suffered by his excesses, and other people by those of Demetrius.

In his conduct to his parents, Demetrius was irreproachable. Antony gave up his mother's brother, in order that he might have leave to kill Cicero, this itself being so cruel and shocking an act that Antony would hardly be forgiven if Cicero's death had been the price of this uncle's safety. In respect of breaches of oaths and treaties, the seizure of Artabazes, and the assassination of Alexander, Antony may urge the plea which no one denies to be true, that Artabazes first abandoned and betrayed him in Media; Demetrius is alleged by many to have invented false pretexts for his act, and not to have retaliated for injuries, but to have accused one whom he injured himself.

The achievements of Demetrius are all his own work. Antony's noblest and greatest victories were won in his absence by his lieutenants. For their final disasters they have both only to thank themselves; not, however, in an equal degree. Demetrius was deserted, the Macedonians revolted from him; Antony deserted others, and ran away while men were fighting for him at the risk of their lives. The fault to be found with the one is that he had thus entirely alienated the affections of his soldiers; the other's condemnation is that he abandoned so much love and faith as he still possessed. We cannot admire the death of either, but that of Demetrius excites our greater contempt. He let himself become a prisoner, and was thankful to gain a three years' accession of life in captivity. He was tamed like a wild beast by his belly, and by wine; Antony took himself out of the world in a cowardly, pitiful, and ignoble manner, but still in time to prevent the enemy having his person in their power.

## DION

If it be true, Sosius Senecio, that, as Simonides tells us—

"Of the Corinthians Troy does not complain"

for having taken part with the Achæans in the siege, because the Trojans also had Corinthians (Glaucus, who sprang from Corinth) fighting bravely on their side, so also it may be fairly said that neither Romans nor Greeks can quarrel with the Academy, each nation being equally represented in the following pair of lives, which will give an account of Brutus and of Dion,—Dion, who was Plato's own hearer, and Brutus, who was brought up in his philosophy. They came from one and the self-same school, where they had been trained alike to run the race of honour; nor need we wonder that in the performance of actions often most nearly allied and akin, they both bore evidence to the truth of what their guide and teacher said, that, without the concurrence of power and success, with justice and prudence, public actions do not attain their proper, great, and noble character. For as Hippomachus the wrestling-master affirmed, he could distinguish his scholars at a distance, though they were but carrying meat from the shambles, so it is very probable that the principles of those who have had the same good education should appear with a resemblance in all their actions, creating in them a certain harmony and proportion, at once agreeable and becoming.

We may also draw a close parallel of the lives of the two men from their fortunes, wherein chance, even more than their own designs, made them nearly alike. For they were both cut off by an untimely death, not being able to accomplish those ends which through many risks and difficulties they aimed at. But, above all, this is most wonderful; that by preternatural interposition both of them had notice given of their approaching death by an unpropitious form, which visibly appeared to them. Although there are people who utterly deny any such thing, and say that no man in his right senses ever yet saw any supernatural phantom or apparition, but that children only, and silly women, or men disordered by sickness, in some aberration of the mind or distemperature of the body, have had empty and extravagant imaginations, whilst the real evil genius, superstition, was in themselves. Yet if Dion and Brutus, men of solid understanding, and philosophers, not to be easily deluded by fancy or discomposed by any sudden apprehension, were thus affected by visions that they forthwith declared to their friends what they had seen, I know not how we can avoid admitting again the utterly exploded opinion of the oldest times, that evil and beguiling spirits, out of envy to good men, and a desire of impeding their good deeds, make efforts to excite in them feelings of terror and distraction, to make them shake and totter in their virtue, lest by a steady and unbiassed perseverance they should obtain a happier condition than these beings after death. But I shall leave these things for another opportunity, and, in this twelfth book of the lives of great men compared one with another, begin with his who was the elder.

Dionysius the First, having possessed himself of the government, at once took to wife the daughter of Hermocrates, the Syracusan. She, in an outbreak which the citizens made before the new power was well settled, was abused in such a barbarous and outrageous manner that for shame she put an end to her own life. But Dionysius, when he was re-established and confirmed in his supremacy, married two wives together, one named Doris, of Locri, the other Aristomache, a native of Sicily, and daughter of Hipparinus, a man of the first quality in Syracuse, and colleague with Dionysius when he was first chosen general with unlimited powers for the war. It is said he married them both in one day, and no one ever knew which of the two he first made his wife; and ever after he divided his kindness equally between them, both accompanying him together at his table, and in his bed by turns. Indeed, the Syracusans were urgent that their own countrywoman might be preferred before the stranger; but Doris, to compensate her for her foreign extraction, had the good fortune to be the mother of the son and heir of the family, whilst Aristomache continued a long time without issue, though Dionysius was very desirous to have children by her, and, indeed, caused Doris's mother to be put to death, laying to her charge that she had given drugs to Aristomache to prevent her being with child.

Dion, Aristomache's brother, at first found an honourable reception for his sister's sake; but his own worth and parts soon procured him a nearer place in his brother-in-law's affection, who, among other favours, gave special command to his treasurers to furnish Dion with whatever money he demanded, only telling him on the same day what they had delivered out. Now, though Dion was before reputed a person of lofty character, of a noble mind, and daring courage, yet these excellent qualifications all received a great development from the happy chance which conducted Plato into Sicily; not assuredly by any human device or calculation, but some supernatural power, designing that this remote cause should hereafter occasion the recovery of the Sicilians' lost liberty and the subversion of the tyrannical government, brought the philosopher out of Italy to Syracuse, and made acquaintance between him and Dion. Dion was, indeed, at this time extremely young in years, but of all the scholars that attended Plato he was the quickest and aptest to learn, and the most prompt and eager to practise, the lessons of virtue, as Plato himself reports of him and his own actions sufficiently testify. For though he had been bred up under a tyrant in habits of submission, accustomed to a life on the one hand of servility and intimidation, and yet on the other of vulgar display and luxury, the mistaken happiness of people that knew no better thing than pleasure and self-indulgence, yet, at the first taste of reason and a philosophy that demands obedience to virtue, his soul was set in a flame, and in the simple innocence of youth, concluding, from his own disposition, that the same reason would work the same effects upon Dionysius, he made it his business, and at length obtained the favour of him, at a leisure hour, to hear Plato.

At this their meeting, the subject-matter of their discourse in general was human virtue, but, more particularly, they disputed concerning fortitude, which Plato proved tyrants, of all men, had the least pretence to; and thence proceeding to treat of justice, asserted the happy estate of the just and the miserable condition of the unjust; arguments which Dionysius would not hear out, but, feeling himself, as it were, convicted by his words, and much displeased to see the rest of the auditors full of admiration for the speaker and captivated with his doctrine, at last, exceedingly exasperated, he asked the philosopher in a rage, what business he had in Sicily. To which Plato answered, " I came to seek a virtuous man." " It seems, then," replied Dionysius, " you have lost your labour." Dion, supposing that this was all, and that nothing further could come of his anger, at Plato's request, conveyed him aboard a galley, which was conveying Pollis, the Spartan, into Greece. But Dionysius privately dealt with Pollis, by all means to kill Plato in the voyage; if not, to be sure to sell him for a slave: he would, of course, take no harm of it, being the same just man as before; he would enjoy that happiness, though he lost his liberty. Pollis, therefore, it is stated, carried Plato to Ægina, and there sold him; the Æginetans, then at war with Athens, having made a decree that whatever Athenian was taken on their coasts should forthwith be exposed to sale. Notwithstanding, Dion was not in less favour and credit with Dionysius than formerly, but was intrusted with the most considerable employments, and sent on important embassies to Carthage, in the management of which he gained very great reputation. Besides, the usurper bore with the liberty he took to speak his mind freely, he being the only man who, upon any occasion, durst boldly say what he thought, as, for example, in the rebuke he gave him about Gelon. Dionysius was ridiculing Gelon's government, and, alluding to his name, said he had been the laughing-stock of Sicily. While others seemed to admire and applaud the quibble, Dion very warmly replied, " Nevertheless, it is certain that you are sole governor here, because you were trusted for Gelon's sake; but for your sake no man will ever hereafter be trusted again." For, indeed, Gelon had made a monarchy appear the best, whereas Dionysius had convinced men that it was the worst of governments.

Dionysius had three children by Doris, and by Aristomache four, two of which were daughters, Sophrosyne and Arete. Sophrosyne was married to his son Dionysius; Arete, to his brother Thearides, after whose death Dion received his niece Arete to wife. Now when Dionysius was sick and like to die, Dion endeavoured to speak with him in behalf of the children he had by Aristomache, but was still prevented by the physicians, who wanted to ingratiate themselves with the next successor, who also, as Timæus reports, gave him a sleeping potion which he asked for, which produced an insensibility only followed by his death.

Nevertheless, at the first council which the young Dionysius

held with his friends, Dion discoursed so well of the present
state of affairs that he made all the rest appear in their politics
but children, and in their votes rather slaves than counsellors,
who timorously and disingenuously advised what would please
the young man, rather than what would advance his interest.
But that which startled them most was the proposal he made
to avert the imminent danger they feared of a war with the
Carthaginians, undertaking, if Dionysius wanted peace, to sail
immediately over into Africa, and conclude it there upon
honourable terms; but, if he rather preferred war, then he
would fit out and maintain at his own cost and charges fifty
galleys ready for the service.

Dionysius wondered much at his greatness of mind, and
received his offer with satisfaction. But the other courtiers,
thinking his generosity reflected upon them, and jealous of
being lessened by his greatness, from hence took all occasions
by private slanders to render him obnoxious to the young man's
displeasure; as if he designed, by his power at sea, to surprise
the government, and by the help of those naval forces confer
the supreme authority upon his sister Aristomache's children.
But, indeed, the most apparent and the strongest grounds for
dislike and hostility existed already in the difference of his
habits, and his reserved and separate way of living. For they,
who, from the beginning by flatteries and all unworthy artifices,
courted the favour and familiarity of the prince, youthful and
voluptuously bred, ministered to his pleasures, and sought how
to find him daily some new amours and occupy him in vain
amusements, with wine or with women, and in other dissipations; by which means, the tyranny, like iron softened in the
fire, seemed, indeed, to the subject, to be more moderate and
gentle, and to abate somewhat of its extreme severity; the edge
of it being blunted, not by the clemency, but rather the sloth
and degeneracy of the sovereign, whose dissoluteness, gaining
ground daily, and growing upon him, soon weakened and broke
those "adamantine chains," with which his father, Dionysius,
said he had left the monarchy fastened and secured. It is
reported of him that, having begun a drunken debauch, he
continued it ninety days without intermission; in all which
time no person on business was allowed to appear, nor was any
serious conversation heard at court, but drinking, singing,
dancing, and buffoonery reigned there without control.

It is likely then they had little kindness for Dion, who never
indulged himself in any youthful pleasure or diversion. And

so his very virtues were the matter of their calumnies, and were represented under one or other plausible name as vices; they called his gravity pride, his plain-dealing self-will, the good advice he gave was all construed into reprimand, and he was censured for neglecting and scorning those in whose misdemeanours he declined to participate. And to say the truth, there was in his natural character something stately, austere, reserved, and unsociable in conversation, which made his company unpleasant and disagreeable not only to the young tyrant, whose ears had been corrupted by flatteries; many also of Dion's own intimate friends, though they loved the integrity and generosity of his temper, yet blamed his manner, and thought he treated those with whom he had to do less courteously and affably than became a man engaged in civil business. Of which Plato also afterwards wrote to him; and, as it were, prophetically advised him carefully to avoid an arbitrary temper, whose proper helpmate was a solitary life. And, indeed, at this very time, though circumstances made him so important, and in the danger of the tottering government he was recognised as the only or the ablest support of it, yet he well understood that he owed not his high position to any good-will or kindness, but to the mere necessities of the usurper.

And, supposing the cause of this to be ignorance and want of education, he endeavoured to induce the young man into a course of liberal studies, and to give him some knowledge of moral truths and reasonings, hoping he might thus lose his fear of virtuous living, and learn to take pleasure in laudable actions. Dionysius, in his own nature, was not one of the worst kind of tyrants, but his father, fearing that if he should come to understand himself better, and converse with wise and reasonable men, he might enter into some design against him, and dispossess him of his power, kept him closely shut up at home; where, for want of other company, and ignorant how to spend his time better, he busied himself in making little chariots, candlesticks, stools, tables, and other things of wood. For the elder Dionysius was so diffident and suspicious, and so continually on his guard against all men, that he would not so much as let his hair be trimmed with any barber's or haircutter's instruments, but made one of his artificers singe him with a live coal. Neither were his brother or his son allowed to come into his apartment in the dress they wore, but they, as all others, were stript to their skins by some of the guard, and, after being seen naked, put on other clothes before they were admitted into the presence. When his brother Leptines was once describing the situation of a place, and took a javelin from one of the guard to draw the plan of it, he was extremely angry with him, and had the soldier who gave him the weapon put to death. He declared the more judicious his friends were the more he suspected them; because he knew that, were it in their choice, they would rather be tyrants themselves than the subjects of a tyrant. He slew Marsyas, one of his captains whom he had preferred to a considerable command, for dreaming that he killed him: without some previous waking thought and purpose of the kind, he could not, he supposed, have had that fancy in his sleep. So timorous was he, and so miserable a slave to his fears, yet very angry with Plato, because he would not allow him to be the valiantest man alive.

Dion, as we said before, seeing the son thus deformed and spoilt in character for want of teaching, exhorted him to study, and to use all his entreaties to persuade Plato, the first of philosophers, to visit him in Sicily, and when he came, to submit himself to his direction and advice; by whose instructions he might conform his nature to the truths of virtue, and, living after the likeness of the Divine and glorious Model of Being, out of obedience to whose control the general confusion is changed into the beautiful order of the universe, so he in like manner might be the cause of great happiness to himself and to all his subjects, who, obliged by his justice and moderation, would then willingly pay him obedience as their father, which now grudgingly, and upon necessity, they are forced to yield him as their master. Their usurping tyrant he would then no longer be, but their lawful king. For fear and force, a great navy and standing army of ten thousand hired barbarians are not, as his father had said, the adamantine chains which secure the regal power, but the love, zeal, and affection inspired by clemency and justice; which, though they seem more pliant than the stiff and hard bonds of severity, are nevertheless the strongest and most durable ties to sustain a lasting government. Moreover, it is mean and dishonourable that a ruler, while careful to be splendid in his dress, and luxurious and magnificent in his habitation, should, in reason and power of speech, make no better show than the commonest of his subjects, nor have the princely palace of his mind adorned according to his royal dignity.

Dion frequently entertaining the king upon this subject, and, as occasion offered, repeating some of the philosopher's sayings, Dionysius grew impatiently desirous to have Plato's company, and to hear him discourse. Forthwith, therefore, he sent letter upon letter to him to Athens, to which Dion added his entreaties; also several philosophers of the Pythagorean sect from Italy sent their recommendations, urging him to come and obtain a hold upon this pliant, youthful soul, which his solid and weighty reasonings might steady, as it were, upon the seas of absolute power and authority. Plato, as he tells us himself, out of shame more than any other feeling, lest it should seem that he was all mere theory, and that of his own good-will he would never venture into action, hoping withal, that if he could work a cure upon one man, the head and guide of the rest, he might remedy the distempers of the whole island of Sicily, yielded to their requests.

But Dion's enemies, fearing an alteration in Dionysius, persuaded him to recall from banishment Philistus, a man of learned education, and at the same time of great experience in the ways of tyrants, and who might serve as a counterpoise to Plato and his philosophy. For Philistus from the beginning had been a great instrument in establishing the tyranny, and for a long time had held the office of captain of the citadel. There was a report that he had been intimate with the mother of Dionysius the first, and not without his privity. And when Leptines, having two daughters by a married woman who he had debauched, gave one of them in marriage to Philistus, without acquainting Dionysius, he, in great anger, put Leptines's mistress in prison, and banished Philistus from Sicily. Whereupon, he fled to some of his friends on the Adriatic coast, in which retirement and leisure it is probable he wrote the greatest part of his history; for he returned not into his country during the reign of that Dionysius.

But after his death, as is just related, Dion's enemies occasioned him to be recalled home, as fitted for their purpose, and a firm friend to the arbitrary government. And this, indeed, immediately upon his return he set himself to maintain; and at the same time various calumnies and accusations against Dion were by others brought to the king: as that he held correspondence with Theodotes and Heraclides, to subvert the government; as, doubtless, it is likely enough, that Dion had entertained hopes, by the coming of Plato, to mitigate the rigid and despotic severity of the tyranny, and to give Dionysius the character of a fair and lawful governor; and had determined, if he should continue averse to that, and were not to be reclaimed, to depose him, and restore the commonwealth to the Syracusans; not that he approved a democratic government, but thought it altogether preferable to a tyranny, when a sound and good aristocracy could not be procured.

This was the state of affairs when Plato came into Sicily, who, at his first arrival, was received with wonderful demonstration of kindness and respect. For one of the royal chariots, richly ornamented, was in attendance to receive him when he came on shore; Dionysius himself sacrificed to the gods in thankful acknowledgment for the great happiness which had befallen his government. The citizens, also, began to entertain marvellous hopes of a speedy reformation, when they observed the modesty which now ruled in the banquets, and the general decorum which prevailed in all the court, their tyrant himself also behaving with gentleness and humanity in all their matters of business that came before him. There was a general passion for reasoning and philosophy, insomuch that the very palace, it is reported, was filled with dust by the concourse of the students in mathematics who were working their problems there. Some few days after, it was the time of one of the Syracusan sacrifices, and when the priest, as he was wont, prayed for the long and safe continuance of the tyranny, Dionysius, it is said, as he stood by, cried out, " Leave off praying for evil upon us." This sensibly vexed Philistus and his party, who conjectured, that if Plato, upon such brief acquaintance, had so far transformed and altered the young man's mind, longer converse and greater intimacy would give him such influence and authority that it would be impossible to withstand him.

Therefore, no longer privately and apart, but jointly and in public, all of them, they began to slander Dion, noising it about that he had charmed and bewitched Dionysius by Plato's sophistry, to the end that when he was persuaded voluntarily to part with his power, and lay down his authority, Dion might take it up, and settle it upon his sister Aristomache's children. Others professed to be indignant that the Athenians, who formerly had come to Sicily with a great fleet and a numerous land army, and perished miserably without being able to take the city of Syracuse, should now, by means of one sophister, overturn the sovereignty of Dionysius; inveighing him to cashier his guard of ten thousand lances, dismiss a navy of four hundred galleys, disband an army of ten thousand horse and many times over that number of foot, and go seek in the schools an unknown and imaginary bliss, and learn by the mathematics how to be happy; while, in the meantime, the substantial enjoyments of absolute power, riches, and pleasure would be handed over to Dion and his sister's children.

By these means, Dion began to incur at first suspicion, and by degrees more apparent displeasure and hostility. A letter, also, was intercepted and brought to the young prince which Dion had written to the Carthaginian agents, advising them that, when they treated with Dionysius concerning the peace, they should not come to their audience without communicating with him: they would not fail to obtain by this means all that they wanted. When Dionysius had shown this to Philistus, and consulted with him, as Timæus relates, about it, he over-reached Dion by a feigned reconciliation, professing, after some fair and reasonable expression of his feelings, that he was at friends with him, and thus, leading him alone to the seaside, under the castle wall, he showed him the letter, and taxed him with conspiring with the Carthaginians against him. And when Dion essayed to speak in his own defence, Dionysius suffered him not; but immediately forced him aboard a boat, which lay there for that purpose, and commanded the sailors to set him ashore on the coast of Italy.

When this was publicly known, and was thought very hard usage, there was much lamentation in the tyrant's own household on account of the women, but the citizens of Syracuse encouraged themselves, expecting that for his sake some disturbance would ensue; which, together with the mistrust others would now feel, might occasion a general change and revolution in the state. Dionysius seeing this, took alarm, and endeavoured to pacify the women and others of Dion's kindred and friends, assuring them that he had not banished, but only sent him out of the way for a time, for fear of his own passion, which might be provoked some day by Dion's self-will into some act which he should be sorry for. He gave also two ships to his relations, with liberty to send into Peloponnesus for him whatever of his property or servants they thought fit.

Dion was very rich, and had his house furnished with little less than royal splendour and magnificence. These valuables his friends packed up and conveyed to him, besides many rich presents which were sent him by the women and his adherents. So that, so far as wealth and riches went, he made a noble appearance among the Greeks, and they might judge, by the affluence of the exile, what was the power of the tyrant.

Dionysius immediately removed Plato into the castle, designing, under colour of an honourable and kind reception, to set a guard upon him, lest he should follow Dion, and declare to the world, in his behalf, how injuriously he had been dealt with. And, moreover, time and conversation (as wild beasts by use grow tame and tractable) had brought Dionysius to endure Plato's company and discourse, so that he began to love the philosopher, but with such an affection as had something of the tyrant in it, requiring of Plato that he should, in return of his kindness, love him only, and attend to him above all other men; being ready to permit to his care the chief management of affairs, and even the government, too, upon condition that he would not prefer Dion's friendship before his. This extravagant affection was a great trouble to Plato, for it was accompanied with petulant and jealous humours, like the fond passions of those that are desperately in love; frequently he was angry and fell out with him, and presently begged and entreated to be friends again. He was beyond measure desirous to be Plato's scholar, and to proceed in the study of philosophy, and yet he was ashamed of it with those who spoke against it and professed to think it would ruin him.

But a war about this time breaking out, he sent Plato away, promising him in the summer to recall Dion, though in this he broke his word at once; nevertheless, he remitted to him his revenues, desiring Plato to excuse him as to the time appointed, because of the war, but, as soon as he had settled a peace, he would immediately send for Dion, requiring him in the interim to be quiet, and not raise any disturbance, nor speak ill of him among the Grecians. This Plato endeavoured to effect, by keeping Dion with him in the academy, and busying him in philosophical studies.

Dion sojourned in the Upper Town of Athens, with Callippus, one of his acquaintance; but for his pleasure he bought a seat in the country, which afterwards, when he went into Sicily, he gave to Speusippus, who had been his most frequent companion while he was at Athens, Plato so arranging it, with the hope that Dion's austere temper might be softened by agreeable company, with an occasional mixture of seasonable mirth. For Speusippus was of the character to afford him this; we find him spoken of in Timon's Silli, as "good at a jest." And Plato himself, as it happened, being called upon to furnish a chorus of boys, Dion took upon him the ordering and management of it, and defrayed the whole expense, Plato giving him this opportunity to oblige the Athenians, which was likely to procure his friend more kindness than himself credit. Dion went also to see several other cities, visiting the noblest and most statesman-like persons in Greece, and joining in their recreations and entertainments in their times of festival. In all which, no sort of vulgar ignorance, or tyrannic assumption, or luxuriousness was remarked in him; but, on the contrary, a great deal of temperance, generosity, and courage, and a well-becoming taste for reasoning and philosophic discourses. By which means he gained the love and admiration of all men, and in many cities had public honours decreed him; the Lacedæmonians making him a citizen of Sparta, without regard to the displeasure of Dionysius, though at that time he was aiding them in their wars against the Thebans.

It is related that once, upon invitation, he went to pay a visit to Ptœodorus, the Megarian, a man, it would seem, of wealth and importance; and when, on account of the concourse of people about his door, and the press of business, it was very troublesome and difficult to get access to him, turning about to his friends, who seemed concerned and angry at it, " What reason," said he, " have we to blame Ptœodorus, when we our-selves used to do no better when we were at Syracuse? "

After some little time, Dionysius, envying Dion, and jealous of the favour and interest he had among the Grecians, put a stop upon his incomes, and no longer sent him his revenues, making his own commissioners trustees of the estate. But, endeavouring to obviate the ill-will and discredit which, upon Plato's account, might accrue to him among the philosophers, he collected in his court many reputed learned men; and am-bitiously desiring to surpass them in their debates, he was forced to make use, often incorrectly, of arguments he had picked up from Plato. And now he wished for his company again, repent-ing he had not made better use of it when he had it, and had given no greater heed to his admirable lessons. Like a tyrant, therefore, inconsiderate in his desires, headstrong and violent in whatever he took a will to, on a sudden he was eagerly set on the design of recalling him, and left no stone unturned, but addressed himself to Archytas, the Pythagorean (his acquaint-ance and friendly relations with whom owed their origin to Plato), and persuaded him to stand as surety for his engage-ments, and to request Plato to revisit Sicily.

Archytas, therefore, sent Archedemus and Dionysius some galleys, with divers friends, to entreat his return; moreover, he wrote to him himself expressly and in plain terms, that Dion must never look for any favour or kindness if Plato would not be prevailed with to come into Sicily; but if Plato did come Dion should be assured of whatever he desired. Dion also received letters full of solicitations from his sister and his wife, urging him to beg Plato to gratify Dionysius in this request, and not give him an excuse for further ill-doing. So that, as Plato says to himself, the third time he set sail for the Strait of Scylla—

> " Venturing again Charybdis's dangerous gulf."

This arrival brought great joy to Dionysius, and no less hopes to the Sicilians, who were earnest in their prayers and good wishes that Plato might get the better of Philistus, and philosophy triumph over tyranny. Neither was he unbefriended by the women, who studied to oblige him; and he had with Dionysius that peculiar credit which no man else ever obtained, namely, liberty to come into his presence without being examined or searched. When he would have given him a considerable sum of money, and, on several repeated occasions, made fresh offers, which Plato as often declined, Aristippus, the Cyrenæan, then present, said that Dionysius was very safe in his munificence, he gave little to those who were ready to take all they could get, and a great deal to Plato, who would accept of nothing.

After the first compliments of kindness were over, when Plato began to discourse of Dion, he was at first diverted by excuses for delay, followed soon after by complaints and disgusts, though not as yet observable to others, Dionysius endeavouring to conceal them, and, by other civilities and honourable usage, to draw him off from his affection to Dion. And for some time Plato himself was careful not to let anything of this dishonesty and breach of promise appear, but bore with it, and dissembled his annoyance. While matters stood thus between them, and, as they thought, they were unobserved and undiscovered, Helicon, the Cyzicenian, one of Plato's followers, foretold an eclipse of the sun, which happened according to his prediction; for which he was much admired by the tyrant, and rewarded with a talent of silver; whereupon Aristippus, jesting with some others of the philosophers, told them, he also could predict something extraordinary; and on their entreating him to declare it, " I foretell," said he, " that before long there will be a quarrel between Dionysius and Plato."

At length, Dionysius made sale of Dion's estate, and converted the money to his own use, and removed Plato from an apartment he had in the gardens of the palace to lodgings among the guards he kept in pay, who from the first had hated Plato, and sought opportunity to make away with him, supposing he advised Dionysius to lay down the government and disband his soldiers.

When Archytas understood the danger he was in, he immediately sent a galley with messengers to demand him of Dionysius; alleging that he stood engaged for his safety, upon the confidence of which Plato had come to Sicily. Dionysius, to palliate his secret hatred, before Plato came away, treated him with great entertainments and all seeming demonstrations of kindness, but could not forbear breaking out one day into the expression, " No doubt, Plato, when you are at home among the philosophers, your companions, you will complain of me, and reckon up a great many of my faults." To which Plato answered with a smile, " The Academy will never, I trust, be at such a loss for subjects to discuss as to seek one in you." Thus, they say, Plato was dismissed; but his own writings do not altogether agree with this account.

Dion was angry at all this, and not long after declared open enmity to Dionysius, on hearing what had been done with his wife; on which matter Plato, also, had had some confidential correspondence with Dionysius. Thus it was. After Dion's banishment, Dionysius, when he sent Plato back, had desired him to ask Dion privately, if he would be averse to his wife's marrying another man. For there went a report, whether true, or raised by Dion's enemies, that his marriage was not pleasing to him, and that he lived with his wife on uneasy terms. When Plato therefore came to Athens, and had mentioned the subject to Dion, he wrote a letter to Dionysius speaking of other matters openly, but on this in language expressly designed to be understood by him alone, to the effect that he had talked with Dion about the business, and that it was evident he would highly resent the affront, if it should be put into execution. At that time, therefore, while there were yet great hopes of an accommodation, he took no new steps with his sister, suffering her to live with Dion's child. But when things were come to that pass, that no reconciliation could be expected, and Plato, after his second visit, was again sent away in displeasure, he then forced Arete, against her will, to marry Timocrates, one of his favourites; in this action coming short even of his father's justice and lenity; for he, when Polyxenus, the husband of his sister, Theste, became his enemy, and fled in alarm out of Sicily, sent for his sister, and taxed her, that, being privy to her husband's flight, she had not declared it to him. But the lady, confident and fearless, made him this reply: " Do you believe me, brother, so bad a wife, or so timorous a woman, that, having known my husband's flight, I would not have borne his company, and shared his fortunes? I knew nothing of it; since otherwise it had been my better lot to be called the wife of the exile Polyxenus than the sister of the tyrant Dionysius." It is said, he admired her free and ready answer, as did the Syracusans also her courage and virtue, insomuch that she retained her dignity and princely retinue after the dissolution of the tyranny, and when she died, the citizens, by public decree, attended the solemnity of her funeral. And the story, though a digression from the present purpose, was well worth the telling.

From this time, Dion set his mind upon warlike measures; with which Plato, out of respect for past hospitalities, and because of his age, would have nothing to do. But Speusippus and the rest of his friends assisted and encouraged him, bidding him deliver Sicily, which with lift-up hands implored his help, and with open arms was ready to receive him. For when Plato was staying at Syracuse, Speusippus, being oftener than he in company with the citizens, had more thoroughly made out how they were inclined; and though at first they had been on their guard, suspecting his bold language, as though he had been set on by the tyrant to trepan them, yet at length they trusted him. There was but one mind and one wish or prayer among them all, that Dion would undertake the design, and come, though without either navy, men, horse, or arms; that he would simply put himself aboard any ship, and lend the Sicilians his person and name against Dionysius. This information from Speusippus encouraged Dion, who, concealing his real purpose, employed his friends privately to raise what men they could; and many statesmen and philosophers were assisting him, as, for instance, Eudemus the Cyprian, on whose death Aristotle wrote his Dialogue of the Soul, and Timonides the Leucadian. They also engaged on his side Miltas the Thessalian, who was a prophet, and had studied in the Academy. But of all that were banished by Dionysius, who were not fewer than a thousand, five and twenty only joined in the enterprise; the rest were afraid, and abandoned it. The rendezvous was in the island Zacynthus, where a small force of not quite eight hundred men came together, all of them, however, persons already distinguished in plenty of previous hard service, their bodies well trained and practised, and their experience and courage amply sufficient to animate and embolden to action the numbers whom Dion expected to join him in Sicily.

Yet these men, when they first understood the expedition was against Dionysius, were troubled and disheartened, blaming Dion, that, hurried on like a madman by mere passion and despair, he rashly threw both himself and them into certain ruin. Nor were they less angry with their commanders and muster-masters that they had not in the beginning let them know the design. But when Dion in his address to them had set forth the unsafe and weak condition of arbitrary government, and declared that he carried them rather for commanders than soldiers, the citizens of Syracuse and the rest of the Sicilians having been long ready for a revolt, and when, after him, Alcimenes, an Achæan of the highest birth and reputation, who accompanied the expedition, harangued them to the same effect, they were contented.

It was now the middle of summer, and the Etesian winds blowing steadily on the seas, the moon was at the full, when Dion prepared a magnificent sacrifice to Apollo, and with great solemnity marched his soldiers to the temple in all their arms and accoutrements. And after the sacrifice, he feasted them all in the race-course of the Zacynthians, where he had made provision for their entertainment. And when here they beheld with wonder the quantity and the richness of the gold and silver plate, and the tables laid to entertain them, all far exceeding the fortunes of a private man, they concluded with themselves that a man now past the prime of life, who was master of so much treasure, would not engage himself in so hazardous an enterprise without good reason of hope, and certain and sufficient assurances of aid from friends over there. Just after the libations were made, and the accompanying prayers offered, the moon was eclipsed; which was no wonder to Dion, who understood the revolutions of eclipses, and the way in which the moon is overshadowed and the earth interposed between her and the sun. But because it was necessary that the soldiers, who were surprised and troubled at it, should be satisfied and encouraged, Miltas the diviner, standing up in the midst of the assembly, bade them be of good cheer, and expect all happy success, for that the divine powers foreshowed that something at present glorious and resplendent should be eclipsed and obscured; nothing at this time being more splendid than the sovereignty of Dionysius, their arrival in Sicily should dim this glory, and extinguish this brightness. Thus Miltas, in public, descanted

upon the incident. But concerning a swarm of bees which
settled on the poop of Dion's ship, he privately told him and
his friends that he feared the great actions they were like to
perform, though for a time they should thrive and flourish,
would be of short continuance, and soon suffer a decay. It is
reported, also, that many prodigies happened to Dionysius at
that time. An eagle, snatching a javelin from one of the guard,
carried it aloft, and from thence let it fall into the sea. The
water of the sea that washed the castle walls was for a whole
day sweet and potable, as many that tasted it experienced.
Pigs were farrowed perfect in all their other parts, but without
ears. This the diviners declared to portend revolt and rebellion,
for that the subjects would no longer give ear to the commands
of their superiors. They expounded the sweetness of the water
to signify to the Syracusans a change from hard and grievous
times into easier and more happy circumstances. The eagle
being the bird of Jupiter, and the spear an emblem of power
and command, this prodigy was to denote that the chief of the
gods designed the end and dissolution of the present government.
These things Theopompus relates in his history.

Two ships of burden carried all Dion's men; a third vessel,
of no great size, and two galleys of thirty oars attended them.
In addition to his soldiers' own arms, he carried two thousand
shields, a very great number of darts and lances, and abundant
stores of all manner of provisions, that there might be no want
of anything in their voyage; their purpose being to keep out at
sea during the whole voyage, and use the winds, since all the
land was hostile to them, and Philistus, they had been told, was
in Iapygia with a fleet, looking out for them. Twelve days
they sailed with a fresh and gentle breeze; on the thirteenth,
they made Pachynus, the Sicilian cape. There Protus, the chief
pilot, advised them to land at once and without delay, for if
they were forced again from the shore, and did not take advantage of the headland, they might ride out at sea many nights
and days, waiting for a southerly wind in the summer season.
But Dion, fearing a descent too near his enemies, and desirous
to begin at a greater distance, and further on in the country,
sailed on past Pachynus. They had not gone far, before stress
of weather, the wind blowing hard at north, drove the fleet
from the coast; and it being now about the time that Arcturus
rises, a violent storm of wind and rain came on, with thunder
and lightning; the mariners were at their wits' end, and ignorant
what course they ran, until on a sudden they found they were

driving with the sea on Cercina, the island on the coast of Africa, just where it is most craggy and dangerous to run upon. Upon the cliffs there they escaped narrowly of being forced and staved to pieces; but, labouring hard at their oars, with much difficulty they kept clear until the storm ceased. Then, lighting by chance upon a vessel, they understood they were upon the Heads, as it is called, of the Great Syrtis; and when they were now again disheartened by a sudden calm, and beating to and fro without making any way, a soft air began to blow from the land, when they expected anything rather than wind from the south, and scarce believed the happy change of their fortune. The gale gradually increasing, and beginning to blow fresh, they clapped on all their sails, and, praying to the gods, put out again into the open seas, steering right from Africa for Sicily. And, running steady before the wind, the fifth day they arrived at Minoa, a little town of Sicily, in the dominion of the Carthaginians, of which Synalus, an acquaintance and friend of Dion's, happened at that time to be governor; who, not knowing it was Dion and his fleet, endeavoured to hinder his men from landing; but they rushed on shore with their swords in their hands, not slaying any of their opponents (for this Dion had forbidden, because of his friendship with the Carthaginians), but forced them to retreat, and, following close, pressed in a body with them into the place, and took it. As soon as the two commanders met, they mutually saluted each other; Dion delivered up the place again to Synalus, without the least damage done to any one therein, and Synalus quartered and entertained the soldiers, and supplied Dion with what he wanted.

They were most of all encouraged by the happy accident of Dionysius's absence at this nick of time; for it appeared that he was lately gone with eighty sail of ships to Italy. Therefore, when Dion was desirous that the soldiers should refresh themselves there, after their tedious and troublesome voyage, they would not be prevailed with, but earnest to make the best use of that opportunity, they urged Dion to lead them straight on to Syracuse. Leaving, therefore, their baggage, and the arms they did not use, Dion desired Synalus to convey them to him as he had occasion, and marched directly to Syracuse.

The first that came in to him upon his march were two hundred horse of the Agrigentines who were settled near Ecnomum, and, after them, the Geloans. But the news soon flying to Syracuse, Timocrates, who had married Dion's wife, the sister of Dionysius, and was the principal man among his friends now remaining in the city, immediately despatched a courier to Dionysius, with letters announcing Dion's arrival; while he himself took all possible care to prevent any stir or tumult in the city, where all were in great excitement, but as yet continued quiet, fearing to give too much credit to what was reported. A very strange accident happened to the messenger who was sent with the letters; for being arrived in Italy, as he travelled through the land of Rhegium, hastening to Dionysius at Caulonia, he met one of his acquaintance, who was carrying home part of a sacrifice. He accepted a piece of the flesh, which his friend offered him, and proceeded on his journey with all speed; having travelled a good part of the night, and being, through weariness, forced to take a little rest, he laid himself down in the next convenient place he came to, which was in a wood near the road. A wolf, scenting the flesh, came and seized it as it lay fastened to the letter-bag, and with the flesh carried away the bag also, in which were the letters to Dionysius. The man, awaking and missing his bag, sought for it up and down a great while, and, not finding it, resolved not to go to the king without his letters, but to conceal himself, and keep out of the way.

Dionysius, therefore, came to hear of the war in Sicily from other hands, and that a good while after. In the meantime, as Dion proceeded in his march, the Camarineans joined his forces, and the country people in the territory of Syracuse rose and joined him in a large body. The Leontines and Campanians, who, with Timocrates, guarded the Epipolæ, receiving a false alarm which was spread on purpose by Dion, as if he intended to attack their cities first, left Timocrates, and hastened off to carry succour to their own homes. News of which being brought to Dion, where he lay near Macræ, he raised his camp by night, and came to the river Anapus which is distant from the city about ten furlongs; there he made a halt, and sacrificed by the river, offering vows to the rising sun. The soothsayers declared that the gods promised him victory; and they that were present, seeing him assisting at the sacrifice with a garland on his head, one and all crowned themselves with garlands. There were about five thousand that had joined his forces in their march; who, though but ill-provided, with such weapons as came next to hand, made up by zeal and courage for the want of better arms; and when once they were told to advance, as if Dion were already conqueror, they ran forward with shouts and acclamations, encouraging each other with the hopes of liberty.

The most considerable men and better sort of the citizens of Syracuse, clad all in white, met him at the gates. The populace set upon all that were of Dionysius's party, and principally searched for those they called setters or informers, a number of wicked and hateful wretches, who made it their business to go up and down the city, thrusting themselves into all companies, that they might inform Dionysius what men said, and how they stood affected. These were the first that suffered, being beaten to death by the crowd.

Timocrates, not being able to force his way to the garrison that kept the castle, took horse, and fled out of the city, filling all the places where he came with fear and confusion, magnifying the amount of Dion's forces that he might not be supposed to have deserted his charge without good reason for it. By this time, Dion was come up, and appeared in the sight of the people; he marched first in a rich suit of arms, and by him on one hand his brother, Megacles, on the other, Callippus the Athenian, crowned with garlands. Of the foreign soldiers, a hundred followed as his guard, and their several officers led the rest in good order; the Syracusans looking on and welcoming them, as if they believed the whole to be a sacred and religious procession, to celebrate the solemn entrance, after an absence of forty-eight years, of liberty and popular government.

Dion entered by the Menitid gate, and, having by sound of trumpet quieted the noise of the people, he caused proclamation to be made, that Dion and Megacles, who were come to overthrow the tyrannical government, did declare the Syracusans and all other Sicilians to be free from the tyrant. But, being desirous to harangue the people himself, he went up through the Achradina. The citizens on each side the way brought victims for sacrifice, set out their tables and goblets, and as he passed by each door threw flowers and ornaments upon him, with vows and acclamations, honouring him as a god. There was under the castle and the Pentapyla a lofty and conspicuous sun-dial, which Dionysius had set up. Getting up upon the top of that, he made an oration to the people, calling upon them to maintain and defend their liberty; who, with great expressions of joy and acknowledgment, created Dion and Megacles generals, with plenary powers, joining in commission with them, at their desire and entreaty, twenty colleagues, of whom half were of those that had returned with them out of banishment. It seemed also to the diviners a most happy omen that Dion, when he made his address to the people, had under his feet the stately monument which Dionysius had been at such pains to erect; but because it was a sun-dial on which he stood when he was made general, they expressed some fears that the great actions he had performed might be subject to change, and admit some rapid turn and declination of fortune.

After this, Dion, taking the Epipolæ, released the citizens who were imprisoned there, and then raised a wall to invest the castle. Seven days after, Dionysius arrived by sea, and got into the citadel, and about the same time came carriages, bringing the arms and ammunition which Dion had left with Synalus. These he distributed among the citizens; and the rest that wanted furnished themselves as well as they could, and put themselves in the condition of zealous and serviceable men-at-arms.

Dionysius sent agents, at first privately, to Dion, to try what terms they could make with him. But he declaring that any overtures they had to make must be made in public to the Syracusans as a free people, envoys now went and came between the tyrant and the people, with fair proposals, and assurances that they should have abatements of their tributes and taxes, and freedom from the burdens of military expeditions, all which should be made according to their own approbation and consent with him. The Syracusans laughed at these offers, and Dion returned answer to the envoys, that Dionysius must not think to treat with them upon any other terms but resigning the government; which if he would actually do, he would not forget how nearly he was related to him, or be wanting to assist him in procuring oblivion for the past, and whatever else was reasonable and just. Dionysius seemed to consent to this, and sent his agents again, desiring some of the Syracusans to come into the citadel and discuss with him in person the terms to which on each side they might be willing, after fair debate, to consent. There were, therefore, some deputed, such as Dion approved of; and the general rumour from the castle was, that Dionysius would voluntarily resign his authority, and rather do it himself as his own good deed than let it be the act of Dion. But this profession was a mere trick to amuse the Syracusans. For he put the deputies that were sent to him in custody, and by break of day, having first to encourage his men made them drink plentifully of raw wine, he sent the garrison of mercenaries out to make a sudden sally against Dion's works. The attack was quite unexpected, and the barbarians set to work boldly with loud cries to pull down the cross-wall, and assailed the Syracusans so furiously that they

were not able to maintain their post.  Only a party of Dion's
hired soldiers, on first taking the alarm, advanced to the rescue;
neither did they at first know what to do, or how to employ
the aid they brought, not being able to hear the commands of
their officers, amidst the noise and confusion of the Syracusans,
who fled from the enemy and ran in among them, breaking
through their ranks, until Dion, seeing none of his orders could
be heard, resolved to let them see by example what they ought
to do, and charged into the thickest of the enemy.  The fight
about him was fierce and bloody, he being as well known by
the enemy as by his own party, and all running with loud cries
to the quarters where he fought.  Though his time of life was
no longer that of the bodily strength and agility for such a
combat, still his determination and courage were sufficient to
maintain him against all that attacked him; but, while bravely
driving them back, he was wounded in the hand with a lance,
his body armour also had been much battered, and was scarcely
any longer serviceable to protect him, either against missiles
or blows hand-to-hand.  Many spears and javelins had passed
into it through the shield, and, on these being broken back, he
fell to the ground, but was immediately rescued, and carried
off by his soldiers.  The command-in-chief he left to Timonides,
and, mounting a horse, rode about the city, rallying the Syracusans that fled; and, ordering up a detachment of the foreign
soldiers out of Achradina, where they were posted on guard, he
brought them as a fresh reserve, eager for battle, upon the tired
and failing enemy, who were already well inclined to give up
their design.  For having hopes at their first sally to take the
whole city, when beyond their expectation they found themselves engaged with bold and practised fighters, they fell back
towards the castle.  As soon as they gave ground, the Greek
soldiers pressed the harder upon them, till they turned and fled
within the walls.  There were lost in this action seventy-four of
Dion's men, and a very great number of the enemy.  This being
a signal victory, and principally obtained by the valour of the
foreign soldiers, the Syracusans rewarded them in honour of it
with a hundred minæ, and the soldiers on their part presented
Dion with a crown of gold.

Soon after, there came heralds from Dionysius bringing Dion
letters from the women of his family, and one addressed outside, "To his father, from Hipparinus;" this was the name of
Dion's son, though Timæus says, he was, from his mother Arete's
name, called Aretæus; but I think credit is rather to be given

to Timonides's report, who was his father's fellow-soldier and confidant. The rest of the letters were read publicly, containing many solicitations and humble requests of the women; that professing to be from his son, the heralds would not have them open publicly, but Dion, putting force upon them, broke the seal. It was from Dionysius, written in the terms of it to Dion, but in effect to the Syracusans, and so worded that, under a plausible justification of himself and entreaty to him, means were taken for rendering him suspected by the people. It reminded him of the good service he had formerly done the usurping government, it added threats to his dearest relations, his sister, son, and wife, if he did not comply with the contents, also passionate demands mingled with lamentations, and, most to the purpose of all, urgent recommendations to him not to destroy the government, and put the power into the hands of men who always hated him, and would never forget their old piques and quarrels; let him take the sovereignty himself, and so secure the safety of his family and his friends.

When this letter was read, the Syracusans were not, as they should have been, transported with admiration at the unmovable constancy and magnanimity of Dion, who withstood all his dearest interests to be true to virtue and justice, but, on the contrary, they saw in this their reason for fearing and suspecting that he lay under an invincible necessity to be favourable to Dionysius; and they began, therefore, to look out for other leaders, and the rather because to their great joy they received the news that Heraclides was on his way. This Heraclides was one of those whom Dionysius had banished, a very good soldier, and well known for the commands he had formerly had under the tyrant; yet a man of no constant purpose, of a fickle temper, and least of all to be relied upon when he had to act with a colleague in any honourable command. He had had a difference formerly with Dion in Peloponnesus, and had resolved, upon his own means, with what ships and soldiers he had, to make an attack upon Dionysius. When he arrived at Syracuse, with seven galleys and three small vessels, he found Dionysius already close besieged, and the Syracusans high and proud of their victories. Forthwith, therefore, he endeavoured by all ways to make himself popular; and, indeed, he had in him naturally something that was very insinuating and taking with a populace that loves to be courted. He gained his end, also, the easier, and drew the people over to his side, because of the dislike they had taken to Dion's grave and stately manner,

which they thought overbearing and assuming; their successes
having made them so careless and confident that they expected
popular arts and flatteries from their leaders before they had
in reality secured a popular government.

Getting, therefore, together in an irregular assembly, they
chose Heraclides their admiral; but when Dion came forward,
and told them that conferring this trust upon Heraclides was
in effect to withdraw that which they had granted him, for he
was no longer their generalissimo if another had the command
of the navy, they repealed their order, and, though much against
their wills, cancelled the new appointment.  When this business
was over, Dion invited Heraclides to his house, and pointed out
to him, in gentle terms, that he had not acted wisely or well to
quarrel with him upon a punctilio of honour, at a time when the
least false step might be the ruin of all; and then, calling a
fresh assembly of the people, he there named Heraclides admiral,
and prevailed with the citizens to allow him a life-guard, as he
himself had.

Heraclides openly professed the highest respect for Dion, and
made him great acknowledgments for this favour, attending
him with all deference, as ready to receive his commands; but
underhand he kept up his dealings with the populace and the
unrulier citizens, unsettling their minds and disturbing them
with his complaints, and putting Dion into the utmost perplexity
and disquiet.  For if he advised to give Dionysius leave to quit
the castle, he would be exposed to the imputation of sparing
and protecting him; if, to avoid giving offence or suspicion, he
simply continued the siege, they would say he protracted the
war to keep his office of general the longer and overawe the
citizens.

There was one Sosis, notorious in the city for his bad conduct
and his impudence, yet a favourite with the people, for the very
reason that they liked to see it made a part of popular privileges to
carry free speech to this excess of licence.  This man, out of a design
against Dion, stood up one day in an assembly, and, having sufficiently railed at the citizens as a set of fools that could not see
how they had made an exchange of a dissolute and drunken for a
sober and watchful despotism, and thus having publicly declared
himself Dion's enemy, took his leave.  The next day he was
seen running through the streets, as if he fled from some that
pursued him, almost naked, wounded in the head, and bloody
all over.  In this condition, getting people about him in the
market-place, he told them that he had been assaulted by Dion's

men; and, to confirm what he said, showed them the wounds he
had received in his head. And a good many took his part, exclaiming loudly against Dion for his cruel and tyrannical conduct,
stopping the mouths of the people by bloodshed and peril of life.
Just as an assembly was gathering in this unsettled and tumultuous state of mind, Dion came before them, and made it appear
how this Sosis was brother to one of Dionysius's guard, and that
he was set on by him to embroil the city in tumult and confusion;
Dionysius having now no way left for his security but to make
his advantage of their dissensions and distractions. The sur-
geons, also, having searched the wound, found it was rather
raised than cut with a downright blow; for the wounds made
with a sword are, from their mere weight, most commonly
deepest in the middle, but this was very slight, and all along of
an equal depth; and it was not one continued wound, as if cut
at once, but several incisions, in all probability made at several
times, as he was able to endure the pain. There were credible
persons, also, who brought a razor, and showed it in the assembly,
stating that they met Sosis, running in the street, all bloody,
who told them that he was flying from Dion's soldiers, who had
just attacked and wounded him; they ran at once to look after
them, and met no one, but spied this razor lying under a hollow
stone near the place from which they observed he came.

Sosis was now likely to come by the worst of it. But, when
to back all this, his own servants came in, and gave evidence
that he had left his house alone before break of day, with the
razor in his hand, Dion's accusers withdrew themselves, and the
people by a general vote condemned Sosis to die, being once again
well satisfied with Dion and his proceedings.

Yet they were still as jealous as before of his soldiers, and the
rather because the war was now carried on principally by sea;
Philistus being come from Iapygia with a great fleet to Dionysius's assistance. They supposed, therefore, that there would be
no longer need of the soldiers, who were all landsmen and armed
accordingly; these were rather, indeed, they thought, in a condition to be protected by themselves, who were seamen, and had
their power in their shipping. Their good opinion of themselves
was also much enhanced by an advantage they got in an engagement by sea, in which they took Philistus prisoner, and used him
in a barbarous and cruel manner. Ephorus relates that when he
saw his ship was taken, he slew himself. But Timonides, who
was with Dion from the very first, and was present at all the
events as they occurred, writing to Speusippus the philosopher,

relates the story thus: that Philistus's galley running aground, he was taken prisoner alive, and first disarmed, then stripped of his corselet, and exposed naked, being now an old man, to every kind of contumely; after which they cut off his head, and gave his body to the boys of the town, bidding them drag it through the Achradina, and then throw it into the Quarries. Timæus, to increase the mockery, adds further, that the boys tied him by his lame leg, and so drew him through the streets, while the Syracusans stood by laughing and jesting at the sight of that very man thus tied and dragged about by the leg, who had told Dionysius that, so far from flying on horseback from Syracuse, he ought to wait till he should be dragged out by the heels. Philistus, however, has stated that this was said to Dionysius by another, and not by himself.

Timæus avails himself of this advantage, which Philistus truly enough affords against himself in his zealous and constant adherence to the tyranny, to vent his own spleen and malice against him. They, indeed, who were injured by him at the time, are perhaps excusable, if they carried their resentment to the length of indignities to his dead body; but they who write history afterwards, and were noways wronged by him in his lifetime, and have received assistance from his writings, in honour should not with opprobrious and scurrilous language upbraid him for those misfortunes which may well enough befall even the best of men. On the other side, Ephorus is as much out of the way in his encomiums. For, however ingenious he is in supplying unjust acts and wicked conduct with fair and worthy motives, and in selecting decorous and honourable terms, yet when he does his best, he does not himself stand clear of the charge of being the greatest lover of tyrants, and the fondest admirer of luxury and power and rich estates and alliances of marriage with absolute princes. He that neither praises Philistus for his conduct, nor insults over his misfortunes, seems to me to take the fittest course.

After Philistus's death, Dionysius sent to Dion, offering to surrender the castle, all the arms, provisions, and garrison soldiers, with full pay for them for five months, demanding in return that he might have safe conduct to go unmolested into Italy, and there to continue, and also to enjoy the revenues of Gyarta, a large and fruitful territory belonging to Syracuse, reaching from the seaside to the middle of the country. Dion rejected these proposals, and referred him to the Syracusans. They, hoping in a short time to take Dionysius alive, dismissed his ambassadors summarily. But he, leaving his eldest son,

Apollocrates, to defend the castle, and putting on board his ships the persons and the property that he set most value upon, took the opportunity of a fair wind, and made his escape, undiscovered by the admiral Heraclides and his fleet.

The citizens loudly exclaimed against Heraclides for this neglect; but he got one of their public speakers, Hippo by name, to go among them, and make proposals to the assembly for a redivision of lands, alleging that the first beginning of liberty was equality, and that poverty and slavery were inseparable companions. In support of this, Heraclides spoke, and used the faction in favour of it to overpower Dion, who opposed it; and in fine, he persuaded the people to ratify it by their vote, and further to decree that the foreign soldiers should receive no pay, and that they would elect new commanders, and so be rid of Dion's oppression. The people, attempting, as it were, after their long sickness of despotism, all at once to stand on their legs, and to do their part, for which they were yet unfit, of freemen, stumbled in all their actions; and yet hated Dion, who, like a good physician, endeavoured to keep the city to a strict and temperate regimen.

When they met in the assembly to choose their commanders, about the middle of summer, unusual and terrible thunders, with other inauspicious appearances, for fifteen days together, dispersed the people, deterring them, on grounds of religious fear, from creating new generals. But, at last, the popular leaders, having found a fair and clear day, and, having got their party together, were proceeding to an election, when a draught-ox, who was used to the crowd and noise of the streets, but for some reason or other grew unruly to his driver, breaking from his yoke, ran furiously into the theatre where they were assembled, and set the people flying and running in all directions before him in the greatest disorder and confusion; and from thence went on, leaping and rushing about, over all that part of the city which the enemies afterwards made themselves masters of. However, the Syracusans, not regarding all this, elected five-and-twenty captains, and, among the rest, Heraclides, and underhand tampered with Dion's men, promising, if they would desert him, and enlist themselves in their service, to make them citizens of Syracuse, with all the privileges of natives. But they would not hear the proposals, but, to show their fidelity and courage, with their swords in their hands, placing Dion for his security in the midst of their battalion, conveyed him out of the city, not offering violence to any one, but upbraiding those they met with their baseness and ingratitude. The citizens, seeing they were but few, and did not offer any violence, despised them; and, supposing that with their large numbers they might with ease overpower and cut them off before they got out of the city, fell upon them in the rear.

Here Dion was in a great strait, being necessitated either to fight against his own countrymen or tamely suffer himself and his faithful soldiers to be cut in pieces. He used many entreaties to the Syracusans, stretching out his hands towards the castle that was full of their enemies, and showing them the soldiers, who in great numbers appeared on the walls and watched what was doing. But when no persuasions could divert the impulse of the multitude, and the whole mass, like the sea in a storm, seemed to be driven before the breath of the demagogues, he commanded his men, not to charge them, but to advance with shouts and clashing of their arms; which being done, not a man of them stood his ground; all fled at once through the streets, though none pursued them. For Dion immediately commanded his men to face about, and led them towards the city of the Leontines.

The very women laughed at the new captains for this retreat; so, to redeem their credit, they bid the citizens arm themselves again, and followed after Dion, and came up with him as he was passing a river. Some of the light-horse rode up and began to skirmish. But when they saw Dion no more tame and calm, and no signs in his face of any fatherly tenderness towards his countrymen, but with an angry countenance, as resolved not to suffer their indignities any longer, bidding his men face round and form in their ranks for the onset, they presently turned their backs more basely than before, and fled to the city, with the loss of some few of their men.

The Leontines received Dion very honourably, gave money to his men, and made them free of their city; sending envoys to the Syracusans, to require them to do the soldiers justice, who, in return, sent back other agents to accuse Dion. But when a general meeting of the confederates met in the town of the Leontines, and the matter was heard and debated, the Syracusans were held to be in fault. They, however, refused to stand to the award of their allies, following their own conceit, and making it their pride to listen to no one, and not to have any commanders but those who would fear and obey the people.

About this time, Dionysius sent in a fleet, under the command of Nypsius the Neapolitan, with provisions and pay for the garri-

son. The Syracusans fought him, had the better, and took four
of his ships; but they made very ill use of their good success, and
for want of good discipline, fell in their joy to drinking and feasting in an extravagant manner, with so little regard to their main
interest that, when they thought themselves sure of taking the
castle, they actually lost their city. Nypsius, seeing the citizens
in this general disorder, spending day and night in their drunken
singing and revelling, and their commanders well pleased with
the frolic, or at least not daring to try and give any orders to
men in their drink, took advantage of this opportunity, made
a sally, and stormed their works; and having made his way
through these, let his barbarians loose upon the city, giving up it
and all that were in it to their pleasure.

The Syracusans quickly saw their folly and misfortune, but
could not, in the distraction they were in, so soon redress it. The
city was in actual process of being sacked, the enemy putting
the men to the sword, demolishing the fortifications, and dragging the women and children, with lamentable shrieks and cries,
prisoners into the castle. The commanders, giving all for lost,
were not able to put the citizens in any tolerable posture of
defence, finding them confusedly mixed up and scattered among
the enemy. While they were in this condition, and the Achradina in danger to be taken, every one was sensible who he was in
whom all their remaining hopes rested, but no man for shame
durst name Dion, whom they had so ungratefully and foolishly
dealt with. Necessity at last forcing them, some of the auxiliary
troops and horsemen cried out, " Send for Dion and his Peloponnesians from the Leontines." No sooner was the venture
made and the name heard among the people, but they gave a
shout for joy, and, with tears in their eyes, wished him there,
that they might once again see that leader at the head of them,
whose courage and bravery in the worst of dangers they well remembered, calling to mind not only with what an undaunted
spirit he always behaved himself, but also with what courage and
confidence he inspired them when he led them against the enemy.
They immediately, therefore, despatched Archonides and Tele-
sides of the confederate troops and of the horsemen, Hellanicus
and four others. These, traversing the road between at their
horses' full speed, reached the town of the Leontines in the evening. The first thing they did was to leap from their horses and
fall at Dion's feet, relating with tears the sad condition the
Syracusans were in. Many of the Leontines and Peloponnesians
began to throng about them, guessing by their speed and the

manner of their address that something extraordinary had occurred.

Dion at once led the way to the assembly, and the people being gathered together in a very little time, Archonides and Hellanicus and the others came in among them, and in short declared the misery and distress of the Syracusans, begging the foreign soldiers to forget the injuries they had received, and assist the afflicted, who had suffered more for the wrong they had done than they themselves who received it would (had it been in their power) have inflicted upon them. When they had made an end, there was a profound silence in the theatre; Dion then stood up, and began to speak, but tears stopped his words; his soldiers were troubled at his grief, but bade him take good courage and proceed. When he had recovered himself a little, therefore, " Men of Peloponnesus," he said, " and of the confederacy, I asked for your presence here, that you might consider your own interests. For myself, I have no interests to consult while Syracuse is perishing, and though I may not save it from destruction, I will nevertheless hasten thither, and be buried in the ruins of my country. Yet if you can find in your hearts to assist us, the most inconsiderate and unfortunate of men, you may to your eternal honour again retrieve this unhappy city. But if the Syracusans can obtain no more pity nor relief from you, may the gods reward you for what you have formerly valiantly done for them, and for your kindness to Dion, of whom speak hereafter as one who deserted you not when you were injured and abused, nor afterwards forsook his fellow-citizens in their afflictions and misfortunes.

Before he had yet ended his speech, the soldiers leapt up, and with a great shout testified their readiness for the service, crying out, to march immediately to the relief of the city. The Syracusan messengers hugged and embraced them, praying the gods to send down blessings upon Dion and the Peloponnesians. When the noise was pretty well over, Dion gave orders that all should go to their quarters to prepare for their march, and having refreshed themselves, came ready armed to their rendezvous in the place where they now were, resolving that very night to attempt the rescue.

Now at Syracuse, Dionysius's soldiers, as long as day continued, ransacked the city, and did all the mischief they could; but when night came on, they retired into the castle, having lost some few of their number. At which the factious ringleaders taking heart, and hoping the enemy would rest content with what they had done and make no further attempt upon them, persuaded the people again to reject Dion, and, if he came with the foreign soldiers, not to admit him; advising them not to yield, as inferior to them in point of honour and courage, but to save their city and defend their liberties and properties themselves. The populace, therefore, and their leaders, sent messengers to Dion to forbid him to advance, while the noble citizens and the horse sent others to him to desire him to hasten his march; for which reason he slacked his pace, yet did not remit his advance. And in the course of the night, the faction that was against him set a guard upon the gates of the city to hinder him from coming in. But Nypsius made another sally out of the castle with a far greater number of men, and those far more bold and eager than before, who quite ruined what of the rampart was left standing, and fell in, pell-mell, to sack and ravage the city. The slaughter was now very great, not only of the men, but of the women, also, and children; for they regarded not so much the plunder, as to destroy and kill all they met. For Dionysius, despairing to regain the kingdom, and mortally hating the Syracusans, resolved to bury his lost sovereignty in the ruin and desolation of Syracuse. The soldiers, therefore, to anticipate Dion's succours, resolved upon the most complete and ready way of destruction, to lay the city in ashes, firing all at hand with torches and lamps, and at distance with flaming arrows, shot from their bows. The citizens fled every way before them; they who, to avoid the fire, forsook their houses, were taken in the streets and put to the sword; they who betook themselves for refuge into the houses were forced out again by the flames, many buildings being now in a blaze, and many falling in ruins upon them as they fled past.

This fresh misfortune by general consent opened the gates for Dion. He had given up his rapid advance, when he received advice that the enemies were retreated into the castle, but, in the morning, some horse brought him the news of another assault, and, soon after, some of those who before opposed his coming fled now to him, to entreat him he would hasten his relief. The pressure increasing, Heraclides sent his brother, and after him his uncle, Theodotes, to beg him to help them; for that now they were not able to resist any longer; he himself was wounded, and the greatest part of the city either in ruins or in flames. When Dion met this sad news, he was about sixty furlongs distant from the city. When he had acquainted the soldiers with the exigency, and exhorted them to behave them-

selves like men, the army no longer marched but ran forwards,
and by the way were met by messengers upon messengers
entreating them to make haste. By the wonderful eagerness
of the soldiers, and their extraordinary speed, Dion quickly
came to the city, and entered what is called the Hecatompedon,
sending his light-armed men at once to charge the enemy, that,
seeing them, the Syracusans might take courage. In the meantime, he drew up in good order his full-armed men and all the
citizens that came in and joined him; forming his battalions
deep, and distributing his officers in many separate commands,
that he might be able to attack from many quarters at once,
and so be more alarming to the enemy.

So, having made his arrangements and offered vows to the
gods, when he was seen in the streets advancing at the head of
his men to engage the enemy, a confused noise of shouts, congratulations, vows, and prayers was raised by the Syracusans,
who now called Dion their deliverer and tutelar deity, and
his soldiers their friends, brethren, and fellow-citizens. And,
indeed, at that moment, none seemed to regard themselves, or
value their safeties, but to be concerned more for Dion's life
than for all their own together, as he marched at the head of
them to meet the danger, through blood and fire and over heaps
of dead bodies that lay in his way.

And indeed the posture of the enemy was in appearance
terrible; for they were flushed and ferocious with victory, and
had posted themselves very advantageously along the demolished
works, which made the access to them very hazardous and
difficult. Yet that which disturbed Dion's soldiers most was
the apprehension they were in of the fire, which made their
march very troublesome and difficult; for the houses being in
flames on all sides, they were met everywhere with the blaze,
and, treading upon burning ruins and every minute in danger
of being overwhelmed with falling houses, through clouds of
ashes and smoke they laboured hard to keep their order and
maintain their ranks. When they came near to the enemy, the
approach was so narrow and uneven that but few of them could
engage at a time; but at length, with loud cheers and much
zeal on the part of the Syracusans, encouraging them and joining with them, they beat off Nypsius's men, and put them to
flight. Most of them escaped into the castle, which was near
at hand; all that could not get in were pursued and picked up
here and there by the soldiers, and put to the sword. The
present exigency, however, did not suffer the citizens to take

immediate benefit of their victory in such mutual congratulations and embraces as became so great a success; for now all were busily employed to save what houses were left standing, labouring hard all night, and scarcely so could master the fire.

The next day, not one of the popular haranguers durst stay in the city, but all of them, knowing their own guilt, by their flight confessed it, and secured their lives. Only Heraclides and Theodotes went voluntarily and surrendered themselves to Dion, acknowledging that they had wronged him, and begging he would be kinder to them than they had been just to him; adding how much it would become him who was master of so many excellent accomplishments to moderate his anger and be generously compassionate to ungrateful men, who were here before him, making their confession that, in all the matter of their former enmity and rivalry against him they were now absolutely overcome by his virtue. Though they thus humbly addressed him, his friends advised him not to pardon these turbulent and ill-conditioned men, but to yield them to the desires of his soldiers, and utterly root out of the commonwealth the ambitious affectation of popularity, a disease as pestilent and pernicious as the passion for tyranny itself. Dion endeavoured to satisfy them, telling them that other generals exercised and trained themselves for the most part in the practices of war and arms; but that he had long studied in the Academy how to conquer anger, and not let emulation and envy conquer him; that to do this it is not sufficient that a man be obliging and kind to his friends, and those that have deserved well of him, but, rather, gentle and ready to forgive in the case of those who do wrong; that he wished to let the world see that he valued not himself so much upon excelling Heraclides in ability and conduct, as he did in outdoing him in justice and clemency; herein to have the advantage is to excel indeed; whereas the honour of success in war is never entire; fortune will be sure to dispute it, though no man should pretend to have a claim. What if Heraclides be perfidious, malicious, and base, must Dion therefore sully or injure his virtue by passionate concern for it? For, though the laws determine it juster to revenge an injury than to do an injury, yet it is evident that both, in the nature of things, originally proceed from the same deficiency and weakness. The malicious humour of men, though perverse and refractory, is not so savage and invincible but it may be wrought upon by kindness, and altered by repeated obligations. Dion, making use of these arguments, pardoned and dismissed Heraclides and Theodotes.

And now, resolving to repair the blockade about the castle, he commanded all the Syracusans to cut each man a stake and bring it to the works; and then, dismissing them to refresh themselves, and take their rest, he employed his own men all night, and by morning had finished his line of palisade; so that both the enemy and the citizens wondered, when day returned, to see the work so far advanced in so short a time. Burying, therefore, the dead, and redeeming the prisoners, who were near two thousand, he called a public assembly, where Heraclides made a motion that Dion should be declared general, with full powers at land and sea. The better citizens approved well of it, and called on the people to vote it so. But the mob of sailors and handicraftsmen would not yield that Heraclides should lose his command of the navy; believing him, if otherwise an ill man, at any rate to be more citizen-like than Dion, and readier to comply with the people. Dion therefore submitted to them in this, and consented Heraclides should continue admiral. But when they began to press the project of the redistribution of lands and houses, he not only opposed it, but repealed all the votes they had formerly made upon that account, which sensibly vexed them. Heraclides, therefore, took a new advantage of him, and, being at Messene, harangued the soldiers and ships' crews that sailed with him, accusing Dion that he had a design to make himself absolute. And yet at the same time he held private correspondence for a treaty with Dionysius by means of Pharax the Spartan. Which, when the noble citizens of Syracuse had intimation of, there arose a sedition in the army, and the city was in great distress and want of provisions; and Dion now knew not what course to take, being also blamed by all his friends for having thus fortified against himself such a perverse and jealous and utterly corrupted man as Heraclides was.

Pharax at this time lay encamped at Neapolis, in the territory of Agrigentum. Dion, therefore, led out the Syracusans, but with an intent not to engage him till he saw a fit opportunity. But Heraclides and his seamen exclaimed against him, that he had delayed fighting on purpose that he might the longer continue his command; so that, much against his will, he was forced to an engagement and was beaten, his loss, however, being inconsiderable, and that occasioned chiefly by the dissension that was in the army. He rallied his men, and, having put them in good order and encouraged them to redeem their credit, resolved upon a second battle. But in the evening, he received advice that Heraclides with his fleet was on his way to Syracuse, with the purpose to possess himself of the city and keep him and his army out. Instantly, therefore, taking with him some of the strongest and most active of his men, he rode off in the dark, and about nine the next morning was at the gates, having ridden seven hundred furlongs that night. Heraclides, though he strove to make all the speed he could, yet, coming too late, tacked and stood out again to sea; and, being unresolved what course to steer, accidentally he met Gæsylus the Spartan, who told him he was come from Lacedæmon to head the Sicilians, as Gylippus had formerly done. Heraclides was only too glad to get hold of him, and fastening him as it might be a sort of amulet to himself, he showed him to the confederates, and sent a herald to Syracuse to summon them to accept the Spartan general. Dion returned answer that they had generals enough, and, if they wanted a Spartan to command them, he could supply that office, being himself a citizen of Sparta. When Gæsylus saw this, he gave up all pretensions, and sailed in to Dion, and reconciled Heraclides to him, making Heraclides swear the most solemn oaths to perform what he engaged, Gæsylus himself also undertaking to maintain Dion's right and inflict chastisement on Heraclides if he broke his faith.

The Syracusans then laid up their navy, which was at present a great charge and of little use to them, but an occasion of differences and dissensions among the generals, and pressed on the siege, finishing the wall of blockade with which they invested the castle. The besieged, seeing no hopes of succour and their provisions failing, began to mutiny; so that the son of Dionysius, in despair of holding out longer for his father, capitulated, and articled with Dion to deliver up the castle with all the garrison soldiers and ammunition; and so, taking his mother and sisters and manning five galleys, he set out to go to his father, Dion seeing him safely out, and scarce a man in all the city not being there to behold the sight, as indeed they called even on those that were not present, out of pity, that they could not be there, to see this happy day and the sun shining on a free Syracuse. And as this expulsion of Dionysius is even now always cited as one of the greatest and most remarkable examples of fortune's vicissitudes, how extraordinary may we imagine their joy to have been, and how entire their satisfaction, who had totally subverted the most potent tyranny that ever was by very slight and inconsiderable means!

When Apollocrates was gone, and Dion coming to take possession of the castle, the women could not stay while he made his entry, but ran to meet him at the gate. Aristomache led Dion's son, and Arete followed after weeping, fearful and dubious how to salute or address her husband, after living with another man. Dion first embraced his sister, then his son; when Aristomache bringing Arete to him, " O Dion," said she, " your banishment made us all equally miserable; your return and victory has cancelled all sorrows, excepting this poor sufferer's, whom I, unhappy, was compelled to be another's while you were yet alive. Fortune has now given you the sole disposal of us; how will you determine concerning her hard fate? In what relation must she salute you, as her uncle, or as her husband? " This speech of Aristomache's brought tears from Dion, who with great affection embraced his wife, gave her his son, and desired her to retire to his own house, where he continued to reside when he had delivered up the castle to the Syracusans.

For though all things had now succeeded to his wish, yet he desired not to enjoy any present advantage of his good fortune, except to gratify his friends, reward his allies, and bestow upon his companions of former time in Athens, and the soldiers that had served him, some special mark of kindness and honour, striving herein to outdo his very means in his generosity. As for himself, he was content with a very frugal and moderate competency, and was indeed the wonder of all men, that when not only Sicily and Carthage, but all Greece looked to him as in the height of prosperity, and no man living greater than he, no general more renowned for valour and success, yet in his guard, his attendance, his table, he seemed as if he rather commoned with Plato in the Academy than lived among hired captains and paid soldiers, whose solace of their toils and dangers it is to eat and drink their fill, and enjoy themselves plentifully every day. Plato indeed wrote to him that the eyes of all the world were now upon him; but it is evident that he himself had fixed his eye upon one place in one city, the Academy, and considered that the spectators and judges there regarded not great actions, courage, or fortune, but watched to see how temperately and wisely he could use his prosperity, how evenly he could behave himself in the high condition he now was in. Neither did he remit anything of his wonted stateliness in conversation or serious charge to the people; he made it rather a point to maintain it, notwithstanding that a little condescension and obliging civility were very necessary for his present affairs;

and Plato, as we said before, rebuked him, and wrote to tell him that self-will keeps house with solitude. But certainly his natural temperament was one that could not bend to complaisance; and, besides, he wished to work the Syracusans back the other way, out of their present excess of license and caprice.

Heraclides began again to set up against him, and, being invited by Dion to make one of the Council, refused to come, saying he would give his opinion as a private citizen in the public assembly. Next he complained of Dion because he had not demolished the citadel, and because he had hindered the people from throwing down Dionysius's tomb and doing despite to the dead; moreover, he accused him for sending to Corinth for counsellors and assistants in the government, thereby neglecting and slighting his fellow-citizens. And indeed he had sent messages for some Corinthians to come to him, hoping by their means and presence the better to settle that constitution he intended; for he designed to suppress the unlimited democratic government, which indeed is not a government, but, as Plato calls it, a market-place of governments, and to introduce and establish a mixed polity, on the Spartan and Cretan model, between a commonwealth and a monarchy, wherein an aristocratic body should preside, and determine all matters of greatest consequence; for he saw also that the Corinthians were chiefly governed by something like an oligarchy, and the people but little concerned in public business.

Now knowing that Heraclides would be his most considerable adversary, and that in all ways he was a turbulent, fickle, and factious man, he gave way to some whom formerly he hindered when they designed to kill him, who, breaking in, murdered Heraclides in his own house. His death was much resented by the citizens. Nevertheless, when Dion made him a splendid funeral, followed the dead body with all his soldiers, and then addressed them, they understood that it would have been impossible to have kept the city quiet, as long as Dion and Heraclides were competitors in the government.

Dion had a friend called Callippus, an Athenian, who, Plato says, first made acquaintance and afterwards obtained familiarity with him, not from any connection with his philosophic studies, but on occasion afforded by the celebration of the mysteries, and in the way of ordinary society. This man went with him in all his military service, and was in great honour and esteem; being the first of his friends who marched by his side into Syracuse, wearing a garland upon his head, having behaved himself very well in all the battles, and made himself remarkable for his gallantry. He, finding that Dion's principal and most considerable friends were cut off in the war, Heraclides now dead, and the people without a leader, and that the soldiers had a great kindness for him, like a perfidious and wicked villain, in hopes to get the chief command of Sicily as his reward for the ruin of his friend and benefactor, and, as some say, being also bribed by the enemy with twenty talents to destroy Dion, inveigled and engaged several of the soldiers in a conspiracy against him, taking this cunning and wicked occasion for his plot. He daily informed Dion of what he heard or what he feigned the soldiers said against him; whereby he gained that credit and confidence, that he was allowed by Dion to consort privately with whom he would, and talk freely against him in any company, that he might discover who were his secret and factious maligners. By this means, Callippus in a short time got together a cabal of all the seditious malcontents in the city; and if any one who would be drawn in advised Dion that he was tampered with, he was not troubled or concerned at it, believing Callippus did it in compliance with his directions.

While this conspiracy was afoot, a strange and dreadful apparition was seen by Dion. As he sat one evening in a gallery in his house, alone and thoughtful, hearing a sudden noise he turned about, and saw at the end of the colonnade, by clear daylight, a tall woman, in her countenance and garb like one of the tragical Furies, with a broom in her hand, sweeping the floor. Being amazed and extremely affrighted, he sent for some of his friends, and told them what he had seen, entreating them to stay with him and keep him company all night; for he was excessively discomposed and alarmed, fearing that if he were left alone the spectre would again appear to him. He saw it no more. But a few days after, his only son, being almost grown up to man's estate, upon some displeasure and pet he had taken upon a childish and frivolous occasion, threw himself headlong from the top of the house and broke his neck.

While Dion was under this affliction, Callippus drove on his conspiracy, and spread a rumour among the Syracusans that Dion, being now childless, was resolved to send for Dionysius's son, Apollocrates, who was his wife's nephew and sister's grandson, and make him his heir and successor. By this time, Dion and his wife and sister began to suspect what was doing, and from all hands information came to them of the plot. Dion being troubled, it is probable, for Heraclides's murder, which was like to be a blot and stain upon his life and actions, in continual weariness and vexation, he had rather die a thousand times, and open his breast himself to the assassin, than live not only in fear of his enemies but suspicion of his friends. But Callippus, seeing the women very inquisitive to search to the bottom of the business, took alarm, and came to them, utterly denying it with tears in his eyes, and offering to give them whatever assurances of his fidelity they desired. They required that he should take the Great Oath, which was after this manner. The juror went into the sanctuary of Ceres and Proserpine, where, after the performance of some ceremonies, he was clad in the purple vestment of the goddess, and, holding a lighted torch in his hand, took his oath. Callippus did as they required, and forswore the fact. And indeed he so little valued the goddesses that he stayed but till the very festival of Proserpine, by whom he had sworn, and on that very day committed his intended murder; as truly he might well enough disregard the day, since he must at any other time as impiously offend her, when he who had acted as her initiating priest should shed the blood of her worshipper.

There were a great many in the conspiracy; and as Dion was at home with several of his friends in a room with tables for entertainment in it, some of the conspirators beset the house around, others secured the doors and windows. The actual intended murderers were some Zacynthians, who went inside in their under-dresses without swords. Those outside shut the doors upon them and kept them fast. The murderers fell on Dion, endeavouring to stifle and crush him; then, finding they were doing nothing, they called for a sword, but none durst open the door. There were a great many within with Dion, but every one was for securing himself, supposing that by letting him lose his life he should save his own, and therefore no man ventured to assist him. When they had waited a good while, at length Lycon the Syracusan reached a short sword in at the window to one of the Zacynthians, and thus, like a victim at a sacrifice, this long time in their power and trembling for the blow, they killed him. His sister, and wife big with child, they hurried to prison, who, poor lady, in her unfortunate condition was there brought to bed of a son, which, by the consent of the keepers, they intended to bring up, the rather because Callippus began already to be embroiled in troubles.

After the murder of Dion, he was in great glory, and had the sole government of Syracuse in his hands; and to that effect

wrote to Athens, a place which, next the immortal gods, being
guilty of such an abominable crime, he ought to have regarded
with shame and fear. But true it is, what is said of that city,
that the good men she breeds are the most excellent, and the bad
the most notorious; as their country also produces the most
delicious honey and the most deadly hemlock. Callippus, however, did not long continue to scandalise fortune and upbraid
the gods with his prosperity, as though they connived at and bore
with the wretched man, while he purchased riches and power by
heinous impieties, but quickly received the punishment he deserved. For, going to take Catana, he lost Syracuse; whereupon
they report he said, he had lost a city and got a bauble. Then
attempting Messene, he had most of his men cut off, and, among
the rest, Dion's murderers. When no city in Sicily would admit
him, but all hated and abhorred him, he went into Italy and took
Rhegium; and there, being in distress and not able to maintain
his soldiers, he was killed by Leptines and Polysperchon, and,
as fortune would have it, with the same sword by which Dion was
murdered, which was known by the size, being but short, as the
Spartan swords, and the workmanship of it very curious and
artificial. Thus Callippus received the reward of his villainies.

When Aristomache and Arete were released out of prison,
Hicetes, one of Dion's friends, took them to his house, and
seemed to intend to entertain them well and like a faithful friend.
Afterwards, being persuaded by Dion's enemies, he provided a
ship and pretended to send them into Peloponnesus, but commanded the sailors, when they came out to sea, to kill them and
throw them overboard. Others say that they and the little boy
were thrown alive into the sea. This man also escaped not the
due recompense of his wickedness, for he was taken by Timoleon
and put to death, and the Syracusans, to revenge Dion, slew his
two daughters: of all which I have given a more particular
account in the life of Timoleon.

## MARCUS BRUTUS

MARCUS BRUTUS was descended from that Junius Brutus to whom the ancient Romans erected a statue of brass in the capitol among the images of their kings with a drawn sword in his hand, in remembrance of his courage and resolution in expelling the Tarquins and destroying the monarchy. But that ancient Brutus was of a severe and inflexible nature, like steel of too hard a temper, and having never had his character softened by study and thought, he let himself be so far transported with his rage and hatred against tyrants that, for conspiring with them, he proceeded to the execution even of his own sons. But this Brutus, whose life we now write, having to the goodness of his disposition added the improvements of learning and the study of philosophy, and having stirred up his natural parts, of themselves grave and gentle, by applying himself to business and public affairs, seems to have been of a temper exactly framed for virtue; insomuch that they who were most his enemies upon account of his conspiracy against Cæsar, if in that whole affair there was any honourable or generous part, referred it wholly to Brutus, and laid whatever was barbarous and cruel to the charge of Cassius, Brutus's connection and familiar friend, but not his equal in honesty and pureness of purpose. His mother, Servilia, was of the family of Servilius Ahala, who when Spurius Mælius worked the people into a rebellion and designed to make himself king, taking a dagger under his arm, went forth into the market-place, and upon pretence of having some private business with him, came up close to him, and, as he bent his head to hear what he had to say, struck him with his dagger and slew him. And thus much, as concerns his descent by the mother's side, is confessed by all; but as for his father's family, they who for Cæsar's murder bore any hatred or ill-will to Brutus say that he came not from that Brutus who expelled the Tarquins, there being none of his race left after the execution of his two sons; but that his ancestor was a plebeian, son of one Brutus, a steward, and only rose in the latest times to office or dignity in the commonwealth. But Posidonius the philosopher writes that it is true indeed what the history relates, that two of the sons of Brutus who were of men's estate were put to death, but that a third, yet an infant, was left alive, from whom the family was propagated down to Marcus Brutus; and further, that there were several famous persons of this house in his time whose looks very much resembled the statue of Junius Brutus. But of this subject enough.

Cato the philosopher was brother to Servilia, the mother of Brutus, and he it was whom of all the Romans his nephew most admired and studied to imitate, and he afterwards married his daughter Porcia. Of all the sects of the Greek philosophers, though there was none of which he had not been a hearer, and in which he had not made some proficiency, yet he chiefly esteemed the Platonists; and not much approving of the modern and middle Academy, as it is called, he applied himself to the study of the ancient. He was all his lifetime a great admirer of Antiochus of the city of Ascalon, and took his brother Aristus into his own house for his friend and companion, a man for his learning inferior indeed to many of the philosophers, but for the evenness of his temper and steadiness of his conduct equal to the best. As for Empylus, of whom he himself and his friends often make mention in their epistles, as one that lived with Brutus, he was a rhetorician, and has left behind him a short but well-written history of the death of Cæsar, entitled Brutus.

In Latin, he had by exercise attained a sufficient skill to be able to make public addresses and to plead a cause; but in Greek, he must be noted for affecting the sententious and short Laconic way of speaking in sundry passages of his epistles; as when, in the beginning of the war, he wrote thus to the Pergamenians: " I hear you have given Dolabella money; if willingly, you must own you have injured me; if unwillingly, show it by giving willingly to me." And another time to the Samians: " Your counsels are remiss and your performances slow; what think ye will be the end? " And of the Patereans thus: " The Xanthians, suspecting my kindness, have made their country the grave of their despair; the Patareans, trusting themselves to me, enjoy in all points their former liberty; it is in your power to choose the judgment of the Patereans or the fortune of the Xanthians." And this is the style for which some of his letters are to be noted.

When he was but a very young man, he accompanied his uncle Cato to Cyprus, when he was sent there against Ptolemy. But when Ptolemy killed himself, Cato, being by some necessary business detained in the isle of Rhodes, had already sent one of his friends, named Canidius, to take into his care and keeping the treasure of the king; but presently, not feeling sure of his honesty, he wrote to Brutus to sail immediately for Cyprus out of Pamphylia, where he then was staying to refresh himself,

being but just recovered of a fit of sickness. He obeyed his
orders, but with a great deal of unwillingness, as well out of
respect to Canidius, who was thrown out of this employment by
Cato with so much disgrace, as also because he esteemed such a
commission mean and unsuitable to him, who was in the prime
of his youth, and given to books and study. Nevertheless,
applying himself to the business, he behaved himself so well in
it that he was highly commended by Cato, and having turned
all the goods of Ptolemy into ready money, he sailed with the
greatest part of it in his own ship to Rome.

But upon the general separation into two factions, when,
Pompey and Cæsar taking up arms against one another, the
whole empire was turned into confusion, it was commonly believed that he would take Cæsar's side; for his father in past
time had been put to death by Pompey. But he, thinking it
his duty to prefer the interest of the public to his own private
feelings, and judging Pompey's to be the better cause, took part
with him; though formerly he used not so much as to salute
or take any notice of Pompey, if he happened to meet him,
esteeming it a pollution to have the least conversation with the
murderer of his father. But now, looking upon him as the
general of his country, he placed himself under his command,
and set sail for Cilicia in quality of lieutenant to Sestius, who
had the government of that province. But finding no opportunity there of doing any great service, and hearing that Pompey
and Cæsar were now near one another and preparing for the
battle upon which all depended, he came of his own accord to
Macedonia to partake in the danger. At his coming it is said
that Pompey was so surprised and so pleased that, rising from
his chair in the sight of all who were about him, he saluted and
embraced him, as one of the chiefest of his party. All the time
that he was in the camp, excepting that which he spent in
Pompey's company, he employed in reading and in study, which
he did not neglect even the day before the great battle. It was
the middle of summer, and the heat was very great, the camp
having been pitched near some marshy ground, and the people
that carried Brutus's tent were a long while before they came.
Yet though upon these accounts he was extremely harassed and
out of order, having scarcely by the middle of the day anointed
himself and eaten a sparing meal, whilst most others were either
laid to sleep or taken up with the thoughts and apprehensions
of what would be the issue of the fight, he spent his time until
the evening in writing an epitome of Polybius.

It is said that Cæsar had so great a regard for him that he ordered his commanders by no means to kill Brutus in the battle, but to spare him, if possible, and bring him safe to him, if he would willingly surrender himself; but if he made any resistance, to suffer him to escape rather than do him any violence. And this he is believed to have done out of a tenderness to Servilia, the mother of Brutus; for Cæsar had, it seems, in his youth been very intimate with her, and she passionately in love with him; and, considering that Brutus was born about that time in which their loves were at the highest, Cæsar had a belief that he was his own child. The story is told that, when the great question of the conspiracy of Catiline, which had like to have been the destruction of the commonwealth, was debated in the senate, Cato and Cæsar were both standing up, contending together on the decision to be come to; at which time a little note was delivered to Cæsar from without, which he took and read silently to himself. Upon this, Cato cried out aloud, and accused Cæsar of holding correspondence with and receiving letters from the enemies of the commonwealth; and when many other senators exclaimed against it, Cæsar delivered the note as he had received it to Cato, who reading it found it to be a love-letter from his own sister Servilia, and threw it back again to Cæsar with the words, " Keep it, you drunkard," and returned to the subject of the debate. So public and notorious was Servilia's love to Cæsar.

After the great overthrow at Pharsalia, Pompey himself having made his escape to the sea, and Cæsar's army storming the camp, Brutus stole privately out by one of the gates leading to marshy ground full of water and covered with reeds, and, travelling through the night, got safe to Larissa. From Larissa he wrote to Cæsar who expressed a great deal of joy to hear that he was safe, and, bidding him come, not only forgave him freely, but honoured and esteemed him among his chiefest friends. Now when nobody could give any certain account which way Pompey had fled, Cæsar took a little journey along with Brutus, and tried what was his opinion herein, and after some discussion which passed between them, believing that Brutus's conjecture was the right one, laying aside all other thoughts, he set out directly to pursue him towards Egypt. But Pompey, having reached Egypt, as Brutus guessed his design was to do, there met his fate.

Brutus in the meantime gained Cæsar's forgiveness for his friend Cassius; and pleading also in defence of the king of the

Lybians, though he was overwhelmed with the greatness of the crimes alleged against him, yet by his entreaties and deprecations to Cæsar in his behalf, he preserved to him a great part of his kingdom. It is reported that Cæsar, when he first heard Brutus speak in public, said to his friends, "I know not what this young man intends, but, whatever he intends, he intends vehemently." For his natural firmness of mind, not easily yielding, or complying in favour of every one that entreated his kindness, once set into action upon motives of right reason and deliberate moral choice, whatever direction it thus took, it was pretty sure to take effectively, and to work in such a way as not to fail in its object. No flattery could ever prevail with him to listen to unjust petitions: and he held that to be overcome by the importunities of shameless and fawning entreaties, though some compliment it with the name of modesty and bashfulness, was the worst disgrace a great man could suffer. And he used to say that he always felt as if they who could deny nothing could not have behaved well in the flower of their youth.

Cæsar, being about to make his expedition into Africa against Cato and Scipio, committed to Brutus the government of Cisalpine Gaul, to the great happiness and advantage of that province. For while people in other provinces were in distress with the violence and avarice of their governors, and suffered as much oppression as if they had been slaves and captives of war, Brutus, by his easy government, actually made them amends for their calamities under former rulers, directing moreover all their gratitude for his good deeds to Cæsar himself; insomuch that it was a most welcome and pleasant spectacle to Cæsar, when in his return he passed through Italy, to see the cities that were under Brutus's command, and Brutus himself increasing his honour and joining agreeably in his progress.

Now several prætorships being vacant, it was all men's opinion that that of the chiefest dignity, which is called the prætorship of the city, would be conferred either upon Brutus or Cassius; and some say that, there having been some little difference upon former accounts between them, this competition set them much more at variance, though they were connected in their families, Cassius having married Junia, the sister of Brutus. Others say that the contention was raised between them by Cæsar's doing, who had privately given each of them such hopes of his favour as led them on, and provoked them at last into this open competition and trial of their interest. Brutus had only the reputation of his honour and virtue to oppose to

the many and gallant actions performed by Cassius against the
thians. But Cæsar, having heard each side, and deliberating
about the matter among his friends, said, "Cassius has the
stronger plea, but we must let Brutus be first prætor." So
another prætorship was given to Cassius; the gaining of which
could not so much oblige him, as he was incensed for the loss
of the other. And in all other things Brutus was partaker of
Cæsar's power as much as he desired: for he might, if he had
pleased, have been the chief of all his friends, and had authority
and command beyond them all, but Cassius and the company
he met with him drew him off from Cæsar. Indeed, he was not
yet wholly reconciled to Cassius, since that competition which
was between them: but yet he gave ear to Cassius's friends,
who were perpetually advising him not to be so blind as to suffer
himself to be softened and won over by Cæsar, but to shun the
kindness and favours of a tyrant, which they intimated that
Cæsar showed him, not to express any honour to his merit or
virtue, but to unbend his strength, and undermine his vigour
of purpose.

Neither was Cæsar wholly without suspicion of him, nor
wanted informers that accused Brutus to him; but he feared,
indeed, the high spirit and the great character and the friends
that he had, but thought himself secure in his moral disposition.
When it was told him that Antony and Dolabella designed some
disturbance, "It is not," said he, "the fat and the long-haired
men that I fear, but the pale and the lean," meaning Brutus and
Cassius. And when some maligned Brutus to him, and advised
him to beware of him, taking hold of his flesh with his hand,
"What," he said, "do you think that Brutus will not wait out
the time of this little body?" as if he thought none so fit to
succeed him in his power as Brutus. And indeed it seems to be
without doubt that Brutus might have been the first man in
the commonwealth, if he had had patience but a little time to be
second to Cæsar, and would have suffered his power to decline
after it was come to its highest pitch, and the fame of his great
actions to die away by degrees. But Cassius, a man of a fierce
disposition, and one that out of private malice, rather than love
of the public, hated Cæsar, not the tyrant, continually fired and
stirred him up. Brutus felt the rule an oppression, but Cassius
hated the ruler; and, among other reasons on which he grounded
his quarrel against Cæsar, the loss of his lions which he had
procured when he was ædile elect was one; for Cæsar, finding
these in Megara, when that city was taken by Calenus, seized

them to himself. These beasts, they say, were a great calamity to the Megarians; for, when their city was just taken, they broke open the lions' dens, and pulled off their chains and let them loose that they might run upon the enemy that was entering the city; but the lions turned upon them themselves, and tore to pieces a great many unarmed persons running about, so that it was a miserable spectacle even to their enemies to behold.

And this, some say, was the chief provocation that stirred up Cassius to conspire against Cæsar; but they are much in the wrong. For Cassius had from his youth a natural hatred and rancour against the whole race of tyrants, which he showed when he was but a boy, and went to the same school with Faustus, the son of Sylla; for, on his boasting himself amongst the boys, and extolling the sovereign power of his father, Cassius rose up and struck him two or three boxes on the ear; which when the guardians and relations of Faustus designed to inquire into and to prosecute, Pompey forbade them, and, sending for both the boys together, examined the matter himself. And Cassius is then reported to have said thus, "Come, then, Faustus, dare to speak here those words that provoked me, that I may strike you again as I did before." Such was the disposition of Cassius.

But Brutus was roused up and pushed on to the undertaking by many persuasions of his familiar friends, and letters and invitations from unknown citizens. For under the statue of his ancestor Brutus, that overthrew the kingly government, they wrote the words, "O that we had a Brutus now!" and, "O that Brutus were alive!" And Brutus's own tribunal, on which he sat as prætor, was filled each morning with writings such as these: "You are alseep, Brutus," and, "You are not a true Brutus." Now the flatterers of Cæsar were the occasion of all this, who, among other invidious honours which they strove to fasten upon Cæsar, crowned his statues by night with diadems, wishing to incite the people to salute him king instead of dictator. But quite the contrary came to pass, as I have more particularly related in the life of Cæsar.

When Cassius went about soliciting friends to engage in this design against Cæsar, all whom he tried readily consented, if Brutus would be head of it; for their opinion was that the enterprise wanted not hands or resolution, but the reputation and authority of a man such as he was, to give as it were the first religious sanction, and by his presence, if by nothing else, to justify the undertaking; that without him they should go about this action with less heart, and should lie under greater suspicions when they had done it; for if their cause had been just and honourable, people would be sure that Brutus would not have refused it. Cassius, having considered these things with himself, went to Brutus and made him the first visit after their falling out; and after the compliments of reconciliation had passed, and former kindnesses were renewed between them, he asked him if he designed to be present on the calends of March, for it was discoursed, he said, that Cæsar's friends intended then to move that he might be made king. When Brutus answered, that he would not be there, " But what," says Cassius, " if they should send for us? " " It will be my business, then," replied Brutus, " not to hold my peace, but to stand up boldly, and die for the liberty of my country." To which Cassius with some emotion answered, " But what Roman will suffer you to die? What, do you not know yourself, Brutus? Or do you think that those writings that you find upon your prætor's seat were put there by weavers and shopkeepers, and not by the first and most powerful men of Rome? From other prætors, indeed, they expect largesses and shows and gladiators, but from you they claim, as an hereditary debt, the extirpation of tyranny; there are all ready to suffer anything on your account, if you will but show yourself such as they think you are and expect you should be." Which said, he fell upon Brutus, and embraced him; and after this, they parted each to try their several friends.

Among the friends of Pompey there was one Caius Ligarius, whom Cæsar had pardoned, though accused for having been in arms against him. This man, not feeling so thankful for having been forgiven as he felt oppressed by that power which made him need a pardon, hated Cæsar, and was one of Brutus's most intimate friends. Him Brutus visited, and finding him sick, " O Ligarius," says he, " what a time you have found out to be sick in! " At which words Ligarius, raising himself and leaning on his elbow, took Brutus by the hand, and said, " But, O Brutus, if you are on any design worthy of yourself, I am well."

From this time they tried the inclinations of all their acquaintances that they durst trust, and communicated the secret to them, and took into the design not only their familiar friends, but as many as they believed bold and brave and despisers of death. For which reason they concealed the plot from Cicero, though he was very much trusted and as well beloved by them all, lest, to his own disposition, which was naturally timorous, adding now the weariness and caution of old age, by his weighing,

as he would do, every particular, that he might not make one
step without the greatest security, he should blunt the edge of
their forwardness and resolution in a business which required
all the despatch imaginable. As indeed there were also two
others that were companions of Brutus, Statilius the Epicurean,
and Favonius the admirer of Cato, whom he left out for this
reason: as he was conversing one day with them, trying them
at a distance, and proposing some such question to be disputed
of as among philosophers, to see what opinion they were of,
Favonius declared his judgment to be that a civil war was worse
than the most illegal monarchy; and Statilius held, that to
bring himself into troubles and danger upon the account of evil
or foolish men did not become a man that had any wisdom or
discretion. But Labeo, who was present, contradicted them
both; and Brutus, as if it had been an intricate dispute, and
difficult to be decided, held his peace for that time, but afterwards discovered the whole design to Labeo, who readily undertook it. The next thing that was thought convenient was to
gain the other Brutus, surnamed Albinus, a man of himself of
no great bravery or courage, but considerable for the number
of gladiators that he was maintaining for a public show, and
the great confidence that Cæsar put in him. When Cassius and
Labeo spoke with him concerning the matter, he gave them no
answer; but, seeking an interview with Brutus himself alone,
and finding that he was their captain, he readily consented to
partake in the action. And among the others, also, the most
and best were gained by the name of Brutus. And, though they
neither gave nor took any oath of secrecy, nor used any other
sacred rite to assure their fidelity to each other, yet all kept their
design so close, were so wary, and held it so silently among
themselves that, though by prophecies and apparitions and
signs in the sacrifices the gods gave warning of it, yet could it
not be believed.

Now Brutus, feeling that the noblest spirits of Rome for
virtue, birth, or courage were depending upon him, and survey-
ing with himself all the circumstances of the dangers they were
to encounter, strove indeed, as much as possible, when abroad,
to keep his uneasiness of mind to himself, and to compose his
thoughts; but at home, and especially at night, he was not the
same man, but sometimes against his will his working care
would make him start out of his sleep, and other times he was
taken up with further reflection and consideration of his difficulties, so that his wife that lay with him could not choose but

take notice that he was full of unusual trouble, and had in agitation some dangerous and perplexing question. Porcia, as was said before, was the daughter of Cato, and Brutus, her cousin-german, had married her very young, though not a maid, but after the death of her former husband, by whom she had one son, that was named Bibulus; and there is a little book, called Memoirs of Brutus, written by him, yet extant. This Porcia, being addicted to philosophy, a great lover of her husband, and full of an understanding courage, resolved not to inquire into Brutus's secrets before she had made this trial of herself. She turned all her attendants out of her chamber, and taking a little knife, such as they use to cut nails with, she gave herself a deep gash in the thigh; upon which followed a great flow of blood, and soon after, violent pains and a shivering fever, occasioned by the wound. Now when Brutus was extremely anxious and afflicted for her, she, in the height of all her pain, spoke thus to him: " I, Brutus, being the daughter of Cato, was given to you in marriage, not like a concubine, to partake only in the common intercourse of bed and board, but to bear a part in all your good and all your evil fortunes; and for your part, as regards your care for me, I find no reason to complain; but from me, what evidence of my love, what satisfaction can you receive, if I may not share with you in bearing your hidden griefs, nor to be admitted to any of your counsels that require secrecy and trust? I know very well that women seem to be of too weak a nature to be trusted with secrets; but certainly, Brutus, a virtuous birth and education, and the company of the good and honourable, are of some force to the forming our manners; and I can boast that I am the daughter of Cato, and the wife of Brutus, in which two titles though before I put less confidence, yet now I have tried myself, and find that I can bid defiance to pain." Which words having spoken, she showed him her wound, and related to him the trial that she had made of her constancy; at which he being astonished, lifted up his hands to heaven, and begged the assistance of the gods in his enterprise, that he might show himself a husband worthy of such a wife as Porcia. So then he comforted his wife.

But a meeting of the senate being appointed, at which it was believed that Cæsar would be present, they agreed to make use of that opportunity; for then they might appear all together without suspicion; and, besides, they hoped that all the noblest and leading men of the commonwealth, being then assembled, as soon as the great deed was done, would immediately stand forward and assert the common liberty. The very place too where the senate was to meet seemed to be by divine appointment favourable to their purpose. It was a portico, one of those joining the theatre, with a large recess, in which there stood a statue of Pompey, erected to him by the commonwealth, when he adorned that part of the city with the porticos and the theatre. To this place it was that the senate was summoned for the middle of March (the Ides of March is the Roman name for the day); as if some more than human power were leading the man thither, there to meet his punishment for the death of Pompey.

As soon as it was day, Brutus, taking with him a dagger, which none but his wife knew of, went out. The rest met together at Cassius's house, and brought forth his son that was that day to put on the manly gown, as it is called, into the forum; and from thence, going all to Pompey's porch, stayed there, expecting Cæsar to come without delay to the senate. Here it was chiefly that any one who had known what they had purposed, would have admired the unconcerned temper and the steady resolution of these men in their most dangerous undertaking; for many of them, being prætors, and called upon by their office to judge and determine causes, did not only hear calmly all that made application to them and pleaded against each other before them, as if they were free from all other thoughts, but decided causes with as much accuracy and judgment as they had heard them with attention and patience. And when one person refused to stand to the award of Brutus, and with great clamour and many attestations appealed to Cæsar, Brutus, looking round about him upon those that were present, said, " Cæsar does not hinder me, nor will he hinder me, from doing according to the laws."

Yet there were many unusual accidents that disturbed them and by mere chance were thrown in their way. The first and chiefest was the long stay of Cæsar, though the day was spent, and he being detained at home by his wife, and forbidden by the soothsayers to go forth, upon some defect that appeared in his sacrifice. Another was this: There came a man up to Casca, one of the company, and, taking him by the hand, " You concealed," said he, " the secret from us, but Brutus has told me all." At which words when Casca was surprised, the other said laughing, " How came you to be so rich of a sudden, that you should stand to be chosen ædile? " So near was Casca to let out the secret, upon the mere ambiguity of the other's expression. Then Popilius Lænas, a senator, having saluted Brutus and Cassius more earnestly than usual, whispered them softly in the ear, and said, "My wishes are with you, that you may accomplish what you design, and I advise you to make no delay, for the thing is now no secret." This said, he departed, and left them in great suspicion that the design had taken wind. In the meanwhile, there came one in haste from Brutus's house and brought him news that his wife was dying. For Porcia, being extremely disturbed with expectation of the event, and not able to bear the greatness of her anxiety, could scarce keep herself within doors; and at every little noise or voice she heard, starting up suddenly, like those possessed with the bacchic frenzy, she asked every one that came in from the forum what Brutus was doing, and sent one messenger after another to inquire. At last, after long expectation and waiting, the strength of her constitution could hold out no longer; her mind was overcome with her doubts and fears, and she lost the control of herself, and began to faint away. She had not time to betake herself to her chamber, but, sitting as she was amongst her women, a sudden swoon and a great stupor seized her, and her colour changed, and her speech was quite lost. At this sight her women made a loud cry, and many of the neighbours running to Brutus's door to know what was the matter, the report was soon spread abroad that Porcia was dead; though with her women's help she recovered in a little while, and came to herself again. When Brutus received this news, he was ex remely troubled, not without reason, yet was not so carried away by his private grief as to quit his public purpose.

For now news was brought that Cæsar was coming, carried in a litter. For, being discouraged by the ill-omens that attended his sacrifice, he had determined to undertake no affairs of any great importance that day, but to defer them till another time, excusing himself that he was sick. As soon as he came out of his litter, Popilius Lænas, he who but a little before had wished Brutus good success in his undertaking, coming up to him, conversed a great while with him, Cæsar standing still all the while, and seeming to be very attentive. The conspirators (to give them this name), not being able to hear what he said, but guessing by what themselves were conscious of that this conference was the discovery of their treason, were again disheartened, and, looking upon one another, agreed from each other's countenances that they should not stay to be taken, but should all kill themselves. And now when Cassius and some others were lay-

ing hands upon their daggers under their robes, and were drawing them out, Brutus, viewing narrowly the looks and gesture of
Lænas, and finding that he was earnestly petitioning and not
accusing, said nothing, because there were many strangers to
the conspiracy mingled amongst them, but by a cheerful countenance encouraged Cassius. And after a little while, Lænas,
having kissed Cæsar's hand, went away, showing plainly that all
his discourse was about some particular business relating to
himself.

Now when the senate was gone in before to the chamber
where they were to sit, the rest of the company placed themselves close about Cæsar's chair, as if they had some suit to
make to him, and Cassius, turning his face to Pompey's statue, is
said to have invoked it, as if it had been sensible of his prayers.
Trebonius, in the meanwhile, engaged Antony's attention at the
door, and kept him in talk outside. When Cæsar entered, the
whole senate rose up to him. As soon as he was sat down, the
men all crowded round about him, and set Tillius Cimber, one of
their own number, to intercede in behalf of his brother that was
banished; they all joined their prayers with his, and took Cæsar
by the hand, and kissed his head and his breast. But he putting
aside at first their supplications, and afterwards, when he saw
they would not desist, violently rising up, Tillius with both
hands caught hold of his robe and pulled it off from his shoulders,
and Casca, that stood behind him, drawing his dagger, gave him
the first, but a slight wound, about the shoulder. Cæsar snatching hold of the handle of the dagger, and crying out aloud in
Latin, " Villain Casca, what do you? " he, calling in Greek to
his brother, bade him come and help. And by this time, finding
himself struck by a great many hands, and looking around about
him to see if he could force his way out, when he saw Brutus
with his dagger drawn against him, he let go Casca's hand, that
he had hold of, and covering his head with his robe, gave up his
body to their blows. And they so eagerly pressed towards the
body, and so many daggers were hacking together, that they cut
one another; Brutus, particularly, received a wound in his hand,
and all of them were besmeared with the blood.

Cæsar being thus slain, Brutus, stepping forth into the midst,
intended to have made a speech, and called back and encouraged
the senators to stay; but they all affrighted ran away in great
disorder, and there was a great confusion and press at the door,
though none pursued or followed. For they had come to an
express resolution to kill nobody beside Cæsar, but to call and

invite all the rest to liberty. It was indeed the opinion of all the others, when they consulted about the execution of their design, that it was necessary to cut off Antony with Cæsar, looking upon him as an insolent man, an affecter of monarchy, and one that, by his familiar intercourse, had gained a powerful interest with the soldiers. And this they urged the rather, because at that time to the natural loftiness and ambition of his temper there was added the dignity of being consul and colleague to Cæsar. But Brutus opposed this counsel, insisting first upon the injustice of it, and afterwards giving them hopes that a change might be worked in Antony. For he did not despair but that so highly gifted and honourable a man, and such a lover of glory as Antony, stirred up with emulation of their great attempt, might, if Cæsar were once removed, lay hold of the occasion to be joint restorer with them of the liberty of his country. Thus did Brutus save Antony's life. But he, in the general consternation, put himself into a plebeian habit, and fled. But Brutus and his party marched up to the capitol, in their way showing their hands all bloody, and their naked swords, and proclaiming liberty to the people. At first all places were filled with cries and shouts; and the wild running to and fro, occasioned by the sudden surprise and passion that every one was in, increased the tumult in the city. But no other bloodshed following, and no plundering of the goods in the streets, the senators and many of the people took courage and went up to the men in the capitol · and a multitude being gathered together, Brutus made an oration to them, very popular, and proper for the state that affairs were then in. Therefore, when they applauded his speech, and cried out to him to come down, they all took confidence and descended into the forum; the rest promiscuously mingled with one another, but many of the most eminent persons, attending Brutus, conducted him in the midst of them with great honour from the capitol, and placed him in the rostra. At the sight of Brutus, the crowd, though consisting of a confused mixture and all disposed to make a tumult, were struck with reverence, and expected what he would say with order and with silence, and, when he began to speak, heard him with quiet and attention. But that all were not pleased with this action they plainly showed when, Cinna beginning to speak and accuse Cæsar, they broke out into a sudden rage, and railed at him in such language that the whole party thought fit again to withdraw to the capitol. And there Brutus, expecting to be besieged, dismissed the most eminent of those that had accompanied them thither, not thinking it just that they who were not partakers of the fact should share in the danger.

But the next day, the senate being assembled in the temple of the Earth, and Antony and Plancus and Cicero having made orations recommending concord in general and an act of oblivion, it was decreed that the men should not only be put out of all fear or danger, but that the consuls should see what honours and dignities were proper to be conferred upon them. After which done, the senate broke up; and, Antony having sent his son as an hostage to the capitol, Brutus and his company came down, and mutual salutes and invitations passed amongst them, the whole of them being gathered together. Antony invited and entertained Cassius, Lepidus did the same to Brutus, and the rest were invited and entertained by others, as each of them had acquaintance or friends. And as soon as it was day, the senate met again, and voted thanks to Antony for having stifled the beginning of a civil war; afterwards Brutus and his associates that were present received encomiums, and had provinces assigned and distributed among them. Crete was allotted to Brutus, Africa to Cassius, Asia to Trebonius, Bithynia to Cimber, and to the other Brutus Gaul about the Po.

After these things, they began to consider of Cæsar's will, and the ordering of his funeral. Antony desired that the will might be read, and that the body should not have a private or dishonourable interment, lest that should further exasperate the people. This Cassius violently opposed, but Brutus yielded to it, and gave leave; in which he seems to have a second time committed a fault. For as before in sparing the life of Antony he could not be without some blame from his party, as thereby setting up against the conspiracy a dangerous and difficult enemy, so now, in suffering him to have the ordering of the funeral, he fell into a total and irrevocable error. For first, it appearing by the will that Cæsar had bequeathed to the Roman people seventy-five drachmas a man, and given to the public his gardens beyond Tiber (where now the temple of Fortune stands), the whole city was fired with a wonderful affection for him, and a passionate sense of the loss of him. And when the body was brought forth into the forum, Antony, as the custom was, making a funeral oration in the praise of Cæsar, and finding the multitude moved with his speech, passing into the pathetic tone, unfolded the bloody garment of Cæsar, showed them in how many places it was pierced, and the number of his wounds. Now there was nothing to be seen but confusion, some cried out to kill the murderers, others (as was formerly done when Clodius led the people) tore away the benches and tables out of the shops round about, and, heaping them altogether, built a great funeral pile, and having put the body of Cæsar upon it, set it on fire, the spot where this was done being moreover surrounded with a great many temples and other consecrated places, so that they seemed to burn the body in a kind of sacred solemnity. As soon as the fire flamed out, the multitude, flocking in some from one part and some from another, snatched the brands that were half burnt out of the pile, and ran about the city to fire the houses of the murderers of Cæsar. But they, having beforehand well fortified themselves, repelled this danger.

There was, however, a kind of poet, one Cinna, not at all concerned in the guilt of the conspiracy, but on the contrary one of Cæsar's friends. This man dreamed that he was invited to supper by Cæsar, and that he declined to go, but that Cæsar entreated and pressed him to it very earnestly; and at last, taking him by the hand, led him into a very deep and dark place, whither he was forced against his will to follow in great consternation and amazement. After this vision, he had a fever the most part of the night; nevertheless in the morning, hearing that the body of Cæsar was to be carried forth to be interred, he was ashamed not to be present at the solemnity, and came abroad and joined the people, when they were already infuriated by the speech of Antony. And perceiving him, and taking him not for that Cinna who indeed he was, but for him that a little before in a speech to the people had reproached and inveighed against Cæsar, they fell upon him and tore him to pieces.

This action chiefly, and the alteration that Antony had wrought, so alarmed Brutus and his party that for their safety they retired from the city. The first stay they made was at Antium, with a design to return again as soon as the fury of the people had spent itself and was abated, which they expected would soon and easily come to pass in an unsettled multitude, apt to be carried away with any sudden and impetuous passion, especially since they had the senate favourable to them; which, though it took no notice of those that had torn Cinna to pieces, yet made a strict search and apprehended in order to punishment those that had assaulted the houses of the friends of Brutus and Cassius. By this time, also, the people began to be dissatisfied with Antony, who they perceived was setting up a kind of monarchy for himself; they longed for the return of Brutus, whose presence they expected and hoped for at the

games and spectacles which he, as prætor, was to exhibit to the
public. But he, having intelligence that many of the old soldiers
that had borne arms under Cæsar, by whom they had had lands
and cities given them, lay in wait for them, and by small parties
at a time had stolen into the city, would not venture to come
himself; however, in his absence there were most magnificent
and costly shows exhibited to the people; for, having brought
up a great number of all sorts of wild beasts, he gave order that
not any of them should be returned or saved, but that all
should be spent freely at the public spectacles. He himself
made a journey to Naples to procure a considerable number of
players, and hearing of one Canutius that was very much
praised for his acting upon the stage, he wrote to his friends
to use all their entreaties to bring him to Rome (for, being a
Grecian, he could not be compelled); he wrote also to Cicero,
begging him by no means to omit being present at the shows.

This was the posture of affairs when another sudden alteration was made upon the young Cæsar's coming to Rome. He
was son to the niece of Cæsar, who adopted him, and left him
his heir by his will. At the time when Cæsar was killed, he was
following his studies at Apollonia, where he was expecting also
to meet Cæsar on his way to the expedition which he had determined on against the Parthians; but, hearing of his death, he
immediately came to Rome, and to ingratiate himself with the
people, taking upon himself the name of Cæsar, and punctually
distributing among the citizens the money that was left them
by the will, he soon got the better of Antony; and by money
and largesses, which he liberally dispersed amongst the soldiers,
he gathered together and brought over to his party a great
number of those that had served under Cæsar. Cicero himself,
out of the hatred which he bore to Antony, sided with young
Cæsar; which Brutus took so ill that he treated with him very
sharply in his letters, telling him that he perceived Cicero could
well enough endure a tyrant, but was afraid that he who hated
him should be the man; that in writing and speaking so well of
Cæsar, he showed that his aim was to have an easy slavery.
"But our forefathers," said Brutus, "could not brook even
gentle masters." Further he added, that for his own part he
had not as yet fully resolved whether he should make war or
peace; but that as to one point he was fixed and settled, which
was, never to be a slave; that he wondered Cicero should fear
the dangers of a civil war, and not be much more afraid of a
dishonourable and infamous peace; that the very reward that

was to be given him for subverting Antony's tyranny was the privilege of establishing Cæsar as tyrant in his place. This is the tone of Brutus's first letters to Cicero.

The city being now divided into two factions, some betaking themselves to Cæsar and others to Antony, the soldiers selling themselves, as it were, by public outcry, and going over to him that would give them most, Brutus began to despair of any good event of such proceedings, and, resolving to leave Italy, passed by land through Lucania and came to Elea by the seaside. From hence it was thought convenient that Porcia should return to Rome. She was overcome with grief to part from Brutus, but strove as much as was possible to conceal it; but, in spite of all her constancy, a picture which she found there accidentally betrayed it. It was a Greek subject, Hector parting from Andromache when he went to engage the Greeks, giving his young son Astyanax into her arms, and she fixing her eyes upon him. When she looked at this piece, the resemblance it bore to her own condition made her burst into tears, and several times a day she went to see the picture, and wept before it. Upon this occasion, when Acilius, one of Brutus's friends, repeated out of Homer the verses, where Andromache speaks to Hector:—

> "But Hector, you
> To me are father and are mother too,
> My brother, and my loving husband true."

Brutus, smiling, replied, " But I must not answer Porcia, as Hector did Andromache:—

> "'Mind you your loom, and to your maids give law.'

"For though the natural weakness of her body hinders her from doing what only the strength of men can perform, yet she has a mind as valiant and as active for the good of her country as the best of us." This narrative is in the memoirs of Brutus written by Bibulus, Porcia's son.

Brutus took ship from hence, and sailed to Athens, where he was received by the people with great demonstrations of kindness, expressed in their acclamation and the honours that were decreed him. He lived there with a private friend, and was a constant auditor of Theomnestus, the Academic, and Cratippus, the Peripatetic, with whom he so engaged in philosophical pursuits that he seemed to have laid aside all thoughts of public business, and to be wholly at leisure for study. But all this while, being unsuspected, he was secretly making preparations for war; in order to which he sent Herostratus into Macedonia to secure the commanders there to his side, and he himself won over and kept at his disposal all the young Romans that were then students at Athens. Of this number was Cicero's son, whom he everywhere highly extols, and says that whether sleeping or waking he could not choose but admire a young man of so great a spirit and such a hater of tyranny.

At length he began to act openly, and to appear in public business, and, being informed that there were several Roman ships full of treasure that in their course from Asia were to come that way, and that they were commanded by one of his friends, he went to meet him about Carystus. Finding him there, and having persuaded him to deliver up the ships, he made a more than usually splendid entertainment, for it happened also to be his birthday. Now when they came to drink, and were filling their cups with hopes for victory to Brutus and liberty to Rome, Brutus, to animate them the more, called for a larger bowl, and holding it in his hand, on a sudden, upon no occasion or fore-thought, pronounced aloud this verse:—

" But fate my death and Leto's son have wrought."

And some writers add that in the last battle which he fought at Philippi, the word that he gave to his soldiers was Apollo, and from thence conclude that this sudden unaccountable ex-clamation of his was a presage of the overthrow that he suffered there.

Antistius, the commander of these ships, at his parting, gave him fifty thousand myriads of the money that he was convey-ing to Italy; and all the soldiers yet remaining of Pompey's army, who after their general's defeat wandered about Thessaly, readily and joyfully flocked together to join him. Besides this, he took from Cinna five hundred horse that he was carrying to Dolabella into Asia. After that, he sailed to Demetrias, and there seized a great quantity of arms that had been provided by the command of the deceased Cæsar for the Parthian war, and were now to be sent to Antony. Then Macedonia was put into his hands and delivered up by Hortensius the prætor, and all the kings and potentates round about came and offered their services. So when news was brought that Caius, the brother of Antony, having passed over from Italy, was marching on directly to join the forces that Vatinius commanded in Dyrrhachium and Apollonia, Brutus resolved to anticipate him, and to seize them first, and in all haste moved forwards with those that he had about him. His march was very difficult, through rugged places and in a great snow, but so swift that he left those that were to bring his provisions for the morning meal a great way behind. And now, being very near to Dyrrhachium, with fatigue and cold he fell into the distemper called Bulimia. This is a disease that seizes both men and cattle after much labour, and especially in a great snow; whether it is caused by the natural heat when the body is seized with cold, being forced all inwards, and consuming at once all the nourishment laid in, or whether the sharp and subtle vapour which comes from the snow as it dissolves cuts the body, as it were, and destroys the heat which issues through the pores; for the sweatings seem to arise from the heat meeting with the cold, and being quenched by it on the surface of the body. But this I have in another place discussed more at large.

Brutus growing very faint, and there being none in the whole army that had anything for him to eat, his servants were forced to have recourse to the enemy, and, going as far as to the gates of the city, begged bread of the sentinels that were upon duty. As soon as they heard of the condition of Brutus, they came themselves, and brought both meat and drink along with them; in return for which Brutus, when he took the city, showed the greatest kindness, not to them only, but to all the inhabitants, for their sakes. Caius Antonius, in the meantime, coming to Apollonia, summoned all the soldiers that were near that city to join him there; but finding that they nevertheless went all to Brutus, and suspecting that even those of Apollonia were inclined to the same party, he quitted that city, and came to Buthrotum, having first lost three cohorts of his men, that in their march thither were cut to pieces by Brutus. After this, attempting to make himself master of some strong places about Byllis which the enemy had first seized, he was overcome in a set battle by young Cicero, to whom Brutus gave the command, and whose conduct he made use of often and with much success. Caius himself was surprised in a marshy place, at a distance from his support; and Brutus having him in his power would not suffer his soldiers to attack, but manœuvring about the enemy with his horse, gave command that none of them should be killed, for that in a little time they would all be of his side; which accordingly came to pass, for they surrendered both themselves and their general. So that Brutus had by this time a very great and considerable army. He showed all marks of honour and esteem to Caius for a long time, and left him the use of the ensigns of his office, though, as some report, he had several letters from Rome, and particularly from Cicero, advising him to put him to death. But at last, perceiving that he began to corrupt his officers, and was trying to raise a mutiny amongst the soldiers, he put him aboard a ship and kept him close prisoner. In the meantime, the soldiers that had been corrupted by Caius retired to Apollonia, and sent word to Brutus, desiring him to come to them thither. He answered that this was not the custom of the Romans, but that it became those who had offended to come themselves to their general and beg forgiveness of their offences; which they did, and accordingly received their pardon.

As he was preparing to pass into Asia, tidings reached him of the alteration that had happened at Rome; where the young Cæsar, assisted by the senate, in opposition to Antony, and having driven his competitor out of Italy, had begun himself to be very formidable, suing for the consulship contrary to law, and maintaining large bodies of troops of which the commonwealth had no manner of need. And then, perceiving that the senate, dissatisfied with the proceedings, began to cast their eyes abroad upon Brutus, and decreed and confirmed the government of several provinces to him, he had taken the alarm. Therefore despatching messengers to Antony, he desired that there might be a reconciliation, and a friendship between them. Then, drawing all his forces about the city, he made himself to be chosen consul, though he was but a boy, being scarce twenty years old, as he himself writes in his memoirs. At the first entry upon the consulship he immediately ordered a judicial process to be issued out against Brutus and his accomplices for having murdered a principal man of the city, holding the highest magistracies of Rome, without being heard or condemned; and appointed Lucius Cornificus to accuse Brutus, and Marcus Agrippa to accuse Cassius. None appearing to the accusation, the judges were forced to pass sentence and condemn them both. It is reported that when the crier from the tribunal, as the custom was, with a loud voice cried Brutus to appear, the people groaned audibly, and the noble citizens hung down their heads for grief. Publicus Silicius was seen to burst out into tears, which was the cause that not long after he was put down in the list of those that were proscribed. After this, the three men, Cæsar, Antony, and Lepidus, being perfectly reconciled, shared the provinces among themselves, and made up the catalogue of proscription, wherein were set those that were designed for slaughter, amounting to two hundred men, in which number Cicero was slain.

The news being brought to Brutus in Macedonia, he was under a compulsion, and sent orders to Hortensius that he should kill Caius Antonius in revenge of the death of Cicero his friend, and Brutus his kinsman, who also was proscribed and slain. Upon this account it was that Antony, having afterwards taken Hortensius in the battle of Philippi, slew him upon his brother's tomb. But Brutus expresses himself as more ashamed for the cause of Cicero's death than grieved for the misfortune of it, and says he cannot help accusing his friends at Rome, that they were slaves more through their own doing than that of those who now were their tyrants; they could be present and see and yet suffer those things which even to hear related ought to them to have been insufferable.

Having made his army, that was already very considerable, pass into Asia, he ordered a fleet to be prepared in Bithynia and about Cyzicus. But going himself through the country by land, he made it his business to settle and confirm all the cities, and gave audience to the princes of the parts through which he passed. And he sent orders into Syria to Cassius to come to him, and leave his intended journey into Egypt; letting him understand that it was not to gain an empire for themselves, but to free their country, that they went thus wandering about and had got an army together whose business it was to destroy the tyrants; that therefore, if they remembered and resolved to persevere in their first purpose, they ought not to be too far from Italy, but make what haste they could thither, and endeavour to relieve their fellow-citizens from oppression.

Cassius obeyed his summons, and returned, and Brutus went to meet him; and at Smyrna they met, which was the first time they had seen one another since they parted at the Piræus in Athens, one for Syria, and the other for Macedonia. They were both extremely joyful and had great confidence of their success at the sight of the forces that each of them had got together, since they who had fled from Italy, like the most despicable exiles, without money, without arms, without a ship or a soldier or a city to rely on, in a little time after had met together so well furnished with shipping and money, and an army both of horse and foot, that they were in a condition to contend for the empire of Rome.

Cassius was desirous to show no less respect and honour to Brutus than Brutus did to him; but Brutus was still beforehand with him, coming for the most part to him, both because he was the elder man, and of a weaker constitution than himself. Men generally reckoned Cassius a very expert soldier, but of a harsh and angry nature, and one that desired to command rather by fear than love, though, on the other side, among his familiar acquaintance he would easily give way to jesting and play the buffoon. But Brutus, for his virtue, was esteemed by the people, beloved by his friends, admired by the best men, and hated not by his enemies themselves. For he was a man of a singularly gentle nature, of a great spirit, insensible of the passions of anger or pleasure or covetousness; steady and inflexible to maintain his purpose for what he thought right and honest. And that which gained him the greatest affection and reputation was the entire faith in his intentions. For it had not ever been supposed that Pompey the Great himself, if he had overcome Cæsar, would have submitted his power to the laws, instead of taking the management of the state upon himself, soothing the people with the specious name of consul or dictator, or some other milder title than king. And they were well persuaded that Cassius, being a man governed by anger and passion, and carried often, for his interest's sake, beyond the bounds of justice, endured all these hardships of war and travel and danger most assuredly to obtain dominion to himself, and not liberty to the people. And as for the former disturbers of the peace of Rome, whether a Cinna, a Marius, or a Carbo, it is manifest that they, having set their country as a stake for him that should win, did almost own in express terms that they fought for empire. But even the enemies of Brutus did not, they tell us, lay this accusation to his charge; nay, many heard Antony himself say that Brutus was the only man that conspired against Cæsar out of a sense of the glory and the apparent justice of the action, but that all the rest rose up against the man himself, from private envy and malice of their own. And it is plain by what he writes himself, that Brutus did not so much rely upon his forces, as upon his own virtue. For thus he speaks in a letter to Atticus, shortly before he was to engage with the enemy: that his affairs were in the best state of fortune that he could wish; for that either he should overcome, and restore liberty to the people of Rome, or die, and be himself out of the reach of slavery; that other things being certain and beyond all hazard, one thing was yet in doubt, whether they should live or die free men. He adds further, that Mark Antony had received a just punishment for his folly, who, when he might have been numbered with Brutus and Cassius and Cato, would join himself to Octavius; that though they should not now be both overcome, they soon would fight between themselves. And in this he seems to have been no ill prophet.

Now when they were at Smyrna, Brutus desired of Cassius that he might have part of the great treasure that he had heaped up, because all his own was expended in furnishing out such a fleet of ships as was sufficient to keep the whole interior sea in their power. But Cassius's friends dissuaded him from this; "for," said they, "it is not just that the money which you with so much parsimony keep, and with so much envy have got, should be given to him to be disposed of in making himself popular, and gaining the favour of the soldiers." Notwithstanding this, Cassius gave him a third part of all that he had; and then they parted each to their several commands. Cassius, having taken Rhodes, behaved himself there with no clemency; though at his first entry, when some had called him lord and king, he answered that he was neither king nor lord, but the destroyer and punisher of a king and lord. Brutus, on the other part, sent to the Lycians to demand from them a supply of money and men, but Laucrates, their popular leader, persuaded the cities to resist, and they occupied several little mountains and hills with a design to hinder Brutus's passage. Brutus at first sent out a party of horse which, surprising them as they were eating, killed six hundred of them, and afterward, having taken all their small towns and villages round about, he set all his prisoners free without ransom, hoping to win the whole nation by good-will. But they continued obstinate, taking in anger what they had suffered, and despising his goodness and humanity; until, having forced the most warlike of them into the city of Xanthus, he besieged them there. They endeavoured to make their escape by swimming and diving through the river that flows by the town, but were taken by nets let down for that purpose in the channel, which had little bells at the top, which gave present notice of any that were taken in them. After that, they made a sally in the night, and seizing several of the battering engines, set them on fire; but being perceived by the Romans, were beaten back to their walls, and there being a strong wind, it carried the flames to the battlements of the city with such fierceness that several of the adjoining houses took fire. Brutus, fearing lest the whole city should be destroyed, commanded his own soldiers to assist and quench the fire.

But the Lycians were on a sudden possessed with a strange

and incredible desperation; such a frenzy as cannot be better expressed than by calling it a violent appetite to die, for both women and children, the bondmen and the free, those of all ages and of all conditions strove to force away the soldiers that came in to their assistance from the walls; and themselves gathering together reeds and wood, and whatever combustible matter they found, spread the fire over the whole city, feeding it with whatever fuel they could, and by all possible means exciting its fury, so that the flame, having dispersed itself and encircled the whole city, blazed out in so terrible a manner that Brutus, extremely afflicted at their calamity, got on horseback and rode round the walls, earnestly desirous to preserve the city, and stretching forth his hands to the Xanthians, begged of them that they would spare themselves and save the town. Yet none regarded his entreaties, but, by all manner of ways, strove to destroy themselves; not only men and women, but even boys and little children, with a hideous outcry, leaped some into the fire, others from the walls, others fell upon their parents' swords, baring their throats and desiring to be struck. After the destruction of the city, there was found a woman who had hanged herself with her young child hanging from her neck, and the torch in her hand with which she had fired her own house.

It was so tragical a sight that Brutus could not endure to see it, but wept at the very relation of it and proclaimed a reward to any soldier that could save a Xanthian. And it is said that an hundred and fifty only were found, to have their lives saved against their wills. Thus the Xanthians after a long space of years, the fated period of their destruction having, as it were, run its course, repeated by their desperate deed the former calamity of their forefathers, who after the very same manner in the Persian war had fired their city and destroyed themselves.

Brutus, after this, finding the Patareans resolved to make resistance and hold out their city against him, was very unwilling to besiege it, and was in great perplexity lest the same frenzy might seize them too. But having in his power some of their women, who were his prisoners, he dismissed them all without any ransom; who, returning and giving an account to their husbands and fathers, who were of the greatest rank, what an excellent man Brutus was, how temperate and how just, persuaded them to yield themselves and put their city into his hands. From this time all the cities round about came into his power, submitting themselves to him, and found him good and merciful even beyond their hopes. For though Cassius at the same time had compelled the Rhodians to bring in all the silver and gold that each of them privately was possessed of, by which he raised a sum of eight thousand talents, and besides this had condemned the public to pay the sum of five hundred talents more, Brutus, not having taken above a hundred and fifty talents from the Lycians, and having done them no other manner of injury, parted from thence with his army to go into Ionia.

Through the whole course of this expedition, Brutus did many memorable acts of justice in dispensing rewards and punishments to such as had deserved either; but one in particular I will relate, because he himself, and all the noblest Romans, were gratified with it above all the rest. When Pompey the Great, being overthrown from his great power by Cæsar, had fled to Egypt, and landed near Pelusium, the protectors of the young king consulted among themselves what was fit to be done on that occasion, nor could they all agree in the same opinion, some being for receiving him, others for driving him from Egypt. But Theodotus, a Chian by birth, and then attending upon the king as a paid teacher of rhetoric, and for want of better men admitted into the council, undertook to prove to them that both parties were in the wrong, those that counselled to receive Pompey, and those that advised to send him away; that in their present case one thing only was truly expedient, to seize him and to kill him; and ended his argument with the proverb, that " dead men don't bite." The council agreed to his opinion, and Pompey the Great (an example of incredible and unforeseen events) was slain, as the sophister himself had the impudence to boast, through the rhetoric and cleverness of Theodotus. Not long after, when Cæsar came to Egypt, some of the murderers received their just reward and suffered the evil death they deserved. But Theodotus, though he had borrowed on from fortune a little further time for a poor, despicable, and wandering life, yet did not lie hid from Brutus as he passed through Asia; but being seized by him and executed, had his death made more memorable than was his life.

About this time, Brutus sent to Cassius to come to him at the city of Sardis, and, when he was on his journey, went forth with his friends to meet him; and the whole army in array saluted each of them with the name of Imperator. Now (as it usually happens in business of great concern, and where many friends and many commanders are engaged), several jealousies of each other and matters of private accusation having passed between Brutus and Cassius, they resolved, before they entered upon any other business, immediately to withdraw into some apartment; where, the door being shut and they two alone, they began first to expostulate, then to dispute hotly, and accuse each other; and finally were so transported into passion as to fall to hard words, and at last burst out into tears. Their friends who stood without were amazed, hearing them loud and angry, and feared lest some mischief might follow, but yet durst not interrupt them, being commanded not to enter the room. However, Marcus Favonius, who had been an ardent admirer of Cato, and, not so much by his learning or wisdom as by his wild, vehement manner, maintained the character of a philosopher, was rushing in upon them, but was hindered by the attendants. But it was a hard matter to stop Favonius, wherever his wildness hurried him; for he was fierce in all his behaviour, and ready to do anything to get his will. And though he was a senator, yet, thinking that one of the least of his excellences, he valued himself more upon a sort of cynical liberty of speaking what he pleased, which sometimes, indeed, did away with the rudeness and unseasonableness of his addresses with those that would interpret it in jest. This Favonius, breaking by force through those that kept the doors, entered into the chamber, and with a set voice declaimed the verses that Homer makes Nestor use—

" Be ruled, for I am older than ye both."

At this Cassius laughed; but Brutus thrust him out, calling him impudent dog and counterfeit Cynic; but yet for the present they let it put an end to their dispute, and parted. Cassius made a supper that night, and Brutus invited the guests; and when they were set down, Favonius, having bathed, came in among them. Brutus called out aloud and told him he was not invited, and bade him go to the upper couch; but he violently thrust himself in, and lay down on the middle one; and the entertainment passed in sportive talk, not wanting either wit or philosophy.

The next day after, upon the accusation of the Sardians, Brutus publicly disgraced and condemned Lucius Pella, one that had been censor of Rome, and employed in offices of trust by himself, for having embezzled the public money. This action did not a little vex Cassius; for but a few days before, two of his own friends being accused of the same crime, he only admonished them in private, but in public absolved them, and continued them in his service; and upon this occasion he accused Brutus of too much rigour and severity of justice in a time which required them to use more policy and favour. But Brutus bade him remember the Ides of March, the day when they killed Cæsar, who himself neither plundered nor pillaged mankind, but was only the support and strength of those that did; and bade him consider that if there was any colour for justice to be neglected, it had been better to suffer the injustice of Cæsar's friends than to give impunity to their own; "for then," said he, "we would have been accused of cowardice only; whereas now we are liable to the accusation of injustice, after all our pain and dangers which we endure." By which we may perceive what was Brutus's purpose, and the rule of his actions.

About the time that they were going to pass out of Asia into Europe, it is said that a wonderful sign was seen by Brutus. He was naturally given to much watching, and by practice and moderation in his diet had reduced his allowance of sleep to a very small amount of time. He never slept in the daytime, and in the night then only when all his business was finished, and when, every one else being gone to rest, he had nobody to discourse with him. But at this time, the war being begun, having the whole state of it to consider, and being solicitous of the event, after his first sleep, which he let himself take after his supper, he spent all the rest of the night in settling his most urgent affairs; which if he could despatch early and so make a saving of any leisure, he employed himself in reading until the third watch, at which time the centurions and tribunes were used to come to him for orders. Thus one night before he passed out of Asia, he was very late all alone in his tent, with a dim light burning by him, all the rest of the camp being hushed and silent; and reasoning about something with himself and very thoughtful, he fancied some one came in, and, looking up towards the door, he saw a terrible and strange appearance of an unnatural and frightful body standing by him without speaking. Brutus boldly asked it, "What are you, of men or gods, and upon what business come to me?" The figure answered, "I am your evil genius, Brutus; you shall see me at Philippi." To which Brutus, not at all disturbed, replied, "Then I shall see you." As soon as the apparition vanished, he called his servants to him, who all told him that they had neither heard any voice nor seen any vision. So then he continued watching till the morning, when he went to Cassius, and told him of what he had seen. He, who followed the principles of Epicurus's philosophy, and often used to dispute with Brutus concerning matters of this nature, spoke to him thus upon this occasion: "It is the opinion of our sect, Brutus, that not all that we feel or see is real and true; but that the sense is a most slippery and deceitful thing, and the mind yet more quick and subtle to put the sense in motion and affect it with every kind of change upon no real occasion of fact; just as an impression is made upon wax; and the soul of man, which has in itself both what imprints, and what is imprinted on, may most easily, by its own operations, produce and assume every variety of shape and figure. This is evident from the sudden changes of our dreams; in which the imaginative principle, once started by any trifling matter, goes through a whole series of most diverse emotions and appearances. It is its nature to be ever in motion, and its motion is fantasy or conception. But besides all this, in your case, the body, being tired and distressed with continual toil, naturally works upon the mind and keeps it in an excited and unusual condition. But that there should be any such thing as supernatural beings, or, if there were, that they should have human shape or voice or power that can reach to us, there is no reason for believing; though I confess I could wish that there were such beings, that we might not rely upon our arms only, and our horses and our navy, all which are so numerous and powerful, but might be confident of the assistance of gods also, in this our most sacred and honourable attempt." With such discourses as these Cassius soothed the mind of Brutus. But just as the troops were going on board, two eagles flew and lighted on the first two ensigns, and crossed over the water with them, and never ceased following the soldiers and being fed by them till they came to Philippi, and there, but one day before the fight, they both flew away.

Brutus had already reduced most of the places and people of these parts; but they now marched on as far as to the coast opposite Thasos, and, if there were any city or man of power that yet stood out, brought them all to subjection. At this point Norbanus was encamped, in a place called the Straits, near Symbolum. Him they surrounded in such sort that they forced him to dislodge and quit the place; and Norbanus narrowly escaped losing his whole army, Cæsar by reason of sickness being too far behind; only Antony came to his relief with such wonderful swiftness that Brutus and those with him did not believe when they heard he was come. Cæsar came up ten days after, and encamped over against Brutus, and Antony over against Cassius.

The space between the two armies is called by the Romans the Campi Philippi. Never had two such large Roman armies

come together to engage each other. That of Brutus was somewhat less in number than that of Cæsar, but in the splendidness
of the men's arms and richness of their equipage it wonderfully
exceeded; for most of their arms were of gold and silver, which
Brutus had lavishly bestowed among them. For though in
other things he had accustomed his commanders to use all
frugality and self-control, yet he thought that the riches
which soldiers carried about them in their hands and on their
bodies would add something of spirit to those that were desirous
of glory, and would make those that were covetous and lovers of
gain fight the more valiantly to preserve the arms which were
their estate.

Cæsar made a view and lustration of his army within his
trenches, and distributed only a little corn and but five drachmas
to each soldier for the sacrifice they were to make. But Brutus,
either pitying this poverty, or disdaining this meanness of spirit
in Cæsar, first, as the custom was, made a general muster and
lustration of the army in the open field, and then distributed a
great number of beasts for sacrifice to every regiment, and fifty
drachmas to every soldier; so that in the love of his soldiers
and their readiness to fight for him Brutus had much the
advantage. But at the time of lustration it is reported that
an unlucky omen happened to Cassius; for his lictor, presenting
him with a garland that he was to wear at sacrifice, gave it him
the wrong way up. Further, it is said that some time before,
at a certain solemn procession, a golden image of Victory, which
was carried before Cassius, fell down by a slip of him that carried
it. Besides this there appeared many birds of prey daily about
the camp, and swarms of bees were seen in a place within the
trenches, which place the soothsayers ordered shut out from the
camp, to remove the superstition which insensibly began to infect
even Cassius himself and shake him in his Epicurean philosophy, and had wholly seized and subdued the soldiers; from
whence it was that Cassius was reluctant to put all to the
hazard of a present battle, but advised rather to draw out the
war until further time, considering that they were stronger in
money and provisions, but in numbers of men and arms inferior.
But Brutus, on the contrary, was still, as formerly, desirous to
come with all speed to the decision of a battle; that so he might
either restore his country to her liberty, or else deliver from
their misery all those numbers of people whom they harassed
with the expenses and the service and exactions of the war.
And finding also his light-horse in several skirmishes still to

have had the better, he was the more encouraged and resolved; and some of the soldiers having deserted and gone to the enemy, and others beginning to accuse and suspect one another, many of Cassius's friends in the council changed their opinions to that of Brutus. But there was one of Brutus's party, named Attellius, who opposed his resolution, advising rather that they should tarry over the winter. And when Brutus asked him in how much better a condition he hoped to be a year after, his answer was, " If I gain nothing else, yet I shall live so much the longer." Cassius was much displeased at this answer; and among the rest, Attellius was had in much disesteem for it. And so it was presently resolved to give battle the next day.

Brutus that night at supper showed himself very cheerful and full of hope, and reasoned on subjects of philosophy with his friends, and afterwards went to his rest. But Messala says that Cassius supped privately with a few of his nearest acquaintance, and appeared thoughtful and silent, contrary to his temper and custom; that after supper he took him earnestly by the hand, and speaking to him, as his manner was when he wished to show affection, in Greek, said, " Bear witness for me, Messala, that I am brought into the same necessity as Pompey the Great was before me, of hazarding the liberty of my country upon one battle; yet ought we to be of courage, relying on our good fortune, which it were unfair to mistrust, though we take evil counsels." These, Messala says, were the last words that Cassius spoke before he bade him farewell; and that he was invited to sup with him the next night, being his birthday.

As soon as it was morning, the signal of battle, the scarlet coat, was set out in Brutus's and Cassius's camps, and they themselves met in the middle space between their two armies. There Cassius spoke thus to Brutus: " Be it as we hope, O Brutus, that this day we may overcome, and all the rest of our time may live a happy life together; but since the greatest of human concerns are the most uncertain, and since it may be difficult for us ever to see one another again, if the battle should go against us, tell me, what is your resolution concerning flight and death? " Brutus answered, " When I was young, Cassius, and unskilful in affairs, I was led, I know not how, into uttering a bold sentence in philosophy, and blamed Cato for killing himself, as thinking it an irreligious act, and not a valiant one among men, to try to evade the divine course of things, and not fearlessly to receive and undergo the evil that shall happen, but run away from it. But now in my own fortunes I am of another mind; for if Providence shall not dispose what we now undertake according to our wishes, I resolve to put no further hopes or warlike preparations to the proof, but will die contented with my fortune. For I already have given up my life to my country on the Ides of March; and have lived since then a second life for her sake, with liberty and honour." Cassius at these words smiled, and, embracing Brutus, said, " With these resolutions let us go on upon the enemy; for either we ourselves shall conquer, or have no cause to fear those that do." After this they discoursed among their friends about the ordering of the battle; and Brutus desired of Cassius that he might command the right wing, though it was thought that this was more fit for Cassius, in regard both of his age and his experience. Yet even in this Cassius complied with Brutus, and placed Messala with the valiantest of all his legions in the same wing, so Brutus immediately drew out his horse, excellently well equipped, and was not long in bringing up his foot after them.

Antony's soldiers were casting trenches from the marsh by which they were encamped across the plain, to cut off Cassius's communications with the sea. Cæsar was to be at hand with his troops to support them, but he was not able to be present himself, by reason of his sickness; and his soldiers, not much expecting that the enemy would come to a set battle, but only make some excursions with their darts and light arms to disturb the men at work in the trenches, and not taking notice of the troops drawn up against them ready to give battle, were amazed when they heard the confused and great outcry that came from the trenches. In the meanwhile Brutus had sent his tickets, in which was the word of battle, to the officers; and himself riding about to all the troops, encouraged the soldiers; but there were but few of them that understood the word before they engaged; the most of them, not staying to have it delivered to them, with one impulse and cry ran upon the enemy. This disorder caused an unevenness in the line, and the legions got severed and divided one from another; that of Messala first, and afterwards the other adjoining, went beyond the left wing of Cæsar; and having just touched the extremity, without slaughtering any great number, passing around that wing, fell directly into Cæsar's camp. Cæsar himself, as his own memoirs tell us, had but just before been conveyed away, Marcus Artorius, one of his friends, having had a dream bidding Cæsar be carried out of the camp. And it was believed that he was slain; for the soldiers had pierced his litter, which was left empty, in many places with their darts and pikes. There was a great slaughter in the camp that was taken; and two thousand Lacedæmonians that were newly come to the assistance of Cæsar were all cut off together.

The rest of the army, that had not gone round, but had engaged the front, easily overthrew them, finding them in great disorder, and slew upon the place three legions; and being carried on with the stream of victory, pursuing those that fled, fell into the camp with them, Brutus himself being there. But they that were conquered took the advantage in their extremity of what the conquerors did not consider. For they fell upon that part of the main body which had been left exposed and separated, where the right wing had broke off from them and hurried away in the pursuit; yet they could not break into the midst of their battle, but were received with strong resistance and obstinacy. Yet they put to flight the left wing, where Cassius commanded, being in great disorder, and ignorant of what had passed on the other wing; and pursuing them to their camp, they pillaged and destroyed it, neither of their generals being present; for Antony, they say, to avoid the fury of the first onset, had retired into the marsh that was hard by; and Cæsar was nowhere to be found after his being conveyed out of the tents; though some of the soldiers showed Brutus their swords bloody, and declared that they had killed him, describing his person and his age. By this time also the centre of Brutus's battle had driven back their opponents with great slaughter; and Brutus was everywhere plainly conqueror, as on the other side Cassius was conquered. And this one mistake was the ruin of their affairs, that Brutus did not come to the relief of Cassius, thinking that he, as well as himself, was conqueror; and that Cassius did not expect the relief of Brutus, thinking that he too was overcome. For as a proof that the victory was on Brutus's side, Messala urges his taking three eagles and many ensigns of the enemy without losing any of his own. But now, returning from the pursuit after having plundered Cæsar's camp, Brutus wondered that he could not see Cassius's tent standing high, as it was wont, and appearing above the rest, nor other things appearing as they had been; for they had been immediately pulled down and pillaged by the enemy upon their first falling into the camp. But some that had a quicker and longer sight than the rest acquainted Brutus that they saw a great deal of shining armour and silver targets moving to and fro in Cassius's camp, and that they thought, by their number and the fashion of their armour, they could not be those that they left to guard the camp; but yet that there did not appear so great a number of dead bodies thereabouts as it was probable there would have been after the actual defeat of so many legions. This first made Brutus suspect Cassius's misfortune, and, leaving a guard in the enemy's camp, he called back those that were in the pursuit, and rallied them together to lead them to the relief of Cassius, whose fortune had been as follows.

First, he had been angry at the onset that Brutus's soldiers made, without the word of battle or command to charge. Then, after they had overcome, he was as much displeased to see them rush on to the plunder and spoil, and neglect to surround and encompass the rest of the enemy. Besides this, letting himself act by delay and expectation, rather than command, boldly and with a clear purpose, he got hemmed in by the right wing of the enemy, and, his horse making with all haste their escape and flying towards the sea, the foot also began to give way, which he perceiving laboured as much as ever he could to hinder their flight and bring them back; and, snatching an ensign out of the hand of one that fled, he stuck it at his feet, though he could hardly keep even his own personal guard together. So that at last he was forced to fly with a few about him to a little hill that overlooked the plain. But he himself, being weak-sighted, discovered nothing, only the destruction of his camp, and that with difficulty. But they that were with him saw a great body of horse moving towards him, the same whom Brutus had sent. Cassius believed these were enemies, and in pursuit of him; however, he sent away Titinius, one of those that were with him, to learn what they were. As soon as Brutus's horse saw him coming, and knew him to be a friend and a faithful servant of Cassius, those of them that were his more familiar acquaintance, shouting out for joy and alighting from their horses, shook hands and embraced him, and the rest rode round about him singing and shouting, through their excess of gladness at the sight of him. But this was the occasion of the greatest mischief that could be. For Cassius really thought that Titinius had been taken by the enemy, and cried out, " Through too much fondness of life, I have lived to endure the sight of my friend taken by the enemy before my face." After which words he retired into an empty tent, taking along with him only Pindarus, one of his freemen, whom he had reserved for such an occasion ever since the disasters in the expedition against the Parthians, when Crassus was slain. From the Parthians he came away in safety; but now, pulling up his mantle over his head, he made his neck bare, and held it forth to Pindarus, commanding him to strike. The head was certainly found lying severed from the body. But no man ever saw Pindarus after, from which some suspected that he had killed his master without his command. Soon after they perceived who the horsemen were, and saw Titinius, crowned with garlands, making what haste he could towards Cassius. But as soon as he understood by the cries and lamentations of his afflicted friends the unfortunate error and death of his general, he drew his sword, and having very much accused and upbraided his own long stay, that had caused it, he slew himself.

Brutus, as soon as he was assured of the defeat of Cassius, made haste to him; but heard nothing of his death till he came near his camp. Then having lamented over his body, calling him " the last of the Romans," it being impossible that the city should ever produce another man of so great a spirit, he sent away the body to be buried at Thasos, lest celebrating his funeral within the camp might breed some disorder. He then gathered the soldiers together and comforted them; and, seeing them destitute of all things necessary, he promised to every man two thousand drachmas in recompense of what he had lost. They at these words took courage, and were astonished at the magnificence of the gift; and waited upon him at his parting with shouts and praises, magnifying him for the only general of all the four who was not overcome in the battle. And indeed the action itself testified that it was not without reason he believed he should conquer; for with a few legions he overthrew all that resisted him; and if all his soldiers had fought, and the most of them had not passed beyond the enemy in pursuit of the plunder, it is very likely that he had utterly defeated every part of them.

There fell of his side eight thousand men, reckoning the servants of the army, whom Brutus calls Briges; and on the other side, Messala says his opinion is that there were slain about twice that number. For which reason they were more out of heart than Brutus, until a servant of Cassius, named Demetrius, came in the evening to Antony, and brought to him the garment which he had taken from the dead body, and his sword; at the sight of which they were so encouraged, that, as soon as it was morning, they drew out their whole force into the field, and stood in battle array. But Brutus found both his camps wavering and in disorder; for his own, being filled with prisoners, required a guard more strict than ordinary over them; and that of Cassius was uneasy at the change of general, besides some envy and rancour, which those that were conquered bore to that part of the army which had been conquerors. Wherefore he thought it convenient to put his army in array, but to abstain from fighting. All the slaves that were taken prisoners, of whom there was a great number that were mixed up, not without suspicion, among the soldiers, he commanded to be slain; but of the freemen and citizens, some he dismissed, saying that among the enemy they were rather prisoners than with him, for with them they were captives and slaves, but with him freemen and citizens of Rome. But he was forced to hide and help them to escape privately, perceiving that his friends and officers were bent upon revenge against them. Among the captives there was one Volumnius, a player, and Sacculio, a buffoon; of these Brutus took no manner of notice, but his friends brought them before him and accused them that even then in that condition they did not refrain from their jests and scurrilous language. Brutus, having his mind taken up with other affairs, said nothing to their accusation; but the judgment of Messala Corvinus was, that they should be whipped publicly upon a stage, and so sent naked to the captains of the enemy, to show them what sort of fellow drinkers and companions they took with them on their campaigns. At this some that were present laughed; and Publius Casca, he that gave the first wound to Cæsar, said, " We do ill to jest and make merry at the funeral of Cassius. But you, O Brutus," he added, " will show what esteem you have for the memory of that general, according as you punish or preserve alive those who will scoff and speak shamefully of him." To this Brutus, in great discomposure, replied, " Why then, Casca, do you ask me about it, and not do yourselves what you think fitting? " This answer of Brutus was taken for his consent to the death of these wretched men; so they were carried away and slain.

After this he gave the soldiers the reward that he had promised them; and having slightly reproved them for having fallen upon the enemy in disorder without the word of battle or command, he promised them, that if they behaved themselves bravely in the next engagement, he would give them up two cities to spoil and plunder, Thessalonica and Lacedæmon. This is the one indefensible thing of all that is found fault with in the life of Brutus; though true it may be that Antony and Cæsar were much more cruel in the rewards that they gave their soldiers after victory; for they drove out, one might almost say, all the old inhabitants of Italy, to put their soldiers in possession of other men's lands and cities. But indeed their only design and end in undertaking the war was to obtain dominion and empire, whereas Brutus, for the reputation of his virtue, could not be permitted either to overcome or save himself but with justice and honour, especially after the death of Cassius, who was generally accused of having been his adviser to some things that he had done with less clemency. But now, as in a ship, when the rudder is broken by a storm, the mariners fit and nail on some other piece of wood instead of it, striving against the danger not well, but as well as in that necessity they can, so Brutus, being at the head of so great an army, in a time of such uncertainty, having no commander equal to his need, was forced to make use of those that he had, and to do and to say many things according to their advice; which was, in effect, whatever might conduce to the bringing of Cassius's soldiers into better order. For they were very headstrong and intractable, bold and insolent in the camp for want of their general, but in the field cowardly and fearful, remembering that they had been beaten.

Neither were the affairs of Cæsar and Antony in any better posture; for they were straitened for provision, and, the camp being in a low ground, they expected to pass a very hard winter. For being driven close upon the marshes, and a great quantity of rain, as is usual in autumn, having fallen after the battle, their tents were all filled with mire and water, which through the coldness of the weather immediately froze. And while they were in this condition, there was news brought to them of their loss at sea. For Brutus's fleet fell upon their ships, which were bringing a great supply of soldiers out of Italy, and so entirely defeated them, that but very few of the men escaped being slain, and they too were forced by famine to feed upon the sails and tackle of the ship. As soon as they heard this, they made what haste they could to come to the decision of a battle, before Brutus should have notice of his good success. For it had so happened that the fight both by sea and land was on the same day, but by some misfortune, rather than the fault of his commanders, Brutus knew not of his victory twenty days after. For had he been informed of this, he would not have been brought to a second battle, since he had sufficient provisions for his army for a long time, and was very advantageously posted, his camp being well sheltered from the cold weather, and almost inaccessible to the enemy, and his being absolute master of the sea, and having at land overcome on that side wherein he himself was engaged, would have made him full of hope and confidence. But it seems the state of Rome not enduring any longer to be governed by many, but necessarily requiring a monarchy, the divine power, that it might remove out of the way the only man that was able to resist him that could control the empire, cut off his good fortune from coming to the ears of Brutus; though it came but a very little too late, for the very evening before the fight, Clodius, a deserter from the enemy, came and announced that Cæsar had received advice of the loss of his fleet, and for that reason was in such haste to come to a battle. But his story met with no credit, nor was he so much as seen by Brutus, being simply set down as one that had no good information, or invented lies to bring himself into favour.

The same night, they say, the vision appeared again to Brutus, in the same shape that it did before, but vanished without speaking. But Publius Volumnius, a philosopher, and one that had from the beginning borne arms with Brutus, makes no mention of this apparition, but says that the first eagle was covered with a swarm of bees, and that there was one of the captains whose arm of itself sweated oil of roses, and, though they often dried and wiped it, yet it would not cease; and that immediately before the battle, two eagles falling upon each other fought in the space between the two armies, that the whole field kept incredible silence and all were intent upon the spectacle, until at last that which was on Brutus's side yielded and fled. But the story of the Ethiopian is very famous, who, meeting the standard-bearer at the opening the gate of the camp, was cut to pieces by the soldiers, that took it for an ill omen.

Brutus, having brought his army into the field and set them in array against the enemy, paused a long while before he would fight; for as he was reviewing the troops, suspicions were excited and informations laid against some of them. Besides, he saw his horse not very eager to begin the action, and waiting to see what the foot would do. Then suddenly Camulatus, a very good soldier, and one whom for his valour he highly esteemed, riding hard by Brutus himself, went over to the enemy, the sight of which grieved Brutus exceedingly. So that partly out of anger, and partly out of fear of some greater treason and desertion, he immediately drew on his forces upon the enemy, the sun now declining, about three of the clock in the afternoon.

Brutus on his side had the better, and pressed hard on the left wing, which gave way and retreated; and the horse too fell in together with the foot, when they saw the enemy in disorder. But the other wing, when the officers extended the line to avoid its being encompassed, the numbers being inferior, got drawn out too thin in the centre, and was so weak here that they could not withstand the charge, but at the first onset fled. After defeating these, the enemy at once took Brutus in the rear, who all the while did all that was possible for an expert general and valiant soldier, doing everything in the peril, by counsel and by hand, that might recover the victory. But that which had been his superiority in the first fight was to his prejudice in the second. For in the first, that part of the enemy which was beaten was killed on the spot; but of Cassius's soldiers that fled, few had been slain, and those that escaped, daunted with their defeat, infected the other and larger part of the army with their want of spirit and their disorder. Here Marcus, the son of Cato, was slain, fighting and behaving himself with great bravery in the midst of the youth of the highest rank and greatest valour. He would neither fly nor give the least ground, but still fighting and declaring who he was and naming his father's name, he fell upon a heap of dead bodies of the enemy. And of the rest, the bravest were slain in defending Brutus.

There was in the field one Lucilius, an excellent man and a friend of Brutus, who, seeing some barbarian horse taking no notice of any other in the pursuit, but galloping at full speed after Brutus, resolved to stop them, though with the hazard of his life; and, letting himself fall a little behind, he told them that he was Brutus. They believed him the rather, because he prayed to be carried to Antony, as if he feared Cæsar, but durst trust him. They, overjoyed with their prey, and thinking themselves wonderfully fortunate, carried him along with them in the night, having first sent messengers to Antony of their coming. He was much pleased, and came to meet them; and all the rest that heard that Brutus was taken and brought alive flocked together to see him, some pitying his fortune, others accusing him of a meanness unbecoming his former glory, that out of too much love of life he would be a prey to barbarians. When they came near together, Antony stood still, considering with himself in what manner he should receive Brutus; but Lucilius, being brought up to him, with great confidence said: " Be assured, Antony, that no enemy either has taken or ever shall take Marcus Brutus alive (forbid it, heaven, that fortune should

ever so much prevail above virtue!), but he shall be found, alive
or dead, as becomes himself. As for me, I am come hither by
a cheat that I put upon your soldiers, and am ready, upon this
occasion, to suffer any severities you will inflict." All were
amazed to hear Lucilius speak these words. But Antony,
turning himself to those that brought him, said: "I perceive,
my fellow-soldiers, that you are concerned, and take it ill that
you have been thus deceived, and think yourselves abused and
injured by it; but know that you have met with a booty better
than that you sought. For you were in search of an enemy,
but you have brought me here a friend. For indeed I am uncertain how I should have used Brutus, if you had brought him
alive; but of this I am sure, that it is better to have such men
as Lucilius our friends than our enemies." Having said this,
he embraced Lucilius, and for the present commended him to
the care of one of his friends, and ever after found him a steady
and a faithful friend.

Brutus had now passed a little brook, running among trees
and under steep rocks, and, it being night, would go no further,
but sat down in a hollow place with a great rock projecting
before it, with a few of his officers and friends about him. At
first, looking up to heaven, that was then full of stars, he repeated
two verses, one of which, Volumnius writes, was this:—

> " Punish, great Jove, the author of these ills."

The other he says he has forgot. Soon after, naming severally
all his friends that had been slain before his face in the battle,
he groaned heavily, especially at the mentioning of Flavius and
Labeo, the latter his lieutenant, and the other chief officer of his
engineers. In the meantime, one of his companions, that was
very thirsty and saw Brutus in the same condition, took his
helmet and ran to the brook for water, when a noise being heard
from the other side of the river, Volumnius, taking Dardanus,
Brutus's armour-bearer, with him, went out to see what it was.
They returned in a short space, and inquired about the water.
Brutus, smiling with much meaning, said to Volumnius, "It is
all drunk; but you shall have some more fetched." But he
that had brought the first water, being sent again, was in great
danger of being taken by the enemy, and having received a
wound, with much difficulty escaped.

Now Brutus guessing that not many of his men were slain in
the fight, Statyllius undertook to dash through the enemy (for
there was no other way), and to see what was become of their

camp; and promised, if he found all things there safe, to hold up a torch for a signal, and then return. The torch was held up, Statyllius got safe to the camp; but when after a long time he did not return, Brutus said, " If Statyllius be alive, he will come back." But it happened that in his return he fell into the enemy's hands, and was slain.

The night now being far spent, Brutus, as he was sitting, leaned his head towards his servant Clitus, and spoke to him; he answered him not, but fell a weeping. After that he drew aside his armour-bearer, Dardanus, and had some discourse with him in private. At last, speaking to Volumnius in Greek, he reminded him of their common studies and former discipline and begged that he would take hold of his sword with him, and help him to thrust it through him. Volumnius put away his request, and several others did the like; and some one saying, that there was no staying there, but they needs must fly, Brutus, rising up, said, " Yes, indeed, we must fly, but not with our feet, but with our hands." Then giving each of them his right hand, with a countenance full of pleasure, he said, that he found an infinite satisfaction in this, that none of his friends had been false to him; that as for fortune, he was angry with that only for his country's sake; as for himself, he thought himself much more happy than they who had overcome, not only as he had been a little time ago, but even now in his present condition; since he was leaving behind him such a reputation of his virtue as none of the conquerors with all their arms and riches should ever be able to acquire, no more than they could hinder posterity from believing and saying, that being unjust and wicked men, they had destroyed the just and the good, and usurped a power to which they had no right. After this, having exhorted and entreated all about him to provide for their own safety, he withdrew from them with two or three only of his peculiar friends; Strato was one of these, with whom he had contracted an acquaintance when they studied rhetoric together. Him he placed next to himself, and, taking hold of the hilt of his sword and directing it with both his hands, fell upon it, and killed himself. But others say, that not he himself, but Strato, at the earnest entreaty of Brutus, turning aside his head, held the sword, upon which he violently throwing himself, it pierced his breast, and he immediately died. This same Strato, Messala, a friend of Brutus, being after reconciled to Cæsar, brought to him once at his leisure, and with tears in his eyes said, " This, O Cæsar, is the man that did the last friendly office to my beloved Brutus." Upon which Cæsar received him kindly; and had good use of him in his labours and his battles at Actium, being one of the Greeks that proved their bravery in his service. It is reported of Messala himself, that, when Cæsar once gave him this commendation, that though he was his fiercest enemy at Philippi in the cause of Brutus, yet he had shown himself his most entire friend in the fight of Actium, he answered, "You have always found me, Cæsar, on the best and justest side."

Brutus's dead body was found by Antony, who commanded the richest purple mantle that he had to be thrown over it, and afterwards the mantle being stolen, he found the thief, and had him put to death. He sent the ashes of Brutus to his mother Servilia. As for Porcia his wife, Nicolaus the philosopher and Valerius Maximus write, that, being desirous to die, but being hindered by her friends, who continually watched her, she snatched some burning charcoal out of the fire, and, shutting it close in her mouth, stifled herself, and died. Though there is a letter current from Brutus to his friends, in which he laments the death of Porcia, and accuses them for neglecting her so that she desired to die rather than languish with her disease. So that it seems Nicolaus was mistaken in the time; for this epistle (if it indeed is authentic and truly Brutus's) gives us to understand the malady and love of Porcia, and the way in which her death occurred.

## THE COMPARISON OF DION AND BRUTUS

THERE are noble points in abundance in the characters of these two men, and one to be first mentioned is their attaining such a height of greatness upon such inconsiderable means; and on this score Dion has by far the advantage. For he had no partner to contest his glory, as Brutus had in Cassius, who was not, indeed, his equal in proved virtue and honour, yet contributed quite as much to the service of the war by his boldness, skill, and activity; and some there be who impute to him the rise and beginning of the whole enterprise, saying that it was he who roused Brutus, till then indisposed to stir, into action against Cæsar. Whereas Dion seems of himself to have provided not only arms, ships, and soldiers, but likewise friends and partners for the enterprise. Neither did he, as Brutus, collect money and forces from the war itself, but, on the contrary, laid out of his own substance, and employed the very means of his private

sustenance in exile for the liberty of his country.  Besides this,
Brutus and Cassius, when they fled to Rome, could not live safe or
quiet, being condemned to death and pursued, and were thus of
necessity forced to take arms and hazard their lives in their own
defence, to save themselves, rather than their country.  On
the other hand, Dion enjoyed more ease, was more safe, and his
life more pleasant in his banishment, than was the tyrant's who
had banished him, when he flew to action, and ran the risk of all
to save Sicily.

Take notice, too, that it was not the same thing for the
Sicilians to be freed from Dionysius, and for the Romans to be
freed from Cæsar.  The former owned himself a tyrant, and
vexed Sicily with a thousand oppressions; whereas Cæsar's
supremacy, certainly, in the process for attaining it, had inflicted
no trouble on its opponents, but, once established and victorious,
it had indeed the name and appearance, but fact that was cruel
or tyrannical there was none.  On the contrary, in the malady
of the times and the need of a monarchical government, he might
be thought to have been sent as the gentlest physician, by no
other than a divine intervention.  And thus the common people
instantly regretted Cæsar, and grew enraged and implacable
against those that killed him.  Whereas Dion's chief offence in
the eyes of his fellow-citizens was his having let Dionysius escape,
and not having demolished the former tyrant's tomb.

In the actual conduct of war, Dion was a commander without
fault, improving to the utmost those counsels which he himself
gave, and where others led him into disaster correcting and
turning everything to the best.  But Brutus seems to have
shown little wisdom in engaging in the final battle, which was
to decide everything, and when he failed not to have done his
business in seeking a remedy; he gave all up, and abandoned
his hopes, not venturing against fortune even as far as Pompey
did, when he had still means enough to rely on in his troops, and
was clearly master of all the seas with his ships.

The greatest thing charged on Brutus is, that he, being saved
by Cæsar's kindness, having saved all the friends whom he chose
to ask for, he moreover accounted a friend, and preferred above
many, did yet lay violent hands upon his preserver.  Nothing
like this could be objected against Dion; quite the contrary;
whilst he was of Dionysius's family and his friend, he did good
service and was useful to him; but driven from his country,
wronged in his wife, and his estate lost, he openly entered upon
a war just and lawful.  Does not, however, the matter turn the

other way? For the chief glory of both was their hatred of tyranny, and abhorrence of wickedness. This was unmixed and sincere in Brutus; for he had no private quarrel with Cæsar, but went into the risk singly for the liberty of his country. The other, had he not been privately injured, had not fought. This is plain from Plato's epistles, where it is shown that he was turned out, and did not forsake the court to wage war upon Dionysius. Moreover, the public good made Brutus Pompey's friend (instead of his enemy as he had been) and Cæsar's enemy; since he proposed for his hatred and his friendship no other end and standard but justice. Dion was very serviceable to Dionysius whilst in favour; when no longer trusted, he grew angry and fell to arms. And, for this reason, not even were his own friends all of them satisfied with his undertaking, or quite asssured that, having overcome Dionysius, he might not settle the government on himself, deceiving his fellow-citizens by some less obnoxious name than tyranny. But the very enemies of Brutus would say that he had no other end or aim, from first to last, save only to restore to the Roman people their ancient government.

And apart from what has just been said, the adventure against Dionysius was nothing equal with that against Cæsar. For none that was familiarly conversant with Dionysius but scorned him for his life of idle amusement with wine, women, and dice; whereas it required an heroic soul and a truly intrepid and unquailing spirit so much as to entertain the thought of crushing Cæsar, so formidable for his ability, his power, and his fortune, whose very name disturbed the slumbers of the Parthian and Indian kings. Dion was no sooner seen in Sicily but thousands ran in to him and joined him against Dionysius; whereas the renown of Cæsar, even when dead, gave strength to his friends; and his very name so heightened the person that took it, that from a simple boy he presently became the chief of the Romans; and he could use it for a spell against the enmity and power of Antony. If any object that it cost Dion great trouble and difficulties to overcome the tyrant, whereas Brutus slew Cæsar naked and unprovided, yet this itself was the result of the most consummate policy and conduct, to bring it about that a man so guarded around, and so fortified at all points, should be taken naked and unprovided. For it was not on the sudden, nor alone, nor with a few, that he fell upon and killed Cæsar; but after long concerting the plot, and placing confidence in a great many men, not one of whom deceived him. For he either at once discerned the best men, or by confiding in them made them good. But Dion, either making a wrong judgment, trusted himself with ill men, or else by his employing them made ill men of good; either of the two would be a reflection on a wise man. Plato also is severe upon him, for choosing such for friends as betrayed him.

Besides, when Dion was killed, none appeared to revenge his death. Whereas Brutus, even amongst his enemies, had Antony that buried him splendidly; and Cæsar also took care his honours should be preserved. There stood at Milan in Gaul, within the Alps, a brazen statue, which Cæsar in aftertimes noticed (being a real likeness, and a fine work of art), and passing by it presently stopped short, and in the hearing of many commanded the magistrates to come before him. He told them their town had broken their league, harbouring an enemy. The magistrates at first simply denied the thing, and, not knowing what he meant, looked one upon another, when Cæsar, turning towards the statue and gathering his brows, said, " Pray is not that our enemy who stands there? " They were all in confusion, and had nothing to answer; but he, smiling, much commended the Gauls, as who had been firm to their friends, though in adversity, and ordered that the statue should remain standing as he found it.

# ARATUS

The Philosopher Chrysippus, O Polycrates, quotes an ancient proverb, not as really it should be, apprehending, I suppose, that it sounded too harshly, but so as he thought it would run best, in these words:—

" Who praise their fathers but the generous sons? "

But Dionysodorus the Trœzenian proves him to be wrong, and restores the true reading, which is thus:—

" Who praise their fathers but degenerate sons? "

telling us that the proverb is meant to stop the mouth of those who, having no merit of their own, take refuge in the virtues of their ancestors, and make their advantage of praising them. But, as Pindar hath it—

" He that by nature doth inherit
From ancestors a noble spirit,"

as you do, who made your life the copy of the fairest originals of your family,—such, I say, may take great satisfaction in being reminded, both by hearing others speak and speaking themselves, of the best of their progenitors. For they assume not the glory of praises earned by others out of any want of worth of their own, but affiliating their own deeds to those of their ancestors, give them honour as the authors both of their descent and manners. Therefore I have sent to you the life which I have written of your fellow-citizen and forefather, Aratus, to whom you are no discredit in point either of reputation or of authority, not as though you had not been most diligently careful to inform yourself from the beginning concerning his actions, but that your sons, Polycrates and Pythocles, may both by hearing and reading become familiar with those family examples which it behoves them to follow and imitate. It is a piece of self-love, and not of the love of virtue, to imagine one has already attained to what is best.

The city of Sicyon, from the time that it first fell off from the pure and Doric aristocracy (its harmony being destroyed, and a mere series of seditions and personal contests of popular leaders ensuing), continued to be distempered and unsettled, changing from one tyrant to another, until, Cleon being slain, Timoclides and Clinias, men of the most repute and power amongst the citizens, were chosen to the magistracy. And the commonwealth now seeming to be in a pretty settled condition, Timoclides died, and Abantidas, the son of Paseas, to possess himself of the tyranny, killed Clinias, and, of his kindred and friends, slew some and banished others. He sought also to kill his son Aratus, whom he left behind him, being but seven years old. This boy in the general disorder getting out of the house with those that fled, and wandering about the city helpless and in great fear, by chance got undiscovered into the house of a woman who was Abantidas's sister, but married to Prophantus, the brother of Clinias, her name being Soso. She, being of a generous temper, and believing the boy had by some supernatural guidance fled to her for shelter, hid him in the house, and at night sent him away to Argos.

Aratus, being thus delivered and secured from this danger, conceived from the first and ever after nourished a vehement and burning hatred against tyrants, which strengthened with his years. Being therefore bred up amongst his father's acquaintance and friends at Argos with a liberal education, and perceiving his body to promise good health and stature, he addicted him-

self to the exercises of the palæstra, to that degree that he competed in the five games, and gained some crowns; and indeed in
his statues one may observe a certain kind of athletic cast, and
the sagacity and majesty of his countenance does not dissemble
his full diet and the use of the hoe. Whence it came to pass
that he less studied eloquence than perhaps became a statesman,
and yet he was more accomplished in speaking than many
believe, judging by the commentaries which he left behind him,
written carelessly and, by the way, as fast as he could do it, and
in such words as first came to his mind.

In the course of time, Dinias and Aristoteles the logician killed
Abantidas, who used to be present in the market-place at their
discussions, and to make one in them; till they taking the
occasion, insensibly accustomed him to the practice, and so had
opportunity to contrive and execute a plot against him. After
him Paseas, the father of Abantidas, taking upon him the government, was assassinated by Nicocles, who himself set up for
tyrant. Of him it is related that he was strikingly like Periander,
the son of Cypselus, just as it is said that Orontes the Persian
bore a great resemblance to Alcmæon, the son of Amphiaraus,
and that Lacedæmonian youth, whom Myrsilus relates to have
been trodden to pieces by the crowd of those that came to see
him upon that report, to Hector.

This Nicocles governed four months, in which, after he had
done all kinds of mischief to the city, he very nearly let it fall
into the hands of the Ætolians. By this time Aratus, being
grown a youth, was in much esteem, both for his noble birth, and
his spirit and disposition, which, while neither insignificant nor
wanting in energy, were solid, and tempered with a steadiness of
judgment beyond his years. For which reason the exiles had
their eyes most upon him, nor did Nicocles less observe his
motions, but secretly spied and watched him, not out of apprehension of any such considerable or utterly audacious attempt,
but suspecting he held correspondence with the kings, who were
his father's friends and acquaintance. And, indeed, Aratus first
attempted this way; but finding that Antigonus, who had
promised fair, neglected him and delayed the time, and that his
hopes from Egypt and Ptolemy were long to wait for, he determined to cut off the tyrant by himself.

And first he broke his mind to Aristomachus and Ecdelus, the
one an exile of Sicyon, the other, Ecdelus, an Arcadian of Megalopolis, a philosopher, and a man of action, having been the
familiar friend of Arcesilaus the Academic at Athens. These

readily consenting, he communicated with the other exiles, whereof some few, being ashamed to seem to despair of success, engaged in the design; but most of them endeavoured to divert him from his purpose, as one that for want of experience was too rash and daring.

Whilst he was consulting to seize upon some post in Sicyonia, from whence he might make war upon the tyrant, there came to Argos a certain Sicyonian, newly escaped out of prison, brother to Xenocles, one of the exiles, who, being by him presented to Aratus, informed him that that part of the wall over which he escaped was, inside, almost level with the ground, adjoining a rocky and elevated place, and that from the outside it might be scaled with ladders. Aratus, hearing this, despatches away Xenocles with two of his own servants, Seuthas and Technon, to view the wall, resolving, if possible, secretly and with one risk to hazard all on a single trial, rather than carry on a contest as a private man against a tyrant by long war and open force. Xenocles, therefore, with his companions, returning, having taken the height of the wall, and declaring the place not to be impossible or indeed difficult to get over, but that it was not easy to approach it undiscovered by reason of some small but uncommonly savage and noisy dogs belonging to a gardener hard by, he immediately undertook the business.

Now the preparation of arms gave no jealousy, because robberies and petty forays were at that time common everywhere between one set of people and another; and for the ladders, Euphranor, the machine-maker, made them openly, his trade rendering him unsuspected, though one of the exiles. As for men, each of his friends in Argos furnished him with ten apiece out of those few they had, and he armed thirty of his own servants, and hired some few soldiers of Xenophilus, the chief of the robber captains, to whom it was given out that they were to march into the territory of Sicyon to seize the king's stud; most of them were sent before, in small parties, to the tower of Polygnotus, with orders to wait there; Caphisias also was despatched beforehand lightly armed, with four others, who were, as soon as it was dark, to come to the gardener's house, pretending to be travellers, and procuring their lodging there, to shut up him and his dogs; for there was no other way to getting past. And for the ladders, they had been made to take in pieces, and were put into chests, and sent before, hidden upon waggons. In the meantime, some of the spies of Nicocles appearing in Argos, and being said to go privately about watching Aratus, he came early in the morning into the market-place, showing himself openly and conversing with his friends; then he anointed himself in the exercise ground, and, taking with him thence some of the young men that used to drink and spend their time with him, he went home; and presently after several of his servants were seen about the market-place, one carrying garlands, another buying flambeaux, and a third speaking to the women that used to sing and play at banquets, all of which things the spies observing were deceived, and said, laughing to one another, "Certainly nothing can be more timorous than a tyrant, if Nicocles, being master of so great a city and so numerous a force, stands in fear of a youth that spends what he has to subsist upon in his banishment in pleasures and day-debauches;" and, being thus imposed upon, they returned home.

But Aratus, departing immediately after his morning meal, and coming to his soldiers at Polygnotus's tower, led them to Nemea; where he disclosed to most of them, for the first time, his true design, making them large promises and fair speeches, and marched towards the city, giving for the word Apollo victorious, proportioning his march to the motion of the moon, so as to have the benefit of her light upon the way, and to be in the garden, which was close to the wall, just as she was setting. Here Caphisias came to him, who had not secured the dogs, which had run away before he could catch them, but had only made sure of the gardener. Upon which most of the company being out of heart and desiring to retreat, Aratus encouraged them to go on, promising to retire in case the dogs were too troublesome; at the same time sending forward those that carried the ladders, conducted by Ecdelus and Mnasitheus, he followed them himself leisurely, the dogs already barking very loud and following the steps of Ecdelus and his companion. However, they got to the wall, and reared the ladders with safety. But as the foremost men were mounting them, the captain of the watch that was to be relieved by the morning guard passed on his way with the bell; and there were many lights, and a noise of people coming up. Hearing which, they clapt themselves close to the ladders, and so were unobserved; but as the other watch also was coming up to meet this, they were in extreme danger of being discovered. But when this also went by without observing them, immediately Mnasitheus and Ecdelus got upon the wall, and, possessing themselves of the approaches inside and out, sent away Technon to Aratus, desiring him to make all the haste he could.

Now there was no great distance from the garden to the wall and to the tower in which latter a large hound was kept. The hound did not hear their steps of himself, whether that he were naturally drowsy, or overwearied the day before, but, the gardener's curs awaking him, he first began to growl and grumble in response, and then as they passed by to bark out aloud. And the barking was now so great, that the sentinel opposite shouted out to the dog's keeper to know why the dog kept such a barking, and whether anything was the matter; who answered, that it was nothing but only that his dog had been set barking by the lights of the watch and the noise of the bell. This reply much encouraged Aratus's soldiers, who thought the dog's keeper was privy to their design, and wished to conceal what was passing, and that many others in the city were of the conspiracy. But when they came to scale the wall, the attempt then appeared both to require time and to be full of danger, for the ladders shook and tottered extremely unless they mounted them leisurely and one by one, and time pressed, for the cocks began to crow, and the country people that used to bring things to the market would be coming to the town directly. Therefore Aratus made haste to get up himself, forty only of the company being already upon the wall, and, staying but for a few more of those that were below, he made straight to the tyrant's house and the general's office, where the mercenary soldiers passed the night, and, coming suddenly upon them, and taking them prisoners without killing any one of them, he immediately sent to all his friends in their houses to desire them to come to him, which they did from all quarters. By this time the day began to break, and the theatre was filled with a multitude that were held in suspense by uncertain reports and knew nothing distinctly of what had happened, until a public crier came forward and proclaimed that Aratus, the son of Clinias, invited the citizens to recover their liberty.

Then at last assured that what they had so long looked for was come to pass, they pressed in throngs to the tyrant's gates to set them on fire. And such a flame was kindled, the whole house catching fire, that it was seen as far as Corinth; so that the Corinthians, wondering what the matter could be, were upon the point of coming to their assistance. Nicocles fled away secretly out of the city by means of certain underground passages, and the soldiers helping the Sicyonians to quench the fire, plundered the house. This Aratus hindered not, but divided also the rest of the riches of the tyrant amongst the citizens. In this exploit, not one of these engaged in it was slain, nor any of the contrary party, fortune so ordering the action as to be clear and free from civil bloodshed. He restored eighty exiles who had been expelled by Nicocles, and no less than five hundred who had been driven out by former tyrants and had endured a long banishment, pretty nearly, by this time, of fifty years' duration. These returning, most of them very poor, were impatient to enter upon their former possessions, and, proceeding to their several farms and houses, gave great perplexity to Aratus, who considered that the city without was envied for its liberty and aimed at by Antigonus, and within was full of disorder and sedition. Wherefore, as things stood, he thought it best to associate it to the Achæan community, and so, although Dorians, they of their own will took upon them the name and citizenship of the Achæans, who at that time had neither great repute nor much power. For the most of them lived in small towns, and their territory was neither large nor fruitful, and the neighbouring sea was almost wholly without a harbour, breaking direct upon a rocky shore. But yet these above others made it appear that the Grecian courage was invincible, whensoever it could only have order and concord within itself and a prudent general to direct it. For though they had scarcely been counted as any part of the ancient Grecian power, and at this time it did not equal the strength of one ordinary city, yet by prudence and unanimity, and because they knew not how to envy and malign, but to obey and follow him amongst them that was most eminent for virtue, they not only preserved their own liberty in the midst of so many great cities, military powers, and monarchies, but went on steadily saving and delivering from slavery great numbers of the Greeks.

As for Aratus, he was in his behaviour a true statesman, high-minded, and more intent upon the public than his private concerns, a bitter hater of tyrants, making the common good the rule and law of his friendships and enmities. So that indeed he seems not to have been so faithful a friend, as he was a reasonable and gentle enemy, ready, according to the needs of the state, to suit himself on occasion to either side; concord between nations, brotherhood between cities, the council and the assembly unanimous in their votes, being the objects above all other blessings to which he was passionately devoted; backward, indeed, and diffident in the use of arms and open force, but in effecting a purpose underhand, and outwitting cities and potentates without observation, most politic and dexterous. There-

fore, though he succeeded beyond hope in many enterprises
which he undertook, yet he seems to have left quite as many
unattempted, though feasible enough, for want of assurance.
For it should seem, that as the sight of certain beasts is strong
in the night but dim by day, the tenderness of the humours of
their eyes not bearing the contact of the light, so there is also
one kind of human skill and sagacity which is easily daunted
and disturbed in actions done in the open day and before the
world, and recovers all its self-possession in secret and covert
enterprises; which inequality is occasioned in noble minds for
want of philosophy, a mere wild and uncultivated fruit of a
virtue without true knowledge coming up; as might be made
out by examples.

Aratus, therefore, having associated himself and his city to
the Achæans, served in the cavalry, and made himself much
beloved by his commanding officers for his exact obedience; for
though he had made so large an addition to the common strength
as that of his own credit and the power of his country, yet he
was as ready as the most ordinary person to be commanded by
the Achæan general of the time being, whether he were a man of
Dynæ, or of Tritæa, or any yet meaner town than these.   Having
also a present of five-and-twenty talents sent him from the king,
he took them, but gave them all to his fellow-citizens, who
wanted money, amongst other purposes, for the redemption of
those who had been taken prisoners.

But the exiles being by no means to be satisfied, disturbing
continually those that were in possession of their estates, Sicyon
was in great danger of falling into perfect desolation; so that,
having no hope left but in the kindness of Ptolemy, he resolved
to sail to him, and to beg so much money of him as might
reconcile all parties.   So he set sail from Mothone beyond Malea,
designing to make the direct passage.   But the pilot not being
able to keep the vessel up against a strong wind and high waves
that came in from the open sea, he was driven from his course,
and with much ado got to shore in Andras, an enemy's land,
possessed by Antigonus, who had a garrison there.   To avoid
which he immediately landed, and, leaving the ship, went up
into the country a good way from the sea, having along with him
only one friend, called Timanthes; and throwing themselves
into some ground thickly covered with wood, they had but an
ill night's rest of it.   Not long after, the commander of the
troops came, and, inquiring for Aratus, was deceived by his
servants, who had been instructed to say that he had fled at

once over into the island of Eubœa. However, he declared the ship, the property on board of her, and the servants, to be lawful prize, and detained them accordingly. As for Aratus, after some few days in his extremity, by good fortune a Roman ship happened to put in just at the spot in which he made his abode, sometimes peeping out to seek his opportunity, sometimes keeping close. She was bound for Syria; but going aboard, he agreed with the master to land him in Caria. In which voyage he met with no less danger on the sea than before. From Caria being after much time arrived in Egypt, he immediately went to the king, who had a great kindness for him, and had received from him many presents of drawings and paintings out of Greece. Aratus had a very good judgment in them, and always took care to collect and send him the most curious and finished works, especially those of Pamphilus and Melanthus.

For the Sicyonian pieces were still in the height of their reputation, as being the only ones whose colours were lasting; so that Apelles himself, even after he had become well known and admired, went thither, and gave a talent to be admitted into the society of the painters there, not so much to partake of their skill, which he wanted not, but of their credit. And accordingly Aratus, when he freed the city, immediately took down the representations of the rest of the tyrants, but demurred a long time about that of Aristratus, who flourished in the time of Philip. For this Aristratus was painted by Melanthus and his scholars, standing by a chariot, in which a figure of Victory was carried, Apelles himself having had a hand in it, as Polemon the geographer reports. It was an extraordinary piece, and therefore Aratus was fain to spare it for the workmanship, and yet, instigated by the hatred he bore the tyrants, commanded it to be taken down. But Neacles the painter, one of Aratus's friends, entreated him, it is said, with tears in his eyes, to spare it, and, finding he did not prevail with him, told him at last he should carry on his war with the tyrants, but with the tyrants alone: " Let therefore the chariot and the Victory stand, and I will take means for the removal of Aristratus; " to which Aratus consenting, Neacles blotted out Aristratus, and in his place painted a palm-tree, not daring to add anything else of his own invention. The feet of the defaced figure of Aristratus are said to have escaped notice, and to be hid under the chariot. By these means Aratus got favour with the king, who, after he was more fully acquainted with him, loved him so much the more, and gave him for the relief of his city one hundred and fifty talents; forty of which he immediately carried away with him, when he sailed to Peloponnesus, but the rest the king divided into instalments, and sent them to him afterwards at different times.

Assuredly it was a great thing to procure for his fellow-citizens a sum of money, a small portion of which had been sufficient, when presented by a king to other captains and popular leaders, to induce them to turn dishonest, and betray and give away their native countries to him. But it was a much greater, that by means of this money he effected a reconciliation and good understanding between the rich and poor, and created quiet and security for the whole people. His moderation, also, amidst so great power was very admirable. For being declared sole arbitrator and plenipotentiary for settling the questions of property in the case of the exiles, he would not accept the commission alone, but, associating with himself fifteen of the citizens, with great pains and trouble he succeeded in adjusting matters, and established peace and good-will in the city, for which good service, not only all the citizens in general bestowed extraordinary honours upon him, but the exiles, apart by themselves, erecting his statue in brass, inscribed on it these elegiac verses:—

> " Your counsels, deeds, and skill for Greece in war
> Known beyond Hercules's pillars are;
> But we this image, O Aratus, gave,
> Of you who saved us, to the gods who save,
> By you from exile to our homes restored,
> That virtue and that justice to record,
> To which the blessing Sicyon owes this day
> Of wealth that's shared alike, and laws that all obey."

By his success in effecting these things, Aratus secured himself from the envy of his fellow-citizens, on account of the benefits they felt he had done them; but King Antigonus being troubled in his mind about him, and designing either wholly to bring him over to his party, or else to make him suspected by Ptolemy, besides other marks of his favour shown to him, who had little mind to receive them, added this too, that, sacrificing to the gods in Corinth, he sent portions to Aratus at Sicyon, and at the feast, where were many guests, he said openly, " I thought this Sicyonian youth had been only a lover of liberty and of his fellow-citizens, but now I look upon him as a good judge of the manners and actions of kings. For formerly he despised us, and, placing his hopes further off, admired the Egyptian riches, hearing so much of their elephants, fleets, and palaces. But after seeing all these at a nearer distance, perceiving them to be but mere stage show and pageantry, he is now come over to us. And for my part I willingly receive him, and, resolving to make great use of him myself, command you to look upon him as a friend." These words were soon taken hold of by those that envied and maligned him, who strove which of them should, in their letters to Ptolemy, attack him with the worst calumnies, so that Ptolemy sent to expostulate the matter with him; so much envy and ill-will did there always attend the so much contended for, and so ardently and passionately aspired to, friendships of princes and great men.

But Aratus, being now for the first time chosen general of the Achæans, ravaged the country of Locris and Calydon, just over against Achæa, and then went to assist the Bœotians with ten thousand soldiers, but came not up to them until after the battle near Chæronea had been fought, in which they were beaten by the Ætolians, with the loss of Abœocritus the Bœotarch, and a thousand men besides. A year after, being again elected general, he resolved to attempt the capture of the Acro-Corinthus, not so much for the advantage of the Sicyonians or Achæans, as considering that by expelling the Macedonian garrison he should free all Greece alike from a tyranny which oppressed every part of her. Chares, the Athenian, having the good fortune to get the better, in a certain battle, of the king's generals, wrote to the people of Athens that this victory was "sister to that at Marathon." And so may this action be very safely termed sister to those of Pelopidas the Theban and Thrasybulus the Athenian, in which they slew the tyrants; except, perhaps, it exceed them upon this account, that it was not against natural Grecians, but against a foreign and stranger domination. The Isthmus, rising like a bank between the seas, collects into a single spot and compresses together the whole continent of Greece; and Acro-Corinthus, being a high mountain springing up out of the very middle of what here is Greece, whensoever it is held with a garrison, stands in the way and cuts off all Peloponnesus from intercourse of every kind, free passage of men and arms, and all traffic by sea and land, and makes him lord of all that is master of it. Wherefore the younger Philip did not jest, but said very true, when he called the city of Corinth "the fetters of Greece." So that this post was always much contended for, especially by the kings and tyrants; and so vehemently was it longed for by Antigonus, that his passion for it came little short of that of frantic love; he was continually occupied with devising how to take it by surprise from those that were then masters of it, since he despaired to do it by open force.

Therefore Alexander, who held the place, being dead, poisoned by him, as is reported, and his wife Nicæa succeeding in the government and the possession of Acro-Corinthus, he immediately made use of his son, Demetrius, and, giving her pleasing hopes of a royal marriage and of a happy life with a youth, whom a woman now growing old might well find agreeable, with this lure of his son he succeeded in taking her; but the place itself she did not deliver up, but continued to hold it with a very strong garrison, of which he seeming to take no notice, celebrated the wedding in Corinth, entertaining them with shows and banquets every day, as one that had nothing else in his mind but to give himself up for a while to indulgence in pleasure and mirth. But when the moment came, and Amœbeus began to sing in the theatre, he waited himself upon Nicæa to the play, she being carried in a royally decorated chair, extremely pleased with her new honour, not dreaming of what was intended. As soon, therefore, as they were come to the turning which led up to the citadel, he desired her to go on before him to the theatre, but for himself, bidding farewell to the music, farewell to the wedding, he went on faster than one would have thought his age would have admitted to the Acro-Corinthus, and, finding the gate shut, knocked with his staff, commanding them to open, which they within, being amazed, did. And having thus made himself master of the place, he could not contain himself for joy; but, though an old man, and one that had seen so many turns of fortune, he must needs revel it in the open streets and the midst of the market-place, crowned with garlands and attended with flute-women, inviting everybody he met to partake in his festivity. So much more does joy without discretion transport and agitate the mind than either fear or sorrow. Antigonus, therefore, having in this manner possessed himself of Acro-Corinthus, put a garrison into it of those he trusted most, making Persæus the philosopher governor.

Now Aratus, even in the lifetime of Alexander, had made an attempt, but, a confederacy being made between Alexander and the Achæans, he desisted. But now he started afresh, with a new plan of effecting the thing, which was this: there were in Corinth four brothers, Syrians born, one of whom, called Diocles, served as a soldier in the garrison, but the three others, having stolen some gold of the king's, came to Sicyon, to one Ægias, a banker, whom Aratus made use of in his business. To him they immediately sold part of their gold, and the rest, one of them, called Erginus, coming often thither, exchanged by parcels. Becoming, by this means, familiarly acquainted with Ægias, and being by him led into discourses concerning the fortress, he told him that in going up to his brother he had observed, in the face of the rock, a side cleft, leading to that part of the wall of the castle which was lower than the rest. At which Ægias joking with him and saying, " So, you wise man, for the sake of a little gold you have broken into the king's treasure; when you might, if you chose, get money in abundance for a single hour's work, burglary, you know, and treason being punished with the same death." Erginus laughed and told him then, he would break the thing to Diocles (for he did not altogether trust his other brothers), and, returning within a few days, he bargained to conduct Aratus to that part of the wall where it was no more than fifteen feet high, and to do what else should be necessary, together with his brother Diocles.

Aratus, therefore, agreed to give them sixty talents if he succeeded, but if he failed in his enterprise, and yet he and they came off safe, then he would give each of them a house and a talent. Now the threescore talents being to be deposited in the hands of Ægias for Erginus and his partners, and Aratus neither having so much by him, nor willing, by borrowing it from others, to give any one a suspicion of his design, he pawned his plate and his wife's golden ornaments to Ægias for the money. For so high was his temper, and so strong his passion for noble actions, that, even as he had heard that Phocion and Epaminondas were the best and justest of the Greeks, because they refused the greatest presents, and would not surrender their duty for money, so he now chose to be at the expense of this enterprise privately, and to advance all the cost out of his own property, taking the whole hazard on himself for the sake of the rest that did not so much as know what he was doing. And who indeed can withhold, even now, his admiration for and his sympathy with the generous mind of one, who paid so largely to purchase so great a risk, and lent out his richest possessions to have an opportunity to expose his own life, by entering among his enemies in the dead of the night, without desiring any other security for them than the hope of a noble success.

Now the enterprise, though dangerous enough in itself, was made much more so by an error happening through mistake in the very beginning. For Technon, one of Aratus's servants, was sent away to Diocles, that they might together view the wall. Now he had never seen Diocles, but made no question of knowing him by the marks Erginus had given him of him; namely, that he had curly hair, a swarthy complexion, and no beard. Being come, therefore, to the appointed place, he stayed waiting for Erginus and Diocles outside the town, in front of the place called Ornis. In the meantime, Dionysius, elder brother to Erginus and Diocles, who knew nothing at all of the matter, but much resembled Diocles, happened to pass by. Technon, upon this likeness, all being in accordance with what he had been told, asked him if he knew Erginus; and on his replying that he was his brother, taking it for granted that he was speaking with Diocles, not so much as asking his name or staying for any other token, he gave him his hand, and began to discourse with him and ask him questions about matters agreed upon with Erginus. Dionysius, cunningly taking the advantage of his mistake, seemed to understand him very well, and returning towards the city, led him on, still talking, without any suspicion. And being now near the gate, he was just about to seize on him, when by chance again Erginus met them, and, apprehending the cheat and the danger, beckoned to Technon to make his escape, and immediately both of them, betaking themselves to their heels, ran away as fast as they could to Aratus, who for all this despaired not, but immediately sent away Erginus to Dionysius to bribe him to hold his tongue. And he not only effected that, but also brought him along with him to Aratus. But when they had him, they no longer left him at liberty, but binding him, they kept him close shut up in a room, whilst they prepared for executing their design.

All things being now ready, he commanded the rest of his forces to pass the night by their arms, and taking with him four hundred chosen men, few of whom knew what they were going about, he led them to the gates by the temple of Juno. It was the midst of summer, and the moon was at full, and the night so clear without any clouds, that there was danger lest the arms glistening in the moonlight should discover them. But as the foremost of them came near the city, a mist came off from the sea, and darkened the city itself and the outskirts about it. Then the rest of them, sitting down, put off their shoes, because men both make less noise and also climb surer if they go up ladders barefooted, but Erginus, taking with him seven young men dressed like travellers, got unobserved to the gate, and killed the sentry with the other guards. And at the same time the ladders were clapped to the walls, and Aratus, having in great haste got up a hundred men, commanded the rest to follow as they could, and immediately drawing up his ladders after him, he marched through the city with his hundred men towards the castle, being already overjoyed that he was undiscovered, and not doubting of the success. But while still they were some way off, a watch of four men came with a light, who did not see them, because they were still in the shade of the moon, but were seen plainly enough themselves as they came on directly towards them. So withdrawing a little way amongst some walls and plots for houses, they lay in wait for them; and three of them they killed. But the fourth, being wounded in the head with a sword, fled, crying out that the enemy was in the city. And immediately the trumpets sounded, and all the city was in an uproar at what had happened, and the streets were full of people running up and down, and many lights were seen shining both below in the town, and above in the castle, and a confused noise was to be heard in all parts.

In the meantime, Aratus was hard at work struggling to get up the rocks, at first slowly and with much difficulty, straying continually from the path, which lay deep, and was overshadowed with the crags, leading to the wall with many windings and turnings; but the moon immediately, and as if by miracle, it is said, dispersing the clouds, shone out and gave light to the most difficult part of the way, until he got to that part of the wall he desired, and there she overshadowed and hid him, the clouds coming together again. Those soldiers whom Aratus had left outside the gate, near Juno's temple, to the number of three hundred, entering the town, now full of tumult and lights, and not knowing the way by which the former had gone, and finding no track of them, slunk aside, and crowded together in one body under a flank of the cliff that cast a strong shadow, and there stood and waited in great distress and perplexity. For, by this time, those that had gone with Aratus were attacked with missiles from the citadel, and were busy fighting, and a sound of cries of battle came down from above, and a loud noise, echoed back and back from the mountain sides, and therefore confused and uncertain whence it proceeded, was heard on all sides. They being thus in doubt which way to turn themselves, Archelaus, the commander of Antigonus's troops, having a great number of soldiers with him, made up towards the castle with great shouts and noise of trumpets to fall upon Aratus's people, and passed by the three hundred, who, as if they had risen out of an ambush, immediately charged him, kill-

ing the first they encountered, and so affrighted the rest, together with Archelaus, that they put them to flight and pursued
them until they had quite broken and dispersed them about the
city. No sooner were these defeated, but Erginus came to them
from those that were fighting above, to acquaint them that
Aratus was engaged with the enemy, who defended themselves
very stoutly, and there was a fierce conflict at the very wall,
and need of speedy help. They therefore desired him to lead
them on without delay, and, marching up, by their shouts
made their friends understand who they were, and encouraged
them; and the full moon, shining on their arms, made them, in
the long line by which they advanced, appear more in number
to the enemy than they were; and the echo of the night multi-
plied their shouts. In short, falling on with the rest, they made
the enemy give way, and were masters of the castle and garrison,
day now beginning to be bright, and the rising sun shining out
upon their success. By this time, also, the rest of his army came
up to Aratus from Sicyon, the Corinthians joyfully receiving
them at the gates and helping them to secure the king's party.

And now, having put all things into a safe posture, he came
down from the castle to the theatre, an infinite number of people
crowding thither to see him and to hear what he would say to
the Corinthians. Therefore drawing up the Achæans on each
side of the stage-passages, he came forward himself upon the
stage, with his corselet still on, and his face showing the effects
of all his hard work and want of sleep, so that his natural exultation and joyfulness of mind were overborne by the weariness of
his body. The people, as soon as he came forth, breaking out
into great applauses and congratulations, he took his spear in
his right hand, and, resting his body upon it with his knee a
little bent, stood a good while in that posture, silently receiving
their shouts and acclamations, while they extolled his valour
and wondered at his fortune; which being over, standing up,
he began an oration in the name of the Achæans, suitable to
the late action, persuading the Corinthians to associate themselves to the Achæans, and withal delivered up to them the keys
of their gates, which had never been in their power since the
time of King Philip. Of the captains of Antigonus, he dismissed
Archelaus, whom he had taken prisoner, and Theophrastus, who
refused to quit his post, he put to death. As for Persæus, when
he saw the castle was lost, he had got away to Cenchreæ, where,
some time after, discoursing with one that said to him that the
wise man only is a true general, " Indeed," he replied, " none

of Zeno's maxims once pleased me better than this, but I have been converted to another opinion by the young man of Sicyon." This is told by many of Persæus. Aratus immediately after made himself master of the temple of Juno and haven of Lechæum, seized upon five-and-twenty of the king's ships, together with five hundred horses and four hundred Syrians: these he sold. The Achæans kept guard in the Acro-Corinthus with a body of four hundred soldiers, and fifty dogs with as many keepers.

The Romans, extolling Philopœmen, called him the last of the Grecians, as if no great man had ever since his time been bred amongst them. But I should call this capture of the Acro-Corinthus the last of the Grecian exploits, being comparable to the best of them, both for the daringness of it, and the success, as was presently seen by the consequences. For the Megarians, revolting from Antigonus, joined Aratus, and the Trœzenians and Epidaurians enrolled themselves in the Achæan community, and issuing forth for the first time, he entered Attica, and passing over into Salamis, he plundered the island, turning the Achæan force every way, as if it were just let loose out of prison and set at liberty. All freemen whom he took he sent back to the Athenians without ransom, as a sort of first invitation to them to come over to the league. He made Ptolemy become a confederate of the Achæans, with the privilege of command both by sea and land. And so great was his power with them, that since he could not by law be chosen their general every year, yet every other year he was, and by his counsels and actions was in effect always so. For they perceived that neither riches nor reputation, nor the friendship of kings, nor the private interest of his own country, nor anything else was so dear to him as the increase of the Achæans' power and greatness. For he believed that the cities, weak individually, could be preserved by nothing else but a mutual assistance under the closest bond of the common interest, and, as the members of the body live and breathe by the union of all in a single natural growth, and on the dissolution of this, when once they separate, pine away and putrify, in the same manner are cities ruined by being dissevered, as well as preserved when, as the members of one great body, they enjoy the benefit of that province and counsel that govern the whole.

Now being distressed to see that, whereas the chief neighbouring cities enjoyed their own laws and liberties, the Argives were in bondage, he took counsel for destroying their tyrant,

Aristomachus, being very desirous both to pay his debt of gratitude to the city where he had been bred up, by restoring it its liberty, and to add so considerable a town to the Achæans. Nor were there some wanting who had the courage to undertake the thing, of whom Æschylus and Charimenes the soothsayer were the chief. But they wanted swords; for the tyrant had prohibited the keeping of any under a great penalty. Therefore Aratus, having provided some small daggers at Corinth and hidden them in the pack-saddles of some pack-horses that carried ordinary ware, sent them to Argos. But Charimenes letting another person into the design, Æschylus and his partners were angry at it, and henceforth would have no more to do with him, and took their measures by themselves, and Charimenes, on finding this, went, out of anger, and informed against them, just as they were on their way to attack the tyrant; however, the most of them made a shift to escape out of the market-place, and fled to Corinth. Not long after, Aristomachus was slain by some slaves, and Aristippus, a worse tyrant than he, seized the government. Upon this, Aratus, mustering all the Achæans present that were of age, hurried away to the aid of the city, believing that he should find the people ready to join with him. But the greater number being by this time habituated to slavery and content to submit, and no one coming to join him, he was obliged to retire, having moreover exposed the Achæans to the charge of committing acts of hostility in the midst of peace; upon which account they were sued before the Mantineans, and, Aratus not making his appearance, Aristippus gained the cause, and had damages allowed him to the value of thirty minæ. And now hating and fearing Aratus, he sought means to kill him, having the assistance herein of King Antigonus; so that Aratus was perpetually dogged and watched by those that waited for an opportunity to do this service. But there is no such safeguard of a ruler as the sincere and steady good-will of his subjects, for where both the common people and the principal citizens have their fears not of, but for, their governor, he sees with many eyes and hears with many ears whatsoever is doing. Therefore I cannot but here stop short a little in the course of my narrative to describe the manner of life which the so much envied arbitrary power and the so much celebrated and admired pomp and pride of absolute government obliged Aristippus to lead.

For though Antigonus was his friend and ally, and though he maintained numerous soldiers to act as his body-guard, and had not left one enemy of his alive in the city, yet he was forced to make his guards encamp in the colonnade about his house; and for his servants, he turned them all out immediately after supper, and then shutting the doors upon them, he crept up into a small upper chamber, together with his mistress, through a trap-door, upon which he placed his bed, and there slept after such a fashion, as one in his condition can be supposed to sleep, that is, interruptedly and in fear. The ladder was taken away by the woman's mother, and locked up in another room; in the morning she brought it again, and putting it to, called up this brave and wonderful tyrant, who came crawling out like some creeping thing out of its hole. Whereas Aratus, not by force of arms, but lawfully and by his virtue, lived in possession of a firmly settled command, wearing the ordinary coat and cloak, being the common and declared enemy of all tyrants, and has left behind him a noble race of descendants surviving among the Grecians to this day; while those occupiers of citadels and maintainers of body-guards, who made all this use of arms and gates and bolts to protect their lives, in some few cases perhaps escaped like the hare from the hunters; but in no instance have we either house or family, or so much as a tomb to which any respect is shown, remaining to preserve the memory of any one of them.

Against this Aristippus, therefore, Aratus made many open and many secret attempts, whilst he endeavoured to take Argos, though without success; once, particularly, clapping scaling ladders in the night to the walls, he desperately got up upon it with a few of his soldiers, and killed the guards that opposed him. But the day appearing, the tyrant set upon him on all hands, whilst the Argives, as if it had not been their liberty that was contended for, but some Nemean game going on for which it was their privilege to assign the prize, like fair and impartial judges, sat looking on in great quietness. Aratus, fighting bravely, was run through the thigh with a lance, yet he maintained his ground against the enemy till night, and, had he been able to go on and hold out that night also, he had gained his point; for the tyrant thought of nothing but flying, and had already shipped most of his goods. But Aratus, having no intelligence of this, and wanting water, being disabled himself by his wound, retreated with his soldiers.

Despairing henceforth to do any good this way, he fell openly with his army into Argolis, and plundered it, and in a fierce battle with Aristippus near the river Chares, he was accused of having withdrawn out of the fight, and thereby abandoned the victory. For whereas one part of his army had unmistakably got the better, and was pursuing the enemy at a good distance from him, he yet retreated in confusion into his camp, not so much because he was overpressed by those with whom he was engaged, as out of mistrust of success and through a panic fear. But when the other wing, returning from the pursuit, showed themselves extremely vexed, that though they had put the enemy to flight and killed many more of his men than they had lost, yet those that were in a manner conquered should erect a trophy as conquerors, being much ashamed he resolved to fight them again about the trophy, and the next day but one drew up his army to give them battle. But, perceiving that they were reinforced with fresh troops, and came on with better courage than before, he durst not hazard a fight, but retired and sent to request a truce to bury his dead. However, by his dexterity in dealing personally with men and managing political affairs, and by his general favour, he excused and obliterated this fault, and brought in Cleonæ to the Achæan association, and celebrated the Nemean games at Cleonæ, as the proper and more ancient place for them. The games were also celebrated by the Argives at the same time, which gave the first occasion to the violation of the privilege of safe conduct and immunity always granted to those that came to compete for the prizes, the Achæans at that time selling as enemies all those they caught going through their country after joining in the games at Argos. So vehement and implacable a hater was he of the tyrants.

Not long after, having notice that Aristippus had a design upon Cleonæ, but was afraid of him, because he then was staying in Corinth, he assembled an army by public proclamation, and commanding them to take along with them provisions for several days, he marched to Cenchreæ, hoping by this stratagem to entice Aristippus to fall upon Cleonæ, when he supposed him far enough off. And so it happened, for he immediately brought his forces against it from Argos. But Aratus, returning from Cenchreæ to Corinth in the dusk of the evening, and setting posts of his troops in all the roads, led on the Achæans, who followed in such good order and with so much speed and alacrity, that they were undiscovered by Aristippus, not only whilst upon their march, but even when they got, still in the night, into Cleonæ, and drew up in order of battle. As soon as it was morning, the gates being opened and the trumpets sounding, he fell upon the enemy with great cries and fury, routed them at once, and kept close in pursuit, following the course which he most imagined Aristippus would choose, there being many turns that might be taken. And so the chase lasted as far as Mycenæ, where the tyrant was slain by a certain Cretan called Tragiscus, as Dinias reports. Of the common soldiers, there fell above fifteen hundred. Yet though Aratus had obtained so great a victory and that too without the loss of a man, he could not make himself master of Argos, nor set it at liberty, because Agias and the younger Aristomachus got into the town with some of the king's forces, and seized upon the government. However, by this exploit he spoiled the scoffs and jests of those that flattered the tyrants, and in their raillery would say that the Achæan general was usually troubled with a looseness when he was to fight a battle, that the sound of a trumpet struck him with a drowsiness and a giddiness, and that when he had drawn up his army and given the word, he used to ask his lieutenants and officers whether there was any further need of his presence now the die was cast, and then went aloof, to await the result at a distance. For indeed these stories were so generally listened to, that, when the philosophers disputed whether to have one's heart beat and to change colour upon any apparent danger be an argument of fear, or rather of some distemperature and chilliness of bodily constitution, Aratus was always quoted as a good general who was always thus affected in time of battle.

Having thus despatched Aristippus, he advised with himself how to overthrow Lydiades, the Megalopolitan, who held usurped power over his country. This person was naturally of a generous temper, and not insensible of true honour, and had been led into this wickedness, not by the ordinary motives of other tyrants, licentiousness and rapacity, but being young, and stimulated with the desire of glory, he had let his mind be unwarily prepossessed with the vain and false applauses given to tyranny, as some happy and glorious thing. But he no sooner seized the government, than he grew weary of the pomp and burden of it. And at once emulating the tranquillity and fearing the policy of Aratus, he took the best resolutions, first, to free himself from hatred and fear, from soldiers and guards, and, secondly, to be the public benefactor of his country. And sending for Aratus, he resigned the government, and incorporated his city into the Achæan community. The Achæans, applauding this generous action, chose him their general; upon which, desiring to outdo Aratus in glory, amongst many other uncalled-for things, he declared war against the Lacedæmonians; which Aratus opposing was thought to do it out of envy; and Lydiades was the second time chosen general, though Aratus acted openly against him, and laboured to have the office conferred upon another. For Aratus himself had the command every other year, as has been said. Lydiades, however, succeeded so well in his pretensions, that he was thrice chosen general, governing alternately, as did Aratus; but at last, declaring himself his professed enemy, and accusing him frequently to the Achæans, he was rejected, and fell into contempt, people now seeing that it was a contest between a counterfeit and a true, unadulterated virtue, and, as Æsop tells us that the cuckoo once, asking the little birds why they flew away from her, was answered, because they feared she would one day prove a hawk, so Lydiades's former tyranny still cast a doubt upon the reality of his change.

But Aratus gained new honour in the Ætolian war. For the Achæans resolving to fall upon the Ætolians on the Megarian confines, and Agis also, the Lacedæmonian king, who came to their assistance with an army, encouraging them to fight, Aratus opposed this determination. And patiently enduring many reproaches, many scoffs and jeerings at his soft and cowardly temper, he would not, for any appearance of disgrace, abandon what he judged to be true common advantage, and suffered the enemy to pass over Geranea into Peloponnesus without a battle. But when, after they passed by, news came that they had suddenly captured Pellene, he was no longer the same man, nor would he hear of any delay, or wait to draw together his whole force, but marched towards the enemy, with such as he had about him, to fall upon them, as they were indeed now much less formidable through the intemperances and disorders committed in their success. For as soon as they entered the city, the common soldiers dispersed and went hither and thither into the houses, quarrelling and fighting with one another about the plunder, and the officers and commanders were running about after the wives and daughters of the Pellenians, on whose heads they put their own helmets, to mark each man his prize, and prevent another from seizing it. And in this posture were they when news came that Aratus was ready to fall upon them. And in the midst of the consternation likely to ensue in the confusion they were in before all of them heard of the danger, the outmost of them, engaging at the gates and in the suburbs with the Achæans, were already beaten and put to flight, and as they came headlong back, filled with their panic those who were collecting and advancing to their assistance.

In this confusion, one of the captives, daughter of Epigethes, a citizen of repute, being extremely handsome and tall, happened to be sitting in the temple of Diana, placed there by the commander of the band of chosen men, who had taken her and put his crested helmet upon her. She, hearing the noise, and running out to see what was the matter, stood in the temple gates, looking down from above upon those that fought, having the helmet upon her head; in which posture she seemed to the citizens to be something more than human, and struck fear and dread into the enemy, who believed it to be a divine apparition; so that they lost all courage to defend themselves. But the Pellenians tell us that the image of Diana stands usually untouched, and when the priestess happens at any time to remove it to some other place, nobody dares look upon it, but all turn their faces from it; for not only is the sight of it terrible and hurtful to mankind, but it makes even the trees, by which it happens to be carried, become barren and cast fruit. This image, therefore, they say, the priestess produced at that time, and holding it directly in the faces of the Ætolians, made them lose their reason and judgment. But Aratus mentions no such thing in his commentaries, but saying that having put to flight the Ætolians, and falling in pell-mell with them into the city, he drove them out by main force, and killed seven hundred of them. And the action was extolled as one of the most famous exploits, and Timanthes the painter made a picture of the battle, giving by his composition a most lively representation of it.

But many great nations and potentates combining against the Achæans, Aratus immediately treated for friendly arrangements with the Ætolians, and, making use of the assistance of Pantaleon, the most powerful man amongst them, he not only made a peace, but an alliance between them and the Achæans. But being desirous to free the Athenians, he got into disgrace and ill-repute among the Achæans, because, notwithstanding the truce and suspension of arms made between them and the Macedonians, he had attempted to take the Piræus. He denies this fact in his commentaries, and lays the blame on Erginus, by whose assistance he took Acro-Corinthus, alleging that he upon his own private account attacked the Piræus, and his ladders happening to break, being hotly pursued, he called out upon Aratus, as if present, by which means deceiving the enemy he got safely off. This excuse, however, sounds very improbable; for it is not in any way likely that Erginus, a private man and a Syrian stranger, should conceive in his mind so great an attempt, without Aratus at his back, to tell him how and when to make it, and to supply him with the means. Nor was it twice or thrice, but very often, that, like an obstinate lover, he repeated his attempts on the Piræus, and was so far from being discouraged by his disappointments, that his missing his hopes but narrowly was an incentive to him to proceed the more boldly in a new trial. One time amongst the rest, in making his escape through the Thrasian plain, he put his leg out of joint, and was forced to submit to many operations with the knife before he was cured, so that for a long time he was carried in a litter to the wars.

And when Antigonus was dead, and Demetrius succeeded him in the kingdom, he was more bent than ever upon Athens, and in general quite despised the Macedonians. And so, being overthrown in battle near Phylacia by Bithys, Demetrius's general, and there being a very strong report that he was either taken or slain, Diogenes, the governor of the Piræus, sent letters to Corinth, commanding the Achæans to quit that city, seeing Aratus was dead. When these letters came to Corinth, Aratus happened to be there in person, so that Diogenes's messengers being sufficiently mocked and derided, were forced to return to their master. King Demetrius himself also sent a ship, wherein Aratus was to be brought to him in chains. And the Athenians, exceeding all possible fickleness of flattery to the Macedonians, crowned themselves with garlands upon the first news of his death. And so in anger he went at once and invaded Attica, and penetrated as far as the Academy, but then suffering himself to be pacified he did no further act of hostility. And the Athenians afterwards, coming to a due sense of his virtue when upon the death of Demetrius they attempted to recover their liberty, called him to their assistance; although at that time another person was general of the Achæans, and he himself had long kept his bed with a sickness, yet rather than fail the city in a time of need, he was carried thither in a litter, and helped to persuade Diogenes the governor to deliver up the Piræus, Munychia, Salamis, and Sunium to the Athenians in consideration of a hundred and fifty talents, of which Aratus himself contributed twenty to the city. Upon this, the Æginetans and the Hermionians immediately joined the Achæans, and the greatest part of Arcadia entered their confederacy; and the Macedonians being occupied with various wars upon their own confines and with their neighbours, the Achæan power, the Ætolians also being in alliance with them, rose to great height.

But Aratus, still bent on effecting his old project, and im-

patient that tyranny should maintain itself in so near a city as
Argos, sent to Aristomachus to persuade him to restore liberty
to that city, and to associate it to the Achæans, and that, following Lydiades's example, he should rather choose to be the
general of a great nation, with esteem and honour, than the
tyrant of one city, with continual hatred and danger. Aristomachus slighted not the message, but desired Aratus to send
him fifty talents, with which he might pay off the soldiers. In
the meantime, whilst the money was providing, Lydiades, being
then general, and extremely ambitious that this advantage might
seem to be of his procuring for the Achæans, accused Aratus to
Aristomachus, as one that bore an irreconcilable hatred to the
tyrants, and, persuading him to commit the affair to his management, he presented him to the Achæans. But there the Achæan
council gave a manifest proof of the great credit Aratus had with
them and the good-will they bore him. For when he, in anger,
spoke against Aristomachus's being admitted into the association, they rejected the proposal, but when he was afterwards
pacified and came himself and spoke in its favour, they voted
everything cheerfully and readily, and decreed that the Argives
and Phliasians should be incorporated into their commonwealth,
and the next year they chose Aristomachus general. He, being
in good credit with the Achæans, was very desirous to invade
Laconia, and for that purpose sent for Aratus from Athens.
Aratus wrote to him to dissuade him as far as he could from
that expedition, being very unwilling the Achæans should be
engaged in a quarrel with Cleomenes, who was a daring man,
and making extraordinary advances to power. But Aristomachus resolving to go on, he obeyed and served in person, on
which occasion he hindered Aristomachus from fighting a battle
when Cleomenes came upon them at Pallantium; and for this
act was accused by Lydiades, and, coming to an open conflict
with him in a contest for the office of general, he carried it by
the show of hands, and was chosen general the twelfth time.

This year, being routed by Cleomenes, near the Lycæum, he
fled, and, wandering out of the way in the night, was believed to
be slain; and once more it was confidently reported so throughout all Greece. He, however, having escaped this danger and
rallied his forces, was not content to march off in safety, but
making a happy use of the present conjuncture, when nobody
dreamed of any such thing, he fell suddenly upon the Mantineans, allies of Cleomenes, and, taking the city, put a garrison
into it, and made the stranger inhabitants free of the city; pro-

curing, by this means, those advantages for the beaten Achæans, which being conquerors, they would not easily have obtained. The Lacedæmonians again invading the Megalopolitan territories, he marched to the assistance of the city, but refused to give Cleomenes, who did all he could to provoke him to it, any opportunity of engaging him in a battle, nor could be prevailed upon by the Megalopolitans, who urged him to it extremely. For besides that by nature he was ill-suited for set battles, he was then much inferior in numbers, and was to deal with a daring leader, still in the heat of youth, while he himself, now past the prime of courage and come to a chastised ambition, felt it his business to maintain by prudence the glory which he had obtained, and the other was only aspiring to by forwardness and daring.

So that though the light-armed soldiers had sallied out and driven the Lacedæmonians as far as their camp, and had come even to their tents, yet would not Aratus lead his men forward, but, posting himself in a hollow water-course in the way thither, stopped and prevented the citizens from crossing this. Lydiades, extremely vexed at what was going on, and loading Aratus with reproaches, entreated the horse that, together with him, they would second them that had the enemy in chase, and not let a certain victory slip out of their hands, nor forsake him that was going to venture his life for his country. And being reinforced with many brave men that turned after him, he charged the enemy's right wing, and routing it followed the pursuit without measure or discretion, letting his eagerness and hopes of glory tempt him on into broken ground, full of planted fruit-trees and cut up with broad ditches, where, being engaged by Cleomenes, he fell, fighting gallantly the noblest of battles, at the gate of his country. The rest, flying back to their main body and troubling the ranks of the full-armed infantry, put the whole army to the rout. Aratus was extremely blamed, being suspected to have betrayed Lydiades, and was constrained by the Achæans, who withdrew in great anger, to accompany them to Ægium, where they called a council, and decreed that he should no longer be furnished with money, nor have any more soldiers hired for him, but that, if he would make war, he should pay them himself.

This affront he resented so far as to resolve to give up the seal and lay down the office of general; but upon second thoughts he found it best to have patience, and presently marched with the Achæans to Orchomenus and fought a battle with Megistonus, the stepfather of Cleomenes, where he got the victory, killing three hundred men and taking Megistonus prisoner. But whereas he used to be chosen general every other year, when his turn came and he was called to take upon him that charge, he declined it, and Timoxenus was chosen in his stead. The true cause of which was not the pique he was alleged to have taken at the people, but the ill circumstances of the Achæan affairs. For Cleomenes did not now invade them gently and tenderly as hitherto, as one controlled by the civil authorities, but having killed the Ephors, divided the lands, and made many of the stranger residents free of the city, he was responsible to no one in his government; and therefore fell in good earnest upon the Achæans, and put forward his claim to the supreme military command. Wherefore Aratus is much blamed, that in a stormy and tempestuous time, like a cowardly pilot, he should forsake the helm when it was even perhaps his duty to have insisted, whether they would or no, on saving them; or if he thought the Achæan affairs desperate, to have yielded all up to Cleomenes, and not to have let Peloponnesus fall once again into barbarism with Macedonian garrisons, and Acro-Corinthus be occupied with Illyric and Gaulish soldiers, and, under the specious name of confederates, to have made those masters of the cities whom he had held it his business by arms and by policy to baffle and defeat, and, in the memoirs he left behind him, loaded with reproaches and insults. And say that Cleomenes was arbitrary and tyrannical, yet was he descended from the Heraclidæ, and Sparta was his country, the obscurest citizens of which deserved to be preferred to the generalship before the best of the Macedonians by those that had any regard to the honour of Grecian birth. Besides, Cleomenes sued for that command over the Achæans as one that would return the honour of that title with real kindnesses to the cities; whereas Antigonus, being declared absolute general by sea and land, would not accept the office unless Acro-Corinthus were by special agreement put into his hands, following the example of Æsop's hunter; for he would not get up and ride the Achæans, who desired him so to do, and offered their backs to him by embassies and popular decrees, till, by a garrison and hostages, they had allowed him to bit and bridle them. Aratus exhausts all his powers of speech to show the necessity that was upon him. But Polybius writes, that long before this, and before there was any necessity, apprehending the daring temper of Cleomenes, he communicated secretly with Antigonus, and that he had beforehand prevailed

with the Megalopolitans to press the Achæans to crave aid from
Antigonus.  For they were the most harassed by the war, Cleomenes continually plundering and ransacking their country.
And so writes also Phylarchus, who, unless seconded by the
testimony of Polybius, would not be altogether credited; for he
is seized with enthusiasm when he so much as speaks a word of
Cleomenes, and as if he were pleading, not writing a history,
goes on throughout defending the one and accusing the other.

The Achæans, therefore, lost Mantinea, which was recovered
by Cleomenes, and being beaten in a great fight near Hecatombæum, so general was the consternation, that they immediately sent to Cleomenes to desire him to come to Argos and
take the command upon him.  But Aratus, as soon as he understood that he was coming, and was got as far as Lerna with his
troops, fearing the result, sent ambassadors to him, to request
him to come accompanied with three hundred only, as to friends
and confederates, and, if he mistrusted anything, he should
receive hostages.  Upon which Cleomenes, saying this was mere
mockery and affront, went away, sending a letter to the Achæans
full of reproaches and accusation against Aratus.  And Aratus
also wrote letters against Cleomenes; and bitter revilings and
railleries were current on both hands, not sparing even their
marriages and wives.  Hereupon Cleomenes sent a herald to
declare war against the Achæans, and in the meantime missed
very narrowly of taking Sicyon by treachery.  Turning off at a
little distance, he attacked and took Pellene which the Achæan
general abandoned, and not long after took also Pheneus and
Penteleum.  Then immediately the Argives voluntarily joined
with him, and the Phliasians received a garrison, and in short
nothing among all their new acquisitions held firm to the
Achæans.  Aratus was encompassed on every side with clamour
and confusion; he saw the whole of Peloponnesus shaking hands
around him, and the cities everywhere set in revolt by men
desirous of innovations.

Indeed no place remained quiet or satisfied with the present
condition; even amongst the Sicyonians and Corinthians themselves, many were well known to have had private conferences
with Cleomenes, who long since, out of desire to make themselves masters of their several cities, had been discontented with
the present order of things.  Aratus, having absolute power
given him to bring these to condign punishment, executed as
many of them as he could find at Sicyon, but going about to
find them out and punish them at Corinth also, he irritated the

people, already unsound in feeling and weary of the Achæan
government. So collecting tumultuously in the temple of Apollo,
they sent for Aratus, having determined to take or kill him
before they broke out into open revolt. He came accordingly,
leading his horse in his hand, as if he suspected nothing. Then
several leaping up and accusing and reproaching him, with mild
words and a settled countenance he bade them sit down, and
not stand crying out upon him in a disorderly manner, desiring
also, that those that were about the door might be let in, and
saying so, he stepped out quietly, as if he would give his horse
to somebody. Clearing himself thus of the crowd, and speaking
without discomposure to the Corinthians that he met, commanding them to go to Apollo's temple, and being now, before
they were aware, got near to the citadel, he leaped upon his
horse, and commanding Cleopater, the governor of the garrison,
to have a special care of his charge, he galloped to Sicyon, followed by thirty of his soldiers, the rest leaving him and shifting
for themselves. And not long after, it being known that he
was fled, the Corinthians pursued him, but not overtaking him,
they immediately sent for Cleomenes and delivered up the city
to him, who, however, thought nothing they could give was so
great a gain, as was the loss of their having let Aratus get away.
Nevertheless, being strengthened by the accession of the people
of the Acte, as it is called, who put their towns into his hands,
he proceeded to carry a palisade and lines of circumvallation
around the Acro-Corinthus.

But Aratus being arrived at Sicyon, the body of the Achæans
there flocked to him, and, in an assembly there held, he was
chosen general with absolute power, and he took about him a
guard of his own citizens, it being now three-and-thirty years
since he first took a part in public affairs among the Achæans,
having in that time been the chief man in credit and power of
all Greece; but he was now deserted on all hands, helpless and
overpowered, drifting about amidst the waves and danger on
the shattered hulk of his native city. For the Ætolians, whom
he applied to, declined to assist him in his distress, and the
Athenians who were well affected to him were diverted from
lending him any succour by the authority of Euclides and
Micion. Now whereas he had a house and property in Corinth,
Cleomenes meddled not with it, nor suffered anybody else to do
so, but calling for his friends and agents, he bade them hold
themselves responsible to Aratus for everything, as to him they
would have to render their account; and privately he sent to

him Tripylus, and afterwards Megistonus, his own stepfather, to offer him, besides several other things, a yearly pension of twelve talents, which was twice as much as Ptolemy allowed him, for he gave him six; and all that he demanded was to be declared commander of the Achæans, and together with them to have the keeping of the citadel of Corinth. To which Aratus returning answer that affairs were not so properly in his power as he was in the power of them, Cleomenes, believing this a mere evasion, immediately entered the country of Sicyon, destroying all with fire and sword, and besieged the city three months, whilst Aratus held firm, and was in dispute with himself whether he should call in Antigonus upon condition of delivering up the citadel of Corinth to him; for he would not lend him assistance upon any other terms.

In the meantime the Achæans assembled at Ægium, and called for Aratus; but it was very hazardous for him to pass thither, while Cleomenes was encamped before Sicyon; besides, the citizens endeavoured to stop him by their entreaties, protesting that they would not suffer him to expose himself to so evident danger, the enemy being so near; the women, also, and children hung about him, weeping and embracing him as their common father and defender. But he, having comforted and encouraged them as well as he could, got on horseback, and being accompanied with ten of his friends and his son, then a youth, got away to the seaside, and finding vessels there waiting off the shore, went on board of them and sailed to Ægium to the assembly; in which it was decreed that Antigonus should be called in to their aid, and should have the Acro-Corinthus delivered to him. Aratus also sent his son to him with the other hostages. The Corinthians, extremely angry at this proceeding, now plundered his property, and gave his house as a present to Cleomenes.

Antigonus being now near at hand with his army, consisting of twenty thousand Macedonian foot and one thousand three hundred horse, Aratus, with the members of council, went to meet him by sea, and got, unobserved by the enemy, to Pegæ, having no great confidence either in Antigonus or the Macedonians. For he was very sensible that his own greatness had been made out of the losses he had caused them, and that the first great principle of his public conduct had been hostility to the former Antigonus. But perceiving the necessity that was now upon him, and the pressure of the time, that lord and master of those we call rulers, to be inexorable, he resolved to put all to the venture. So soon, therefore, as Antigonus was told that Aratus was coming up to him, he saluted the rest of the company after the ordinary manner, but him he received at the very first approach with especial honour, and finding him afterwards to be both good and wise, admitted him to his nearer familiarity. For Aratus was not only useful to him in the management of great affairs, but singularly agreeable also as the private companion of a king in his recreations. And therefore, though Antigonus was young, yet as soon as he observed the temper of the man to be proper for a prince's friendship, he made more use of him than of any other, not only of the Achæans, but also of the Macedonians that were about him. So that the thing fell out to him just as the god had foreshown in a sacrifice. For it is related that, as Aratus was not long before offering sacrifice, there were found in the liver two gall-bags inclosed in the same caul of fat; whereupon the soothsayer told him that there should very soon be the strictest friendship imaginable between him and his greatest and most mortal enemies; which prediction he at that time slighted, having in general no great faith in soothsayings and prognostications, but depending most upon rational deliberation. At an after time, however, when, things succeeding well in the war, Antigonus made a great feast at Corinth, to which he invited a great number of guests, and placed Aratus next above him, and presently calling for a coverlet, asked him if he did not find it cold, and on Aratus's answering, "Yes, extremely cold," bade him come nearer, so that when the servants brought the coverlet, they threw it over them both, then Aratus, remembering the sacrifice, fell a laughing, and told the king the sign which had happened to him, and the interpretation of it. But this fell out a good while after.

So Aratus and the king, plighting their faith to each other at Pegæ, immediately marched toward the enemy, with whom they had frequent engagements near the city, Cleomenes maintaining a strong position, and the Corinthians making a very brisk defence. In the meantime Aristoteles the Argive, Aratus's friend, sent privately to him to let him know that he would cause Argos to revolt, if he would come thither in person with some soldiers. Aratus acquainted Antigonus, and taking fifteen hundred men with him, sailed in boats along the shore as quickly as he could from the Isthmus to Epidaurus. But the Argives had not patience till he could arrive, but, making a sudden insurrection, fell upon Cleomenes's soldiers, and drove them into the citadel. Cleomenes having news of this, and fearing lest, if the enemy should possess themselves of Argos, they might cut off his retreat home, leaves the Acro-Corinthus and marches away by night to help his men. He got thither first, and beat off the enemy, but Aratus appearing not long after, and the king approaching with his forces, he retreated to Mantinea, upon which all the cities again came over to the Achæans, and Antigonus took possession of the Acro-Corinthus. Aratus, being chosen general by the Argives, persuaded them to make a present to Antigonus of the property of the tyrants and the traitors. As for Aristomachus, after having put him to the rack in the town of Cenchreæ, they drowned him in the sea; for which, more than anything else, Aratus was reproached, that he could suffer a man to be so lawlessly put to death, who was no bad man, had been one of his long acquaintance, and at his persuasion had abdicated his power and annexed the city to the Achæans.

And already the blame of the other things that were done began to be laid to his account; as that they so lightly gave up Corinth to Antigonus, as if it had been an inconsiderable village; that they had suffered him, after first sacking Orchomenus, then to put into it a Macedonian garrison; that they made a decree that no letters nor embassy should be sent to any other king without the consent of Antigonus, that they were forced to furnish pay and provision for the Macedonian soldiers, and celebrated sacrifices, processions, and games in honour of Antigonus, Aratus's citizens setting the example and receiving Antigonus, who was lodged and entertained at Aratus's house. All these things they treated as his fault, not knowing that having once put the reins into Antigonus's hands and let himself be borne by the impetus of regal power, he was no longer master of anything but one single voice, the liberty of which it was not so very safe for him to use. For it was very plain that Aratus was much troubled at several things, as appeared by the business about the statues. For Antigonus replaced the statues of the tyrants of Argos that had been thrown down, and on the contrary threw down the statues of all those that had taken the Acro-Corinthus, except that of Aratus, nor could Aratus, by all his entreaties, dissuade him. Also, the usage of the Mantineans by the Achæans seemed not in accordance with the Grecian feelings and manners. For being master of their city by the help of Antigonus, they put to death the chief and most noted men amongst them; and of the rest, some they sold, others they sent, bound in fetters, into Macedonia, and made slaves of their wives and children; and of the money thus raised, a third part they divided among themselves, and the other two-thirds were distributed among the Macedonians. And this might seem to have been justified by the law of retaliation; for although it be a barbarous thing for men of the same nation and blood thus to deal with one another in their fury, yet necessity makes it, as Simonides says, sweet and something excusable, being the proper thing, in the mind's painful and inflamed condition, to give alleviation and relief. But for what was afterwards done to that city, Aratus cannot be defended on any ground either of reason or necessity. For the Argives having had the city bestowed on them by Antigonus, and resolving to people it, he being then chosen as the new founder, and being general at that time, decreed that it should no longer be called Mantinea, but Antigonea, which name it still bears. So that he may be said to have been the cause that the old memory of the " beautiful Mantinea " has been wholly extinguished and the city to this day has the name of the destroyer and slayer of its citizens.

After this, Cleomenes, being overthrown in a great battle near Sellasia, forsook Sparta and fled into Egypt, and Antigonus, having shown all manner of kindness and fair-dealing to Aratus, retired into Macedonia. There, falling sick, he sent Philip, the heir of the kingdom, into Peloponnesus, being yet scarce a youth, commanding him to follow above all the counsel of Aratus, to communicate with the cities through him, and through him to make acquaintance with the Achæans; and Aratus, receiving him accordingly, so managed him as to send him back to Macedon both well affected to himself and full of desire and ambition to take an honourable part in the affairs of Greece.

When Antigonus was dead, the Ætolians, despising the sloth and negligence of the Achæans, who having learnt to be defended by other men's valour and to shelter themselves under the Macedonian arms, lived in ease and without any discipline, now attempted to interfere in Peloponnesus. And plundering the land of Patræ and Dyme in their way, they invaded Messene and ravaged it; at which Aratus being indignant, and finding that Timoxenus, then general, was hesitating and letting the time go by, being now on the point of laying down his office, in which he himself was chosen to succeed him, he anticipated the proper term by five days, that he might bring relief to the Messenians. And mustering the Achæans, who were both in their persons unexercised in arms and in their minds relaxed and averse to war, he met with a defeat at Caphyæ. Having thus begun the war, as it seemed, with too much heat and passion, he then ran into the other extreme, cooling again and desponding so much that he let pass and overlooked many fair opportunities of advantage given by the Ætolians, and allowed them to run riot, as it were, throughout all Peloponnesus, with all manner of insolence and licentiousness. Wherefore, holding forth their hands once more to the Macedonians, they invited and drew in Philip to intermeddle in the affairs of Greece, chiefly hoping, because of his affection and trust that he felt for Aratus, they should find him easy-tempered, and ready to be managed as they pleased.

But the king, being now persuaded by Apelles, Megaleas, and other courtiers, that endeavoured to ruin the credit Aratus had with him, took the side of the contrary faction and joined them in canvassing to have Eperatus chosen general by the Achæans. But he being altogether scorned by the Achæans, and, for the want of Aratus to help, all things going wrong, Philip saw he had quite mistaken his part, and, turning about and re-conciling himself to Aratus, he was wholly his; and his affairs, now going on favourably both for his power and reputation, he depended upon him altogether as the author of all his gains in both respects; Aratus hereby giving a proof to the world that he was as good a nursing father of a kingdom as he had been of a democracy, for the actions of the king had in them the touch and colour of his judgment and character. The moderation which the young man showed to the Lacedæmonians, who had incurred his displeasure, and his affability to the Cretans, by which in a few days he brought over the whole island to his obedience, and his expedition against the Ætolians, so wonderfully successful, brought Philip reputation for hearkening to good advice, and to Aratus for giving it; for which things the king's followers envy-ing him more than ever and finding they could not prevail against him by their secret practices, began openly to abuse and affront him at the banquets and over their wine, with every kind of petulance and impudence; so that once they threw stones at him as he was going back from supper to his tent. At which Philip being much offended, immediately fined them twenty talents, and finding afterwards that they still went on disturbing matters and doing mischief in his affairs, he put them to death.

But with his run of good success, prosperity began to puff him up, and various extravagant desires began to spring and show themselves in his mind; and his natural bad inclinations break-ing through the artificial restraints he had put upon them, in a little time laid open and discovered his true and proper character. In the first place, he privately injured the younger Aratus in his wife, which was not known of a good while, because he was lodged and entertained at their house; then be began to be more rough and untractable in the domestic politics of Greece, and showed plainly that he was wishing to shake himself loose of Aratus. This the Messenian affairs first gave occasion to suspect. For they falling into sedition, and Aratus being just too late with his succours, Philip, who got into the city one day before him, at once blew up the flame of contention amongst them, asking privately, on the one hand, the Messenian generals, if they had not laws whereby to suppress the insolence of the common people, and on the other, the leaders of the people, whether they had not hands to help themselves against their oppressors. Upon which gathering courage, the officers attempted to lay hands on the heads of the people, and they on the other side, coming upon the officers with the multitude, killed them, and very near two hundred persons with them.

Philip having committed this wickedness, and doing his best to set the Messenians by the ears together more than before, Aratus arrived there, and both showed plainly that he took it ill himself, and also he suffered his son bitterly to reproach and revile him. It should seem that the young man had an attachment for Philip, and so at this time one of his expressions to him was, that he no longer appeared to him the handsomest, but the most deformed of all men, after so foul an action. To all which Philip gave him no answer, though he seemed so angry as to make it expected he would, and though several times he cried out aloud while the young man was speaking. But as for the elder Aratus, seeming to take all that he said in good part, and as if he were by nature a politic character and had a good command of himself, he gave him his hand and led him out of the theatre, and carried him with him to the Ithomatas, to sacrifice there to Jupiter, and take a view of the place, for it is a post as fortifiable as the Acro-Corinthus, and, with a garrison in it, quite as strong and as impregnable to the attacks of all around it. Philip therefore went up hither, and having offered sacrifice, receiving the entrails of the ox with both his hands from the priest, he showed them to Aratus and Demetrius the Pharian, presenting them sometimes to the one and sometimes to the other, asking them what they judged, by the tokens in the sacrifice, was to be done with the fort; was he to keep it for himself, or restore it to the Messenians. Demetrius laughed and answered, " If you have in you the soul of a soothsayer, you will restore it, but if of a prince you will hold the ox by both the horns," meaning to refer to Peloponnesus, which would be wholly in his power and at his disposal if he added the Ithomatas to the Acro-Corinthus. Aratus said not a word for a good while; but Philip entreating him to declare his opinion, he said: " Many and great hills are there in Crete, and many rocks in Bœotia and Phocis, and many remarkable strongholds both near the sea and in the midland in Acarnania, and yet all these people obey your orders, though you have not possessed yourself of any one of those places. Robbers nest themselves in rocks and precipices; but the strongest fort a king can have is confidence and affection. These have opened to you the Cretan sea; these make you master of Peloponnesus, and by the help of these, young as you are, are you become captain of the one, and lord of the other." While he was still speaking, Philip returned the entrails to the priest, and drawing Aratus to him by the hand, " Come, then," said he, " let us follow the same course; " as if he felt himself forced by him, and obliged to give up the town.

From this time Aratus began to withdraw from court, and retired by degrees from Philip's company; when he was preparing to march into Epirus, and desired him that he would accompany him thither, he excused himself and stayed at home, apprehending that he should get nothing but discredit by having anything to do with his actions. But then, afterwards, having shamefully lost his fleet against the Romans and miscarried in all his designs, he returned into Peloponnesus, where he tried once more to beguile the Messenians by his artifices, and failing in this, began openly to attack them and to ravage their country, then Aratus fell out with him downright, and utterly renounced his friendship; for he had begun then to be fully aware of the injuries done to his son in his wife, which vexed him greatly, though he concealed them from his son, as he could but know he had been abused, without having any means to revenge himself. For, indeed, Philip seems to have been an instance of the greatest and strangest alteration of character; after being a mild king and modest and chaste youth, he became a lascivious man and most cruel tyrant; though in reality this was not a change of his nature, but a bold unmasking, when safe opportunity came, of the evil inclinations which his fear had for a long time made him dissemble.

For that the respect he at the beginning bore to Aratus had a great alloy of fear and awe appears evidently from what he did to him at last. For being desirous to put him to death, not thinking himself, whilst he was alive, to be properly free as a man, much less at liberty to do his pleasure as king or tyrant, he durst not attempt to do it by open force, but commanded Taurion, one of his captains and familiars, to make him away secretly by poison, if possible, in his absence. Taurion, therefore, made himself intimate with Aratus, and gave him a dose not of your strong and violent poisons, but such as cause gentle, feverish heats at first, and a dull cough, and so by degrees bring on certain death. Aratus perceived what was done to him, but, knowing that it was in vain to make any words of it, bore it patiently and with silence, as if it had been some common and usual distemper. Only once, a friend of his being with him in his chamber, he spat some blood, which his friend observing and wondering at, " These, O Cephalon," said he, " are the wages of a king's love."

Thus died he in Ægium, in his seventeenth generalship. The Achæans were very desirous that he should be buried there with a funeral and monument suitable to his life, but the Sicyonians treated it as a calamity to them if he were interred anywhere but in their city, and prevailed with the Achæans to grant them the disposal of the body.

But there being an ancient law that no person should be buried within the walls of their city, and besides the law also a strong religious feeling about it, they sent to Delphi to ask counsel of the Pythoness, who returned this answer:—

" Sicyon, whom oft he rescued, ' Where,' you say,
' Shall we the relics of Aratus lay? '
The soil that would not lightly o'er him rest,
Or to be under him would feel opprest,
Were in the sight of earth and seas and skies unblest."

This oracle being brought, all the Achæans were well pleased at it, but especially the Sicyonians, who, changing their mourning into public joy, immediately fetched the body from Ægium, and in a kind of solemn procession brought it into the city, being crowned with garlands, and arrayed in white garments, with singing and dancing, and, choosing a conspicuous place, they buried him there, as the founder and saviour of their city. The place is to this day called Aratium, and there they yearly make two solemn sacrifices to him, the one on the day he delivered the city from tyranny, being the fifth of the month Dæsius, which the Athenians call Anthesterion, and this sacrifice they call Soteria; the other in the month of his birth, which is still remembered. Now the first of these was performed by the priest of Jupiter Soter, the second by the priest of Aratus, wearing a band around his head, not pure white, but mingled with purple. Hymns were sung to the harp by the singers of the feasts of Bacchus; the procession was led up by the president of the public exercises, with the boys and young men; these were followed by the councillors wearing garlands, and other citizens such as pleased. Of these observances, some small traces, it is still made a point of religion not to omit on the appointed days; but the greatest part of the ceremonies have through time and other intervening accidents been disused.

And such, as history tells us, was the life and manners of the elder Aratus. And for the younger, his son, Philip, abominably wicked by nature and a savage abuser of his power, gave him such poisonous medicines, as though they did not kill him indeed, yet made him lose his senses, and run into wild and absurd attempts and desire to do actions and satisfy appetites that were ridiculous and shameful. So that his death, which happened to him while he was yet young and in the flower of his age, cannot be so much esteemed a misfortune as a deliverance and end of his misery. However Philip paid dearly, all through the rest of his life, for these impious violations of friendship and hospitality. For, being overcome by the Romans, he was forced to put himself wholly into their hands, and, being deprived of his other dominions and surrendering all his ships except five, he had also to pay a fine of a thousand talents, and to give his son for hostage, and only out of mere pity he was suffered to keep Macedonia and its dependencies; where continually putting to death the noblest of his subjects and the nearest relations he had, he filled the whole kingdom with horror and hatred of him. And whereas amidst so many misfortunes he had but one good chance, which was the having a son of great virtue and merit, him, through jealousy and envy at the honour the Romans had for him, he caused to be murdered, and left his kingdom to Perseus, who, as some say, was not his own child, but supposititious, born of a sempstress Gnathænion. This was he whom Paulus Æmilius led in trumph, and in whom ended the succession of Antigonus's line and kingdom. But the posterity of Aratus continued still in our days at Sicyon and Pellene.

# ARTAXERXES

THE first Artaxerxes, among all the kings of Persia the most remarkable for a gentle and noble spirit, was surnamed the Long-handed, his right hand being longer than his left, and was the son of Xerxes. The second, whose story I am now writing, who had the surname of the Mindful, was the grandson of the former, by his daughter Parysatis, who brought Darius four sons, the eldest Artaxerxes, the next Cyrus, and two younger than these, Ostanes and Oxathres. Cyrus took his name of the ancient Cyrus, as he, they say, had his from the sun, which, in the Persian language, is called Cyrus. Artaxerxes was at first called Arsicas; Dinon says Oarses; but it is utterly improbable that Ctesias (however otherwise he may have filled his books with a perfect farrago of incredible and senseless fables) should be ignorant of the name of the king with whom he lived as his physician, attending upon himself, his wife, his mother, and his children.

Cyrus, from his earliest youth, showed something of a head-strong and vehement character; Artaxerxes, on the other side, was gentler in everything, and of a nature more yielding and soft in its action. He married a beautiful and virtuous wife, at the desire of his parents, but kept her as expressly against their wishes. For King Darius, having put her brother to death, was purposing likewise to destroy her. But Arsicas, throwing himself at his mother's feet, by many tears, at last, with much ado, persuaded her that they should neither put her to death nor divorce her from him. However, Cyrus was his mother's favourite, and the son whom she most desired to settle in the throne. And therefore, his father Darius now lying ill, he, being sent for from the sea to the court, set out thence with full hopes that by her means he was to be declared the successor to the kingdom. For Parysatis had the specious plea in his behalf, which Xerxes on the advice of Demaratus had of old made use of, that she had borne him Arsicas when he was a subject, but Cyrus, when a king. Notwithstanding, she prevailed not with Darius, but the eldest son, Arsicas, was proclaimed king, his name being changed into Artaxerxes; and Cyrus remained satrap of Lydia, and commander in the maritime provinces.

It was not long after the decease of Darius that the king, his

successor, went to Pasargadæ, to have the ceremony of his
inauguration consummated by the Persian priests.  There is a
temple dedicated to a warlike goddess, whom one might liken
to Minerva, into which when the royal person to be initiated
has passed, he must strip himself of his own robe, and put on
that which Cyrus the first wore before he was king; then, having
devoured a frail of figs, he must eat turpentine, and drink a cup
of sour milk.  To which if they superadd any other rites, it is
unknown to any but those that are present at them.  Now
Artaxerxes being about to address himself to this solemnity,
Tisaphernes came to him, bringing a certain priest, who, having
trained up Cyrus in his youth in the established discipline of
Persia, and having taught him the Magian philosophy, was
likely to be as much disappointed as any man that his pupil did
not succeed to the throne.  And for that reason his veracity
was the less questioned when he charged Cyrus as though he
had been about to lie in wait for the king in the temple, and to
assault and assassinate him as he was putting off his garment.
Some affirm that he was apprehended upon this impeachment,
others that he had entered the temple and was pointed out
there, as he lay lurking by the priest.  But as he was upon the
point of being put to death, his mother clasped him in her arms,
and, entwining him with the tresses of her hair, joined his neck
close to her own, and by her bitter lamentation and intercession
to Artaxerxes for him, succeeded in saving his life; and sent
him away again to the sea and to his former province.  This,
however, could no longer content him; nor did he so well
remember his delivery as his arrest, his resentment for which
made him more eagerly desirous of the kingdom than before.

Some say that he revolted from his brother, because he had
not a revenue allowed him sufficient for his daily meals; but
this is on the face of it absurd.  For had he had nothing else,
yet he had a mother ready to supply him with whatever he could
desire out of her own means.  But the great number of soldiers
who were hired from all quarters and maintained, as Xenophon
informs us, for his service, by his friends and connections, is in
itself a sufficient proof of his riches.  He did not assemble them
together in a body, desiring as yet to conceal his enterprise;
but he had agents everywhere, enlisting foreign soldiers upon
various pretences; and, in the meantime, Parysatis, who was
with the king, did her best to put aside all suspicions, and Cyrus
himself always wrote in a humble and dutiful manner to him,
sometimes soliciting favour, sometimes making countercharges

against Tisaphernes, as if his jealousy and contest had been wholly with him. Moreover, there was a certain natural dilatoriness in the king, which was taken by many for clemency. And, indeed, in the beginning of his reign, he did seem really to emulate the gentleness of the first Artaxerxes, being very accessible in his person, and liberal to a fault in the distribution of honours and favours. Even in his punishments, no contumely or vindictive pleasure could be seen; and those who offered him presents were as much pleased with his manner of accepting, as were those who received gifts from him with his graciousness and amiability in giving them. Nor truly was there anything, however inconsiderable, given him, which he did not deign kindly to accept of; insomuch that when one Omises had presented him with a very large pomegranate, " By Mithras," said he, " this man, were he intrusted with it, would turn a small city into a great one."

Once when some were offering him one thing, some another, as he was on a progress, a certain poor labourer, having got nothing at hand to bring him, ran to the river side, and, taking up water in his hands, offered it to him; with which Artaxerxes was so well pleased that he sent him a goblet of gold and a thousand darics. To Euclidas, the Lacedæmonian, who had made a number of bold and arrogant speeches to him, he sent word by one of his officers, " You have leave to say what you please to me, and I, you should remember, may both say and do what I please to you." Teribazus once, when they were hunting, came up and pointed out to the king that his royal robe was torn; the king asked him what he wished him to do; and when Teribazus replied, " May it please you to put on another and give me that," the king did so, saying withal, " I give it you, Teribazus, but I charge you not to wear it." He, little regarding the injunction, being not a bad, but a lightheaded, thoughtless man, immediately the king took it off, put it on, and bedecked himself further with royal golden necklaces and women's ornaments, to the great scandal of everybody, the thing being quite unlawful. But the king laughed and told him, " You have my leave to wear the trinkets as a woman, and the robe of state as a fool." And whereas none usually sat down to eat with the king besides his mother and his wedded wife, the former being placed above, the other below him, Artaxerxes invited also to his table his two younger brothers, Ostanes and Oxathres. But what was the most popular thing of all among the Persians was the sight of his wife Statira's chariot, which always appeared with its curtains down, allowing her country-women to salute and approach her, which made the queen a great favourite with the people.

Yet busy, factious men, that delighted in change, professed it to be their opinion that the times needed Cyrus, a man of great spirit, an excellent warrior, and a lover of his friends, and that the largeness of their empire absolutely required a bold and enterprising prince. Cyrus, then, not only relying upon those of his own province near the sea, but upon many of those in the upper countries near the king, commenced the war against him. He wrote to the Lacedæmonians, bidding them come to his assistance and supply him with men, assuring them that to those who came to him on foot he would give horses, and to the horsemen chariots; that upon those who had farms he would bestow villages, and those who were lords of villages he would make so of cities; and that those who would be his soldiers should receive their pay, not by count, but by weight. And among many other high praises of himself, he said he had the stronger soul; was more a philosopher and a better Magian; and could drink and bear more wine than his brother, who, as he averred, was such a coward and so little like a man, that he could neither sit his horse in hunting nor his throne in time of danger. The Lacedæmonians, his letter being read, sent a staff to Clearchus, commanding him to obey Cyrus in all things. So Cyrus marched towards the king, having under his conduct a numerous host of barbarians, and but little less than thirteen thousand stipendiary Grecians; alleging first one cause, then another, for his expedition. Yet the true reason lay not long concealed, but Tisaphernes went to the king in person to declare it. Thereupon, the court was all in an uproar and tumult, the queen-mother bearing almost the whole blame of the enterprise, and her retainers being suspected and accused. Above all, Statira angered her by bewailing the war and passionately de-manding where were now the pledges and the intercession which saved the life of him that conspired against his brother; " to the end," she said, " that he might plunge us all into war and trouble." For which words Parysatis hating Statira, and being naturally implacable and savage in her anger and revenge, con-sulted how she might destroy her. But since Dinon tells us that her purpose took effect in the time of the war, and Ctesias says it was after it, I shall keep the story for the place to which the latter assigns it, as it is very unlikely that he, who was actually present, should not know the time when it happened, and there was no motive to induce him designedly to misplace its date in his narrative of it, though it is not infrequent with him in his history to make excursions from truth into mere fiction and romance.

As Cyrus was upon the march, rumours and reports were brought him, as though the king still deliberated, and were not minded to fight and presently to join battle with him; but to wait in the heart of his kingdom until his forces should have come in thither from all parts of his dominions. He had cut a trench through the plain ten fathoms in breadth, and as many in depth, the length of it being no less than four hundred furlongs. Yet he allowed Cyrus to pass across it, and to advance almost to the city of Babylon. Then Teribazus, as the report goes, was the first that had the boldness to tell the king that he ought not to avoid the conflict, nor to abandon Media, Babylon, and even Susa, and hide himself in Persis, when all the while he had an army many times over more numerous than his enemies, and an infinite company of governors and captains that were better soldiers and politicians than Cyrus. So at last he resolved to fight, as soon as it was possible for him. Making, therefore, his first appearance, all on a sudden, at the head of nine hundred thousand well-marshalled men, he so startled and surprised the enemy, who with the confidence of contempt were marching on their way in no order, and with their arms not ready for use, that Cyrus, in the midst of such noise and tumult, was scarcely able to form them for battle. Moreover, the very manner in which he led on his men, silently and slowly, made the Grecians stand amazed at his good discipline; who had expected irregular shouting and leaping, much confusion and separation between one body of men and another, in so vast a multitude of troops. He also placed the choicest of his armed chariots in the front of his own phalanx over against the Grecian troops, that a violent charge with these might cut open their ranks before they closed with them.

But as this battle is described by many historians, and Xenophon in particular as good as shows it us by eyesight, not as a past event, but as a present action, and by his vivid account makes his hearers feel all the passions and join in all the dangers of it, it would be folly in me to give any larger account of it than barely to mention any things omitted by him which yet deserve to be recorded. The place, then, in which the two armies were drawn out is called Cunaxa, being about five hundred furlongs distant from Babylon. And here Clearchus be-

seeching Cyrus before the fight to retire behind the combatants,
and not expose himself to hazard, they say he replied, " What
is this, Clearchus? Would you have me, who aspire to empire,
show myself unworthy of it? " But if Cyrus committed a great
fault in entering headlong into the midst of danger, and not
paying any regard to his own safety, Clearchus was as much to
blame, if not more, in refusing to lead the Greeks against the
main body of the enemy, where the king stood, and in keeping
his right wing close to the river, for fear of being surrounded.
For if he wanted, above all other things, to be safe, and considered it his first object to sleep in a whole skin, it had been
his best way not to have stirred from home. But, after marching in arms ten thousand furlongs from the sea-coast, simply on
his choosing, for the purpose of placing Cyrus on the throne, to
look about and select a position which would enable him, not
to preserve him under whose pay and conduct he was, but himself to engage with more ease and security, seemed much like
one that through fear of present dangers had abandoned the
purpose of his actions, and been false to the design of his expedition. For it is evident from the very event of the battle
that none of those who were in array around the king's person
could have stood the shock of the Grecian charge; and had they
been beaten out of the field, and Artaxerxes either fled or fallen,
Cyrus would have gained by the victory, not only safety, but a
crown. And, therefore, Clearchus by his caution must be considered more to blame for the result in the destruction of the
life and fortune of Cyrus, than he by his heat and rashness.
For had the king made it his business to discover a place, where
having posted the Grecians, he might encounter them with the
least hazard, he would never have found out any other but that
which was most remote from himself and those near him; of
his defeat in which he was insensible, and, though Clearchus
had the victory, yet Cyrus could not know of it, and could take
no advantage of it before his fall. Cyrus knew well enough
what was expedient to be done, and commanded Clearchus with
his men to take their place in the centre. Clearchus replied
that he would take care to have all arranged as was best, and
then spoiled all.

For the Grecians, where they were, defeated the barbarians
till they were weary, and chased them successfully a very great
way. But Cyrus being mounted upon a noble but a headstrong
and hard-mouthed horse, bearing the name, as Ctesias tells us,
of Pasacas, Artagerses, the leader of the Cadusians, galloped up

to him, crying aloud, " O most unjust and senseless of men, who are the disgrace of the honoured name of Cyrus, are you come here leading the wicked Greeks on a wicked journey, to plunder the good things of the Persians, and this with the intent of slaying your lord and brother, the master of ten thousand times ten thousand servants that are better men than you? **as** you shall see this instant; for you shall lose your head here, before you look upon the face of the king." Which when he had said, he cast his javelin at him. But his coat of mail stoutly repelled it, and Cyrus was not wounded; yet the stroke falling heavy upon him, he reeled under it. Then Artagerses turning his horse, Cyrus threw his weapon, and sent the head of it through his neck near the shoulder bone. So that it is almost universally agreed to by all the authors that Artagerses was slain by him.

But as to the death of Cyrus, since Xenophon, as being himself no eye-witness of it, has stated it simply and in few word, it may not be amiss perhaps to run over on the one hand what Dinon, and on the other, what Ctesias had said of it.

Dinon then affirms that, after the death of Artagerses, Cyrus, furiously attacking the guard of Artaxerxes, wounded the king's horse, and so dismounted him, and when Teribazus had quickly lifted him up upon another, and said to him, " O king, remember this day, which is not one to be forgotten," Cyrus, again spurring up his horse, struck down Artaxerxes. But at the third assault the king being enraged and saying to those near him that death was more eligible, made up to Cyrus, who furiously and blindly rushed in the face of the weapons opposed to him. So the king struck him with a javelin, as likewise did those that were about him. And thus Cyrus falls, as some say, by the hand of the king; as others by the dart of a Carian, to whom Artaxerxes for a reward of his achievement gave the privilege of carrying ever after a golden cock upon his spear before the first ranks of the army in all expeditions. For the Persians call the men of Caria cocks, because of the crests with which they adorn their helmets.

But the account of Ctesias, to put it shortly, omitting many details, is as follows: Cyrus, after the death of Artagerses, rode up against the king, as he did against him, neither exchanging a word with the other. But Ariæus, Cyrus's friend, was beforehand with him, and darted first at the king, yet wounded him not. Then the king cast his lance at his brother, but missed him, though he both hit and slew Satiphernes, a noble man and a faithful friend to Cyrus. Then Cyrus directed his lance against the king, and pierced his breast with it quite through his armour, two inches deep, so that he fell from his horse with the stroke. At which those that attended him being put to flight and disorder, he, rising with a few, among whom was Ctesias, and making his way to a little hill not far off, rested himself. But Cyrus, who was in the thick enemy, was carried off a great way by the wildness of his horse, the darkness which was now coming on making it hard for them to know him, and for his followers to find him. However, being made elate with victory, and full of confidence and force, he passed through them, crying out, and that more than once, in the Persian language, " Clear the way, villains, clear the way; " which they indeed did, throwing themselves down at his feet. But his tiara dropped off his head, and a young Persian, by name Mithridates, running by, struck a dart into one of his temples near his eye, not knowing who he was; out of which wound much blood gushed, so that Cyrus, swooning and senseless, fell off his horse. The horse escaped, and ran about the field; but the companion of Mithridates took the trappings which fell off, soaked with blood. And as Cyrus slowly began to come to himself, some eunuchs who were there tried to put him on another horse, and so convey him safe away. And when he was not able to ride, and desired to walk on his feet, they led and supported him, being indeed dizzy in the head and reeling, but convinced of his being victorious, hearing, as he went, the fugitives saluting Cyrus as king, and praying for grace and mercy. In the meantime, some wretched, poverty-stricken Caunians, who in some pitiful employment as camp followers had accompanied the king's army, by chance joined these attendants of Cyrus, supposing them to be of their own party. But when, after a while, they made out that their coats over their breastplates were red, whereas all the king's people wore white ones, they knew that they were enemies. One of them, therefore, not dreaming that it was Cyrus, ventured to strike him behind with a dart. The vein under the knee was cut open, and Cyrus fell, and at the same time struck his wounded temple against a stone, and so died. Thus runs Ctesias's account, tardily, with the slowness of a blunt weapon effecting the victim's death.

When he was now dead, Artasyras, the king's eye, passed by on horseback, and, having observed the eunuchs lamenting, he asked the most trusty of them, " Who is this, Pariscas, whom you sit here deploring? " He replied, " Do not you see, O Artasyras, that it is my master, Cyrus? " Then Artasyras wondering, bade the eunuch be of good cheer, and keep the dead body safe. And going in all haste to Artaxerxes, who had now given up all hope of his affairs, and was in great suffering also with his thirst and his wound, he with much joy assured him that he had seen Cyrus dead. Upon this, at first, he set out to go in person to the place, and commanded Artasyras to conduct him where he lay. But when there was a great noise made about the Greeks, who were said to be in full pursuit, conquering and carrying all before them, he thought it best to send a number of persons to see; and accordingly thirty men went with torches in their hands. Meantime, as he seemed to be almost at the point of dying from thirst, his eunuch Satibarzanes ran about seeking drink for him; for the place had no water in it and he was at a good distance from his camp. After a long search he at last met one of those poor Caunian camp-followers, who had in a wretched skin about four pints of foul and stinking water, which he took and gave to the king; and when he had drunk all off, he asked him if he did not dislike the water; but he declared by all the gods that he never so much relished either wine, or water out of the lightest or purest stream. " And therefore," said he, " if I fail myself to discover and reward him who gave it to you, I beg of heaven to make him rich and prosperous."

Just after this, came back the thirty messengers, with joy and triumph in their looks, bringing him the tidings of his unexpected fortune. And now he was also encouraged by the number of soldiers that again began to flock in and gather about him; so that he presently descended into the plain with many lights and flambeaux round about him. And when he had come near the dead body, and, according to a certain law of the Persians, the right hand and head had been lopped off from the trunk, he gave orders that the latter should be brought to him, and, grasping the hair of it, which was long and bushy, he showed it to those who were still uncertain and disposed to fly. They were amazed at it, and did him homage; so that there were presently seventy thousand of them got about him, and entered the camp again with him. He had led out to the fight, as Ctesias affirms, four hundred thousand men. But Dinon and Xenophon aver that there were many more than forty myriads actually engaged. As to the number of the slain, as the catalogue of them was given up to Artaxerxes, Ctesias says, they were nine thousand, but that they appeared to him no fewer than twenty thousand. Thus far there is something to be said on both sides. But it is a flagrant untruth on the part of

Ctesias to say that he was sent along with Phalinus the Zacyn-
thian and some others to the Grecians. For Xenophon knew
well enough that Ctesias was resident at court; for he makes
mention of him, and had evidently met with his writings. And,
therefore, had he come, and been deputed the interpreter of
such momentous words, Xenophon surely would not have struck
his name out of the embassy to mention only Phalinus. But
Ctesias, as is evident, being excessively vainglorious and no less
a favourer of the Lacedæmonians and Clearchus, never fails to
assume to himself some province in his narrative, taking opportunity, in these situations, to introduce abundant high praise
of Clearchus and Sparta.

When the battle was over, Artaxerxes sent goodly and magnificent gifts to the son of Artagerses, whom Cyrus slew. He
conferred likewise high honours upon Ctesias and others, and,
having found out the Caunian who gave him the bottle of water,
he made him—a poor, obscure man—a rich and an honourable
person. As for the punishments he inflicted upon delinquents,
there was a kind of harmony betwixt them and the crimes. He
gave order that one Arbaces, a Mede, that had fled in the fight
to Cyrus and again at his fall had come back, should, as a
mark that he was considered a dastardly and effeminate, not a
dangerous or treasonable man, have a common harlot set upon
his back, and carry her about for a whole day in the market-
place. Another, besides that he had deserted to them, having
falsely vaunted that he had killed two of the rebels, he decreed
that three needles should be struck through his tongue. And
both supposing that with his own hand he had cut off Cyrus,
and being willing that all men should think and say so, he sent
rich presents to Mithridates, who first wounded him, and charged
those by whom he conveyed the gifts to him to tell him, that
" the king has honoured you with these his favours, because
you found and brought him the horse-trappings of Cyrus."
The Carian, also, from whose wound in the ham Cyrus died,
suing for his reward, he commanded those that brought it him
to say that " the king presents you with this as a second re-
muneration for the ·good news told him; for first Artasyras,
and, next to him, you assured him of the decease of Cyrus."
Mithridates retired without complaint, though not without resentment. But the unfortunate Carian was fool enough to give
way to a natural infirmity. For being ravished with the sight
of the princely gifts that were before him, and being tempted
thereupon to challenge and aspire to things above him, he

deigned not to accept the king's present as a reward for good news, but indignantly crying out and appealing to witnesses, he protested that he, and none but he, had killed Cyrus, and that he was unjustly deprived of the glory. These words, when they came to his ear, much offended the king, so that forthwith he sentenced him to be beheaded. But the queen mother, being in the king's presence, said, " Let not the king so lightly discharge this pernicious Carian; let him receive from me the fitting punishment of what he dares to say." So when the king had consigned him over to Parysatis, she charged the executioners to take up the man, and stretch him upon the rack for ten days, then, tearing out his eyes, to drop molten brass into his ears till he expired.

Mithridates, also, within a short time after, miserably perished by the like folly; for being invited to a feast where were the eunuchs both of the king and of the queen mother, he came arrayed in the dress and the golden ornaments which he had received from the king. After they began to drink, the eunuch that was the greatest in power with Parysatis thus speaks to him: " A magnificent dress, indeed, O Mithridates, is this which the king has given you; the chains and bracelets are glorious, and your scymetar of invaluable worth; how happy has he made you, the object of every eye!" To whom he, being a little overcome with the wine, replied, " What are these things, Sparamizes? Sure I am, I showed myself to the king in that day of trial to be one deserving greater and costlier gifts than these." At which Sparamizes smiling, said, " I do not grudge them to you, Mithridates; but since the Grecians tell us that wine and truth go together, let me hear now, my friend, what glorious or mighty matter was it to find some trappings that had slipped off a horse, and to bring them to the king?" And this he spoke, not as ignorant of the truth, but desiring to unbosom him to the company, irritating the vanity of the man, whom drink had now made eager to talk and incapable of controlling himself. So he forbore nothing, but said out, " Talk you what you please of horse-trappings and such trifles; I tell you plainly, that this hand was the death of Cyrus. For I threw not my darts as Artagerses did, in vain and to no purpose, but only just missing his eye, and hitting him right on the temple, and piercing him through, I brought him to the ground; and of that wound he died." The rest of the company, who saw the end and the hapless fate of Mithridates as if it were already completed, bowed their heads to the ground; and he

who entertained them said, "Mithridates, my friend, let us eat
and drink now, revering the fortune of our prince, and let us
waive discourse which is too weighty for us."

Presently after, Sparamizes told Parysatis what he said, and
she told the king, who was greatly enraged at it, as having the
lie given him, and being in danger to forfeit the most glorious
and most pleasant circumstance of his victory. For it was his
desire that every one, whether Greek or barbarian, should believe
that in the mutual assaults and conflicts between him and his
brother, he, giving and receiving a blow, was himself indeed
wounded, but that the other lost his life. And, therefore, he
decreed that Mithridates should be put to death in boats; which
execution is after the following manner: Taking two boats
framed exactly to fit and answer each other, they lay down in
one of them the malefactor that suffers, upon his back; then,
covering it with the other, and so setting them together that
the head, hands, and feet of him are left outside, and the rest
of his body lies shut up within, they offer him food, and if he
refuse to eat it, they force him to do it by pricking his eyes;
then, after he has eaten, they drench him with a mixture of
milk and honey, pouring it not only into his mouth, but all over
his face. They then keep his face continually turned towards
the sun: and it becomes completely covered up and hidden by
the multitude of flies that settle on it. And as within the boats
he does what those that eat and drink must needs do, creeping
things and vermin spring out of the corruption and rottenness
of the excrement, and these entering into the bowels of him,
his body is consumed. When the man is manifestly dead, the
uppermost boat being taken off, they find his flesh devoured,
and swarms of such noisome creatures preying upon and, as it
were, growing to his inwards. In this way Mithridates, after
suffering for seventeen days, at last expired.

Masabates, the king's eunuch, who had cut off the hand and
head of Cyrus, remained still as a mark for Parysatis's vengeance.
Whereas, therefore, he was so circumspect, that he gave her no
advantage against him, she framed this kind of snare for him.
She was a very ingenious woman in other ways, and was an
excellent player at dice, and, before the war, had often played
with the king. After the war, too, when she had been reconciled to him, she joined readily in all amusements with him,
played at dice with him, was his confidant in his love matters,
and in every way did her best to leave him as little as possible
in the company of Statira, both because she hated her more

than any other person, and because she wished to have no one so powerful as herself. And so once when Artaxerxes was at leisure, and inclined to divert himself, she challenged him to play at dice with her for a thousand darics, and purposely let him win them, and paid him down in gold. Yet, pretending to be concerned for her loss, and that she would gladly have her revenge for it, she pressed him to begin a new game for a eunuch; to which he consented. But first they agreed that each of them might except five of their most trusty eunuchs, and that out of the rest of them the loser should yield up any the winner should make choice of. Upon these conditions they played. Thus being bent upon her design, and thoroughly in earnest with her game, and the dice also running luckily for her, when she had got the game, she demanded Masabates, who was not in the number of the five excepted. And before the king could suspect the matter, having delivered him up to the tormentors, she enjoined them to flay him alive, to set his body upon three stakes, and to stretch his skin upon stakes separately from it.

These things being done, and the king taking them ill, and being incensed against her, she with raillery and laughter told him, " You are a comfortable and happy man indeed, if you are so much disturbed for the sake of an old rascally eunuch, when I, though I have thrown away a thousand darics, hold my peace and acquiesce in my fortune." So the king, vexed with himself for having been thus deluded, hushed up all. But Statira both in other matters openly opposed her, and was angry with her for thus, against all law and humanity, sacrificing to the memory of Cyrus the king's faithful friend and eunuch.

Now after that Tisaphernes had circumvented and by a false oath had betrayed Clearchus and the other commanders, and, taking them, had sent them bound in chains to the king, Ctesias says that he was asked by Clearchus to supply him with a comb; and that when he had it, and had combed his head with it, he was much pleased with this good office, and gave him a ring, which might be a token of the obligation to his relatives and friends in Sparta; and that the engraving upon this signet was a set of Caryatides dancing. He tells us that the soldiers, his fellow-captives, used to purloin a part of the allowance of food sent to Clearchus, giving him but little of it; which thing Ctesias says he rectified, causing a better allowance to be conveyed to him, and that a separate share should be distributed to the soldiers by themselves; adding that he ministered to and

supplied him thus by the interest and at the instance of Parysatis. And there being a portion of ham sent daily with his
other food to Clearchus, she, he says, advised and instructed
him, that he ought to bury a small knife in the meat, and thus
send it to his friend, and not leave his fate to be determined by
the king's cruelty; which he, however, he says, was afraid to
do. However, Artaxerxes consented to the entreaties of his
mother, and promised her with an oath that he would spare
Clearchus; but afterwards, at the instigation of Statira, he put
every one of them to death except Menon. And thenceforward,
he says, Parysatis watched her advantage against Statira and
made up poison for her; not a very probable story, or a very
likely motive to account for her conduct, if indeed he means
that out of respect to Clearchus she dared to attempt the life of
the lawful queen, that was mother of those who were heirs of
the empire. But it is evident enough, that this part of his
history is a sort of funeral exhibition in honour of Clearchus.
For he would have us believe that, when the generals were
executed, the rest of them were torn in pieces by dogs and birds;
but as for the remains of Clearchus, that a violent gust of wind,
bearing before it a vast heap of earth, raised a mound to cover
his body, upon which, after a short time, some dates having
fallen there, a beautiful grove of trees grew up and overshadowed
the place, so that the king himself declared his sorrow, concluding
that in Clearchus he put to death a man beloved of the gods.

Parysatis, therefore, having from the first entertained a secret
hatred and jealousy against Statira, seeing that the power she
herself had with Artaxerxes was founded upon feelings of honour
and respect for her, but that Statira's influence was firmly and
strongly based upon love and confidence, was resolved to contrive her ruin, playing at hazard, as she thought, for the greatest
stake in the world. Among her attendant women there was
one that was trusty and in the highest esteem with her, whose
name was Gigis; who, as Dinon avers, assisted in making up
the poison. Ctesias allows her only to have been conscious of
it, and that against her will; charging Belitaras with actually
giving the drug, whereas Dinon says it was Melantas. The two
women had begun again to visit each other and to eat together;
but though they had thus far relaxed their former habits of
jealousy and variance, still, out of fear and as a matter of
caution, they always ate of the same dishes and of the same
parts of them. Now there is a small Persian bird, in the inside
of which no excrement is found, only a mass of fat, so that they

suppose the little creature lives upon air and dew. It is called *rhyntaces*. Ctesias affirms, that Parysatis, cutting a bird of this kind into two pieces with a knife one side of which had been smeared with the drug, the other side being clear of it, ate the untouched and wholesome part herself, and gave Statira that which was thus infected; but Dinon will not have it to be Parysatis, but Melantas, that cut up the bird and presented the envenomed part of it to Statira; who, dying with dreadful agonies and convulsions, was herself sensible of what had happened to her, and aroused in the king's mind suspicion of his mother, whose savage and implacable temper he knew. And therefore proceeding instantly to an inquest, he seized upon his mother's domestic servants that attended at her table and put them upon the rack. Parysatis kept Gigis at home with her a long time, and though the king commanded her, she would not produce her. But she, at last herself desiring that she might be dismissed to her own home by night, Artaxerxes had intimation of it, and lying in wait for her, hurried her away, and adjudged her to death. Now poisoners in Persia suffer thus by law. There is a broad stone, on which they place the head of the culprit, and then with another stone beat and press it, until the face and the head itself are all pounded to pieces; which was the punishment Gigis lost her life by. But to his mother, Artaxerxes neither said nor did any other hurt, save that he banished and confined her, not much against her will, to Babylon, protesting that while she lived he would not come near that city. Such was the condition of the king's affairs in his own house.

But when all his attempts to capture the Greeks that had come with Cyrus, though he desired to do so no less than he had desired to overcome Cyrus and maintain his throne, proved unlucky, and they, though they had lost both Cyrus and their own generals, nevertheless escaped, as it were, out of his very palace, making it plain to all men that the Persian king and his empire were mighty indeed in gold and luxury and women, but otherwise were a mere show and vain display, upon this all Greece took courage and despised the barbarians; and especially the Lacedæmonians thought it strange if they should not now deliver their countrymen that dwelt in Asia from their subjection to the Persians, nor put an end to the contumelious usage of them. And first having an army under the conduct of Thimbron, then under Dercyllidas, but doing nothing memorable, they at last committed the war to the management of their King Agesilaus, who, when he had arrived with his men in Asia, as soon as he had landed them, fell actively to work, and got himself great renown. He defeated Tisaphernes in a pitched battle, and set many cities in revolt. Upon this, Artaxerxes, perceiving what was his wisest way of waging the war, sent Timocrates the Rhodian into Greece, with large sums of gold, commanding him by a free distribution of it to corrupt the leading men in the cities, and to excite a Greek war against Sparta. So Timocrates following his instructions, the most considerable cities conspiring together, and Peloponnesus being in disorder, the ephors remanded Agesilaus from Asia. At which time, they say, as he was upon his return, he told his friends that Artaxerxes had driven him out of Asia with thirty thousand archers; the Persian coin having an archer stamped upon it.

Artaxerxes scoured the seas, too, of the Lacedæmonians, Conon the Athenian and Pharnabazus being his admirals. For Conon, after the battle of Ægospotami, resided in Cyprus; not that he consulted his own mere security, but looking for a vicissitude of affairs with no less hope than men wait for a change of wind at sea. And perceiving that his skill wanted power, and that the king's power wanted a wise man to guide it, he sent him an account of his projects, and charged the bearer to hand it to the king, if possible, by the mediation of Zeno the Cretan or Polycritus the Mendæan (the former being a dancing-master, the latter a physician), or, in the absence of them both, by Ctesias; who is said to have taken Conon's letter, and foisted into the contents of it a request, that the king would also be pleased to send over Ctesias to him, who was likely to be of use on the sea-coast. Ctesias, however, declares that the king, of his accord, deputed him to his service. Artaxerxes, however, defeating the Lacedæmonians in a sea-fight at Cnidos, under the conduct of Pharnabazus and Conon, after he had stripped them of their sovereignty by sea, at the same time brought, so to say, the whole of Greece over to him, so that upon his own terms he dictated the celebrated peace among them, styled the peace of Antalcidas. This Antalcidas was a Spartan, the son of one Leon, who, acting for the king's interest, induced the Lacedæmonians to covenant to let all the Greek cities in Asia and the islands adjacent to it become subject and tributary to him, peace being upon these conditions established among the Greeks, if indeed the honourable name of peace can fairly be given to what was in fact the disgrace and betrayal of Greece, a treaty more inglorious than had ever been the result of any war to those defeated in it.

And therefore Artaxerxes, though always abominating other Spartans, and looking upon them, as Dinon says, to be the most impudent men living, gave wonderful honour to Antalcidas when he came to him into Persia; so much so that one day, taking a garland of flowers and dipping it in the most precious ointment, he sent it to him after supper, a favour which all were amazed at. Indeed he was a person fit to be thus delicately treated, and to have such a crown, who had among the Persians thus made fools of Leonidas and Callicratidas. Agesilaus, it seems, on some one having said, " O the deplorable fate of Greece, now that the Spartans turn Medes! " replied, " Nay, rather it is the Medes who become Spartans." But the subtilty of the repartee did not wipe off the infamy of the action. The Lacedæmonians soon after lost their sovereignty in Greece by their defeat at Leuctra; but they had already lost their honour by this treaty. So long then as Sparta continued to be the first state in Greece, Artaxerxes continued to Antalcidas the honour of being called his friend and his guest; but when, routed and humbled at the battle of Leuctra, being under great distress for money, they had despatched Agesilaus into Egypt, and Antalcidas went up to Artaxerxes, beseeching him to supply their necessities, he so despised, slighted, and rejected him, that finding himself, on his return, mocked and insulted by his enemies, and fearing also the ephors, he starved himself to death. Ismenias, also, the Theban, and Pelopidas, who had already gained the victory at Leuctra, arrived at the Persian court; where the latter did nothing unworthy of himself. But Ismenias, being commanded to do obeisance to the king, dropped his ring before him upon the ground, and so, stooping to take it up, made a show of doing him homage. He was so gratified with some secret intelligence which Timagoras the Athenian sent in to him by the hand of his secretary Beluris, that he bestowed upon him ten thousand darics, and because he was ordered, on account of some sickness, to drink cow's milk, there were fourscore milch kine driven after him; also, he sent him a bed, furniture, and servants for it, the Grecians not having skill enough to make it, as also chairmen to carry him, being infirm in body, to the seaside. Not to mention the feast made for him at court, which was so princely and splendid that Ostanes, the king's brother, said to him, " O Timogoras, do not forgot the sumptuous table you have sat at here; it was not put before you for nothing; " which was indeed rather a reflection upon his treason than to remind him of the king's bounty. And indeed the Athenians condemned Timagoras to death for taking bribes.

But Artaxerxes gratified the Grecians in one thing in lieu of the many wherewith he plagued them, and that was by taking off Tisaphernes, their most hated and malicious enemy, whom he put to death; Parysatis adding her influence to the charges made against him. For the king did not persist long in his wrath with his mother, but was reconciled to her, and sent for her, being assured that she had wisdom and courage fit for royal power, and there being now no cause discernible but that they might converse together without suspicion or offence. And from thenceforward humouring the king in all things according to his heart's desire, and finding fault with nothing that he did, she obtained great power with him, and was gratified in all her requests. She perceived he was desperately in love with Atossa, one of his own two daughters, and that he concealed and checked his passion chiefly for fear of herself, though, if we may believe some writers, he had privately given way to it with the young girl already. As soon as Parysatis suspected it, she displayed a greater fondness for the young girl than before, and extolled both her virtue and beauty to him, as being truly imperial and majestic. In fine she persuaded him to marry her and declare her to be his lawful wife, overriding all the principles and the laws by which the Greeks hold themselves bound, and regarding himself as divinely appointed for a law to the Persians, and the supreme arbitrator of good and evil. Some historians further affirm, in which number is Heraclides of Cuma, that Artaxerxes married not only this one, but a second daughter also, Amestris, of whom we shall speak by and by. But he so loved Atossa when she became his consort, that when leprosy had run through her whole body, he was not in the least offended at it; but putting up his prayers to Juno for her, to this one alone of all the deities he made obeisance, by laying his hands upon the earth; and his satraps and favourites made such offerings to the goddess by his direction, that all along for sixteen furlongs, betwixt the court and her temple, the road was filled up with gold and silver, purple and horses, devoted to her.

He waged war out of his own kingdom with the Egyptians, under the conduct of Pharnabazus and Iphicrates, but was unsuccessful by reason of their dissensions. In his expedition against the Cadusians, he went himself in person with three hundred thousand footmen and ten thousand horse, and making an incursion into their country, which was so mountainous as

scarcely to be passable, and withal very misty, producing no
sort of harvest of corn or the like, but with pears, apples, and
other tree-fruits feeding a war-like and valiant breed of men, he
unawares fell into great distresses and dangers. For there was
nothing to be got, fit for his men to eat, of the growth of that
place, nor could anything be imported from any other. All they
could do was to kill their beasts of burden, and thus an ass's
head could scarcely be bought for sixty drachmas. In short,
the king's own table failed; and there were but few horses left;
the rest they had spent for food. Then Teribazus, a man often
in great favour with his prince for his valour and as often out of
it for his buffoonery, and particularly at that time in humble
estate and neglected, was the deliverer of the king and his army.
There being two kings amongst the Cadusians, and each of them
encamping separately, Teribazus, after he had made his application to Artaxerxes and imparted his design to him, went to one
of the princes, and sent away his son privately to the other. So
each of them deceived his man, assuring him that the other prince
had deputed an ambassador to Artaxerxes, suing for friendship
and alliance for himself alone; and, therefore, if he were wise,
he told him, he must apply himself to his master before he had
decreed anything, and he, he said, would lend him his assistance
in all things. Both of them gave credit to these words, and
because they supposed they were each intrigued against by the
other, they both sent their envoys, one along with Teribazus,
and the other with his son. All this taking some time to transact,
fresh surmises and suspicions of Teribazus were expressed to the
king, who began to be out of heart, sorry that he had confided in
him, and ready to give ear to his rivals who impeached him. But
at last he came, and so did his son, bringing the Cadusian agents
along with them, and so there was a cessation of arms and a peace
signed with both the princes. And Teribazus, in great honour
and distinction, set out homewards in the company of the king;
who, indeed, upon this journey made it appear plainly that
cowardice and effeminacy are the effects, not of delicate and
sumptuous living, as many suppose, but of a base and vicious
nature, actuated by false and bad opinions. For notwithstanding his golden ornaments, his robe of state, and the rest of that
costly attire, worth no less than twelve thousand talents, with
which the royal person was constantly clad, his labours and toils
were not a whit inferior to those of the meanest persons in his
army. With his quiver by his side and his shield on his arm, he
led them on foot, quitting his horse, through craggy and steep

ways, insomuch that the sight of his cheerfulness and unwearied strength gave wings to the soldiers, and so lightened the journey, that they made daily marches of above two hundred furlongs.

After they had arrived at one of his own mansions, which had beautiful ornamented parks in the midst of a region naked and without trees, the weather being very cold, he gave full commission to his soldiers to provide themselves with wood by cutting down any, without exception, even the pine and cypress. And when they hesitated and were for sparing them, being large and goodly trees, he, taking up an axe himself, felled the greatest and most beautiful of them. After which his men used their hatchets, and piling up many fires, passed away the night at their ease. Nevertheless, he returned not without the loss of many and valiant subjects, and of almost all his horses. And supposing that his misfortunes and the ill-success of his expedition made him despised in the eyes of his people, he looked jealously on his nobles, many of whom he slew in anger, and yet more out of fear. As, indeed, fear is the bloodiest passion in princes; confidence, on the other hand, being merciful, gentle, and unsuspicious. So we see among wild beasts, the intractable and least tamable are the most timorous and most easily startled; the nobler creatures, whose courage makes them trustful, are ready to respond to the advances of men.

Artaxerxes, now being an old man, perceived that his sons were in controversy about his kingdom, and that they made parties among his favourites and peers. Those that were equitable among them thought it fit, that as he had received it, so he should bequeath it, by right of age, to Darius. The younger brother, Ochus, who was hot and violent, had indeed a considerable number of the courtiers that espoused his interest, but his chief hope was that by Atossa's means he should win his father. For he flattered her with the thoughts of being his wife and partner in the kingdom after the death of Artaxerxes. And truly it was rumoured that already Ochus maintained a too intimate correspondence with her. This, however, was quite unknown to the king; who, being willing to put down in good time his son Ochus's hopes, lest, by his attempting the same things his uncle Cyrus did, wars and contentions might again afflict his kingdom, proclaimed Darius, then twenty-five years old, his successor, and gave him leave to wear the upright hat, as they called it. It was a rule and usage of Persia, that the heir apparent to the crown should beg a boon, and that he that declared him so should give whatever he asked, provided it were within the sphere of his power. Darius therefore requested Aspasia, in former time the most prized of the concubines of Cyrus, and now belonging to the king. She was by birth a Phocæan, of Ionia, born of free parents, and well educated. Once when Cyrus was at supper, she was led in to him with other women, who, when they were sat down by him, and he began to sport and dally and talk jestingly with them, gave way freely to his advances. But she stood by in silence, refusing to come when Cyrus called her, and when his chamberlains were going to force her towards him, said, " Whosoever lays hands on me shall rue it; " so that she seemed to the company a sullen and rude-mannered person. However, Cyrus was well pleased, and laughed, saying to the man that brought the women, " Do you not see to a certainty that this woman alone of all that came with you is truly noble and pure in character? " After which time he began to regard her, and loved her, above all of her sex, and called her the Wise. But Cyrus being slain in the fight, she was taken among the spoils of his camp.

Darius, in demanding her, no doubt much offended his father, for the barbarian people keep a very jealous and watchful eye over their carnal pleasures, so that it is death for a man not only to come near and touch any concubine of his prince, but likewise on a journey to ride forward and pass by the carriages in which they are conveyed. And though, to gratify his passion, he had against all law married his daughter Atossa, and had besides her no less than three hundred and sixty concubines selected for their beauty, yet being importuned for that one by Darius, he urged that she was a free-woman, and allowed him to take her, if she had an inclination to go with him, but by no means to force her away against it. Aspasia, therefore, being sent for, and, contrary to the king's expectation, making choice of Darius, he gave him her indeed, being constrained by law, but when he had done so, a little after he took her from him. For he consecrated her priestess to Diana of Ecbatana, whom they name Anaitis, that she might spend the remainder of her days in strict chastity, thinking thus to punish his son, not rigorously, but with modera-tion, by a revenge checkered with jest and earnest. But he took it heinously, either that he was passionately fond of Aspasia, or because he looked upon himself as affronted and scorned by his father. Teribazus, perceiving him thus minded, did his best to exasperate him yet further, seeing in his injuries a representation of his own, of which the following is the account: Artaxerxes, having many daughters, promised to give Apama to

Pharnabazus to wife, Rhodogune to Orontes, and Amestris to Teribazus; whom alone of the three he disappointed, by marrying Amestris himself. However, to make him amends, he betrothed his youngest daughter Atossa to him. But after he had, being enamoured of her too, as has been said, married her, Teribazus entertained an irreconcilable enmity against him. As indeed he was seldom at any other time steady in his temper, but uneven and inconsiderate; so that whether he were in the number of the choicest favourites of his prince, or whether he were offensive and odious to him, he demeaned himself in neither condition with moderation, but if he was advanced he was intolerably insolent, and in his degradation not submissive and peaceable in his deportment, but fierce and haughty.

And therefore Teribazus was to the young prince flame added upon flame, ever urging him, and saying, that in vain those wear their hats upright who consult not the real success of their affairs, and that he was ill-befriended of reason if he imagined, whilst he had a brother, who, through the women's apartments, was seeking a way to the supremacy, and a father of so rash and fickle a humour, that he should by succession infallibly step up into the throne. For he that out of fondness to an Ionian girl has eluded a law sacred and inviolable among the Persians is not likely to be faithful in the performance of the most important promises. He added, too, that it was not all one for Ochus not to attain to, and for him to be put by his crown; since Ochus as a subject might live happily, and nobody could hinder him; but he, being proclaimed king, must either take up his sceptre or lay down his life. These words presently inflamed Darius: what Sophocles says being indeed generally true:—

> " Quick travels the persuasion to what's wrong."

For the path is smooth, and upon an easy descent, that leads us to our own will; and the most part of us desire what is evil through our strangeness to and ignorance of good. And in this case, no doubt, the greatness of the empire and the jealousy Darius had of Ochus furnished Teribazus with material for his persuasions. Nor was Venus wholly unconcerned in the matter, in regard, namely, of his loss of Aspasia.

Darius, therefore, resigned himself up to the dictates of Teribazus; and many now conspiring with them, a eunuch gave information to the king of their plot and the way how it was to be managed, having discovered the certainty of it, that they had resolved to break into his bed-chamber by night, and there to kill him as he lay. After Artaxerxes had been thus advertised, he did not think fit, by disregarding the discovery, to despise so great a danger, nor to believe it when there was little or no proof of it. Thus then he did: he charged the eunuch constantly to attend and accompany the conspirators wherever they were; in the meanwhile, he broke down the party-wall of the chamber behind his bed, and placed a door in it to open and shut, which he covered up with tapestry; so the hour approaching, and the eunuch having told him the precise time in which the traitors designed to assassinate him, he waited for them in his bed, and rose not up till he had seen the faces of his assailants and recognised every man of them. But as soon as he saw them with their swords drawn and coming up to him, throwing up the hanging, he made his retreat into the inner chamber, and, bolting the door, raised a cry. Thus when the murderers had been seen by him, and had attempted him in vain, they with speed went back through the same doors they came in by, enjoining Teribazus and his friends to fly, as their plot had been certainly detected. They, therefore, made their escape different ways; but Teribazus was seized by the king's guards, and after slaying many, while they were laying hold on him, at length being struck through with a dart at a distance, fell. As for Darius, who was brought to trial with his children, the king appointed the royal judges to sit over him, and because he was not himself present, but accused Darius by proxy, he commanded his scribes to write down the opinion of every one of the judges, and show it to him. And after they had given their sentences, all as one man, and condemned Darius to death, the officers seized on him, and hurried him to a chamber not far off. To which place the executioner, when summoned, came with a razor in his hand, with which men of his employment cut off the heads of offenders. But when he saw that Darius was the person thus to be punished he was appalled and started back, offering to go out, as one that had neither power nor courage enough to behead a king; yet at the threats and commands of the judges who stood at the prison door, he returned and grasping the hair of his head and bringing his face to the ground with one hand, he cut through his neck with the razor he had in the other. Some affirm that sentence was passed in the presence of Artaxerxes; that Darius, after he had been convicted by clear evidence, falling prostrate before him, did humbly beg his pardon; that instead of giving it, he rising up in rage and drawing his scymetar, smote him till he had killed him; and then, going forth into the court, he worshipped

the sun, and said, " Depart in peace, ye Persians, and declare to
your fellow-subjects how the mighty Oromasdes hath dealt out
vengeance to the contrivers of unjust and unlawful things."

Such, then, was the issue of this conspiracy.  And now Ochus
was high in his hopes, being confident in the influence of Atossa;
but yet was afraid of Ariaspes, the only male surviving, besides
himself, of the legitimate offspring of his father, and of Arsames,
one of his natural sons.  For indeed Ariaspes was already
claimed as their prince by the wishes of the Persians, not because
he was the elder brother, but because he excelled Ochus in
gentleness, plain dealing, and good-nature;  and on the other
hand Arsames appeared, by his wisdom, fitted for the throne, and
that he was dear to his father Ochus well knew.   So he laid
snares for them both, and being no less treacherous than bloody,
he made use of the cruelty of his nature against Arsames, and of
his craft and wiliness against Ariaspes.  For he suborned the
king's eunuchs and favourites to convey to him menacing and
harsh expressions from his father, as though he had decreed to
put him to a cruel and ignominious death.   When they daily communicated these things as secrets, and told him at one time that
the king would do so to him ere long, and at another, that the
blow was actually close impending, they so alarmed the young
man, struck such a terror into him, and cast such a confusion
and anxiety upon his thoughts, that, having prepared some
poisonous drugs, he drank them, that he might be delivered from
his life.  The king, on hearing what kind of death he died,
heartily lamented him, and was not without a suspicion of the
cause of it.  But being disabled by his age to search into and
prove it, he was, after the loss of this son, more affectionate than
before to Arsames, did manifestly place his greatest confidence in
him, and made him privy to his counsels.  Whereupon Ochus
had no longer patience to defer the execution of his purpose, but
having procured Arpates, Teribazus's son, for the undertaking,
he killed Arsames by his hand.  Artaxerxes at that time had
but a little hold on life, by reason of his extreme age, and so, when
he heard of the fate of Arsames, he could not sustain it at all, but
sinking at once under the weight of his grief and distress, expired,
after a life of ninety-four years, and a reign of sixty-two.   And
then he seemed a moderate and gracious governor, more especially
as compared to his son Ochus, who outdid all his predecessors in
blood-thirstiness and cruelty.

# GALBA

IPHICRATES the Athenian used to say that it is best to have a mercenary soldier fond of money and of pleasures, for thus he will fight the more boldly, to procure the means to gratify his desires. But most have been of opinion, that the body of an army, as well as the natural one, when in its healthy condition, should make no efforts apart, but in compliance with its head. Wherefore they tell us that Paulus Æmilius, on taking command of the forces in Macedonia, and finding them talkative and impertinently busy, as though they were all commanders, issued out his orders that they should have only ready hands and keen swords, and leave the rest to him. And Plato, who can discern no use of a good ruler or general if his men are not on their part obedient and conformable (the virtue of obeying, as of ruling, being, in his opinion, one that does not exist without first a noble nature, and then a philosophic education, where the eager and active powers are allayed with the gentler and humaner sentiments), may claim in confirmation of his doctrine sundry mournful instances elsewhere, and, in particular, the events that followed among the Romans upon the death of Nero, in which plain proofs were given that nothing is more terrible than a military force moving about in an empire upon uninstructed and unreasoning impulses. Demuades, after the death of Alexander, compared the Macedonian army to the Cyclops after his eye was out, seeing their many disorderly and unsteady motions. But the calamities of the Roman government might be likened to the motions of the giants that assailed heaven, convulsed as it was, and distracted, and from every side recoiling, as it were, upon itself, not so much by the ambition of those who were proclaimed emperors, as by the covetousness and licence of the soldiery, who drove commander after commander out, like nails one upon another.

Dionysius, in raillery, said of the Pheræan who enjoyed the government of Thessaly only ten months, that he had been a tragedy-king, but the Cæsars' house in Rome, the Palatium, received in a shorter space of time no less than four emperors, passing, as it were, across the stage, and one making room for another to enter.

This was the only satisfaction of the distressed, that they

need not require any other justice on their oppressors, seeing them thus murder each other, and first of all, and that most justly, the one that ensnared them first, and taught them to expect such happy results from a change of emperors, sullying a good word by the pay he gave for its being done and turning revolt against Nero into nothing better than treason.

For, as already related, Nymphidius Sabinus, captain of the guards, together with Tiggelinus, after Nero's circumstances were now desperate, and it was perceived that he designed to fly into Egypt, persuaded the troops to declare Galba emperor, as if Nero had been already gone, promising to all the court and prætorian soldiers, as they are called, seven thousand five hundred drachmas apiece, and to those in service abroad twelve hundred and fifty drachmas each; so vast a sum for a largess as it was impossible any one could raise, but he must be infinitely more exacting and oppressive than ever Nero was. This quickly brought Nero to his grave, and soon after Galba too; they murdered the first in expectation of the promised gift, and not long after the other because they did not obtain it from him; and then, seeking about to find some one who would purchase at such a rate, they consumed themselves in a succession of treacheries and rebellions before they obtained their demands. But to give a particular relation of all that passed would require a history in full form; I have only to notice what is properly to my purpose, namely, what the Cæsars did and suffered.

Sulpicius Galba is owned by all to have been the richest private person that ever came to the imperial seat. And besides the additional honour of being of the Servii, he valued himself more especially for his relationship to Catulus, the most eminent citizen of his time both for virtue and renown, however he may have voluntarily yielded to others as regards power and authority. Galba was also akin to Livia, the wife of Augustus, by whose interest he was preferred to the consulship by the emperor. It is said of him that he commanded the troops well in Germany, and, being made proconsul in Libya, gained a reputation that few ever had. But his quiet manner of living and his sparingness in expenses and his disregard of appearances gave him, when he became emperor, an ill-name for meanness, being, in fact, his worn-out credit for regularity and moderation. He was entrusted by Nero with the government of Spain, before Nero had yet learned to be apprehensive of men of great repute. To the opinion, moreover, entertained of his mild natural temper, his old age added a belief that he would never act incautiously.

There while Nero's iniquitous agents savagely and cruelly harassed the provinces under Nero's authority, he could afford no succour, but merely offer this only ease and consolation, that he seemed plainly to sympathise, as a fellow-sufferer, with those who were condemned upon suits and sold. And when lampoons were made upon Nero and circulated and sung everywhere about, he neither prohibited them, nor showed any indignation on behalf of the emperor's agents, and for this was the more beloved; as also that he was now well acquainted with them, having been in chief power there eight years at the time when Junius Vindex, general of the forces in Gaul, began his insurrection against Nero. And it is reported that letters came to Galba before it fully broke out into an open rebellion, which he neither seemed to give credit to, nor on the other hand to take means to let Nero know; as other officers did, sending to him the letters which came to them, and so spoiled the design, as much as in them lay, who yet afterwards shared in the conspiracy, and confessed they had been treacherous to themselves as well as him. At last Vindex, plainly declaring war, wrote to Galba, encouraging him to take the government upon him, and give a head to this strong body, the Gaulish provinces, which could already count a hundred thousand men in arms, and were able to arm a yet greater number if occasion were. Galba laid the matter before his friends, some of whom thought it fit to wait, and see what movement there might be and what inclinations displayed at Rome for the revolution. But Titus Vinius, captain of his prætorian guard, spoke thus: " Galba, what means this inquiry? To question whether we shall continue faithful to Nero is, in itself, to cease to be faithful. Nero is our enemy, and we must by no means decline the help of Vindex: or else we must at once denounce him, and march to attack him, because he wishes you to be the governor of the Romans, rather than Nero their tyrant." Thereupon Galba, by an edict, appointed a day when he would receive manumissions, and general rumour and talk beforehand about his purpose brought together a great crowd of men so ready for a change, that he scarcely appeared, stepping up to the tribunal, but they with one consent saluted him emperor. That title he refused at present to take upon him; but after he had a while inveighed against Nero, and bemoaned the loss of the more conspicuous of those that had been destroyed by him, he offered himself and service to his country, not by the titles of Cæsar or emperor, but as the lieutenant of the Roman senate and people.

Now that Vindex did wisely in inviting Galba to the empire, Nero himself bore testimony; who, though he seemed to despise Vindex and altogether to slight the Gauls and their concerns, yet when he heard of Galba (as by chance he had just bathed and sat down to his morning meal), at this news he overturned the table.   But the senate having voted Galba an enemy, presently, to make his jest, and likewise to personate a confidence among his friends, "This is a very happy opportunity," he said, "for me, who sadly want such a booty as that of the Gauls, which must all fall in as lawful prize; and Galba's estate I can use or sell at once, he being now an open enemy."   And accordingly he had Galba's property exposed to sale, which when Galba heard of, he sequestered all that was Nero's in Spain, and found far readier bidders.

Many now began to revolt from Nero, and pretty nearly all adhered to Galba; only Clodius Macer in Africa, and Virginius Rufus, commander of the German forces in Gaul, followed counsel of their own; yet these two were not of one and the same advice, for Clodius, being sensible of the rapines and murders to which he had been led by cruelty and covetousness, was in perplexity, and felt it was not safe for him either to retain or quit his command.   But Virginius, who had the command of the strongest legions, by whom he was many repeated times saluted emperor and pressed to take the title upon him, declared that he neither would assume that honour himself, nor see it given to any other than whom the senate should elect.

These things at first did not a little disturb Galba, but when presently Virginius and Vindex were in a manner forced by their armies, having got the reins, as it were, out of their hands, to a great encounter and battle, in which Vindex, having seen twenty thousand of the Gauls destroyed, died by his own hand, and when the report straight spread abroad, that all desired Virginius, after this great victory, to take the empire upon him, or else they would return to Nero again, Galba, in great alarm at this, wrote to Virginius, exhorting him to join with him for the preservation of the empire and the liberty of the Romans, and so retiring with his friends into Clunia, a town in Spain, he passed away his time, rather repenting his former rashness, and wishing for his wonted ease and privacy, than setting about what was fit to be done.

It was now summer, when on a sudden, a little before dusk, comes a freedman, Icelus by name, having arrived in seven days from Rome; and being informed where Galba was reposing himself in private, he went straight on, and pushing by the servants of the chamber, opened the door and entered the room, and told him, that Nero being yet alive but not appearing, first the army, and then the people and senate, declared Galba emperor; not long after, it was reported that Nero was dead; "but I," said he, "not giving credit to common fame, went myself to the body and saw him lying dead, and only then set out to bring you word." This news at once made Galba great again, and a crowd of people came hastening to the door, all very confident of the truth of his tidings, though the speed of the man was almost incredible. Two days after came Titus Vinius with sundry others from the camp, who gave an account in detail of the orders of the senate, and for this service was considerably advanced. On the freedman, Galba conferred the honour of the gold ring, and Icelus, as he had been before, now taking the name of Marcianus, held the first place of the freedmen.

But at Rome, Nymphidius Sabinus, not gently, and little by little, but at once, and without exception, engrossed all power to himself; Galba, being an old man (seventy-three years of age), would scarcely, he thought, live long enough to be carried in a litter to Rome; and the troops in the city were from old time attached to him, and now bound by the vastness of the promised gift, for which they regarded him as their benefactor, and Galba as their debtor. Thus presuming on his interest, he straightway commanded Tigellinus, who was in joint commission with himself, to lay down his sword; and giving entertainments, he invited the former consuls and commanders, making use of Galba's name for the invitation; but at the same time prepared many in the camp to propose that a request should be sent to Galba that he should appoint Nymphidius sole prefect for life without a colleague. And the modes which the senate took to show him honour and increase his power, styling him their benefactor, and attending daily at his gates, and giving him the compliment of heading with his own name and confirming all their acts, carried him on to a yet greater degree of arrogance, so that in a short time he became an object, not only of dislike, but of terror, to those that sought his favour. When the consuls themselves had despatched their couriers with the decrees of the senate to the emperor, together with the sealed diplomas, which the authorities in all the towns where horses or carriages are changed look at, and on that certificate hasten the couriers forward with all their means, he was highly displeased that his seal had not been used, and none of his soldiers employed on the errand. Nay, he even deliberated what course to take with the consuls themselves, but upon their submission and apology he was at last pacified. To gratify the people, he did not interfere with their beating to death any that fell into their hands of Nero's party. Amongst others, Spiclus, the gladiator, was killed in the forum by being thrown under Nero's statues, which they dragged about the place over his body. Aponius, one of those who had been concerned in accusations, they knocked to the ground, and drove carts loaded with stones over him. And many others they tore in pieces, some of them no way guilty, insomuch that Mauriscus, a person of great account and character, told the senate that he feared, in a short time, they might wish for Nero again.

Nymphidius, now advancing towards the consummation of his hopes, did not refuse to let it be said that he was the son of Caius Cæsar, Tiberius's successor; who, it is told, was well acquainted with his mother in his early youth, a woman indeed handsome enough, the offspring of Callistus, one of Cæsar's freedmen, and a certain sempstress. But it is plain that Caius's familiarity with his mother was of too late date to give him any pretensions, and it was suspected he might, if he pleased, claim a father in Martianus, the gladiator, whom his mother, Nymphidia, took a passion for, being a famous man in his way, whom also he much more resembled. However, though he certainly owned Nymphidia for his mother, he ascribed meantime the downfall of Nero to himself alone, and thought he was not sufficiently rewarded with the honours and riches he enjoyed (nay, though to all was added the company of Sporus, whom he immediately sent for while Nero's body was yet burning on the pile, and treated as his consort with the name of Poppæa), but he must also aspire to the empire. And at Rome he had friends who took measures for him secretly, as well as some women and some members of the senate also, who worked underhand to assist him. And into Spain he despatched one of his friends, named Gellianus, to view the posture of affairs.

But all things succeeded well with Galba after Nero's death; only Virginius Rufus, still standing doubtful, gave him some anxiety, lest he should listen to the suggestions of some who encouraged him to take the government upon him, having, at present, besides the command of a large and warlike army, the new honours of the defeat of Vindex and the subjugation of one considerable part of the Roman empire, namely, the entire Gaul, which had seemed shaking about upon the verge of open revolt.

Nor had any man indeed a greater name and reputation than
Virginius, who had taken a part of so much consequence in the
deliverance of the empire at once from a cruel tyranny and a
Gallic war. But he, standing to his first resolves, reserved to
the senate the power of electing an emperor. Yet when it was
now manifest that Nero was dead, the soldiers pressed him hard
to it, and one of the tribunes, entering his tent with his drawn
sword, bade him either take the government or that. But after
Fabius Valens, having the command of one legion, had first
sworn fealty to Galba, and letters from Rome came with tidings
of the resolves of the senate, at last with much ado he persuaded
the army to declare Galba emperor. And when Flaccus Hordeonius came by Galba's commission as his successor, he handed
over to him his forces, and went himself to meet Galba on his
way, and having met him turned back to attend him; in all
which no apparent displeasure nor yet honour was shown him.
Galba's feelings of respect for him prevented the former; the
latter was checked by the envy of his friends, and particularly
of Titus Vinius, who, acting in the desire of hindering Virginius's
promotion, unwittingly aided his happy genius in rescuing him
from those hazards and hardships which other commanders were
involved in, and securing him the safe enjoyment of a quiet life
and peaceable old age.

Near Narbo, a city in Gaul, the deputation of the senate met
Galba, and after they had delivered their compliments, begged
him to make what haste he could to appear to the people that
impatiently expected him. He discoursed with them courteously and unassumingly, and in his entertainment, though Nymphidius had sent him royal furniture and attendance of Nero's,
he put all aside, and made use of nothing but his own, for which
he was well spoken of, as one who had a great mind, and was
superior to little vanities. But in a short time, Vinius, by declaring to him that these noble, unpompous, citizen-like ways
were a mere affectation of popularity and a petty bashfulness at
assuming his proper greatness, induced him to make use of Nero's
supplies, and in his entertainments not to be afraid of a regal
sumptuosity. And in more than one way the old man let it
gradually appear that he had put himself under Vinius's disposal.

Vinius was a person of an excessive covetousness, and not
quite free from blame in respect to women. For being a young
man, newly entered into the service under Calvisius Sabinus,
upon his first campaign, he brought his commander's wife, a
licentious woman, in a soldier's dress, by night into the camp,

and was found with her in the very general's quarters, the *principia*, as the Romans call them. For which insolence Caius Cæsar cast him into prison, from whence he was fortunately delivered by Caius's death. Afterwards, being invited by Claudius Cæsar to supper, he privily conveyed away a silver cup, which Cæsar hearing of, invited him again the next day, and gave order to his servants to set before him no silver plate, but only earthenware. And this offence, through the comic mildness of Cæsar's reprimand, was treated rather as a subject of jest than as a crime. But the acts to which now, when Galba was in his hands and his power was so extensive, his covetous temper led him were the causes, in part, and in part the provocation, of tragical and fatal mischiefs.

Nymphidius became very uneasy upon the return out of Spain of Gellianus, whom he had sent to pry into Galba's actions, understanding that Cornelius Laco was appointed commander of the court guards, and that Vinius was the great favourite, and that Gellianus had not been able so much as to come nigh, much less have any opportunity to offer any words in private, so narrowly had he been watched and observed. Nymphidius, therefore, called together the officers of the troops, and declared to them that Galba of himself was a good, well-meaning old man, but did not act by his own counsel, and was ill-guided by Vinius and Laco; and lest, before they were aware, they should engross the authority Tigellinus had with the troops, he proposed to them to send deputies from the camp, acquainting him that if he pleased to remove only these two from his counsel and presence, he would be much more welcome to all at his arrival. Wherein, when he saw he did not prevail (it seeming absurd and unmannerly to give rules to an old commander what friends to retain or displace, as if he had been a youth newly taking the reins of authority into his hands), adopting another course, he wrote himself to Galba letters in alarming terms, one while as if the city were unsettled, and had not yet recovered its tranquillity; then that Clodius Macer withheld the corn-ships from Africa; that the legions in Germany began to be mutinous, and that he heard the like of those in Syria and Judæa. But Galba not minding him much or giving credit to his stories, he resolved to make his attempt beforehand, though Clodius Celsus, a native of Antioch, a person of sense, and friendly and faithful to Nymphidius, told him he was wrong, saying he did not believe one single street in Rome would ever give him the title of Cæsar. Nevertheless many also derided Galba, amongst the rest Mithridates of Pontus, saying, that as soon as this wrinkled, bald-headed man should be seen publicly at Rome, they would think it an utter disgrace even to have had such a Cæsar.

At last it was resolved, about midnight, to bring Nymphidius into the camp, and declare him emperor. But Antonius Hono-ratus, who was first among the tribunes, summoning together in the evening those under his command, charged himself and them severely with their many and unreasonable turns and alterations, made without any purpose or regard to merit, simply as if some evil genius hurried them from one reason to another. "What though Nero's miscarriages," said he, "gave some colour to your former acts, can you say you have any plea for betraying Galba in the death of a mother, the blood of a wife, or the degradation of the imperial power upon the stage and amongst players? Neither did we desert Nero for all this, until Nymphidius had persuaded us that he had first left us and fled into Egypt. Shall we, therefore, send Galba after, to appease Nero's shade, and, for the sake of making the son of Nymphidia emperor, take off one of Livia's family, as we have already the son of Agrippina? Rather, doing justice on him, let us revenge Nero's death, and show ourselves true and faithful by preserving Galba."

The tribune having ended his harangue, the soldiers assented, and encouraged all they met with to persist in their fidelity to the emperor, and, indeed, brought over the greatest part. But presently hearing a great shout, Nymphidius, imagining, as some say, that the soldiers called for him, or hastening to be in time to check any opposition and gain the doubtful, came on with many lights, carrying in his hand a speech in writing, made by Cingonius Varro, which he had got by heart, to deliver to the soldiers. But seeing the gates of the camp shut up, and large numbers standing armed about the walls, he began to be afraid. Yet drawing nearer he demanded what they meant, and by whose orders they were then in arms; but hearing a general acclamation, all with one consent crying out that Galba was their emperor, advancing towards them, he joined in the cry, and likewise commanded those that followed him to do the same. The guard notwithstanding permitted him to enter the camp only with a few, where he was presently struck with a dart, which Septimius, being before him, received on his shield; others, however, assaulted him with their naked swords, and on his flying, pursued him into a soldier's cabin, where they slew him. And dragging his body thence, they placed a railing about it, and exposed it next day to public view. When Galba heard of the end which Nymphidius had thus come to, he commanded that all his confederates who had not at once killed themselves should immediately be despatched; amongst whom were Cingonius, who made his oration, and Mithridates, formerly mentioned. It was, however, regarded as arbitrary and illegal, and though it might be just, yet by no means popular, to take off men of their rank and equality without a hearing. For every one expected another scheme of government, being deceived, as is usual, by the first plausible pretences; and the death of Petronius Turpilianus, who was of consular dignity, and had remained faithful to Nero, was yet more keenly resented. Indeed, the taking off of Macer in Africa by Trebonius, and Fonteius by Valens in Germany, had a fair pretence, they being dreaded as armed commanders, having their soldiers at their bidding; but why refuse Turpilianus, an old man and unarmed, permission to try to clear himself, if any part of the moderation and equity at first promised were really to come to a performance? Such were the comments to which these actions exposed him. When he came within five-and-twenty furlongs or thereabouts of the city, he happened to light on a disorderly rabble of the seamen, who beset him as he passed. These were they whom Nero made soldiers, forming them into a legion. They so rudely crowded to have their commission confirmed that they did not let Galba either be seen or heard by those that had come out to meet their new emperor; but tumultuously pressed on with loud shouts to have colours to their legion, and quarters assigned them. Galba put them off until another time, which they interpreted as a denial, grew more insolent and mutinous, following and crying out, some with their drawn swords in their hands. Upon seeing which, Galba commanded the horse to ride over them, when they were soon routed, not a man standing his ground, and many of them were slain, both there and in the pursuit; an ill-omen, that Galba should make his first entry through so much blood and among dead bodies. And now he was looked upon with terror and alarm by any one who had entertained contempt of him at the sight of his age and apparent infirmities.

But when he desired presently to let it appear what a change would be made from Nero's profuseness and sumptuosity in giving presents, he much missed his aim, and fell so short of magnificence, that he scarcely came within the limits of decency. When Canus, who was a famous musician, played at supper for him, he expressed his approbation, and bade the bag be brought to him; and taking a few gold pieces, put them in with this remark, that it was out of his own purse, and not on the public account. He ordered the largesses which Nero had made to actors and wrestlers and such like to be strictly required again, allowing only the tenth part to be retained; though it turned to very small account, most of those persons expending their daily income as fast as they received it, being rude, improvident livers; upon which he had further inquiry made as to those who had bought or received from them, and called upon these people to refund. The trouble was infinite, the exactions being prosecuted far, touching a great number of persons, bringing disrepute on Galba, and general hatred on Vinius, who made the emperor appear base-hearted and mean to the world, whilst he himself was spending profusely, taking whatever he could get, and selling to any buyer. Hesiod tells us to drink without stinting of—

> " The end and the beginning of the cask."

And Vinius, seeing his patron old and decaying, made the most of what he considered to be at once the first of his fortune and the last of it.

Thus the aged man suffered in two ways, first, through the evil deeds which Vinius did himself, and, next, by his preventing or bringing into disgrace those just acts which he himself designed. Such was the punishing Nero's adherents. When he destroyed the bad, amongst whom were Helius, Polycletus, Petinus, and Patrobius, the peoples mightily applauded the act, crying out, as they were dragged through the forum, that it was a goodly sight, grateful to the gods themselves, adding, however, that the gods and men alike demanded justice on Tigellinus, the very tutor and prompter of all the tyranny. This good man, however, had taken his measures beforehand, in the shape of a present and a promise to Vinius. Turpilianus could not be allowed to escape with life, though his one and only crime had been that he had not betrayed or shown hatred to such a ruler as Nero. But he who had made Nero what he became, and afterwards deserted and betrayed him whom he had so corrupted, was allowed to survive as an instance that Vinius could do anything, and an advertisement that those that had money to give him need despair of nothing. The people, however, were so possessed with the desire of seeing Tigellinus dragged to execution, that they never ceased to require it at the theatre, and in the race-course, till they were checked by an edict from the emperor himself, announcing that Tigellinus could not live

long, being wasted with a consumption, and requesting them not
to seek to make his government appear cruel and tyrannical.
So the dissatisfied populace were laughed at, and Tigellinus made
a splendid feast, and sacrificed in thanksgiving for his deliverance; and after supper, Vinius, rising from the emperor's table,
went to revel with Tigellinus, taking his daughter, a widow,
with him; to whom Tigellinus presented his compliments, with
a gift of twenty-five myriads of money, and bade the super-
intendent of his concubines take off a rich necklace from her
own neck and tie it about hers, the value of it being estimated
at fifteen myriads.

After this, even reasonable acts were censured; as, for
example, the treatment of the Gauls who had been in the conspiracy with Vindex. For people looked upon their abatement
of tribute and admission to citizenship as a piece, not of
clemency on the part of Galba, but of money-making on that of
Vinius. And thus the mass of the people began to look with
dislike upon the government. The soldiers were kept on a
while in expectation of the promised donative, supposing that
if they did not receive the full, yet they should have at least as
much as Nero gave them. But when Galba, on hearing they
began to complain, declared greatly, and like a general, that he
was used to enlist and not to buy his soldiers, when they heard
of this, they conceived an implacable hatred against him; for
he did not seem to defraud them merely himself in their present
expectations, but to give an ill precedent, and instruct his
successors to do the like. This heart-burning, however, was as
yet at Rome a thing undeclared, and a certain respect for Galba's
personal presence somewhat retarded their motions, and took
off their edge, and their having no obvious occasion for beginning a revolution curbed and kept under, more or less, their
resentments. But those forces that had been formerly under
Virginius, and now were under Flaccus in Germany, valuing
themselves much upon the battle they had fought with Vindex,
and finding now no advantage of it, grew very refractory and
intractable towards their officers; and Flaccus they wholly disregarded, being incapacitated in body by unintermitted gout,
and, besides, a man of little experience in affairs. So at one of
their festivals, when it was customary for the officers of the
army to wish all health and happiness to the emperor, the
common soldiers began to murmur loudly, and on their officers
persisting in the ceremony, responded with the words, " If he
deserves it."

When some similar insolence was committed by the legions under Vitellius, frequent letters with the information came to Galba from his agents; and taking alarm at this, and fearing that he might be despised not only for his old age, but also for want of issue, he determined to adopt some young man of distinction, and declare him his successor. There was at this time in the city Marcus Otho, a person of fair extraction, but from his childhood one of the few most debauched, voluptuous, and luxurious livers in Rome. And as Homer gives Paris in several places the title " of fair Helen's love," making a woman's name the glory and addition to his, as if he had nothing else to distinguish him, so Otho was renowned in Rome for nothing more than his marriage with Poppæa, whom Nero had a passion for when she was Crispinus's wife. But being as yet respectful to his own wife, and standing in awe of his mother, he engaged Otho underhand to solicit her. For Nero lived familiarly with Otho, whose prodigality won his favour, and he was well pleased when he took the freedom to jest upon him as mean and penurious. Thus when Nero one day perfumed himself with some rich essence and favoured Otho with a sprinkle of it, he, entertaining Nero next day, ordered gold and silver pipes to disperse the like on a sudden freely, like water, throughout the room. As to Poppæa, he was beforehand with Nero, and first seducing her himself, then, with the hope of Nero's favour, he prevailed with her to part with her husband, and brought her to his own house as his wife, and was not content afterwards to have a share in her, but grudged to have Nero for a claimant, Poppæa herself, they say, being rather pleased than otherwise with this jealousy; she sometimes excluded Nero, even when Otho was not present, either to prevent his getting tired with her, or, as some say, not liking the prospect of an imperial marriage, though willing enough to have the emperor as her lover. So that Otho ran the risk of his life, and strange it was he escaped, when Nero, for this very marriage, killed his wife and sister. But he was beholden to Seneca's friendship, by whose persuasions and entreaty Nero was prevailed with to despatch him as prætor into Lusitania, on the shores of the Ocean; where he behaved himself very agreeably and indulgently to those he had to govern, well knowing this command was but to colour and disguise his banishment.

When Galba revolted from Nero, Otho was the first governor of any of the provinces that came over to him, bringing all the gold and silver he possessed in the shape of cups and tables, to be coined into money, and also what servants he had fitly qualified to wait upon a prince. In all other points, too, he was faithful to him, and gave him sufficient proof that he was inferior to none in managing public business. And he so far ingratiated himself, that he rode in the same carriage with him during the whole journey, several days together. And in this journey and familiar companionship he won over Vinius also, both by his conversation and presents, but especially by conceding to him the first place, securing the second, by his interest, for himself. And he had the advantage of him in avoiding all odium and jealousy, assisting all petitioners, without asking for any reward, and appearing courteous and of easy access towards all, especially to the military men, for many of whom he obtained commands, some immediately from the emperor, others by Vinius's means, and by the assistance of the two favourite freedmen, Icelus and Asiaticus, these being the men in chief power in the court. As often as he entertained Galba, he gave the cohort on duty, in addition to their pay, a piece of gold for every man there, upon pretence of respect to the emperor, while really he undermined him, and stole away his popularity with the soldiers.

So Galba consulting about a successor, Vinius introduced Otho, yet not even this gratis, but upon promise that he would marry his daughter if Galba should make him his adopted son and successor to the empire. But Galba, in all his actions, showed clearly that he preferred the public good before his own private interest, not aiming so much to pleasure himself as to advantage the Romans by his selection. Indeed he does not seem to have been so much as inclined to make choice of Otho had it been but to inherit his own private fortune, knowing his extravagant and luxurious character, and that he was already plunged in debt five thousand myriads deep. So he listened to Vinius, and made no reply, but mildly suspended his determination. Only he appointed himself consul, and Vinius his colleague, and it was the general expectation that he would declare his successor at the beginning of the new year. And the soldiers desired nothing more than that Otho should be the person.

But the forces in Germany broke out into their mutiny whilst he was yet deliberating, and anticipated his design. All the soldiers in general felt much resentment against Galba for not having given them their expected largess, but these troops made a pretence of a more particular concern, that Virginius Rufus was cast off dishonourably, and that the Gauls who had fought

with them were well rewarded, while those who had refused to
take part with Vindex were punished; and Galba's thanks
seemed all to be for him, to whose memory he had done honour
after his death with public solemnities as though he had been
made emperor by his means only. Whilst these discourses
passed openly throughout the army, on the first day of the
first month of the year, the Calends, as they call it, of January,
Flaccus summoning them to take the usual anniversary oath of
fealty to the emperor, they overturned and pulled down Galba's
statues, and having sworn in the name of the senate and people
of Rome, departed. But the officers now feared anarchy and
confusion, as much as rebellion; and one of them came forward
and said: "What will become of us, my fellow-soldiers, if we
neither set up another general, nor retain the present one?
This will be not so much to desert from Galba as to decline all
subjection and command. It is useless to try and maintain
Flaccus Hordeonius, who is but a mere shadow and image of
Galba. But Vitellius, commander of the other Germany, is
but one day's march distant, whose father was censor and thrice
consul, and in a manner co-emperor with Claudius Cæsar; and
he himself has the best proof to show of his bounty and largeness
of mind, in the poverty with which some reproach him. Him
let us make choice of, that all may see we know how to choose
an emperor better than either Spaniards or Lusitanians."
Which motion whilst some assented to, and others gainsaid, a
certain standard-bearer slipped out and carried the news to
Vitellius, who was entertaining much company by night. This
taking air, soon passed through the troops, and Fabius Valens,
who commanded one legion, riding up next day with a large
body of horse, saluted Vitellius emperor. He had hitherto
seemed to decline it, professing a dread he had to undertake
the weight of the government; but on this day, being fortified,
they say, by wine and a plentiful noon-day repast, he began to
yield, and submitted to take on him the title of Germanicus they
gave him, but desired to be excused as to that of Cæsar. And
immediately the army under Flaccus also, putting away their
fine and popular oaths in the name of the senate, swore obedience
to Vitellius as emperor, to observe whatever he commanded.

Thus Vitellius was publicly proclaimed emperor in Germany;
which news coming to Galba's ear, he no longer deferred his
adoption; yet knowing that some of his friends were using their
interest for Dolabella, and the greatest number of them for
Otho, neither of whom he approved of, on a sudden, without any

one's privity, he sent for Piso, the son of Crassus and Scribonia,
whom Nero slew, a young man in general of excellent disposition
for virtue, but his most eminent qualities those of steadiness
and austere gravity. And so he set out to go to the camp to
declare him Cæsar and successor to the empire. But at his very
first going forth many signs appeared in the heavens, and when
he began to make a speech to the soldiers, partly extempore,
and partly reading it, the frequent claps of thunder and flashes
of lightning, and the violent storm of rain that burst on both
the camp and the city, were plain discoveries that the divine
powers did not look with favour or satisfaction on this act of
adoption that would come to no good result. The soldiers,
also, showed symptoms of hidden discontent, and wore sullen
looks, no distribution of money being even now made to them.
However, those that were present and observed Piso's countenance and voice could not but feel admiration to see him so little
overcome by so great a favour, of the magnitude of which at the
same time he seemed not at all insensible. Otho's aspect, on
the other hand, did not fail to let many marks appear of his
bitterness and anger at his disappointment; since to have been
the first man thought of for it, and to have come to the very
point of being chosen, and now to be put by, was in his feelings
a sign of the displeasure and ill-will of Galba towards him. This
filled him with fears and apprehensions, and sent him home with
a mind full of various passions, whilst he dreaded Piso, hated
Galba, and was full of wrath and indignation against Vinius.
And the Chaldeans and soothsayers about him would not permit
him to lay aside his hopes or quit his design, chiefly Ptolemæus,
insisting much on a prediction he had made, that Nero should
not murder Otho, but he himself should die first, and Otho
succeed as emperor; for the first proving true, he thought he
could not distrust the rest. But none perhaps stimulated him
more than those that professed privately to pity his hard fate
and compassionate him for being thus ungratefully dealt with
by Galba; especially Nymphidius's and Tigellinus's creatures,
who, being now cast off and reduced to low estate, were eager to
put themselves upon him, exclaiming at the indignity he had
suffered, and provoking him to revenge himself.

Amongst these were Veturius and Barbius, the one an *optio*,
the other a *tesserarius* (these are men who have the duties of
messengers and scouts), with whom Onomastus, one of Otho's
freedmen, went to the camp, to tamper with the army, and
brought over some with money, others with fair promises, which

was no hard matter, they being already corrupted, and only
wanting a fair pretence. It had been otherwise more than the
work of four days (which elapsed between the adoption and
murder), so completely to infect them as to cause a general
revolt. On the sixth day ensuing, the eighteenth, as the Romans
call it, before the Calends of February, the murder was done.
On that day, in the morning, Galba sacrificed in the Palatium
in the presence of his friends, when Umbricius, the priest, taking
up the entrails, and speaking not ambiguously, but in plain
words, said that there were signs of great troubles ensuing, and
dangerous snares laid for the life of the emperor. Thus Otho
had even been discovered by the finger of the god; being there
just behind Galba, hearing all that was said, and seeing what
was pointed out to them by Umbricius. His countenance
changed to every colour in his fear, and he was betraying no
small discomposure, when Onomastus, his freedman, came up
and acquainted him that the master builders had come, and
were waiting for him at home. Now that was the signal for
Otho to meet the soldiers. Pretending then that he had
purchased an old house, and was going to show the defects to
those that had sold it to him, he departed; and passing through
what is called Tiberius's house, he went on into the forum, near
the spot where a golden pillar stands, at which all the several
roads through Italy terminate.

Here, it is related, no more than twenty-three received and
saluted him emperor; so that, although he was not in mind as
in body enervated with soft living and effeminacy, being in his
nature bold and fearless enough in danger, nevertheless, he was
afraid to go on. But the soldiers that were present would not
suffer him to recede, but came with their swords drawn around
his chair, commanding the bearers to take him up, whom he
hastened on, saying several times over to himself, " I am a lost
man." Several persons overheard the words, who stood by
wondering, rather than alarmed, because of the small number
that attempted such an enterprise. But as they marched on
through the forum, about as many more met him, and here and
there three or four at a time joined in. Thus returning towards
the camp, with their bare swords in their hands, they saluted
him as Cæsar; whereupon Martialias, the tribune in charge of
the watch, who was, they say, noways privy to it, but was simply
surprised at the unexpectedness of the thing, and afraid to refuse,
permitted him entrance. And after this, no man made any
resistance; for they that knew nothing of the design, being

purposely encompassed by the conspirators, as they were straggling here and there, first submitted for fear, and afterwards were persuaded into compliance. Tidings came immediately to Galba in the Palatium, whilst the priests were still present and the sacrifices at hand, so that persons who were most entirely incredulous about such things, and most positive in their neglect of them, were astonished, and began to marvel at the divine event. A multitude of all sorts of people now began to run together out of the forum; Vinius and Laco and some of Galba's freedmen drew their swords and placed themselves beside him; Piso went forth and addressed himself to the guards on duty in the court; and Marius Celsus, a brave man, was despatched to the Illyrian legion, stationed in what is called the Vipsanian chamber, to secure them.

Galba now consulting whether he should go out, Vinius dissuaded him, but Celsus and Laco encouraged him by all means to do so, and sharply reprimanded Vinius. But on a sudden a rumour came hot that Otho was slain in the camp; and presently appeared one Julius Atticus, a man of some distinction in the guards, running up with his drawn sword, crying out that he had slain Cæsar's enemy; and pressing through the crowd that stood in his way, he presented himself before Galba with his bloody weapon, who, looking on him, demanded, " Who gave you your orders? " And on his answering that it had been his duty and the obligation of the oath he had taken, the people applauded, giving loud acclamations, and Galba got into his chair and was carried out to sacrifice to Jupiter, and so to show himself publicly. But coming into the forum, there met him there, like a turn of wind, the opposite story, that Otho had made himself master of the camp. And as usual in a crowd of such a size, some called to him to return back, others to move forwards; some encouraged him to be bold and fear nothing, others bade him to be cautious and distrust. And thus whilst his chair was tossed to and fro, as it were on the waves, often tottering, there appeared first horse, and straightway heavy-armed foot, coming through Paulus's court, and all with one accord crying out, " Down with this private man." Upon this, the crowd of people set off running, not to fly and disperse, but to possess themselves of the colonnades and elevated places of the forum, as it might be to get places to see a spectacle. And as soon as Atillius Vergilio knocked down one of Galba's statues, this was taken as the declaration of war, and they sent a discharge of darts upon Galba's litter, and missing their aim, came up and attacked him nearer hand with their naked swords. No man resisted or offered to stand up in his defence, save one only, a centurion, Sempronius Densus, the single man among so many thousands that the sun beheld that day act worthily of the Roman empire, who, though he had never received any favour from Galba, yet out of bravery and allegiance endeavoured to defend the litter. First, lifting up his switch of vine, with which the centurions correct the soldiers when disorderly, he called aloud to the aggressors, charging them not to touch their emperor. And when they came upon him hand-to-hand, he drew his sword, and made a defence for a long time, until at last he was cut under the knees and brought to the ground.

Galba's chair was upset at the spot called the Lacus Curtius, where they ran up and struck at him as he lay in his corselet. He, however, offered his throat, bidding them " Strike, if it be for the Romans' good." He received several wounds on his legs and arms, and at last was struck in the throat, as most say, by one Camurius, a soldier of the fifteenth legion. Some name Terentius, others Lecanius; and there are others that say it was Fabius Fabulus, who it is reported cut off the head and carried it away in the skirt of his coat, the baldness making it a difficult thing to take hold of. But those that were with him would not allow him to keep it covered up, but bade him let every one see the brave deed he had done; so that after a while he stuck upon the lance the head of the aged man that had been their grave and temperate ruler, their supreme priest and consul, and, tossing it up in the air, ran like a bacchanal, twirling and flourishing with it, while the blood ran down the spear. But when they brought the head to Otho, " Fellow-soldiers," he cried out, " this is nothing, unless you show me Piso's too," which was presented him not long after. The young man, retreating upon a wound received, was pursued by one Murcus, and slain at the temple of Vesta. Titus Vinius was also despatched, avowing himself to have been privy to the conspiracy against Galba by calling out that they were killing him contrary to Otho's pleasure. However, they cut off his head, and Laco's too, and brought them to Otho, requesting a boon.

And as Archilochus says—

> " When six or seven lie breathless on the ground,
> 'Twas I, 'twas I, say thousands, gave the wound."

Thus many that had no share in the murder wetted their hands and swords in blood, and came and showed them to Otho, pre-

senting memorials suing for a gratuity. Not less than one hundred and twenty were identified afterwards from their written
petitions; all of whom Vitellius sought out and put to death.
There came also into the camp Marius Celsus, and was accused
by many voices of encouraging the soldiers to assist Galba, and
was demanded to death by the multitude. Otho had no desire
for this, yet, fearing an absolute denial, he professed that he did
not wish to take him off so soon, having many matters yet to
learn from him; and so committed him safe to the custody of
those he most confided in.

Forthwith a senate was convened, and as if they were not the
same men, or had other gods to swear by, they took that oath in
Otho's name which he himself had taken in Galba's and had
broken; and withal conferred on him the titles of Cæsar and
Augustus; whilst the dead carcasses of the slain lay yet in their
consular robes in the market-place. As for their heads, when
they could make no other use of them, Vinius's they sold to his
daughter for two thousand five hundred drachmas; Piso's was
begged by his wife, Verania; Galba's they gave to Patrobius's
servants; who when they had it, after all sorts of abuse and
indignities, tumbled it into the place where those that suffer
death by the emperor's orders are usually cast, called Sessorium.
Galba's body was conveyed away by Priscus Helvidius by Otho's
permission, and buried in the night by Argius, his freedman.

Thus you have the history of Galba, a person inferior to few
Romans, either for birth or riches, rather exceeding all of his
time in both, having lived in great honour and reputation in the
reigns of five emperors, insomuch that he overthrew Nero rather
by his fame and repute in the world than by actual force and
power. Of all the others that joined in Nero's deposition, some
were by general consent regarded as unworthy, others had only
themselves to vote them deserving of the empire. To him the
title was offered, and by him it was accepted; and simply lending
his name to Vindex's attempt, he gave to what had been called
rebellion before, the name of a civil war, by the presence of
one that was accounted fit to govern. And therefore, as he
considered that he had not so much sought the position as the
position had sought him, he proposed to command those whom
Nymphidius and Tigellinus had wheedled into obedience no
otherwise than Scipio formerly and Fabricius and Camillus had
commanded the Romans of their times. But being now overcome with age, he was indeed among the troops and legions an
upright ruler upon the antique model; but for the rest, giving

himself up to Vinius, Laco, and his freedmen, who make their gain of all things, no otherwise than Nero had done to his insatiate favourites, he left none behind him to wish him still in power, though many to compassionate his death.

# OTHO

THE new emperor went early in the morning to the capitol, and sacrificed; and, having commanded Marius Celsus to be brought, he saluted him, and with obliging language desired him rather to forget his accusation than remember his acquittal; to which Celsus answered neither meanly nor ungratefully, that his very crime ought to recommend his integrity, since his guilt had been his fidelity to Galba, from whom he had never received any personal obligations. Upon which they were both of them admired by those that were present, and applauded by the soldiers.

In the senate, Otho said much in a gentle and popular strain. He was to have been consul for part of that year himself, but he gave the office to Virginius Rufus, and displaced none that had been named for the consulship by either Nero or Galba. Those that were remarkable for their age and dignity he promoted to the priesthoods; and restored the remains of their fortunes, that not yet been sold, to all those senators that were banished by Nero, and recalled by Galba. So that the nobility and chief of the people, who were at first apprehensive that no human creature, but some supernatural, or penal vindictive power had seized the empire, began now to flatter themselves with hopes of a government that smiled upon them thus early.

Besides, nothing gratified or gained the whole Roman people more than his justice in relation to Tigellinus. It was not seen how he was in fact already suffering punishment, not only by the very terror of retribution which he saw the whole city requiring as a just debt, but with several incurable diseases also; not to mention those unhallowed frightful excesses among impure and prostitute women, to which, at the very close of life, his lewd nature clung, and in them gasped out, as it were, its last; these, in the opinion of all reasonable men, being themselves the extremest punishment, and equal to many deaths. But it was felt like a grievance by people in general that he continued yet to see the light of day, who had been the occasion of the loss of it to so many persons, and such persons, as had died by his means. Wherefore Otho ordered him to be sent for, just as he was contriving his escape by means of some vessels that lay ready for him on the coast near where he lived, in the neighbourhood of Sinuessa. At first he endeavoured to corrupt the messenger, by a large sum of money, to favour his design; but when he found this was to no purpose, he made him as considerable a present as if he had really connived at it, only entreating him to stay till he had shaved; and so took that opportunity, and with his razor despatched himself.

And while giving the people this most righteous satisfaction of their desires, for himself he seemed to have no sort of regard for any private injuries of his own. And at first, to please the populace, he did not refuse to be called Nero in the theatre, and did not interfere when some persons displayed Nero's statues to public view. And Cluvius Rufus says, imperial letters, such as are sent with couriers, went into Spain with the name of Nero affixed adoptively to that of Otho; but as soon he perceived this gave offence to the chief and most distinguished citizens, it was omitted.

After he had begun to model the government in this manner, the paid soldiers began to murmur, and endeavoured to make him suspect and chastise the nobility, either really out of a concern for his safety, or wishing, upon this pretence, to stir up trouble and warfare. Thus, whilst Crispinus, whom he had ordered to bring him the seventeenth cohort from Ostia, began to collect what he wanted after it was dark, and was putting the arms upon the waggons, some of the most turbulent cried out that Crispinus was disaffected, that the senate was practising something against the emperor, and that those arms were to be employed against Cæsar, and not for him. When this report was once set afoot, it got the belief and excited the passions of many; they broke out into violence; some seized the waggons, and others slew Crispinus and two centurions that opposed them; and the whole number of them, arraying themselves in their arms, and encouraging one another to stand by Cæsar, marched to Rome. And hearing there that eighty of the senators were at supper with Otho, they flew into the palace, and declared it was a fair opportunity to take off Cæsar's enemies at one stroke. A general alarm ensued of an immediate coming sack of the city. All were in confusion about the palace, and Otho himself in no small consternation, being not only concerned for the senators (some of whom had brought their wives to supper thither), but also feeling himself to be an object of alarm and suspicion to them, whose eyes he saw fixed on him in silence and terror. Therefore he gave orders to the prefects to address the soldiers and do their best to pacify them, while he bade the guests rise, and leave by another door. They had only just made their way out, when the soldiers rushed into the room, and called out, " Where are Cæsar's enemies? " Then Otho, standing up on his couch, made use both of arguments and entreaties, and by actual tears at last, with great difficulty, persuaded them to desist. The next day he went to the camp, and distributed a bounty of twelve hundred and fifty drachmas a man amongst them; then commended them for the regard and zeal they had for his safety, but told them that there were some who were intriguing among them, who not only accused his own clemency, but had also misrepresented their loyalty; and, therefore, he desired their assistance in doing justice upon them. To which, when they all consented, he was satisfied with the execution of two only, whose deaths he knew would be regretted by no one man in the whole army.

Such conduct, so little expected from him, was regarded by some with gratitude and confidence; others looked upon his behaviour as a course to which necessity drove him, to gain the people to the support of the war. For now there were certain tidings that Vitellius had assumed the sovereign title and authority, and frequent expresses brought accounts of new accessions to him; others, however, came, announcing that the Pannonian, Dalmatian, and Mœsian legions, with their officers, adhered to Otho. Ere long also came favourable letters from Mucianus and Vespasian, generals of two formidable armies, the one in Syria, the other in Judæa, to assure him of their firmness to his interest: in confidence whereof he was so exalted, that he wrote to Vitellius not to attempt anything beyond his post; and offered him large sums of money and a city, where he might live his time out in pleasure and ease. These overtures at first were responded to by Vitellius with equivocating civilities; which soon, however, turned into an interchange of angry words; and letters passed between the two, conveying bitter and shameful terms of reproach, which were not false indeed, for that matter, only it was senseless and ridiculous for each to assail the other with accusations to which both alike must plead guilty. For it were hard to determine which of the two had been most profuse, most effeminate, which was most a novice in military affairs, and most involved in debt through previous want of means.

As to the prodigies and apparitions that happened about this time, there were many reported which none could answer for, or which were told in different ways; but one which everybody actually saw with their eyes, was the statue, in the capitol, of Victory carried in a chariot, with the reins dropped out of her hands, as if she were grown too weak to hold them any longer; and a second, that Caius Cæsar's statue in the island of Tiber, without any earthquake or wind to account for it, turned round from west to east; and this, they say, happened about the time when Vespasian and his party first openly began to put themselves forward. Another incident, which the people in general thought an evil sign, was the inundation of the Tiber; for though it happened at a time when rivers are usually at their fullest, yet such height of water and so tremendous a flood had never been known before, nor such a destruction of property, great part of the city being under water, and especially the corn market, so that it occasioned a great dearth for several days.

But when news was now brought that Cæcina and Valens, commanding for Vitellius, had possessed themselves of the Alps, Otho sent Dolabella (a patrician, who was suspected by the soldiery of some evil purpose); for whatever reason, whether it were fear of him or of any one else, to the town of Aquinum, to give encouragement there; and proceeding then to choose which of the magistrates should go with him to the war, he named amongst the rest Lucius, Vitellius's brother, without distinguishing him by any new marks either of his favour or displeasure. He also took the greatest precautions for Vitellius's wife and mother, that they might be safe, and free from all apprehension for themselves. He made Flavius Sabinus, Vespasian's brother, governor of Rome, either in honour to the memory of Nero, who had advanced him formerly to that command, which Galba had taken away, or else to show his confidence in Vespasian by his favour to his brother.

After he came to Brixillum, a town of Italy near the Po, he stayed behind himself, and ordered the army to march under the conduct of Marius Celsus, Suetonius Paulinus, Gallus, and Spurina, all men of experience and reputation, but unable to carry their own plans and purposes into effect, by reason of the ungovernable temper of the army, which would take orders from none but the emperor whom they themselves had made their master. Nor was the enemy under much better discipline, the soldiers there also being haughty and disobedient upon the same account, but they were more experienced and used to hard work; whereas Otho's men were soft from their long easy living and

lack of service, having spent most of their time in the theatres
and at state shows and on the stage; while moreover they tried
to cover their deficiencies by arrogance and vain display, pretending to decline their duty, not because they were unable to do
the thing commanded, but because they thought themselves
above it. So that Spurina had like to have been cut in pieces
for attempting to force them to their work; they assailed him
with insolent language, accusing him of a design to betray and
ruin Cæsar's interest; nay, some of them that were in drink
forced his tent in the night, and demanded money for the expenses of their journey, which they must at once take, they said,
to the emperor, to complain of him.

However, the contemptuous treatment they met with at
Placentia did for the present good service to Spurina, and to the
cause of Otho. For Vitellius's men marched up to the walls,
and upbraided Otho's upon the ramparts, calling them players,
dancers, idle spectators of Pythian and Olympic games, but
novices in the art of war, who never so much as looked on at a
battle; mean souls, that triumphed in the beheading of Galba,
an old man unarmed, but had no desire to look real enemies in
the face. Which reproaches so inflamed them that they kneeled
at Spurina's feet, entreated him to give his orders, and assured
him no danger or toil should be too great or too difficult for them.
Whereupon when Vitellius's forces made a vigorous attack on
the town, and brought up numerous engines against the walls,
the besieged bravely repulsed them, and, repelling the enemy
with great slaughter, secured the safety of a noble city, one of
the most flourishing places in Italy.

Besides, it was observed that Otho's officers were much more
inoffensive, both towards the public and to private men, than
those of Vitellius; among whom was Cæcina, who used neither
the language nor the apparel of a citizen, an overbearing, foreign-
seeming man, of gigantic stature, and always dressed in trews
and sleeves, after the manner of the Gauls, whilst he conversed
with Roman officials and magistrates. His wife, too, travelled
along with him, riding in splendid attire on horseback, with a
chosen body of cavalry to escort her. And Fabius Valens, the
other general, was so rapacious that neither what he plundered
from enemies, nor what he stole or got as gifts and bribes from
his friends and allies, could satisfy his wishes. And it was said
that it was in order to have time to raise money that he had
marched so slowly that he was not present at the former attack.
But some lay the blame on Cæcina, saying, that out of a desire to

gain the victory by himself before Fabius joined him, he committed sundry other errors of lesser consequence, and by engaging unseasonably and when he could not do so thoroughly, he very nearly brought all to ruin.

When he found himself beat off at Placentia, he set off to attack Cremona, another large and rich city. In the meantime, Annius Gallus marched to join Spurina at Placentia; but having intelligence that the siege was raised, and that Cremona was in danger, he turned to its relief, and encamped just by the enemy, where he was daily reinforced by other officers. Cæcina placed a strong ambush of heavy infantry in some rough and woody country, and gave orders to his horse to advance, and if the enemy should charge them, then to make a slow retreat, and draw them into the snare. But his stratagem was discovered by some deserters to Celsus, who attacked with a good body of horse, but followed the pursuit cautiously, and succeeded in surrounding and routing the troops in the ambuscade; and if the infantry which he ordered up from the camp had come soon enough to sustain the horse, Cæcina's whole army, in all appearance, had been totally routed. But Paulinus, moving too slowly, was accused of acting with a degree of needless caution not to have been expected from one of his reputation. So that the soldiers incensed Otho against him, accused him of treachery, and boasted loudly that the victory had been in their power, and that if it was not complete, it was owing to the mismanagement of their generals; all which Otho did not so much believe as he was willing to appear not to disbelieve. He therefore sent his brother Titianus, with Proculus, the prefect of the guards, to the army, where the latter was general in reality, and the former in appearance. Celsus and Paulinus had the title of friends and counsellors, but not the least authority or power. At the same time, there was nothing but quarrel and disturbance amongst the enemy, especially where Valens commanded; for the soldiers here, being informed of what had happened at the ambuscade, were enraged because they had not been permitted to be present to strike a blow in defence of the lives of so many men that had died in that action; Valens, with much difficulty, quieted their fury, after they had now begun to throw missiles at him, and quitting his camp, joined Cæcina.

About this time, Otho came to Bedriacum, a little town near Cremona, to the camp, and called a council of war; where Proculus and Titianus declared for giving battle, while the soldiers were flushed with their late success, saying they ought not to lose their time and opportunity and present height of strength, and wait for Vitellius to arrive out of Gaul. But Paulinus told them that the enemy's whole force was present, and that there was no body of reserve behind; but that Otho, if he would not be too precipitate, and chose the enemy's time, instead of his own, for the battle, might expect reinforcements out of Mœsia and Pannonia, not inferior in numbers to the troops that were already present. He thought it probable, too, that the soldiers, who were then in heart before they were joined, would not be less so when the forces were all come up. Besides, the deferring battle could not be inconvenient to them that were sufficiently provided with all necessaries; but the others, being in an enemy's country, must needs be exceedingly straitened in a little time. Marius Celsus was of Paulinus's opinion; Annius Gallus, being absent and under the surgeon's hands through a fall from his horse, was consulted by letter, and advised Otho to stay for those legions that were marching from Mœsia. But after all he did not follow the advice; and the opinion of those that declared for a battle prevailed.

There are several reasons given for this determination, but the most apparent is this; that the prætorian soldiers, as they are called, who serve as guards, not relishing the military discipline which they now had begun a little more to experience, and longing for their amusements and unwarlike life among the shows of Rome, would not be commanded, but were eager for a battle, imagining that upon the first onset they should carry all before them. Otho also himself seems not to have shown the proper fortitude in bearing up against the uncertainty, and, out of effeminacy and want of use, had not patience for the calculations of danger, and was so uneasy at the apprehension of it that he shut his eyes, and like one going to leap from a precipice, left everything to fortune. This is the account Secundus the rhetorician, who was his secretary, gave of the matter. But others would tell you that there were many movements in both armies for acting in concert; and if it were possible for them to agree, then they should proceed to choose one of their most experienced officers that were present; if not, they should convene the senate, and invest it with the power of election. And it is not improbable that, neither of the emperors then bearing the title having really any reputation, such purposes were really entertained among the genuine, serviceable, and sober-minded part of the soldiers. For what could be more odious and unreasonable than that the evils which the Roman citizens had formerly thought it so lamentable to inflict upon each other for the sake of a Sylla or a Marius, a Cæsar or a Pompey, should now be undergone anew, for the object of letting the empire pay the expenses of the gluttony and intemperance of Vitellius, or the looseness and effeminacy of Otho? It is thought that Celsus, upon such reflections, protracted the time in order to a possible accommodation; and that Otho pushed on things to an extremity to prevent it.

He himself returned to Brixillum, which was another false step, both because he withdrew from the combatants all the motives of respect and desire to gain his favour which his presence would have supplied, and because he weakened the army by detaching some of his best and most faithful troops for his horse and foot guards.

About the same time also happened a skirmish on the Po. As Cæcina was laying a bridge over it, Otho's men attacked him, and tried to prevent it. And when they did not succeed, on their putting into their boats torchwood, with a quantity of sulphur and pitch, the wind on the river suddenly caught their material that they had prepared against the enemy, and blew it into a light. First came smoke, and then a clear flame, and the men, getting into great confusion and jumping overboard, upset the boats, and put themselves ludicrously at the mercy of their enemies. Also the Germans attacked Otho's gladiators upon a small island in the river, routed them, and killed a good many.

All which made the soldiers at Bedriacum full of anger, and eagerness to be led to battle. So Proculus led them out of Bedriacum to a place fifty furlongs off, where he pitched his camp so ignorantly and with such a ridiculous want of foresight that the soldiers suffered extremely for want of water, though it was the spring time, and the plains all around were full of running streams and rivers that never dried up. The next day he proposed to attack the enemy, first making a march of not less than a hundred furlongs; but to this Paulinus objected, saying they ought to wait, and not immediately after a journey engage men who would have been standing in their arms and arranging themselves for battle at their leisure, whilst they were making a long march, with all their beasts of burden and their camp followers to encumber them. As the generals were arguing about this matter, a Numidian courier came from Otho with orders to lose no time, but give battle. Accordingly they consented, and moved. As soon as Cæcina had notice, he was much surprised, and quitted his post on the river to hasten to the camp. In the meantime, the men had armed themselves mostly, and were receiving the word from Valens; so while the legions took up their position, they sent out the best of their horse in advance.

Otho's foremost troops, upon some groundless rumour, took up the notion that the commanders on the other side would come over; and accordingly, upon their first approach, they saluted them with the friendly title of fellow-soldiers. But the others returned the compliment with anger and disdainful words; which not only disheartened those that had given the salutation, but excited suspicions of their fidelity amongst the others on their side, who had not. This caused a confusion at the very first onset. And nothing else that followed was done upon any plan; the baggage-carriers, mingling up with the fighting men, created great disorder and division; as well as the nature of the ground, the ditches and pits in which were so many that they were forced to break their ranks to avoid and go round them, and so to fight without order, and in small parties. There were but two legions, one of Vitellius's called The Ravenous, and another of Otho's, called The Assistant, that got out into the open out-spread level and engaged in proper form, fighting, one main body against the other, for some length of time. Otho's men were strong and bold, but had never been in battle before; Vitellius's had seen many wars, but were old and past their strength. So Otho's legion charged boldly, drove back their opponents, and took the eagle, killing pretty nearly every man in the first rank, till the others, full of rage and shame, returned the charge, slew Orfidius, the commander of the legion, and took several standards. Varus Alfenus, with his Batavians, who are the natives of an island of the Rhine, and are esteemed the best of the German horse, fell upon the gladiators, who had a reputation both for valour and skill in fighting. Some few of these did their duty, but the greatest part of them made towards the river, and, falling in with some cohorts stationed there, were cut off. But none behaved so ill as the prætorians, who, without ever so much as meeting the enemy, ran away, broke through their own body that stood, and put them into disorder. Notwithstanding this, many of Otho's men routed those that were opposed to them, broke right into them, and forced their way to the camp through the very middle of their conquerors.

As for their commanders, neither Proculus nor Paulinus ventured to re-enter with the troops; they turned aside, and avoided the soldiers, who had already charged the miscarriage upon their officers. Annius Gallus received into the town and rallied the scattered parties, and encouraged them with an assurance that the battle was a drawn one and the victory had in many parts been theirs. Marius Celsus, collecting the officers, urged the public interest; Otho himself, if he were a brave man, would not, after such an expense of Roman blood, attempt anything further; especially since even Cato and Scipio, though the liberty of Rome was then at stake, had been accused of being too prodigal of so many brave men's lives as were lost in Africa, rather than submit to Cæsar after the battle of Pharsalia had gone against them. For though all persons are equally subject to the caprice of fortune, yet all good men have one advantage she cannot deny, which is this, to act reasonably under misfortunes.

This language was well accepted amongst the officers, who sounded the private soldiers, and found them desirous of peace; and Titianus also gave directions that envoys should be sent in order to a treaty. And accordingly it was agreed that the conference should be between Celsus and Gallus on one part, and Valens with Cæcina on the other. As the two first were upon their journey, they met some centurions, who told them the troops were already in motion, marching for Bedriacum, but that they themselves were deputed by their generals to carry proposals for an accommodation. Celsus and Gallus expressed their approval, and requested them to turn back and carry them to Cæcina. However, Celsus, upon his approach, was in danger from the vanguard, who happened to be some of the horse that had suffered at the ambush. For as soon as they saw him, they hallooed, and were coming down upon him; but the centurions came forward to protect him, and the other officers crying out and bidding them desist, Cæcina came up to inform himself of the tumult, which he quieted, and giving a friendly greeting to Celsus, took him in his company and proceeded towards Bedriacum. Titianus, meantime, had repented of having sent the messengers; and placed those of the soldiers who were more confident upon the walls once again, bidding the others also go and support them. But when Cæcina rode up on his horse and held out his hand, no one did or said to the contrary; those on the walls greeted his men with salutations, others opened the gates and went out, and mingled freely with those they met; and instead of acts of hostility, there was nothing but mutual shaking of hands and congratulations, every one taking the oaths and submitting to Vitellius.

This is the account which the most of those that were present at the battle give of it, yet own that the disorder they were in, and the absence of any unity of action, would not give them leave to be certain as to particulars. And when I myself travelled afterwards over the field of battle, Mestrius Florus, a man of consular degree, one of those who had been, not willingly, but by command, in attendance on Otho at the time, pointed out to me an ancient temple, and told me, that as he went that way after the battle, he observed a heap of bodies piled up there to such a height that those on the top of it touched the pinnacles of the roof. How it came to be so, he could neither discover himself nor learn from any other person; as indeed, he said, in civil wars it generally happens that greater numbers are killed when an army is routed, quarter not being given, because captives are of no advantage to the conquerors; but why the carcasses should be heaped up after that manner is not easy to determine.

Otho, at first, as it frequently happens, received some uncertain rumours of the issue of the battle. But when some of the wounded that returned from the field informed him rightly of it, it is not, indeed, so much to be wondered at that his friends should bid him not give all up as lost or let his courage sink; but the feeling shown by the soldiers is something that exceeds all belief. There was not one of them would either go over to the conqueror or show any disposition to make terms for himself, as if their leader's cause was desperate; on the contrary, they crowded his gates, called out to him the title of emperor, and as soon as he appeared, cried out and entreated him, catching hold of his hand, and throwing themselves upon the ground, and with all the moving language of tears and persuasion, besought him to stand by them, not abandon them to their enemies, but employ in his service their lives and persons, which would not cease to be his so long as they had breath; so urgent was their zealous and universal importunity. And one obscure and private soldier, after he had drawn his sword, addressed himself to Otho: " By this, Cæsar, judge our fidelity; there is not a man amongst us but would strike thus to serve you; " and so stabbed himself. Notwithstanding this, Otho stood serene and unshaken, and, with a face full of constancy and composure, turned himself about and looked at them, replying thus: " This day, my fellow-soldiers, which gives me such proofs of your affection, is preferable even to that on which you saluted me emperor; deny me not, therefore, the yet higher satisfaction of laying down my life for the preservation of so many brave men; in this, at least, let me be worthy of the empire, that is, to die for it. I am of opinion the enemy has neither gained an entire nor a decisive victory; I have advice that the Mœsian army is not many days' journey distant, on its march to the Adriatic; Asia, Syria, and Egypt, and the legions that are serving against the Jews, declare for us; the senate is also with us, and the wives and children of our opponents are in our power; but alas, it is not in defence of Italy against Hannibal or Pyrrhus or the Cimbri that we fight; Romans combat here against Romans, and, whether we conquer or are defeated our country suffers and we commit a crime: victory, to whichever it fall, is gained at her expense. Believe it many times over, I can die with more honour than I can reign. For I cannot see at all how I should do any such great good to my country by gaining the victory, as I shall by dying to establish peace and unanimity and to save Italy from such another unhappy day."

As soon as he had done, he was resolute against all manner of argument or persuasion, and taking leave of his friends and the senators that were present, he bade them depart, and wrote to those that were absent, and sent letters to the towns, that they might have every honour and facility in their journey. Then he sent for Cocceius, his brother's son, who was yet a boy, and bade him be in no apprehension of Vitellius, whose mother and wife and family he had treated with the same tenderness as his own; and also told him that this had been his reason for delaying to adopt him, which he had meant to do as his son; he had desired that he might share his power, if he conquered, but not be involved in his ruin if he failed. " Take notice," he added, " my boy, of these my last words, that you neither too negligently forget, nor too zealously remember, that Cæsar was your uncle." By and by he heard a tumult amongst the soldiers at the door, who were treating the senators with menaces for preparing to withdraw; upon which, out of regard to their safety, he showed himself once more in public, but not with a gentle aspect and in a persuading manner as before; on the contrary, with a countenance that discovered indignation and authority, he commanded such as were disorderly to leave the place, and was not disobeyed.

It was now evening, and feeling thirsty, he drank some water, and then took two daggers that belonged to him, and when he had carefully examined their edges, he laid one of them down, and put the other in his robe, under his arm, then called his servants, and distributed some money amongst them, but not inconsiderately, nor like one too lavish of what was not his own; for to some he gave more, to others less, all strictly in moderation, and distinguishing every one's particular merit. When this was done, he dismissed them, and passed the rest of the night in so sound a sleep that the officers of his bed-chamber heard him snore. In the morning, he called for one of his freedmen, who had assisted him in arranging about the senators, and bade him bring him an account if they were safe. Being informed they were all well and wanted nothing, " Go then," said he, " and show yourself to the soldiers, lest they should cut you to pieces for being accessory to my death." As soon as he was gone, he held his sword upright under him with both his hands, and falling upon it expired with no more than one single groan to express his sense of the pang, or to inform those that waited without. When his servants, therefore, raised their exclamations of grief, the whole camp and city were at once filled with lamentation; the soldiers immediately broke in at the doors with a loud cry, in passionate distress, and accusing themselves that they had been so negligent in looking after that life which was laid down to preserve theirs. Nor would a man of them quit the body to secure his own safety with the approaching enemy; but having raised a funeral pile, and attired the body, they bore it thither, arrayed in their arms, those among them greatly exulting who succeeded in getting first under the bier and becoming its bearers. Of the others, some threw themselves down before the body and kissed his wound, others grasped his hand, and others that were at a distance knelt down to do him obeisance. There were some who, after putting their torches to the pile, slew themselves, though they had not, so far as appeared, either any particular obligations to the dead, or reason to apprehend ill-usage from the victor. Simply, it would seem, no king, legal or illegal, had ever been possessed with so extreme and vehement a passion to command others, as was that of these men to obey Otho. Nor did their love of him cease with his death; it survived and changed ere long into a mortal hatred to his successor, as will be shown in its proper place.

They placed the remains of Otho in the earth, and raised over them a monument which neither by its size nor the pomp of its inscription might excite hostility. I myself have seen it, at Brixillum; a plain structure, and the epitaph only this: To the memory of Marcus Otho. He died in his thirty-eighth year, after a short reign of about three months, his death being as much applauded as his life was censured; for if he lived not better than Nero, he died more nobly. The soldiers were displeased with Pollio, one of their two prefects, who bade them immediately swear allegiance to Vitellius; and when they understood that some of the senators were still upon the spot, they made no opposition to the departure of the rest, but only disturbed the tranquillity of Virginius Rufus with an offer of the government, and moving in one body to his house in arms, they first entreated him, and then demanded of him to accept of the empire, or at least to be their mediator. But he, that refused to command them when conquerors, thought it ridiculous to pretend to it now they were beat, and was unwilling to go as their envoy to the Germans, whom in past time he had compelled to do various things that they had not liked; and for these reasons he slipped away through a private door. As soon as the soldiers perceived this, they owned Vitellius, and so got their pardon, and served under Cæcina.

# INDEX

# Index

# EVERYMAN'S LIBRARY: A Selected List

## BIOGRAPHY

**Baxter, Richard** (1615–91).
    THE AUTOBIOGRAPHY OF RICHARD BAXTER.   868
**Boswell, James** (1740–95). *See* Johnson.
**Brontë, Charlotte** (1816–55).
    LIFE, 1857. By *Mrs Gaskell*. Introduction by *May Sinclair*. (*See also* Fiction.) 318
**Burns, Robert** (1759–96).
    LIFE, 1828. By *J. G. Lockhart* (1794–1854). With Introduction by *Prof. James Kinsley*, M.A., PH.D.   (*See also* Poetry and Drama.) 156
**Byron, Lord** (1788–1824).
    LETTERS. Edited by *R. G. Howarth*, B.LITT., and with an Introduction by *André Maurois*.   (*See also* Poetry and Drama.) 931
**Canton, William** (1845–1926).
    A CHILD'S BOOK OF SAINTS, 1898.   (*See also* Essays.) 61
**Cellini, Benvenuto** (1500–71).
    THE LIFE OF BENVENUTO CELLINI, written by himself. Translated by *Anne Macdonell*. Introduction by *William Gaunt*.   51
**Cowper, William** (1731–1800).
    SELECTED LETTERS. Edited, with Introduction, by *W. Hadley*, M.A.   774
    (*See also* Poetry and Drama.)
**Dickens, Charles** (1812–70).
    LIFE, 1874. By *John Forster* (1812–76). Introduction by *G. K. Chesterton*. 2 vols.
    (*See also* Fiction.) 781–2
**Evelyn, John** (1620–1706).
    DIARY. Edited by *William Bray*, 1819. Intro. by *G. W. E. Russell*. 2 vols.   220–1
**Fox, George** (1624–91).
    JOURNAL, 1694. Revised by *Norman Penney*, with Account of Fox's last years. Introduction by *Rufus M. Jones*.   754
**Franklin, Benjamin** (1706–90).
    AUTOBIOGRAPHY, 1817. With Introduction and Account of Franklin's later life by *W. Macdonald*. Reset new edition (1949), with a newly compiled Index.   316
**Goethe, Johann Wolfgang von** (1749–1832).
    LIFE, 1855. By *G. H. Lewes* (1817–78). Introduction by *Havelock Ellis*. Index.
    (*See also* Poetry and Drama.) 269
**Hudson, William Henry** (1841–1922).
    FAR AWAY AND LONG AGO, 1918. Intro. by *John Galsworthy*.   956
**Johnson, Samuel** (1709–84).
    LIVES OF THE ENGLISH POETS, 1781. Introduction by *Mrs L. Archer-Hind*. 2 vols.
    (*See also* Essays, Fiction.) 770–1
    BOSWELL'S LIFE OF JOHNSON, 1791. A new edition (1949), with Introduction by *S. C. Roberts*, M.A., LL.D., and a 30-page Index by Alan Dent. 2 vols.   1–2
**Keats, John** (1795–1821).
    LIFE AND LETTERS, 1848. By *Lord Houghton* (1809–85). Introduction by *Robert Lynd*. Note on the letters by Lewis Gibbs.   (*See also* Poetry and Drama.) 801
**Lamb, Charles** (1775–1834).
    LETTERS. New edition (1945) arranged from the Complete Annotated Edition of the Letters. 2 vols.   (*See also* Essays and Belles-Lettres, Fiction.) 342–3
**Napoleon Buonaparte** (1769–1821).
    HISTORY OF NAPOLEON BUONAPARTE, 1829. By *J. G. Lockhart* (1794–1854).   3
    (*See also* Essays and Belles-Lettres.)
**Nelson, Horatio, Viscount** (1758–1805).
    LIFE, 1813. By *Robert Southey* (1774–1843).   (*See also* Essays.) 52
**Outram, General Sir James** (1803–63), 'the Bayard of India.'
    LIFE, 1903. Deals with important passages in the history of India in the nineteenth century. By *L. J. Trotter* (1827–1912).   396
**Pepys, Samuel** (1633–1703).
    DIARY. Newly edited (1953), with modernized spelling, by *John Warrington*, from the edition of Mynors Bright (1875–9). 3 vols.   53–5
**Plutarch** (46?–120).
    LIVES OF THE NOBLE GREEKS AND ROMANS. Dryden's edition, 1683–6. Revised, with Introduction, by *A. H. Clough* (1819–61). 3 vols.   407–9
**Rousseau, Jean Jacques** (1712–78).
    CONFESSIONS, 1782. 2 vols. Complete and unabridged English translation. New Introduction by *Prof. R. Niklaus*, B.A., PH.D., of Exeter University.   859–60
    (*See also* Essays, Theology and Philosophy.)
**Scott, Sir Walter** (1771–1832).
    LOCKHART'S LIFE OF SCOTT. An abridgement by *J. G. Lockhart* himself from the original 7 volumes. New Introduction by *W. M. Parker*, M.A.   39

**Swift, Jonathan** (1667–1745).
JOURNAL TO STELLA, 1710–13. Deciphered by *J. K. Moorhead*. Introduction by *Sir Walter Scott*. Sir Walter Scott's essay 'Swift, Stella and Vanessa' is included.    757
(*See also* Essays, Fiction.)
**Walpole, Horace** (1717–97).
SELECTED LETTERS. Edited, with Introduction, by *W. Hadley*, M.A.    775
**Wellington, Arthur Wellesley, Duke of** (1769–1852).
LIFE, 1862. By *G. R. Gleig* (1796–1888).    341

# CLASSICAL

**Aeschylus** (525–455 B.C.).
PLAYS. Translated into English Verse by *G. M. Cookson*. New Introduction by *John Warrington*, and notes on each play.    62
**Aristophanes** (450?–385? B.C.).
THE COMEDIES. Translated by *J. Hookham Frere*, etc. Edited, with Introduction, by *J. P. Maine* and *J. H. Frere*. 2 vols.    (*Vol. 1 temporarily out of print.*) 516
**Aristotle** (384–322 B.C.).
POLITICS and THE ATHENIAN CONSTITUTION. Edited and translated by *John Warrington*.    605
METAPHYSICS. Edited and translated by *John Warrington*. Introduction by *Sir David Ross*, K.B.E., M.A., D.LITT.    1000
**Caesar, Julius** (102?–44 B.C.).
WAR COMMENTARIES. 'The Gallic Wars' and 'The Civil War.' Newly translated and edited by *John Warrington*.    702
**Cicero, Marcus Tullius** (106–43 B.C.).
THE OFFICES (translated by *Thomas Cockman*, 1699); LAELIUS, ON FRIENDSHIP; CATO, ON OLD AGE; AND SELECT LETTERS (translated by *W. Melmoth*, 1753). With Note on Cicero's Character by De Quincey. Introduction by *John Warrington*. 345
**Demetrius** (fl. late first century A.D.). (*See under* Aristotle.)
**Demosthenes** (384–322 B.C.). (*See under* Oratory, p. 11.)
**Epictetus** (*b. c.* A.D. 60).
MORAL DISCOURSES. THE ENCHIRIDION AND FRAGMENTS. Translated by *Elizabeth Carter* (1717–1806). Edited by *W. H. D. Rouse*, M.A.    404
**Euripides** (484?–407 B.C.).
PLAYS. New Introduction by *John Warrington*. Translated by *A. S. Way*, D.LITT. 2 vols.    63, 271
**Herodotus** (484?–425? B.C.).
HISTORY. The 'History' deals with the period covering the Persian invasion of Greece, 492–480 B.C. Rawlinson's Translation, additional notes and Introduction by *E. H. Blakeney*. 2 vols. (*Vol. II temporarily out of print.*)    405–6
**Homer** (? ninth century B.C.).
ILIAD. New verse translation by *S. O. Andrew* and *Michael Oakley*.    453
ODYSSEY. The new verse translation (first published 1953) by *S. O. Andrew*. Introduction by *John Warrington*.    454
**Juvenal** (*c.* A.D. 50–*c.* 130).
SATIRES; with THE SATIRES OF PERSIUS. Introduction by *Prof. H. J. Rose*, M.A., F.B.A. William Gifford Translation, 1802. Revised by *John Warrington*.    997
**Lucretius** (*c.* 99?–50? B.C.).
ON THE NATURE OF THINGS. Metrical Translation by *W. E. Leonard*.    750
**Ovid** (43 B.C.–A.D. 18).
SELECTED WORKS. Chosen by *J. C.* and *M. J. Thornton*. Selections from the *Metamorphoses*, *Heroical Epistles*, the *Festivals*, the *Ibis*, and his epistles written in exile: also his *Art of Love*.    955
**Persius** (34–62). *See* Juvenal.
**Plato** (427–347 B.C.).
THE REPUBLIC. Translated, with an Introduction, by *A. D. Lindsay*, C.B.E., LL.D. The greatest achievement of the Greek intellect in philosophy.    64
SOCRATIC DISCOURSES OF PLATO AND XENOPHON. Introduction by *A. D. Lindsay*, C.B.E., LL.D.    457
THE LAWS. The last of Plato's dialogues is here printed in the A. E. Taylor (1869–1945) Translation.    275
**Sophocles** (496?–406 B.C.).
DRAMAS. This volume contains the seven surviving dramas.    114
**Thucydides** (*c.* 460–401 B.C.).
HISTORY OF THE PELOPONNESIAN WAR. Translation by *Richard Crawley*. Introduction by *John Warrington*. Index and five plans.    455
**Virgil** (70–19 B.C.).
AENEID. Verse translation by *Michael Oakley*. Introduction by *E. M. Forster*.    161
ECLOGUES AND GEORGICS. Verse Translation by *T. F. Royds*. The 'Eclogues' were inspired by Theocritus; the 'Georgics' describe a countryman's life.    222
**Xenophon** (430?–360? B.C.). (*See under* Plato.)

# ESSAYS AND BELLES-LETTRES

3

**Lamb, Charles** (1775–1834).
ESSAYS OF ELIA AND LAST ESSAYS OF ELIA, 1823–33. Introduction by *Augustine Birrell*. Includes the first and the last Essays of Elia. 14
*(See also* Biography, Fiction.)

**Landor, Walter Savage** (1775–1864).
IMAGINARY CONVERSATIONS, AND POEMS, 1824–9, 1853. Edited, with Introduction by *Havelock Ellis*. 890

**Lawrence, David Herbert** (1885–1930).
STORIES, ESSAYS AND POEMS. Selected by *Desmond Hawkins*. Poetry, Essays, Travel Sketches and Letters. 958
*(See also* Fiction.)

**Locke, John** (1632–1704).
AN ESSAY CONCERNING HUMAN UNDERSTANDING, 1690. Abridged and edited by *Raymond Wilburn*, presenting the whole sweep of the work. 984
*(See also* Theology and Philosophy.)

**Lynd, Robert** (1879–1949).
ESSAYS ON LIFE AND LITERATURE. Introduction by *Desmond MacCarthy*. 990

**Macaulay, Thomas Babington, Lord** (1800–59).
CRITICAL AND HISTORICAL ESSAYS, 1843. New Introduction by *Douglas Jerrold*. 2 vols. 225–6
MISCELLANEOUS ESSAYS, 1823–59; LAYS OF ANCIENT ROME, 1842; and MISCELLANEOUS POEMS, 1812–47. Introduction by *Prof. G. M. Trevelyan*, O.M. 439
*(See also* History.)

**Machiavelli, Niccolò** (1469–1527).
THE PRINCE, 1513. New Introduction by *Prof. H. Butterfield*, M.A., HON. D.LITT. Translated by *W. K. Marriott*. 280

**Mazzini, Joseph** (1805–72).
THE DUTIES OF MAN (translated by *Miss E. Noyes*); and OTHER ESSAYS. New Introduction by *Dr Thomas Jones*, C.H., LL.D. 224

**Milton, John** (1608–74).
PROSE WRITINGS. Introduction by *K. M. Burton*, M.A. The contents of this volume include 'Areopagitica,' 1644, and other important prose works. 795
*(See also* Poetry, etc.)

**Mitford, Mary Russell** (1787–1855).
OUR VILLAGE, 1824–32. Edited, with an Introduction, by *Sir John Squire*. 927

**Modern Humour.** An Anthology in Prose and Verse from over sixty authors. 957

**Montaigne, Michel de** (1533–92).
ESSAYS, 1580–8. John Florio's version, 1603. Edited (from the third edition, 1632), with Intro. by *A. R. Waller*, 3 vols. *(Vol. I temporarily out of print.)* 440–2

**Napoleon Buonaparte** (1769–1821).
LETTERS. Some 300 of the most interesting of the Emperor's letters, chosen and translated by *J. M. Thompson*, F.B.A., F.R.HIST.S. *(See also* Biography.) 995

**Nelson, Horatio, Viscount** (1758–1805).
NELSON'S LETTERS. Compiled by *Geoffrey Rawson*. *(See also* Biography.) 244

**Newman, John Henry** (1801–90).
ON THE SCOPE AND NATURE OF UNIVERSITY EDUCATION; and CHRISTIANITY AND SCIENTIFIC INVESTIGATION, 1852. Introduction by *Wilfrid Ward*. 723
*(See also* Theology and Philosophy.)

**Poe, Edgar Allan** (1809–49).
ESSAYS. *(See* Poetry.)

**Quiller-Couch, Sir Arthur** (1863–1944).
CAMBRIDGE LECTURES, from 'Q.'s' well-known books *The Art of Reading*, 1920; *The Art of Writing*, 1916; *Studies in Literature*, 1918; and *Shakespeare's Workmanship*, 1918. *(See also* Fiction.) 974

**Rousseau, Jean Jacques** (1712–78).
ÉMILE; OR, EDUCATION. Translated by *Barbara Foxley*, M.A. Intro. (1955) by *Prof. André Boutet de Monvel*. *(See also* Biography, Theology and Philosophy.) 518

**Ruskin, John** (1819–1900).
SESAME, AND LILIES, 1864; THE TWO PATHS, 1859; and THE KING OF THE GOLDEN RIVER; or THE BLACK BROTHERS, 1851. Introduction by *Sir Oliver Lodge*. 219
THE SEVEN LAMPS OF ARCHITECTURE, 1849. With an Introduction (1956) by *Sir Arnold Lunn*. Illustrated with 14 plates of engravings. 207

**Sévigné, Marie de Rabutin-Chantal, Marquise de** (1626–96).
SELECTED LETTERS. Selected and translated by *H. T. Barnwell*, M.A. 98

**Spectator, The,** 1711–14. By Joseph Addison (1672–1719), Sir Richard Steele (1672–1729) and Others. Edited by *Prof. Gregory Smith*. New Introduction by *P. Smithers*, D.PHIL., M.P., and a Biographical and General Index by *Prof. Gregory Smith*. Reset with minor revisions, 1945. 4 vols. *(See also* Essays *under* Steele.) 164–7

**Spencer, Herbert** (1820–1903).
ESSAYS ON EDUCATION, 1861. Introduction by *C. W. Eliot*. 504

**Steele, Sir Richard** (1672–1729).
THE TATLER, 1709–11. 993

**Sterne, Laurence** (1713–68).
A SENTIMENTAL JOURNEY THROUGH FRANCE AND ITALY, 1768; JOURNAL TO ELIZA, written in 1767; and LETTERS TO ELIZA, 1766–7. Introduction by *Daniel George*. *(See also* Fiction.) 796

**Collins, Wilkie** (1824–89).
  THE MOONSTONE, 1868. Introduction by *Dorothy L. Sayers.*      979
  THE WOMAN IN WHITE, 1860. New Introduction by *Maurice Richardson.*      464
**Conrad, Joseph** (1857–1924).
  LORD JIM, 1900. Characteristically set in the East Indies. Introduction by *R. B. Cunninghame Graham.*      925
  THE NIGGER OF THE 'NARCISSUS,' 1897; TYPHOON, 1903; and THE SHADOW LINE, 1917. Introduction by *A. J. Hoppé.* Three of Conrad's best-known stories.      980
  NOSTROMO, 1904. New edition of Conrad's greatest novel with an Introduction by *Richard Curle.*      38
**Cooper, James Fenimore** (1789–1851).
  THE LAST OF THE MOHICANS, 1826, A NARRATIVE OF 1757. With an Introduction by *Ernest Rhys.*      79
  THE PRAIRIE, 1827. The last of the 'Leatherstocking Tales.'      172
**Craik, Mrs.** *See* Mulock.
**Daudet, Alphonse** (1840–97).
  TARTARIN OF TARASCON, 1872; and TARTARIN ON THE ALPS, 1885. Two light episodic novels, some of the funniest episodes ever written in French.      423
**Defoe, Daniel** (1661?–1731).
  THE FORTUNES AND MISFORTUNES OF MOLL FLANDERS, 1722. Introduction by *G. A. Aitken.* One of Defoe's greatest books, famous for its picture of low life.      837
  JOURNAL OF THE PLAGUE YEAR, 1722. Introduction by *G. A. Aitken.*      289
  LIFE, ADVENTURES AND PIRACIES OF THE FAMOUS CAPTAIN SINGLETON, 1720. Introduction by *Edward Garnett.* A supposed record of a journey across Africa.      74
  ROBINSON CRUSOE, 1719. Parts 1 and 2 complete. Introduction by *Guy N. Pocock.*
      (*See also* Travel.) 59
**De Rojas, Fernando** (15th century).
  CELESTINA: OR THE TRAGI-COMEDY OF CALISTO AND MELIBEA, attributed to Fernando de Rojas. Translated, with an Introduction, by *Phyllis Hartnoll*, M.A., L. ÉS L. This is a new translation (1958).      100
**Dickens, Charles** (1812–70). Each of the following volumes of Dickens's works has an Introduction by *G. K. Chesterton*:

| | | | |
|---|---|---|---|
| BARNABY RUDGE, 1841. | 76 | LITTLE DORRIT, 1857. | 293 |
| BLEAK HOUSE, 1852–3. | 236 | MARTIN CHUZZLEWIT, 1843–4. | 241 |
| CHRISTMAS BOOKS, 1843–8. | 239 | NICHOLAS NICKLEBY, 1838–9. | 238 |
| CHRISTMAS STORIES, 1850–67. | 414 | OLD CURIOSITY SHOP, 1841. | 173 |
| DAVID COPPERFIELD, 1849–50. | 242 | OLIVER TWIST, 1838. | 233 |
| DOMBEY AND SON, 1846–8. | 240 | OUR MUTUAL FRIEND, 1864–5. | 294 |
| GREAT EXPECTATIONS, 1861. | 234 | PICKWICK PAPERS, 1836–7. | 235 |
| HARD TIMES, 1854. | 292 | A TALE OF TWO CITIES, 1859. | 102 |

      (*See also* Biography.)
**Disraeli, Benjamin.** *See* Beaconsfield.
**Dostoyevsky, Fyodor** (1821–81).
  THE BROTHERS KARAMAZOV, 1879–80. Translated by *Constance Garnett.* Introduction by *Edward Garnett.* 2 vols.      802–3
  CRIME AND PUNISHMENT, 1866. *Constance Garnett* translation.      501
  THE IDIOT, 1873. Translated by *Eva M. Martin.* New Introduction by *Richard Curle.*      682
  LETTERS FROM THE UNDERWORLD, 1864; and OTHER TALES (THE GENTLE MAIDEN; THE LANDLADY). Translated, with Introduction, by *C. J. Hogarth.*      654
  POOR FOLK, 1845; and THE GAMBLER, 1867. Translated, with Introduction, by *C. J. Hogarth.*      711
  THE POSSESSED, 1871. Translated by *Constance Garnett.* Introduction by *Nikolay Andreyev*, PH.D., M.A. 2 vols.      861–2
**Dumas, Alexandre** (1802–70).
  THE BLACK TULIP, 1850. The brothers De Witt in Holland, 1672–5. New Introduction by *Prof. Marcel Girard.*      174
  COUNT OF MONTE CRISTO, 1844. 2 vols. Napoleon's later phase. New Introduction by *Prof. Marcel Girard.*      393–4
  MARGUERITE DE VALOIS, 1845. The Eve of St Bartholomew.      326
  THE THREE MUSKETEERS, 1844. The France of Cardinal Richelieu.      81
**Du Maurier, George Louis Palmella Busson** (1834–96).
  TRILBY, 1894. Illustrated by the author. Preface by *Sir Gerald Du Maurier. Trilby* breathes the air of Paris in the eighties and is drawn largely from the author's own experience.      863
**Edgeworth, Maria** (1767–1849).
  CASTLE RACKRENT, 1800; and THE ABSENTEE, 1812. Introduction by *Prof. Brander Matthews.*      410
**Eliot, George** (pseudonym of Mary Ann Evans, 1819–80).
  ADAM BEDE, 1859. New Introduction by *Robert Speaight.*      27
  MIDDLEMARCH, 1872. New Introduction by *Gerald Bullett.* 2 vols.      854–5
  THE MILL ON THE FLOSS, 1860. Introduction by *Sir W. Robertson Nicoll.*      325
  ROMOLA, 1863. Intro. by *Rudolph Dircks.* The Florence of Savonarola.      231
  SILAS MARNER, THE WEAVER OF RAVELOE, 1861. Introduction by *A. Matheson.* 12

7

**Manzoni, Alessandro** (1785–1873).
  THE BETROTHED (*I Promessi Sposi*, 1840, rev. ed.). Translated (1951) from the Italian by *Archibald Colquhoun*, who also adds a preface. 999
**Marryat, Frederick** (1792–1848).
  MR MIDSHIPMAN EASY. New Introduction by *Oliver Warner*. 82
  THE SETTLERS IN CANADA, 1844. Introduction by *Oliver Warner*. 370
**Maugham, W. Somerset** (*b.* 1874).
  CAKES AND ALE, 1930. The finest novel of the author's inter-war period. 932
**Maupassant, Guy de** (1850–93).
  SHORT STORIES. Translated by *Marjorie Laurie*. Intro. by *Gerald Gould*. 907
**Melville, Herman** (1819–91).
  MOBY DICK, 1851. Intro. by *Prof. Sherman Paul*. 179
  TYPEE, 1846; and BILLY BUDD (*published* 1924). South Seas adventures. New Introduction by *Milton R. Stern*. 180
**Meredith, George** (1828–1909).
  THE ORDEAL OF RICHARD FEVEREL, 1859. Introduction by *Robert Sencourt*. 916
**Mickiewicz, Adam** (1798–1855).
  PAN TADEUSZ, 1834. Translated into English prose, with Introduction, by *Prof. G. R. Noyes*. Poland's epic of Napoleonic wars. 842
**Modern Short Stories.** Selected by *John Hadfield*. Twenty stories. 954
**Moore, George** (1852–1933).
  ESTHER WATERS, 1894. The story of Esther Waters, the servant girl who 'went wrong.' Introduction by *C. D. Medley*. 933
**Mulock [Mrs Craik], Maria** (1826–87).
  JOHN HALIFAX, GENTLEMAN, 1856. Introduction by *J. Shaylor*. 123
**Pater, Walter** (1839–94).
  MARIUS THE EPICUREAN, 1885. Introduction by *Osbert Burdett*. 903
**Poe, Edgar Allan** (1809–49).
  TALES OF MYSTERY AND IMAGINATION. Introduction by *Padraic Colum*. 336
  (*See also* Poetry and Drama.)
**Priestley, J. B.** (*b.* 1894).
  ANGEL PAVEMENT, 1931. A finely conceived novel of London. 938
**Quiller-Couch, Sir Arthur** (1863–1944).
  HETTY WESLEY, 1903. Introduction by the author. (*See also* Essays.) 864
**Radcliffe, Mrs Ann** (1764–1823).
  THE MYSTERIES OF UDOLPHO, 1794. Intro. by *R. A. Freeman*. 2 vols. 865–6
**Reade, Charles** (1814–84).
  THE CLOISTER AND THE HEARTH, 1861. Introduction by *Swinburne*. 29
**Richardson, Samuel** (1689–1761).
  PAMELA, 1740. Introduction by *George Saintsbury*. 2 vols. 683–4
  CLARISSA, 1747–8. Introduction by *Prof. W. L. Phelps*. 4 vols. 882–5
**Russian Short Stories.** Translated, with Introduction, by *Rochelle S. Townsend*. Stories by Pushkin, Gogol, Tolstoy, Korolenko, Chehov, Chirikov, Andreyev, Kuprin, Gorky, Sologub. 758
**Scott, Sir Walter** (1771–1832).
  The following Waverley Novels each contain an Introduction, biographical and bibliographical, based upon Lockhart's *Life*:
  THE ANTIQUARY, 1816. Introduction by *W. M. Parker*, M.A. 126
  THE BRIDE OF LAMMERMOOR, 1819. A romance of life in East Lothian, 1695. New Introduction by *W. M. Parker*, M.A. 129
  GUY MANNERING, 1815. A mystery story of the time of George III. New Introduction by *W. M. Parker*, M.A. 133
  THE HEART OF MIDLOTHIAN, 1818. Period of the Porteous Riots, 1736. New Introduction by *W. M. Parker*, M.A. 134
  IVANHOE, 1820. A romance of the days of Richard I. 16
  KENILWORTH, 1821. The tragic story of Amy Robsart, in Elizabeth I's time. New Preface and Glossary by *W. M. Parker*, M.A. 135
  OLD MORTALITY, 1817. Battle of Bothwell Bridge, 1679. New Introduction by *W. M. Parker*, M.A. 137
  QUENTIN DURWARD, 1823. A tale of adventures in fifteenth-century France. New Introduction by *W. M. Parker*, M.A. 140
  REDGAUNTLET, 1824. A tale of adventure in Cumberland, about 1763. New Introduction by *W. M. Parker*, M.A. 141
  ROB ROY, 1818. A romance of the Rebellion of 1715. 142
  THE TALISMAN, 1825. Richard Cœur-de-Lion and the Third Crusade, 1191. New Preface by *W. M. Parker*, M.A. (*See also* Biography.) 144
**Shchedrin** (M. E. Saltykov, 1826–92).
  THE GOLOVLYOV FAMILY. Translated by *Natalie Duddington*. Introduction by *Edward Garnett*. 908
**Shelley, Mary Wollstonecraft** (1797–1851).
  FRANKENSTEIN, 1818. With Mary Shelley's own Preface. 616
**Shorter Novels.**
  Vol. I: ELIZABETHAN. Introduction by *George Saintsbury* and Notes by *Philip Henderson*. Contains: Deloney's 'Jack of Newberie' and 'Thomas of Reading'; Nashe's 'The Unfortunate Traveller'; Green's 'Carde of Fancie.' 824

# HISTORY

# ORATORY

# POETRY AND DRAMA

## REFERENCE

*Many volumes formerly included in Everyman's Library reference section are now included in Everyman's Reference Library and are bound in larger format.*

# ROMANCE

**Aucassin and Nicolette, with other Medieval Romances.** Translated, with Introduction, by *Eugene Mason*. 497

**Boccaccio, Giovanni** (1313–75).
DECAMERON, 1471. Translated by *J. M. Rigg*, 1903. Introduction by *Edward Hutton*, 2 vols. Unabridged. 845–6

**Bunyan, John** (1628–88).
PILGRIM'S PROGRESS, Parts I and II, 1678–84. Reset edition. Introduction by *Prof. G. B. Harrison*, M.A., PH.D. (*See also* Theology and Philosophy.) 204

**Cervantes, Saavedra Miguel de** (1547–1616).
DON QUIXOTE DE LA MANCHA. Translated by *P. A. Motteux*. Notes by *J. G. Lockhart*. Introduction and supplementary Notes by *L. B. Walton*, M.A., B.LITT. 2 vols. 385–6

**Chrétien de Troyes** (fl. 12th cent.).
ARTHURIAN ROMANCES ('Erec et Enide'; 'Cligés'; 'Yvain' and 'Lancelot'). Translated into prose, with Introduction, notes and bibliography, by *William Wistar Comfort*. 698

**Kalevala, or The Land of Heroes.** Translated from the Finnish by W. F. Kirby. 2 vols. 259–60

**Mabinogion, The.** Translated with Introduction by *Thomas Jones*, M.A., D.LITT., and *Gwyn Jones*, M.A. 97

**Malory, Sir Thomas** (fl. 1400 ?–70).
LE MORTE D'ARTHUR. Introduction by *Sir John Rhys*. 2 vols. 45–6

**Marie de France** (12th century), LAYS OF, AND OTHER FRENCH LEGENDS. Eight of Marie's 'Lais' and two of the anonymous French love stories of the same period translated with an Introduction by *Eugene Mason*. 557

**Njal's Saga.** THE STORY OF BURNT NJAL (written about 1280–90). Translated from the Icelandic by *Sir G. W. Dasent* (1861). Introduction (1957) and Index by *Prof. Edward Turville-Petre*, B.LITT., M.A. 558

**Rabelais, François** (1494 ?–1553).
THE HEROIC DEEDS OF GARGANTUA AND PANTAGRUEL, 1532–5. Introduction by *D. B. Wyndham Lewis*. 2 vols. A complete unabridged edition of Urquhart and Motteux's translation, 1653–94. 826–7

# SCIENCE

**Boyle, Robert** (1627–91).
THE SCEPTICAL CHYMIST, 1661. Introduction by *M. M. Pattison Muir*. 559

**Darwin, Charles** (1809–82).
THE ORIGIN OF SPECIES, 1859. The sixth edition embodies Darwin's final additions and revisions. New Introduction (1956) by *W. R. Thompson*, F.R.S. 811

**Eddington, Arthur Stanley** (1882–1944). (*See also* Travel and Topography.)
THE NATURE OF THE PHYSICAL WORLD, 1928. Introduction by *Sir Edmund Whittaker*, F.R.S., O.M. 922

**Euclid** (fl. *c*. 330–*c*. 275 B.C.).
THE ELEMENTS OF EUCLID. Edited by *Isaac Todhunter*, with Introduction by *Sir Thomas L. Heath*, K.C.B., F.R.S. 891

**Faraday, Michael** (1791–1867).
EXPERIMENTAL RESEARCHES IN ELECTRICITY, 1839–55. With Plates and Diagrams, and an appreciation by *Prof. John Tyndall*. 576

**Harvey, William** (1578–1657).
THE CIRCULATION OF THE BLOOD. Introduction by *Ernest Parkyn*. 262

**Howard, John** (1726 ?–90).
THE STATE OF THE PRISONS, 1777. Intro. and Notes by *Kenneth Ruck*. 835

**Marx, Karl** (1818–83).
CAPITAL, 1867. Translated by *Eden* and *Cedar Paul*. 2 vols. Introduction by *Prof. G. D. H. Cole*. 848–9

**Mill, John Stuart** (1806–73). *See* Wollstonecraft.

**Owen, Robert** (1771–1858).
A NEW VIEW OF SOCIETY, 1813; and OTHER WRITINGS. Introduction by *G. D. H. Cole*. 799

**Pearson, Karl** (1857–1936).
THE GRAMMAR OF SCIENCE, 1892. 939

**Ricardo, David** (1772–1823).
THE PRINCIPLES OF POLITICAL ECONOMY AND TAXATION, 1817. Introduction by *Prof. Michael P. Fogarty*, M.A. 590

**Smith, Adam** (1723–90).
THE WEALTH OF NATIONS, 1766. Intro. by *Prof. Edwin Seligman*. 2 vols. 412–13

**White, Gilbert** (1720–93).
A NATURAL HISTORY OF SELBORNE, 1789. New edition (1949). Introduction and Notes by *R. M. Lockley*. 48

**Wollstonecraft, Mary** (1759–97), THE RIGHTS OF WOMAN, 1792; and Mill, John Stuart (1806–73), THE SUBJECTION OF WOMEN, 1869. New Introduction by *Pamela Frankau*. 825

# THEOLOGY AND PHILOSOPHY

**Robinson, Wade** (1838–76).
 THE PHILOSOPHY OF ATONEMENT, AND OTHER SERMONS, 1875. Introduction by
 *F. B. Meyer.* 637
**Rousseau, Jean Jacques** (1712–78).
 THE SOCIAL CONTRACT, 1762; and OTHER ESSAYS. Introduction by *G. D. H. Cole.*
 (*See also* Biography, Essays.) 660
**Saint Augustine** (353–430).
 CONFESSIONS. Dr Pusey's Translation, 1838, with Introduction by *A. H. Arm-
 strong,* M.A. 200
 THE CITY OF GOD. Complete text of John Healey's Elizabethan Translation, 1610.
 Edited by *R. V. G. Tasker,* M.A., B.D., with an Introduction by *Sir Ernest Barker.*
 2 vols. 982–3
**Saint Francis** (1182–1226).
 THE LITTLE FLOWERS; THE MIRROR OF PERFECTION (by Leo of Assisi); and THE
 LIFE OF ST FRANCIS (by St Bonaventura). Introduction by *Thomas Okey.* 485
**Spinoza, Benedictus de** (1632–77).
 ETHICS, 1677; and ON THE CORRECTION OF THE UNDERSTANDING, 1687. Translated
 by *Andrew Boyle.* New Introduction by *T. S. Gregory.* 481
**Swedenborg, Emanuel** (1688–1772).
 THE TRUE CHRISTIAN RELIGION, 1771. New and unabridged translation by *F.
 Bayley.* Introduction by *Dr Helen Keller.* 960 pages. 893
**Thomas à Kempis** (1380 ?–1471).
 THE IMITATION OF CHRIST, 1471. 484
**Thomas Aquinas** (1225–74).
 SELECTED WRITINGS. Selected and edited by *Father M. C. D'Arcy.* 953

# TRAVEL AND TOPOGRAPHY

**Borrow, George** (1803–81).
 THE BIBLE IN SPAIN, 1842. Introduction by *Edward Thomas.* 151
 WILD WALES: the People, Language and Scenery, 1862. Introduction by *David
 Jones,* C.B.E., the painter and Borrovian. (*See also* Fiction.) 49
**Boswell, James** (1740–95).
 JOURNAL OF A TOUR TO THE HEBRIDES WITH SAMUEL JOHNSON, 1786. Edited, with
 a new Introduction, by *Lawrence F. Powell,* M.A., HON. D.LITT. 387
**Calderón de la Barca, Mme** (1804–82).
 LIFE IN MEXICO, 1843. Introduction by *Manuel Romero De Terreros.* 664
**Cobbett, William** (1762–1835).
 RURAL RIDES, 1830. Introduction by *Asa Briggs,* M.A., B.SC. 2 vols. 638–9
**Cook, James** (1728–79).
 VOYAGES OF DISCOVERY. Edited by *John Barrow,* F.R.S., F.S.A. Introduction by
 *Guy Pocock,* M.A. 99
**Crèvecœur, J. Hector St John de** (1735–1813).
 LETTERS FROM AN AMERICAN FARMER, 1782. Intro. and Notes by *W. Barton Blake.*
 640
**Darwin, Charles** (1809–82).
 THE VOYAGE OF THE 'BEAGLE,' 1839. (*See also* Science.) 104
**Defoe, Daniel** (1661 ?–1731).
 A TOUR THROUGH ENGLAND AND WALES, 1724–6. Intro. by *G. D. H. Cole.* 2 vols.
 (*See also* Fiction.) 820–1
**Kinglake, Alexander** (1809–91).
 EOTHEN, 1844. Introduction by *Harold Spender.* 337
**Lane, Edward William** (1801–76).
 MANNERS AND CUSTOMS OF THE MODERN EGYPTIANS, 1836. With a new Introduction
 by *Moursi Saad el-Din,* of the Egyptian Ministry of Education. 315
**Park, Mungo** (1771–1806).
 TRAVELS. Introduction (1954) by *Prof. Ronald Miller,* M.A., PH.D. 205
**Polo, Marco** (1254–1324).
 TRAVELS. Introduction by *John Masefield.* 306
**Portuguese Voyages,** 1498–1663. Edited by *Charles David Ley.* 986
**Stevenson, Robert Louis** (1850–94).
 AN INLAND VOYAGE, 1878; TRAVELS WITH A DONKEY, 1879; and THE SILVERADO
 SQUATTERS, 1883. New Introduction by *M. R. Ridley,* M.A. 766
 (*See also* Essays, Poetry, Fiction.)
**Stow, John** (1525 ?–1605).
 THE SURVEY OF LONDON. The fullest account of Elizabethan London. 589
**Wakefield, Edward Gibbon** (1796–1862).
 A LETTER FROM SYDNEY, AND OTHER WRITINGS ON COLONIZATION. Introduction
 by *Prof. R. C. Mills.* 828
**Waterton, Charles** (1782–1865).
 WANDERINGS IN SOUTH AMERICA, 1825. Introduction by *Edmund Selous.* 772